ACTIVEPERL
DEVELOPER'S
GUIDE

ActivePerl Developer's Guide

Martin C. Brown

McGraw-Hill

New York   San Francisco   Washington, D.C.
Auckland   Bogotá   Caracas   Lisbon   London   Madrid
Mexico City   Milan   Montreal   New Delhi   San Juan
Singapore   Sydney   Tokyo   Toronto

McGraw-Hill

A Division of The McGraw·Hill Companies

1 2 3 4 5 6 7 8 9 0   AGM/AGM   5 4 3 2 1 0

P/N 212337-0
part of
ISBN 0-07-212339-7

ActiveState, ActivePerl, and PerlScript are trademarks of ActiveState Tool Corp.

*The sponsoring editor for this book was Rebekah Young, the editing supervisor
was Scott Amerman, and the production supervisor was Claire Stanley. It was
set in Century Schoolbook by Priscilla Beer of McGraw-Hill's desktop composi-
tion unit in cooperation with Spring Point Publishing Services.*

Printed and bound by Quebecor World Martinsburg.

To Sharon,
who still listens
to my rants and frustrations.

CONTENTS

Contents

Contents

ACKNOWLEDGEMENTS

First of all, thanks to Simon Yates, who offered the book in the first place, and Rebekah Young, who helped me finish it in it's final incarnation. Behind the scenes, I should also thank Bob Bolick for the coffee and biscuits, and Sharon Linsenbach for dealing with DHL. Thanks, too, to Scott Amerman and the rest of the production team for turning the manuscript into the final book, and for correcting my mistakes.

Neil Salkind, my agent, deserves a mention for his negotiating skills. He also deserves a slap on the back for continuing to secure me even more work so that, heaven forbid, I don't get bored.

For the sterling work on technically editing the book and making sure that I've got everything right, I give thanks to Ann-Marie Mallon. How she spots things that I should never have got wrong in the first place still escapes me.

Finally, a big thanks to the people who develop Perl and the people who develop Windows extensions for Perl that have helped to make this book a possibility. This includes those people at ActiveState who have, on occasion, offered a solution to a problem, starting with the production of a Windows version of Perl in the first place.

If there's anybody I've forgotten to acknowledge, I apologize unreservedly in advance now. I have done my best to check and verify all sources and contact all parties involved but it's perfectly possible for me to make a mistake.

INTRODUCTION

About This Book

ActivePerl Application Development has three main focus areas. The first is to help programmers already familiar with Perl under Unix to migrate to the new platform. There are differences between the platforms, both from an architecture and supported function point of view. This book should help you bridge the gap from Perl programming to Windows programming, either by providing a Perl workaround, or by giving you the Windows-specific alternative.

The second focus area is on developing applications with the ActivePerl development system. ActivePerl is the version of Perl produced by ActiveState, which is already compiled and optimized for the Windows platform. ActivePerl is supplied as an installable application, thereby overcoming the biggest hurdle, that of compiling Perl on the Windows platform. ActivePerl also provides us with some features not offered in the standard Perl, including an extensive Windows specific library, a Perl Package Manager (similar to the CPAN module), an interactive GUI debugger, and some neat abilities that help you develop Perl-based websites on Windows servers.

The last focus area concentrates on helping people already familiar with programming Windows using Visual Basic and provides a guide for migrating their programming skills from VB to Perl.

What this book is not is a tutorial guide to programming with Perl under Windows, or a complete reference to Perl for Windows programmers; many of the Perl functions and library are ignored if there are no differences between Unix and Windows implementations. Furthermore, it is not a complete guide to applications development. We won't be covering algorithms or providing solutions to your development problems.

We will, on the other hand, provide you with all the information you should ever need to enable you to develop applications using ActivePerl and the Win32 specific Perl libraries. Armed with that information, and provided that you have an existing understanding about how to program with Perl, you should then be able to produce any application you like using this book and ActivePerl.

Who Is the Book For?

The target audience is directly split into two groups: existing Unix Perl programmers who need to develop a Windows-specific or -compatible application, and Visual Basic programmers who want to learn how to program in Perl.

If you are in the former category, you'll need to know Perl to a reasonable level already. The book is not a tutorial guide (although the last section may help). We have made the assumption that you already know how to program in Perl and know the basic operations and development processes behind writing a Perl script. For Visual Basic programmers, you will need to be well versed in VB, but not necessarily an expert. The last section gives a quick introduction to the Perl language, so provided that you know how to program, you should be able to pick up the Perl language quite quickly.

How to Use This Book

If you are a Unix programmer, I suggest you use it as a reference in combination with another guide, such as *Perl: The Complete Reference*, to enable you to program in Perl under Windows. You should be able to find everything you need for successfully migrating your Unix Perl applications to Windows. If there's something missing, let me know, and I'll see what I can do.

For Visual Basic programmers, skip to the last section, which gives an outline and overview of the differences and then follows with a number of different aspects that are different between the two languages. Armed with this information, and the function migration guide in Appendix C, you should be up and running as a Perl programmer in no time at all.

Chapter Breakdown

The book is split into five main sections. The first covers the basic differences between the two platforms and the basics of using the Win32 libraries. Section 2 covers different aspects of Perl programming and provides a complete guide to developing applications on the Windows platform using Win32 specific extensions. Section 3 covers some of the tools available with the ActivePerl and Perl Development Kit distribution that can help with your Perl programming. Section 4 covers the migration from Visual Basic programming to ActivePerl programming. Section 5 consists of appendixes.

The chapter specific contents are as follows:

Chapter 1: Introduction, looks at Perl and the ActivePerl distribution, including ActivePerl's history and how the core development of Perl interacts with the Perl distribution supplied by ActiveState.

Chapter 2: Compatibility Fundamentals covers the basics of the Windows version of Perl, how Windows differs from Unix, and how to avoid many of the problems associated with the core differences between the two platforms while programming in Perl.

Chapter 3: Database Access examines the two base database types supported internally by Perl, text files and DBM, including information on how to convert from the Unix formats to Windows. This chapter also includes extensive information on how to use the Win32::ODBC driver for accessing ODBC-compliant databases such as Oracle and Microsoft SQL Server.

Chapter 4: File Management provides a guide to using files and obtaining file information such as the file statistics and information, both at a simple level and also for accessing the security and extended property information supported by the Windows filesystems.

Chapter 5: Process Management looks at the basics of starting new processes within Windows, and at the problems associated with starting applications using some of the Perl built-in functions.

Chapter 6: Interprocess Communication gives an overview of the interprocess communication services offered by Windows and how to migrate Unix-specific IPC to your Windows applications.

Chapter 7: Networking provides information on how to share and communicate with other machines over the network using a combination of the built-in tools, the LWP and libnet modules available from CPAN, and the Windows-specific modules such as Win32::Internet.

Chapter 8 Systems Information and Administration covers the use of

Perl as a tool for obtaining information about a system, including the registry, and for administrating a machine through the supplied extensions, and the `Win32::AdminMisc` extension from Dave Roth.

Chapter 9: Web Development examines some of the more unusual things of which one is capable when using Perl as a scripting solution under Windows. We start with a basic look at how to use Perl as a scripting solution, and then at ways in which we can use Perl for server side and client scripting.

Chapter 10: Interface Development covers the production of a user interface using Perl, first using the text-based `Win32::Console` module and then using the Tk GUI interface system, which has an advantage in that it is truly cross-platform.

Chapter 11: Beyond Compatibility completely ignores Perl's Unix roots and instead looks at the features offered by ActivePerl that aren't supported by default in the Unix core distribution. This includes the playing of sounds and how to control and communicate with other Windows applications through the `Win32::OLE` interface.

Chapter 12: Perl Package Managers provides information on using the package management tools provided by ActiveState to replace the functionality of the CPAN module.

Chapter 13: ActiveState Perl Debugger covers the debugging tool available with the Perl Development kit.

Chapter 14: Creating Applications with PerlApp offers some solutions to those people wanting to produce standalone executable applications using the ActivePerl and Perl Development Kit suites.

Chapter 15: A Difference of Approach provides some overview material for those users wanting to migrate from Visual Basic to Perl.

Chapter 16: Data Types and Operator gives a quick guide to the basic data types and statements provided by Perl and how they relate to Visual Basic's solutions.

Chapter 17: Functions, Packages, and Modules examines the processes behind abstracting your scripts into the various subcomponents that make up a Perl script in relation to the structures normally offered under Visual Basic.

Chapter 18: Data Manipulation looks at the basic mechanics of manipulating information in Perl, including reading and writing files and regular expressions.

Appendix A: Resource Guide gives you a quick guide of the other books, websites, mailing lists, and Usenet newsgroups that are available for solving your Perl problems.

Appendix B: Tk Quick Reference covers the basic method and properties for the main widgets supported by the Tk GUI interface builder and is designed to augment the information in Chapter 10.

Appendix C: VB/Perl Function Cross Reference is a complete guide to all of the functions in Visual Basic and how to achieve the same results in Perl, either by using the internal functions, a custom function, or one of the many extensions available from CPAN.

Appendix D: Windows Error Messages provides a organized list of the message constants and errors returned under Windows. These can be used in combination with the information in Chapter 8 to more closely monitor errors in your code.

Conventions Used in This Book

All Perl keywords are highlighted in a special font, `like this`, but functions are listed without parentheses. This is because the C functions on which the Perl versions may be based are also shown like this `()`.

```
Examples and code are displayed using a fixed-width font.
```

Function descriptions are formatted using the same fixed-width font.

NOTE.   *Notes are formatted like this and include additional information about a particular topic. You'll also find similarly formatted "Warnings," which highlight possible dangerous tools or tricks to watch out for when programming.*

Contacting the Author

I'm always willing to help you out if you are having problems with any of the scripts and solutions offered in this guide. Despite the best efforts of me, my tech editors, and the team at McGraw-Hill, errors do sometimes occur. Sometimes they can be blamed on a lack of sleep, other times, we've just slipped up! If you are having problems, please check the website (details below) which will always contain the latest information on any errors and bugs found in the book and its code.

I also welcome comments and suggestions on my work. Despite programming in Perl for more than five years, there's still a lot to lean. In particular, if you think you've got a better way of doing things, let me know, and I'll to incorporate it into the next book and post a summary on the website.

If you do need to get in touch, I prefer to be contacted by email. You can use either books@mcwords.com (preferred) or mc@whoever.com. Alternatively, visit my website, http://www.mcwords.com, which contains resources and updated information about the scripts and contents of this book.

ActivePerl
Introduction

## CHAPTER 1

Introduction and Background

Perl is short for Practical Extraction and Reporting Language, or Practically Eclectic Rubbish Lister, depending on your point of view. Primarily, Perl has been a tool for parsing and processing text, either for conversion or for formatting purposes. In fact, Perl is a much more practical language and can be used for a number of different processes, from simple utilities right up to full-blown application development.

Perl is probably best known for its skills within the arena of web programming. Because Perl has some very strong text-handling abilities, it is ideally suited to processing the information that is supplied by forms from websites, and also for formatting and returning information using HTML (Hypertext Markup Language). A number of famous and many quite ordinary sites use Perl behind the scenes on their web server to support input from forms, to produce reports, and even to run complete online stores—for instance, Amazon (http://www.amazon.com) uses Perl to handle their shopping facilities.

This book concentrates on the development of applications using Perl under Windows 95/98, NT, and 2000. These platforms are more commonly known collectively as Win32. Primarily, we'll be looking at the development of code that is portable between Unix and Win32. Initially, we'll be concentrating on how you can write code that takes advantage of Perl's cross-platform capabilities, then we'll look more closely at the Win32-specific extensions that can enhance the applications you develop.

We'll start this chapter by looking at why you might use Perl in the first place and then move on to the history of Perl and, more specifically, the history and availability of Perl on the Windows platform.

Why Use Perl?

Perl is a very flexible language that allows you to develop applications very quickly with little fuss or complication. It has a number of very strong features, including the built-in ability to handle text and regular expressions in a natural fashion without requiring external libraries. Perl is also supported on a number of platforms and has one of the largest "user" followings on the Internet. The Perl community works very hard to help Perl users and programmers. There is even a global repository for Perl libraries and extensions called CPAN (Comprehensive Perl Archive Network) that users can investigate when they start to write their own applications.

Because of this wide support, and because Perl is such a practical language with many abilities, it can be used to program all sorts of applications. Unlike languages such as C/C++ and Pascal, Perl does not need to be compiled before it is used, which helps to reduce the development time. It also does preclude the need for a defined structure—we can write a program in one line without worrying about importing any modules or making any explicit definitions.

Some of the other main features of the Perl language are outlined in the following sections.

Perl Is Free

It may not seem like a major feature, but in fact being free is very important. Some languages, such as C (which is free with compilers such as GNU's gcc), have been commercialized by Metrowerks, Microsoft, and other companies. Other languages, such as Visual Basic, are entirely commercial. Perl's source code is open and free—anybody can download the C source that constitutes a Perl interpreter. Furthermore, you can easily extend the core functionality of Perl both within the realms of the interpreted language and by modifying the Perl source code.

Perl Is Simple to Learn, Concise, and Easy to Read

Because of its history and roots, most people with any programming experience will be able to program with Perl. It has a syntax similar to C and shell script, among others, but with a less restrictive format. Many things are more quickly written in Perl because of the number of built-in functions and logical assumptions that the Perl interpreter makes during execution. It's also easy to read, because the code can be written in a clear and concise format that almost reads like an English sentence.

Perl Is Fast

As we will see shortly, Perl is not an interpreter in the strictest sense—the code is compiled before it is executed. Compared to most scripting languages, this makes execution almost as fast as writing compiled C code. But because the code is still interpreted, there is no compilation process, and applications can be written much faster than with other languages without any of the performance problems normally associated with an interpreted language.

Perl Is Extensible

You can write Perl-based packages and modules that extend the functionality of the language. You can also use external C code that can be called directly by Perl to extend the functionality further. The reverse is also true: The Perl interpreter can be incorporated directly into many languages, including C. This allows your C programs to use the functionality of the Perl interpreter without calling an external program.

Perl Has Flexible Data Types

You can create simple variables that contain text or numbers, and Perl will treat the variable data accordingly at the time it is used. You can increment text values (such as hexadecimal) directly, without any conversion, and strings can be interpolated with each other without requiring external functions to concatenate, or combine, the results.

You can also handle arrays of values as simple lists, as typical indexed arrays, and even as stacks of information. Finally, you can model complex data using hashes—a form of associative array where the list of the information is indexed via strings instead of numbers.

Perl Is Object-Oriented

Perl supports all of the object-oriented features—inheritance, polymorphism, and encapsulation. There are no restrictions on when or where you make use of object-oriented features. Unlike C and C++, there is no boundary.

Perl Is Collaborative

A huge network of Perl programmers exists worldwide. Most programmers supply, and use, the modules and scripts supplied via the Comprehensive Perl Active Network (CPAN). This is a repository of the best modules and scripts available. Using an existing prewritten module can save you hundreds, perhaps even thousands, of hours of development time.

Why Use Perl on Windows?

One of the commonly held myths about Perl is that it is a Unix tool, available only to Unix programmers. Although this is indeed the root of Perl's heritage, the Perl language has been supported on multiplatforms for many years. The Perl interpreter is, in fact, written in the C language, so the porting process only really revolves around the compatibility of the operating system.

One of the fundamental problems with Windows from a user, administrator, and programmer perspective is that it does not come with any form of programming language. The only application that comes close to a programming language is the batch file, a feature of the DOS command prompt that is severely limited not only internally but also externally where there is a lack of suitable utilities. For repetitive tasks or even for apparently very simple operations, there is no solution. We have no way of controlling the environment in which we work unless we do it interactively as part of the Windows GUI (graphical user interface).

The problem affects everybody in different ways. For the administrator, creating users, managing services, and even monitoring your systems is an arduous task if conducted using the normal tools. With Perl we can solve all of these problems by writing scripts that operate on the operating system directly, rather than having to use the GUI for every single operation.

For the user, the needs are less extravagant, but nonetheless very important. We can use Perl to download web pages, clean up hard disks, or just to automate a task that they do every day, such as printing a set of reports.

As a programmer, you can use Perl as a prototyping tool. Because we can avoid the normal compilation and linking stages, Perl can build an application in seconds. Of course, there is no reason why we should use Perl only for prototyping—once you've prototyped the application in Perl, why not complete it in Perl? With Perl we can access databases, use network sockets, or manage systems and devices. We can even use Perl to control other applications. In addition, Perl can be used as a programmer's tool, extracting, organizing, or managing the source files and headers used in an application's development. To make the whole process easier, Perl uses the same Win32 API (application programming interface) that you use with Pascal or C/C++, so you don't need to worry about "translating" Perl functions and calls to their respective C/C++ versions.

Perl History

Perl itself is older than you might think. The first version released to the public, Perl 1, was launched in 1988. This is surprising to many people, since many believe Perl to be an Internet and more specifically a web development language. Yet the first version was available long before Tim Berners-Lee came up with the idea for HTML (June 1993) and the subsequent explosion of the World Wide Web—what many consider to be the real content of the Internet.

The main version that started to be used in earnest by most programmers was Perl 4. Development of Perl 4 was actually targeted toward making the production of the "Camel" book, better known as *Programming Perl*, 2nd edition, by Larry Wall, Tom Christiansen, and Randal L. Schwartz (O'Reilly & Associates, 1996). The last version of Perl 4 to be released was 4.036 in 1992.

The main development effort is now focused on Perl v5; the latest stable version, at this writing, is v5.005_03. Development for Perl is split between the developmental versions and the currently stable version. Development versions progress at a relatively rapid rate, fixing bugs and introducing minor features and updates in the process. The stable versions are those that should be used in commercial installations. You can identify a development version by the sequence after the underscore character—values above 50 are developmental.

There are two basic Perl distributions available to the Windows user: the core distribution, which requires compilation, and the ActiveState distribution, which is available as an installer in a similar format to other Windows-based applications.

Perl Win32 History

The original Win32 port of Perl was ported in 1997 by Dick Hardt, from a company called Hip Communications. Contrary to popular belief, this original port was actually funded by Microsoft because they wanted to include Perl within the Windows NT Resource Kit. Microsoft needed a scripting language to allow administrators to have the same level of scripting ability as was available to Unix users who have the shell. Although Windows NT has the command shell, this is really nothing more advanced than a DOS window with batch file capability—Microsoft wanted a proper language, and Perl seemed to fit the bill. Perl was, in fact, the first scripting language available under Windows NT that included OLE (object linking and embedding). This is the system that allows different Windows applications to communicate directly with each other and even control each other.

Hip later became ActiveWare and is now better known as ActiveState, renamed after a collaboration between the ActiveWare team and O'Reilly and Associates, the publisher best known for supporting the core Perl development and for publishing a series of books written by the authors of Perl. The Perl Porters Group, a selection of individuals that control and manage the porting of the Perl interpreter to new platforms, has been working with ActiveState to allow the core distribution to compile under Win32 without further modification. Development still continues in two threads, with the core, Unix-derived version and the ActiveState versions being developed in parallel.

At the basic level, there are no differences between the core and ActiveState versions of Perl, most programs will run unmodified on both Perl interpreters. However, because of the obvious platform differences, some features and functions either don't work or don't work quite as they should (we'll be looking at those more closely in the rest of this book).

The ActiveState version may lag behind the core distribution for a small period whilst the port to Win32 is completed, but on the whole, the Perl interpreter is updated roughly every 6 months, so the changes are not that significant. The time difference allows any bugs or changes that have been made to the core language to be tested on the new platform. Changes to the core distribution are obviously incorporated into the ActiveState version eventually.

In fact, ActiveState releases its own versions and revisions of its Perl interpreter under different build numbers. At this writing, the latest build was 522, which is based on v5.005_03 of the core Perl distribution and so is concurrent with the current stable core version. New releases (builds) of ActiveState's version are released fairly frequently, with the new versions incorporating bug fixes or improvements to the ActiveState tools rather than making modifications to the Perl interpreter.

ActiveState Tools

The most important distinction between the core and ActiveState versions is that ActiveState Perl is in part a commercial effort. ActiveState supports a number of different packages. The main *ActivePerl* package is free and consists of the core Perl distribution, including the main libraries and extensions, precompiled and ready to run on your machine.

In addition to the main ActivePerl product, ActiveState also sells other tools that enhance the development process on a commercial basis. The most obvious additional tool set is the *Perl Development Kit* (PDK), which includes additional tools for aiding the development of Perl programs. The additional features include a visual debugger and an interface to the Windows Component Object Model (COM).

The *PerlEx* tool is more specific. It provides the fastest methods available for executing Perl scripts on Windows NT-based web servers. It uses a method similar to the Apache mod_perl module to ensure that Perl scripts execute as quickly as possible by precompiling each script into its bytecode format for direct execution by the Perl virtual machine.

We'll be looking in more detail at some of these components throughout this book. Additional information on the basic package contents in each case is given in the following sections.

ActivePerl

The main ActivePerl package is free and consists of the Perl binary and libraries for Win32, *Perl for ISAPI*, *PerlScript*, and *Perl Package Manager*. The interpreter is precompiled and comes with the same basic library as the core distribution. In addition, it comes with a number of additional modules and extensions specific to the Win32 platform. These provide additional interfaces to the operating system in addition to plugging the gaps where the core distribution is missing a particular function that is supported under Unix.

Perl for ISAPI (Internet Server Application Programming Interface) is a plug-in for Microsoft's Internet Information Server (v2.0 and above) or any ISAPI-compatible web browser. The plug-in provides a quick method for executing Perl scripts within the confines of a Win32 web server. Although not as slick as the mod_perl module for Apache, it's a similar basic idea. If you want mod_perl style speed, you should look at the

PerlEx tool. The Perl for ISAPI is just a DLL (dynamic link library) that provides a direct interface to the core Perl interpreter, but because it is loaded once by the web server, Perl scripts execute more quickly than they would if the actual Perl interpreter was loaded each time.

PerlScript is also a plug-in, but it provides an interface to allow Perl to be used for ActiveX scripting. ActiveX is a technology supported by Microsoft's IIS (Internet Information Server) web servers and other applications that allows you to embed scripts into documents that are supported by ActiveX Scripting Host applications. Most people will have come across this technology within the realm's Active Server Pages (ASP) on web hosts. A basic installation allows you to embed VBScript (Visual Basic) and JScript (Microsoft's Java/JavaScript language) into the pages. With PerlScript, you can now also embed Perl scripts into the same documents.

The Perl Package Manager is a simplified interface for installing new packages and extensions. If you have used the CPAN module under Unix, then it is a similar basic principle.

Perl Development Kit

The Perl Development Kit is designed as an extension to the basic ActivePerl package. It provides the additional features that professional developers often need in a single installable application. The kit includes the *Perl Debugger*, *PerlCOM*, *PerlCtrl*, *PerlApp*, the *Visual Package Manager*, the *Network Installer*, and *Perl WSAPI*.

The ActiveState Perl Debugger is an interactive debugger in a similar vein to other debuggers you will find within the Microsoft's Visual Studio environments for Visual Basic and C++. It is a complete replacement for the debugger supplied as standard with the core Perl distribution. Like other debuggers, you can set watch points and breakpoints, and interactively control the progress of your scripts. We'll be taking a close look at the ActiveState Perl Debugger later in this book.

Although PerlScript allows you to use Perl within ActiveX scripts, if you want to use Perl within any ActiveX application, you need to use PerlCOM. PerlCOM exposes Perl as an ActiveX component, which means you can include Perl scripts and objects within any application that supports ActiveX development. In addition, you can use DCOM, the Distributed Component Object Model, to create distributed applications that include the features of Perl.

When supporting an application that uses COM controls, you can use the PerlCtrl application to convert a Perl script into a standalone COM control. You can then use the control in any COM-supporting application, such as Visual Basic.

One of the fundamental problems with Perl and other similar scripting languages is that when you distribute an application, you distribute its source code. Although for many systems this is an advantage rather than a problem, it presents potential headaches for copyright and intellectual property rights. You can get around this by distributing a standalone Perl application by converting it from the script using PerlApp. This can be used to convert a Perl script into a completely freestanding application that can be used on any Windows machine without it requiring the Perl interpreter.

The Visual Package Manager provides a browser-based interface to adding packages and extensions to the Perl interpreter. This is a friendlier interface than the basic Perl Package Manager that comes with the ActivePerl kit.

When installing Perl within a network environment, going around and installing Perl on each machine individually, is a tedious and time-consuming process. The Network Installer can install Perl and additional extensions and modules onto a number of workstations automatically—it can even be configured to install the application the next time a user logs in to the workstation.

The Perl WSAPI is an embedded version of the Perl interpreter designed to execute within the O'Reilly WebSite free web server. It provides a familiar CGI-style interface for Unix developers but without the overhead normally associated with running a Perl interpreter for each Common Gateway Interface (CGI) script invocation.

Comparing Perl to Other Languages

We've already looked at why you might want to use Perl on your Windows systems from a generic point of view. But how about the specific advantages of Perl over other languages? The truth is that it all comes down to a question of suitability for the purpose and personal preference. The personal preference angle is difficult to quantify, since it relies on the sometimes arbitrary partiality of the programmer.

The advantages over other languages, on the other hand, are easier to describe. Perl is a very clean language to use, and the extensions and interfaces that come with Perl make it an ideal companion when you want to do a variety of different tasks. Perl uses the same API as the other C/C++-based applications written natively for the Windows platform. This means we can directly access and control features of the operating system. This is something not offered by many of the languages—even Python, which comes with an extensive set of Windows modules, does not offer the same level of integration as Perl.

If it uses the same libraries and API, then why not use C/C++? The answer to that is very simple: time. With C/C++, Java, even Visual Basic, there are a number of hurdles to overcome before you can even start programming. Once you've written your application, it has to be compiled and linked before it can be used. With Perl, you essentially tell it what you want to do, and then you execute the program. You can write in Perl in 5 minutes what it would take even a hardened C programmer to write in 30 minutes, and you can guarantee your Perl application will be more flexible.

In this book we'll be primarily looking at the difference between Perl and Visual Basic (VB)—since it's the language that most programmers and users will have experience with. VB is essentially not much more than an interface-building tool and probably shouldn't be officially classed as a "language" as such, but it does have its strengths. Most significant of these is the fact that it is available in an extended format called VB for Applications. This is the embedded language for many applications, including the Microsoft Office suite.

Since we'll be looking at these differences more extensively in Section 4, we'll ignore a comparison of the Perl and Visual Basic for the moment. However, there are some other languages that you should probably be aware of when comparing Perl to other Windows-supported languages.

Tcl

Tcl (Tool Command Language) was developed as an embeddable scripting language. A lot of the original design centered around a macrolike language for helping with shell-based applications. Tcl was never really developed as a general-purpose scripting language, although many people use it as such. In fact, Tcl was designed with the philosophy that you should actually use two or more languages when developing large software systems.

Tcl's variables are very different from those in Perl. Because it was designed with the typical shell-based string handling in mind, strings are null-terminated (as they are in C). This means that Tcl cannot be used for handling binary data. Compared to Perl, Tcl is also generally slower on iterative operations over strings. You cannot pass arrays by value or by reference; they can only be passed by name. This makes programming more complex, although not impossible.

Lists in Tcl are actually stored as a single string, and arrays are stored within what Perl would treat as a hash. Accessing a true Tcl array is therefore slightly slower, as it has to look up associative entries in order to decipher the true values. The data-handling problems also extend to numbers, which Tcl stores as strings and converts to numbers only when a calculation is required. This slows mathematical operations significantly.

Unlike Perl, which parses the script first before optimizing and then executing, Tcl is a true interpreter, and each line is interpreted and optimized individually at execution time. This reduces the optimization options available to Tcl. Perl, on the other hand, can optimize source lines, code blocks, and even entire functions if the compilation process allows. The same Tcl interpretation technique also means that the only way to debug Tcl code and search for syntactic errors is to actually execute the code. Because Perl goes through the precompilation stage, it can check for syntactic and other possible/probable errors without actually executing the code.

Finally, the code base of the standard Tcl package does not include many of the functions and abilities of the Perl language. This is especially important if you are trying to write a cross-platform POSIX-compliant application. Perl supports the entire POSIX function set, but Tcl supports a much smaller subset of the POSIX function set, even using external packages.

It should be clear from this description that Perl is a better alternative to Tcl in situations where you want easy access to the rest of the OS. Most significantly, Tcl will never be a general-purpose scripting language. Tcl will, on the other hand, be a good solution if you want to embed a scripting language inside another language.

Python

Python was developed as an object-oriented language and is well thought out, interpreted, byte-compiled, extensible, and a largely procedural programming language. Like Perl, it's good at text processing and even general-purpose programming. Python also has a good history in the realm of GUI-based application development. Compared to Perl, Python has fewer users, but it is gaining acceptance as a practical rapid application development (RAD) tool.

Unlike Perl, Python does not resemble C, and it doesn't resemble Unix-style tools like awk either. Python was designed from scratch to be object-oriented and has clear module semantics. This can make it confusing to use, as the namespaces get complex to resolve. On the other hand, this makes it much more structured, which can ease development for those with structured minds.

I'm not aware of anything that is better in Python than in Perl. They both share object features, and the two are almost identical in execution speed. However, the reverse is not true: Perl has better regular expression features, and the level of integration between Perl and the Unix environment is hard to beat (although it can probably be solved within Python using a suitably written external module).

In general, there is not a lot to tip the scales in favor of one of the two languages. Perl will appeal to those people who already know C or Unix shell utilities. Perl is also older and more widespread, and there is a much larger library of contributed modules and scripts. Python, on the other hand, may appeal to those people who have experience with more object-oriented languages such as Java or Modula-2.

Both languages provide easy control and access with regard to the external environment in which they work. Perl arguably fills the role better though, because many of the standard system functions you are used to are supported natively by the language, without requiring external modules. The technical support for the two languages is also very similar, with both using websites and newsgroups to help users program in the new language.

Finally, it's worth mentioning that of all the scripting languages available, Perl and Python are two of the most stable platforms for development. There are, however, some minor differences. First, Perl provides quite advanced functions and mechanisms for tracking errors and faults in the scripts. However, making extensive use of these facilities can still cause problems. For example, calling the system `truncate()` function within Perl will cause the whole interpreter to crash. Python, on the other hand, uses a system of error trapping that will immediately identify a problem like this before it occurs, allowing you to account for it in your applications. This is largely due to the application development nature of the language.

Java

At first viewing, Java seems to be a friendlier, interpreted version of C++. Depending on your point of view, this can either be an advantage or a disadvantage. Java probably inherits less than a third of the complexity of C++, but it retains much of the complexity of its brethren.

Java was designed primarily as an implementation-independent language, originally with web-based intentions, but now as a more general-purpose solution to a variety of problems. Like Perl, Java is byte-compiled, but unlike Perl, programs are supplied in byte-compiled format and then executed via a Java virtual machine at execution time.

Because of its roots and its complexity, Java cannot really be considered as a direct competitor to Perl. It is difficult to use Java as a rapid development tool and virtually impossible to use it for most of the simple text processing and system administration tasks that Perl is best known for.

C/C++

Perl itself is written in C. You can download and view the Perl source code if you so wish, but it's definitely not for the fainthearted. Many of the structures and semantics of the two languages are very similar. For example, both C and Perl use semicolons as end-of-line terminators. They also share the same code block and indentation features. However, Perl tends to be stricter when it comes to code block definitions—you always require curly brackets, for example—but most C programmers will be comfortable with the Perl environment.

Like C++, Perl is object-oriented. Both share the same abilities of inheritance, polymorphism, and encapsulation. However, object orientation in Perl is easier to use compared to the complexities of constructors and inheritance found in C++. In addition to all this, there is no distinction between the standard and object-oriented implementations of Perl as there is with C and C++. This means you can mix and match different variables, objects, and other data types within a single Perl application—something that would be difficult to achieve easily with C and C++.

Because Perl is basically an interpreted language (as mentioned earlier), development is generally quicker than writing in native C. Perl also has many more built-in facilities and abilities that would otherwise need to be handwritten in C/C++. For example, regular expressions and many of the data-handling features would require a significant amount of programming to reproduce in C with the same ease of use available in Perl.

Because of Perl's roots in C, it is also possible to extend Perl with C source code and vice versa: You can embed Perl programs in C source code. We won't be looking at any specific examples in this book, but check out my book *Perl: The Complete Reference* (McGraw-Hill, 1999) if you want further information on this process.

2

Using Perl for Windows

The core and ActiveState versions of Perl are basically identical at a programming language level to the Unix version. There are, however, some differences relating to the way in which scripts are executed and the way in which some of the core elements of this process are affected by the platform differences. Most of the time, the differences are minor, or they are effectively hidden by the Perl interpreter or the C libraries on which they are built.

Most of the differences, of course, relate to the fundamental differences between Unix, Perl's original development platform, and Windows. Some are purely terminology-based—the terms UNC (Universal Naming Convention) and DLL (Dynamic Link Library) will be new to some people. Other differences are more complex and relate to the underlying library support of the Windows platform. These can cause untold problems if you're not aware of them before you start the programming process.

In this chapter, we'll look at the basics of getting Perl installed onto your machine and how to run some Perl scripts. Then we'll move on to the basics of the development process under Windows and how they differ from Unix. We'll also use this opportunity to look at some of the basic tools and extensions supported by the ActivePerl Development Kit that help to bridge the gap.

Installing Perl on Windows

There are two ways of installing Perl on Windows. The core distribution can be compiled with any C compiler on a Windows machine, including Microsoft's Visual C++, Borland C++ Builder, and free compilers such as gcc and egcs. The core distribution does not come with the Win32-specific extension libraries, so I recommend you use the ActiveState installers unless you need to make specific changes to the source code.

Compiling the Core Perl Distribution

Since the core distribution is now Windows-compatible, it is possible to compile your own version of the Perl compiler from source code. Although some people prefer this version, it's important to note that core distribution does not come with any of the Win32-specific modules. You will need to download and install those modules separately.

If you want to install a version of the Perl binary based on the latest source code, you will need to find a C compiler capable of compiling the application. It's then a case of following the instructions relevant to your C and development environment. The supported C compilers are described here. Other versions and C compilers may work, but it's not guaranteed.

- *Borland C++, version 5.02 or later.* With the Borland C++ compiler you will need to use a different make command, since the one supplied does not work very well and certainly doesn't support MakeMaker extensions. The documentation recommends the dmake application, available from http://dmake.wticorp.com.

- *Microsoft Visual C++, version 4.2 or later.* You can use the nmake application that comes with Visual C++ to build the distribution correctly.

- *Mingw32 with egcs, versions 1.0.2 and 1.1 or Mingw32 with gcc, version 2.8.1.* Both egcs and gcc supply their own make command. You can download a copy of the egcs version (preferred) from ftp://ftp.xraylith.wisc.edu/pub/khan/gnu-win32/mingw32/. The gcc version is available from http://agnes.dida.physik.uni-essen.de/~janjaap/mingw32/.

Also be aware that Windows 95 as a compilation platform is not supported. This is because the command shell available under Windows 95 is not capable of working properly with the scripts and make commands required during the building process. The best platform for building from the core source code is Windows NT using the standard cmd shell.

In all cases, ignore the Configure utility that you would normally use when compiling under Unix and Unix-like operating systems. Instead, change to the win32 directory and run the make command for your installation. For example:

```
c:\perl\win32> dmake
```

For Microsoft's Visual C++, you will need to execute the vcvars32.bat batch file, which sets up the environment for using the Visual C++ on the command line. For example:

```
c:\perlsrc\win32> c:\progra~1\micros~~1\vc98\bin\vcvars32.bat
```

You may need to increase the environment memory on your command.com for this batch file to work properly; you can do this by modifying the properties for the MS-DOS Prompt shortcut. Select the shortcut within the Start menu, and then choose the *Program* tab. You should modify the Cmd Line field to read

```
C:\WINDOWS\COMMAND.COM /E:4096
```

This boosts the environment memory for the command prompt up to 4KB, more than enough for all the variables you should need.

Remember that compiling and installing Perl from the source distribution does not give you the integration facilities or modules that are included as standard within the ActiveState version.

You will need to manually update your PATH variable so that you have access to the Perl interpreter on the command line. You can do this within Windows 95/98 by modifying the autoexec.bat file. You will need to add a line like

```
SET PATH=C:\PERL\BIN\;%PATH%
```

This will update your search path without replacing the pre-existing contents. The C:\PERL\BIN\ is the default install location; you should modify this to wherever you have installed the binary.

On Windows NT, you will need to update the PATH variable by using the System control panel.

Installing ActiveState Perl

You can download the latest installers for the ActiveState tools from http://www.activestate.com. The ActivePerl installer is downloadable for free, but for the Perl Development Kit and PerlEx toolkits, you will either need to purchase a full license or obtain a trial license key.

All of the ActiveState Perl tools are available as simple package installers. To install the software, double-click on the installer file once you have downloaded it, and follow the onscreen instructions. Unless you want to install the product on a different disk, I recommend you use the default installation path, which is C:\perl. This will also set up the necessary file associations and modify your PATH environment variable so that you can execute Perl within a command prompt.

The Win32 Libraries

Perl has a large library of modules available that extend its capabilities. The full range of modules is too large to list here in detail, but it includes modules from simple processing facilities to complete tools for managing and monitoring your websites and servers. The place to look for modules is the CPAN archive; see Appendix A for details.

The ActiveState version of Perl already comes with a large suite of additional modules, including a series of Windows-specific modules known as the *LibWin32 library*. The full list of modules installed by default can be seen in Table 2-1.

TABLE 2-1

Default Modules Installed by ActivePerl.

Module	Description
Archive::Tar	A toolkit for opening and using UNIX TAR files.
Compress::Zlib	An interface for decompressing information entirely within Perl.
LWP	Gisle Aas's Lib WWW Perl (LWP) toolkit. This includes modules for processing HTML, URLs (Uniform Resource Locator), and MIME-encoded (Multipurpose Internet Mail Extensions) information and the necessary code for downloading files by HTTP (Hypertext Transfer Protocol) and FTP (File Transfer Protocol).
Win32::ChangeNotify	Interface to the NT Change/Notify system for monitoring the status of files and directories transparently.
Win32::Clipboard	Access to the global system clipboard. You can add/remove objects from the clipboard directory.
Win32::Console	Terminal control of an MS-DOS or Windows NT command console.
Win32::Event	Interface to the Win32 event system for IPC (interprocess communication).
Win32::EventLog	Interface to reading from and writing to the Windows NT event log system.
Win32::File	Allows you to access and set the attributes of a file.
Win32::FileSecurity	Interface to the extended file security options under Windows NT.
Win32::Internet	Interface to Win32's built-in Internet access system for downloading files.

(Continued)

TABLE 2-1

(Continued)

Module	Description
Win32::IPC	Base methods for the different IPC techniques supported under Win32.
Win32::Mutex	Interface to the mutex (mutual/exclusive) locking and access mechanism.
Win32::NetAdmin	Network administration functions for individual machines and entire domains.
Win32::NetResource	Provides a suite of Perl functions for accessing and controlling the individual Net resources.
Win32::ODBC	ODBC (Open database connectivity) interface for accessing databases.
Win32::OLE	Interface to OLE automation.
Win32::PerfLib	Supports an interface to the Windows NT performance system.
Win32::Pipe	Named pipes and assorted functions.
Win32::Process	Allows you to create manageable Win32 processes within Perl.
Win32::Registry	Provides an interface to the Windows Registry. See the Win32API::Registry module and the Win32::TieRegistry module for a tied interface.
Win32::Semaphore	Interface to the Win32 semaphores.
Win32::Service	Allows the control and access of Windows NT services.
Win32::Shortcut	Access (and modification) of Win32 shortcuts.
Win32::Sound	Allows you to play WAV and other file formats within a Perl script.
Win32::TieRegistry	A tied interface to the Win32 Registry system.
Win32::WinError	Access to the Win32 error system.
Win32API::Net	Provides a complete interface to the underlying C++ functions for managing accounts with the NT LanManager.
Win32API::Registry	Provides a low-level interface to the core API used for manipulating the Registry.

Installing Third-Party Modules

For many third-party modules it should just be a simple case of running the Perl Makefile and then executing the make application for the module to install it into the right location. Note that some modules include C source code, and for those, you will require a C compiler to build them.

Use the links above to download a compiler if you don't have one already.

The Perl `Makefile` uses the `MakeMaker` module to correctly configure a `Makefile` to copy the module files into the right location. If you don't already own a copy of `make`, such as `dmake` or `nmake`, you can download a copy of the `nmake` from Microsoft at ftp://ftp.microsoft.com/Softlib/MSLFILES/nmake15.exe.

Once you have a copy of `make`, the typical sequence goes like this:

```
C:\> perl Makefile.PL
C:\> nmake
C:\> nmake test
C:\> nmake install
```

The `MakeMaker` module will make all the necessary decisions regarding file locations and install the module into a suitable directory.

Documentation

Documentation for Perl under Windows comes in the form of HTML documents. These have been converted from the core POD—Plain Old Documentation—format by a Perl script into their HTML versions. You can view these files in any browser. If you have installed ActiveState Perl, you should be able to access the documentation by accessing the Documentation entry in the ActivePerl folder within your Start menu.

The web page presents you with a comprehensive interface to not only the core language reference files but also the ActiveState and Win32 reference and FAQ documentation.

Running Perl Scripts

Once installed correctly, there are two basic ways of executing a Perl script. You can either type

```
C:\> perl hello.pl
```

in a command window, or you can double-click on a script in Windows Explorer. The former method allows you to specify command-line arguments; the latter method will require that you ask the user for any required information.

Under Windows NT, if you want a more Unix-like method of executing scripts, you can modify the `PATHEXT` environment variable (in the

System control panel) to include *.pl* as a recognized extension. This allows you to call a script just like any other command on the command line, but with limitations. The following will work:

```
C:\> hello readme.txt
```

However, redirection and pipes to the Perl script will not work. This means that the following examples, although perfectly valid under Unix, will not work under Windows:

```
C:\> hello <readme.txt
C:\> hello readme.txt|more
```

The other alternative, which works on all platforms, is to use the pl2bat utility. This wraps the call to your Perl script within a Windows batch file. For example, we could use it to convert our hello.pl utility:

```
C:\> pl2bat hello.pl
C:\> hello
```

The big advantage here is that because we are using batch file, it works on any platform, and we can even add command-line options to the Perl interpreter within the batch file to alter the behavior. Furthermore, pipes and redirection work correctly with batch files, which, therefore, also means the options work with our Perl script.

If you want to specify any additional command-line options, you can use the normal "shebang" line to specify these options. Although Windows will ignore this line, the Perl interpreter still has to read the file, and so it will extract any information from the line that it needs. So, for example, to turn warnings on within a script, you might use a line such as:

```
#!perl -w
```

Note that you must still comment-out the line using a leading hash character.

Data and File Formats

The Win32 port of Perl does its best to eliminate many of the incompatibilities inherent between the Unix and Windows platform. The more significant of these differences is the line termination characters. These affect not only the data you use with your script, they can also affect some aspects of the script itself. Other problems include the fact that Windows treats binary files different from text files and that filenames and paths are specified differently.

Line Termination

Text files under Windows are terminated with \r\n (a carriage-return and a newline character; \015\012 in octal), and files are terminated by the SUB (^Z, \032) character. However, within the C libraries that are used to build Perl, the end-of-line characters are converted to a single newline, \n, as you would expect in Unix. This affects input, where the terminators are stripped to a single newline, and output, where a newline is converted to carriage-return newline on output. Thus, for most situations, you should not need to modify text-processing Perl scripts between the two platforms.

Where the line termination may make a difference is with the script source itself. When you are copying files from Unix to Windows, you must ensure that you transfer the files as text rather than binary files. Also, be careful when editing files within a Windows editor to ensure that a single blank line is added to the end of the source file. This is to prevent Perl from incorrectly identifying lines when it is extracting bare content.

For example, if you have a script like the following that uses a "here" document to print information out to the screen, it may report an error under Windows:

```
print <<"END";
Hello World!
END
```

This is because Perl will be looking for the word "END" but won't see it if the line is not terminated with a newline or carriage-return newline sequence.

Files and Pathnames

Unlike Unix, which uses a single hierarchical structure emanating from the "root" partition, Windows addresses files with a combination of drives and directories. Every path on a Windows system may start with a drive letter prefix. Each drive letter refers to a different physical disk. The drive letter is separated from the rest of the filename and path by a colon, so be careful if you have chosen colons as field separators in text files.

Directories and files are by default separated by the backslash (\). However, the Win32 libraries also allow the use of the forward slash (/), so you do not need to modify the file paths within your programs, beyond adding drive letters or changing directory locations as necessary.

However, be aware that using a backslash within a file specification in Perl holds hidden dangers. Although the line

```
print "Exists\n" if (-f "C:\autoexec.bat");
```

in theory should work, in fact, it fails because the double quotes indicate to Perl that the string should be interpolated and so the \a at the start is translated into a control character. There are two ways around this; the easiest is to use single quotes for file paths:

```
print "Exists\n" if (-f 'C:\autoexec.bat');
```

Because there is no interpolation, the string will be interpreted exactly as it is written.

The other option is to escape the backslashes by replacing single instances with doubles:

```
print "Exists\n" if (-f "C:\\autoexec.bat");
```

Also, remember that because files may reside on a different physical disk you should be storing an absolute rather than relative pathname. Windows interprets relative paths with reference to the current disk drive—i.e., the one active in the command prompt—or as set by the host program (such as a web server). This means that running a script that uses a relative path from C: will work, but from D: may not.

Another point to consider when using files under Windows is that the operating system does not differentiate between case. Although by tradition you can access the autoexec.bat file, you could access the file using AUTOEXEC.BAT or even AuToExEc.BaT. This has both advantages and disadvantages. The main disadvantage is that you cannot use differently cased names within the same directory. The major advantage is that you no longer have to be so strict when specifying filenames. This is particularly useful if you accept filename information from the user.

The final note regarding files relates to the use of file extensions. Under Unix, although there are some conventions such as .pl for Perl files and .o for object files, they have no special meaning to the operating system. Within Windows, file extensions are used by the operating system to identify the type of file. When you double-click on a document ending with the extension .doc, the operating system uses the file association table to identify this as a Microsoft Word document.

Within Windows you should, as we've already seen, continue to use the .pl extension for your Perl scripts. This will ensure that when the scripts are double-clicked they are executed by the Perl interpreter. Within your scripts, care should be taken to ensure that any files you do create work with the extension mapping system. For example, if you are creating a text file, use the extension .txt and for a comma-separated data file, use .csv. These associations are vital if you expect your users to be able to open the files created by your Perl scripts in other applications.

You can check the extensions used for a particular type of file by examining the Save dialog within the application. Alternatively, you can view the associations between file extensions and the applications used to open them within Windows Explorer. You do this by going to the File Types tab of the Folder Options window, available from the View menu. Here you can not only view the file types, you can also modify the associations and the icon used to display the file within the Explorer window.

Time

Under Unix, the value returned by the `time` function is given in seconds since the epoch. Under both Unix and Win32 operating systems, the epoch is identical: 00:00:00 on 1 January 1970. You therefore shouldn't have any worries regarding time translation of epoch-referenced values.

That said, if you want to store date and time information in a more architecture-neutral format, consider storing the date and time as a date/time string and not an epoch value. The best format is the universal time string format `YYYYMMDDHHMMSS`. For example, when writing this the time was 18/10/99 10:11:38 a.m., which we could express as `19991018101138`.

Executing External Programs

You can execute external programs within Perl using the normal `system` and related functions. However, be warned that only `system` spawns a normal command shell. Certain operations, such as pipes and redirection, will only work with programs that are executed by the shell or that otherwise support pipes and redirection.

Another thing to be careful of is running external commands when using Perl within a web server under Windows. You may have problems running commands within Perl for ISAPI, Perl WSAPI, and PerlScript. We'll look at ways of getting around this when we look at using Perl with web servers later in this book.

Chapters 5 and 6 will look at the different ways in which we can communicate with other processes.

Determining Host Information

There are some things you can do to protect yourself from the difference in the environment when moving from Unix to Windows. The most obvious way to start when developing on a new platform is to sound out your environment. By this I don't mean knowing that you are working under Windows NT instead of 95; I am referring to the discovery within your scripts about the machine they are running on.

You can determine the platform on which you are working by using the $^O variable. This will return a name referring to the current platform. If you want to obtain the name of the operating system on which the current Perl interpreter was compiled, use the value of $Config{'archname'}, which is available to you when the Config module has been imported. In all cases the value of $^O is probably of more use than the architecture name for writing cross-platform scripts. The other thing you might want to do is determine the version of the Perl language that you are using. The core Perl language version number is stored in the $] variable. You can obtain other version information about Perl and the operating system on which you are running by using the Win32 module. I use the following script to give me an idea of the operating system on which I am running:

```
use strict;
use Config;

print "Current OS Platform: $^O\n";
print "Interpreter built on: $Config{'archname'}\n";

print "Core Perl Version: $]\n";

use Win32;

print "Processor: ",Win32::GetChipName,"\n";
```

```
my ($sp, $major, $minor, $build, $id) = Win32::GetOSVersion;
print "Windows 95/98\n" if Win32::IsWin95;
print "Windows NT\n" if Win32::IsWinNT;
print "OS Version: $major.$minor, Build $build\n";
print "Build Number: ",Win32::BuildNumber,"\n";
print "Service Pack: $sp\n";
```

This outputs the following on a Windows 98 machine:

```
C:\> perl 01.pl
Current OS Platform: MSWin32
Interpreter built on: MSWin32-x86-object
Core Perl Version: 5.00503
Processor: 586
Windows 95/98
OS Version: 4.10, Build 67766222
Build Number: 521
Service Pack:
```

Under Windows NT, with the same version of Perl installed, we get a slightly different story:

```
C:\> perl 01.pl
Current OS Platform: MSWin32
Interpreter built on: MSWin32-x86-object
Core Perl Version: 5.00503
Processor: 586
Windows NT
OS Version: 4.0, Build 1381
Build Number: 521
Service Pack: Service Pack 5
```

Note here that the OS version includes not only the Windows NT version number but also the service pack number.

Obviously, there is nothing to stop you from continuing to use the `require` format to specify a required version number, but it will only apply to the core version, not the ActiveState build number. You will need to write a separate function to check this information and `die` accordingly.

Function Support

As mentioned, Perl is a Unix-derived programming language, and as such, many of the functions are Unix-specific. As a general rule, these functions fall into one of the following groups:

■ Functions that involve looking up details in one of the Unix files contained in /*etc*. These are

```
endgrent            getprotobynumber
endhostend          getprotoent
endnetent           getpwent
endprotoent         getpwnam
endpwent            getpwuid
endservent          getservent
getgrent            getservbyport
getgrgid            setgrent
getgrnam            sethostent
gethostent          setnetent
getlogin            setpgrp
getnetbyaddr        setprotoent
getnetbyname        setpwent
getnetent           setservent
```

■ Functions that adjust elements of a file system. Although all the basic file interfacing options will work, those that don't work are

```
chown       readlink
chroott     symlink
fcntl link  umask
```

■ Access to the internals of the Unix operating system, or Unix process-specific data:

```
dump          setpgrp
getpgrp       setpriority
getppid       syscall
getpriority
```

■ Unix-specific utility functions are also generally unimplemented, in particular, the IPC systems such as shm*, msg*, and sem*.

■ The socketpair function does not work because it is not natively supported under Windows, but there is nothing to stop you from creating your own pairs of sockets manually.

You will find details in the remaining chapters of this book about how to use functions supplied in the Win32 modules to act as substitutes for many of these functions.

The Base Win32 Library

Although the Win32 library consists of many different application-specific modules, the library also includes a generic base module, called simply `Win32`. This module, supplied with ActivePerl, includes a number of functions that can help to provide additional information within the Win32 environment. Most of the functions supplement or provide direct replacements for functions in the core language.

As a general rule for all of the modules within the Win32 library, none of them export any symbols by default into the current package space. This means that you need to use the fully qualified names for functions and variables. For example, to call the `FormatMessage` function, you must use

```
Win32::FormatMessage();
```

and not

```
FormatMessage();
```

Details on the functions supplied by default in the `Win32` module are shown in the following sections.

Win32::GetLastError

The `GetLastError` function is a vital part of the overall Win32 interface. It provides the extended error information returned by the Win32 subsystem when an error occurs. The value returned is a number, and it should be extracted as soon as an error occurs. You should be using this to augment the errors normally placed into the `$!` variable, which will normally only contain details on the library errors, not the underlying OS errors.

Win32::FormatMessage

In order to convert the error number returned by the `Win32::GetLastError` function into a message string, you must use the `FormatMessage` function:

```
Win32::FormatMessage ERRORCODE
```

I generally use the functions `Win32::GetLastError` and `Win32::FormatMessage` as part of a custom subroutine that acts as an alternative to the normal `$!` and `die` handling supported by Perl:

```
sub win32die
{
    my $error=Win32::GetLastError();
    if ($error ne 0)
    {
        die $_[0] . Win32::FormatMessage($error);
    }
    return 1;
}
```

You can then call this directly within a function as a wrapper around the whole Win32 error-reporting process:

```
Win32::Spawn('dir') || win32die;
```

This is more practical than doing the testing manually, but be careful about using the functions without testing the return values from functions in the first place. Also, always make sure you call the Win32::GetLastError function immediately after an error occurs; otherwise, you may get an unexpected return value.

You can see the different types of errors generated using the following script:

```
use Win32;

unless(open(FILE,"NOTINHERE"))
{
    my $perlerror = $!;
    my $winerror = Win32::GetLastError;

    print "Perl Error: $!\n";
    print "Perl Extended OS Error:$^E\n";
    print "Win32 Error Number: $winerror\n";
    print "Win32 Error String: ",Win32::FormatMessage($winerror),"\n";
}
```

If you run the following script, you get a list of the different error messages:

```
C:\>perl 03.pl
Perl Error: No such file or directory
Perl Extended OS Error:The system cannot find the file specified
Win32 Error Number: 2
Win32 Error String: The system cannot find the file specified.
```

Note how the special $^E variable is actually populated with the information normally only available with Win32::FormatMessage. Personally, I prefer to use the functions rather than using the $^E variable, but it's up to you which you use.

Win32::LoginName

This function returns the name of the owner of the current Perl interpreter. Under Windows 95/98, this is either the name registered within the "multiple users" system within the OS or that registered with an NT domain. Under NT, it's either the local user name or the registered name from a domain. Use the Win32::DomainName module to determine the domain name to which the user is currently connected.

Win32::NodeName

This function returns the node name of the current machine. Note that this is not the same as the Internet host name.

Win32::DomainName

This function returns the name of the domain in which the current Win32:LoginName is currently connected. Under Windows 95/98, if the user is not connected to a domain, then it returns an empty string. Under Windows NT, the function returns the name of the node if the user is not connected to a domain. The following script will output the basic information about a user:

```
use Win32;

print "Login: ",Win32::LoginName(),"\n";
print "Node: ",Win32::NodeName(),"\n";
print "Domain: ",Win32::DomainName(),"\n";
```

On a standalone Windows 98 machine, this outputs the following:

```
C:\> perl 04.pl
Login: MC
Node: MC
Domain:
```

On a Windows NT Workstation not connected to a domain, this outputs

```
C:\> perl 04.pl
Login: MC
Node: INCONTINENT
Domain: INCONTINENT
```

And on an NT Workstation connected to a local domain, it outputs

```
C:\> perl 04.pl
Login: MC
Node: INCONTINENT
Domain: MCSLP
```

Win32::GetOSVersion

This function returns the current OS version as an array:

```
($sp, $major, $minor, $build, $id) = Win32::GetOSVersion;
```

See Table 2-2 for details of the returned information.

You can also use Win32::IsWin95 and Win32::IsWin98 to determine the main OS version.

Win32::IsWinNT

This function returns True if the machine on which the interpreter is running is using Windows NT.

Win32::IsWin95

The Win32::IsWin95 function returns True if the machine on which the interpreter is running is using Windows 95.

TABLE 2-2

Information returned by **Win32:: GetOSVersion**.

Element	Description
$sp	The service pack number for the current OS. Under Windows 95/98, this string is empty.
$major	The major version number—under Windows NT 4, this would be 4.
$minor	The minor version number.
$build	The build number for this version.
$id	Indicates the operating system type: 1 for Windows 95/98 and 2 for Windows NT.

Win32::GetChipName

The Win32::GetChipName function returns a string defining the type of the machine's processor. For example, on a Pentium machine, it returns 586; on a Digital Alpha machine, it returns alpha.

 NOTE.   *The* Win32::GetChipName *function is unreliable under Windows NT, although the function does work. It's expected to be removed in future revisions.*

Win32::GetCwd

This function returns the current working directory. You should use this in preference to the Cwd module that is part of the core Perl distribution.

Win32::SetCwd

You can set the current working directory by using the SetCwd function. This accepts a single argument—the name of the directory to which you want to change. It returns True if the change succeeded.

Win32::FsType

The Win32::FsType function returns information defining the underlying file system type for the current drive, based on the current working directory. Since different file systems have different abilities, it is sometimes useful to know the limitations of the file system before you start using it.

You can use this function in two ways, depending on the context:

```
$filetype = Win32::FsType();
($filetype, $flags, $length) = Win32::FsType();
```

The $filetype is the string referring to the file system type. This will be either FAT or FAT32 or NTFS. File systems belonging to remote network drivers are returned according to their published type. For example, a shared Windows NT directory will return NTFS, but a directory shared from an AppleShare IP server is published as FAT.

The different $flags relate to different file system abilities, while the $length parameter shows the longest filename supported by the file system. This is the longest filename rather than pathname—since a path can consist of many different individual file and directory names. Note that because the function examines the current working directory, you will need to change directories, using Win32::SetCwd or chdir to the file system you want to examine. The following script gets information for all drives from C: to Z:

```
use Win32;

foreach $drive ('C'..'Z')
{
    next unless Win32::SetCwd("$drive:\\");
    ($type,$flags,$length) = Win32::FsType();
    print "$drive: $type, $length\n";
}
```

On my Windows 98 machine, this outputs the following:

```
C:\>
C: FAT32, 255
D: CDFS, 221
E: FAT, 31
F: FAT, 31
G: FAT, 31
H: FAT, 31
I: FAT, 31
J: NTFS, 255
```

Win32::GetNextAvailableDrive

When you click on the Map Network Drive button in Windows Explorer, you are automatically presented with a probable drive letter choice. The Win32::GetNextAvailableDrive function returns the next drive letter that has not already been allocated either to a local physical drive or to a mapped network drive. In early versions this function actually returned B:, since most machines have only a floppy drive. More recent versions only look for an available drive in letters C: to Z:.

Win32::GetTickCount

This function returns an integer giving the number of milliseconds that the machine has currently been running—that is, the number of milliseconds since the last reboot. This is roughly identical to the time information returned by the `uptime` command under Unix, although it is more precise. To convert the information into a useful string, use the `localtime` function:

```
use Win32;

($secs,$mins,$hours,$days)
    = (localtime((Win32::GetTickCount()/1000)))[0,1,2,7];
print("System up for: $days days, ",
      $hours,'h, ',$mins,'m, ',$secs,"s\n");
```

The output will look something like this:

```
C:\> perl 07.pl
System up for: 0 days, 21h, 17m, 40s
```

For systems administrators, this can be useful information, since it provides an instant view of how long a machine has been running—particularly useful on servers when you want to measure their reliability. The figure is also sufficiently random so that it could be used with the `srand` function to seed the random-number generator.

Win32::Spawn

`Win32::Spawn` spawns a new process, running COMMAND, using the command line COMMANDLINE. The PID should be a reference to a scalar, which will contain the process ID of the newly created process.

```
Win32::Spawn COMMAND, COMMANDLINE, PID
```

Note that the COMMAND should only be the name or path to the command or program that you want to execute. The PATH environment variable is not searched, and you must specify the full filename, for example, `edit.exe` instead of `edit`.

The COMMANDLINE should contain the actual command that you would type into a command shell in order, for example, `edit myfile.txt`.

The specified program is run concurrently. The process does not block while the program is running, so it is essentially the same as using the `start` command within a command shell under Windows NT.

Win32::InitiateSystemShutdown

On a Windows 95/98 machine, any logged in user can start a system shutdown. Under Windows NT, you must have been granted the necessary permissions to allow you to shut down the machine. In either case, you can shut down a machine using the `Win32::InitiateSystem Shutdown` function:

```
Win32::InitiateSystemShutdown(MACHINE, MESSAGE, COUNT, FORCE, REBOOT)
```

The descriptions of the different arguments are shown in Table 2-3.

The `Win32::InitiateSystemShutdown` function returns `True` if the shutdown request was successful, or `False` (zero) if the request failed. You can abort a shutdown during the countdown period by calling `Win32::AbortSystemShutdown`.

TABLE 2-3

Arguments when shutting a machine down.

Argument	Description
MACHINE	The name of the machine to shut down. On Windows NT machines with an account with suitable privileges, this allows you to remotely shut the machine down without having to physically sit at the machine to do it. The name should be specified either in UNC format, as the machine's name, or an empty string if you want to shut down the local machine.
MESSAGE	The message string to be displayed to the user when the system shutdown starts.
COUNT	The number of seconds to delay before the shutdown actually takes place. The dialog displaying the MESSAGE also displays a countdown, starting at COUNT, showing the amount of time remaining. If zero, the shutdown will start immediately and no message will be displayed.
FORCE	If true, the shutdown doesn't ask any of the applications politely to save their documents; instead, the applications are just killed.
REBOOT	If true, the machine will reboot instead of shutting down.

Win32::AbortSystemShutdown

`Win32::AbortSystemShutdown` aborts a shutdown during the count-down period. It accepts a single argument, the name of the machine to be aborted:

```
Win32::AbortSystemShutdown(MACHINE)
```

The function will return `True` if the abort request is successful—irrespective of whether the machine was asked to shut down by the `Win32::InitiateSystemShutdown` function. Otherwise, the function returns `False` (zero).

Using Function Overloading

When you want to support a particular function or operation within a script that is not normally supported under Windows, you may want to consider developing a special module that provides a personal interface to the built-in Perl functions. Another alternative is to provide your own set of "built-in" functions and then overload the real built-in functions with your own versions. You can do this through the use of a `BEGIN` block in your script and the `use subs` pragma.

The following code fragment shows the method required to determine which functions are supported:

```
BEGIN
{
    eval { chown() };
    push @functions,'chown' if $@;
}

use subs @functions;
use MyBuiltin @functions;

chown();
```

Note that the actual test must be done within the `BEGIN` block so that it is executed at compile time rather than runtime; then by the time compilation reaches the `use subs` pragma, the contents of `@functions` has already been populated with the required information.

The definition for `chown`, either for performing the action directly or by acting as an alias to the Win32 version of the function, should then be placed into the MyBuiltin package, which is defined just like any other:

```
package MyBuiltin;

require Exporter;
@ISA = qw/Exporter/;
@EXPORT = ();
@EXPORT_OK = qw/chown/;

sub chown
{
    print "Changed mode!";
    return 1;
}
```

The contents of @EXPORT should be empty, since you don't want to import anything as standard. The value of @EXPORT_OK contains the list of built-in functions that you want to support and overload if necessary. Thus, when you call MyBuiltin with a list of unsupported built-in functions, you import your own list of replacements. In this example, a simple print statement is used to show that the overloading is working. In a real case, you'll probably want to put some real functionality into the functions you want to overload.

If you are testing a lot of functions, you will need to use loops and references to test the functions you want to overload:

```
BEGIN
{
    @subtest = qw/chown exec/;
    foreach $function (@subtest)
    {
        eval { &$function };
        push @functions,$function if $@;
    }
}
```

It's not possible in this to optimize the loop by placing the foreach loop within the eval block, since you're using each eval invocation to test the existence of each function. Although this is a performance hit, the overall process aids in compatibility.

2

Programming with the Win32 Library

## CHAPTER 3

Database Access

Virtually all modern applications use some form of database to store information. Everything from the lowly utility through to the full-blown accounting system requires some access to some form of data storage. For many applications, even storing the preferences becomes a minor database exercise. Of course, there are also those situations where you need to process information that has been extracted from a database or that is generically in a database format, such as the logs and other information output by a particular application or process.

There are two main types of database—those that are textual-based and use either fixed-length fields and records or those that use variable-length information in combination with some form of field and record delimiter character. The latter types are accessed via some sort of interface, such as DBM, Oracle, and ODBC.

Within Perl, text databases are easy to use; you read lines or blocks of characters from the file and process the line or block using `split` or `pack` to extract the individual field and other information from the file. You can use text databases in places where you do not have access to a full database system or when processing information from a database that does not support a more complex format.

There are downsides to text databases: With the delimited form, you have to choose a delimiter character that will not appear and therefore not interfere with the information that you are trying to store. With fixed-length databases, you are limited by the amount of information you can store, although you can overcome the delimiter problem. With both databases, the time required to add information to the database is relatively short, but the time required to search or update the database is prohibitive for most online purposes, since you must search to a specific point and then copy or overwrite the information.

Within Win32 implementations, it is unlikely that you will want to use a text database for anything but a log report. However, you may be required to access and process information that has originated on a Unix platform, or you may be transferring a system from Unix to Windows. In both these cases, you will need to take additional precautions when using Perl to process the data.

When you are interfacing to commercial or other external database systems, there are many options available to you. The option chosen by many programmers for small amounts of immediate storage is the DBM database. This uses a key/value pairing system, and Perl provides an interface to the database by using `tie` to associate a hash with the underlying DBM structure. Since a hash also uses the same key/value structure, this makes processing a DBM database very easy. Under Windows there is only one DBM implementation—SDBM, which comes as standard with the Perl interpreter. We'll look in this chapter at the basic ways of using this type of DBM database and how we can access information stored in other DBM implementations.

In many cases, however, you will probably choose or need to use a commercial database system such as Microsoft's Access, SQL Server, FileMaker Pro, or Oracle. In these instances, it's possible to use a module that is supplied as standard with the ActivePerl distribution called ODBC, short for open database connectivity.

ODBC interfaces are now supported by most commercial database systems. The ODBC system allows you to retrieve data from information sources using SQL, or the Structured Query Language. You can use SQL to query and update databases that are traditionally accessed using SQL, such as SQL Server, Sybase, and Oracle. The ODBC systems also allow other databases, such as Access, FileMaker Pro, and FoxPro to be queried using SQL. You can even use ODBC to access information stored within less-well-used sources, such as Excel spreadsheets. In addition, ODBC will allow you to access delimited text files.

We'll be looking in this chapter at accessing information from all of these different sources, paying particular attention to how you can transfer and use data from Unix platforms when you are migrating applications.

Variable-Length (Delimited) Databases

The simplest form of database is a simple text file that uses some form of delimiter to separate individual fields in each record and to separate individual records. The normal format under Unix is to use the newline character to separate individual records and then a colon, comma, or other punctuation character to separate the individual fields.

There are no fundamental differences between accessing a text database under Windows or Unix—the I/O libraries will take care of the line termination issue, and you can continue to use the `split` and other functions to extract the data.

For example, to display the information in a database delimited with commas, you might use a script like this:

```
open(D,"<C:/DATA/USERS.DAT") || die "Can't open file, $!";
while(<D>)
{
    chomp;
    @fields = split /,/;
    print join(' ', @fields),"\n";
}
close(D) || dir "Couldn't close file, $!";
```

As an alternative, you can also use the Win32::ODBC module, which provides a Data Source driver for comma-separated files. See the section later in this chapter for details on how to use the ODBC driver to extract information.

Fixed-Length Databases

A fixed-length database uses a predefined format to describe the content type of the individual fields that go to make up each record. You can then place the data into a binary string using the pack function and extract the individual fields from the binary string using unpack.

For example, you might have a task database that is made up of the task name, composed of 40 characters, the date it is required to be completed, and the date when it was actually completed. The date values we can store as integers by converting the date and time into a numerical value. This would require a format string of A40LL, which means that a full record is 48 bytes long.

To read a record from the file, you read 48 bytes and then pass the format string and field string to the unpack command to extract the data. To write a record to the file, we need to store the field information in a suitable binary string, using pack, and merely append that string to the file. If we want to search for data in the file, then we can move to a specific record by using seek. For example, to go to the seventh record, we need to move to a point just beyond the sixth record, so we use seek to move to a point 288 bytes within the file.

All of the practical elements for doing this under Win32 are identical to the processes required under Unix, except for one point. When we open the data file, we must ensure that it is opened in binary format (using binmode) to make certain that no line termination processing is executed on the data stream. If we didn't open the file in binary mode, we run the risk of corrupting the data that we read from the file. This is because the line-termination translation could potentially retrieve one fewer character than normal from the file, making the extraction of data difficult, if not impossible, without some form of data loss or corruption.

The following first script shows how we might add information to our database:

```
my ($taskfile) = "tasks.db";
my ($taskformat) = "A40LL";

die "Usage: $0 title required-date\n" if (@ARGV<2);

($mday,$mon,$year) = split '/',pop;
$reqdate = ($year*10000)+($mon*100)+$mday;

$task = join(" ",@ARGV);

open(DATA,">$taskfile") || die "Couldn't open the task file, $!\n";
binmode(DATA);

print DATA pack($taskformat,$task,$reqdate,0);

close(DATA);
```

Note that we convert the date into a numerical format. Aside from making it shorter to store, from the point of view of using a 4-byte integer instead of an 8-byte string, it has other advantages. First of all, it's platform-independent. We can take the data file produced and use it on a Mac or Unix implementation without changing anything—we're not relying on the epoch to store the date value. Second, it's easier to sort a date in this format; we'll see why in the next script.

You can now add tasks to the database:

```
C:\> perl 02.pl Write Book 30/11/1999
```

To report the information, we need to read in each record and decode the information back into a displayable format. We do that with a combination of unpack to extract the fields and regular expressions to put the date back into a normal format. You can see this in the following script:

```
use Getopt::Std;

my $taskfile   = "tasks.db";
my $taskformat = "A40LL";
my $tasklength = length(pack($taskformat,));
my $ref=0;
my %lref;
use vars qw /$opt_d $opt_r $opt_c/;

getopts('drc');

open(DATA,"<$taskfile") || die "Couldn't open the task file, $!\n";
```

```perl
binmode(DATA);

while(read(DATA,$_,$tasklength))
{
    my ($title,$reqdate,$compdate) = unpack($taskformat,$_);
    $lref{$ref} = $title;
    $lref{$ref} = "$reqdate" if ($opt_r);
    $lref{$ref} = "$compdate" if ($opt_c);
    $lref{$ref}{title} = $title;
    $lref{$ref}{reqdate} = $reqdate;
    $lref{$ref}{compdate} = $compdate;
    $ref++;
}

close(DATA);

printf("%-40s  %-10s  %-10s\n","Title","Req. Date","Comp. Date");

foreach my $key (sort_values(\%lref))
{
    $lref{$key}{reqdate} =~ s#(....)(..)(..)#$3/$2/$1#;
    if ($lref{$key}{compdate}>0)
    {
        next if ($opt_d);
        $lref{$key}{compdate} =~ s#(....)(..)(..)#$3/$2/$1#;
    }
    else
    {
        $lref{$key}{compdate}="";
    }
    printf("%-40s  %10s  %10s\n",
            $lref{$key}{title},
            $lref{$key}{reqdate},
            $lref{$key}{compdate});
}

sub sort_values
{
    my $lref = shift;

    if ($opt_r)
    {
        sort {$lref{$a}{reqdate} <=> $lref{$b}{reqdate}} keys %$lref;
    }
    elsif ($opt_c)
    {
        sort {$lref{$a}{compdate} <=> $lref{$b}{compdate}} eys %$lref;
    }
    else
    {
        sort {$lref{$a}{title} cmp $lref{$b}{title}} keys %$lref;
    }
}
```

Note in the main while loop of the script that we use read to place
each record byte string into the $_ special variable, and then use unpack
to split it into its constituent parts.

To aid in the display of the information, we put the records and fields into a hash of hashes. We can then sort the individual records into the individual fields. You can now see the reason for the date conversion. By translating into a number, you can perform a simple comparison test; later dates will have larger numbers and can therefore be sorted just like any other number.

To just display a simple list, just execute the script (02.pl):

```
C:\> perl 02.pl
Title                           Req. Date    Comp. Date
Finish Article                  11/11/1999
Shop for Christmas              17/12/1999
Write Book                      30/11/1999
```

Or, to get a list sorted by the required date, use the -r option:

```
C:\> perl 02.pl -r
Title                           Req. Date    Comp. Date
Finish Article                  11/11/1999
Write Book                      30/11/1999
Shop for Christmas              17/12/1999
```

You can see how the list is now sorted by the required date.

Updating a fixed-length database requires searching through the database for the correct record and then moving to the exact point within the file where you want to overwrite the data. For our Task Manager, we key against the task title, making comparisons and remembering our current location within the file until we find a match. Then we move back and write out an updated version of the record.

The following script shows the method for updating the task database and setting the "completed date" to the desired value.

```
use Fcntl;

my ($taskfile) = "tasks.db";
my ($taskformat) = "A40LL";
my $tasklength = length(pack($taskformat,));
my $lastseek = 0;

die "Usage: modtask.pl title completed-date\n" if (@ARGV<2);

($mday,$mon,$year) = split '/',pop;
$compdate = ($year*10000)+($mon*100)+$mday;

$matchtask = join(' ',@ARGV);

open(DATA,"+<$taskfile") || die "Couldn't open the task file, $!\n";
binmode(DATA);

while(read(DATA,$_,$tasklength))
```

```
{
    ($title,$reqdate,$olddate) = unpack($taskformat,$_);
    last if (($title eq $matchtask) && ($olddate eq 0));
    $lastseek=tell(DATA);
}

if ($lastseek >= (-s $taskfile))
{
    die "Couldn't find the task specified\n";
}
seek(DATA,$lastseek,SEEK_SET);

print DATA pack($taskformat,$title,$reqdate,$compdate);

close(DATA) || die "Couldn't close the database\n";
```

For example, to set the completion date on the "Finish Article" task:

```
C:\> perl 03.pl Finish Article 27/11/1999
```

Looking at the database contents again using the `02.pl` script:

```
Title                           Req. Date   Comp. Date
Finish Article                  11/11/1999  27/11/1999
Shop for Christmas              17/12/1999
Write Book                      30/11/1999
```

In all cases, the only major differences between these scripts and the Unix versions (which are featured in my *Perl: The Complete Reference* title) is the inclusion of the `binmode` function, required to ensure that Perl doesn't inadvertently start translating the line termination sequences. This would only really matter if you were storing information that might contain line termination characters, but it's good practice to enforce binary mode operation on all files that are not accessed on a line-by-line basis.

DBM

The original DBM (known as ODBM under Perl) was developed as a quick method of storing information in a direct way under Unix. The main focus behind the system was to be able to access a piece of information by name from a file with a single system call. The database system therefore uses a complex hash table that is kept in memory while the database is open. When you request a key, the DBM system looks up the data location in the hash and reads all of the data from that position in one go.

This has advantages in that the system is very fast, but it also has a number of limitations. The maximum amount of information you can store in a key/value pair is called the *bucket size*. Original implementations of DBM only supported a bucket size of 1 KB, newer implementations such as NDBM and SDBM (which comes as part of the Perl source code distribution) supported bucket sizes of up to 2 KB. Alternative implementations like GDBM (from GNU) and the Berkeley DB system support unlimited bucket sizes, while still retaining most of the single-system call functionality. Of course, as the amount of information that is stored in the database increases, the possibilities of extracting all of that information in a single system call reduce quite considerably.

Under Unix, the basic choices available to you are ODBM, NDBM, and SDBM. If you have the GNU and Berkeley DB libraries installed, then you have access to all the DBM suites that Perl supports within the default distribution. You can see the relative merits of the different DBM implementations in Table 3-1.

Unfortunately, the Win32 platform supports only the SDBM system in the standard implementation, and then only because the SDBM database was written exclusively for use with Perl. This presents us with something of a limitation if you choose to use DBM as your database system. Note that the ActivePerl installation supports a maximum bucket size of only 1024 bytes—you can change this figure only if you are build-

TABLE 3-1

Available Unix DBM implementations.

Implementation	DBM/ ODBM	NDBM	SDBM	GDBM	Berkeley DB
Module	ODBM_File	NDBM_File	SDBM_File	GDBM_File	DB_File
Bucket limit	1–2 KB	1–4 KB	1 KB (none)	None	None
Disk usage	Varies	Varies	Small	Big	Big
Speed	Slow	Slow	Slow	OK	Fast
Data files distributable	No	No	Yes	Yes	Yes
Byte-order independent	No	No	No	No	Yes
User defined sort order	No	No	No	No	Yes
Wildcard lookups	No	No	No	No	Yes

ing and compiling the core distribution. You cannot modify the bucket size of the SDBM system as supplied with the ActivePerl distribution.

In most cases, this shouldn't be too much of a problem, since you can use an ODBC database in those situations where a DBM database might be required. In fact, for most production-level systems, it's recommended that you rebuild your databases using an ODBC data container of some kind; DBM was never meant for high volumes of data; and certainly not for e-commerce. Probably most significant of all, DBM was never really designed for use on the Win32 platform. The SDBM implementation that is supported is only provided for compatibility purposes.

Transferring DBM Databases

One of the fundamental problems with the DBM format is that the data files are very wasteful—it is highly likely that there will be holes in the data file that are simply empty and unused. These exist because of the way information is placed into the blocks that make up the database. An individual bucket (key/value combination) will be placed into as small a number of blocks (normally the same size as the bucket size) as possible. However, if you only store a bucket of 2 bytes, the remaining 1022 bytes will be allocated but never used. This means that a DBM database may, for example, appear to be 48 KB in size on disk, but in actuality it only contains 8 KB of valid data, the remaining 40 KB is wasted, empty space.

Although this does not normally cause a problem, when transferring the database from one platform to another, the "empty" portions of the database can fool many transfer processes to simply ignore the empty bytes. Thus, when you transfer our sample 48 KB DBM file, you end up with a file that is in fact only 9.6 KB long and therefore completely unreadable. The SDBM implementation gets around this problem by using a different "fill" character to ensure that the transfer process transfers all of the data, not just what it thinks is valid. Since you'll need to transfer your data to an SDBM database in order for it to be accessible on the Windows platform, we can probably ignore this particular aspect of the compatibility process.

Further, like all DBM-based implementations, the SDBM implementation uses two files, the DIR and the PAG files. The file with the *.dir* suffix is a directory table containing a bit-based representation of the buckets and their index location. The second file contains all the data for the database and has *.pag* as its suffix.

When you transfer a database, you must transfer both these files. I've found the best method to use is to create an archive using tar and gzip on the Unix host and then transfer this file, either by using the binary mode and FTP or by copying the file over a network connection. You then use WinZip to extract the archive into its two constituent parts. This ensures the file format is correct and also improves the performance for transferring large database files.

Copying Between DBM Databases

Because you cannot use most of the DBM databases directly under Windows, you must instead convert the database from its original format into SDBM format. We can do this by using tie to associate two hashes—one with the source DBM implementation and the other with SDBM. We can then copy the records from one database into the other.

The following script will convert key and value pairs from the GDBM to the SDBM format. Note that this script does not get over any size limitation between the formats—nor does it solve your transfer problems, although SDBM files are easier to transport than other DBM systems.

```
use GDBM_File;
use SDBM_File;
use Fcntl;

die "Usage:$0 old new\n" if (@ARGV<2);

my($old,$new) = @ARGV;

tie (%oldhash, 'GDBM_File', $old, O_RDONLY, 0444)
    || die "$0: Error opening source $old: $!\n";
tie (%newhash, 'SDBM_File', $new, O_CREAT|O_RDWR, 0666)
    || die "$0: Error opening dest $new: $!\n";

while(($key, $value) = each(%oldhash))
{
    $newhash{$key} = $value;
}

untie %oldhash || die "$0: Error closing old DBM file, $!\n";
untie %newhash || die"$0: Error closing new DBM file, $!\n:";
```

Note that the script uses each, rather than a simple assignation. This helps to reduce the memory requirement while copying the data, although it will be slower.

The `dbmopen` and `dbmclose` Functions

The old method for using DBM databases was to use the `dbmopen` and `dbmclose` functions to create an association between a hash and a DBM file. Although this method is currently still supported, you should really be using the `tie` discussed below. The `dbmopen` function provides a direct method for opening the database but does not adhere to the new object-oriented approach of the `tie` system. For reference purposes, the format of the `dbmopen` command is as follows:

```
dbmopen(HASH, FILE, MODE)
```

where `HASH` is the hash to which you want to make the association, `FILE` is the path to the file that you want to open (or create), and `MODE` is the octal file mode that the new database files should have. Under Win32 this last option is ignored. See Chapter 4 for information on restricting access to files within Perl under Win32.
For example, to open a DBM file called *mydata*:

```
dbmopen(%data, 'mydata', 0666) || die "Can't open DB: $!";
```

The dbmclose function then cancels the association:

```
dbmclose(%data) || die "Couldn't close file properly: $!";
```

NOTE.   Support for these two functions is expected to be removed in either the next major release or the following major release. You should really use the tie *method, which provides a more stable, practical, and extendable solution.*

Opening DBM Databases in Windows

Under both Unix and Windows, the preferred method for opening DBM databases is to use the `tie` method to associate a hash with the database file. The `tie` function associates a new object class with the specified variable. With DBM files, the association is between the file and a hash, just as with the now deprecated `dbmopen` function.

You must import the `SDBM_File` module in order to obtain the class definitions for the `tie` function. The `SDBM_File` class accepts the following arguments when opening/creating a database:

```
tie(HASH, 'SDBM_File', FILENAME, FLAGS, MODE)
```

The `HASH` is the hash to which you want the DBM database associated. The `FILENAME` is the name of the file to open or the name of the file to create if the database is new. Note that you should not specify either of the *.dir* or *.pag* extensions to the name; the `SDBM` libraries will open the appropriate file or create new ones as necessary.

The `FLAGS` is a list of constants combined using the logical OR. You can obtain the necessary constants by importing the `Fcntl` module, which defines the constants shown in Table 3-2. Note that you must specify the `O_CREAT` flag if you want to create a file. If the file does not exist and you have not specified this flag, the function will return `False`. The `MODE` is the octal mode of the new file.

For example, to create the files that make up the "mydata" database, you might call `tie` like this:

```
tie(%hash, 'SDBM_File', 'mydata', O_RDWR|O_CREAT, 0666)
    || die "Cannot open DB: $!";
```

TABLE 3-2

File access flags.

Flag	Description
O_APPEND	Appends information to the given file.
O_CREAT	Creates a new file if it doesn't already exist.
O_EXCL	Causes the open to fail if the file already exists when used with O_CREAT.
O_NDELAY	Opens the file without blocking. Reads or writes to the file will not cause the process to wait for the operation to be complete.
O_NONBLOCK	Behaves as O_NDELAY.
O_RDONLY	Opens the file read-only.
O_RDWR	Opens the file for reading and writing.
O_TRUNC	Opens the file, truncating (emptying) the file if it already exists.
O_WRONLY	Opens the file write-only.

Here's a full example that calculates the maximum bucket size for key/value pairs:

```perl
#!/bin/perl -w
use SDBM_File;
use Fcntl;
use strict;

my %hash;

tie (%hash, 'SDBM_File', 'sizetest', O_RDWR|O_CREAT, 0666)
    || die "Can't create DB: $!";

my $x;
eval {
    for($x=256;$x<=8192;$x+=16)
    {
        $hash{'TEST'} = 'x' x ($x-4);
    }
};
print "Maximum bucket size: $x\n" if $@;

untie %hash;
```

If you run this script, it will report the maximum amount of information that you can store within a key value pair:

```
$ perl 04.pl
Maximum bucket size: 1024
```

Using DBM Databases to Store Data

Once a DBM database has been associated with a hash, you can use the DBM hash just as if it was a normal internal hash variable. This means you can use the keys and formatting that you might use internally within the DBM file. The only difference is that updating the hash updates the file to which it is associated. Creating new entries, updating their values, and deleting keys from the hash will have the corresponding effect on the data file.

Storing Complex Data　The simplest model for storing information in a DBM database is identical to the model used for a Perl hash. You have a unique key of information and use that key to refer to a single piece of data. However, this is a fairly flat model if you want to store complex pieces of information in a structured format. Instead, you can use the key/value pairs to store the more traditional records used in a database system.

By using a formatted key or value, you can store the information for individual fields within a DBM file. The entire record can be stored either in multiple keys or within a single key with a structure value. For example, imagine the following simple record structure:

```
Firstname, 10 characters
Lastname, 10 characters
Email, 40 characters
```

You could use a formatted key value of the form field-id, such that a single record could be entered into the database as:

```
$db{'firstname-1'} = 'Martin';
$db{'lastname-1'} = 'Brown';
$db{'email-1'} = 'mc@mcwords.com';
```

The first name of the next person in the table would be stored in the key firstname-2, the last name in lastname-2, and so on. Although this seems like a practical method, it is a relatively complex system to implement, and it is wasteful of database keys, which will need to be processed individually.

An alternative solution is to use one of the methods described earlier for text-based databases. By using delimiters or fixed-length records, you can store an entire record within a single key/value pair. Using delimiters, the above information could be written into the database and then recovered from it using the following Perl code:

```
use Fcntl;
use SDBM_File;

tie %db, 'SDBM_File', 'Test_SDBM', O_CREAT|O_RDWR, 0644
    || die "Can't open DB File, $!";;

$db{'1'} = join(',',qw/Brown Martin mc@mcwords.com/);
$db{'2'} = join(',',qw/Foo Bar foo@foobar.com/);
$db{'3'} = join(',',qw/Bar Foo bar@barfoo.com/);

foreach $id (sort keys %db)
{
    ($lastname, $firstname, $email) = split(/,/,$db{$id});
    print "$id: lastname: $lastname\n";
    print "$id: firstname: $firstname\n";
    print "$id: email: $email\n";
}

untie %db || die "Can't close DB File, $!";
```

In this example, the database is populated using a simple numeric key, with the data added via a join using a comma as the delimiter. To print the information you've just stored, you work through the database and, using split, place the fields data into individual variables, which you then print.

As you know, however, delimited text requires very careful selection of the delimiter to ensure that the information is stored correctly. Here is the same result using pack and fixed-length records, which gets around this problem.

```
use Fcntl;
use SDBM_File;

tie %db, 'SDBM_File', 'Test_SDBM', O_CREAT|O_RDWR, 0644
    || die "Can't open DB File, $!";

$db{'email-pstr'}   = 'a10a10a30';
$db{'email-fields'} = join(',', qw/Lastname Firstname Email/);

$db{'email-1'} = pack($db{'email-pstr'},qw/Brown Martin   mc@mcwords.com/);
$db{'email-2'} = pack($db{'email-pstr'},qw/Foo Bar foo@foobar.com/);
$db{'email-3'} = pack($db{'email-pstr'},qw/Bar Foo bar@barfoo.com/);

@fieldnames = split(/,/,$db{'email-fields'});

foreach $id (sort grep(/^email-[0-9]+/,keys %db))
{
    @fields = unpack($db{'email-pstr'},$db{$id});
    for($i=0;$i<@fields;$i++)
    {
        $id =~ s/email\-//;
        print "$id: $fieldnames[$i]: $fields[$i]\n";
    }
}

untie %db || die "Can't close DB File, $!"
```

Note in this example that you also manage to keep track of the field names and sizes by recording this information into keys within the database. This makes the format of the database and its contents completely database-defined. Also note that I've used a prefix in the base keys. Although it's relatively useless here, it can be useful if you want to store multiple tables within a single database file. Each table has its own name and, in turn, its own pack string, field list, and sequence.

There is still a problem with this particular solution. It is even more wasteful of space than a flat text file using fixed-length records. This is because of the internal storage method used for DBM databases and the problems associated with fixed-length records. In this example, every record will take up at least 60 bytes. A more complex record structure will take up significantly more.

Of course, Perl allows you to do more than just use simple key/value pairs. You can build complex data structures that will enable you to model information using nested Perl variables such as hashes of hashes and arrays of hashes. Unfortunately, you cannot use normal DBM implementations to create nested hashes of hashes and hashes of arrays. If we return to our first solution, we can demonstrate this by using a hash of hashes to store the data in a more structured format:

```
use Fcntl;

use SDBM_File;

tie %db, 'SDBM_File', 'Test_SDBM', O_CREAT|O_RDWR, 0644;
    || die "Can't open DB File, $!";

$db{1} = 'Record';
$db{1}{lastname} = 'Brown';
$db{1}{firstname} = 'Martin';
$db{1}{email} = 'mc@mcwords.com';

$db{2}{lastname} = 'Foo';
$db{2}{firstname} = 'Bar';
$db{2}{email} = 'foo@foobar.com';

$db{3}{lastname} = 'Bar';
$db{3}{firstname} = 'Foo';
$db{3}{email} = 'bar@barfoo.com';
foreach (sort keys %db)
{
    foreach $field (sort keys %{$db{$_}})
    {
        print "$_: $field: $db{$_}{$field}\n";
    }
}
untie %db || die "Can't close DB File, $!"
```

Within the confines of the script, this database will work, since the internal hash structures used to store the information are still held in memory. The information written to disk, however, is useless. The standard DBM implementations don't know how to translate the references contained within the internal hash structure into the keys and values used in the DBM file.

However, the MLDBM module by Gurusamy Sarathay (available from CPAN) uses existing DBM modules and the Data::Dumper module to convert the complex references into a simple format that can be stored within an ordinary hash file. It uses the same basic idea, using the tie function to associate a hash with hash file—the MLDBM object handles all of the complexity for you:

```
use SDBM_File;
use MLDBM qw(SDBM_File);
use Fcntl;
tie (%db, 'MLDBM', 'Test_MLDBM', O_CREAT|O_RDWR, 0644) || die $!;
```

This overcomes all the previous problems. The data is stored in a structured format, which can be accessed simply by using standard hash techniques. Furthermore, the storage space used for this system is significantly lower than the fixed-length database example shown earlier. The storage space is still slightly higher than the delimited system due to the use of a secondary-level key, but it overcomes the problem of choosing a suitable delimiter.

Relational Databases

The *relational* element of a relational database that most people think of is actually the automatic lookup of information. When you report from a database that is composed of many tables, you can choose to print out the "merged" information from all of the linked tables in order to produce the desired set of results. The clever bit is the linking between the individual tables, and this is something that is actually possible to do manually using any database system—text, DBM, or otherwise. With DBM, you have the advantage over text databases of convenient random access, which is the only practical way of achieving a "flat" relational system.

You can model relational data in any database system. The only requirement for using it is that you are able to access all of the tables simultaneously. The actual method of linking between the tables can be done automatically or manually. With the `tie` interface, you can have as many physical DBM databases open at any one time as you like (operating system limits permitting). Through the use of the principles you saw in the previous section, there is no reason why you couldn't actually model the information in a single database with structured key/value pairs.

The most critical part of the development of a relational system is the modeling of the data. Once you have decided on the format of the information and how it is going to be linked, you also need to consider how the links will work. Let's look briefly at a relational system for storing multiple contact information for multiple people using a DBM database. The list below shows the information we need to store, extracted from a raw text file.

The first list (and therefore table) is the list of contact names. This has three fields: first name, last name, and a list of record numbers for the second table, numbers. The numbers table has two fields: the number type and the number itself. "Number" can mean pager, phone, fax, mobile, e-mail, and so on.

The first table might be populated like this:

```
$db{'contact-1'} = "Martin;Brown;1,3,4";
$db{'contact-2'} = "Bob;Smith;2,5";
```

The key is made up of the table name and a unique ID within that table. The information is stored using delimited text fields in the value portion of the key/value pair. Note that semicolons separate the individual fields, but commas separate the link data in the third field.

The numbers table could be populated with the following information:

```
$db{'numbers-1'} = "Email;mc@mcwords.com";
$db{'numbers-2'} = "Email;bsmith@foobar.com";
$db{'numbers-3'} = "Fax;01234 456789";
$db{'numbers-4'} = "Phone;09876 543210";
$db{'numbers-5'} = "Mobile;0789 123456";
```

To access the complete contact information for Martin Brown, you need to access record number 1 of the contact table and then access the related information listed in field 3 of that record. In this case this is records 1, 3, and 4 from the numbers table. To dump the information from the database in a formatted formation, you might use a script like this:

```
use Fcntl;
use SDBM_File;

tie %db, 'SDBM_File', 'Test_Rel', O_CREAT|O_RDWR, 0644
    || die "Can't open DB File, $!";;

foreach $id (sort grep(/^contact-[0-9]+/,keys %db))
{
    ($lastname, $firstname, $relations) = split(/;/,$db{$id});
    print "$firstname $lastname\n";
    foreach $subid (sort split(/,/,$relations))
    {
        ($type,$num) = $db{"numbers-$subid"}
            if (exists($db{"numbers-$subid"}));
        print "    $type: $num\n";
    }
}

untie %db || die "Can't close DB File, $!";
```

The method is basically very similar to the tricks you saw in the previous section for modeling complex data structures within a DBM database. When run on the database above, it produces the following:

```
Brown Martin
    Email: mc@mcwords.com
    Fax: 01234 456789
    Phone: 09876 543210
Smith Bob
    Email: bsmith@foobar.com
    Mobile: 0789 123456
```

If you want to use some of the earlier techniques for including information in the database about the database, you can even begin to drive the links using formatted structures. I've developed a simple relational database system originally designed for complex contact management, using this type of relational system. It needed to be ultimately portable to a variety of platforms, and the client wanted to keep away from proprietary database systems.

Before that, I used a simple NDBM database within Perl 4 (before the tie function) to develop a relational system for configuring Hewlett-Packard Unix workstations and servers online. The system has since been removed from the website, so contact me (see the preface) if you want more information on this system.

DBM Limitations

As we've already seen, you must be careful when using DBM databases to store complex structures. A DBM database can only store data at the first hash level. Nested hashes of arrays and hashes of hashes cannot be stored directly within a DBM database, but we can get by with the MLDBM module. The limitations of the default SDBM implementation mean that it's unlikely that you will be able to store any useful amount of data using this system, but it may enable you to fill a temporary gap until you migrate to a more robust Win32-based database system.

If you are converting data from a nested DBM structure hosted on a Unix platform, then you will need to write a script to extract the data from its source format into the different tables you will be using on the host system, and then either import the data using the host application (Access, FileMaker, etc.), or you can use a Perl script with the Win32::ODBC module to import the data directly.

The ODBC Database Interface

One of the fundamental problems with most database systems is that they all have different interfaces and different methods for executing queries, obtaining information, and updating the database. When using a single database within a project, this is often not a problem, but in these modern times, things are slightly more complex. It is relatively common to use more than one data source during a project's development, and even more common is the migration from one database platform to another.

If you had previously designed your database to use Oracle for data storage, then moving to SQL Server would mean completely rewriting a lot of your code. No matter how hard you had tried to isolate your data access from the top level of your application, there would be at least some level of rewrite.

Perl has always been able to support the different database platforms, either using individual database interfaces or through the use of a unified interface such as DBI, short for Database Interface. The DBI toolkit provides access to a variety of database systems using DBD's database drivers. Drivers exist for connecting to most commercial systems such as SQL Server, Sybase, Oracle, and to free databases such as MySQL. There are even drivers for using CSV files and accessing the data using normal SQL queries.

While the DBI module provides one solution to the data access problem, there is a much better overall solution to accessing databases hosted on Win32 platforms. ODBC is a database interface designed and developed by a consortium of database organizations and commercial developers. These include the X/Open SQL Access Group, ISO (International Organization for Standardization), ANSI (American National Standards Institute), Oracle, IBM, Sybase, and many others. Although the technology is primarily seen as a Microsoft product, they were just one of the first companies to take on the idea and integrate both into their operating system and their database products.

ODBC Overview

ODBC is a system that allows database software companies to produce libraries that support access to their databases through the ODBC service. ODBC provides a consistent and simple interface to any database system that has supplied a suitable ODBC driver. At all times, however, it is important to remember that ODBC is only an interface that provides a method for an application to access a database in a uniform way. ODBC is not a language, application, or utility—merely an interface and a set of standards.

Figure 3-1

The ODBC system overview.

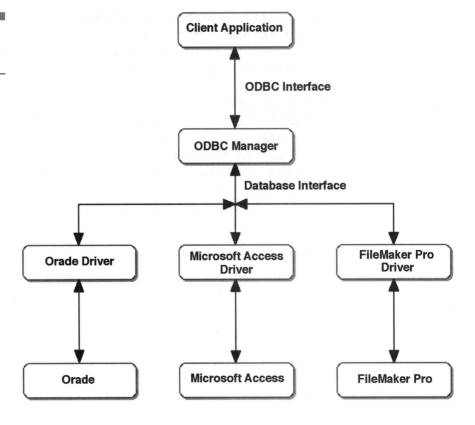

When a program wants to use an ODBC database, the application talks to the ODBC Manager. On Windows, the ODBC Manager is a DLL (dynamic link library) that decides how to service the request of the application. However, the ODBC Manager does not provide any actual functionality, other than to act as an interface or pipe between the user's application and the database system that he or she has requested to use. The general overview of the system can be seen in Figure 3-1.

Once you have connected to a database, you need to be able to communicate your requests to the database system to access and edit information. The ODBC system would not be truly open unless this particular aspect had also been standardized. The ODBC standard uses SQL to perform queries and update and add records. The ODBC system handles the translation between the SQL statements and the underlying database system, using the ODBC driver supplied by the database developer. For example, the FileMaker Pro database does not normally support

SQL queries, but it does supply an SQL interface to the FileMaker database format. We'll return to the specifics of making queries shortly.

Database Tiers

The ODBC system works on three basic models, based on the number of tiers, or steps, between the ODBC Manager and the actual database system. Theoretically, you could have as many tiers between the ODBC Manager and the database as you like, but in practice there are really only three tiers, numbered one, two, and three.

In the one-tier model, the application talks to the ODBC Manager, and it is the ODBC Manager that opens the database using the ODBC driver installed by the database application. This removes the requirement for the database application, since the ODBC Manager does all of the work for which an application would normally be required. The one-tier model is most often used with database applications that are essentially single-user or accessed on the local machines, such as Excel and Access.

With the two-tier model, the ODBC Manager talks to one of the supplied drivers, which in turn talks to a database application. This model is the one used by applications that want to talk to databases on remote systems. Databases that support a network-based client/server model such as SQL Server and Oracle would operate using the two-tier model in most networks, although it's also possible that an Oracle database might be accessed at tier one.

When you want to access a remote database using some form of gateway, then you use the three-tier model. The application talks to the ODBC Manager, which in turn talks to another process, which then talks to the database source. The eventual source can be any database—although normally a tier-three-level access would be to a database that doesn't ordinarily support the ODBC interface.

Setting Up an ODBC Database

In order to access a database using ODBC, you must set up the database within the ODBC Manager. The database type, the file location, and other metadata regarding the database is placed into a single ODBC structure, called a Data Source Name, or DSN. The DSN defines all of the information required to open a database using the ODBC interface. Beyond the name or location of the data file or database connection, the DSN can also include other information such as the login name and password and configuration data about the threads and performance aspect of using the database.

Each DSN is unique—it provides a simple name by which you can access a given database. The name is merely a reference point, so it's perfectly possible to have a DSN that points to an Excel database, and then is later modified to point to an Access database. You can continue to use the same DSN (although you will need to change the ODBC driver), and because access to the database is via SQL, there is no need to modify the commands and expressions you use to extract data from the database. You can therefore develop an application on a platform without SQL Server, safe in the knowledge that when installed on an SQL Server machine, the application will work with only trivial modifications to the SQL statements.

By using a DSN as the identifier in this manner, the ODBC system completely separates the physical process of connecting to a database from the complexities of supplying queries and processing results, and instead resolves the issue down to a simple one of expressions. You supply SQL expressions to the DSN connection and let ODBC handle all of the complexity.

You set up DSNs using the ODBC Data Sources control panel, as seen in Figure 3-2.

User DSNs are user databases that you want to have access to via the ODBC system. Generally, a User DSN fits into the one-tier model. Two- and three-tier model databases are usually configured as System DSNs, since they require additional configuration on the host that controls the database. There are a number of generic DSNs available, for example, with Microsoft Office you get drivers for Excel, Access, FoxPro, and CSV files.

To add a new DSN, click on the Add button. This presents you with a list of the ODBC drivers supported on the current machine. You can see a sample list in Figure 3-3.

Let's create a new DSN, called "Acronym," that will provide us with connectivity to a Microsoft Access database on the desktop. Figure 3-4 shows the configuration window for a new DSN.

The Name field is the name you want to use for the DSN, and the Description is used as a reference point. We'll see how you can obtain this information when we look at the `Win32::ODBC` module later in this chapter. The buttons in the middle of the window allow you to select, create, repair, or compact the database. Note that the exact list of options listed here depends on the database driver you are using. For a database

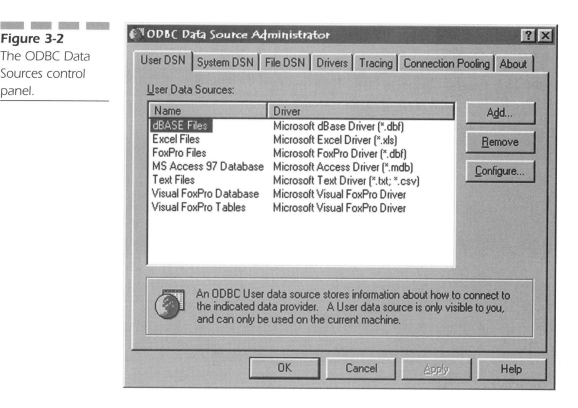

Figure 3-2
The ODBC Data Sources control panel.

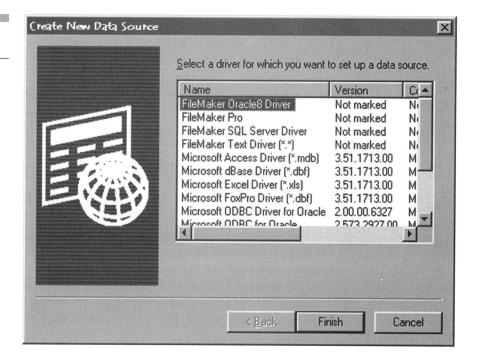

Figure 3-3
ODBC drivers.

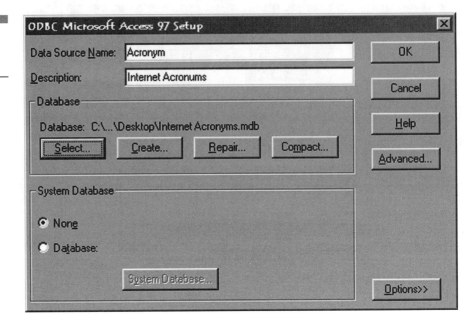

that can be accessed via a file such as FileMaker Pro, you'll get a similar interface that allows you to select the name of the FileMaker Pro data file to be opened.

For Excel spreadsheets you are offered a simple selection interface to enable you to choose the Excel file and worksheet. For a connection to an SQL Server database, you are given a completely different screen that requests the server name or IP address information. In this instance, the database name is less important, since once you have connectivity to the SQL Server host, you can access the different tables provided by the server—if you have suitable permissions.

Note that however you make the database selection, it does not affect the name of the DSN. You could modify the DSN from Excel to Access to Oracle using the exact same DSN.

For our Access database, the buttons provide a similar set of features to that available within the Tools menu of the Access application. The Select button gives you a simple file browser dialog box so you can select the location of the existing database file you want to use. The Create button provides a similar dialog, only now you can create a new, empty database file to store information. Note that this new file will be empty and without any tables or other information. Since the SQL language allows you to create new tables, this option means that you will need to create the tables pragmatically.

The Repair and Compact options will repair an Access database if it has been corrupted or compact it to save space. The act of compaction permanently deletes records from the data file, since merely deleting a record from the database only marks the record for deletion—the information is not actually deleted from the file until it is compacted. Compaction can take some time, especially on large databases, but aside from saving space, it can also improve performance.

These options are unique to the Access database and therefore unique to this particular ODBC driver. Other ODBC drivers may supply different tools to aid in the support of the ODBC interface to the database in question. Also note that these options are supported by the ODBC Manager and aren't supported via the ODBC driver or the Perl interface to the ODBC system.

Database Terminology

Before we get started looking at the specifics of accessing databases using ODBC, it's worth going over some simple terminology. Since the ODBC system is primarily used to communicate with relational information, these terms are specific to relational databases. However, most of these terms are also perfectly valid for other databases. If you know your database terminology, you might want to skip this section.

Database   The term *database* refers to a collection of information. However, this is not isolated to a single source of information. A database may consist of multiple sources of information, whether they are tables, files, or remote sources, such as audio or video streams or network connections.

Tables   A *table* is the basic storage container for information within a relational database. A table is generally used to define a single sequence of information. For example, you might store a list of customers in a table or a list of orders. Tables store information in a combination of rows and columns. Each row refers to an individual record, whereas each column defines an individual field. You can select either an entire row—and therefore a record from a table—or an entire column (field).

Record   A *record* is a collection of fields that make up a piece of information about a single person, place, object, or other entity. A record is typically a single row from a single table. However, if you take joins into account, a record can also span multiple tables. For example, an order record may consist of a single order information record and links to customer and supplier records, and a list of order lines.

Field A *field* is the smallest storage container within a database. It holds a single piece of information within a record. Fields are generally used to hold a very specific piece of information. For example, if you had a database of people's names, you might have separate fields for the first name, last name, and any initials.

Query A *query* is a statement that obtains information from a database. A query can request information either from a single table or from multiple tables. It can also request multiple records and any number of fields from the tables specified in the query. Queries can also be used to update or create information in a database and even to create new tables. The query language for ODBC databases is SQL.

Joins A *join* is where the individual rows of one or more tables are merged by an identifying value. For example, you might have two tables, one with a list of companies and the other with a list of contacts at those companies. Each company record has a unique ID, and each contact has a field that contains the ID of the company to which they belong. By joining the list of contacts to the list of companies using the company ID, you can get a list of contacts and the company name to which they belong without having to manually look up the information.

Data set A *data set* is a collection of rows and columns from a database. The data set can span multiple tables. Returning to our earlier order example, one order (and all the associated rows from the different tables) is not strictly a data set; but a data set would contain a list of order records.

Cursor A *cursor* defines your position within a database. The cursor defines a set of rows (as returned from a query), the order of those rows, and the current row within that order.

SQL Refresher

To help keep ODBC as a completely independent interface to different database systems, we need to use a standard language that could be used to query and update an ODBC database. SQL has been around for many years; it was the standard query language supported by many of the early relational systems and was actually designed and developed by IBM. Other companies, perhaps now better known for their database systems, such as Oracle and Microsoft, have adopted SQL as their main query language. SQL is now further developed by a consortium of database developers, led primarily by IBM, Microsoft, and Oracle, the leading players in the database market.

The role of the consortium is to define the SQL language standard. Although some companies have their own extensions to the SQL language, the core operations of creating, updating, and querying tables remain the same across all the different database systems.

Actually, this isn't entirely true; there are some semantics of the language that are optional on some systems. These can occasionally cause problems when you are migrating between different database systems. Often, the differences relate to how the databases have been developed over the years. As a classic example, examine these two CREATE statements:

```
CREATE table AUDIO (ID numeric (10,0) identity,
                    TITLE varchar (30) not null,
                    ARTIST varchar (30) not null)
```

And:

```
CREATE table AUDIO (ID number,
                    TITLE varchar2(30),
                    ARTIST varchar2(30))
```

The two statements create the same table, AUDIO, with a numeric ID field, and two character fields for TITLE and ARTIST. The first is valid on Microsoft SQL Server 7, while the second version works on an Oracle8 database. The differences here have to do with the supported data types. We'll look at data types later in this chapter when we look at creating new tables. We'll also look at other places where there are possible differences as we work through the different basic statements.

Also note in the examples given above that certain words are in uppercase. Although SQL is not case-sensitive, by convention, certain words are typed in uppercase so that you can identify different portions of an SQL statement more quickly. Those that are normally specified in uppercase are leading statement keywords (CREATE, INSERT, SELECT), any additional keywords for the statement (WHERE, INTO, FROM, etc.). All other elements such as the filenames are specified in title or lowercase.

SQL Statements

Although it's difficult to summarize all of the different operations available via SQL into a number of distinct statements, essentially there are four main SQL statements that can be executed on an SQL database: SELECT, INSERT, UPDATE, and DELETE. You might also want to use a fifth statement, CREATE, which creates new objects (tables, indexes) within a database file. We'll look at all five statements before moving on to the topic of executing these statements within Perl.

SELECT

When you want to extract information from the database, you use the SELECT statement. The SELECT statement retrieves a set of rows and columns from the database, returning a data set. The basic format of the SELECT statement is as follows:

```
SELECT [ALL|DISTINCT] field [, field, ...]
FROM table
[WHERE condition]
ORDER BY field [ASC|DESC] [, field [ASC|DESC]]
```

The field is the name (or names) of the fields from the table that you want to select. Because the SELECT statement allows you to specify the individual fields from the table that you want to extract, you can avoid many of the problems normally associated with extracting data from a database. Instead of manually ignoring the fields you don't want to access, you can instead only select the fields you want. You can also specify an asterisk as the field name, and this will select all fields within the table.

The optional ALL prefix tells the SQL engine to select all of the columns from the table matching the condition, and is equivalent to the * specification detailed above. The optional DISTINCT prefix forces the SELECT statement to only return a list of distinct (unique) rows from the database. This removes any duplicates from the table column, irrespective of their location in relation to each other. For example, if you wanted a list of all the acronyms in our database, you could use

```
SELECT Acronym from Acronyms
```

But the list returned contains a lot of duplicates:

```
AAMOF
AFAIC
AFAIK
...
RSN
RTFM
RTFM
RTFM
RTFM
RTFMA
...
```

To just get a list of the acronyms without any duplicates, change the SELECT query to include the DISTINCT keyword:

```
SELECT DISTINCT Acronym from Acronyms
```

which now returns

```
AAMOF
AFAIC
AFAIK
...
RSN
RTFM
RTFMA
...
```

The use of the DISTINCT keyword is especially useful in situations where you want to give a user a list of possible values, but you don't want to use a separate table to hold the information. Instead, just use DISTINCT to reduce all of the values already in the table to a list of accepted values.

You can select fields from multiple tables by specifying the table and field name in the query, separated by a single period. For example, to extract the contact name and business from the contact and company tables:

```
SELECT contact.name, company.name FROM contact, company
WHERE contact.companyid = companyid
```

The *condition* is an expression that refines the selection of rows from the table. If the WHERE keyword is not specified, then all rows from the table are selected. Most of the syntax for conditions are identical to those you will find within Perl. See Table 3-3 for a list of valid conditional operators. Note that in all cases in the table, A is normally the name of a field from one of the selected tables, and B (or C) are either constants, or further SELECT statements. For example, to select all of the addresses where the city is London, you might use the condition city = "London".

For example, to extract the acronym and expansion from our acronyms database, but only for acronyms that match RTFM, we could use the query:

```
SELECT Acronym,Expansion from Acronyms
WHERE Acronym = 'RTFM'
```

TABLE 3-3

Conditional
operators for the
SELECT
statement.

Operator	Description
A = B	A is equal to B.
A > B	A is greater than B.
A >= B	A is greater than or equal to B.
A < B	A is less than B.
A <= B	A is less than or equal to B.
A <> B	A does not equal B.
A [NOT] BETWEEN B AND C	Value of A is (is NOT) between the range of values specified by B and C.
A [NOT] LIKE B	Value of A is (is NOT) like the value of B. The value of B should be a string using the standard wildcard characters (see the discussion on wildcards below).
EXISTS (B)	Returns True for every row returned by the subquery specified by B.
A IS [NOT] NULL	Value A is (is NOT) null (empty).
A [NOT] IN (B, C, ...)	Value A is (is NOT) in the list of values specified within the parentheses.
A <operator> {ALL|ANY} (B)	Value A is compared to all or any of the records returned by the subquery B. If the ALL keyword is used, then all the returned rows must match the operator condition. If ANY is specified, then only one of the returned values must match.

You can also combine multiple statements using the AND and OR keywords to perform logical comparisons with individual conditions:

```
SELECT Acronym, Expansion from Acronyms
WHERE Acronym = 'RTFM' AND Expansion = 'Read The Factual Manual'
```

Note that you can nest logical comparisons using parentheses to group comparisons and conditions together. You can also get more complex and perform wildcard searches. Imagine you are looking for an acronym that contains the word *Fact*. You might use the following query:

```
SELECT Acronym,Expansion from Acronyms
WHERE Expansion LIKE '%Fact%'
```

The % character is a wildcard; it matches zero or more characters, and any character. Think of it as shorthand for the . * you would normally use in a regular expression.

Conversely, the underscore (_) matches any one character, thus we can look for all three letter abbreviations using this query:

```
SELECT Acronym from Acronyms WHERE Acronym LIKE '___'
```

If you want to include either of the two wildcard characters in your queries, you can escape the character with the familiar backslash:

```
SELECT Salespc from Sales WHERE Salespc LIKE '__\%'
```

Not all SQL engines support the escaping of the wildcard characters. You can work out whether the ODBC driver supports escaping and what character to use using the following script:

```
use Win32::ODBC;
$db = new Win32::ODBC("Acronym");

if ($db->GetInfo($db->SQL_LIKE_ESCAPE_CLAUSE()) eq 'Y')
{
    print "ODBC Driver supports wildcard escapes\n";
    $char = $db->GetInfo($db->SQL_SEARCH_PATTERN_ESCAPE());
    print "Escape Character is: $char\n";
}
```

See below for more information on the GetInfo function.

SQL accepts single quotes as delimiters to text strings. The single quotes tell SQL to treat anything between them as text rather than a keyword. For most queries within Perl, it's best to use the double quotes to specify the query, so that you can use single quotes within the string. For example:

```
$db->Sql("SELECT Acronym from Acronyms WHERE Acronym LIKE '___'");
```

However, be careful when using the single quote in text strings where the quote has its normal, apostrophe meaning. The following query would raise an error:

```
SELECT Acronym, Expansion from Acronyms WHERE Expansion LIKE '%I'm%'
```

The error would be raised even if you embed the query in a string within Perl, since you are still including three single quotes into the query you are supplying to the SQL engine. The trick is to use the escape character for SQL. Confusingly, the escape character for most

SQL interfaces is the single quote, so you would rewrite the above query as:

```
SELECT Acronym, Expansion from Acronyms WHERE Expansion LIKE '%I''m%'
```

Since you can't always control the query strings that you are supplying to the SQL engine, you should probably create a simple function to replace single quotes in query strings to double quotes:

```
sub SqlEscape($)
{
    $_[0] =~ s/'/''/g;
}
```

Now you can use the function inline to the queries you supply to the database:

```
$db->Sql("SELECT Acronym, Expansion from Acronyms " .
        "WHERE Expansion LIKE " . SqlEscape("%I'm%"));
```

The last thing to be aware of is that double quotes can be used to quote identifiers. For example, imagine you have created a table called Audio Tapes. If you tried to select data from this table using the following query, an error would be raised:

```
SELECT * FROM Audio Tapes
```

Instead, you need to quote the table name by using quoted identifiers. SQL accepts the double quote as a delimiter for quoted identifiers:

```
SELECT * FROM "Audio Tapes"
```

Within a Perl statement, you'll need to escape the double quotes using the backslash character:

```
$db->Sql("SELECT * FROM \"Audio Tapes\"");
```

The final part of the SELECT statement is the ORDER BY clause. This allows you to specify the order in which information will be returned, according to the normal sorting orders. You can order the entire data set by one or more fields within the tables you have selected. The default operation is to sort in ascending order (lowest to highest number, and A to Z), or you can explicitly request ascending order by using the ASC keyword. You can also sort in descending order by using the DESC keyword. For example, to sort our acronyms, we might use

```
SELECT Acronym, Expansion FROM Acronyms ORDER BY Acronym
```

JOINS   Joins are a critical part of the relational process. A *join* is where you create a logical connection between two columns in two different tables. For example, in an order processing system you might have two tables. One contains the list of orders; the other contains a list of order lines. A join between the two would enable you to obtain all of the information from a single order.

You specify a logical join using the WHERE clause to the SELECT statement, specifying an expression that links the two tables together. For example:

```
SELECT Order.Order_ID, Item.Order_ID, Item.Item_ID, Item.PLU,
Order.Total FROM Order, Item
WHERE Order.Order_ID = Item.Order_ID
```

The join can be to another table or to the same table, in the case of nested information such as staff and their supervisors. There are other types of joins such as inner and outer joins and left, right, and full outer joins. For more information on the different types of joins and the results they produce see *SQL from the Ground Up* by Mary Pyefinch (Osborne, 1999).

INSERT

The INSERT statement adds a row of information to a table. An INSERT statement has the following syntax:

```
INSERT INTO table
[(colname [, colname ] ... )]
VALUES (value [, value ] ... )
```

The table is the name of a table into which the data will be inserted, and colname and value are the fields and values that you want to insert. The order of the field names and the data must match in order for the information to be inserted correctly. The specification of field names is optional if you want to insert information into all the columns of the database.

For example, to add a new record to our acronym database, we might use the following SQL statement:

```
INSERT INTO Acronyms (Acronym, Expansion)
VALUES ('PDQ', 'Pretty Darn Quick')
```

Since we are creating entries in both columns, we can simplify the statement to

```
INSERT INTO Acronyms VALUES ('PDQ', 'Pretty Darn Quick')
```

UPDATE

The UPDATE statement updates the information for one or more rows in a table. The syntax for the UPDATE statement is as follows:

```
UPDATE table
SET column=value
[, column=value ...]
[WHERE condition]
```

The table is the name of the table in the database. The column and value are the column names and values that you want to assign to those columns. If the WHERE keyword is included, then the statement will only update those columns that match condition. The condition uses the same operators and syntax as the SELECT statement. Note that if the condition matches multiple rows, all of the rows will be updated with the given information.

For example, to modify the entry for IIRC in our Acronyms database:

```
UPDATE Acronyms SET Expansion='If I Recall Correctly'
WHERE Acronym='IIRC'
```

Note, of course, that this would update all of the IIRC entries in the table. We could supply a more specific statement to ensure we update the correct row:

```
UPDATE Acronyms SET Expansion='If I Recall Correctly'
WHERE Acronym='IIRC' AND Expansion='If I Remember Correctly'
```

DELETE

The DELETE statement is essentially identical to the SELECT statement, except that instead of returning a matching list of rows from a table, it deletes the rows from the database:

```
DELETE [FROM] table [WHERE condition]
```

The `table` is the name of the table that you want to delete rows from, and `condition` is the expression to use to find the rows to be deleted. Note that the FROM keyword is not really optional; some data sources require it, and others do not.

For example, to delete all of the IIRC entries from the Acronyms table:

```
DELETE FROM Acronyms WHERE Acronym = 'IIRC'
```

You can also delete all of the rows in a table by omitting the search condition:

```
DELETE FROM Acronyms
```

CREATE

If you are developing a database system, then there may be times when you need to build your tables pragmatically within Perl. One major benefit of creating databases in this way is that you can transport an application to another machine and have the script create the tables it needs to operate. For turnkey solutions this is invaluable—it automates the process of installing a new application, right down to the creation of the storage mechanisms required.

Not all databases support the creation of database tables. Many have some constraints or limitations on what can be done with a CREATE statement. However, for those that do, the basic format for a CREATE statement is as follows. Not all of the options are included here. If you need to use a more complex SQL statement to create your tables, use a guide such as *SQL from the Ground Up* by Mary Pyefinch (Osborne, 1999).

```
CREATE TABLE table
(field type[(size)] [NOT NULL] [index]
[, field type[(size)] [NOT NULL] [index], ...])
```

The `table` is the name of the table to be created. The `field` is the name of the field to be created in the table, and `type` and `size` define the field's type and width. The NOT NULL keywords indicate that the field must contain a value; INSERT and UPDATE statements that do not populate a NOT NULL field will fail.

The valid data types depend on the ODBC driver that you are using, but there are some generic types that should work on most systems. See Table 3-4 for a list of the base types that should be translated by most drivers into the local format.

TABLE 3-4

Generic SQL data types.

Data Type	Specification Size	Description
Char	(x)	A simple character field, with the width determined by the value of x
Integer	N/A	A field of whole numbers, positive or negative
Decimal	(x,y)	A field of decimal numbers, where x is the maximum length in digits for the number, and y is the maximum number of digits after the decimal point
Date	N/A	A date field (see "Formatting Dates" below)
Logical	N/A	A field that can have only two values, true or false

For example, to create a table that will hold the time information for a task:

```
CREATE TABLE Tasktime (TaskID Integer NOT NULL,
                       TaskName Char(40),
                       StartDate Date,
                       CompDate Date,
                       TotalHours Decimal(4.2),
                       Completed Logical)
```

NOTE. *The base ActivePerl* Win32::ODBC *module does not include the* GetTypeInfo *method that is supported by the version available directly from Dave Roth (see Appendix A). This method returns information about the supported types and the names used by the local driver in the form of a data set that can be accessed via the usual* FetchRow *and* Data *functions.*

FORMATTING DATES Although the SQL language is standardized, the format for storing specific data strings such as dates are not. Different systems record dates in different orders (d/m/y, m/d/y, y/m/d, etc.) and to different precisions (2- and 4-digit years). To get around this, the SQL language allows for an escape clause that accepts a standard format that is translated by the ODBC driver into the database's native format.

You use the escape sequence just as you would a quoted text block:

```
SELECT Date, Event FROM Event WHERE Date > {d '1999-03-26'}
```

SQL supports three such formats: one for dates, one for times, and a final one for dates and times called the *timestamp*. The formats for each are as follows:

```
{d 'yyyy-mm-dd'}              # Date
{t 'hh:mm:ss'}               # Time
{ts 'yyyy-mm-dd hh:mm:ss'} # Timestamp
```

Note that the formats are explicit, you must specify all the digits, using zeros to fill the gaps where necessary.

Using the `Win32::ODBC` Module

The `Win32::ODBC` module provides a direct method for accessing ODBC databases via an object-oriented interface. You start by creating a new `Win32::ODBC` object, then methods on that object perform the different functions, such as executing queries and extracting the data from individual rows of the returned information. The general sequence of operation is therefore

1. Connect to the database
2. Submit query
3. Extract data
4. Close database

You open a new connection like this:

```
$database = new Win32::ODBC("DSN" [, CONNECT_OPTION, ...]);
```

The DSN (data source name) should be a recognized DSN, or it can be a DSN string. The optional CONNECT_OPTION arguments set additional options to be enabled when connecting to the database. The available options are ODBC driver-specific, so you will need to use the GetConnectOption method to obtain the list of options for the specific driver. See Table 3-7 later in this chapter for a list of valid option constants.

To connect to a predefined DSN (see "Setting Up an ODBC Database" earlier in the chapter) just specify the DSN name, in quotes; for example, to connect to our Acronym DSN, you would use the following line:

```
$db = new Win32::ODBC("Acronym");
```

The string form of the DSN allows you to specify additional information when connecting to a DSN. The options are supplied as a list of *key-*

TABLE 3-5

DSN string key-words.

Keyword	Value
DSN	The name of an existing, preconfigured DSN.
FILEDSN	The path to a DSN file, which contains the list of configured options to allow you to connect to an ODBC database. A DSN file must have the extension *.DSN.*
DRIVER	The name of the driver to use for opening this connection. You can get a list of drivers by calling the `Win32::ODBC::Drivers()` function.
UID	The user ID to use to connect to the ODBC database.
PWD	The password to use to connect to the ODBC database.
SAVEFILE	The path to a file in which to save the DSN string information as a DSN file. This file can then be used with the FILEDSN option.

word=value pairs, each pair separated by a semicolon. See Table 3-5 for details of the keywords you can use.

For example, to connect to an Access database that requires a login and password:

```
$db = new Win32::ODBC("DSN=Acronym;UID=MC;PWD=Hello");
```

The new object will be undefined if the connection to the database fails. To trap errors, enclose the call in an `if` statement or check the value of the new object after you try to connect. You can use the `Win32::ODBC::Error` function to get the extended error from the ODBC interface:

```
$db = new Win32::ODBC("Acronym");
if ($db)
{
    # Do some querying
}
else
{
    die "Couldn't connect to DB:" . Win32::ODBC::Error();
}
```

The `Win32::ODBC::Error` function returns a string or a list, depending on the context in which it is called. In a list context, the function returns the error number, error text, and the connection number:

```
(ERROR_ID, ERROR_TEXT, CONN_ID) = Win32::ODBC::Error();
```

The error number and text string are unique to the database driver, so don't rely on them to be consistent across different database implementations. In a scalar context, the `Win32::ODBC::Error` function returns a string containing the above information, in the form:

```
"[ERROR_ID] [CONN_ID] [ERROR_TEXT]"
```

For convenience, you can also use the `Error` method to a `Win32::ODBC` object. You must close the connection to the database when you have finished with it. You can do this by calling the `Close` method:

```
$db->Close();
```

If you fail to close the connection, you can sometimes end up with a number of "zombie" connections. Eventually, these connections should timeout and get disconnected by the ODBC driver. For mission-critical applications where you may be supporting a number of simultaneous accesses to a database, you should ensure that you have the maximum number of free connections available. For databases such as SQL Server and Oracle, which manage the number of connections according to the license, you will need to take extra care.

You might consider adding the following END block to your script to ensure that the connection is closed wherever your script terminates:

```
END
{
    if (defined($db))
    {
        $db->Close();
    }
}
```

Because you cannot always be sure that the database connection has been opened, make sure you test the validity of the objects before you call the `Close` method.

Executing a Query   You execute a query to the current ODBC connection by using the `Sql` method:

```
$db->Sql("SELECT * from Acronyms");
```

This places the data returned by the query into the current cursor. The return value of the call is true (greater than zero) if the query failed, or if the query succeeded, the undefined value. Because of this, you'll need to take care when running the query to make certain you check the success correctly.

The best format is to use an `if` statement and then call the error handler when the function returns `True`:

```
if($db->Sql("select * from Acronyms"))
{
    die "Can't select: " . Win32::ODBC::Error();
}
```

The `Sql` method can be used to execute any SQL query; we'll look at some other examples shortly.

To extract the information returned by the query, you need to use either the `Data` or `DataHash` methods in combination with the `FetchRow` method. `FetchRow` obtains a single row of data from the returned query, but it does not actually return the data. Instead, it returns `True` if there was another row available in the query, or `False` if the end of the data set has been reached. To extract the field data from the current row of the data set, you use the `Data` function, which returns the information as a list, or the `DataHash` function, which returns the information as a hash, with the field names as the keys.

For example, you might select and print some data from a table like this:

```
$db->Sql("SELECT * from Acronyms");
while($db->FetchRow())
{
    print join(": ", $db->Data()),"\n";
}
```

The script runs the query and then works through the rows returned by the data set, printing out each field of data. The only problem with this method is that it assumes that you know the sequence of data that is returned. If you use a specific SELECT statement, the fields will be returned in order. In other words, we can modify the above script to:

```
$db->Sql("SELECT Acronym,Expansion from Acronyms");
while($db->FetchRow())
{
    ($acronym,$expansion) = $db->Data();
    print "$acronym: $expansion\n";
}
```

Alternatively, you can specify the field order in the call to the `Data` method:

```
$db->Sql("SELECT * from Acronyms");
while($db->FetchRow())
{
    ($expansion, $acronym) = $db->Data('Expansion', 'Acronym');
    print "$acronym: $expansion\n";
}
```

Because you can select the fields that you want returned, you could also perform the extraction on a field-by-field basis:

```
$db->Sql("SELECT * from Acronyms");
while($db->FetchRow())
{
    $expansion = $db->Data('Expansion');
    $acronym = $db->Data('Acronym');
    print "$acronym: $expansion\n";
}
```

The other alternative is to use the DataHash method:

```
$db->Sql("SELECT * from Acronyms");
while($db->FetchRow())
{
    %row = $db->DataHash();
    print "$row{Acronym}: $row{Expansion}\n";
}
```

The DataHash function also supports the supply of field names, although this seems pointless in most situations, since once you have the hash, you can select the field names you want to extract.

If you are not sure what field names are available, you can use the FieldNames function:

```
$db->Sql("SELECT * from Acronyms");
@fields = $db->FieldNames();
while($db->FetchRow())
{
    %row = $db->DataHash();
    foreach(@fields)
    {
        print "$_: $row{$_}\n";
    }
    print "\n";
}
```

The FetchRow function supports two optional arguments:

```
$db->FetchRow([ROW [,TYPE]]);
```

The ROW is the record number from the returned data set that you want to extract data from. Note that unless the TYPE is specified, the defini-

TABLE 3-6

Fetch row types.

Type	Description
SQL_FETCH_NEXT	Fetch the next record from the data set. The ROW argument is ignored.
SQL_FETCH_FIRST	Fetch the first record from the data set. The ROW argument is ignored.
SQL_FETCH_LAST	Fetch the last record from the data set. The ROW argument is ignored.
SQL_FETCH_PRIOR	Fetch the previous record from the data set. The ROW argument is ignored.
SQL_FETCH_ABSOLUTE	Fetch the record from the data set specified by ROW. Selection is absolute; a ROW value of 10 will return the tenth record from the data set.
SQL_FETCH_RELATIVE	Fetch the record from the data set that is ROW records away from the current record. This is the default operation.
SQL_FETCH_BOOKMARK	Fetch the record at the location defined by the last bookmark setting. The ROW value is ignored.

tion is relative; if you have already accessed five rows and specify a value of 10 for ROW, then you will actually access row 15, not row 10.

The TYPE defines the type of fetch to perform. The list of supported types is not consistent across databases: only some support a TYPE at all; others only support some functions. You specify the type using a constant; see Table 3-6 for a list of valid types.

NOTE. Constants within the Win32::ODBC *module should be specified either as functions, or as methods to open database objects and treated as functions. For example, in Table 3-6,* SQL_FETCH_BOOKMARK *should ideally be accessed as* $db->SQL_FETCH_BOOKMARK(), *or as* Win32::ODBC::SQL_FETCH_BOOKMARK().

Note that the use of arguments causes the ODBC interface to use the SQLExtendedFetch function instead of the SQLFetch function. Not all databases support the SQLExtendedFetch function, and use of the function is not always recommended. Furthermore, even if the database does support the SQLExtendedFetch function, you should not mix extended and standard calls.

Two further methods are only available with certain ODBC drivers. The RowCount method returns the number of rows within the current data set. Individual drivers may return valid information either for all SQL statements or only for individual statements such as UPDATE, INSERT, and DELETE, but not for SELECT. The method returns -1 if the function is not supported within the ODBC driver.

The MoreResults method (not supported on all drivers) returns True if there is an additional data set of information after the first (or previous) data set has been processed. Certain database engines allow you to supply multiple SELECT statements to the SQL engine at the same time, thus returning multiple data sets. MoreResults returns undef if there are no more results.

Inserting and Updating Data The processing of inserting, updating, and deleting information from an ODBC database is just a case of creating the correct SQL statement and executing the statement using the Sql method. In all cases, the Sql method continues to return a true value if the statement failed to execute properly, and you can still use the Win32::ODBC::Error function or the more convenient Error method to find out what the problem was. We'll look at some examples shortly.

Sample Script

The script below is a complete command-line interface to our simple Acronym database, using the Win32::ODBC module. The script allows you to query, add, and delete entries from the database. It also takes into account a number of tricks, including handling the duplication of acronym entries (there is more than one expansion for some acronyms) and demonstrates three of the four main query types.

The build_acrohash function queries the database, using the list of supplied acronyms as a reference point, and then builds an internal hash that can be queried more easily. It also serves as a useful reference for verifying whether an acronym exists in the table so it can be deleted. A lot of the function contents are related to the error checking to ensure that we get information from the database, but the rest is dedicated to building the hash table.

Because there may be multiple entries for the same acronym, we need to be careful about how we add acronyms to the hash. One of the main benefits of a hash is that you cannot have duplicate entries. To get around this, we check the acronym hash to see if the acronym already exists. If it does, then we add a number, enclosed in parentheses, to the hash key and repeat the process until we have a hash key that is not already in use. Building the hash this way also has advantages when we come to display the expanded acronyms.

Expanding acronyms is then just a case of extracting the data from the hash, making sure that we account for the multiple entries by using a regular expression. This is the one step that could have been eliminated with a direct database access format. We could have just used a simple loop like the following for each acronym that we wanted:

```
if ($db->Sql("SELECT * FROM Acronyms WHERE Acronym = '$acronym'"))
{
    print "$acronym: Not found in the database\n";
}
else
{
    while($db->FetchRow())
    {
        ($acronym, $expansion) = $db->Data();
        print "$acronym: $expansion\n";
    }
}
```

Instead, what we do is build a query that searches the table for each of the acronyms that we want, and then we build the hash from that list. This removes the need to import the whole database and maximizes the use of the search capabilities of the database engine, and not Perl, to get the list of acronyms we want.

The remaining functions, expand_acronym, del_acronym, and add_acronym, provide an interface for the process of selecting the acronyms from the hash and deleting or inserting new entries accordingly. Note that we haven't got a routine for updating an acronym—this is because identifying an individual acronym when there are multiple possible matches is messy within a command-line interface.

```
#!perl
use Win32::ODBC;
use strict;

unless (@ARGV)
{
    print <<EOF;
Usage: $0 ACRONYM [ACRONYM...]
or:    $0 -a ACRONYM EXPANSION
or:    $0 -d ACRONYM
EOF
    exit(1);
}

if ($ARGV[0] =~ m/^-a$/i)
{
    shift @ARGV;
```

```perl
    my $acronym = shift @ARGV;
    map { $_ = uc($_) } @ARGV;
    add_acronym($acronym,join(' ',@ARGV));
}
elsif ($ARGV[0] =~ m/^-d$/i)
{
    shift @ARGV;
    my $acronym = shift @ARGV;
    map { $_ = uc($_) } @ARGV;
    del_acronym($acronym,join(' ',@ARGV));
}
else
{
    map { $_ = uc($_) } @ARGV;
    expand_acronym(@ARGV);
}

sub del_acronym
{
    my ($acronym, $expansion) = @_;
    my ($db,$subacro);
    my %acronyms = build_acrohash($acronym);

    my @acrolist = (grep /^$acronym$|^$acronym\(\d+\)$/,
                    keys %acronyms);
    foreach $subacro (@acrolist)
    {
        if ($acronyms{$subacro} =~ /^$expansion$/i)
        {
            if ($db = new Win32::ODBC("Acronym"))
            {
                unless($db->Sql("DELETE FROM Acronyms "
                            . "WHERE Acronym='$acronym' AND "
                            . "expansion='$acronyms {$subacro}'"))
                {
                    print "Acronym '$acronym' deleted\n";
                }
                else
                {
                    die "Error: Couldn't delete data; " . $db->Error();
                }
                $db->Close();
            }
        }
    }
}

sub add_acronym
{
    my ($acronym, $expansion) = @_;
    my ($db,$query,$mode,$query);
    my %acronyms = build_acrohash($acronym);

    if ($db = new Win32::ODBC("Acronym"))
    {
        unless($db->Sql("INSERT INTO Acronyms (Acronym, "
                    . "Expansion) VALUES ('$acronym',"
                    . "'$expansion')"))
```

```perl
        {
            print "Acronym '$acronym' added\n";
        }
        else
        {
            die "Error: Couldn't insert data; " . $db->Error();
        }
        $db->Close();
    }
}

sub build_acrohash
{
    my @acrolist = @_;
    my (%acronyms,$db,$acronym,$expansion,$query);
    $query = "SELECT Acronym, expansion FROM acronyms ";

    if (@acrolist)
    {
        $acronym = shift @acrolist;
        $query .= "WHERE Acronym = '$acronym' ";
        foreach $acronym (@acrolist)
        {
            $query .= "OR Acronym = '$acronym' ";
        }
    }
    $query .= "ORDER BY acronym";

    if ($db = new Win32::ODBC("Acronym"))
    {
        unless($db->Sql($query))
        {
            while(($db->FetchRow()))
            {
                my ($acronym,$expansion) = $db->Data();
                if (exists($acronyms{$acronym}))
                {
                    my $id = 1;
                    while(exists($acronyms{"$acronym($id)"}))
                    {
                        $id++;
                    }
                    $acronyms{"$acronym($id)"} = $expansion;
                }
                else
                {
                    $acronyms{$acronym} = $expansion;
                }
            }
        }
        else
        {
            die "Error: Couldn't get any information from the DB"
                . $db->Error();
        }
    }
    else
    {
```

```
            die "Error: Couldn't open the DB; " . $db->Error();
        }

    $db->Close();
    return %acronyms;
}

sub expand_acronym
{
    my @acronyms = @_;
    my %acronyms = build_acrohash(@acronyms);
    my $acronym;
    foreach $acronym (sort @acronyms)
    {
        my @acrolist = grep(/^$acronym$|^$acronym\(\d+\)$/,
                            keys %acronyms);
        if (@acrolist)
        {
            foreach my $subacro (sort @acrolist)
            {
                print "$subacro: $acronyms{$subacro}\n";
            }
        }
        else
        {
            print "Not found: $acronym\n";
        }
    }
}
```

To get a list of expansions for a list of acronyms:

```
C:\> perl acronym.pl aamof iirc ftfm
AAMOF: As a matter of fact
IIRC: Not found
RTFM: Read The Farging Manual!
RTFM: Read The Fershlugginer Manual!
RTFM: Read The Freaking Manual!
RTFM: Read The Friggin' Manual!
RTFM: Read The Flaming Manual!
```

Adding a new entry just means supplying the acronym and the expansion on the command line:

```
C:\> perl acronym.pl -a iirc If I Remember Correctly
Acronym 'IIRC' Added
```

Because there are multiple entries, to delete an entry, we must specify both the acronym and the expansion:

```
C:\> perl acronym.pl -d RTFM Read The Freaking Manual!
```

Other SQL Features

There are some other features that may be used within SQL that are also accessible through the `Win32::ODBC` module. Many of these relate to specific processes available when processing data or when updating and inserting information into tables.

Cursors   A cursor is a simple record of the current location within a returned data set. The information within a cursor includes the rows in the data set, the number of rows in the current data set, and the current row within the data set. Because cursors store this information, they can be handy if you want to return to the same list of information a number of times. For example, a list of keywords could be accessed and used within an application. Although you could update the list manually each time you wanted to use the list, it would be much easier if you could just reread the data from the data set. Even if the data within the data set had changed, the cursor would still refer to the required list of rows within the table.

The `Win32::ODBC` module normally controls the operation of cursors automatically. When you call a method that returns a data set, such as `Sql` or `Catalog`, the module automatically drops the current cursor (if there is one) and creates a new cursor, ready to store the information about the new query.

If you want to reuse the information within a cursor, then you don't want the cursor to be dropped. You can control whether the current cursor is automatically dropped by setting the statement close type using the `SetStmtCloseType` method to an active `Win32::ODBC` object:

```
$db->SetStmtCloseType(CLOSETYPE [, CONNECTION]);
```

where `CLOSETYPE` is the type of closure to be used after each statement has been executed, and `CONNECTION` is the optional connection number. If `CONNECTION` is not specified, then the current connection is used. See Table 3-7.

For example, to ensure that cursors are not destroyed when new SQL statements are executed:

```
$db->SetStmtCloseType($db->SQL_DONT_CLOSE());
```

The function returns a string indicating the current setting. You can

TABLE 3-7

Statement close types.

Constant	Description
SQL_CLOSE	The cursor will be dropped, but the currently active SQL statement will not be destroyed.
SQL_DROP	Both the statement and cursor are destroyed.
SQL_DONT_CLOSE	Neither the cursor nor the statement will be destroyed when a new SQL statement is parsed.

also use the GetStmtCloseType method to obtain the current setting, either for the current connection or for the connection ID supplied:

```
$db->GetStmtCloseType([CONN_ID]);
```

Cursors can also be useful when you want to use the results of a search within another SELECT or UPDATE statement. For example:

```
UPDATE Acronyms SET Acronym='IIRC' WHERE CURRENT OF cursor
```

In order for this to work, you will need to know the current name of the cursor, which is obtainable by the GetCursorName method:

```
$cursor = $db->GetCursorName();
```

The function returns the name of the cursor, or undef if there is no current cursor. The ODBC driver automatically gives cursors a name, but for convenience, you can also manually set the name of the current cursor:

```
$db->SetCursor('ACRONYMS');
```

To forcibly drop an active cursor, you can use the DropCursor method:

```
$db->DropCursor([CLOSETYPE]);
```

The CLOSETYPE optionally accepts the SQL_DROP and SQL_CLOSE constants. If none is specified, then the SQL_DROP method is used by default.

Transactions Transactions allow a process to make modifications to a database and then either finally accept them (commit) or dump the changes and return the database to its previous state (roll back). Many databases don't support transaction processing—they are in autocommit mode, and all modifications and deletions update the database in real time.

In many situations, the autocommit becomes a problem, automatically accepting modifications when you are updating a number of tables simultaneously can be dangerous. If one modification to one of the tables you are updating fails, you have what amounts to a corrupted database. You'll have to manually delete the data you inserted into other tables just to get the database back to its original state.

For systems that do support transaction processing, you will need to use the `Transact` method to finally commit or roll back your changes:

```
$db->Transact(TYPEF);
```

The `TYPE` is a constant, either one of `SQL_COMMIT`, to commit and save the changes you have made or `SQL_ROLLBACK`, which ignores the changes you have made and returns the database to the state it was in before you started making modifications, or since the last `SQL_COMMIT` within the current connection.

Note that if you don't deliberately use transaction processing, your data will normally be automatically committed when you close the connection to the ODBC driver.

Support Functions and Methods

As well as the object-oriented approach to obtaining information, the ODBC interface also provides functions and methods for obtaining additional information about the supported drivers, the drivers' abilities, or the available data sources. The functions are split below into *global functions* and *object information* functions. Global functions are those that can affect or are available directly within the interface without opening a connection. Object information functions are those that obtain additional data about the connection or driver currently in use.

Global Functions The use of the ODBC system relies on the drivers that are configured for the current machine. The supported drivers define the availability and, more specifically, your ability to access a particular database. You can get a list of drivers by using the `Win32::ODBC::Drivers` function:

```
use Win32::ODBC;

%drivers = Win32::ODBC::Drivers();

foreach(sort keys %drivers)
{
    print "$_\n";
    foreach $pair (split /;/,$drivers{$_})
    {
        my ($attrib,$value) = split /=/,$pair;
        print "   $attrib: $value\n";
    }
    print "\n";
}
```

The function returns a hash, with each key being the name of the driver. The corresponding value is a list of attributes for the given driver, separated by semicolons. Each attribute is in the form of key/value pair, separated by equal signs. Following is some sample output:

```
FileMaker Oracle8 Driver
  UsageCount: 3
  APILevel: 1
  ConnectFunctions: YYY
  DriverODBCVer: 03.50
  FileUsage: 0
  SQLLevel: 1
  CPTimeout: 60
FileMaker Pro
  UsageCount: 1
  APILevel: 1
  ConnectFunctions: YYY
  DriverODBCVer: 03.00
  FileUsage: 0
  SQLLevel: 0
...
 SQL Server
  DSNConverted: F
  UsageCount: 4
  SQLLevel: 1
  FileUsage: 0
  DriverODBCVer: 02.50
  ConnectFunctions: YYY
  APILevel: 2
```

Most of the attributes returned should be self-explanatory.

You can get a list of the databases available on a machine (i.e., the list of configured DSNs) by using the Win32::ODBC::DataSources function. The function returns a hash, where the keys are the DSN names, and the values are the driver details for the DSN. The following will print out a list of the available data sources:

```
use Win32::ODBC;

%sources = Win32::ODBC::DataSources();

foreach (sort keys %sources)
{
    print "$_: $sources{$_}\n";
}
```

This will output a list of information similar to the following:

```
Acronym: Microsoft Access Driver (*.mdb)
Excel Files: Microsoft Excel Driver (*.xls)
FoxPro Files: Microsoft FoxPro Driver (*.dbf)
MQIS: SQL Server
MS Access 97 Database: Microsoft Access Driver (*.mdb)
Text Files: Microsoft Text Driver (*.txt; *.csv)
Visual FoxPro Database: Microsoft Visual FoxPro Driver
Visual FoxPro Tables: Microsoft Visual FoxPro Driver
dBASE Files: Microsoft dBase Driver (*.dbf)
```

You can get the configuration information for an individual DSN using the getDSN function:

```
use Win32::ODBC;
%dsninfo = Win32::ODBC::GetDSN("Acronym");

foreach(sort keys %dsninfo)
{
    print "$_: $dsninfo{$_}\n";
}
```

The information returned will be the options configured for the DSN, according to the ODBC control panel:

```
DBQ: C:\WINDOWS\Desktop\Acronyms.mdb
Description: Internet Acronums
Driver: C:\WINDOWS\SYSTEM\odbcjt32.dll
DriverId:
FIL: MS Access;
SafeTransactions:
UID:
```

If you do not supply the name of a DSN, the function will return the configuration information for the currently active database connection.

The version numbers of the Perl side of the ODBC interface are available via the Version function:

```
print "Module: ",Win32::ODBC::Version('ODBC.PM'),"\n";
```

The output, confusingly, is the version number of the Perl loadable library (PLL) that is in use:

```
C:\> perl version.pl
Module: ODBC.PLL:970208 Beta
```

Object Information You can get the ID number of the current connection to the ODBC driver using the Connection method to a valid database object. The returned value is just a reference number to the currently active connection. You can use this information to help identify which connections are active or to use within a log file to aid the tracing of problems.

```
$db->Connection();
```

The connection ID is unique for a process; connections are given a sequential ID until the script exits. Note that the ID is not unique across an entire machine—it's possible for two scripts to have the same ID. If you are using this information in a log, then you should also store the process ID, obtainable via the $$special variable.

You can also use the Win32::ODBC::GetConnections() function to obtain a list of the currently active connection IDs:

```
print join "\n",Win32::ODBC::Connections();
```

The list returned will be in reverse order, with the most recently opened connection ID first. You will also always get a list of at least one element with a value of zero. This is the control connection.

CONTROLLING YOUR CONNECTION The GetConnectOption and SetConnectOption methods get and set information about the current connection. These can be used to control the connection, including enabling tracing and logging functions, setting transactions, and controlling the parameters of the underlying ODBC connection, including buffer sizes.

To get the current value of a connection option you use the GetConnectOption method, while the SetConnectOption method sets the option to a specific value:

```
$db->GetConnectOption(OPTION)
$db->SetConnectOption(OPTION, VALUE)
```

The GetConnectOption returns the current value for the specified option; the return type is option-specific. As with other functions and methods, the OPTION is a constant, as defined with the Win32::ODBC module and/or the corresponding ODBC driver libraries. The exact list of

TABLE 3-8

Options for the
GetConnect
Option and
SetConnect
Option
functions.

Option	Description
SQL_ACCESS_MODE	Accepts/returns the constants SQL_MODE_READ_ONLY or SQL_MODE_READ_WRITE. You can use this option to modify the connection so that it is impossible to perform any updates. However, be warned that the exact response is entirely ODBC driver-specific, there is no requirement for the ODBC driver to reject the updates even in read-only mode.
SQL_AUTOCOMMIT	Specifies whether the driver should use manual or automatic commit mode. The constants SQL_AUTOCOMMIT_OFF and SQL_AUTOCOMMIT_ON turn autocommit off and on, respectively.
SQL_CURRENT_QUALIFIER	A null-terminated string containing the name of the qualifer to be used by the data source.
SQL_LOGIN_TIMEOUT	The number of seconds to wait for a login request to complete before returning to the caller with a failure. The default is ODBC driver-dependent and should be a nonzero integer.
SQL_ODBC_CURSORS	Specifies how the ODBC Manager should use the cursor interface when handling queries. If set to SQL_CUR_USE_IF_NEEDED, then the driver will determine if the requested driver supports cursors. If it does, then the driver cursor system is used. If not, then an internal ODBC Manager cursor system is used instead. You can also force the driver or ODBC cursor implementations using the SQL_CUR_USE_DRIVER and SQL_CUR_USE_ODBC constants, respectively.
SQL_OPT_TRACE	Switches on or off the tracing of queries and connections to the ODBC Manager. You can use the SQL_OPT_TRACE_OFF and SQL_OPT_TRACE_ON constants to control the behavior; the default is for tracing to be switched off. The location of the file is defined by the SQL_OPT_TRACEFILE option.
SQL_OPT_TRACEFILE	The name of the file in which trace statements will be written (see SQL_OPT_TRACE). Defaults to \SQL.LOG on the current drive.
SQL_PACKET_SIZE	An integer defining the size of the network packets to be used when communicating with network-based DSNs.
SQL_QUIET_MODE	Specifies the window, in terms of a 32-bit window handle, that should be used to display any dialog boxes prompted by the ODBC Manager. If set to a null pointer, then no dialog boxes are shown. The default operation is to show dialog boxes as normal.
SQL_TRANSLATE_DLL	The name of the DLL that contains the necessary driver functions required by the ODBC interface.

options supported is dependent on the options supported by your ODBC driver. The generic connection options are shown in Table 3-8.

GETTING COLUMN INFORMATION When you have selected a range of information, you might want to know about the abilities (attributes) of a specific column in order to make the best use of the storage field. You can get this information by calling the ColAttributes method on an open database object:

```
$db->ColAttributes(ATTRIBUTE [, FIELD_NAME]);
```

The ATTRIBUTE is a constant, defined within the Win32::ODBC module. The list of constants supported by the function is shown in Table 3-9.

TABLE 3-9

Attributes supported by Win32::ODBC:: ColAttributes.

Attribute	Description
SQL_COLUMN_AUTO_INCREMENT	True if the column auto-increments its value when new data is inserted into the table. You can insert data into an auto-incremented column, but you cannot update the information.
SQL_COLUMN_CASE_SENSITIVE	True if the column is collated and compared in a case-sensitive fashion.
SQL_COLUMN_COUNT	The number of columns available in the result set.
SQL_COLUMN_DISPLAY_SIZE	Maximum number of characters required to display the data in the column.
SQL_COLUMN_LABEL	The column label or title. This is different from the column name. If the column does not have a label, then the column label is returned instead.
SQL_COLUMN_LENGTH	The amount of information, in bytes, returned by the previous SQLFetch method call. Note that numerical or binary information may return a different length than what you expect.
SQL_COLUMN_MONEY	True if the column is used to store monetary rather than plain numerical information.
SQL_COLUMN_NAME	The column name.
SQL_COLUMN_NULLABLE	Returns a value equal to SQL_NO_NULLS if the column does not accept NULL values, SQL_NUL-LABLE if the column accepts NULL values, SQL_NULLABLE_UNKNOWN if the column's ability to accept NULL values is unknown.

(Continued)

TABLE 3-9

(Continued)

Attribute	Description
SQL_COLUMN_OWNER_NAME	The owner of the table from which the column was selected.
SQL_COLUMN_PRECISION	The precision information for the column.
SQL_COLUMN_QUALIFIER_NAME	The qualifier of the table that contains the column.
SQL_COLUMN_SCALE	The scale of the column on the data source.
SQL_COLUMN_SEARCHABLE	Returns a value according to whether the column is searchable. The returned value will match one of the following constants: SQL_UNSEARCHABLE if the column cannot be in a WHERE clause, SQL_LIKE_ONLY if the column can only be used with the LIKE predicate, SQL_ALL_EXCEPT_LIKE if the column can be used in every statement except LIKE, and SQL_SEARCHABLE if the column can be searched with any operator.
SQL_COLUMN_TABLE_NAME	The name of the table from which the column has been selected.
SQL_COLUMN_TYPE	The SQL data type (see Table 3-4).
SQL_COLUMN_TYPE_NAME	The data type according to the types supported by the ODBC driver.
SQL_COLUMN_UNSIGNED	Returns True if the column is unsigned (or non-numeric).
SQL_COLUMN_UPDATABLE	The return value according to one of the following constants: SQL_ATTR_READONLY, SQL_ATTR_WRITE, SQL_ATTR_READWRITE_UNKNOWN.

For example, to obtain the maximum width of the fields, you might use a script like this:

```
use Win32::ODBC;

$db = new Win32::ODBC("Acronym");
$db->Sql("Select * from Acronyms");

%colinfo = $db->ColAttributes($db->SQL_COLUMN_DISPLAY_SIZE());

foreach (sort keys %colinfo)
{
    print "$_: $colinfo{$_}\n";
}
```

You can also get a catalog of all the available resources (tables, indexes, etc.) within a DSN using the Catalog method:

```
$db->Catalog(QUALIFIER, OWNER, NAME, TYPE);
```

The arguments define the range of the information to be returned. You can select to only retrieve tables or indexes, or only those objects within the DSN that are owned by a specific user. If you want to select all of the objects within a certain class, just supply an empty string.

The QUALIFIER is the name of the source of the information. This might be the database file, in which case you would supply the path to the file, or the database name. The OWNER is the login or user name of the owner of the database. The NAME is the name of the table that you want to retrieve information about.

The last argument, TYPE, is the name of a database-specific type to select from the catalog. Valid values are TABLE, VIEW, SYSTEM TABLE, GLOBAL TEMPORARY, LOCAL TEMPORARY, ALIAS, or SYNONYM. Other values may be available. Check the documentation for the ODBC driver.

In all cases, you can use the normal SQL wildcards to select items from the catalog.

The information is returned as a data set, so you will need to use FetchRow and Data or DataHash to get the information. For example, to list all of the objects within our Acronym database:

```
use Win32::ODBC;

$db = new Win32::ODBC("Acronym");

$db->Catalog('','','','');

while($db->FetchRow())
{
    %row = $db->DataHash();
    foreach $field (sort keys %row)
    {
        print "$field: $row{$field}\n";
    }
    print "\n";
}
$db->Close();
```

The output can be quite revealing:

```
REMARKS:
TABLE_NAME: MSysACEs
TABLE_OWNER:
TABLE_QUALIFIER: C:\WINDOWS\Desktop\Acronyms
TABLE_TYPE: SYSTEM TABLE
...
REMARKS:
TABLE_NAME: Acronyms
TABLE_OWNER:
```

```
TABLE_QUALIFIER: C:\WINDOWS\Desktop\Acronyms
TABLE_TYPE: TABLE
```

You can also use the `TableList` method to an open object to get a list of the available tables:

```
@tables = $db->TableList(QUALIFIER, OWNER, NAME, TYPE);
```

Again, you can supply empty strings if you want to select all of the tables within a current range. Note that the return type is a list. You do not need to obtain the information via `FetchRow`, so it should be safe to use this function without it affecting the currently active data set. You can supply a single % string to the `TYPE` to get a list of all the available table types supported by the ODBC driver.

The `GetFunctions` method returns information about the functions and options supported by the current ODBC driver:

```
$db->GetFunctions([FUNCTION, .... ]);
```

where `FUNCTION` is a constant that refers to the function you want to check.

If you don't specify any functions, then the method returns a hash of all the supported functions. For example, to check whether the current ODBC driver supports transaction processing:

```
%functions = $db-GetFunctions($db->SQL_API_SQLTRANSACT);
print "Transactions Supported\n"
    if ($functions{$db->SQL_API_SQLTRANSACT});
```

The list of possible constants is shown below. You can supply any of the constants shown in the table, irrespective of whether the database supports the function or not; the returned hash will not contain a key for an unsupported option.

```
SQL_API_SQLALLOCCONNECT
SQL_API_SQLALLOCENV
SQL_API_SQLALLOCSTMT
SQL_API_SQLBINDCOL
SQL_API_SQLBINDPARAMETER
SQL_API_SQLBROWSECONNECT
SQL_API_SQLCANCECL
SQL_API_SQLCOLATTRIBUTES
SQL_API_SQLCOLUMNPRIVILEGES
SQL_API_SQLCOLUMNS
SQL_API_SQLCONNECT
SQL_API_SQLDATASOURCES
SQL_API_SQLDESCRIBECOL
SQL_API_SQLDESCRIBEPARAM
```

```
SQL_API_SQLDISCONNECT
SQL_API_SQLDRIVERCONNECT
SQL_API_SQLDRIVERS
SQL_API_SQLERROR
SQL_API_SQLEXECDIRECT
SQL_API_SQLEXECUTE
SQL_API_SQLEXTENDEDFETCH
SQL_API_SQLFETCH
SQL_API_SQLFOREIGNKEYS
SQL_API_SQLFREECONNECT
SQL_API_SQLFREEENV
SQL_API_SQLFREESTMT
SQL_API_SQLGETCONNECTOPTION
SQL_API_SQLGETCURSORNAME
SQL_API_SQLGETDATA
SQL_API_SQLGETFUNCTIONS
SQL_API_SQLGETINFO
SQL_API_SQLGETSTMTOPTION
SQL_API_SQLGETTYPEINFO
SQL_API_SQLMORERESULTS
SQL_API_SQLNATIVESQL
SQL_API_SQLNUMPARAMS
SQL_API_SQLNUMRESULTCOLS
SQL_API_SQLPARAMDATA
SQL_API_SQLPARAMOPTIONS
SQL_API_SQLPREPAR
SQL_API_SQLPRIMARYKEYS
SQL_API_SQLPROCEDURECOLUMNS
SQL_API_SQLPROCEDURES
SQL_API_SQLPUTDATA
SQL_API_SQLROWCOUNT
SQL_API_SQLSETCONNECTOPTION
SQL_API_SQLSETCURSORNAME
SQL_API_SQLSETPARAM
SQL_API_SQLSETPOS
SQL_API_SQLSETSCROLLOPTIONS
SQL_API_SQLSETSTMTOPTION
SQL_API_SQLSPECIALCOLUMNS
SQL_API_SQLSTATISTICS
SQL_API_SQLTABLEPRIVILEGES
SQL_API_SQLTABLES
SQL_API_SQLTRANSACT
```

The `GetInfo` method returns information about the current ODBC connection. To use the method, you supply a constant that specifies the information that you want to obtain. The return value is the information that you requested—normally a `Y` or `N` to indicate whether a particular feature is available or not on the current connection. For example, here is an earlier example for determining whether the ODBC driver supports escape clauses, and if so, what character to use:

```
use Win32::ODBC;

$db = new Win32::ODBC("Acronym");

if ($db->GetInfo($db->SQL_LIKE_ESCAPE_CLAUSE()) eq 'Y')
```

```
{
    print "ODBC Driver supports wildcard escapes\n";
    $char = $db->GetInfo($db->SQL_SEARCH_PATTERN_ESCAPE());
    print "Escape Character is: $char\n";
}
```

A selection of the most commonly used constants to the GetInfo method is shown in Table 3-10. For a full list, refer to the documentation for the database system.

TABLE 3-10

Sample Constants for the GetInfo method.

Info Constant	Description
SQL_ACCESSIBLE_PROCEDURES	Y if the user can execute the available procedures; N if any of the procedures are not executable by the current user.
SQL_ACCESSIBLE_TABLES	Y if the user can execute SELECT statements on the available tables; N if there are tables that cannot be accessed by the current user.
SQL_CATALOG_NAME	Y if the ODBC driver supports catalog names, or N if it does not.
SQL_DATA_SOURCE_NAME	A string containing the current data source name used during the connection. Normally, this should equal the DSN string.
SQL_DATA_SOURCE_READ_ONLY	Y if the data source is in read-only mode.
SQL_DATABASE_NAME	A string containing the name of the current database in use.
SQL_DBMS_NAME	A string containing the name of the database product being used. Note that this is a shortened name. For example, Microsoft Access simply returns ACCESS.
SQL_DBMS_VER	A string, in the format ##.##.####, which defines the current version number for the database product being used. The first two digits are the major version, the second two digits the minor version, and the last four the current release or patch version.
SQL_DRIVER_NAME	A string containing the name of the current driver used to access the data source.
SQL_DRIVER_ODBC_VER	The ODBC version number that the current driver supports.
SQL_DRIVER_VER	A string containing the version number of the SQL driver in the form ##.##.####.

TABLE 3-10

(Continued)

Info Constant	Description
SQL_KEYWORDS	A comma-separated list of all the data source resource keywords.
SQL_LIKE_ESCAPE_CLAUSE	Y if the driver supports an escape character for the % and _ wildcard characters.
SQL_ODBC_VER	A string defining the version of ODBC that the driver conforms to.
SQL_PROCEDURES	Y if the driver supports procedures using the ODBC procedure invocation syntax; N otherwise.
SQL_SERVER_NAME	A string containing the name of the server for the current data source.
SQL_SPECIAL_CHARACTERS	A string containing a list of all the nonalphanumeric characters (including underscores) that are supported within an identifier (table, column, etc.).
SQL_TABLE_TERM	A string defining the name used by a data source to refer to a table. For example, Access would return table, whereas FileMaker Pro would return file.
SQL_USER_NAME	A string containing the name of the current user—not necessarily identical to the login name.

Requests to the ODBC interface are buffered to improve performance. Each column in a returned row of data is given its own buffer. Because the information that has been retrieved from the database is stored in a local buffer, we don't have to get more information from the database each time, which would be a comparatively slow process.

The only problem with the ODBC buffer implementation is that it bases the size of the buffer on the size of the column being returned. For most fields, the field width is enough information for ODBC to be able to approximate the size, but not fields that support a fixed width, so the buffer created for an Oracle BLOB (binary large object) or Access Memo field is often inadequate to store the returned information. Instead, ODBC uses the default value configured within the DSN properties.

You can obtain the current buffer size using the GetMaxBufferSize function:

```
$bufsize = $db->GetMaxBufSize();
```

You can also increase the maximum buffer size by calling the `SetMaxBufferSize` function:

```
$db->SetMaxBufSize(2048);
```

Both functions return the current size of the buffer. You'll need to compare the returned value against the value you tried to set to determine whether the operation was successful.

Debugging

Although it's possible to use one of the more traditional methods to debug your ODBC scripts, no amount of the normal debugging will provide you with information about what is going on behind the scenes within the ODBC interface. As such, there are a number of functions that can be used to debug the ODBC interface directly.

The most basic of these is the `GetSQLState` method. This returns the current state of the SQL interpreter for the ODBC driver. The value returned is a string and will have been generated either by the ODBC Manager, if the problem occurred before the connection to the database had been completed, or the ODBC driver after an SQL statement has been parsed. The information returned is more extensive than that returned by the individual functions, such as `Sql`, and can be used to provide more-detailed information about the level of success of a particular statement's execution:

```
$db->GetSQLState();
```

The returned string is the error number (usually an alphanumeric string) specific to the ODBC driver or the ODBC Manager. You'll need to refer to the documentation for the database driver to identify the meaning of the error code.

You can also switch on debugging, which returns additional information while the ODBC connection is in use. You can switch debugging on and off on a connection basis, allowing you to control which connections return additional information. The `Debug` method to the database object turns debugging on and off. So, to turn debugging on:

```
$db->Debug(1);
```

To turn it off:

```
$db->Debug(0);
```

Turning debugging on also causes the `Win32::ODBC::Error` function to return two additional fields of information: the `FUNCTION` and the `LEVEL`. The `FUNCTION` is the name of the internal function within the ODBC interface in which the error occurred, and `LEVEL` defines any additional error information supplied by that function. Thus, in a list context, the function returns

```
(ERROR_ID, ERROR_TEXT, CONN_ID, FUNCTION, LEVEL) =
    Win32::ODBC::Error();
```

The `DumpData` method dumps the fields and rows from the current data set directly to the standard output; you cannot control or capture the information output (without redirection of some form). Because it cannot be controlled, the function is only useful within the sphere of debugging:

```
use Win32::ODBC;

$db = new Win32::ODBC("Acronym");

$db->Sql("select * from Acronyms");
$db->DumpData();

$db->Close();
```

The output looks like a simplified version of our own Acronym script:

```
Dumping Data for connection: 1
Error: ""
Acronym Expansion
——- ——-
AAMOF As a matter of fact
AFAIC As Far As I'm Concerned
AFAIK As Far As I Know
AFK Away From Keyboard
AIJ Am I Jesus?
AISI As I See It
...
WYSIWYG What You See Is What You Get
YAOTM Yet Another Off-Topic Message
IMNNAHAISBO in my not-nearly-as-humble-as-I-should-be opinion
```

To get some simple indication of the success or otherwise of an SQL statement, you can use the `Run` method. This works in exactly the same fashion as the `Sql` method, except that `Run` also dumps the connection ID, executed statement, and a returned error direct to the standard output after it has executed the statement. The line

```
$db->Run("SELECT * FROM Acronyms");
```

produces

```
Executing connection 1
sql statement: "select * from Acronyms"
Error: ""
```

When closing the connection to a database, you can also get further information about the current database state by calling the `Shutdown` method, rather than the normal `Close` method:

```
$db->ShutDown();
```

Configuring DSNs using `Win32::ODBC`

Aside from using the ODBC Manager in Control Panel, you can also pragmatically create DSNs using Perl and the `Win32::ODBC` module. The format of the function call is

```
ConfigDSN(OPTION, DRIVER, (ATTRIBUTE1 [, ATTRIBUTE2, ATTRIBUTE3,
    ...]))
```

This configures the DSN. `OPTIONS` can be `ODBC_ADD_DSN`, which adds a new DSN; `ODBC_MODIFY_DSN`, which modifies an existing DSN; `ODBC_REMOVE_DSN`, which removes an existing DSN. The `DRIVER` is the name of a valid driver. Use `DataSources` or `Drivers` to determine the available list.

The attributes should be in the normal "ATTR=VALUE" format associated with DSN connections. For example, to create the DSN that connects to our Acronym database:

```
use Win32::ODBC;

Win32::ODBC::ConfigDSN(Win32::ODBC::ODBC_ADD_DSN(),
                       'Microsoft Access Driver (*.mdb)',
                       'DSN=Acronyms',
                       'DBQ=C:\WINDOWS\Desktop\Acronyms.mdb');
```

If you modify a DSN, you must supply the DSN and the remaining attributes that you want to update. To delete a DSN, you only need to specify the DSN string.

Using OLE Automation

You can use OLE to extract information from another application, usually even if it doesn't support an ODBC driver. Rather than go into the process here, we'll return to the topic of OLE in Chapter 11.

## CHAPTER 4

File
Management

Many of the fundamental aspects of using files and directories are identical under Windows and Unix. The major differences lie with the additional information stored along with the directory entry, such as modification times and user/group ownership and permission information. Windows supports some of these features. Each file has simple attributes, and Windows NT machines have even more complex file permission and ownership attributes; others, such as the access time information, are simply not stored by the operating system.

We'll take a look in this chapter at the differences between the Unix and Win32 implementations of the function set that Perl provides for managing files and directories. We'll start by looking at the Win32 file systems, and how they differ at a fundamental level from the Unix interface supported by Perl.

The Windows File System

You should already be aware of the naming conventions employed by Windows machines. Unlike Unix, which uses a single mount point under which all other physical and logical drives can be found, Windows distinguishes between individual drives, whether local physical or logical drives or those mounted over the network. Each drive is given a letter, starting at A: for the floppy drive and C: for the first hard drive.

Further drives—fixed, removable, or network-mounted—are given additional letters up to Z:. Directories within a drive are separated from the drive letter by a colon, and then individual components of the path are separated by the backslash (\) character.

In fact, this is only a convention. The Win32 platform also allows you to use the forward slash to separate individual path components. For example, the main Windows operating system directory could be referenced as "C:/Windows". This means that you can continue to use forward slashes as path separators in your programs on both platforms without worrying about determining which platform on which the script is currently executing.

Care should also be taken when introducing path constants that incorporate the backslash. Within single quotes no special processing occurs. But within double quotes and other operators that interpolate strings, the backslash is used to indicate an escape character sequence. For example, the line

```
unlink("C:\newfile.txt");
```

actually looks for a file in the current working directory of the C: drive that starts with the newline character, followed by `ewfile.txt`. You should either use \\ for the backslash in your paths, use a forward slash, or use the `File::Spec` module. This translates a given path split into its component parts into a platform-specific path according to the current operating system requirements. See "Cross Platform Pathnames" later in this chapter for a description of how to use this module.

Current directory information is retained for both the current drive and the current working directory. Changing drives implies a change to the current directory of the new drive. For example, if you are currently in C:\Windows and change to D:\Temp, changing back to C: would place you in C:\Windows. See "Navigating Directories" later in this chapter for more information on changing directories under Windows.

Filenames and Lengths   Windows directory names are not case-sensitive. Although you can name files with mixed case, you cannot have a file with the same name but different case. For example, the file TheOnion.doc would be correctly displayed with case as shown, but it could not reside in the same directory as theonion.doc; the two filenames are identical to Windows.

The length of a Windows filename is effectively unlimited, but the maximum length of a Windows file path is 255 characters.

The Windows Desktop   The Windows operating system uses the notion of a "Desktop." This should be considered to be the root directory as far as the user is concerned. Moving to the desktop, within a file selection dialog box shows the list of files and icons available on the user's desktop, including the My Computer icon, which provides access to the physical and logical drives available on the machine. In fact, the desktop is just a special directory within the Windows directory.

The actual physical location of the Desktop directory depends on the version of Windows you are using. For Windows 95 and 98, the file is normally to be found within the main C:\Windows directory, as in C:\Windows\Desktop. Note that this folder only contains the files that have been copied to the desktop by the user; the other components of the Windows desktop are added by the operating system.

For Windows NT, the location is unique to each user, with each local user directory located in C:\Winnt\Profiles. Within this directory you will find directories for the configurable components of the Windows NT environment, including the Desktop folder and the Start menu.

File Extensions Under Windows, the extension of a file is a critical component of the identification process. Using a built-in table, you can specify what application opens a document with a specific extension when it is double-clicked. For example, the extension *.doc* indicates a Microsoft Word document.

The extension of a file is therefore a vital part of the naming process and will affect the accessibility of any files generated by your Perl applications.

File Permissions and Ownership Ignoring Windows NT systems for the moment, note that Windows does not provide any form of locking or security mechanism, even when used in a so-called multi-user mode. Under Unix, individual files have an owner, a group owner, and a permission mode that define the accessibility of a file in terms of user, group, and other, nonqualified users. For example, the file shown below is owned by the user bin and has a group owner of root. The file is readable and executable by the user bin, members of the group root, and everybody else:

```
-r-xr-xr-x   3 bin      root      86140 Jul 16  1994 /bin/sh*
```

For each entity (user, group, other) there are three permission bits: Read, Write, and Execute. The Read permission bit determines whether the file can be read, the Write bit determines whether the file can be written to or deleted, and the Execute permission defines whether the file can be executed or whether a directory can be traversed.

Under Windows 95/98, individual files do not have user or group owners. Nor do they have a complex set of permissions. Instead, they have a list of attributes that specify whether the file has been archived or marked as read-only. See the "File Attributes" section later in this chapter for more information.

The file permissions are also used to determine whether a file is executable or whether the current user or group should be changed before the application is executed. Windows uses a predefined list of extensions to determine whether a file is executable. This includes files ending in *.exe*, *.com*, and *.bat*. Under Windows NT, this list can be modified, which allows us to create an entry for *.pl* files so that when double-clicked, they are executed by the Perl interpreter.

In addition, although it is possible to identify an individual user, within the confines of Windows 95 and Windows 98, there are no user-level restrictions on the files you have access to on the local machine.

Windows NT/2000, on the other hand, supports a far more complex set of file permissions that support much more complicated masks and access rights than those offered by the Unix file system. See "NT File Security" later in the chapter for more information.

The Universal Naming Convention (UNC)

The term *files* is actually a generic term for anything that can be accessed through the file system. Although primarily this includes physical files, either on local drives or on mounted network drives, it can also include network resources accessed by a UNC (Universal Naming Convention). A UNC name is a naming convention for describing servers and share points on those servers. UNC names start with two backslashes (\\) and are followed by the server name, share name, subdirectory, and file, according to the following layout:

```
\\server\share\subdirectory\filename
```

You can use a UNC name in any of the locations within this chapter when we refer to a file—a UNC name is just another form of the usual file path. We'll be looking more closely at UNC and shared network resources in Chapter 6.

Deleting and Renaming Files

You can delete files under Win32 using the `unlink` function. Although the `unlink` name actually refers to the process of unlinking a directory name from an inode under Unix, the operation of the function under Win32 remains identical: it deletes a file. Note that because you cannot create multiple links to the same file, the `unlink` function deletes both the directory entry and the file:

```
unlink('C:\TEMP\myfile.doc');
```

Also note that use of the function deletes the file immediately; once a file is deleted via Perl, it is permanent. If you want to move a file to the Recycle Bin, use the `rename` function to move the file to the \Recycled directory on the same drive as the file. For example, to move the above file to the Recycle Bin, we would call

```
rename('C:\TEMP\myfile.doc','C:\Recycled');
```

You can rename files using the `rename` function. The function will rename the file, moving it either within the confines of the same logical Windows drive or across drives by copying the file. So, the following lines will work as you would expect:

```
rename("E:/oldfile","E:/Projects/newfile");
rename("E:/Projects/newfile","F:/otherfile");
```

Navigating Directories

Because Windows supports more than one logical drive, the act of changing directories is slightly more complex. Windows retains a current working directory for each drive, in addition to a global current working directory. This means that when you change directories, you should use absolute pathnames and always specify the drive letter. If you change to a different drive without specifying a path, then you will change to the current working directory for that drive.

For example, in the following script, the absolute directory is changed for two drives, C: and E:

```
use Win32;
chdir("c:/Windows");
print Win32::GetCwd,"\n";
chdir("e:/Projects ");
print Win32::GetCwd,"\n";
chdir("c:/");
print Win32::GetCwd,"\n";
chdir("e:");
print Win32::GetCwd,"\n";
```

if you run this script:

```
C:> perl 03.pl
C:\Windows
E:\Projects
C:\
E:\Projects
```

Using `chdir` to change to another drive without also specifying the path does not change the current working directory on either the original or destination drive. Note as well in this example that we are using the

Win32::GetCwd function from the main Win32 library. See Chapter 2 for more details on this function. The standard Cwd module and getcwd function will work, but the information returned is in Unix (forward slash) format.

If you do not supply an argument to the chdir function, then under Unix, you change to the home directory for the current user. Although Windows NT supports the notion of home directories, this is not a generic Windows feature. Therefore, if you call chdir with no arguments within ActivePerl, nothing happens—no directory change is made.

Also note that the chroot function does not work under Windows and will cause a fatal error if used.

Making and Removing Directories

The mkdir and rmdir operations work as they do under Unix. However, given the notes above regarding the current working directory, care should be taken to ensure that the correct drive and directory are used. As before, the best approach is to use a fully qualified directory name wherever possible.

The mkdir function normally accepts both the directory name and the octal permissions to use for the newly created directory. The mode is meaningless under Windows, so you can supply any value to the function to create a new directory. You can remove any directory providing it is already empty. For example:

```
mkdir("newdira", 0666) or die "Couldn't create the directory: $!";
mkdir("newdirb", 0777) or die "Couldn't create the directory: $!";
open(FILE, ">newdira/filea") or die "Couldn't create the file: $!";
close(FILE);
rmdir("newdirb") or die "Couldn't delete the directory: $!";
rmdir("newdira") or die "Couldn't delete the directory: $!";
```

Note that you can continue to use the standard error reporting. You do not need to employ the Win32::GetLastError function.

File Globbing

When using a Unix shell, *file globbing*, the action of converting a file specification using wildcards and other data into a list of valid filenames on the command line, is actually handled by the shell itself. The information is then passed to the application via the ARGV variable (@ARGV in Perl). Under Windows, the shell does not do any form of file globbing and instead relies on the abilities of the command in question to translate a file specification into a valid list of files.

So with a simple script such as:

```
print join("\n",@ARGV);
```

when we execute it

```
C:\> perl 05.pl *
```

you'll simply get *—not exactly what you want. Instead, if you want to accept wildcards on the command line for file specifications, you must do the globbing manually using either the glob function or the <*> operator.

Both the function and the operator work in a similar fashion to the Unix version, so the fragments

```
@filelist = glob("*");
```

and

```
@filelist = <*>;
```

are too small.

However, the globbing expression syntax supported by Windows is slightly different when compared to the Unix version. The standard syntax supported by most Windows commands only supports two basic forms of wildcard selection: You can use either * or ? to indicate multiple or single characters respectively. For example:

```
@filelist = <*.txt>;
```

would select all files with an extension of *.txt* and

```
@filelist = <chk????.txt>;
```

would select all files starting with *chk* and followed by four characters.

You cannot use regular expression style specifications under Windows. They simply do not work. For example:

```
@filelist = glob("[A-Z]*");
```

This is largely because the globbing process is actually performed by the external command `perlglob.exe` supplied as part of the ActivePerl distribution. This program uses the Microsoft library function to expand the given arguments into a list of matching files, using the same algorithm as other Windows applications. Aside from the level of simplicity that this system supports, it also has a number of inherent problems. For example, the specification `*let*` will actually list all the files, whether or not the name contains *let* or not.

The solution to the globbing difference problem is to use the `grep` function with the returned list from the `glob` call. For example, to obtain a list of all the files starting with a number:

```
@filelist = grep { m/^[0-9]/; } glob("*");
```

Using this method should allow you to support most of the file selections that you are familiar with. Alternatively, you can use the `opendir` suite of functions with a regular expression to select the files you want. Using `opendir` is faster, because it does not rely on an external program to perform the globbing process. See the following section, "Reading Directories," for more details.

The final alternative is to replace the default `perlglob.exe` with the `perlglob.bat` batch file. The batch calls a Perl script that performs the same basic operation as above and allows a more extensive set of wildcards.

Reading Directories

ActivePerl supports the same directory handle system as the Unix version. The directory handle is supported by the `opendir`, `readdir`, and `closedir` suite of functions. The `opendir` functions are actually supported directly by the Windows operating system, since they are part of the POSIX standard. If you want to remain ultimately compatible across platforms, then you should use the following:

```
opendir    DIRHANDLE, EXPR
readdir    DIRHANDLE
rewinddir  DIRHANDLE
telldir    DIRHANDLE
seekdir    DIRHANDLE, POS
closedir   DIRHANDLE
```

The directory system is much like the basic file interface. You open a directory, specifying the path you want to open, and then you use successive calls to `readdir` to get a name from the directory. Alternatively, in a list context, the `readdir` function returns a list of all the files in the specified directory. For example, for a simple directory listing:

```
opendir (DIR, '.') or die "Couldn't open directory, $!";
while ($file = readdir DIR)
{
    print "$file\n";
}
close DIR;
```

Going through each file entry individually sidesteps the problems of allocating large blocks of memory to store the list temporarily. Alternatively, you can ignore the memory requirements and filter the list directly using `grep`:

```
opendir(DIR, '.') or die "Couldn't open directory, $!";
foreach (sort grep(/^.*\.c$/,readdir(DIR)))
{
    print "$_\n";
}
closedir DIR;
```

Cross-Platform Pathnames

We already know that pathnames under Windows are different from those under other platforms. We also saw in Chapter 1 how the basic premise of the pathname under Windows is compatible with the Unix style. For example, you can use \Windows as well as /Windows within ActivePerl.

However, when you use or specify a path that may be used by another application, you need to ensure that the path is in the correct format. Perl supports a standard module, `File::Spec`, which provides a simple interface to the process of building paths. By using the `File::Spec` module in your scripts, you can ensure cross-platform compatibility.

The module is supported behind the scenes by a number of platform-specific modules that are imported as required, depending on the platform on which the script is running. You shouldn't need to import the support modules individually; instead, import the `File::Spec` module and let it decide which module is required.

The module supports one main function, `catfile`, which combines individual path elements into a single pathname using the correct path separators. For example, the fragment

```
print File::Spec->catfile('C:','Projects'),"\n";
```

will print

```
C:\Projects
```

You can use the `canonpath` function to clean an existing path into a Windows-friendly version. For example, the fragment

```
print File::Spec->canonpath("C:/Windows//./System/"),"\n";
```

would correctly output `C:\Windows\System`

Getting File Information

There are a number of ways of getting information about a file. Some of the information can be obtained by using the `-X` series of tests. However, for more-detailed information you must use one of the functions that obtain information directly from the operating system for a specific file.

The -x Tests

Most of the basic file tests supported by the `-X` tests work as you would expect, the exceptions to the rule being those tests that are linked directly to the Unix file system, such as file and group ownership. The supported list of functions therefore matches Table 4-1.

For example, you can use the following script to identify a file:

```
foreach(@ARGV)
{
    fileinfo($_);
}

sub fileinfo
{
    my ($file) = @_;
    my (@description,$size);
    if (-e $file)
```

```
    {
        push @description, 'binary' if (-B $file);
        push @description, 'a socket' if (-S $file);
        push @description, 'a text file' if (-T $file);
        push @description, 'a directory' if (-d $file);
        push @description, 'executable' if (-x $file);
        push @description, (($size = -s $file))
                                ? "$size bytes" : 'empty';
        print "$file is ", join(', ',@description),"\n";
    }
}
```

Note, however, that the _ special filehandle does not work in the current version; you must use the full path to the file in each call.

Windows does not support hard or symbolic (soft) links. However, it does support "shortcuts," which are similar in principle to symbolic links.

TABLE 4-1

File test operators.

Operator	Description
-B	Returns True if the file is in binary format.
-C	Number of days since the last inode change.
-M	Number of days since the script was started.
-R, -r	Returns True if the file is readable.
-S	Returns True if the file is a socket.
-T	Returns True if the file is in text format.
-W,-w	Returns True if the file is writable.
-X,-X	Returns True if the file is executable.
-b	Returns True if the file is a block special file.
-c	Returns True if the file is a character special file.
-d	Returns True if the path is a directory.
-e	Returns True if the file exists.
-f	Returns True if the file is a plain file.
-o	Returns True if the file is owned by the effective user ID.
-s	Returns the size of the file, with zero referring to an empty file.
-t	Returns True if the file is opened by a TTY (terminal).
-x	Returns True if the file is executable (checks the valid extension list, *.exe*, *.bat*, *.com*, etc.).
-z	Returns True if the file size is zero.

All shortcuts have the extension *.lnk*, so you can easily identify if a file is a link using a regular expression or substring match:

```
print "String Link!\n" if (substr($link,-4,4) eq '.lnk');
print "Regexp Link!\n" if ($link =~ /\.lnk$/);
```

A shortcut defines more than a link to a file and can consist of additional information, such as the arguments to supply to the command and details of the icon to use when displaying the shortcut within the Explorer. See the "Shortcuts" section later in this chapter for more details on using the Win32::Shortcut module to access, create, and modify Windows shortcuts.

chmod **and** umask

Because Windows does not support the normal notions of file modes (the octal file permissions under Unix), neither the chmod or umask functions work under Windows NT. For changing the attributes, the closest thing to file permissions available under Windows, see the Win32::File module under "File Attributes" later in this chapter. For Windows NT security, see the Win32::FileSecurity module detailed later in this chapter.

There is no equivalent to the umask function.

File Statistics

The basic file information, such as the file mode, owner, and modification times, can be obtained using the stat function. This returns a list of parameters for a given file. The following definition is from the Unix version:

```
($dev,  $inode, $mode,  $nlink, $uid,   $gid,     $rdev,
 $file, $size,  $atime, $mtime, $ctime, $blksize, $blocks) = stat
```

The information returned by Windows is slightly different due to the difference in file system data stored. The Windows version returns only 11 elements, not 13; the $blksize and $blocks elements are omitted. Details of the information returned by Windows can be seen in Table 4-2.

TABLE 4-2

Data returned by
the Stat function.

Element	Short Name	Description
0	dev	Device number of file system, starting at zero for A:, one for B:, and so on.
1	inode	Inode number, irrelevant on Win32, always returns zero.
2	mode	File mode (type and permissions). Although this returns what appears to be a valid value, the figures are meaningless. Use the -X tests or Win32::File module to get precise details on the format and/or accessibility of a file.
3	nlink	Number of (hard) links to the file. Always returns 1.
4	uid	Numeric user ID of the file's owner. Always returns 0. See Win32::FileSecurity, coming up in the chapter, for information on file ownership information for Windows NT platforms.
5	gid	Numeric group ID of file's owner. Always returns zero. See Win32::FileSecurity for information on file ownership information for Windows NT platforms.
6	rdev	The device identifier; returns the same value as element zero, dev.
7	size	File size, in bytes.
8	atime	Last access time, in seconds, since the epoch. Note that this figure will only be updated by some applications.
9	mtime	Last modification time, in seconds, since the epoch.
10	ctime	The last inode change time, in seconds, since the epoch.

Timestamps

We already know that we can obtain the creation, modification, and access timestamps using the stat function. Those figures can also be modified using the utime function. Unlike the Unix version, however, you cannot explicitly modify the access time and the modification time. Setting one value implicitly sets the other. This effectively changes the general format of the command from

```
utime ATIME, MTIME, LIST
```

to

```
utime MTIME, MTIME, LIST
```

For the example below, the time specified is taken from the `time` function, which returns the number of seconds since the epoch at the time executed. The following emulates the Unix `touch` command:

```
$now = time;
utime $now, $now+(24*3600), 'C:\Temp\MyDocument.txt';
```

If we now examine the file, both the modification and access time are the same, even though we set the modification time a day ahead.

This particular operational change should not cause any major problems. It's likely that you will only be adjusting the modification rather than the access time; you should be aware of the difference.

File Attributes

Perl is very Unix-centric when it comes to the file modes that are used to define the access to individual files and directories. We already know that the octal permission mode available for Unix files is meaningless under Windows. In essence, this means that all files can be read, written, or deleted by any user or application on a Windows 95 or 98 system.

Windows 95/98/NT and 2000 all support a basic set of attributes for each file or directory on the system. The attributed system was inherited from DOS, and each attribute allows you to define specific characteristics for each file or directory on the system. All attributes have only two states: on or off. Some of the attributes affect the way in which the operating system provides access to the file; other attributes are simply indicators. See Table 4-3 for a list of valid attributes.

You can change the attributes of a file using the `Win32::File` module. This supports two functions, `Win32::File::GetAttributes` and `Win32::File::SetAttributes`. In addition, it also exports constants for each attribute.

```
Win32::File::GetAttributes(FILE, ATTR);
Win32::File::SetAttributes(FILE, ATTR);
```

To obtain the attributes for a file, you use the `Win32::File::GetAttributes` function and then use logic to identify the different attributes. The following script displays all of the attributes for a given file:

```
use Win32::File;

foreach $file (@ARGV)
{
    print "$file: ",join(", ",show_attr($file)),"\n";
```

TABLE 4-3

Windows attributes.

Attribute	Description
ARCHIVE	This bit is set automatically by the operating system if the file has been modified since the last time it was backed up. The resetting of this attribute to "off" must be conducted by the application that backed the file. It is not reset automatically.
COMPRESSED	The file has been compressed by the operating system to conserve space. Note that this doesn't indicate files compressed by PKZIP, Lharc, or similar applications, only those compressed by a system such as DriveSpace. This attribute is read-only and cannot be modified.
DIRECTORY	The file is a directory. This attribute is read-only and cannot be modified.
HIDDEN	The file is hidden. This restricts which applications can see the file. By default, Windows Explorer and the DOS prompt are unable to see hidden files. Within the Explorer, it is possible to show hidden files (via the Options item in the View menu). Note that the opendir suite of functions automatically list all files, irrespective of this attribute setting.
NORMAL	The file is an ordinary file that can be read or written to. This attribute is read-only and cannot be modified.
READONLY	The file has been marked as read-only. System calls to write or delete the file will fail, although there is nothing to stop an application from modifying this attribute to allow the file to be modified.
SYSTEM	The file is a system file. Similar in principle to READONLY, a system file cannot be deleted, irrespective of the setting of READONLY attribute. Again, there is nothing to stop an application from resetting the SYSTEM flag to enable the file to be deleted.

```perl
}

sub show_attr
{
    my ($file) = @_;
    my @attr;

    if (Win32::File::GetAttributes($file,$attr))
    {
        push @attr,"Archive" if ($attr & ARCHIVE);
        push @attr,"Directory" if ($attr & DIRECTORY);
        push @attr,"Compressed" if ($attr & COMPRESSED);
        push @attr,"Hidden" if ($attr & HIDDEN);
        push @attr,"Normal" if ($attr & NORMAL);
        push @attr,"Read-Only" if ($attr & READONLY);
        push @attr,"System" if ($attr & SYSTEM);

        return @attr;
    }
    else
    {
        die "Error: " . Win32::FormatMessage(Win32::GetLastError());
    }
}
```

Running this script on a couple of files yields the following:

```
C:\> perl 08.pl 08.pl c:\config.sys c:\io.sys
08.pl: Archive
c:\config.sys: Normal
c:\io.sys: Hidden, Read-Only, System
```

To modify the attributes of a file, you use the Win32::File:SetAttributes, with the second argument containing a value relating to the individual attributes logically OR'd together. For example, to reset the archive status of a file:

```perl
use Win32::File;

foreach $file (@ARGV)
{
    print "Setting Archive attribute for $file\n";
}

sub set_attr
{
    my ($file) = @_;
    my @attr;

    if (Win32::File::GetAttributes($file,$attr))
    {
        unless (Win32::File::SetAttributes($file, $attr | RCHIVE))
        {
            w32_error();
        }
    }
    else
    {
        w32_error();
    }
}

sub w32_error
{
    die "Error: " . Win32::FormatMessage(Win32::GetLastError());
}
```

We can now reset the attribute on c:\config.sys:

```
$ perl 09.pl c:\config.sys
Setting Archive attribute for c:\config.sys
```

And we can check the status with our previous script:

```
$ perl 08.pl c:\config.sys
c:\config.sys: Archive
```

Note, of course, that we cannot modify those attributes that are read-only, such as DIRECTORY and COMPRESSED. You might also have noticed that the NORMAL and ARCHIVE tags are a toggle for each other—a file will have one of the two attributes, but not both.

NT File Security

Aside from the simple attributes configurable via the Win32::File module, file systems formatted using the NTFS format—available under Windows NT—support extended security via *discretionary access control lists*, or ACLs. These allow more-complex security options than are offered either via the standard attributes or even via the file modes applied to Unix file systems. For example, you can restrict users so that they are able to delete a file but not actually access or modify it.

NOTE. *ACLs under Windows are similar in principle to the ACLs available in HP-UX, although the individual rights supported are slightly different.*

Rather than using a simple mode that can only define one of four possible values to either the owner, group owner, or everybody else, ACLs

Figure 4-1

The security properties for a directory.

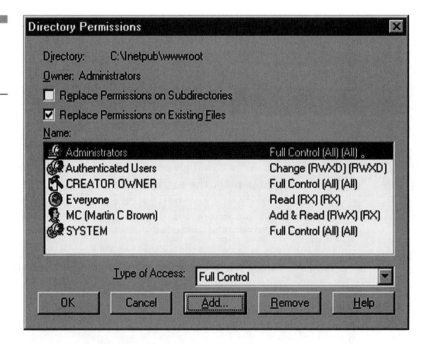

work by supporting a list of permissions that can be assigned to a specific user or group. You can have as many of these entries against a file or directory as necessary. Thus, you can have an individual user that does not have access to a file, while a group to which that user belongs does have access. For example, Figure 4-1 shows a sample security properties window that specifies that guests have the ability to change information but not delete it, while administrators have full access.

Within Perl, the way to access and modify this information is to use the `Win32::FileSecurity` module. The system works via a simple set of functions and constants that define the different security options available, as defined in Table 4-4.

TABLE 4-4

Access control constants.

Constant	Description
DELETE	User/group can delete the object.
READ_CONTROL	User/group can read the access control list. If the individual has not been given these permissions, then they cannot discover what their access level is.
WRITE_DAC	User/group can update the discretionary access control lists. Unless the user/group has this ability, the ACL cannot be updated by the user/group.
WRITE_OWNER	User/group can modify the owner of the file.
SYNCHRONIZE	A synchronization object can signal the file. See `Win32::Mutex` or `Win32::ChangeNotify` later in this chapter.
STANDARD_RIGHTS_READ	Read permission for a directory.
STANDARD_RIGHTS_WRITE	Write permission for a directory.
STANDARD_RIGHTS_EXECUTE	Directory can be opened/traversed.
STANDARD_RIGHTS_ALL	All basic permissions (Read/Write/Execute).
SPECIFIC_RIGHTS_ALL	Full access for all objects.
GENERIC_READ	Read permission for a file.
GENERIC_WRITE	Write permission for a file.
GENERIC_EXECUTE	Execute permission for a file.
GENERIC_ALL	Basic access (Read, Write, Execute, Delete) for a file.
FULL, F	Full access, equal to GENERIC_READ, GENERIC_WRITE, DELETE, WRITE_DAC, and WRITE_OWNER.
READ, R	Read access.
CHANGE, C	Change (modification) access.

The module supports a number of different functions used to both obtain and set the permissions, in addition to functions that extract or build an access control list. The main operations are supported by the Get and Set functions, which, respectively, get and set the access control lists for a single file or directory:

```
Win32::FileSecurity::Get(FILE, PERMISSIONS)
Win32::FileSecurity::Set(FILE, PERMISSIONS)
```

The access control information is placed into or taken from the hash pointed to by PERMISSIONS. The information placed into the hash is not quite as useful as it first appears. The keys contain the user or group for the permission, and the value contains a numerical representation of the permissions for that user, otherwise called a *mask*.

For example, if we want to print out the ACLs for our earlier sample directory, we might use a simple script like this:

```
use Win32::FileSecurity;

Win32::FileSecurity::Get('C:\inetpub\wwwroot',\%acl);

foreach(sort keys %acl)
{
    print "$_: $acl{$_}\n";
}
```

When run, it outputs the following on my NT workstation:

```
C:\>10.pl
BUILTIN\Administrators: 270467583
CREATOR OWNER: 270467583
Everyone: -1609432641
INCONTINENT\MC: -1609432641
NT AUTHORITY\Authenticated Users: -535625281
NT AUTHORITY\SYSTEM: 270467583
```

To convert the mask into a list of constants, you need to use the EnumerateRights function:

```
use Win32::FileSecurity;

Win32::FileSecurity::Get('C:\inetpub\wwwroot',\%acl);

foreach(sort keys %acl)
{
  Win32::FileSecurity::EnumerateRights($acl{$_},\@acllist);
    print "$_: ",join(' ',@acllist),"\n";
}
```

which more usefully outputs a textual list of access rights for the file:

```
BUILTIN\Administrators: DELETE READ_CONTROL WRITE_DAC WRITE_OWNER
   SYNCHRONIZE STANDARD_RIGHTS_REQUIRED STANDARD_RIGHTS_READ
   STANDARD_RIGHTS_WRITE STANDARD_RIGHTS_EXECUTE STANDARD_RIGHTS_ALL
   GENERIC_ALL READ CHANGE ADD FULL
CREATOR OWNER: DELETE READ_CONTROL WRITE_DAC WRITE_OWNER SYNCHRONIZE
   STANDARD_RIGHTS_REQUIRED STANDARD_RIGHTS_READ STANDARD_RIGHTS_WRITE
   STANDARD_RIGHTS_EXECUTE STANDARD_RIGHTS_ALL GENERIC_ALL READ CHANGE
   ADD FULL
Everyone: READ_CONTROL SYNCHRONIZE STANDARD_RIGHTS_READ
   STANDARD_RIGHTS_WRITE STANDARD_RIGHTS_EXECUTE GENERIC_READ
   GENERIC_EXECUTE READ ADD
INCONTINENT\MC: READ_CONTROL SYNCHRONIZE STANDARD_RIGHTS_READ
   STANDARD_RIGHTS_WRITE STANDARD_RIGHTS_EXECUTE GENERIC_READ
   GENERIC_EXECUTE READ ADD
NT AUTHORITY\Authenticated Users: DELETE READ_CONTROL SYNCHRONIZE
   STANDARD_RIGHTS_READ STANDARD_RIGHTS_WRITE STANDARD_RIGHTS_EXECUTE
   GENERIC_READ GENERIC_WRITE GENERIC_EXECUTE READ CHANGE ADD
NT AUTHORITY\SYSTEM: DELETE READ_CONTROL WRITE_DAC WRITE_OWNER
   SYNCHRONIZE STANDARD_RIGHTS_REQUIRED STANDARD_RIGHTS_READ
   STANDARD_RIGHTS_WRITE STANDARD_RIGHTS_EXECUTE STANDARD_RIGHTS_ALL
   GENERIC_ALL READ CHANGE ADD FULL
```

Note that the information is returned with the user or group name defined within one of the preset domains or system security directories. For example, the user "MC" is located within INCONTINENT, which is the name of the machine, while the Authenticated Users group is located within the NT AUTHORITY system domain. Other possible locations include registered NT domains and generic NT users and groups.

To set the permissions for a file, you need to use the MakeMask function. This accepts a list of constants, as defined in Table 4-4, and returns the correct numeric mask that you can then assign to a key of a suitable hash. For example, to create a mask to enable Read access to a file or directory, you might use a line like this:

```
$mask = Win32::FileSecurity::MakeMask(qw/READ_CONTROL GENERIC_READ/);
```

Now let's assign this value to the user "MC" within our previous example. First of all, we need to update the hash we obtained earlier with the Win32::FileSecurity::Get function:

```
$acl{'INCONTINENT\MC'} = $mask;
```

To actually modify the permissions, you need to use the Win32::FileSecurity::Set function, which applies the access control list defined within the hash to the file you specify. In our case, that means using a simple call:

```
Win32::FileSecurity::Set('C:\inetpub\wwwroot',\%acl);
```

Note that the act of setting a file with a given hash is absolute—if you only want to update the permissions for a single user or group, you will first need to obtain the current settings before updating the value for a given user. To delete the permissions for a user or group, you must use the `delete` function to remove the corresponding key/value pair from the hash, and then set the file permissions to match that of the modified hash.

To put this system into action, imagine that you want to create a script that will set a directory to a standard set of permissions. The script will exclusively configure the directory so that there is no access to the Guest account or to members of the Guests group. The following script does exactly that:

```
use Win32::FileSecurity;

foreach $file (@ARGV)
{
    set_permissions($file);
}

sub set_permissions
{
    my ($file) = @_;

    if (Win32::FileSecurity::Get($file,\%acl))
    {
        @guests = grep(/Guests?$/,keys %acl);
        foreach $guest (@guests)
        {
            print "Removing permissions for $guest on file\n";
            delete $acl{$guest};
        }
        if (Win32::FileSecurity::Set($file,\%acl))
        {
            print "Modified $file\n";
        }
        else
        {
            win32_die();
        }
    }
    else
    {
        win32_die();
    }
}

sub win32_die
{
    die Win32::FormatMessage(Win32::GetLastError());
}
```

You can now use this script to remove the permissions for one or more files and directories given on the command line:

```
C:\>11.pl c:\private
Removing permissions for INCONTINENT\Guest on c:\private
Removing permissions for BUILTIN\Guests on c:\private
Modified c:\private
```

If you want to modify the individual permissions for a given user, then you will need to examine the contents of the list returned by the `EnumerateRights` function. Remember that the list is returned as strings, so you will need to make direct comparisons and then remove individual rights by using `splice` or by copying across the rights you do want to a new list.

Additional File Information

As well as the basic file and security information stored with a file, Windows also supports the ability to store additional information against certain systems and applications, such as the version and copyright data. The information is stored within the file, rather than in a separate attribute storage system, and it can normally only be applied to binary files that support the embedded data. Thus, the information is generally restricted only to executables, DLLs, and other system-related files.

To obtain the additional information within Perl requires the use of Dave Roth's `Win32::AdminMisc` module. The module only works under Windows NT, so you cannot obtain the information from within Windows 95/98, even though both platforms support the ability to store the data. The information returned is identical to that shown in the Version tab of the Properties dialog for a file, as shown in Figure 4-2.

The module supports a single function, `Win32::AdminMisc::GetFileInfo`.

```
GetFileInfo(FILE [, INFO])
```

The function places the information for `FILE` into the hash pointed to by the hash reference pointed to by `INFO`. The keys of the hash are the field titles; the values are the corresponding field contents.

For example, the following script outputs the same information for the file shown in Figure 4-2:

```
use Win32::AdminMisc;

my %info;

$file = "$ENV{SYSTEMROOT}/regedit.exe";
```

Figure 4-2

Additional file
information.

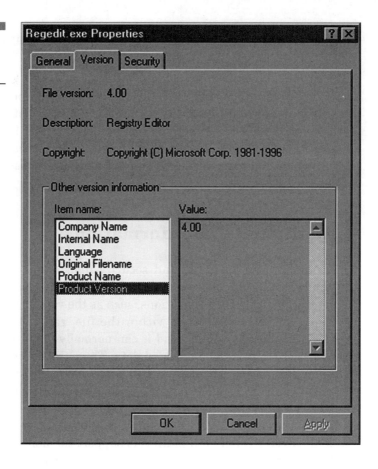

```
if (Win32::AdminMisc::GetFileInfo($file, \%info))
{
    print_hash($file,0,%info);
}
else
{
    print Win32::FormatMessage(Win32::GetLastError());
}

sub print_hash
{
    my ($title,$indent,%hash) = @_;

    print "$title:\n";

    foreach $key (sort keys %hash)
    {
        if (ref($hash{$key}) eq 'HASH')
        {
```

```
            print_hash($key,$indent+4,%{$hash{$key}});
        }
        else
        {
            print ' ' x $indent ,"$key: $hash{$key}\n";
        }
    }
}
```

When executed, you get the following output:

```
C:\WINNT/regedit.exe:
0x0409:
    CompanyName: Microsoft Corporation
    FileDescription: Registry Editor
    FileVersion: 4.00
    InternalName: REGEDIT
    LangID: 0x0409
    Language: English (United States)
    LegalCopyright: Copyright (C) Microsoft Corp. 1981-1996
    OriginalFilename: REGEDIT.EXE
    ProductName: Microsoft(R) Windows NT(TM) Operating System
    ProductVersion: 4.00
CompanyName: Microsoft Corporation
FileDescription: Registry Editor
FileInfo:
    DateStamp: 0
    Debug: 0
    FileType: application
    FileVersion: 4.0.1371.1
    OS: nt
    Patched: 0
    PreRelease: 0
    ProductVersion: 4.0.1371.1
    SpecialBuild: 0
FileVersion: 4.00
InternalName: REGEDIT
LangID: 0x0409
Language: English (United States)
LegalCopyright: Copyright (C) Microsoft Corp. 1981-1996
OriginalFilename: REGEDIT.EXE
ProductName: Microsoft(R) Windows NT(TM) Operating System
ProductVersion: 4.00
```

Note that information output is nested to display the embedded hash contained within some of the fields retrieved by the function. In this case there is an embedded hash using a key of 0x0409. This is the reference key for the U.S. English language version of the file information. Had we been viewing the information in an alternative language, then we would have found a different language key. The individual fields supported by the main and embedded hashes should be self-explanatory. However, see Table 4-5 for the main keys and Table 4-6 for the hash information embedded in the FileInfo key.

TABLE 4-5

Information returned by `GetFileInfo`.

Hash Key	Description
CompanyName	The name of the company that created the file.
FileDescription	A description of the file contents.
FileInfo	A hash containing extended information about the file version. See Table 4-6.
FileVersion	A simple file version number.
InternalName	The name used by the application internally—normally set by the developer.
LangID	The hexadecimal language ID for the file. These are the language IDs used by the operating system. If you have a copy of Visual C++, check the *LANGCODE.CPP* file for a complete list. As a quick reference, 0x0409 refers to U.S. English, and 0x0809 refers to British English.
Language	The language for the file, as a string, such as "English (United States)" or "English (British)."
LegalCopyright	The copyright notice for the file.
OriginalFilename	The real name of the file as it was generated, rather than its current name.
ProductName	The product name or product family name.
ProductVersion	The product or product family version.

TABLE 4-6

Information within the embedded `FieldInfo` hash element.

Hash Key	Description
DateStamp	The date and time when the file was generated.
Debug	Indicates whether the file was compiled with debugging switched on.
FileType	The file type, for example, "application."
FileVersion	The full file version number, including any patch and subversion numbers.
OS	Valid operating systems under which the application will run.
Patched	Indicates whether the file has been updated or patched since it was installed.
PreRelease	Indicates whether the file is a prerelease version.
ProductVersion	The product version number. When an application is part of a larger product, this may show a different version than `FileVersion`.
SpecialBuild	Indicates whether the file is part of a special unique build. Zero means the file is a standard version.

Note that in the `FileVersion` and `ProductVersion` numbers for system files, the number will be in the form

```
major.minor.build.servicepack
```

In our example above, the file was for version 4.0 of Windows NT, Build 1371, Service Pack 1 (original build).

I've used this information in the past to determine the version numbers of all the applications on a particular machine. When managing a network of machines, it is often difficult to keep track of which machines have had the various updates and patches applied. The script below provides a complete tool for extracting the information from a machine for all of the applications and libraries. It will also compare the file with a previous execution or against a file generated by another machine so that you can compare the version numbers.

```perl
use File::Find;
use Win32::AdminMisc;
use Getopt::Std;

unless(getopts("dc:u:"))
{
    print "Usage: 13.pl [-c file]|[-u file] [-d]\n";
}

my (%filever,$id) = ((),0);

if ($opt_c)
{
    open(FILE,"$opt_c") || die "Couldn't open $opt_c: $!";
    while(<FILE>)
    {
        chomp;
        my ($file,$version) = split /~/;
        $filever{$file} = $version;
    }
}
else
{
    open(FILE,">$opt_u") || die "Couldn't open $opt_u: $!";
}

find(\&process_file,'c:/Program Files');

close(FILE);

print "\n";
sub process_file
{
    my $file = $File::Find::name;
    return unless ($file =~ m/(dll)$/);
    my %info;
    unless(Win32::AdminMisc::GetFileInfo($file,\%info))
    {
```

```
        warn "$file: " . Win32::FormatMessage(Win32::GetLastError())
            if ($opt_d);
        return;
    }
    print "Processing ",$id++,"\r";
    if ($opt_c)
    {
        unless (exists($filever{$file}))
        {
            print "$file is not in stat file\n";
            return;
        }
        if ($info{FileVersion} ne $filever{$file})
        {
            print("$file does not match that on record, was ",
                $filever{$file},
                " currently ",
                $info{FileVersion},
                "\n");
        }
    }
    if ($opt_u)
    {
        print FILE "$file~$info{FileVersion}\n";
    }
}
```

To create a new version file, call the script with -u and the name of the file in which you want to store the information:

```
C:\> 13.pl -u stat.ver
Processing 34
```

Once you have a file, you can use the same script to compare the files with the versions kept on record:

```
C:\> 13.pl -c stat.ver
c:/Program Files/Microsoft FrontPage Express/bin/fp20htp.dll does
  not match that on record, was 2.0.2.1119 currently 2.0.2.1130
c:/Program Files/Microsoft FrontPage Express/bin/fp20tl.dll does
  not match that on record, was 2.0.2.1119 currently 2.0.2.1130
c:/Program Files/Microsoft FrontPage Express/bin/fp20utl.dll
  does not match that on record, was 2.0.2.1119 currently 2.0.2.1130
```

You can tell from the output given that what we need to do on this machine is to update FrontPage Express.

Shortcuts

Shortcuts are more complex than the hard or symbolic links available under Unix. Instead of being simple pointers to a file or directory, a shortcut is actually a special type of file that points to another file or directory. Each shortcut file has an extension of *.lnk*, and the contents of the file define the parameters to use when the shortcut is accessed.

However, instead of being a simple pointer to the file or directory, a shortcut actually enables you to specify additional information, such as the arguments to the program you are linking to and a working directory. You can even assign keyboard sequences to shortcuts to provide a quick method for opening a file or directory.

Because shortcuts are more complex and practical than simple links, they are used all over the operating system to support different features. At the simplest level, you'll find shortcuts on your desktop that will open applications or take you to different folders, either on your local hard disk or to network volumes. Shortcuts are also used to provide the list of applications available via the Start menu.

Finally, because shortcuts can include additional command-line arguments, they are also used to support a number of different options or configurations while continuing to use the same application. For example, if you have Quake II installed on your machine, you will find that you have Start menu items called Quake II and Quake II—Compatibility Mode. Both run the same physical application, but the latter shortcut includes the command-line arguments that switch the application into 640x480, software video mode.

You can see the information stored in a shortcut by looking at its Properties. See Figure 4-3 for a sample.

Unlike the previous modules that we have seen, access to shortcut information is via an object rather than a function/hash-based interface:

```
use Win32::Shortcut;

$link = new Win32::Shortcut();
```

The above code creates a new `Win32::Shortcut` object but does not automatically associate it with an existing file. For that you use the `Load` method:

```
$link->Load("C:\Everything.lnk");
```

Or you can combine the two by specifying the name of the link you want to load during object creation:

```
$link = new Win32::Shortcut("C:\Everything.lnk");
```

The above method also works when you want to create a new shortcut; you will need to manually assign the different values to the object in order to set up the shortcut for use.

Figure 4-3

Properties for an application shortcut.

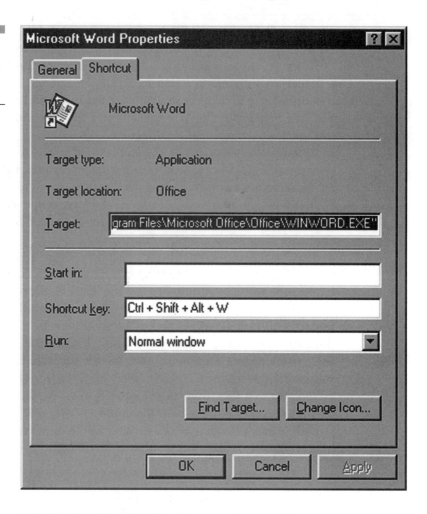

NOTE.   *You must specify the .lnk extension to the file; the module doesn't add the extension for you.*

To extract or set the information, you call the corresponding method for the property that you want to access. Calling the method without any arguments causes the method to return the current value. Supplying an argument to the methods sets the property to the supplied value. For example, the following script obtains the information for the "Microsoft Word" alias in the Start menu:

```
use Win32::Shortcut;

$file = 'C:\WINDOWS\Start Menu\Programs\Office\Microsoft Word.lnk';
```

```
my $sc = new Win32::Shortcut;

if ($sc->Load($file))
{
    print "File:              ", $file,"\n";
    print "IconNumber:        ", $sc->IconNumber,"\n";
    print "IconLocation:      ", $sc->IconLocation,"\n";
    print "Hotkey:            ", $sc->Hotkey,"\n";
    print "Description:       ", $sc->Description,"\n";
    print "ShowCmd:           ", $sc->ShowCmd,"\n";
    print "WorkingDirectory:  ", $sc->WorkingDirectory,"\n";
    print "Arguments:         ", $sc->Arguments,"\n";
    print "ShortPath:         ", $sc->ShortPath,"\n";
    print "Path:              ", $sc->Path,"\n";
}
else
{
    warn "Warning: $file: " .
      Win32::FormatMessage(Win32::GetLastError());
}
```

If I run this on my machine, the script outputs the following information:

```
File:              C:\WINDOWS\Start Menu\Programs\Office\Microsoft
                   Word.lnk
IconNumber:        0
IconLocation:
Hotkey:            1879
Description:
ShowCmd:           1
WorkingDirectory:
Arguments:
ShortPath:         C:\PROGRA~~1\MICROS-~~\OFFICE\WINWORD.EXE
Path:              C:\Program Files\Microsoft Office\Office\WINWORD.EXE
```

You can see a list of the properties and their purpose in Table 4-7.

Once you have set the values for a shortcut, you need to save the changes to the Shortcut file. You do this by using the `Save` method, which writes out the information to the file but does not close. You can make further modifications; just ensure you use the `Save` method to record those details back to the file once you have finished.

```
$link->Save("C:\Nothing.lnk");
```

The `Save` method accepts a single argument: the name of the file that you want to save the shortcut information to. This overrides the value of the `File` property and is useful in those situations where you want to generate the information for a shortcut but don't know until the last minute where the shortcut is to be created. If you omit the filename in the method call, the method will take the name from the `File` property.

TABLE 4-7

Shortcut
properties.

Property	Description
Arguments	The arguments to the file or command being linked to. This is the second half of the Target box in the Properties dialog. Not used for shortcuts pointing to simple files or directories.
Description	An optional description.
File	The name of the Shortcut file. This is the location of the actual shortcut on disk, *not* the name of the file you are linking to. It *must* have an *.lnk* extension.
Hotkey	The 2-byte shortcut key, returned as a decimal value. See the "Hotkeys" section later in this chapter for details on how to encode and decode a hotkey sequence.
IconLocation	The path to the file that contains the icon you want to use for the shortcut.
IconNumber	The number of the icon within the IconLocation file.
Path	The path to the target file.
ShortPath	The DOS 8.3 character-compatible version of Path. This value is set by the operating system. It has to be unique and is therefore not modifiable by the user (this is to ensure that DOS programs are still able to access multiple files starting with the same string—for example, Document, which fills the normal eight-character limit).
ShowCmd	The style of window in which the command will be executed. Can be one of SW_SHOWNORMAL, SW_SHOWMAXIMIZED, or SW_SHOWMINNOACTIVE, for normal, maximized, and minimized windows.
WorkingDirectory	The directory in which Path will be executed. Identical to the Start In field in the Properties dialog.

If you want to obtain the path to which a shortcut points without actually accessing the properties for the object, you can use the Resolve method:

```
$real=$link->Resolve();
```

This also accepts an argument; if the supplied argument is the numerical value 2, then a dialog will be displayed to allow the user to resolve the shortcut if the current file location cannot be found.

The Set method enables you to set the properties for a shortcut without using the methods shown in Table 4-7:

```
$link->Set(PATH, ARGS, WORKINGDIR, DESC,
          SHOWCMD, HOTKEY, ICONFILE, ICONNUMBER);
```

Once you have finished with the object, you can explicitly close it with the `Close` method or just let it run out of scope.

Hotkeys

When we looked at the properties of the Microsoft Word shortcut earlier, the `Hotkey` property had a value of 1879. This is a decimal that we need to convert into its hexadecimal equivalent before we can start to decode what the code refers to. To convert the value into hex, we need to use `printf` **or** `sprintf`:

```
printf("Keycode: 0x%04x\n",$sc->Hotkey);
```

This gives a four-digit hex value. From our sample, the value output is

```
0x0757
```

The first two digits refer to the modifier key, a combination of Control, Alt, or Shift, whereas the third and fourth digits refer to the keycode—the code generated when you press a specific key on the keyboard.

The modifier keys are easy to decode. The value is just a simple mask, so we can work out which keys were pressed by using logic against the predefined mask values. The values for each key are given in Table 4-8.

For example, Control-Shift would have a value of 0x03.

The keycodes for the remaining keys are unique to each key. Each key on the keyboard is given a unique number; for example, the hexadecimal value 0x57 is equivalent to pressing the W key. Note that these values are different from the ASCII value. This is because it doesn't actually output ASCII characters—the keyboard just sends a keycode to the computer. How the computer interprets the code is dependent on the operating system and any localization or other customization that might have been applied.

TABLE 4-8

Modifier key values.

Modifier Key	Keycode Value
Shift	0x01
Control	0x02
Alt	0x04

TABLE 4-9

Key codes for special keys.

Description	Value	Description	Value
Backspace key	0x08	End key	0x23
Tab key	0x09	Home key	0x24
Clear key	0x0c	Left Arrow key	0x25
Enter key	0x0d	Up Arrow key	0x26
Shift key	0x10	Right Arrow key	0x27
Ctrl key	0x11	Down Arrow key	0x28
Menu key	0x12	Print Screen key	0x2a
Pause key	0x13	Execute key	0x2b
Caps Lock key	0x14	Ins key	0x2d
Esc key	0x1b	Del key	0x2e
Spacebar key	0x20	Help key	0x2f
Page Up key	0x21	Num Lock key	0x90
Page Down key	0x22		

For example, when you press Shift-3 on a keyboard attached to a machine configured for a U.S. keyboard, a dollar will be displayed, while a UK-configured keyboard will generate a pound sign. The ASCII values for these two characters are completely different. However, the keyboard is not aware of the configuration; it sends the same keycode no matter what language the keyboard is configured for. All the keyboard knows is to send the keycode for Shift-3 (which would be 0x0133).

Tables 4-9 through 4-12 show the keycode generated by the special keys, alphanumeric keys, number-keypad keys, and function keys, respectively.

Using this information, we can now see that the 0x0757 code configured for the Microsoft Word shortcut equates to Control-Alt-Shift-W.

Many people use shortcut hotkeys because they find the keyboard quicker to use than the mouse for simple things like opening an application. The problem is, you can have so many keyboard shortcuts for different applications that it gets difficult to remember them all. You could keep a manual record of the information, but this is time-consuming, and it means that you would have to update the data each time.

Instead, you could use the following script, which examines all of the shortcuts in the Start menu, extracts the hotkey information, and then decodes the hotkey number into a real keyboard combination.

TABLE 4-10

Key codes for the
standard keys.

Description	Value	Description	Value
0 key	0x30	I key	0x49
1 key	0x31	J key	0x4A
2 key	0x32	K key	0x4B
3 key	0x33	L key	0x4C
4 key	0x34	M key	0x4D
5 key	0x35	N key	0x4E
6 key	0x36	O key	0x4F
7 key	0x37	P key	0x50
8 key	0x38	Q key	0x51
9 key	0x39	R key	0x52
A key	0x41	S key	0x53
B key	0x42	T key	0x54
C key	0x43	U key	0x55
D key	0x44	V key	0x56
E key	0x45	W key	0x57
F key	0x46	X key	0x58
G key	0x47	Y key	0x59
H key	0x48	Z key	0x5A

TABLE 4-11

Key codes for the
numeric keys.

Description	Value	Description	Value
0 key	0x60	8 key	0x68
1 key	0x61	9 key	0x69
2 key	0x62	Multiplication sign (*) key	0x6A
3 key	0x63	Plus sign (+) key	0x6B
4 key	0x64	Enter (keypad) key	0x6C
5 key	0x65	Minus sign (-) key	0x6D
6 key	0x66	Decimal point (.) key	0x6E
7 key	0x67	Division sign (/) key	0x6F

```perl
use Win32::Shortcut;
use File::Find;
use strict;

my %keys = init_keys();
my $sc = new Win32::Shortcut;

find(\&wanted,"C:/WINDOWS/Start Menu/");

sub wanted
{
    my $file = $File::Find::name;

    return unless($file =~ m/\.lnk$/);

    if ($sc->Load($file))
    {
        my ($realfile) = ($file =~ m#.*/(.*)\.lnk$#);
        if ($sc->Hotkey > 0)
        {
            printf("%-40s: %s\n",$realfile,decode_key($sc->Hotkey));
        }
    }
    else
    {
        warn "Warning: $file: " .
            Win32::FormatMessage(Win32::GetLastError());
    }
}

sub decode_key
{
    my ($key) = @_;

    my (@mods,@keys);

    my ($mod,$realkey) = unpack("a2a2", sprintf("%04x",$key));

    push @mods,'Shift' if ($mod & 0x01);
    push @mods,'Control' if ($mod & 0x02);
    push @mods,'Alt' if ($mod & 0x04);

    return(join('-',@mods) . " " . $keys{hex($realkey)});
}

sub init_keys()
{
    my %keys;

    open(KEYS,"keylist.txt") || die "Cannot open keylist.txt: $!";

    while(<KEYS>)
    {
        chomp;
        my ($key, $desc) = split(/\t/,$_,2);
        $keys{hex($key)} = $desc;
    }

    close(KEYS);

    return(%keys);
}
```

TABLE 4-12

Key codes for the
function keys.

Description	Value	Description	Value
F1 key	0x70	F9 key	0x78
F2 key	0x71	F10 key	0x79
F3 key	0x72	F11 key	0x7A
F4 key	0x73	F12 key	0x7B
F5 key	0x74	F13 key	0x7C
F6 key	0x75	F14 key	0x7D
F7 key	0x76	F15 key	0x7E
F8 key	0x77	F16 key	0x7F

If I run this on my machine, I get output like this:

```
Internet Explorer              : Shift-Control-Alt I
Microsoft Excel                : Shift-Control-Alt E
Microsoft Outlook              : Shift-Control-Alt M
Microsoft Word                 : Shift-Control-Alt W
Acrobat Reader 4.0             : Shift-Control-Alt A
Quicken Deluxe 2000            : Shift-Control-Alt Q
```

File Locking

Neither Windows 95 nor Windows 98 directly supports any form of file locking. Under Windows NT, via the POSIX compatibility layer, you can use `flock` to do file locking for you. The `fcntl` function is not supported, but you can still import the necessary constants from the `Fcntl` module. You can see the list of valid constants in Table 4-13.

The format for the `flock` command is

```
flock FILEHANDLE, OPERATION
```

Here is an example of locking a file before writing:

```
use Fcntl qw/LOCK_SH LOCK_EX LOCK_UN LOCK_NB/;
flock DATA, LOCK_EX;
print DATA $message;
flock DATA, LOCK_UN;
```

Note that `flock` will block process execution until such time as the requested lock can be achieved. The way to get around this is to use $LOCK_NB, which attempts to lock the filehandle without blocking.

TABLE 4-13

Locking operations.

Operation	Result
LOCK_SH	Set shared lock.
LOCK_EX	Set exclusive lock.
LOCK_UN	Unlock specified file.
LOCK_NB	Set lock without blocking.

However, caution should be used here: You must make sure you test the result of the lock before you start using the file. When using $LOCK_NB, the result from flock will be True, irrespective of whether the lock succeeded.

When using the flock function, the file locking offered is advisory rather than guaranteed. The fact that the lock has been set does not guarantee that another application will not be able to access or overwrite the file. This is because all the applications that use the file need to use the same file-locking mechanism, and without a coherent Windows standard for file locking, there is no way to enforce the locking mechanism. You should also be aware that flock will not work over a networked file system.

File Locking without flock

Unfortunately, Windows 95 and 98 do not support either the flock or fcntl function, so you cannot use these functions to provide file-level locking. This means there are only two possible solutions: Either you use a separate lock file to indicate the locked status of a file, or you use the operating system option of a mutex. A *mutex* is a mutually exclusive object that you can use to indicate a lock on any network-accessible resource, including files, printers, and network connections.

The Win32::Mutex module provides mechanisms for creating, working, and destroying with mutexes. The method is similar to file locks: A process creates a mutex attached to a particular resource. Only one process can own a mutex at any one time, and while the process owns it, it has exclusive access to the specified resource. The following code

```
Use Win32::Mutex;
$mutex = new Win32::Mutex([INITIAL, [NAME]])
```

creates a new mutex. If INITIAL is true, immediate ownership of the mutex is assumed. NAME is the name of the mutex you want to create, or it opens an existing mutex if one with the same name already exists. Alternatively, you can use the following method:

```
$mutex = Win32::Mutex->open(NAME)
```

In this instance you must specify the name of an existing mutex. For a file-based resource, the name you use is the file path or UNC name for a file or directory.

The following code

```
$mutex->release
```

releases ownership of the mutex. It returns True if successful.

This code

```
$mutex->wait([TIMEOUT])
```

waits for the mutex to be released by another process and immediately sets ownership of it. If TIMEOUT is specified, it waits for that number of seconds. If the timeout expires, the function returns False. The wait queue is ordered in first-in, first-out (FIFO) mode—the first process to wait on a mutex will be the first in a queue and the first to obtain the mutex when the previous process has finished with it.

NOTE. *My experience with mutexes has not been satisfactory. Although the theory works well, the mutex system was designed to support shared access to UNC-based resources, not to individual files. Although in an ideal world, the* Win32::Mutex *system should work, in my tests the practice is very different.*

Monitoring Directory Changes

There are times when it is useful to be able to monitor whether the contents of a directory change. For example, imagine you have a publicly shared folder and want to know immediately when someone has placed a new file in the folder. Although you could study the file list, after a given period, this would be terribly inefficient.

Windows provides a solution in the form of the "change notification" system. This notifies a process when a specific directory changes for any reason. The Active Perl distribution includes a module to access this system, Win32::ChangeNotify, which is an interface to the operating system's ChangeNotify system that is used by many parts of the operating to control its operation, including the printer queues. For example, the following code

```
use Win32::ChangeNotify;

$notify = Win32::ChangeNotify->new(PATH, SUBTREE, EVENTS);
```

creates a new object configured to monitor the PATH specified, which can either be a file or directory. If it is a directory, you can set SUBTREE to 1, which causes the new monitor object to include all of the subdirectories within PATH as well as the main directory. The EVENTS argument is a string of the constants listed in Table 4-14. The constants should be separated either by white space or the | character.

Once created, two methods control the operation of the object. The reset method resets the system so that the object will be notified when a change occurs. It must be called before you start the loop to monitor for changes. No notification will take place until this function is called:

```
$notify->reset();
```

The reset method actually resets the change notification object, clearing any previous values that would have been returned by the Wait method (see below). This means that it must be used each time you start

TABLE 4-14

Events to monitor.

Constant	Description
FILE_NOTIFY_CHANGE_ATTRIBUTES	Any changes to the file's/directory's attributes.
FILE_NOTIFY_CHANGE_DIR_NAME	Any directory name change.
FILE_NOTIFY_CHANGE_FILE_NAME	Any change to a file's name.
FILE_NOTIFY_CHANGE_LAST_WRITE	Any change to the file, which implies an update of the file's last modification time, or the directory's last content change.
FILE_NOTIFY_CHANGE_SECURITY	Implements changes to the security of the directory or file.
FILE_NOTIFY_CHANGE_SIZE	Implements changes to the file's size or to additions to a directory contents. However, it doesn't detect deletions from a given directory.

waiting for a change, including the state after a change has previously been detected.

The Wait takes a single argument, the timeout value, and blocks the process until the timeout expires or when a change occurs on the specified object:

```
$notify->Wait(60);
```

This line would block the process and wait for 60 seconds for a change to the directory to occur. If no change takes place, then the Wait method returns 0. If you want to wait forever, then use the constant INFINITE. If the call returns because of a timeout, you can call Wait again until a change is detected.

If Wait returns True, then it indicates that a modification has taken place, and you need to examine the directory contents. Note though that the queue length for change notifications is only 1—even if a number of changes have taken place, the change notification system will only be aware of a single change. When you have processed the changes, you need to reset the current state by calling reset. This will immediately place the current queue value into the current state. To clear both the current and queue state, call reset twice.

When you have finished monitoring an object, you should use the Close method. This frees up memory and processor cycles—once the object is destroyed, the directory is no longer monitored.

The following script sets up a simple watch to monitor when a new file is copied into a specific directory:

```
$watch = Win32::Change Notify->new(

$watchdir = 'c:/incoming';

$watch = Win32::ChangeNotify->new
                        $watchdir,
                        1,
                        FILE_NOTIFY_CHANGE_ATTRIBUTES
                        | FILE_NOTIFY_CHANGE_SIZE);

$result = Win32::GetLastError();

%watchlist = ();

foreach(glob("$watchdir/*.*"))
{
    $watchlist{$_} = 1;
}

if ($watch)
{
```

```perl
while(1)
{
    while($watch->FindNext())
    {
        my (@add,@delete,%newlist);
        print "Watching...\n";
        $watch->Wait(INFINITE);
        print "Somethings changed, calculating...\n";
        foreach $file (glob("$watchdir/*.*"))
        {
            $newlist{$file} = 1;
            next if (exists($watchlist{$file}));
            push @add, $file;
        }
        foreach $file (keys %watchlist)
        {
            next if (exists($newlist{$file}));
            push @delete, $file;
        }
        %watchlist = %newlist;
        print("The following files have been added\n",
            join("\n",@add),"\n");
        print("The following files have been deleted\n",
            join("\n",@delete),"\n");
    }
}
else
{
    die "Error!: " . Win32::FormatMessage($result);
}
```

Note that although in this example we output the information about which files have been deleted, we cannot monitor that operation. The Win32::ChangeNotify object will only be updated when a new file has been added to the directory.

Opening and Using Files

Most of the file functions you are used to using under Unix work in an identical fashion. For reference, the list of valid modes is shown in Table 4-15.

The only two that do not work are "-|" and "|-". This is because both these expressions open a pipe to a forked process, and Windows does not use the fork function. For most instances you can use a piped expression in place of one of these two options; however, this is less secure, so care should be taken when using pipes with tainted information.

TABLE 4-15

Options for opening files.

Expression	Result
`"filename"`	Opens the file for reading only.
`"<filename"`	Opens the file for reading only.
`">filename"`	Truncates and opens the file for writing.
`"+<filename"`	Opens the file for reading and writing.
`"+>filename"`	Truncates and opens the file for reading and writing.
`"|command"`	Runs the command and pipes the output to the filehandle.
`"command|"`	Pipes the output from the filehandle to the input of command.
`"-"`	Opens STDIN.
`">-"`	Opens STDOUT.
`"<&FILEHANDLE"`	Duplicates specified FILEHANDLE or file descriptor, if numeric, for reading.
`">&FILEHANDLE"`	Duplicates specified FILEHANDLE or file descriptor, if numeric, for writing.
`"<&=N"`	Opens the file descriptor matching N; essentially identical to C's `fdopen()`.

Working with Binary Files

You must specify to the Perl interpreter when you are expecting to read or write files in binary rather than text format by using the `binmode` function. The problem is that Windows does not use ^Z to signify the end of a binary file, so it cannot be used to detect the end of file. In addition to the end-of-file problems, because the libraries automatically convert between \r\n and \n, you may end up corrupting data.

For example, consider the following code:

```
open(SRC, "infile") or die "Can't open source $!";
open(DEST, ">outfile") or die "Can't open destination $!";
while(read(SRC,$buffer,1024))
{
    print DEST $buffer;
}
close(SRC);
close(DEST);
```

This script will work fine on text files, but for binary files, it's highly likely it will corrupt the destination copy of the file.

Instead, you must specify the binary operation on both the source and destination files:

```
open(SRC, "infile") or die "Can't open source $!";
open(DEST, ">outfile") or die "Can't open destination $!";
binmode(SRC);
binmode(DEST);
while(read(SRC,$buffer,1024))
{
    print DEST $buffer;
}
close(SRC);
close(DEST);
```

Note that the change only occurs at the point at which you specify the binary operation for the filehandle; any reads or writes that occur before the call to binmode will be in text mode.

Another point to note with the difference between binary and text mode files is that pointers within files may be different when using the same file in the two different modes. This shouldn't affect functions like seek, which is a binary operation and therefore ignores line translation, but it may alter the effects of figures given to functions such as read.

For example, the script:

```
open(SRC,"TEXT");
seek(SRC,100,0);
read(SRC,$buffer,100);
print "Text mode\n";
print $buffer;
close(SRC);

open(SRC,"TEXT");
binmode(SRC);
seek(SRC,100,0);
print "Binary mode\n";
read(SRC,$buffer,100);
print $buffer;
close(SRC);
```

locates to the same position within the file, but it doesn't output the same text:

```
Text mode
 just some sample text
This is just some sample text
This is just some sample text
This is just some
Binary mode
 just some sample text
This is just some sample text
This is just some sample text
This is just s
```

You can see here that in text mode, the `read` function has correctly translated the \r\n lines, and it has read 100 bytes of text, excluding the \r line termination characters. In binary mode, the \r characters are included in the count of 100 bytes that has been read from the file.

As a general rule, of course, you should not be using hard-coded values anyway. If you are porting across a text-processing application, then most of these problems will not affect you, provided you have remembered to transfer the documents as text, not binary.

`truncate`

The `truncate` function truncates a file to a specific size. Under Windows you must be careful when using the function; there may be conflicts between open files and filehandles. If supplied a filehandle, the file must have been opened with Write access; otherwise, the call will fail. If supplied a filename, it should not be opened by the same or another application.

File and IO Control

The `fcntl` function is not supported under Windows. Aside from the file-locking solution mentioned above, there are no workarounds for the functionality supported by `fcntl`. The `ioctl` function is only supported on network sockets.

## CHAPTER 5

Process Management

Using external programs is often a practical way of getting information about a machine when more direct methods are unavailable. Most of the time you probably don't even think about the mechanics of creating a new process even when using `system` or `open` to obtain information from the host.

Although most of the functions supported by Perl for starting applications, including `system`, backticks, `open`, and `exec`, work as normal, they do not always provide the functionality you need. The ActivePerl distribution comes with the `Win32::Process` module, which provides direct access to the Windows API used for creating new processes. However, to understand how to migrate your Unix applications to Windows, you need to appreciate how processes on the two operating systems differ.

Many of the difficulties associated with migrating Unix applications that employ process creation and management are related to the way in which Windows treats individual processes. Reading the Windows 95/98 and Windows NT SDK (software development kit) information will provide you with the best idea of how the system works, but we'll take a quick look here and compare it to the Unix equivalents. We'll primarily deal with Windows NT here, as much of the core technology developed for NT is now a part of all the current Windows revisions, including to some degree Windows 2000.

Under Unix, a *process* is an addressable area of memory that is executed by the processor. Control of the process is normally only offered through the use of predefined signals. These allow you to suspend, resume, and kill a process, as well as providing methods for the process itself to communicate with its parent—for example, when the process raises a `SIGFPE` signal, which indicates a floating-point math error. Through the kernel scheduler, you can also control the priority of the process. All of the methods rely on individual functions that communicate with different parts of the OS in order to achieve their objectives.

Processes can be logically grouped into process groups, and parent processes can have related child processes. The process group and parent information can be used both as a method of control (you can kill a process group or parent and all of its children). Individual processes are also created by a specific user—it is not possible to create a "general" process. User processes can only be controlled by the user or by the system administrator.

Although it's impossible to generalize, most modern Unix systems also allow individual processes to have a number of individual threads. These are directly controlled by the parent process and can be executed on more than one processor simultaneously. Like processes, they can also be controlled by a number of functions, but their treatment is again individual and their control does not rely on communicating with the parent process.

Under Windows, a process and its associated threads are exposed to the programmer as an object. Methods are available for controlling a process, from creation through to suspension and priority and finally to termination. Like Unix, each process has its own priority, controllable through object methods, and the process object also has a security profile that controls not only what the process can access, but also who has access to the process. Unlike Unix, Windows processes can be generic—that is, the security profile is left wide open so that potentially anybody can modify the processes' execution, including terminating them.

A process object contains information about the process's virtual address space, the process's security profile, a set of threads that execute within the process's address space, and a set of resources that are available to all threads within the process. Windows also allows processes to be collated into process groups, but new groups can only be created when starting a new process—it cannot be done within the application. A Windows process does not have a strict sense of its parent, but an application that creates a process can control the child process, only because it has direct access to the process's object information.

Communication with a process can only take place through the process's object. Although signals are supported, it is a reduced set included only for POSIX compliance and not actually used for communication within Windows. It's also impossible to use signals to control other processes; you can only raise signals to processes that you have created.

Because the generation of new processes is based on executing new code using threads, operations like `fork`—which duplicate the current application—do not work. Under Unix, `fork` is often used to spawn a new process to handle communication with a client. For example, many web servers use `fork` to duplicate themselves when responding to a client's request. In most cases, the `fork` function is used to provide an easy way of duplicating the parent process's open file handles. Windows actually supports the inheritance of file handles for new processes during process creation, making `fork` unnecessary in many situations.

Although `fork` is not natively supported by any Windows operating system, Perl 5.6 and beyond does include `fork` support. The support is fairly limited, due to the fact that the emulation is occurring within Perl, rather than using an OS function (which would make life significantly easier!). We'll look at some of the limitations in this chapter.

One final difference is that Windows does not support the notion of `setuid` programs. The Unix `setuid` system allows an application to be started by one user but actually executed as it was run by another. This is the way in which `passwd` changes the password of a user. Normally the user does not have write access to the `/etc/passwd` and `/etc/shadow` files. Because `passwd` is `setuid` root, users can change their passwords by momentarily appearing to have the privileges of the systems administrator.

The `setuid` system is not supported by Windows directly, but it does allow applications to be run with the security permissions of another user by making use of the `CreateProcessAsUser` function. Unlike the main `CreateProcess` function, which creates a generic process with no user-specific security profile, the `CreateProcessAsUser` function creates a new process with the security profile of the current user. When used in conjunction with the `LogonAsUser` function (which changes the current user profile), it enables you to run an application as another user within the confines of a single script. The standard ActivePerl libraries do not support these two functions, but they are available through Dave Roth's `Win32::AdminMisc` module.

In this chapter, we'll look at the basics of creating new processes using the built-in Perl functions before moving on to the Windows-specific `Win32::Process` module and the `Win32::AdminMisc::CreateProcessAsUser` function. We'll also look at ways in which processes can be controlled once created.

Finally, we'll take a look at the environment variables, which play an important part both in providing information about the current environment and also defining the `PATH`, which is used when searching for applications.

Running External Programs

There are basically four ways of executing external programs: using the `system` function, backticks, the `open` function, and the `exec` function. As a general rule, most functions work identically to the Unix implementations, but there are some minor differences related to the environment that is available to you when you run applications in this way.

Using system

The `system` function has two forms: either you supply a single scalar argument or a list. In its former format, it executes the statement you supply using a command shell (usually COMMAND.COM) and outputs the result. The standard input, output, and error handles are inherited by the command. For example:

```
system('dir *.pl');
```

In fact, Perl does its best to identify the contents of the argument and only calls the command via a shell when it detects any metacharacters that would need to be parsed by the shell interpreter.

The list format executes the program, taking the first argument as the name of the program to execute and the remainder of the arguments as arguments to the program:

```
system('dir','*.pl');
```

The more astute will have noticed that we are actually still running a command that is embedded into the command interpreter. There is no application called `dir`, and you won't find `dir.exe` on a Windows machine. This is in deference to the Unix implementation, which tries to run the command directly, ignoring any shell interpreter.

The `system` function calls the program, which inherits the environment and standard input, output, and error file handles from the Perl interpreter. It also pauses the interpreter until the application you have called has completed. For example, the script

```
system('notepad file.txt');
```

will run the Notepad application, but until you exit the application, the Perl script will not continue.

If you want to "spawn" a new application but not wait for it, then you can add the word *start* to the beginning of the program call:

```
system('start notepad file.txt');
```

The `start` keyword creates a new process that is independent of the Perl interpreter; in fact, the Perl script can end with the spawned program still running. If you want a more explicit function for spawning, rather than calling, external programs, see the `Win32::Spawn` function later in this chapter.

Backticks

Backticks (also known as "backquotes" or the `qx{}` operator) run the command specified through a command interpreter just like `system`, except that the standard output from the command is returned to the Perl interpreter. You can use this to get the information from an application without redirecting it and then opening the redirected file:

```
@dirlist = 'dir';
```

Using open

The `open` function can also be used to run an external program and accept its output (as with backticks) or provide information through the program's own standard input. For example, we could rewrite the script

```
@dirlist = 'dir';
foreach $dir (@dirlist)
{
    print $dir;
}
```

with

```
open(DIRLIST,"dir|") or die "Can't open pipe to dir: $!";
while(<DIRLIST>)
{
    print $_;
}
```

Both are overly long-winded for what we are trying to achieve, but you should get the idea. The trick is that the pipe symbol | at the end of the filename argument to the `open` function indicates to Perl that it should accept the standard output of the function as the source of information when reading from the `DIRLIST` file handle.

If you place the pipe symbol at the beginning of the file definition, then the file handle can be used to write to the standard input of the program. For example, you could print a sorted list of words to the screen by piping the output through the `sort` program, writing to the program's file handle:

```
open(SORT,"|sort") or die "Couldn't pipe to sort: $!";
print SORT join(@words,"\n");
```

In general, you can use the `open` function in much the same was you would under Unix. The only trick to be wary of is that Windows does not have as wide a range of command-line programs. Commands you may be familiar with under Unix cannot be guaranteed to be available, even in another form, under Windows.

In particular, one of the most often requested programs under Windows is `sendmail`, used under Unix for sending e-mail. Normally you'd call the program like this:

```
open(MAIL,"sendmail -t") or die "Couldn't send mail: $!";
```

Unfortunately, there is no standard program for sending e-mail under Windows, although there are tools that will make the process appear as easy as the above solution. In general, you should probably be using the `Net::SMTP` module (which comes with ActivePerl) or use sockets to talk directly to an SMTP server. See *Perl: The Complete Reference* for details.

As another alternative, under Windows you could use OLE to communicate with a client mail program such as Microsoft Outlook to send the e-mail. However, this would rely on you knowing what the machine's e-mail software was and how to communicate with the program to send the e-mail.

Creating New Processes

We've differentiated here between running an external program and waiting for it to complete and the action of creating a new process that is not considered to be a child of the parent Perl script. Using `system` or `open`, we execute a program explicitly for use in combination with the Perl script that we've called. For example, we might call `dir` to execute a directory listing, but we still want to wait and display that information to the user.

When spawning a new process, we are probably using the system to execute an external application as part of a management environment. Imagine, for example, a Perl script that allows us to start a number of applications simultaneously. In theory, we could use the `start` keyword with the `system` function, but being able to control the process that is created can be useful. The ability to change a process's priority, or even to suspend a process altogether, can be useful when creating a management script.

Using `fork`

The obvious solution to starting new processes within a Perl program—for instance, when you want to spawn a new server to handle a client request—is to use the `fork` function. At the time of writing, in the current releases, the `fork` function was not supported under any version of Windows.

This is due to the way in which the Windows system operates and not actually a limitation of the Perl language. Windows was not designed to be able to duplicate the currently executing process (which is essentially what `fork` does). Instead, most Windows applications use threads rather than `fork` to provide a number of services simultaneously from the same host application.

Although there are threading systems built into current versions of Perl, they are highly experimental. The Perl language was never designed for multithreaded operation; in fact, the core code is not even thread-safe, leading to all sorts of potential problems when performing seemingly trivial operations within a Perl script. Even accessing a hash using the `each`, `keys`, or `values` functions should probably not be considered a thread-safe operation within Perl.

With all that in mind, a `fork` function has been developed that works under the Windows platform. Support is currently fairly limited, and some of the more useful tricks of the `fork` system are not implemented, but the core purpose of the function—to duplicate the currently executing interpreter—does work. This means that it's now possible to do most operations that rely on the `fork` function within ActivePerl.

Rather than creating a child process in the strict sense, the Windows `fork` function creates a pseudo-process. The pseudo-process is actually a duplication of the current interpreter created within a new thread of the main interpreter. This means that using `fork` does not create a new process—the new interpreter will not appear within the process list. This means that killing the "parent" kills the parent and all its "children," since the children are just additional threads within the parent.

The ActivePerl `fork` function returns the pseudo-process ID to the parent and 0 to the child process, just like the real `fork` function. The pseudo-process ID is separate from the real process ID given to genuine additional processes. The `undef` value is returned if the `fork` operation fails.

For those readers who have not used the `fork` function before, you need to give some careful consideration within the Perl script when using `fork`. The execution contents of the new process are part of the current script; you do not call an external script or function to initiate the new process. For example, you can see from the comments in the following code where the boundaries of the child and parent lie:

```
#Parent Process

print "Starting the parent\n";

unless ($pid = fork)
{
#Start of Child Process
    sleep 2;
    for (1..10)
    {
        print "Child, Count $_\n";
        sleep 1;
    }
    exit 0;
}
#End of Child
#Continuation of Parent
for (1..5)
{
    print "Parent, Count $_\n";
    sleep 2;
}

waitpid($pid,0);

#End of Parent
```

As soon as the `fork` function returns, the child starts execution, running the script elements in the following block. You can do anything within this block. All the functions, modules, and variables are inherited by the child. However, you cannot use an inherited variable to share information with the parent. We'll cover the method for that shortly.

Also note that execution of the parent continues as soon as the `fork` function returns; so you get two simultaneously executing processes. If you run the above script, you should get output similar to this:

```
Starting the parent
Parent, Count 1
Child, Count 1
Parent, Count 2
Child, Count 2
Child, Count 3
Parent, Count 3
Child, Count 4
Child, Count 5
```

```
Parent, Count 4
Child, Count 6
Child, Count 7
Parent, Count 5
Child, Count 8
Child, Count 9
Child, Count 10
```

Within Unix, this has the effect of introducing a quasi-multithreading system. Within Windows, the `fork` function makes use of the threads within the OS to support the function. Although in practice we are creating new threads, we don't have control over the new processes we create.

ActivePerl `fork` Limitations   There are some limitations and considerations that you should keep in mind when using the `fork` function under ActivePerl, all due to the way the system works. Following is a brief list of these issues:

- Open file handles are inherited; so had you redirected STDOUT to a different file, the child would also have written to this file automatically. This can be used for parent–child communication. Note, however, that unlike Unix `fork`, any shared file handles also share their position, as reported by `seek`. This means that changing the position within a parent will also change the position within the child. You should separately open the file in the child if you want to maintain separate file pointers.

- The `$$` and `$PROCESS_ID` variables in the pseudo-process are given a unique process ID. This is separate from the main process ID list.

- All pseudo-processes inherit the environment (i.e., `%ENV`) from the parent and maintain their own copy. Changes to the pseudo-process environment do not affect the parent.

- All pseudo-processes have their own current directory.

- The `wait` and `waitpid` functions accept pseudo-process IDs and operate normally.

- The `kill` function can be used to kill a pseudo-process if it has been supplied with the pseudo-process's ID. However, the function should be used with caution, as killed pseudo-processes may not clean up their environment before dying.

- Using `exec` within a forked process actually calls the program in a new external process. This then returns the program's exit code to the pseudo-process, which then returns the code to the parent. This has two effects. First, the process ID returned by `fork` will not match that of the `exec`'d process. Second, the `-|` and `|-` formats to the `open` command do not work. See "Safer Pipes with `open`" in Chapter 6 for more information on how to get around this limitation.

Since the operation of `fork` is likely to change before this book goes to print, you should check the details on the `fork` implementation at the ActiveState web site. See Appendix A for details.

Using `wait` and `waitpid` In order to acknowledge the completion of the child process, you need to use one of the two available functions, `wait` and `waitpid`. The ActiveState implementation of `fork` supports the use of both `wait` and `waitpid` when waiting for child processes to exit.

Both functions block the parent process until the child process (or processes) have exited cleanly. This should not cause problems if the functions are used as part of a signal handler, or if they are called as the last function within a parent that knows its children should have exited, probably because it sent a suitable signal. For example:

```
wait
waitpid PID, FLAGS
```

The `wait` function simply waits for a child process to terminate. The `waitpid` function enables you to wait for a specific process ID and condition.

Valid flags are defined in the `POSIX` module, and they are summarized here in Table 5-1.

TABLE 5-1

Flags for `waitpid`

Flag	Description
WIFEXITED	Wait for processes that have exited.
WIFSIGNALED	Wait for processes that received a signal.
WNOHANG	Non-blocking wait.
WSTOPSIG	Wait for processes that received STOP signal.
WTERMSIG	Wait for processes that received TERM signal.
WUNTRACED	Wait for processes stopped by signals.

Using exec

The exec function replaces the current process (the Perl script) with the name of the program that you specify:

```
exec LIST
```

The first element is taken as the name of the program that you want to execute; the remaining arguments are passed as arguments to the program.

Note that execution is immediate and complete. The Perl interpreter will be killed and the application will be executed; no remaining statements (including any END block statements) will be executed.

For example, we can create a wrapper around the dir command:

```
exec('dir','*.doc');
```

Now when we run the script, what it actually does is replace the interpreter with the dir command and provide a list of all the files ending with ".doc".

Using Win32::Spawn

The easiest way to start a new application is to use the Win32::Spawn function to spawn (create) a new process. The basic format for the function is as follows:

```
Win32::Spawn(COMMAND, CMDLINE, PID)
```

This spawns a new process, running the COMMAND using the command line CMDLINE. The environment variable PATH is *not* searched for the command called; use a fully qualified path name if you need to. Also note that you need to include the extension of the program. The PID should be a scalar, which will contain the process ID of the newly created process.

Note the terminology here: COMMAND is the full name of the application to be executed, but it's the information in CMDLINE that is used to spawn the application. For example, to open a document in the built-in WordPad application:

```
use Win32;

Win32::Spawn('wordpad.exe', 'wordpad myfile.txt', $pid)
    or die "Couldn't run application: "
        . Win32::Formatmessage (Win32::GetLastError());
```

NOTE.   The first word in CMDLINE *is completely ambiguous. Although in theory the argument should be what you enter on the command line, Windows actually ignores the first word of the second argument, using the value of the first argument in its place.*

The problem with Win32::Spawn is that, once created, we have no control over the process that has been created. You can use the built-in kill function to send a signal to the process. Windows is POSIX-compliant, so most of the signal levels should work (see "Process Control" later in this chapter).

The Win32::Process Module

If you want a more manageable approach to creating new processes, you can use the Win32::Process module. Unlike the generic functions and methods, processes created via the Win32::Process module can be controlled. The control is limited to starting, killing, suspending/resuming, and controlling the priority of the process that is created.

You start a new process using the Create function:

```
use Win32;
use Win32::Process;

Win32::Process::Create(PROCESS, APPL, CMDLINE,
                       IHANDLES, OPTIONS, DIR)
```

The above line creates a new object, placing the object reference into the scalar pointed to by PROCESS. The APPL argument is the full path name of the application you want to run. Note that you cannot use a short name—the PATH environment variable will not be searched.

The CMDLINE is how the command line would appear if you were to execute it within the cmd shell. The IHANDLES argument specifies whether the new process should inherit the file handles of the caller. A value of one (1) indicates that the new process should inherit the standard input, output, and error handles of the caller.

The OPTIONS argument takes a logically OR'd list of flags that will control the execution options of the process you are calling. We'll look at the flags and the constants that you can use to define these options shortly.

The DIR argument is the working directory of the new process. For example:

```
Win32::Process::Create($process,
             "C:\\WinNT\\system32\\notepad.exe",
             "notepad source.txt",
             0,
             NORMAL_PRIORITY_CLASS,
             .");
```

The flags that you can apply to the OPTIONS argument are shown in
Table 5-2. You can also apply *one* priority class, as defined by the constants in Table 5-3, to the options. When you are specifying more than
one option, they should be logically OR'd together. For example:

```
Win32::Process::Create($process,
             "C:\\WinNT\\system32\\notepad.exe",
             "notepad source.txt",
             0,
             CREATE_SUSPENDED|NORMAL_PRIORITY_CLASS,
             ".");
```

Process Security   When you create a new process using the
Win32::Process module, there is no security on the process itself,
meaning that any user can potentially kill, suspend, or otherwise control
your process. Currently there is no way to modify the security of a
process started in this way. See the Win32::AdminMisc::
CreateProcessAsUser function later in this chapter for more information on how to create more secure processes.

Controlling the Process   Once created, the new process can be controlled using methods against the object that was created when the new
process was started. The Suspend method suspends (pauses) execution
of the process. For example:

```
$count = $process->Suspend()
```

This pauses the process's thread, effectively allocating no CPU time to
the process. The return value is a count of the number of times that the
process has been paused. The number of times that you can suspend a
process is limited by the OS, with each call to Suspend incrementing the
count by one. The current limit is 127 suspensions before the method
returns an error (-1). Use the $^E variable or the Win32::
GetLastError function to get the precise error.

When you suspend a process, you will only suspend the process's
thread, not any child threads that it may have created. If you want to
start a suspended process, then use the CREATE_SUSPENDED flag when
creating the process.

TABLE 5-2

Option flags when creating a new process.

Flag	Description
CREATE_DEFAULT_ERROR_MODE	The new process does not inherit the error mode of the calling process. Instead, the new process is given the default error mode.
CREATE_NEW_CONSOLE	The new process has a new console window created for it. This cannot be used with the DETACHED_PROCESS flag.
CREATE_NEW_PROCESS_GROUP	The new process is the root of a new process group. The process group includes all processes that are descendants of this root process.
CREATE_SEPARATE_WOW_VDM	Valid only when starting a 16-bit Windows-based application. If set, then the new process runs in its own 16-bit Virtual DOS Machine (VDM) compartment. By default, all 16-bit applications run in a single shared VDM. The advantage of running them separately is that a crash only kills the single VDM, not all the other 16-bit processes running in the same VDM. Applications that run in their own VDM also have their own input queues, which prevents the execution of other 16-bit applications, pausing while the applications accept input.
CREATE_SUSPENDED	Starts the new process in a suspended (nonexecuting) state. The suspend counter is incremented to 1. Use the Resume method to resume processing.
CREATE_UNICODE_ENVIRONMENT	The new process environment contains support for Unicode characters. The default is to use ANSI characters.
DEBUG_PROCESS	Sets up the called process (and any children) to be debugged, using the calling Perl script as the debugger.
DEBUG_ONLY_THIS_PROCESS	If not set, and the calling process (Perl) is not being debugged, then the new process becomes another process being debugged by the calling process's debugger.
DETACHED_PROCESS	For console processes only. The new process does not have access to the console of the parent process. However, the new process can create its own console (see Chapter 10). Cannot be used in conjunction with the CREATE_NEW_CONSOLE option.

TABLE 5-3

Available priority
classes for
processes.

Priority Class	Description
IDLE_PRIORITY_CLASS	The process will only run when the system is idle, soaking up all the available processor time that is left. Any threads of any other process running at a higher priority will preempt the process.
NORMAL_PRIORITY_CLASS	Standard process scheduling.
HIGH_PRIORITY_CLASS	Process runs at a higher-than-normal level and should be used for processes that have time-critical elements or that must be executed immediately. Processes with this priority preempt the processes of NORMAL and IDLE priority processes.
REALTIME_PRIORITY_CLASS	Runs at the highest available priority, with priority over both other user- and system-level processes. A time-consuming task with this priority level may affect disk writes, mouse responsiveness, and other core system elements. Should be used with caution: It may cause a machine lockup if the process is not otherwise controlled properly, since it will suck up all available processor time. Only available to users with suitable access (under Windows NT this normally only means Administrators or members of the Administrator group).

You decrement the suspension counter using the Resume method.

```
$process->Resume()
```

Each call to Resume decrements the suspension counter by one—the process will only start executing again when the counter reaches zero. Assuming that the current counter value is zero, this means that

```
$process->Suspend();
$process->Resume();
```

will suspend and then resume the execution, but

```
$process->Suspend();
$process->Suspend();
$process->Resume();
```

will not.

The Resume method returns the value of the suspend counter before it is decremented. This means that a value of 1 indicates that the current suspend counter is at zero. The method returns -1 if there was an error.

Because others can control your process, including suspending it, you might want to put a wrapper around the Resume method to ensure that your Resume call really does resume execution:

```
sub ResumeProcess
{
    my ($process) = @_;
    while(1)
    {
        $suspendcount = $process->Resume();
        next if ($suspendcount>1);
        return 0 if ($suspendcount == 1);
        return -1 if ($suspendcount == < 0);
    }
}
```

Note that because Resume can return a negative value, we need to be more choosy about how we check the return values.

Controlling the Process Priority   You can get the current priority of a process using the GetPriorityClass method. This will return a value that will correspond to the constants shown in Table 5-3. For example:

```
$priority = $process->GetPriorityClass()
```

To change the priority of a process you use the SetPriorityClass method:

```
$process->SetPriorityClass(CLASS)
```

This sets the priority class of the process to the value of CLASS, according to the constants defined in Table 5-3.

Under Windows NT on systems with multiple processors, you can also control the processors on which a thread can execute. This allows a greater level of control over the main thread of the process, but unless you know the processor usage of the machine, the information is largely useless. The list of processors on which a process is allowed to run is called the *process affinity mask* and is returned as a bit vector, with each subsequent bit (from low to high order) indicating the processors the process is currently configured for.

The GetProcessAffinitymask method gets the current process affinity mask, as well as the system affinity mask, which defines which processors in a system are available for use. For example:

```
$process->GetProcessAffinitymask(PROCESSMASK, SYSTEMMASK)
```

The information is placed into the scalars pointed to by PROCESSMASK and SYSTEMMASK, respectively. With one single call, you can get an idea of the processors available within a system.

To actually set the process affinity mask, use the SetProcessAffinitymask, supplying a single argument, the bit vector of the process mask you want the process to use:

```
$process->SetProcessAffinitymask(PROCESSMASK)
```

To obtain and set the process mask information, you'll need to use the vec function (see Appendix C).

Getting Process Information   You can get the current process ID (as used by the OS) using the GetProcessID method, which returns the integer ID:

```
$process->GetProcessID()
```

When a process exits, you can use the GetExitCode function to obtain the exit code returned by the application:

```
$process->GetExitCode($ExitCode)
```

Killing and Waiting for a Process   You can kill a currently executing process using the Kill method, which accepts a single argument, the exit code to be returned:

```
$process->Kill(EXITCODE)
```

When you use the Win32::Process:Create function, the execution of the script continues, unlike the native system function built into Perl. To actually force the script to wait for the process's completion, you should use the Wait method.

```
$process->Wait(TIMEOUT)
```

This waits for the specified process to exit, waiting for a maximum of TIMEOUT seconds. The return value of Wait is false if the wait times out, setting the error code in $! to WAIT_FAILED (see the Win32::WinError module in Chapter 8.). If you want to wait for an infinite amount of time, you can use the predefined constant INFINITE.

Using `Win32::AdminMisc::CreateProcessAsUser`

The `CreateProcessAsUser` function, which comes as part of the `Win32::AdminMisc`, creates a new process using the security profile of the current user. This means that the new process will have access to the same resources as the new user, including access to shared resources, files, and directories. Obviously, within the confines of executing a process, there is little difference between using `CreateProcessAsUser` and the facilities offered by the `Win32::Process` module.

The `CreateProcessAsUser` function does provide more control over the process that is created, including the ability to specify the process's window size and location, and the startup mode of the process's window (maximized, minimized, etc.). The real benefit of the function is only really felt when used in conjunction with the `Win32::AdminMisc::LogonAsUser` function. This function allows you to impersonate another user within the confines of an application. In effect, this is the same as the `setuid` function provided within Unix.

Unfortunately, `Win32::AdminMisc::CreateProcessAsUser` is only available under Windows NT and Windows 2000, since these are the only OSs that support impersonation and honor the required security permissions for the new process.

The basic format of the function is as follows:

```
use Win32;
use Win32::AdminMisc
Win32::AdminMisc::CreateProcessAsUser(APP [, DIRECTORY][, CONFIG]);
```

where the `APP` argument is the name of the application to be executed. This should be defined using the full application name (including the extension) and any arguments you want to pass to the application, just as if you were running the application on the command line. For example, to run WordPad, you'd use:

```
Win32::AdminMisc::CreateProcessAsUser("Wordpad.exe myfile.txt");
```

The next two arguments are optional, and you can specify either argument as the second argument to the function—it will automatically identify what you have supplied. If you want to supply all three, then you should use the order shown above. The `DIRECTORY` is the path to the directory that will be used as the default by the application.

The `OPTION` is a hash (not a reference to a hash) that should define the options to be used when the process is created. The list of supported options is shown in Table 5-4.

Note that the `Flags` and `Priority` options use the constants defined in Tables 5-2 and 5-3. The `Fill` option defines the color to be used when creating the console used by a new console application. To specify a color, use

TABLE 5-4

Options when creating a new process using `CreateProcess AsUser.`

Option	Description
Title	For console applications only, the title of the process's window.
Desktop	The name of the virtual desktop to be used for displaying the process. Should be avoided unless you know what you are doing.
X	The X coordinate of the upper left corner of the process's window (in pixels, from the top left corner of the corner of the screen).
Y	The Y coordinate of the upper left corner of the process's window (in pixels, from the top left corner of the corner of the screen).
Xsize	The width of the new process's window in pixels.
Ysize	The height of the new process's window in pixels.
Xbuffer	For console processes, the number of characters wide that the buffer should be (see Chapter 10 for more details on console buffers).
Ybuffer	For console processes, the number of characters high that the buffer should be (see Chapter 10 for more details on console buffers).
Fill	For console processes, the foreground and background color to use when filling the window. See Table 5-5 for details.
Priority	The priority of the new process. Uses the same constants defined in Table 5-3.
Flags	The flags to use when starting the process. See Table 5-2 for details of valid values.
ShowWindow	Sets the visibility of the window during startup. See Table 5-6 for details.
StdInput	Specifies the numerical file handle to be used for the process's standard input. Note that if specified, you must also specify values for StdOutput and StdError.
StdOutput	Specifies the numerical file handle to be used for the process's standard output. Note that if specified, you must also specify values for StdInput and StdError.
StdError	Specifies the numerical file handle to be used for the process's standard error. Note that if specified, you must also specify values for StdInput and StdOutput.
Inherit	If set to 1, then the process inherits the standard input, output, and error handles from the current process.
Directory	Specifies the directory that will be used as the current directory by the process.

TABLE 5-5

Color constants for the fill color of the new console.

Constant	Description
BACKGROUND_RED	The background color will have a red component.
BACKGROUND_BLUE	The background color will have a blue component.
BACKGROUND_GREEN	The background color will have a green component.
BACKGROUND_INTENSITY	The background color will be intensified or brightened.
FOREGROUND_RED	The foreground text color will have a red component.
FOREGROUND_BLUE	The foreground text color will have a blue component.
FOREGROUND_GREEN	The foreground text color will have a green component.
FOREGROUND_INTENSITY	The foreground text color will be intensified or brightened.

the constants shown in Table 5-5 logically OR'd together. For example, to create a window with a red foreground and blue background, use BACK-GROUND_BLUE|FOREGROUND_RED. For a more complete list of supported colors and how to produce them using the constants shown in the table, see the discussion on "Writing with Color" within the Win32::Console section of Chapter 10.

The ShowWindow option defines how the window will be displayed during startup. The constants shown in Table 5-5 allow you to specify the mode in which the window will appear. The SW_MAXIMIZE will display the window as full screen, while SW_MINIMIZE starts the process but only displays the new process within the taskbar. Note that you can only specify one of the constants shown in Table 5-6.

For example, to start a new process as another user, you might use a script like this:

```
use Win32;
use Win32::AdminMisc;

my ($user, $domain, $password, $cmd);

unless (@ARGV >= 3)
{
    die "Usage: runuser.pl USER PASSWD CMD...\n";
}

$user = shift;
if ($user =~~ m#\\#)
{
    ($user,$domain) = ($user =~~ m#^(.*)\\(.*)$#);
}
$password = shift;
$cmd = join(' ',@ARGV);

if (Win32::AdminMisc::LogonAsUser($domain,
```

TABLE 5-6

Options for the window state of the new process.

Constant	Description
SW_HIDE	The process is created but never shown (always hidden).
SW_MAXIMIZE	The initial window of the application is maximized (fills the screen).
SW_MINIMIZE	The initial window of the application is minimized (shown only in the taskbar).
SW_RESTORE	The initial window is shown as it was last used.
SW_SHOW	The process is shown once created. This is the default for all applications and is only negated when SW_HIDE is used.
SW_SHOWMAXIMIZED	**Alias for** SW_MAXIMIZE.
SW_SHOWMINIMIZED	**Alias for** SW_MINIMIZE.
SW_SHOWMINNOACTIVE	The process is created in the minimized state, but the currently active application (focus) is not changed to the new process.
SW_SHOWNOACTIVATE	The process is created as normal, but the currently active application (focus) is not changed to the new process.
SW_SHOWNORMAL	The process is created and shown as normal.

```
                                $user,
                                $password,
                                LOGON32_LOGON_INTERACTIVE))
{
    if (Win32::AdminMisc::CreateProcessAsUser(
                        $cmd,
                        'Flags' => CREATE_NEW_CONSOLE,
                        'Title' => "User: $user process"
                        ))
    {
        print('Couldnt start program ($cmd):\n\t',
                Win32::FormatMessage(Win32::GetLastError()),
                "\n");
    }
}
else
{
    print("Couldnt logon as $user to $domain:\n\t",
            Win32::FormatMessage(Win32::GetLastError()),
            "\n");
}
```

NOTE. *I've never been able to get these two functions to work correctly, even in the script shown above or Dave Roth's sample script.*

Process Control

Most of the process control functions supported under the Unix implementation of Perl do not work under the Win32 implementation because of the difference in the way the systems operate.

The `kill` function is the only function that works under Windows. Despite its name, `kill` merely sends a signal to a process. For example:

```
kill EXPR, LIST
```

sends a signal of the numerical value `EXPR` to the process IDs specified in `LIST`. You can also use quoted strings to `EXPR`. Windows supports a reduced set of signals compared to most Unix implementations; see Table 5-7 for details. Note that the process group functionality of `kill` (available by supplying a negative value for `EXPR`) is not available in Windows, since it doesn't support process groups.

The remaining process control functions are not supported within Windows at all. Table 5-8 shows a list of unsupported functions and pointers to alternative functions.

Accessing the Environment

Just like Unix, the environment variables are available via the `%ENV` hash. Under Windows 95/98, these variables are set initially by the values in AUTOEXEC.BAT. If you execute a script from a DOS prompt, then values could also have been introduced within the local confines of the command interpreter—when the prompt is closed, the values will be lost.

TABLE 5-7

Signals supported by Windows.

Name	Effect
SIGABRT	Aborts the process (abnormal termination).
SIGFPE	Arithmetic (floating-point) exception.
SIGILL	Illegal instruction.
SIGINT	Interrupt (Control-C).
SIGSEGV	Segmentation (illegal storage access) fault.
SIGTERM	Termination request.

TABLE 5-8

Unsupported
process control
functions.

Function	Description
getpriority	Gets the priority of the current process. See `Win32::Process` and the `GetPriorityClass` function for details on getting the priority of a spawned process.
setpriority	Sets the priority of the current process. See `Win32::Process` and the `GetPriorityClass` function for details on setting the priority of a spawned process.
getppid	Gets the parent process ID for the current process. No Windows equivalent.
getpgrp	Gets the parent process group for the current process. No Windows equivalent.
setpgrp	Sets the parent process group for the current process. No Windows equivalent.

Under Windows NT, environment variables are handled slightly differently. The basics of the environment variables remain the same, and most are set as part of the startup process. But the environment variables available within the command prompt, or to other DOS-based programs including Perl, are configured slightly differently. There are two levels of environment variable: the System variable and the User variable. Variables are set first by the System variables, then by AUTOEXEC.BAT, and finally the User variables defined within the user's profile.

System variables are global and are configured either via the AUTOEXEC.BAT, the host command prompt, or by the settings configured in the Environment tab of the System control panel. System variables cannot be modified by anybody except administrators for the domain. The settings in the System variable class include the default path, processor values, and core system directories, including the special WINDIR variable, which defines the location of the Windows operating system.

User variables, on the other hand, are those created and modifiable by individual users. These are created as normal through the command prompt, or the user's profile and startup script, and dynamically by the system as the user logs in.

Unfortunately, there is no way of determining whether an environment variable is system- or user-generated. Even if you could determine that information, it probably wouldn't be helpful. Note as well that although Windows appears to support mixed-case environment variable names, they are only accessible using uppercase names.

The following simple script will output the environment variables on any machine:

```perl
for my $env (sort keys %ENV)
{
    print "$env=$ENV{$env}\n";
}
```

On a typical Windows 95/98 machine, the output will look similar to the following:

```
CLASSPATH=C:\WINDOWS\SYSTEM\QTJava.zip
CMDLINE=perl env.pl
COMSPEC=C:\WINDOWS\COMMAND.COM
PATH=C:\WINDOWS\COMMAND;C:\;C:\PROGRA~~1\EMACS-
~1.1\BIN;C:\PERL\BIN;C:\WINDOWS;C:\WINDOWS\COMMAND;C:\PROGRA~~1\TCL\
  BIN;C:\PROGRA~~1\PYTHON;C:\PROGRA~~1\MICROS~4\VC98\BIN;C:\
  PROGRA~~1\MICROS~4\COMMON\MSDEV98\BIN
PROMPT=$p$g
QTJAVA=C:\WINDOWS\SYSTEM\QTJava.zip
TEMP=C:\WINDOWS\TEMP
TMP=C:\WINDOWS\TEMP
WINBOOTDIR=C:\WINDOWS
WINDIR=C:\WINDOWS
```

On Windows NT, it will look like this:

```
COMPUTERNAME=INCONTINENT
COMSPEC=C:\WINNT\system32\cmd.exe
HOMEDRIVE=C:
HOMEPATH=\
INCLUDE=C:\Program Files\Microsoft Visual
Studio\VC98\atl\include;C:\Program Files\Microsoft Visual
Studio\VC98\mfc\include;C:\Program Files\Microsoft Visual
Studio\VC98\include
LIB=C:\Program Files\Microsoft Visual Studio\VC98\mfc\lib;C:\Program
Files\Microsoft Visual Studio\VC98\lib
LOGONSERVER=\\INCONTINENT
MSDEVDIR=C:\Program Files\Microsoft Visual Studio\Common\MSDev98
NUMBER_OF_PROCESSORS=1
OS=Windows_NT
OS2LIBPATH=C:\WINNT\system32\os2\dll;
PATH=C:\Oracle\Ora81\bin;C:\Program
Files\Oracle\jre\1.1.7\bin;C:\Perl\bin;C:\WINNT\system32;C:\WINNT;;
  C:\Program Files\Mts;C:\Program Files\Microsoft Visual
Studio\Common\Tools\WinNT;C:\Program Files\Microsoft Visual
  Studio\Common\MSDev98\Bin;C:\Program Files\Microsoft Visual
  Studio\Common\Tools;C:\Program Files\Microsoft Visual
  Studio\VC98\bin
PATHEXT=.COM;.EXE;.BAT;.CMD;.VBS;.JS
PROCESSOR_ARCHITECTURE=x86
PROCESSOR_IDENTIFIER=x86 Family 6 Model 3 Stepping 3, GenuineIntel
```

```
PROCESSOR_LEVEL=6
PROCESSOR_REVISION=0303
PROMPT=$P$G
SYSTEMDRIVE=C:
SYSTEMROOT=C:\WINNT
TEMP=C:\TEMP
TMP=C:\TEMP
USERDOMAIN=INCONTINENT
USERNAME=MC
USERPROFILE=C:\WINNT\Profiles\MC
WINDIR=C:\WINNT
```

Windows 2000 defines the following environment variables:

```
ALLUSERSPROFILE=D:\Documents and Settings\All Users
COMPUTERNAME=INCONTINENT
COMSPEC=D:\WINNT\system32\cmd.exe
HOMEDRIVE=D:
HOMEPATH=\
LOGONSERVER=\\INCONTINENT
NUMBER_OF_PROCESSORS=1
OS=Windows_NT
OS2LIBPATH=D:\WINNT\system32\os2\dll;
PATH=D:\WINNT\system32;D:\WINNT
PATHEXT=.COM;.EXE;.BAT;.CMD;.VBS;.JS;.WS
PROCESSOR_ARCHITECTURE=x86
PROCESSOR_IDENTIFIER=x86 Family 6 Model 3 Stepping 3, GenuineIntel
PROCESSOR_LEVEL=6
PROCESSOR_REVISION=0303
PROGRAMFILES=D:\Program Files
PROMPT=$P$G
SYSTEMDRIVE=D:
SYSTEMROOT=D:\WINNT
TEMP=D:\DOCUME~1\ADMINI~1\LOCALS~1\Temp
TMP=D:\DOCUME~1\ADMINI~1\LOCALS~1\Temp
USERDNSDOMAIN=mchome.com
USERDOMAIN=MCSLP
USERNAME=Administrator
USERPROFILE=D:\Documents and Settings\Administrator
WINDIR=D:\WINNT
```

NOTE.   *Environment variables within the command interpreter are available by "quoting" the variable name in percent signs—for example,* %PATH%.

Like Unix, some of the environment variables have special significance, as shown in Table 5-9.

Although some of the variables supply some useful information, they are only available under Windows NT and 2000. Theoretically, you could use this information within your applications, but there is no guarantee that all this information will be set. If you do want to rely on the values

TABLE 5-9

Standard environ-
ment variables.

Variable	Platform	Description
ALLUSERSPROFILE	2000	The location of the generic profile currently in use.
CMDLINE	95/98	The command line, including the name of the application executed.
COMPUTERNAME	NT, 2000	The name of the computer.
COMSPEC	All	The path to the command interpreter (usually COMMAND.COM) used when opening a command prompt.
HOMEDRIVE	NT, 2000	The drive letter (and colon) of the user's home drive.
HOMEPATH	NT, 2000	The path to the users home directory.
HOMESHARE	NT, 2000	The UNC name of the user's home directory. Note that this value will be empty if the user's home directory is unset or set to local drive.
LOGONSERVER	NT, 2000	The domain name server the user was authenticated on.
NUMBER_OF_PROCESSORS	NT, 2000	The number of processors active in the current machine.
OS	NT, 2000	The name of the operating system.
OS2LIBPATH	NT, 2000	The path to the OS/2 compatibility libraries.
PATH	All	The path searched for applications within the command prompt and for programs executed via a system, backtick, or open function.
PATHEXT	NT, 2000	The list of extensions that will be used to identify an executable program.
PROCESSOR_ARCHITECTURE	NT, 2000	The processor architecture of the current machine.
PROCESSOR_IDENTIFIER	NT, 2000	The identifier (the information tag returned by the CPU when queried).
PROCESSOR_LEVEL	NT, 2000	The processor level: 3 refers to a 386, 4 to a 486, and 5 to the Pentium. Values of 3000 and 4000 refer to MIPS processors, and 21064 would refer to an Alpha processor.
PROCESSOR_REVISION	NT, 2000	The processor revision.

(Continued)

TABLE 5-9

(Continued)

Variable	Platform	Description
PROMPT	All	The prompt used within the command prompt.
SYSTEMDRIVE	NT, 2000	The drive holding the currently active operating system.
SYSTEMROOT	NT, 2000	The root directory of the active operating system.
TEMP	All	The user-specified path to a directory used for temporary files.
TMP	All	The user-specified path to a directory used for temporary files.
USERDOMAIN	NT, 2000	The domain the current user is connected to.
USERDNSDOMAIN	2000	The DNS domain for the user (used by the Active Directory service).
USERNAME	NT, 2000	The name of the current user.
USERPROFILE	NT, 2000	The location of the user's profile.
WINBOOTDIR	NT, 2000	The location of the Windows operating system that was used to boot the machine.
WINDIR	All	The location of the active Windows operating system; this is the directory when searching for DLLs and other OS information.

of these environment variables, check the platform you are running under first use, using the tricks in Chapter 2.

If you do intend to use these variables, consider having a backup solution in place—use the Win32 and Win32::AdminMisc modules, for example.

Environment Application

Although all of the environment variables can be used to provide some level of useful information, the only one that you can guarantee will be available is the PATH variable. As with Unix, this contains a semicolon-separated list of directories that will be searched when a program is executed, either on the command line or via the system or the qx/backtick operator.

The PATH is formed automatically by the operating system (see the sidebar "How the Path Is Built" for information on how this variable is populated). If you want to modify the contents of the PATH, remember that direct modification via assignment will update the environment of the host. For programs executed via double-clicking or through a web server, this will not have any significant effect.

How the Path Is Built

The PATH environment variable is actually built based on the operating system configuration. Under Windows 95 this consists solely of the settings defined in AUTOEXEC.BAT. Under Windows NT and 2000, the path is based first on those settings defined within the System portion of the Environment tab in the System control panel, then those defined in the User portion of the System control panel, and finally the information from the AUTOEXEC.BAT file is used.

This means that the path contains directories specified in the order System, User, and then AUTOEXEC.BAT. Therefore, by default, System-defined locations are searched in preference to all others.

Scripts executed through a command prompt are different, however. You will modify the path for all future executions via the command interpreter. The trick is to use a block and the local operator to localize a copy of the environment variable to the block and then modify that.

For example:

```
{

    local $ENV{'PATH'} = 'C:\Mybin';
    system("dothing");
}
```

When the block completes, the value of PATH will return to normal, and no modification will have been made.

Incidentally, when you are specifying directories, the temptation is to use forward slashes—which will work—or to automatically use a double backslash, for example, C:\\MYBIN. Although it works, the double backslash just makes things more difficult to read. If you are writing a cross-platform script, use the forward slash and let the Windows libraries handle the difference.

If you are writing a Windows-only script, use single quotes and a single backslash. For a start, it's faster to type, and it's also faster to execute (although admittedly the effect is negligible), because Perl doesn't try to do interpolation on the string. More importantly, it's easier to read when you come to use the script.

## CHAPTER 6

Interprocess Communication

We've already seen some examples of communicating with other processes when using `system` or `open`. There are, of course, more direct ways to communicate directly with another process by using one of the built-in libraries. They are all forms of *interprocess communication* (IPC), a system often used to provide a conduit for communicating either data between processes or for indicating to another process that a resource or event has completed.

Unfortunately, the base IPC methods built into Perl rely on the features of Unix. More specifically, they rely on the features of System V Release 4. In most instances, the use of these functions was sparse at best, largely due to the lack of the suitable libraries on many Unix-based platforms.

Instead, most IPC systems actually use the pipe to communicate between two processes. There are two basic forms of pipe: the *anonymous pipe* and the *named pipe*. The difference between the two is that a named pipe exists as a file within a file system and therefore allows multiple client processes to communicate with a server process using the pipe.

There is no built-in support for named pipes within Perl; the normal method for creating a named pipe within Perl is to use `system` to call the Unix `mknod` command to create a pipe. The Win32 libraries do, however, include their own named pipe system, which is supported in Perl using the `Win32::Pipe` module.

In addition to `Win32::Pipe`, there are some other base modules and extensions that provide some form of IPC. In this chapter, we'll look at the supported Win32 IPC modules, the standard Perl functions and modules that work under Windows, and at how to migrate from the System V IPC functions built into the Perl language.

Using the Win32 IPC Libraries

The Windows system is built upon a number of technologies that require the use of IPC in order for them to function correctly. Some of the functionality of the OS is actually supported by the IPC APIs that are made available to Perl programmers through a series of modules. Some of these modules we have already seen. The `Win32::ChangeNotify` and `Win32::Mutex` modules both make use of the IPC features of Windows.

The other two modules—`Win32::Event` and `Win32::Semaphore`—are much simpler and only offer an indication of an event, not the events type. All four modules are supported by the `Win32::IPC` module, which

provides the base classes used by the other modules to provide the functionality.

Because these modules use the Win32 APIs, you can communicate
with other software using the same APIs using Perl. The Windows system uses a simple text string to identify IPC resources, so if you know
that an event or semaphore has been provided, you need only know its
name to access the information using Perl.

Win32::IPC

The `Win32::IPC` module supports the base classes and methods used to
support all the different forms of IPC supported by the Win32 platform.
You shouldn't ever need to use or call it directly, since it's automatically
imported by the other IPC modules when it's required.

The Win32 IPC system forms a core part of many of the systems used
under Windows. As well as being used by the `Win32::Event` and
`Win32::Semaphore` modules detailed in this chapter, it is also used by
`Win32::ChangeNotify` and `Win32::Mutex`, which we examined in
Chapter 4.

The module provides one base method, `wait`. This method allows you
to wait for a particular object to become free. This method is automatically inherited by the modules that use the `Win32::IPC` module, so we'll
cover those later.

If you do specifically import the module, then you'll also have access to
two functions that allow you to wait for groups of objects, only returning
when any or all of the objects have been signaled. You must specifically
import the `wait_any` and `wait_all` functions; they are not exported by
the module by default. For example:

```
use Win32::IPC qw/wait_any wait_all/;
```

The `wait_any` function waits until any of the objects in the supplied
array have been signaled. The `wait_all` function returns only when all
of the specified objects have been signaled. For example:

```
wait_any(OBJECTS [, TIMEOUT])
wait_all(OBJECTS [, TIMEOUT])
```

where OBJECTS is the array of objects to be checked and TIMEOUT is the
optional maximum time to wait before continuing. Note that the format
of OBJECTS is an array. Since the function returns an index to the object

signaled, you will need to populate an array with the objects before you call the function:

```
my @objects = ($obja, $obja);
$index = wait_any(@objects);
```

The TIMEOUT should be specified in seconds. If it is not specified, then the function waits forever (i.e., until any or all of the events have been signaled). If it is supplied and is zero, then the function returns immediately.

The return value depends on the conditions of the supplied objects. If the functions return undef, then it means that there was an error—use Win32::GetLastError to determine the error that occurred. If the return value was 0, then the function timed out. If the return value was a negative value, then it means one of the objects was destroyed before the function completed. A return value of -1 indicates the object that was destroyed.

If the return value is a positive number, then it indicates the index number of the object that caused the function to return. For wait_any this will indicate the object that was signaled. If more than one object is signaled at the same time, the function returns the object with the lowest index. For wait_all it will indicate the last object to be signaled. See Table 6-1 for a summary of these return values.

The objects themselves must have been created using one of the IPC modules.

Win32::Event

A Windows event is a basic flip-flop value that can be accessed by multiple processes. The most obvious use is to indicate that a process or operation should continue. The state of a named event can be set and read by multiple threads and processes. The state of a specific event can be sig-

TABLE 6-1

Return values from the wait_any and wait_all functions.

Return Value	Description
undef	An error occurred.
0	The function timed out.
+N	The object at index N-1 was signaled.
-N	The object at index N-1 was destroyed/abandoned.

naled or reset, and different threads can wait for a particular event to signal. The effect is similar to that of a semaphore (see the next section, "Win32::Semaphore") but with a maximum value of 1.

Each event has two states, either unsignaled or signaled, and the current setting of the event can be set via a set of methods. When the event is set, the event is in the signaled state; when reset, the event is switched to its unsignaled state.

Creating and Opening Events   The following code:

```
$event = Win32::Event->new([MANUAL [, INITIAL [, NAME]]])
```

creates a new event object. If MANUAL is true (1), then the event must be manually reset after it has been signaled. If false (0), the event will automatically reset itself to the unsignaled state. The MANUAL setting also affects how threads and processes that are waiting for the event are signaled when using the pulse method. See below for more details.

If INITIAL is true, then the initial state of the event is to be signaled, the default value is zero. The NAME is the string you want to use to identify the event. This will also create an object that refers to an existing event if NAME matches that of an existing entry. Note that the name is optional—if you do not supply a value, then an anonymous event will be created. For example, to create an event called 'PROCESS', with an initial value of unsignaled, use the following:

```
$event = Win32::Event->new(0,0,'PROCESS');
```

To open an existing event created by another process, you must know its name. You then use the open function to create a new object and open the event:

```
$event = Win32::Event->open(NAME)
```

where NAME is the name of an existing object.

Changing the Event Status   There are three methods for setting the state of an event. To simply set the state of the event to its signaled state, use the set method:

```
$event->set();
```

To reset the event back to its unsignaled state, use the reset method:

```
$event->reset();
```

The `pulse` method signals (sets) the event, and then immediately resets the event to its unsignaled state. The effect is to release a single thread if the event was created as an autoreset event. For manually reset events, it releases all threads and processes waiting on the event.

```
$event->pulse();
```

Waiting for an Event   The `wait` method, inherited from the `Win32::IPC` module, blocks the current process and returns only when the corresponding event has been set to its signaled state, or until the optional timeout value has been reached:

```
$event->wait([TIMEOUT])
```

If `TIMEOUT` is not specified, then the function waits forever. The return value matches the basic list shown in Table 6-1, except for a single object. That is, the return value is 0 if the function timed out, or `undef` if there was an error. If negative, the return value indicates that the object was destroyed, and a positive value indicates that the object was signaled.

The most obvious use of the `Win32::Event` module is to act as a control for another process when processing information. For example, imagine that you have a program that accepts data from a remote host and then places it into a folder to be parsed by another process. Only once the information has been written to the file completely do you want the second process to start parsing the file. You can use events to control this, while still keeping both processes in memory.

Sample Script   The example script demonstrates the process. When run in server mode, it accepts user input. Once received, the information is written to a file and an event is signaled. The process then waits until the event is signaled again by the client. When run in client mode, the process waits for the server to signal an event. Then the process opens the file, prints out the contents, and sets the event so that the server can continue.

```
#perl -w

use Win32::Event;

if ($ARGV[0] eq '-s')
{
    $parseevent = Win32::Event->new(0,0,'PARSE');
```

```
      while(1)
      {

          my $info = '';
          open(DATA,">parse.txt") || die "Cant open parse.txt: $!";
          print "Enter your message:\n";
          while(<STDIN>)
          {
              $info .= $_;
          }
          print DATA $info;
          close(DATA);
          print "Sending message\n";
          $parseevent->pulse();
          $parseevent->wait();

      }
}
elsif ($ARGV[0] eq '-c')
{
      while(1)
      {
          $parseevent = Win32::Event->open('PARSE');
          $parseevent->wait();
          print "Received a message:\n";
          open(DATA,"parse.txt") || die "Cant open parse.txt: $!";
          while(<DATA>)
          {
              print;
          }
          close(DATA);
          print "End of message\n";
          $parseevent->pulse();
      }
}
```

To use the script, open two command prompts and use the server in one and the client in the other. For example, in one command prompt, run the following:

```
C:\> perl 01.pl -s
Enter your message:
Hello, this is a test!
Sending message
Enter your message:
```

In the other, run the client:

```
C:\> perl 01.pl -c
Received a message:
Hello, this is a test!
End of message
```

Of course, events can be used for more complex operations, and the

`Win32::Event` interface uses the core Windows libraries, so you can access Windows events created by the OS or another non-Perl application.

Win32::Semaphore

The `Win32::Semaphore` module provides access to the Win32 semaphore system. Semaphores are essentially identical to `Win32::Event` objects, except that a semaphore can have a specific numerical value, rather than having an on/off state. For the most part, the operation is identical to the System V semaphore system but is not compatible.

Unlike a `Win32::Event` object, you cannot set specific values. Instead, you increment the value of the semaphore by a specific value to indicate status. The `wait` function waits for a semaphore to become nonzero and decrements the value by 1. Therefore, you can increment a semaphore by a specific value and then cause a process to execute a statement a particular number of times according to the value of the semaphore.

Creating and Opening Semaphores   To create a new semaphore object, you use the `new` method:

```
$sobj = Win32::Semaphore->new(INITIALCOUNT, MAXCOUNT [, NAME]);
```

The new object reference is placed into `$sobj`. The INITIALCOUNT argument defines the initial semaphore value, and MAXCOUNT specifies the maximum value for the semaphore. The optional NAME is the name to be given to the new semaphore, and the name that can be used to open an existing semaphore from another process. Note that if you supply a NAME that refers to an existing semaphore object, then the INITIALCOUNT and MAXCOUNT arguments are ignored and the semaphore is opened as if you were using the `open` method. If you do not supply a NAME, then an anonymous semaphore is created.

The `open` method creates an object pointing to an existing semaphore:

```
$sobj = Win32::Semaphore->open(NAME);
```

where NAME is the name of an existing semaphore.

Changing the Semaphore Value   You set the value of a semaphore using the `release` method:

```
$sobj->release([RELEASECOUNT [, LASTCOUNT]]);
```

The value of the semaphore is increased by the value of RELEASECOUNT, a value of 1 is used if the RELEASECOUNT argument is not supplied. The LASTCOUNT argument should be a reference to a scalar that will be populated with the previous value of the semaphore. If RELEASECOUNT plus LASTCOUNT is greater than the MAXCOUNT value specified when the semaphore was created, then the semaphore value is not modified.

Waiting for a Semaphore   The wait method waits for the semaphore value to become nonzero and then decrements the semaphore value by 1. For example:

```
$sobj->wait([TIMEOUT]);
```

The optional TIMEOUT value specifies the period, in seconds, to wait for the semaphore value to increase. If not specified, the method waits indefinitely.

Note the difference in operation between Win32::Event and Win32::Semaphore. A semaphore has a value, rather than being a toggle. In essence, the semaphore wait method works in the same way as the Win32::Event method; it waits for the value to be nonzero—the equivalent of the Win32::Event signaled state. This also means that if you call wait and the semaphore has a value greater than 1, then the method will immediately return to the caller. Also note that the semaphore's value is decremented automatically by the wait call.

For example, if you create a semaphore and then increment it by 5, you will need to call wait five times to clear the semaphore:

```
$semaphore = Win32::Semaphore->new(0,16,'My Semaphore');
$semaphore->release(5);
$count=1;
while($semaphore->wait())
{
    print "Count: $count\n";
}
```

Using Pipes

Unlike events and semaphores, which only allow simple indication of events, pipes provide a way for two or more processes to communicate with each other. Pipes are a one-way communication channel that can be used to transfer information between two processes. Because they are one-way, they can only be used to communicate information to or from a process. You can get around this by opening pipes that provide a conduit for the individual I/O channels (i.e., STDIN, STDOUT, and STDERR).

The most typical use of pipes is within the open function when you want to read from and write to a particular command, instead of a typical file. This class of pipe is called an *anonymous pipe*. Within Unix, you can also have *named pipes*. Named pipes allow communication between two processes using a file as the connection—one process writes to the file (the client), while the other reads from the file (the server). Windows supports a similar system via the Win32::Pipe module. Windows' named pipes are different in that they are two-way channels that are network-capable.

Finally, you can use the pipe function, which is built into the Perl interpreter, in combination with the fork function to provide a communications channel between a parent and a child process.

Using open

We've already seen a number of examples of using the open function to communicate with external programs. As just mentioned, this type of pipe is called an anonymous pipe. An anonymous pipe is one implied through the use of the pipe symbol at the beginning or end of an open statement. For example, to read the output from the dir command:

```
open(DIR, "dir *.doc|") or die "Can't run dir: $!";
while(<DIR>)
{
    print;
}
close(DIR) or die "Error in dir: $!";
```

You can also write information through an external command. For example, the GNU gzip command compresses information. Normally, you would use the command after you have created the file, but using open, you can write a compressed file directly:

```
open(COMPRESS, "|gzip - >file.gz") or die "Can't run gzip: $!";
print COMPRESS "Compressed Data";
close(COMPRESS) or die "Gzip didn't work: $!";
```

When using pipes, you must check the return status of both open and close. This is because each function returns an error from a different element of the piped command. The open function forks a new process and executes the specified command. The return value of this operation trapped by `open` is the return value of the `fork` function. The new process is executed within a completely separate process, and there is no way for `open` to obtain that error. This effectively means that the `open` will return `True` if the new process could be forked, irrespective of the status of the command you are executing. The `close` function, on the other hand, picks up any errors generated by the executed process because it monitors the return value received from the child process.

Therefore, in the first example, you could actually read nothing from the command, and without checking the return status of `close`, you might assume that the command failed to return any valid data. In the second example, where you are writing to a piped command, you need to be more careful. There is no way of determining the status of the opened command without immediately calling `close`, which rather defeats the purpose.

Safer Pipes with `open`

Under Unix, you can use the `"-|"` and `"|-"` options to the `open` command to open a safer pipe to a command. The execution with this method is safer because the command called specifically runs in a forked process and is therefore subject to the same environment of the parent. This is especially useful when working with a Perl script accessed via a website.

NOTE.   The techniques shown here do not work on the prerelease version of Perl 5.6, which was still in beta at this writing. Although ActivePerl 5.6 is the first version of Perl to support the `fork` *function on the Windows platform, this is one of the limitations of the pseudoprocess system. See the section on* `fork` *in Chapter 5 for more information. Also see the section "Using* `pipe`*", coming up in this chapter, for an alternative.*

For example:

```
open(GZDATA,"-|") or exec 'gzcat', 'file.gz';
```

This example forks a new process and immediately executes `gzcat`, with its standard output redirected to the GZDATA filehandle. The method is simple to remember. If you open a pipe to minus, then you can write to the filehandle, and the child process will receive the information in its STDIN. Opening a pipe from minus enables you to read information that the child sends to its STDOUT from the opened filehandle.

Using `IPC::Open2` and `IPC::Open3`

Although the `open` function is very useful when working with a single process, it is not two-way. As convenient as it may seem, you can't do the following:

```
open(MORE, "|more file|");
```

This is because a pipe is unidirectional—it either reads from or writes to a piped command. Although in theory this should work, it can result in a deadlocked process where neither the parent nor piped command know whether they should be reading from or writing to the MORE filehandle.

The solution is to use the `open2` function that comes as part of the `IPC::Open2` module, which is part of the standard distribution:

```
use FileHandle;
use IPC::Open2;
$pid = open2(\*READ, \*WRITE, "more file");
WRITE->autoflush();
```

You can now communicate in both directions with the `more` command, reading from it with the READ filehandle and writing to it with the WRITE filehandle. This will receive data from the standard output of the piped command and write to the standard input of the piped command.

There is a danger with this system, however, in that it assumes the information is always available from the piped command and that it is always ready to accept information. But accesses either way will block until the piped command is ready to accept or to reply with information. This is due to the buffering supported by the standard I/O functions. There isn't a complete solution to this if you are using off-the-shelf commands; if you are using your own programs, then you'll have control over the buffering, and it shouldn't be a problem.

The `IPC::Open3` module is essentially identical to `IPC::Open2`, but it opens a command for reading, writing, and error handling. For example:

```
use IPC::Open3;

$pid = open3(WRITER, READER, ERROR, LIST);
```

The WRITER, READER, and ERROR should be references to existing filehandles to be used for standard input, standard output, and standard error from the command and arguments supplied in LIST. Note that the order of the READER and WRITER arguments is different from that in open2. If " is given as the argument for ERROR, then ERROR and READER use the same filehandle.

Note that this function still exhibits the deadlocking problem associated with the open2 function.

Using pipe

The underlying functionality of the open2 function is made possible using the pipe function, which creates a pair of connected pipes, one for reading and one for writing:

```
pipe READHANDLE, WRITEHANDLE
```

The way to use the function is to create the two new pipes and then fork a new process. Because the filehandles will have been duplicated, you can then just read and write to the two filehandles to allow communication between the child and parent. For example:

```perl
use IO::Handle;
pipe(PARENTREAD, PARENTWRITE);
pipe(CHILDREAD, CHILDWRITE);

PARENTWRITE->autoflush(1);
CHILDWRITE->autoflush(1);

if ($child = fork)      # Parent code
{
    close CHILDREAD;   # We don't need these in the parent
    close PARENTWRITE;
    print CHILDWRITE "34+56;\n";
    chomp($result = <PARENTREAD>);
    print "Got a value of $result from child\n";
    close PARENTREAD;
    close CHILDWRITE;
    waitpid($child,0);
}
else
{

    close PARENTREAD;   # We don't need these in the child
    close CHILDWRITE;
    chomp($calculation = <CHILDREAD>);
    print "Got $calculation\n";
    $result = eval "$calculation";
    print PARENTWRITE "$result\n";
    close CHILDREAD;
    close PARENTWRITE;
    exit;
}
```

Now we can communicate between the child and the parent by reading and writing to and from the corresponding filehandle. If you run this script, you get the following output:

```
Got a value of 90 from child
Got 34+56;
```

Win32::Pipe

A named pipe is essentially just a special type of file. It resides, just like any other file, within the file system (or within the UNC under Windows) and provides a method for two-way communication between two otherwise unrelated processes. Once a named pipe has been created, you can read and write to and from the pipes just like they were any other type of file. The named pipe system has been in use for some time within Unix as a way of accepting print jobs. A specific printer interface creates and monitors the file while users send data to the named pipe. The printer interface accepts the data, spools the accepted file to disk, and then spawns a new process to send it out to the printer.

The Win32::Pipe module works in an almost identical fashion to normal Unix named pipes created using the mknod or mkfifo commands. One of the biggest differences between Unix and Windows' named pipes is that in Windows they are network-compliant. You can use named pipes on Win32 systems to communicate across a network only knowing the UNC of the pipe—we don't need to use TCP/IP sockets or know the server's IP address or name to communicate. Better still, we don't need to implement any type of communications protocol to enable safe communication across the network; the named pipe API handles that for us.

The Windows implementation also works slightly differently from the point of view of handling the named pipe. The server creates the named pipe using the API, supplied through Perl using the Win32::Pipe module. Once created, the server uses the new pipe object to send and receive information. Clients can connect to the named pipe either using the normal open function or the Win32::Pipe module.

Creating Named Pipes   When you create a named pipe, you need to use the new method to create a suitable Win32::Pipe object:

```
$pipe = new Win32::Pipe(NAME);
```

The NAME should be the name of the pipe that you want to create. The name you give here can be a short name; it does not have to be fully qualified (see the "Pipe Naming Conventions" sidebar for more information).

Pipe Naming Conventions

When you are creating a new pipe you give it a simple name. For example, you can create a pipe called "Status." Any clients wishing to access the pipe must, however, use the full UNC name of the pipe. Pipes exist within a simple structure that includes the server name and the special "pipe" shared resource. For example, on a machine called "Insentient," our pipe would be available for use from a client via the name \\INSENTIENT\pipe\Status.

If you do not know the name, then you should be able to use \\.\pipe\Status, where the single dot refers to the current machine.

You can also nest pipes in their own structure. For example, you could have two pipes: one in "\\INSENTIENT\pipe\Status\Memory" and the other in "\\INSENTIENT\ pipe\Status\Disk".

The structure is not an actual directory, nor is it stored on the filesystem. It's just another shared resource made available by the Windows operating system that is accessible using the UNC system.

There are some limitations to creating and using pipes:

- There is a limit of 256 client/server connections to a named pipe. This means you can have one server and 255 client machines talking to it through a single pipe at any one time.

- There is no limit (aside from the disk/memory) resources of the machine to the number of named pipes that you can create.

- The default buffer size is 512 bytes; you can change this with the ResizeBuffer method.

- All named pipes created using this module are streams, rather than message based (see the following Note).

▬ ▬ ▬ ▬ ▬ ▬ ▬ ▬ ▬ ▬ ▬ ▬ ▬ ▬ ▬ ▬ ▬

NOTE.   Dave Roth, the original author of this module, has updated the module, but the updated version is not included as standard in the ActivePerl distribution. The new version allows for message-based communication, where client and server communicate using fixed-size messages, where the buffer size determines the message size.

Opening Named Pipes   The easiest way to open an existing pipe is to use the `open` function:

```
open(DATA,NAME);
```

where `NAME` is the UNC of the pipe to open. For example:

```
open(DATA,"\\\\INSENTIENT\\pipe\\MCStatus");
```

Alternatively, and in my experience more reliably, you can use the `Win32::Pipe` module to open an existing pipe by supplying the UNC name instead of the short name:

```
$pipe = new Win32::Pipe("\\\\INSENTIENT\\pipe\\MCStatus");
```

Note in both cases the use of double backslashes. These are required to ensure that the first backslash is not parsed by the Perl interpreter.

Accepting Connections   Once the pipe has been created, you need to listen to tell the server to wait for a connection from a client. The `Connect` method blocks the current process and returns only when a new connection from a client has been received. For example:

```
$pipe->Connect();
```

Once connected, you can start to send or receive information through the pipe using the `Read` and `Write` methods.

Note that you do not need to call this method from a client. The `new` method implies a connection when accessing an existing pipe.

Reading and Writing Pipes   If you have opened the pipe using `open`, then you can continue to use the standard `print` and `<FILEHANDLE>` formats to write and read information to and from the filehandle pointing to the pipe.

If you have used the module to open a pipe, or to create one when developing a server, then you need to use the `Read` and `Write` methods.

The Read method returns the information read from the pipe, or undef if no information could be read:

```
$pipe->Read();
```

Note that you will need to call Read multiple times until all the information within the pipe's buffer has been read. When the method returns undef, it indicates the end of the data stream from the pipe.

To write to a pipe, you need to use the Write method. This writes the supplied string to the pipe:

```
$pipe->Write(EXPR);
```

The method returns True if the operation succeeded, or undef if the operation failed—usually because the other end of the pipe (client or server) disconnected before the information could be written.

The Pipe Buffer   The information written to and read from the pipe is held in a buffer. The default buffer size if 512 bytes. You can verify the current buffer size using the BufferSize method:

```
$pipe->BufferSize()
```

This returns the current size, or undef if the pipe is invalid.

To change the buffer size, use the ResizeBuffer method. For most situations you shouldn't need to change the buffer size. The following code sets the buffer size to SIZE.

```
$pipe->ResizeBuffer(SIZE)
```

Disconnecting and Closing Pipes   Once the server end of a pipe has finished using the open pipe connection to the client, it should call the Disconnect method. This is the logical opposite of the Connect method. You should only use this method on the server of a connection. Although it's valid to call it from a client script, it has no effect, since clients do not require the Connect method:

```
$pipe->Disconnect();
```

To actually close a pipe because you have finished using it, you should use the Close method. From a client this destroys the local pipe object and closes the connection. From a server the Close method destroys the pipe object and also destroys the pipe itself. Further client connections to the pipe will raise an error.

```
$pipe->Close();
```

Getting Pipe Errors   You can get the last error message raised by the pipe system for a specific pipe using the `Error` method:

```
$pipe->Error();
```

When used on a pipe object, it returns the error code of the last operation. An error code of 0 indicates a success. When used directly from the module, (i.e., `Win32::Pipe::Error()`), the function returns a list containing the error code and associated error string for the last operation, irrespective of the pipe on which it occurred.

In general, you should probably use the `$^E` variable or the `Win32::GetLastError` functions to obtain an error from a function. For example:

```
$pipe = new Win32::Pipe('MCStatus') or die "Creating pipe: $^E ($!)";
```

Sample Scripts   The two scripts below demonstrate a very simple system that creates a server that accepts status information from other machines. In the form it's in here, the information is just printed out, although it's perfectly practical to actually supply and record the information in a more useful format for later processing and viewing.

NOTE.   *This script is a modified version of the ntstat.pl script that is featured in Chapter 11 of my* Perl Annotated Archives *book.*

The first script is the server. This simply opens a new pipe and then waits for connections:

```perl
#perl -w

use Win32::Pipe;
my $debug = 1;

$pipe = new Win32::Pipe('MCStatus') || die "Creating Pipe: $^E ($!)";
if (defined($pipe))
{
    print "Pipe created\n" if $debug;
    while(1)
    {
    print "Waiting for a new connection\n" if $debug;
    if ($pipe->Connect())
    {
        print "Accepted connection\n" if $debug;
        while($data = $pipe->Read())
```

```
            {
                print $data;
            }
            print "Closing connection\n" if $debug;
            $pipe->Disconnect()
                || die "Couldn't disconnect properly: $^E ($!)";
            }
        }
    }
    END {
    $pipe->Close();
    }
```

The client is more complex, since it has to obtain and then send the information. The pipe interaction is probably the easiest part of the entire script. We use the `Win32::AdminMisc` script to obtain the disk and memory usage on the machine, and then we report that information back to the server process using the named pipe. Because a named pipe is network-compatible, we can use this to accept information from any number of machines without having to resort to sockets or, as in the case of the original system on which this is based, an FTP client.

```perl
use Win32::Pipe;
use Win32::AdminMisc;
use Win32;

use strict;

my $time = scalar localtime();
my $node = Win32::NodeName();

my $pipe = new Win32::Pipe("\\\\INCONCEIVABLE\\pipe\\MCStatus")
    || die "Creating pipe: $^E ($!)";

$pipe->Write ("$node, $time\n====\n");
$pipe->Write ("Disk Space\n");

my @drives = Win32::AdminMisc::GetDrives(DRIVE_FIXED);

my $totalfree;
foreach my $let (@drives)
{
    my ($tot,$free) = Win32::AdminMisc::GetDriveSpace($let);
    my $reallet = $let;
    $reallet =~7E s/:\\//g;
    $tot = int($tot/1024);
    $free = int($free/1024);
    my $used=$tot-$free;
    $totalfree += $free;
    $pipe->Write ("$reallet: Used: $used, Free: $free\n");
}
$pipe->Write ("Total Free Disk: $totalfree\n");

my %Data;
```

```
if (%Data = Win32::AdminMisc::GetMemoryInfo())
{

    $pipe->Write ("Memory: Used: " .
                  (($Data{PageTotal}-$Data{PageAvail})/1024) .
                  ", Free: " .
                  ($Data{PageAvail}/1024) . "\n");
}
$pipe->Write("====END\n");
$pipe->Close();
```

If you run the server you can then monitor the information as it comes in from each machine when the client script is executed:

```
Pipe created
Waiting for a new connection
Accepted connection
INCONTINENT, Wed Mar  8 15:47:05 2000
=====
Disk Space
C: Used: 1582488, Free: 13068788
D: Used: 48880, Free: 8199048
Total Free Disk: 21267836
Memory: Used: 143652, Free: 328376
====END
Waiting for a new connection
Accepted connection
INSENTIENT, Wed Mar  8 15:49:11 2000
=====
Disk Space
C: Used: 212569, Free: 14438707
Total Free Disk: 21267836
Memory: Used: 112659, Free: 359369
====END
```

Migrating from the System V IPC Functions

The System V flavor of Unix introduced three different methods for interprocess communication. The IPC centers around three basic premises: messages, semaphores, and shared memory. The messaging system operates a simple message queue for the exchange of information. Semaphores provide shared counters across processes and are usually used to indicate the availability of shared resources. Shared memory allows for segments of memory to be shared among processes.

The messaging system is not duplicated directly within Windows. There is a separate Win32::Message module that provides the facility

TABLE 6-2

Compatibility functions for IPC under Windows.

Function	Win32-Compatible Solution
msg*	No direct equivalent. For simple messaging, consider using the Win32::Pipe module to communicate across Win32 machines. For cross-platform solutions, use sockets.
semctl	The Win32::Semaphore module provides methods for creating and modifying semaphores within the Windows system.
semget	No direct equivalent, but you could use Win32::Semaphore->Release(0,\$last) and then use the value in $last.
semop	No direct equivalent. See the Win32::Semaphore module for a similar system.
shm*	No Windows equivalent. Probably best to consider using the Win32::Pipe module for low-volume transfers.

to send messages to other machines on a network, but this presents a dialog box at the client end suitable for supplying a message to a user and cannot really be used for exchanging information.

The shared memory is not supported under Windows in any form. This is unfortunate because it provides one of the best ways of exchanging information in large quantities between processes. It is for exactly this reason that shared memory is often used by Unix database applications—you can share large chunks of data between a server and client process without having to worry about the usual client/server handling routines.

The Win32::Semaphore module provides an almost identical toolkit for sharing counter information across Win32 processes. The operation is very similar to the System V semaphore system. The Win32::Event system is very similar, except that the event object has only two states, unsignaled and signaled.

Table 6-2 gives a list of the built-in Perl IPC functions and their Windows equivalents, or suggestions for implementing equivalent functionality.

Other Forms of IPC

From a practical point of view, all forms of IPC rely entirely on the host operating system. Named pipes, while theoretically similar on the two platforms, actually exhibit minor differences that would make them incompatible in most situations. It's also becoming less important to communicate between processes on the same machine, since most applications make use of threads or `fork` to handle multiple requests to clients over a network.

Although not strictly classed as an IPC tool, normal networking sockets available through `socket` and the `Win32::Internet` module provide a much more practical cross-platform solution for sharing information. We'll look at the use of sockets, along with the additional modules and protocols supported by the base ActivePerl installation, in the next chapter.

## CHAPTER 7

Networking

For many years now, the network has become as important as the computers that use it. Sharing information and communicating between two or more machines has become not just a useful ability but a necessity. With the introduction of the Internet, the process has become even more complex. Not only is there a transport protocol to handle (TCP or UDP), you also need to know how to use the session protocol (FTP, HTTP).

Under Windows, TCP/IP (Transmission Control Protocol/Internet Protocol) is the primary protocol used for communication. It's used as the transport protocol for file and printer sharing and also as the underlying protocol for providing other communication channels for SQL Server and Internet services.

In this chapter we'll look at the two main networking services. First, we'll look at the use of standard TCP/IP sockets for communicating with other machines. Then we'll cover raw socket access using built-in functions, as well as communication with Internet servers using the supplied `CPAN` modules and the `Win32::Internet` module, which uses the Windows Internet library.

Using Standard Sockets

Sockets provide a simple way of communicating between two machines. The socket system is easy to understand if you think logically about what the term *socket* actually means. In this section, we'll take a quick look at how to communicate with other machines by using raw sockets. First, however, we'll look at how sockets work. If you already know this, skip to the next section.

If you specifically want to talk with an Internet server, then use the `LWP` or `libnet` toolkits, which we look at later in this chapter.

Socket Refresher

The BSD socket system was introduced in BSD 4.2 as a way of providing a consistent interface to the different available protocols. A socket provides a connection between an application and the network. You must have a socket at each end of the connection in order to communicate between the machines. One machine is the local machine—the current machine—and other is the peer—the remote machine to which you are talking.

Socket-based networking actually refers to a generic system for communicating using a standard set of functions. There are two common socket-based networking families. The Internet family communicates across a network (between one or more machines) using the TCP/IP or UDP/IP (User Datagram Protocol/Internet Protocol) protocols. The Unix family allows communication between two processes on a single machine and is frequently used as a form of interprocess communication (IPC) on Unix machines. It's not, unfortunately, supported under Windows, but see Chapter 6 for other forms of IPC.

The difference between TCP/IP and UDP/IP is that TCP/IP is connection-oriented and UDP/IP is connectionless. A connection-oriented network relies on the fact that two computers that want to talk to each other must go through some form of connection process, usually called a *handshake*. This handshake is similar to using the telephone: the caller dials a number and the receiver picks up the phone. In this way, the caller immediately knows whether the recipient has received the message, because the recipient will have answered the call. This type of connection is supported by TCP/IP and is the main form of communication over the Internet and local area networks (LANs).

In a connectionless network, information is sent to the recipient without first setting up the connection; no attempt is made to actually connect with the remote host. This type of network is also known as a *datagram*, or packet-oriented network, because the data is sent in discrete packets. Each packet will consist of the sender's address, the recipient's address, and the information, but no response will be provided once the message has been received. A connectionless network is therefore more like the postal service—you compose and send a letter, although you have no guarantee that the letter will reach its destination or that the information was received correctly. Connectionless networking is supported by UDP/IP.

In either case, the "circuit" is not open permanently between the two machines. Data is sent in individual packets that may take different paths and routes to the destination. The routes may involve local area networks, dial-up connection, ISDN routers, and even satellite links. Within the UDP protocol, the packets can arrive in any order, and it is up to the client program to reassemble them into the correct sequence—if there is one. With TCP, the packets are automatically reassembled into the correct sequence before they are represented to the client as a single data stream. With UDP, the packets are not reassembled into the correct sequence—doing this manually is avoided by generally using only one packet to supply the information.

There are advantages and disadvantages to both types of networks. A connectionless network is fast, because there is no requirement to acknowledge the data or enter into any dialog to set up the connection to receive the data. However, a connectionless network is also unreliable, because there is no way to ensure the information reached its destination. A connection-oriented network is slow (in comparison to a connectionless network) because of the extra dialog involved, but it guarantees the data sequence, providing end-to-end reliability.

The *IP* element of the TCP/IP and UDP/IP protocols refers to the *Internet Protocol*, which is a set of standards for specifying the individual addresses of machines within a network. Each machine within the networking world has a unique IP address. This is made up of a sequence of 4 bytes typically written in dot notation, for example, 198.10.29.145. These numbers relate both to individual machines within a network and to entire collections of machines.

Because humans are not very good at remembering numbers, a system called DNS (Domain Name System) relates easy-to-remember names to IP addresses—for example, the name www.mcgraw-hill.com relates to a single IP address. You can also have a single DNS name pointing to a number of IP addresses and multiple names pointing to the same name. It is also possible to have a single machine that has multiple interfaces, and each interface can have multiple IP addresses assigned to it. However, in all cases, if the interfaces are connected to the Internet in one form or another, then the IP addresses of each interface will be unique.

However, the specification for socket communication does not end there. Many different applications can be executed on the same machine, and so communication must be aimed not only at the machine but also at a particular application. This is known as the *port number*. If the IP address is a telephone number, the port number is the equivalent of an extension number. The first 1024 port numbers are assigned to well-known Internet protocols, and different protocols have their own unique port number. For example, HTTP, which is used to transfer information between your web browser and a web server, has a port number of 80. To connect to a server application, you need both the IP address (or machine name) and the port number on which the server is "listening."

There are many different methods for controlling this two-way communication, although none is ultimately reliable. The most obvious is to "best-guess" the state that each end of the connection should be in. For example, if one end sends a piece of information, then it might be safe to assume it should then wait for a response. If the opposite end makes the same assumption, then it can send information after it has just received some. This is not necessarily reliable, because if both ends decide to wait for information at the same time, then both ends of the connection are effectively dead. Alternatively, if both ends decide to send information at the same time, the two processes will not lock; but because they use the same send-receive system, once they have both sent information, they will both return to the wait state, expecting a response.

A better solution to the problem is to use a protocol that places rules and restrictions on the communication method and order. This is how SMTP (Simple Main Transfer Protocol) and similar protocols work. The client sends a command to the server, and the immediate response from the server tells the client what to do next. The response may include data and will definitely include an end-of-data string. In effect, it's similar to the technique used when communicating by radio. At the end of each communication, you say "Over" to indicate to the recipient that you have finished speaking. In essence, it still uses the same best-guess method for communication. Provided the communication starts off correctly, and each end sends the end-of-communication signal, the communication should continue correctly.

Perl provides a basic toolkit for communicating over sockets in the form of the `socket`, `accept`, and `bind` built-in functions. These support the low-level interface for talking over a communication pipe. Once the communication channel is open, Perl uses standard file handles for transferring information.

Resolving Network Information

Most of the functions that provide information about the TCP/IP network, including resolving protocol, service, and network numbers, work as normal under Windows. The functions rely on the files /etc/hosts, /etc/protocols, /etc/services, and /etc/networks. The Windows versions are actually in the root folder of the Windows installation—by default, C:\Windows or C:\Winnt.

The ones that don't work are the functions that make progressive calls to iterate through the files, such as `gethostent` and `getnetent`. This is because unlike the Unix functions, the Windows functions don't actually directly access the files.

If you are migrating from Unix, you shouldn't have any problems using these functions, and the summary of how to use them is included for reference.

Hosts   The gethostbyname function calls the system-equivalent function. Under Unix the system functions use the configuration of the nsswitch.conf file, which defines the order in which hosts should be resolved. Usually this involves the local host's file and then the DNS server, followed by other network services such as NIS/NIS+ and Netinfo. With Windows, as soon as a DNS server is configured within the TCP/IP properties, all further requests are made through the DNS server, ignoring the host's file altogether.

In a scalar context, the function returns the host's IP address packed into a four-character string. In a list context, the gethostbyname function returns the host name, aliases, address type, length, and physical IP addresses for the host defined in NAME. They can be extracted like this:

```
($name, $aliases, $addrtype, $length, @addresses)
    = gethostbyname($host);
```

The $aliases scalar is a space-separated list of alternative aliases for the specified name. The @addresses array contains a list of addresses in a packed format, which you will need to extract with unpack.

For example, you can get the IP address of a host as a string with

```
$address = join('.',unpack("C4",
                    scalar gethostbyname("www.mchome.com")));
```

To perform the opposite—that is, getting the name of a host based on its IP address—use the gethostbyaddr:

```
gethostbyaddr ADDR, ADDRTYPE
```

In a list context this returns the same information as gethostbyname, except that it accepts a packed IP address as its first argument. The ADDRTYPE should be AF_Unix for Unix sockets and AF_INET for Internet sockets. These constants are defined within the Socket module. In a scalar context it just returns the host name as a string.

For example, to obtain the host name for an IP address:

```
use Socket;
print scalar gethostbyaddr(pack("C4",198,112,10,135),AF_INET);
```

The following functions are not supported under Windows:

```
gethostent
sethostent
endhostent
```

You might also want to check the `gethostbyname` and `gethost-byaddr` functions contained within the `Win32::AdminMisc` module. See Chapter 8 for more details.

Protocols   The entries returned by the `proto` series of functions are the top-level protocols such as TCP or UDP. Like the host functions, the Windows implementation works in an identical fashion.

The `getprotobyname` function translates a specific protocol name into a protocol number in a scalar context, or returns the following in a list context:

```
($name, $aliases, $protocol) = getprotobyname('tcp');
```

Alternatively, you can resolve a protocol number into a protocol name with the `getprotobynumber` function.

```
getprotobynumber NUMBER
```

This returns the protocol name in a scalar context, and the same name, aliases, and protocol number information in a list context:

```
($name, $aliases, $protocol) = getprotobyname(6);
```

The following built-in Perl functions are not supported under Windows:

```
getprotoent
setprotoent
endprotoent
```

Services   The services are the service-specific protocols such as FTP or HTTP. The `getservbyname` function resolves NAME for the specified protocol PROTO into the following fields:

```
($name, $aliases, $port, $protocol_name) = getservbyname 'http', 'tcp';
```

The PROTO should be either `'tcp'` or `'udp'`, depending on what protocol you want to use. In a scalar context, the function just returns the service port number.

```
getservbyport PORT, PROTO
```

This resolves the port number PORT for the PROTO protocol, returning the same fields as `getservbyname`:

```
($name, $aliases, $port, $protocol_name) = getservbyport 80, 'tcp';
```

The following functions are not supported under Windows.

```
getservent
setservent
endservent
```

Networks   The network functions are unsupported under Windows, even though Windows does actually have a networks file where it stores the network name and IP address information. If you need to use these files, open the file directly and parse it manually using something like:

```
open(NETWORKS,"C:\WINDOWS\NETWORKS") || die "Error: $!";
while(<NETWORKS>)
{
    chomp;
    ($network,$address) = split;
...
}
```

This means that the following functions are not supported under Windows:

```
getnetbyname
getnetbyaddr
getnetent
setnetent
endnetent
```

Using Sockets

The core socket functions built-in to Perl—socket, bind, and so on—should operate as normal. However, in practice, many of the functions fail for unexpected reasons, and operations that may work on one Windows platform (95/98, NT) cannot be guaranteed to work on another. The built-in socket functions are as follows:

accept	bind	connect	getpeername
getsockname	getsockopt	listen	recv
send	setsockopt	shutdown	socket

The only function that is known not to operate under Windows is socketpair. This opens a pair of sockets that can be used for two-way communication with another machine or for IPC on the same machine. See Chapter 6 for more reliable forms of IPC.

In addition to the unstable built-in support for sockets, some of the functions that you may use in combination with sockets also do not operate. For example, using the `alarm` function to time out requests and services such as simple `ping` scripts will not work, since Windows doesn't support the `alarm` function.

The `IO::Socket` Module For a more compatible cross-platform solution, you should really be using the `IO::Socket` module. This provides all of the functionality offered by the built-in functions but uses an object-based interface. Because the module is built for a specific platform, it also guarantees that the module will work under Windows.

Using the module is straightforward—since it hides most of the complexity of the process required with the `socket` and other functions into a single class. The new object created by the module is also compatible with the other `IO::*` modules such as `IO::Select` and inherits the methods of the `IO::Handle` class.

The `IO::Socket` module is logically split into two submodules: `IO::Socket::INET` and `IO::Socket::Unix`. The base `IO::Socket` module supports the base methods for the class, `IO::Socket::INET` supports the methods for Internet domain sockets, and `IO::Socket::Unix` supports Unix domain sockets, which are unsupported under Windows.

To create a new `IO::Socket` object, you use the `new` class method:

```
$socket = IO::Socket->new(Domain => 'Unix');
```

The constructor supports only one option, `Domain`, which defines the domain in which to create the socket. All the other arguments supplied to the constructor will be passed on to the corresponding module for parsing. The alternative is to use the correct class when creating the new object, in other words:

```
$socket = IO::Socket::INET->new(PeerAddr => 'www.mcwords.com:80');
```

The base `IO::Socket` class supports a number of methods common to both socket families.

The return value in either case is a new socket handle object. This is actually derived from the `IO::Handle` module and acts as a normal file handle within Perl. You can send information to a socket using `print`:

```
print $socket ("GET /index.html\n\n");
```

You can also read using the <FILEHANDLE> operator:

```
$info = <$socket>;
```

They can also be used in combination with the IO::Select handle when manipulating multichannel I/O (see the server example later in this section).

━ ━ ━ ━ ━ ━ ━ ━ ━ ━ ━ ━ ━ ━ ━ ━ ━ ━ ━ ━

NOTE.   By default, all new sockets created with IO::Socket *have* autoflush *switched on, so there is no buffering on sockets. See the documentation on* IO::Handle *for more information.*

IO::Socket Methods   The accept method accepts a new socket connection just like the built-in accept function, returning a new IO::Socket handle of the appropriate type:

```
$object = $socket->accept([PKG]);
($object, $peeraddr) = accept([PKG]);
```

If you specify PKG, the new object will be of the specified class, rather than that of the parent handle. In a scalar context, only the new object is returned; in a list context, both the object and the peer (remote) address are returned. The method will return undef or an empty list on failure.

The timeout method sets the timeout value for connecting to remote hosts or for accepting incoming connections:

```
$socket->timeout([VALUE]);
```

If supplied without any arguments, the current timeout setting is returned. If called with an argument, it sets the timeout value. The timeout value is used by various other methods.

The sockopt method provides the functionality of the built-in getsockopt and setsockopt functions:

```
$socket->sockopt(OPT [, VALUE]);
```

If supplied with only one argument, then the method returns the current socket option. If supplied with two arguments, then it sets the value of OPT to VALUE. Valid socket options are shown in Table 7-1.

To finally close a socket, use the close method:

```
$socket->close();
```

TABLE 7-1

Socket options.

Option	Description
SO_DEBUG	Enable/disable recording of debugging information.
SO_REUSEADDR	Enable/disable local address reuse.
SO_KEEPALIVE	Enable/disable keep connections alive.
SO_DONTROUTE	Enable/disable routing bypass for outgoing messages.
SO_LINGER	Linger on close if data is present.
SO_BROADCAST	Enable/disable permission to transmit broadcast messages.
SO_OOBINLINE	Enable/disable reception of out-of-band data in band.
SO_SNDBUF	Set buffer size for output.
SO_RCVBUF	Set buffer size for input.

The remainder of the methods return information about the current socket connection:

```
$socket->sockdomain();
```

returns the numerical value of the socket domain type.

```
$socket->socktype();
```

returns the numerical value of the socket type.

```
$socket->protocol();
```

returns the numerical value of the protocol being used on the socket. If the protocol is unknown, 0 is returned.

```
$socket->peername();
```

returns the packed socket address of the remote host attached to the socket.

```
$socket->sockname();
```

returns the packed socket address of the local host. Note that this may be different to the default IP address of the host if the host has multiple IP addresses. Also note that this method will only work if the socket is connected to the remote host.

TABLE 7-2

Options for
creating an
IO::Socket::
INET object.

Option	Format	Description
PeerAddr	hostname[:port]	Remote host address (and port). The address can be specified as a name (which will be resolved) or as an IP address. The port (if specified) should be a valid service name and/or port number as defined in PeerPort.
PeerPort	service(port)|port	The service port name and number, or number only.
LocalAddr	hostname[:port]	Local host address to bind to.
LocalPort	service(no)|no	The local service port name and number, or number only.
Proto	"tcp"|"udp"|...	The protocol name or number. If this is not specified and you give a service name in the PeerPort option, then the constructor will attempt to derive Proto from the given service name. If it cannot be resolved, then "tcp" is used.
Type	SOCK_STREAM|SOCK_DGRAM|...	The socket type, specified using a constant as exported by Socket. This will be deduced from Proto if not otherwise specified.
Listen		The queue size for listening to requests.
Timeout		Timeout value for various operations.
Reuse		If true, then it sets the SO_REUSEADDR option before binding to the local socket.

The IO::Socket::INET Module   The IO::Socket::INET class provides a constructor to create a socket within the Internet family/domain. The constructor accepts a hash that takes the options shown in Table 7-2.

If passed a single argument, the constructor assumes that it's a PeerAddr specification. For example, to create a connection to a web server on port 80:

```
$socket = IO::Socket::INET->new('www.mcwords.com:http(80)');
```

Or, to create a local socket for listening:

```
$socket = IO::Socket::INET->new(LocalAddr => 'localhost',
                                LocalPort => '7000',
                                Listen    => '5',
                                Proto     => 'tcp');
```

Note that by specifying `LocalAddr` and `Listen`, the constructor builds a local socket suitable for acting as a server-side socket. You must use the `accept` method (inherited from `IO::Socket`) to accept new connections.

`IO::Socket::INET` **Methods.** Beyond the methods inherited from `IO::Socket` and `IO::Handle`, the `IO::Socket::INET` class also supports the following methods:

`sockaddr`

returns the 4-byte packed address of the local socket.

`sockport`

returns the port number used for the local socket.

`sockhost`

returns the IP address in the form `xxx.xxx.xxx.xxx` for the local socket.

`peeraddr`

returns the 4-byte packed address of the remote socket.

`peerport`

returns the port number used for the remote socket.

`peerhost`

returns the IP address in the form `xxx.xxx.xxx.xxx` for the remote socket.

Examples We'll take a look at two examples that use the `IO::Socket` module. The first is a simple client that queries a remote host for the time of day. The `daytime` port returns the date and time on the local machine as a simple string. It's not supported by Windows 95/98 machines, but the service is supported by default on Windows 2000 machines, and of course most Unix machines.

```perl
use IO::Socket;

$socket = IO::Socket::INET->new(PeerAddr => $ARGV[0],
                                PeerPort => 13);

if (defined($socket))
{
    $_ = <$socket>;
    print "The time on $ARGV[0] is $_";
    close($socket);
}
else
{
    die "Couldn't open socket: $!";
}
```

You can see here how I've used the basic file handle to get the information from the remote host. If you run the script and supply a suitable host, you should get something like this:

```
C:\>perl 02.pl incontinent
The time on incontinent is 12:37:35 26/03/2000
```

The second example shows an IO::Socket-based server that uses select to accept connections from multiple hosts (bypassing the requirement for fork). This was originally written as a quick way of passing messages into a log file from any machine—all I had to do was use telnet from any machine to the server port and type the message. It evolved first into a way of accepting todo entries from multiple machines, and then to the MediaWeb system, which monitors remote machines (see *Perl: Annotated Archives* for details).

```perl
use IO::Socket;
use IO::Select;
use strict;

my $port = 4004;

#Create the listening socket

my $listen = IO::Socket::INET->new(LocalPort => 4004,
                                   Listen => 5,
                                   Reuse => 1 );

#Make sure the socket works

if (defined($listen))
```

```
{
    print "Listening for connections on $port\n";
}
else
{
    die "Error creating socket for listening: $!";
}
#Create a new select object and add our
#listening socket to it

my $socketlist = IO::Select->new;
$socketlist->add($listen);

#Open a file to log the incoming text

open(LOGGER,"+>logger.txt") || die "Couldn't create log file";

#Enter an infinite loop

while(1) {
    # Check if there are any active sockets with waiting data

    my ($ready) = IO::Select->select($socketlist, undef,
                                      undef, undef);

    # Work through each socket

    foreach my $socket (@$ready)
    {
        # If it's our listening socket then there's a
        # new incoming connection

        if ($socket == $listen)
        {
            my $newsocket = $listen->accept();
            if (defined($newsocket))
            {
                # Add the new client to the list of sockets
                # in the select object, and greet the client

                $socketlist->add($newsocket);
                my $host = $newsocket->peerhost();
                print $newsocket "Hello ",$host,"\n";
                print("Accepted new connection from $host\n");
            }
            else
            {
                print "Error: Couldn't accept the connection\n";
            }
        }
        else
        {
            my $line = <$socket>;
            my $host = $socket->peerhost();

            # If we've received a line of data...

            if (defined($line))
            {
```

```
                        # If the command is quit, the client wants to
                        # disconnect, so remove them from the
                        # select list and close the socket
                        if ($line =~ /^quit/i)
                        {
                            $socketlist->remove($socket);
                            $socket->close();
                            print("$host has left the building\n");
                        }
                        else
                        {
                            # Otherwise, print the line to the log file
                            print LOGGER (scalar localtime(), ':',
                                        $host, ':', $line);
                        }
                    }
                    else
                    {
                        # If there wasn't any data, then the waiting
                        # data identified by select was a disconnect
                        $socketlist->remove($socket);
                        $socket->close();
                        print("$host left without saying goodbye\n");
                    }
                }
            }
        }
```

By using IO::Select **we avoid having to** fork **new processes, or in
the case of the ActivePerl 5.6 distribution, new Windows threads to handle each incoming connection. For a low-volume server like this it's not a
problem, but if you want to implement a high-volume server, then you'd
have to use** fork **in order to achieve a reasonable level of performance.**

For a simple client, refer to the following:

```
use IO::Socket;


my $port = 4004;
my $message;

my $socket = IO::Socket::INET->new(PeerAddr => 'insentient',
                                    PeerPort => $port);

if (defined($socket))
{
    $greeting = <$socket>;
    print $greeting;
    while(<STDIN>)
    {
        print $socket $_;
    }
    print $socket "quit\n";
    $socket->close();
}
```

```
else
{
    die "Couldn't open socket: $!";
}
```

CPAN Toolkits

Most modern socket communication is geared toward communicating with servers and other machines using standard protocols such as FTP and SMTP. Although you can program these yourself, it's much better to use one of the existing toolkits that exist on CPAN for this purpose.

The ActivePerl distribution comes with the LWP bundle (libwww-Perl) as part of the standard library. Other, similar modules include the lib-net bundle from Graham Barr and the Net::DNS modules from Michael Fuhr. All of the modules work in an identical fashion under Windows as they do under Unix. For people not familiar with the LWP module, we'll quickly look at some of the main features.

The LWP Modules

The libwww-Perl library from Gisla Aas combines a number of different modules to provide a complete service for downloading and parsing web-related content. The LWP modules allow you to create a new "user agent" that will download a given URL to a local file. In addition, the LWP library includes the HTML::* series of modules, which parse HTML and can be used to extract image and link references, and URI::*, which parses and identifies the components of URLs.

The library is far too big to be discussed in this book, but let's look at two scripts that download URLs to the local machine. The first one downloads a single URL to a file. This can be used either to get a single web page or to download a file from the Web without using a web browser:

```
#!/usr/local/bin/perl -w


use LWP::Simple;

$url  = shift or usage();
$file = shift or usage();
$rc = mirror($url, $file);
```

```perl
unless(is_success($rc))
{
    print STDERR ("$0: $rc ",
        status_message($rc),
        "    ($url)\n");
    exit 1;
}

sub usage
{
    print "geturl.pl URL FILE";
    exit;
}
```

To use, supply the URL and the file in which you want it to be saved:

```
C:\> perl geturl.pl http://www.mcwords.com index.html
```

The script uses the LWP::Simple module. This module exports a single function, mirror, which copies a URL to a file.

The other modules in the LWP set allow you to further URLs and HTML to extract the individual components. Using that premise, we can extrapolate from the example above so that we can download an entire website to the local machine, all through Perl. The example mirrors an entire site.

```perl
#!/usr/local/bin/perl

use LWP::Simple;
use LWP::UserAgent;
use HTML::LinkExtor;
use URI::URL;
use Getopt::Long;
use File::Basename;

my ($file,$host,$localdir,$curhost);
my ($url, $specdir, $quiet, $silent, $inchost, $unrestrict)
    = (undef, undef, undef, undef, undef);

usage() unless(GetOptions("d=s" => \$specdir,
                           "s"   => \$silent,
                           "q"   => \$quiet,
                           "h"   => \$inchost,
                           "u"   => \$unrestrict
                           ));

usage() unless($url=shift);
$specdir = '.' unless defined($specdir);
$specdir = "$specdir/" unless ($specdir =~ m#/$#);
$quiet = 1 if ($silent);

my %fullurl;
my @urlstack = ($url);
```

```perl
my @urls = ();
my $p = HTML::LinkExtor->new(\&callback);
my $ua = new LWP::UserAgent;
my $res = $ua->request(HTTP::Request->new(GET => $url));
my $base = $res->base;
$curhost = $host = url($url,'')->host;

print "Retrieving from $url to $specdir",
    ($inchost ? "$host\n" : "\n")
        unless ($silent);

while ($url = pop(@urlstack))
{

    $host = url($url,'')->host;
    if ($host ne $curhost)
    {
        my $ua = new LWP::UserAgent;
        my $res = $ua->request(HTTP::Request->new(GET => $url));
        my $base = $res->base;
        $host = url($url,'')->host;
        $curhost = $host;
        print "Changing host to $host\n" unless $quiet;
    }
    $localdir = ($inchost ? "$specdir$host/" : "$specdir/");

    $file = url($url,$base)->full_path;
    $file .='index.html' if ($file =~ m#/$#);
    $file =~ s#^/#$localdir#;

    print "Retrieving: $url to $file\n" unless ($quiet);
    my $dir = dirname($file);
    unless (-d $dir)
    {
        mkdirhier($dir);
    }
    getfile($url,$file);
    if (-e $file)
    {

        $p->parse_file($file);
        @urls = map { $_ = url($_, $base)->abs; } @urls;
        addtostack(@urls);
    }
}

sub addtostack
{
    my (@urllist) = @_;

    for my $url (@urllist)
    {
        next if ($url =~ /#/);
        next unless ($url =~ m#^http#);
        my $urlhost = url($url,$base)->host;
        unless (defined($unrestrict))
            { next unless ($urlhost eq $host); };
        push(@urlstack,$url) unless(defined($fullurl{$url}));
        $fullurl{$url} = 1;
```

```
        }
}

sub callback
{
    my($tag, %attr) = @_;
    push(@urls, values %attr);
}

sub getfile
{

    my ($url,$file) = @_;
    my $rc = mirror($url, $file);

    if ($rc == 304)
    {
        print "File is up to date\n" unless ($quiet);
    }
    elsif (!is_success($rc))
    {
        warn "sitemirr: $rc ", status_message($rc), " ($url)\n"
            unless ($silent);
        return(0);
    }
}

sub mkdirhier
{
    my ($fullpath) = @_;
    my $path;

    for my $dir (split(m#/#,$fullpath))
    {
        unless (-d "$path$dir")
        {
            mkdir("$path$dir",0777)
                or die "Couldn't make directory $path/$dir: $!";
        }
        $path .= "$dir/";
    }
}

sub usage
{
    die <<EOF;
Usage:
    sitemirr.pl [-d localdir] [-s] [-q] [-u] URL

Where:

localdir is the name of the local directory you want
        files copied to (default: .)
h       Include host in local directory path
q       Retrieve quietly (show errors only)
s       Retrieve silently (no output)
u       Unrestrict site match (will download ALL
        URL's, including those from other hosts)
EOF
```

The important part here is the HTML::LinkExtor module. It parses the HTML downloaded by the LWP::UserAgent module, builds a list of images and other HTML pages linked within the downloaded page, and then downloads each of those.

To use, you can simply supply the URL on the command line:

```
C:\> perl sitemirr.pl http://www.mcslp.com
Retrieving from http://www.mcslp.com to ./
Retrieving: http://www.mcslp.com to .//index.html
Retrieving: http://www.mcslp.com/projects/nelsi to .//projects/nelsi
Retrieving: http://www.mcslp.com/projects/spip to .//projects/spip
Retrieving: http://www.mcslp.com/img/elsewhere.gif to .//img/else-
where.gif
```

See the documentation for more details on using the LWP, HTML, and URI modules.

The libnet Bundle

Graham Barr's libnet bundle provides access to standard Internet servers. These augment, rather than replace, the features of the LWP bundle. You can download the libnet bundle using the Perl Package Manager (see Chapter 12).

Most usefully, the libnet bundle allows you to send e-mail by talking to SMTP servers directly—thereby bypassing the sendmail or similar tools often required by Unix machines to send e-mail. For example, a simple e-mail script is as follows:

```
#!/usr/local/bin/perl5

use Net::SMTP;
use Net::Domain qw/hostdomain/;
use Getopt::Long;
my ($subject,$from,$message,$msgbody,$smtp,$realsubject);

GetOptions("s=s" => \$subject,
           "f=s" => \$from);

if (@ARGV < 1)
{
    die "No recipients specified";
}

print "Enter message: \n";
while(<STDIN>)
{
    last if (/^\.$/);
    $message .= $_;
}
```

```
$smtp = Net::SMTP->new('mail.mchome.com');
die "Couldn't open connection to server" unless $smtp;
$from = defined($from) ?
    $from : Win32::LoginName() . '@' . hostdomain();

$smtp->mail($from)
    || die "Bad 'from' address";

foreach my $recipient (@ARGV)
{
    warn "Couldn't set recipient $recipient"
        unless($smtp->to($recipient));
}

$realsubject = "Subject: ";
$realsubject .= defined($subject) ? $subject : "<no subject>";
$realsubject .= "\n\n";
$smtp->data();
$smtp->datasend("From: $from\n");
$smtp->datasend('To: ' . join(', ',@ARGV) . "\n");
$smtp->datasend($realsubject);
$smtp->datasend($message);
die "Connection wouldn't accept data"
    unless($smtp->dataend());

die "Couldn't close connection to server"
    unless($smtp->quit());
```

Using this script, we can now send e-mail from the command line:

```
C:\> perl 08.pl -f mc@mcwords.com mc@mcwords.com
Enter Message:
Just a reminder...
.
```

For our final example, here is a script that will upload an entire directory structure to a remote machine using FTP, even allowing for file formats:

```
#!/usr/local/bin/perl5

use Net::FTP;
use Getopt::Long;
use File::Find;
use Cwd;

my $debug       = 1;
my $remserver   = undef;
my $remport     = '21';
my $user        = 'anonymous';
my $password    = 'me@foo.bar';
my $dir         = '.';
my $localdir    = './';
my $curxfermode = 'ASCII';

unless (GetOptions("d" => \$debug,
```

```
                              "s=s" => \$remserver,
                              "r=s" => \$dir,
                              "p=i" => \$remport,
                              "u=s" => \$user,
                              "w=s" => \$password,
                              "l=s" => \$localdir
                              ))
{
 usage();
}

usage() unless $remserver;

$localdir = './' unless ($localdir);
my $ftp = Net::FTP->new($remserver, 'Port' => $remport);
die "Could not connect to $remserver" unless $ftp;
$ftp->login($user, $password)
    or die "Couldn't login to $remserver";
$ftp->cwd($dir)
    or die "Invalid directory ($dir) on FTP Server";
$ftp->ascii()
    or warn "Couldn't change default xfer mode, continuing";

chdir($localdir);
my $currentdir = getcwd();
find(\&sendfile,'.');

$ftp->quit();

sub sendfile
{

    my $file      =  $File::Find::name;
    $file         =~ s#^\./##g;
    my $localfile =  "$currentdir/$file";
    $localfile    =~ s#//#/#g;
    my $remfile   =  $file;

    print "Processing $localfile rem($remfile)\n" if $debug;

    if (-d $localfile)
    {

        my $remcurdir = $ftp->pwd();
        unless($ftp->cwd($remfile))
        {
            unless ($localfile eq '..')
            {
                print "Attempting to make directory $remfile\n";
                $ftp->mkdir($remfile,1) or
                    die "Couldn't make directory $remfile";
            }
        }
        else
        {
            $ftp->cwd($remcurdir) or
                die "Couldn't change to directory $currentdir";
        }
    }
```

```perl
else
{
    my ($remtime,$localtime,$upload) = (undef,undef,0);
    unless($remtime = $ftp->mdtm($remfile))
    {
        $remtime = 0;
    }
    $localtime = (stat($file))[9];
    if (defined($localtime) and defined($remtime))
    {
        if ($localtime > $remtime)
        {
            $upload=1;
        }
    }
    else
    {
        $upload=1;
    }
    if ($upload)
    {
        if (-B $localfile)
        {
            if ($curxfermode eq 'ASCII')
            {
                if ($ftp->binary())
                {
                    $curxfermode = 'BIN';
                    print "Changed mode to BINary\n"
                        if $debug;
                }
                else
                {
                    warn "Couldn't change transfer mode";
                }
            }
        }
        else
        {
            if ($curxfermode eq 'BIN')
            {
                if ($ftp->ascii())
                {
                    $curxfermode = 'ASCII';
                    print "Changed mode to ASCII\n"
                        if $debug;
                }
                else
                {
                    warn "Couldn't change transfer mode";
                }
            }
        }
        print "Uploading $localfile to $remfile\n" if $debug;
        $ftp->put($localfile,$remfile)
            or warn "Couldn't upload $remfile";
    }
    else
    {
```

```
                     print "File $remfile appears to be up to date\n"
                       if $debug;
               }
         }
}

sub usage
{
     print <<EOF;
Usage:

     uplsite.pl [-d] [-r remdir] [-p remport] [-u user]
               [-w password] [-l localdir] -s server

Description:

Uploads a directory structure to the server using FTP.

Where:

-d  Switch on debugging output
-r  Remote directory to upload to (defaults to .)
-p  The remote port to use (defaults to 21)
-u  The user name to login as (defaults to anonymous)
-w  The password to use (defaults to me\@foo.bar)
-l  The local directory to upload from (defaults to .)
-s  The remote server address to upload to (required)

EOF
     exit 1;
}
```

For example, you can use the script to upload an entire website to your service provider:

```
C:\> perl uplsite.pl -s myhost -u mylogin -w password ./website
Processing C:/Website/index.html rem(index.html)
Processing C:/Website/projects rem(projects)
Attempting to make directory projects
Processing C:/Website/projects/index.html rem(projects/index.html)
...
```

This script was originally developed under Linux to demonstrate cross-platform facilities offered by the Net::FTP module. It's been tested and reproduced here without modification.

Other modules in the libnet bundle are shown in Table 7-3.

Using the Win32::Internet Module

The Win32::Internet module was developed by Aldo Calpini and takes a different path to the process of downloading Internet data. While the

TABLE 7-3

Modules included in the `libnet` bundle.

Module	Description
`Net::Cmd`	Provides a standard toolkit for talking to any command-based Internet servers (used as a base class for `Net::SMTP`, `Net::FTP`, and others).
`Net::Domain`	Exports three functions for determining the local host's name, domain name, and a fully qualified hostname (includes the domain).
`Net::DummyInetd`	Enables you to set up a dummy `Inetd` daemon that will listen for connections from a specified port and then supply the information to a specific script or other program.
`Net::FTP`	An interface to an FTP server; allows you to traverse a remote FTP directory structure and upload and download files.
`Net::Netrc`	Allows you to control the .netrc files used by the `ftp` program.
`Net::NNTP`	Supports a communication channel for talking to NNTP (Usenet) news servers.
`Net::PH`	Interface to PH servers, which provide name and e-mail address expansion and lookup services.
`Net::POP3`	Provides objects and methods for accessing e-mail on Post Office Protocol (POP) servers.
`Net::SMTP`	Interface to SMTP-based servers used for sending and routing e-mail.
`Net::SNPP`	Interface to SNPP (Simple Network Pager Protocol) servers for sending messages to pagers.
`Net::Time`	Supports functions for querying time servers (supports both the `time` and `daytime` protocols).

LWP/libnet modules make use of the `IO::Socket` module and some Perl programming, the `Win32::Internet` module uses the WININET.DLL shared library used by Windows itself for communicating over the Internet.

Although the `Win32::Internet` module is obviously not cross-platform-compliant, it does offer some advantages over LWP. First and foremost is that because it uses the Windows libraries, connectivity to the Internet is assured; you don't have to worry about connecting to dial-up-based services, as Windows will automatically make the connection for you.

For cross-platform compatibility, you should probably use the LWP or `Net::*` modules, since these ensure operation on all platforms. The two modules also provide a much more extensive toolkit than that offered by the `Win32::Internet` module, which is limited to FTP and HTTP requests.

The module itself is huge and provides both low-level and high-level interfaces to the underlying Internet libraries supported under Win32. The start of all operations is to create a new `Win32::Internet` object:

```
use Win32::Internet;
$internet = new Win32::Internet();
```

This creates a generic Internet object. You can use the remainder of the methods and techniques discussed here to actually download pages using HTTP and files using FTP. If all you want to do is download a specific URL (without the interactivity offered by HTTP- or FTP-specific sessions) see the "Data Transfer" section below.

Data Transfer

To download the content of a URL to a scalar variable, use the `FetchURL` method:

```
FetchURL(URL)
```

The method returns the URL content or `undef` on error. For example:

```
$internet = new Win32::Internet();
$index = $internet->FetchURL('http://www.mcwords.com');
```

Alternatively, for larger downloads, you can create a new URL object, and then use URL methods to read bytes from the connection. The starting point is the `OpenURL` method:

```
$url = $internet->OpenURL(URL)
```

This creates a new object for downloading URL, or it returns `undef` if the URL could not be accessed.

The `ReadFile` method returns data from the buffer that contains the URL object:

```
$file = $url->ReadFile([EXPR]);
```

The method returns up to `EXPR` bytes from the download buffer. If

EXPR is not specified, all the bytes from the buffer are read. To determine the actual number of bytes waiting in the buffer, use the QueryDataAvailable method:

```
$bytes = $url->QueryDataAvailable();
```

Once you have finished using a URL object, you should use the close method to disconnect from the remote server. The following code:

```
$url->Close();
```

closes the Internet connection. This is implied when the object is destroyed; you do not need to explicitly close an open connection.

Configuration

All Win32::Internet objects can be controlled through a series of methods outlined below. All the methods work in a similar fashion: The method always returns the current value, but if supplied an argument, it will set the option to that value and return the new value. The methods are as follows:

```
$internet->ConnectBackoff([VALUE]);
```

reads (or sets) the value of the connection timeout, defined in milliseconds.

```
$internet->ConnectRetries([VALUE]);
```

reads (or sets) the number of times a connection is retried.

```
$internet->ConnectTimeout([VALUE]);
```

reads (or sets) the connection timeout value in milliseconds before a connection is defined as a failure.

```
$internet->ControlReceiveTimeout([VALUE]);
```

reads or sets the timeout value in milliseconds. Used for FTP control connections.

```
$internet->ControlSendTimeout([VALUE]);
```

reads or sets the timeout value in milliseconds. Used for FTP send requests.

```
$internet->DataReceiveTimeout([VALUE]);
```

sets the timeout value, in milliseconds, for use when receiving data.

```
$internet->DataSendTimeout([VALUE]);
```

sets the timeout value, in milliseconds, for use when sending data.

```
$internet->Password([PASSWORD]);
```

reads or sets the password used during an FTP or HTTP connection.

```
$internet->QueryOption(OPTION);
```

queries an Internet option. See the Microsoft documentation, available on http://msdn.microsoft.com/library/devprods/vs6/visualc/vccore/_core_wininet_.28.http.2c_.ftp.2c_.gopher.29.htm for more information.

```
$internet->SetOption(OPTION, VALUE);
```

sets the Internet option OPTION to VALUE.

```
$internet->UserAgent([NAME]);
```

reads or sets the user agent (the browser name) used for HTTP requests.

```
$internet->Username([NAME]);
```

reads or sets the user name in use for the current HTTP or FTP connection. Used in conjunction with the Password option to set the authorization when connecting to a site.

```
$internet->Version();
```

returns the version numbers for the Win32::Internet module and the corresponding DLL version number for the Internet library.

URL Formatting

To format the URLs used with the rest of the interface, the module supplies a series of functions (not methods) for building and extracting the elements of a URL.

The following code:

```
$url = CanonicalizeURL(URL, [flags]);
```

cleans a URL format, accounting for special characters (which are converted to the correct escape sequences), returning the new URL, or undef on error.

This code:

```
$url = CombineURL(BASE, RELATIVE [, FLAGS]);
```

combines the URL in BASE with the relative URL in RELATIVE and returns the final result. For example:

```
print CombineURL('http://www.mcwords.com/projects',
                 '/projects/index.shtml');
```

would return 'http://www.mcwords.com/projects/index.shtml'.

This code:

```
($protocol, $host, $port, $login, $password, $path, $extrainfo)
    = CrackURL(URL [, FLAGS]);
```

returns an array containing the individual elements of a URL.

Finally, the following code:

```
CreateURL(PROTOCOL, HOST, PORT, LOGIN,
          PASSWORD, PATH, EXTRA [,    FLAGS])
CreateURL(HASH [, FLAGS]);
```

returns a URL based on the individual arguments. With the hash version, you must supply a reference to a hash containing the information. If supplied a hash, then the keys of the hash are used to build the URL. In the same order as the first version, the fields supported are scheme, hostname, port, username, password, path, and extrainfo.

Error Handling

The Win32::Internet module provides its own error numbering system, which integrates with the main Win32::GetLastError function. The main function is Error.

For example:

```
$error = $internet->Error();
```

```
$error = Win32::Internet::Error();
```

returns the last error returned by the Win32 Internet subsystem. If the error contains additional information, this is returned as additional elements of the list. There are three levels of error: 1 indicates a trivial module-related error; numbers 1..11999 indicate a generic system error, which can be obtained using the Win32::GetLastError function; numbers above 12000 indicate an Internet subsystem error—additional information should have been returned.

Because there is no way of determining the error type until the call has been made, you will need to extract the error number and text when calling and determine later whether the second argument returned should be ignored.

FTP Interface

Beyond the basic FetchURL method offered by the module, there are also two further classes supported that provide interface access for the FTP and HTTP protocols. The first, FTP, allows you to conduct interface conversations with an FTP server in a similar fashion to the Net::FTP module. For example:

```
$internet->FTP(FTPOBJECT, SERVER, USERNAME, PASSWORD,
               [PORT, PASV, CONTEXT]);
$internet->FTP(FTPOBJECT, HASHREF);
```

This opens a connection to an FTP server, using the server and other information provided. Note that it must be used as a method call to an existing Win32::Internet object. Once the connection is complete, a new object is placed in FTPOBJECT. The new object can then be used to control the communication with the FTP server, and individual FTP commands are implemented as methods to the new object. If you use the hash method, the names of the hash keys are the lowercase equivalents of the arguments to the scalar version.

The supported methods for the new object match the commands available within any FTP client. The methods are given in Table 7-4.

HTTP Interface

The HTTP protocol is not interactive; however, you can control the information sent to the HTTP server during a request and request the addi-

TABLE 7-4

Methods for FTP
objects.

Method	Description
Ascii	Sets ASCII (text) transfer mode.
Asc	
Binary	Sets binary transfer mode.
Bin	
Cd PATH	Changes the remote directory to PATH.
Cwd PATH	
Chdir PATH	
Delete FILE	Deletes the remote FILE.
Del FILE	
Get REMOTE, [LOCAL, OVERWRITE]	Gets the remote file REMOTE. If supplied, the file is downloaded to the file LOCAL, and only overwritten if OVERWRITE is true.
List [PATTERN [, MODE]]	Lists the remote files matching PATTERN, or all files if no pattern is supplied. If MODE is unspecified or 1, then a simple name is listed for each file. If MODE is 2, then an array (or arrays) is returned, with each element of the subarray containing the full name, DOS name, size, attributes, creation time, access time, and modification time.
	If MODE is 3, then the information for mode 2 is returned, but as a hash with the keys name, altname, size, attr, ctime, atime, and mtime.
	In all cases, times are returned as a comma-separated list of numbers referring to the second, hour, minute, day, month, and year.
Ls [PATTERN [, MODE]]	
Dir [PATTERN [, MODE]]	
Mkdir NAME	Makes the directory on the remote server with the name NAME.
Md NAME	
Mode [mode]	Returns the current transfer mode. If MODE is supplied as 'asc', sets the current mode to ASCII, while bin sets the mode to binary.

Method	Description
Put LOCAL [, REMOTE]	Puts the file LOCAL onto the remote server as REMOTE.
Pwd	Returns the current directory.
Rename OLD, NEW	Renames the remote file OLD to NEW.
Ren OLD, NEW	
Rmdir NAME	Removes the remote directory NAME.
Rd NAME	

tional information that is sent back by the server when an item has been requested. For example:

```
$internet->HTTP(HTTPOBJECT, SERVER, USERNAME, PASSWORD
              [,PORT, FLAGS, CONTEXT]);
$internet->HTTP(HTTPOBJECT, HASHREF);
```

opens an HTTP connection to a remote machine using the information provided. You can supply undef for USERNAME and PASSWORD if you want guest access to the server. The hash version uses lowercase versions of the above arguments. The function creates the new object in the scalar pointed to by HTTPOBJECT, and you can then use the newly created object to access the remote server.

The main method for a new object is Request, which sends a request to the HTTP server. The method has two formats:

```
$http->Request([path, method, version, referer, accept]);
$http->Request(hashref);
```

This sends the request to the server. All arguments are optional. If specified, the PATH is the path to the file you want to access. The METHOD is the HTTP method supported—the default is GET. The function returns undef on error or the contents of the URL requested. For descriptions of the remainder of the arguments, see the OpenRequest method below.

For example, to open a page:

```
$file = $http->Request('index.html');
```

The Request method is a one-step procedure that calls OpenRequest, SendRequest, QueryInfo, ReadFile, and, finally, Close.

Complex Requests   If you want to perform more complex requests, then you need to use the OpenRequest method. This creates a new request object, through which you can supply not only the object you want to download but also additional header information and the HTTP header information returned by the server.

The format of the OpenRequest method is as follows:

```
($statuscode, $headers, $file)
    = $http->OpenRequest(requestobject,
                         [path, method, version, referer, accept,
                             FLAGS,CONTEXT]);
($statuscode, $headers, $file)
    = $http->OpenRequest(requestobject, hashref);
```

The method creates a new request object in the scalar pointed to by REQUESTOBJECT. The remainder of the arguments to the method are described in Table 7-5.

The return value is an array containing the status code of the request, the HTTP headers, and the contents of the URL requested.

The other methods allow you to configure additional headers or request additional information about the request you are making. The request is not actually sent until the SendRequest method is called on the new request object. The following code:

```
$request->AddHeader(header);
```

adds the HTTP header HEADER to the request. For example:

```
$http->OpenRequest($request,"/index.html");
$request->AddHeader("Accept: text/html");
$request->SendRequest();
```

TABLE 7-5

HTTP request
arguments.

Argument	Description
PATH	The URL to request.
METHOD	The HTTP method to use; can actually be GET, POST, HEAD, or PUT.
VERSION	The HTTP version. The default is HTTP/1.0.
REFERER	The URL of the document from which the URL in the request was obtained.
ACCEPT	The content types accepted. They must be separated by a \0 (ASCII zero).

The `SendRequest` method actually sends a request to the remote HTTP server:

```
($statuscode, $headers, $file) = $request->SendRequest([DATA]);
```

The optional `DATA` is some additional data that is sent between the HTTP headers and the actual request. This is used when supplying information that would ordinarily be supplied by a form.

To actually supply the information, you need to tell the server to accept form data by specifying the content type of the request:

```
$request->AddHeader("Content-Type: application/x-www-form-
    urlencoded");
$request->SendRequest("name=Martin%20Brown&email=mc@whoever.com");
```

Once the request has been sent, you can get additional information sent back by the server using the `QueryInfo` method:

```
$header = $request->QueryInfo(header);
```

The `HEADER` argument is the name of the response field to access. For example, to get the format of the file returned:

```
print "Type is: ", $request("Content-type");
```

Managing Shared Resources

Under Windows, you can share resources over the network. The principles are very similar to the Network File System (NFS) used under Unix, except that it applies to both files and printers. Also, in line with the domain system employed by Windows for identifying resources, they are described using a UNC, or Universal Naming Convention, which allows you to refer to a shared resource on the network using a strict format. For example:

```
\\server\share
```

where `server` is the name of the server on which the object is shared and `share` is the name of the shared object. Unfortunately, from the name alone, there is not enough information to determine whether a share is a shared disk or a shared printer—although the distinction is made through the network browser in Windows.

The `Win32::NetResource` module provides a suite of Perl functions for accessing and using the shared resources on a network. Note that the module does not export the functions by default. You will have to select the functions you want to use during import, as in the following:

```
use Win32::NetResource qw/:DEFAULT GetSharedResources/;
```

But remember to import the default symbols, which include the constants you'll need when using the functions!

Using Shared Resources

The `Win32::NetResource` module provides functions for determining which resources are available on the network. This is handled by a Windows library, which is normally used to traverse the network using the Network Neighborhood icon on the Windows desktop. The functions all rely on a "Net Resource" hash, which contains information about the shared resources. The keys for the hash are listed in Table 7-6.

Getting a list of Shared Resources   The main function is `GetSharedResources`, which populates an array with net resource hashes containing each of the shared items on the network. In the following code:

```
GetSharedResources(NETRESOURCES, TYPE)
```

the function places the information into the array pointed to by NETRE-SOURCES and selects only the resource type defined by TYPE (see Table 7-6). The function returns `True` if it completed successfully or `False` if it failed. See "Error Handling" at the end of the chapter for more information.

For example, the script below outputs a list of the shared resources:

```
use Win32::NetResource qw/:DEFAULT GetSharedResources/;

GetSharedResources(\@resources,RESOURCETYPE_ANY);

foreach $resource (@resources)
{
    if ($resource->{DisplayType} == RESOURCEDISPLAYTYPE_DOMAIN)
    {
        print "Domain: $resource->{RemoteName}\n";
    }
    elsif ($resource->{DisplayType} == RESOURCEDISPLAYTYPE_SERVER)
```

TABLE 7-6

Net resource info.

Key	Value
Scope	The scope of the shared resource, which can be one of the following:
	RESOURCE_CONNECTED—Resources currently connected.
	RESOURCE_GLOBALNET—Resources on the network.
	RESOURCE_REMEMBERED—Remembered (persistent) connections—for example, those set to automatically reconnect at logon.
Type	The type of resource to list; see Table 7-7 for a list of suitable constants.
DisplayType	The format of the returned resource information, which can be set using one of the constants listed in Table 7-8.
Usage	Defines the resource's usage, as follows:
	RESOURCEUSAGE_CONNECTABLE—It's a normal resource to which you can connect.
	RESOURCEUSAGE_CONTAINER—The resource is a container for other shared resources.
LocalName	The name of the local device the resource is connected to.
RemoteName	The network name/address of the resource.
Comment	The comment for the resource.
Provider	The name of the provider of the resource.

TABLE 7-7

Resource types.

Resource Type	Description
RESOURCETYPE_ANY	Any type of resource.
RESOURCETYPE_DISK	Shared disks/folders.
RESOURCETYPE_PRINT	Shared printers/spoolers.

TABLE 7-8

Resource display types.

Display Type	Description
RESOURCEDISPLAYTYPE_DOMAIN	The object should be displayed as a domain.
RESOURCEDISPLAYTYPE_GENERIC	The display type does not matter.
RESOURCEDISPLAYTYPE_SERVER	The object should be displayed as a server.
RESOURCEDISLPAYTYPE_SHARE	The object should be displayed as a share point.

```
{
    print "Server: $resource->{RemoteName}\n";
}
elsif ($resource->{DisplayType} == RESOURCEDISPLAYTYPE_SHARE)
{
    print "Shared ";
    print "Printer: "      //if ($resource->{Type} == RESOURCETYPE_PRINT);
    print "Disk:    " if ($resource->{Type} == RESOURCETYPE_DISK);
    print "$resource->{RemoteName} ";
    print "($resource->{Comment})" if ($resource->{Comment});
    print "\n";
}
}
```

On my network this outputs the following:

```
Domain: MCHOME
Server: \\INCONTINENT
Shared Disk:     \\INCONTINENT\Websites
Shared Disk:     \\INCONTINENT\NETLOGON (Logon server are )
Shared Printer: \\INCONTINENT\Deskjet (Deskjet 340)
Shared Printer: \\INCONTINENT\OfficeJet (OfficeJet 635)
Shared Disk:     \\INCONTINENT\SYSVOL (Logon server share
Shared Disk:     \\INCONTINENT\Incoming
Shared Printer: \\INCONTINENT\Laserwriter (Laserwriter)
Server: \\INFURIATE
Shared Disk:     \\INFURIATE\Perl
Server: \\INSENTIENT
Server: \\LINUX
```

Note that the shared resources include the domains and servers on the network—even if the servers do not share any resources.

Connecting to a Shared Resource   To add a new connection (to a shared disk), use the AddConnection function. This does the same as the "Map Network Drive" option in Windows Explorer. For example:

```
AddConnection(NETRESOURCE, PASSWORD, USERNAME, CONNECTION)
```

This creates a connection to the network resource specified by the NETRE-SOURCE hash. Note that this should be a reference to a net resource hash, not a flat hash variable. The connection uses the PASSWORD and USERNAME for authorization—use undef if the shares allow guest access. The value of CONNECTION should be either 1, for a connection that should be reactivated the next time the user logs on, or zero for a temporary mount.

To actually use the function, you must build a hash with the correct keys. The most important keys are RemoteName for the UNC name of the share and LocalName for the drive letter of the disk to which the share should be associated. The following script mounts all of the available shares:

```
use Win32;
use Win32::NetResource qw/:DEFAULT AddConnection GetSharedResources/;

$letter = substr(Win32::GetNextAvailDrive(),0,1);

GetSharedResources(\@resources,RESOURCETYPE_DISK);

foreach $resource (@resources)
{
    if (($resource->{Type} == RESOURCETYPE_DISK) &&
        ($resource->{Usage} == RESOURCEUSAGE_CONNECTABLE))
    {
        next if ($resource->{RemoteName} =~ /(SYSVOL|NetLogon)$/i);
        print "$letter -> $resource->{RemoteName}\n";
        $resource->{LocalName} = "$letter:";
        $letter++;
        unless (AddConnection($resource, 'PASSWD', 'USER', 1))
        {
            print Win32::FormatMessage(Win32::GetLastError());
        }
    }
}
```

This script outputs the following:

```
I-> \\INCONTINENT\Websites
J-> \\INCONTINENT\Incoming
K-> \\INFURIATE\Perl
L-> \\INFURIATE\temp
```

Disconnecting a Shared Resource   Once a connection is open, you can disconnect it with `CancelConnection` function. The following code:

```
CancelConnection(NAME, CONNECTION, FORCE)
```

cancels the connection with the local drive letter NAME. If FORCE is 1, then the connection is canceled even if any errors that require intervention occur. The CONNECTION argument should specify the status of the shared resource as it was configured when the original connection was made. For example:

```
CancelConnection('I:', 1, 1);
```

Translating Folders into UNCs   To translate the path of a local folder into the UNC by which the folder can be accessed, you can use the `GetUNCName` function:

```
GetUNCName(UNCNAME, LOCALPATH)
```

This places the UNC of `LOCALPATH` into `UNCNAME`. For example, to check the UNC for our shared disk above:

```
GetUNCName($unc,'I:\MCHOME');
print "$unc\n";
```

this might output the following:

```
\\INCONTINENT\Websites\MCHOME
```

Sharing Resources

You can also set resources to be shared using the remainder of the functions in the `Win32::NetResource` module. These functions rely on a second hash, the "Share Info" hash, which defines the information shared resources. The keys of the Share Info hash is shown in Table 7-9. Because these functions are directly related to share information you can use them to get information about any shared resource—not just disks and folders.

Permission information is only supplied on Windows 95/98 machines. Under Windows NT the permission system utilizes user-level security and will always return a value of zero. Don't confuse this with the value of zero returned under Windows 95 or 98.

TABLE 7-9

Elements of the Share Info hash.

Key	Description
netname	The name of the share (not the UNC).
type	The share type (see Table 7-7).
remark	The comment for the shared resource.
permissions	The share permissions—see Table 7-10.
maxusers	The maximum number of users able to connect to the shared resource, if -1, then there is no limit.
current-users	The current number of users accessing the shared resource.
path	The absolute path to the shared resource.
passwd	The password required to use the shared resource.

TABLE 7-10

*Share permission
values.*

Value	Description
0x00	No permissions.
0x01	Permission to read or execute data from the resource.
0x02	Permission to write data to the resource.
0x04	Permission to create data within the resource.
0x08	Permission to execute the resource.
0x10	Permission to delete the resource.
0x20	Permission to modify the resource attributes (date, time, etc. See Chapter 4).
0x40	Permission to modify the permissions of the resource.
0x7f	Permission to do anything with the resource.

For Windows 95/98 machines, the values in the permissions key are a bitmask composed of the values shown in Table 7-10. Note that you cannot set the permissions for any resource using the Win32::NetResource module regardless of the platform.

Getting Share Information To get the information for a share, use the NetShareGetInfo function, which populates a share hash with the information. The following code:

```
NetShareGetInfo(NETNAME, SHARE, SERVER)
```

inserts the information for the share called NETNAME on SERVER into the Share Info hash pointed to by SHARE. By using this in combination with the GetSharedResources function, you can get all of the information about the shares on the network:

```
use Win32::NetResource qw/:DEFAULT NetShareGetInfo
GetSharedResources/;

GetSharedResources(\@resources,RESOURCETYPE_DISK);

printf("%-12s %-20s %-20s %3s %4s\n",
        'Server',
        'Share',
        'Path',
        'Max',
        'Users');
```

```
foreach $resource (@resources)
{
    if (($resource->{Type} == RESOURCETYPE_DISK) &&
        ($resource->{Usage} == RESOURCEUSAGE_CONNECTABLE))
    {
        next if ($resource->{RemoteName} =~ /(SYSVOL|NetLogon)$/i);
        my ($server,$name)
            = ($resource->{RemoteName} =~ m/\\\\(.*)\\(.*)/);
        unless(NetShareGetInfo($name, $share, $server))
        {
            print Win32::FormatMessage(Win32::GetLastError());
            next;
        }
        printf("%-12s %-20s %-20s %3d %4d\n",
                $server,
                $name,
                $share->{path},
                $share->{maxusers},
                $share->{current-users});
    }
}
```

which outputs something like this:

```
Server        Share          Path                      Max
Users
INCONTINENT   Websites       D:\Shared\Websites        -1    0
INCONTINENT   Incoming       D:\Shared\Incoming        -1    0
INFURIATE     Perl           C:\Perl                    5    0
```

Setting Share Information　You can also update the information about an existing hash using the NetShareSetInfo function. For example:

```
NetShareSetInfo(NETNAME, SHARE, ERROR, SERVER)
```

sets the information for the shared resource NETNAME to the values configured in SHARE on SERVER. Any errors are placed into ERROR (see "Error Handling" at the end of the chapter for more information).

Creating New Shares　To add a new shared resource, use the NetShareAdd function:

```
NetShareAdd(SHARE, ERROR [, SERVERNAME])
```

This adds a share using the information in the Share Info hash pointed to by SHARE. Errors are placed into ERROR. If the optional SERVERNAME is supplied, then it's used as the name of a machine in the local domain. If an empty string is specified or undef, then the local machine is used.

For example, the following script will share the directories supplied on the command line:

```perl
use Win32;
use Win32::WinError;
use Win32::NetResource qw/:DEFAULT
                          GetError
                          WNetGetLastError
                          NetShareGetInfo
                          NetShareAdd/;

unless(@ARGV)
{
    print "Usage:\n$0 directory";
}

foreach $dir (@ARGV)
{
    unless (-d $dir)
    {
        print "Making $dir\n";
        mkdir($dir,0755) || die "Couldn't make directory $dir: $!";
    }
    my ($base) = ($dir =~ m/(?:\\|\/)(.*)/);
    %share = (
                'path' => $dir,
                'maxusers' => -1,
                'netname' => $base,
                'remark' => '',
                'passwd' => '',
                'permissions' => 0,
                );
    unless(NetShareAdd(\%share,$paramerror))
    {
        if(GetError($error))
        {
            my $errormsg;
            if ($error == ERROR_EXTENDED_ERROR)
            {
                WNetGetLastError($error,$text, $provider);
                $errormsg = "$text ($provider)";
            }
            else
            {
                $errormsg = Win32::FormatMessage($error);
            }
            die $errormsg;
        }
    }
}
```

Removing Shares   To delete a shared resource, use the `NetShareDel` function. The following code:

```perl
NetShareDel(NETNAME, SERVER)
```

removes the share named NETNAME from SERVER. Note that it's the *name* of the share, not the path. For example, to delete a share called 'Temp' you'd use the following:

```
NetShareDel('Temp');
```

Checking Shared Devices   You can also check if a device (disk) has been shared using the NetShareCheck function. For example:

```
NetShareCheck(DEVICE, TYPE [, SERVER])
```

checks if a share is active on the disk referred to by DEVICE; this should be the drive letter of the disk you want to check. Only the first character of the string supplied is actually checked. If the share is active, then TYPE will be populated with the type of share on the device. The SERVER argument is optional, but if specified, it checks the disk on the remote machine.

Error Handling

All the functions within the Win32::NetResource module return False if the function fails. To get further information on the failure, you need to use the GetError function, which places the error code for the last error into the scalar supplied as its only argument:

```
GetError(ERRORCODE)
```

If the value of ERRORCODE returned matches the ERROR_EXTENDED_ ERROR constant exported by the Win32::WinError function, then you will need to obtain the extended information using the WnetGetLast Error function:

```
WNetGetLastError(ERRORCODE, DESCRIPTION, NAME)
```

This places the error description and source into DESCRIPTION and NAME, respectively, according to the error code supplied in the first argument.

## CHAPTER 8

Systems Information and Administration

In this chapter we'll look at how you can manage the machines on your network from Perl. Systems management is really split into two parts: information and administration. The information portion concerns understanding and determining the important facts about your machine and its environment. Administration is the act of using that information in combination with a series of functions and commands to modify the current configuration.

Under Unix, there are a variety of ways of accessing different pieces of system information. A lot of configuration is placed into /etc, but individual application preferences are spread right over the disk. Determining whether the current machine has a particular piece of software installed is near impossible, as all the different platforms install tools into different directories and different structures. To further complicate matters, with the use of free software, the tools, utilities, and configuration could be installed anywhere.

Administration is equally difficult. Although it's safe to assume that the user information is in /etc/passwd, there are other details and restrictions on what information you can obtain through direct access. The functions that are made available for accessing these details are limited and platform-specific.

This is one of the areas in which Windows has an advantage. For all the criticisms of the operating system architecture, it does have a central location for the bulk of the configuration data for the entire machine. This includes everything from the OS setup, any installed extensions—right down to the settings of individual applications.

In addition, the Windows API includes functions and interfaces for accessing a lot of the internal information about both the OS and the user and group information. At a simplistic level it means that we can automate some of the most common operations, such as creating a user or modifying the permissions for a given resource. On a more complex level, we can use Perl to start and stop Windows NT services both on the local machine and remotely.

Windows is actually a client/server-oriented operating system that is completely network-aware. We've already seen many examples of the network-level interaction offered by Windows. When Windows machines are configured within a domain, you can access other machines and resources within that domain very easily (see Chapter 7). Furthermore, with a domain-managed network, we can also control domain users and groups across the network by talking remotely to the NT or Windows 2000 server and requesting changes.

In this chapter we will look first at how to get system information from the Windows Registry. Then we'll move on to accessing and adding entries to the Windows NT Event Log and how to extract information from the performance monitoring tools built into NT. The last section concentrates on administering a network using the Windows API and Perl. Although the bulk of this chapter is targeted at a Windows NT or Windows 2000 network, many of the principles shown here can be used on Windows 95/98 machines.

Error Handling

The most obvious method is to use the `Win32::GetLastError` and the `Win32::FormatMessage` functions, as described in Chapter 2. These two functions return the error number and the error string, respectively, when called. The normal use is to embed one function call into the other to get an error message suitable for passing to the `die` or `print` functions. For example:

```
Wn32::FormatMessage(Win32::GetLastError());
```

Some, but not all, Win32 modules also attempt to set the $\$^E$ extended OS error with the error information that would normally be returned by `Win32::GetLastError`, but you shouldn't rely on the $\$^E$ variable. It's also worth remembering that the $\$!$ variable is unlikely to give any information about an error relating to a Win32 library call. However, $\$!$ will continue to return errors relating to the built-in Perl, which uses C or POSIX calls.

Other modules within the library provide their own error methods and functions that return specific information about errors relating to the module or API in question. You can see a breakdown of the modules that offer this in Table 8-1.

Win32::WinError

Although the `Win32::FormatMessage` and other functions and methods are useful for printing a fixed error message, they are not very useful if you want to trap a specific error condition. The `Win32::WinError` module defines the constants that relate to specific errors so that you can make judgments based on the error response, instead of blindly failing and displaying an error message when an operation fails.

TABLE 8-1

Module-specific error reporting functions.

Module	Method/Function	Description
Win32::ODBC	Error()	Returns a text string in scalar context, or the error number, description, connection number, and SQL statement in a list context.
Win32::NetResource	GetError(ERROR)	Always returns 1, placing the error string into the scalar pointed to by ERROR.
Win32::OLE	LastError()	Returns the error number or string detailing the error that occurred.
Win32::Internet	Error()	Returns an error string describing the last error.

For example, the following code would get an extended error from the `Win32::NetResource` module, printing a suitable error message according to the type of error that occurred.:

```
use Win32::WinError;
use Win32::NetResource;
Win32::NetResource::NetShareGetInfo("multimedia",\%share,"\\atuin");

Win32::NetResource::GetError($error);

if ($error == ERROR_BAD_NETPATH)
{
    print "Error: Couldn't find the network path\n";
}
```

See Appendix D for a complete list of error constants exported by the `Win32::WinError` module.

Accessing the Registry

The Windows Registry is used to store all sorts of information in a structured format. Since the introduction of Windows 95, Microsoft has been promoting the use of the registry for storing information in place of the INI files used under Windows 3.x. The registry is huge, and because it is used both for system and application configuration, information can be difficult to navigate.

On the plus side, the use of a central registry means that there is a single resource that can be accessed when you want to determine configuration information for a machine. Instead of trying to find the INI file for an application, you can look in the registry for the information.

Within Perl there are three ways to access the registry. At the basic level you can use the `Win32API::Registry` module. This provides low-level access to the system routines that access and update registry entries. Using this is not recommended, since it relies on knowing the details of the registry. The module does provide other utility functions for controlling a machine, but these are also offered elsewhere in other modules.

The `Win32::Registry` module also provides a low-level interface to the Win32 Registry. Although it does a better job of hiding the underlying complexities, using it still feels slightly alien compared to the normal interfaces and systems offered within Perl for accessing complex data. We will be looking at the `Win32::Registry` module very briefly in this chapter.

The most convenient method for accessing the registry is to use the `Wsin32::TieRegistry` module. This exports a tied object (actually a hash) to the caller, which can then be used to access entries within the registry using the structure format. By accessing keys within the hash, you can extract data and update the information stored within the registry. We'll have a detailed look at the module in this chapter.

WARNING. *The Windows Registry is a complex informational source, and using it without knowledge of its layout and the dangers associated with making modifications is not advised.*

Win32::Registry

The `Win32::Registry` module provides an object and functional interface to the Win32 Registry. The objects exported by default from the module are shown in Table 8-2.

Each object within the module inherits the same set of methods. The `Open` method opens a registry key on the local machine, while the `Create` method creates a new registry key. Most usefully though, the `Connect` method opens a key on a remote machine.

The format of the `Open` method is as follows:

```
$object->Open(PATH, KEY);
```

TABLE 8-2

Registry objects exported by the Win32:: Registry module.

Registry Object	Description
$HKEY_LOCAL_MACHINE	Points to the root that contains configuration information about the computer. This includes extension mappings, application data, and device drivers.
$HKEY_CURRENT_USER	Points to the root of information about an individual user. This key is unavailable when accessing the registry remotely, since there is no concept of a "current" remote user.
$HKEY_CLASSES_ROOT	The root key for the OLE/COM-related objects and classes exported by the system (see Chapter 11). This is actually a link to the key located at HKEY_LOCAL_MACHINE\Software\Classes. This key is unavailable when you are accessing the registry remotely.
$HKEY_USERS	The root key for all uses. The HKEY_CURRENT_USER contains links to the user currently logged into the computer, which is actually a link to the user information stored in this key.
$HKEY_PERFORMANCE_DATA	The performance data for the machine. This is the key available on Windows NT machines. Use the HKEY_DYN_DATA root for Windows 95/98.
$HKEY_CURRENT_CONFIG	Points to the current configuration of the machine.
$HKEY_DYN_DAT	The Windows 95/98 performance data.

The PATH is the path to the registry key you want to access. Registry paths are like directory paths; individual branches of the registry tree are named and separated by a backslash. The resulting registry object is placed into the scalar pointed to by KEY.

For example, to create a new root key that points to the root of Microsoft software configuration:

```
$HKEY_LOCAL_MACHINE->Open('Software\Microsoft',$msroot);
```

NOTE.   *Registry keys are not case-sensitive, so "MICROSOFT" and "microsoft" are treated as identical.*

The Create method looks like this:

```
$object->Create(PATH, KEY);
```

For example, to create a new registry key for your own software root:

```
$HKEY_LOCAL_MACHINE->Create('Software\MyApplication',$approot);
```

The new object acts just like an object opened via the Open method. We'll look at how to access and update information shortly.

To delete a registry key, you use the DeleteKey method:

```
$object->DeleteKey(PATH);
```

where PATH is the path to the key that you want to delete. For example, to delete the key we just created:

```
$HKEY_LOCAL_MACHINE->DeleteKey('Software\MyApplication');
```

To open the registry on a remote machine, you can use the Connect method, which opens the registry remotely over the network. You don't have to worry about the communication with the remote machine—the Win32 API handles that for you. The format is as follows:

```
$object->Connect(MACHINE, ROOT);
```

MACHINE is the network path to the machine you want to access, and ROOT is a reference to the object that you want to use to store the new root registry. The actual root entry you open on the remote machine is taken from the $object root that you specify. For example, to open the user configuration information for a remote machine:

```
$HKEY_USERS->Connect("\\\Insentient", $userroot);
```

Once you have finished working with a registry key, you need to close the connection to the registry by using the Close method:

```
$object->Close();
```

Extracting Registry Data   To get a list of values within a registry key, you can use the GetValues method. This places the values for the current key into a hash:

```
$object->GetValues(VALUES);
```

where VALUES is referenced to a hash to store the information. The structure of the resulting hash is a list of keys relating to the registry object key; the corresponding value is an array that contains the name of the value, the data type of the values data, and the data itself.

To extract an individual piece of information from a registry key, you need to use the QueryValue method:

```
$object->QueryValue(PATH, VALUE);
```

This places the data from the registry key at PATH into the scalar pointed to by VALUE. Unfortunately, this method actually only returns the default data value for a registry key. Since the 32-bit versions of Windows, individual registry keys have been able to hold more than one piece of information. To get this information, you need to use the QueryValueEx function:

```
$object->QueryValueEx(PATH, DATATYPE, VALUE);
```

This gets the value of the key pointed to by PATH of the type DATATYPE into the variable pointed to by VALUE. Valid data types are shown in Table 8-3.

TABLE 8-3

Registry data types.

Data Type	Description
REG_SZ	A character string.
REG_EXPAND_SZ	A character string with embedded environmental variables that need to be expanded.
REG_MULTI_SZ	An array of null-terminated strings. The end of the list will be terminated by two null characters, one which terminates the string, and the second which terminates the list.
REG_BINARY	A binary string.
REG_DWORD	A 32-bit number.
REG_DWORD_LITTLE_ENDIAN	A 32-bit number in little endian format (you can use pack to extract it).
REG_DWORD_BIG_ENDIAN	A 32-bit number in big endian format.
REG_LINK	A symbolic link in the registry to another registry key.
REG_NONE	No defined value.
REG_RESOURCE_LIST	A device driver resource list.

For example, to extract the location of the ActivePerl debugger installed by the Perl Development Kit:

```
use Win32::Registry;

if ($HKEY_LOCAL_MACHINE->Open("Software\\ActiveState\\Perl
Debugger\\1.0\\General\\",$perlroot))
{
    $perlroot->QueryValueEx('Executable',REG_SZ,$path);
    print "$path\n";
}
```

To actually set a value, you use the SetValue method.

```
$object->SetValue(PATH, DATATYPE, VALUE);
```

NOTE.   *There is a* SetValueEx *method, but it actually does nothing different than the* SetValue *method.*

The only value for DATATYPE that is directly supported is the REG_SZ. There are no tools for converting between the Windows embedded types and the internal Perl types.

So to update the path to the Perl debugger, perhaps because we've moved it:

```
use Win32::Registry;

if ($HKEY_LOCAL_MACHINE->Open("Software\\ActiveState\\Perl
Debugger\\1.0\\General\\",$perlroot))
{
    $perlroot->SetValue('Executable',
                        REG_SZ,
                        'D:\PERL\DEBUGGER\PERLDB.EXE');
}
```

Win32::TieRegistry

The Win32::TieRegistry supports a combination object/tied hash interface to the registry information that is more flexible and more Perl-like in its usage than the functional/object-based solution offered by the Win32::Registry module. The method for using it is to import the Win32::TieRegistry module, which exports the $Registry object:

```
use Win32::TieRegistry(Delimiter => '/');
```

Registry Root	TieRegistry Root
HKEY_CLASSES_ROOT	Classes
HKEY__CURRENT_USER	CUser
HKEY_LOCAL_MACHINE	LMachine
HKEY_USERS	Users
HKEY_PERFORMANCE_DATA	PerfData
HKEY_CURRENT_CONFIG	CConfig
HKEY_DYN_DATA	DynData

The delimiter argument defines the character you want to use as a delimiter between registry keys when accessing registry elements. To access a registry entry:

```
$swroot = $Registry->{"LMachine/Software/"};
```

The root of the registry is split into seven sections, for which the TieRegistry module uses aliases, as shown in Table 8-4. See Table 8-2 for a description of the individual key roots.

The return value is a new object/hash reference that can be used to select further keys within a specific class. For example, to access the "Hewlett-Packard" key within the "Software" key:

```
$hpkeyroot = $swroot->{"Hewlett-Packard/"};
```

The trailing delimiter is required to indicate that you are accessing a root key and want an object returned, rather than the relevant key value, as in:

```
$installdir = $hpkeyroot->{"OfficeJet Series 600/Env/InstallRoot"};
```

If you want to obtain the data type for the specified value, then you must call the ArrayValues method. This switches the return type when accessing a given registry key to return the data and the data type:

```
$hpkeyroot->ArrayValues(1);
($installdir, $type)
    = $hpkeyroot->{"OfficeJet Series 600/Env/InstallRoot"};
```

The $type variable will now contain one of the registry types already seen in the Win32::Registry module above.

To update a value, you can simply assign the new value:

```
$hpkeyroot->{"OfficeJet Series 600/Env/InstallRoot"} = "E:\TEMP";
```

This assumes a data type of REG_SZ. If you want to assign a different data type, you can supply the data and type as an array reference:

```
$hpkeyroot->{"OfficeJet Series 600/Env/InstallRoot"}
                      = [ "E:\TEMP", "REG_MULTI_SZ" ];
```

Remember, though, if you want to assign a BINARY or DWORD value, you'll need to use pack to convert the value into a suitable format.

Other features work as you would expect for an object reference. You can extract all the keys and values for a class, using keys and values, and then use grep to extract the individual elements you're looking for. For example:

```
@swkeys = grep(/Microsoft/, keys (%{$swroot->{"/"}}));
```

Accessing the Windows NT Logs

Windows NT writes significant events—that is, errors, warnings, and informational detail—into an event log. These event logs can be viewed within Windows using the Event Viewer. From here you can export the information for later processing.

Alternatively, you can read entries directly from the NT event log system using this module:

```
use Win32::EventLog;
$object = new Win32::EventLog(EVENTLOG [, SERVER])
```

The new class method returns an event log object, opening the EVENTLOG on SERVER. The default event logs on an NT machine are System, Application, and Security; however, if you give a new name at this point, then a new server log will be created. If SERVER is not specified or blank then the log is opened on the local machine.

The main method is Read, which gets an individual record from the specified event log:

```
$eventlog = new Win32::EventLog('Application');
$eventlog->Read(FLAG, RECORD, EVENT);
```

Flag	Description
EVENTLOG_FORWARDS_READ	Reads the log in chronological order.
EVENTLOG_BACKWARDS_READ	Reads the log in reverse chronological order.
EVENTLOG_SEEK_READ	Reads from the record number specified in RECORD. This option must be used in conjunction with the EVENTLOG_FORWARDS_READ or EVENT-LOG_BACKWARDS_READ.
EVENTLOG_SEQUENTIAL_READ	Reads the next record after a previous Read function, retaining the position and directional information.

This reads a single record, populating the hash pointed to by EVENT. The FLAG should be a combination of the flags shown in Table 8-5. The RECORD is the record number to be retrieved. Records start at one (see the GetNumber and the GetOldest methods in this section).

Note that the EVENTLOG_FORWARDS_READ and EVENTLOG_BACK-WARDS_READ flags are mutually exclusive.

The keys of the hash that are returned by the Read method are listed in Table 8-6.

Event types—as returned in the EventType key, are given in Table 8-7.

To add an event entry to the log, use the Report method:

```
$eventlog->Report(EVENT)
```

This adds the event in the hash EVENT to the log. You'll need to have populated a suitable hash before supplying the information. Use the GetNumber method to populate the RecordNumber key with a suitable record number.

The GetNumber method places the next record number for an event into the scalar pointed to by NUMBER:

```
$eventlog->GetNumber(NUMBER)
```

The GetOldest method places the oldest record number in the log into the scalar pointed to by NUMBER:

```
$eventlog->GetOldest(NUMBER)
```

Once you have finished using the log, you should close it using the CloseEventLog function:

```
Win32::EventLog::CloseEventLog(HANDLE);
```

TABLE 8-6

Event log fields.

Key	Description
Category	An application-specific category number.
ClosingRecordNumber	The last record number in a multirecord entry.
Computer	The name of the computer from which the event was reported.
Data	The event data reported.
EventID	An application-specific ID number.
EventType	An integer relating to one of the constants shown in Table 8-7.
Length	The length of the application data.
Message	A short message string for the event.
RecordNumber	The record number within the event log.
Source	The name of the application or service that reported the entry.
Strings	Application-specific text strings.
TimeGenerated	The number of seconds since the epoch when the event was generated.
TimeWritten	The number of seconds since the epoch when the event was added to the log.
User	The user name of the application that reported the event, if applicable.

TABLE 8-7

Event log entry types.

Event Type	Description
EVENTLOG_ERROR_TYPE	The event was an error.
EVENTLOG_WARNING_TYPE	The event was a warning.
EVENTLOG_INFORMATION_TYPE	The event indicates a particular piece of information but is not a warning or error.
EVENTLOG_AUDIT_SUCCESS	The event was a successful audit. Events of this type are only recorded if the administrator has configured an object (file, directory, etc.) to be audited. The entry will include the information about the user who successfully accessed the object.
EVENTLOG_AUDIT_FAILURE	An attempt was made to access an object, but the attempt was unsuccessful.

where HANDLE is the handle for an open event log object that is stored in the handle property for the object. For example:

```
Win32::EventLog::CloseEventLog($object->{handle});
```

For example, to report the entire error event log entries for the System log:

```
use Win32::EventLog;

$log = new Win32::EventLog('System');

while($log-
>Read(EVENTLOG_SEQUENTIAL_READ|EVENTLOG_BACKWARDS_READ,0,\%record))
{
    if ($record{EventType} == EVENTLOG_ERROR_TYPE)
    {
        print(scalar(localtime($record{TimeGenerated})),
            ": $record{Source}: $record{Strings}\n");
    }
}
```

Monitoring Windows NT Performance

The Win32::PerfLib module provides access to the internal counters used to store performance and other monitoring data. This information is ordinarily available through the Windows NT Performance Monitor. If you've used the tool, you will know the wide range of different types of information that are recorded by the system into a series of logs. This module provides direct access to the data so that you can process it for yourself.

To actually open the performance logs for a machine, you need to create a new Win32::PerfLib object:

```
$perflib = new Win32::PerfLib([SERVER]);
```

This creates a new performance object, connecting to the optional SERVER if supplied. The data structures and contents are exceedingly complex and way beyond the scope of this book. However, we will look at the base structures that make up the system. Refer to the documentation for more information on these structures.

The core of the performance library are the counters used to store information. Each counter has a unique number and a name associated. Different versions of the Windows NT operating system may use different numerical sequences—indeed, they may even have different sets of counters. To get a list of counter names, use the `GetCounterNames` function to place the counter numbers (keys) and names (values) into a hash:

```
Win32::PerfLib::GetCounterNames(SERVER, HASH)
```

Note that you do not have to have opened a performance object to get at this information. To get a more extensive description of the counters available you can use the `GetCounterHelp` function. This places the counter numbers into the keys and their descriptions into the values. For example:

```
Win32::PerfLib::GetCounterHelp(SERVER, HASH)
```

To actually get the counter information for a specific counter, use the `GetObjectList` method:

```
$perflib->GetObjectList(COUNTER,HASH)
```

This places the counter information for the counter number in COUNTER and places it into the hash pointed to by HASH. See the documentation for details on the structure, which is a heavily nested hash of hashes and arrays, which contain the performance information for a period of time.

The following code:

```
$perflib->Close($hashref)
```

closes the connection to the performance library. Use the following:

```
Win32::PerfLib::GetCounterType(COUNTERTYPE)
```

to convert the counter identified by the number COUNTERTYPE to a readable string.

Controlling Windows NT Services

Windows NT services are similar in principle to Unix daemons. They provide a particular service or functionality and can be started and stopped at will. They can also be configured to start up automatically or manually, and it's possible that one service can specifically rely on another service for its operation. For example, the file sharing service provides file sharing abilities to other Windows computers, but it will not run unless the Server service, which provides network registration and networking protocol services, is also running.

You can control Windows NT services directly within Perl using the `Win32::Service` module. This provides a functional interface to the Service Manager on a Windows NT machine, normally available through the control panels. However, because of NT's ability to communicate with other machines on the network, we can also monitor and control the services for other machines on the network—provided, of course, that the current user has suitable privileges (administrator access) within the domain to which the machine belongs.

The `Win32::Service` module supports six functions, outlined below. You can use the `GetLastError` function to determine the level of error that occurred. Functions return `False` on error. The module does not export these functions into the calling package's name space; you must use the fully qualified names in your scripts.

Services are identified by their names, rather than an arbitrary ID. You can get a list of current services using the `GetServices` function:

```
GetServices(HOST, SERVICES)
```

The function gets the list of configured services from `HOST` and places the list into the hash referred to by `SERVICES`. If `HOST` is `undef` or an empty string, then the current host is used. The keys of the hash returned contain the full service name, which is used to identify the service, and the values of the shortened service name.

To start and stop a service, you use its service name with the `StartService` and `StopService` functions:

```
StartService(HOST, SERVICE)
StopService(HOST, SERVICE)
```

Again, if `HOST` is blank or empty, then the current host is used. The `SERVICE` should be the service name, as returned in the keys of the `GetServices` function.

To pause and then resume a service, use the `PauseService` and `ResumeService` function:

```
PauseService(HOST, SERVICE)
ResumeService(HOST, SERVICE)
```

TABLE 8-8

*Status information
for a running
service.*

Key	Description
ServiceType	The type of service. You can identify the service type using one of the predefined constants, exported by the module. SERVICE_WIN32_OWN_PROCESS SERVICE_WIN32_SHARE_PROCESS SERVICE_KERNEL_DRIVER SERVICE_FILE_SYSTEM_DRIVER
CurrentState	The status of the service. This is a combination of the "Status" and "Startup" information provided in the Services control panel. See Table 8-9 for more details.
ControlsAccepted	The list of control codes accepted by the command.
Win32ExitCode	The generic error code returned when the service starts or stops.
ServiceSpecificExitCode	A service-specific error code.
CheckPoint	A simple increment that increases as the service runs; usually zero.
WaitHint	An estimate, in milliseconds, of the time left before the current state completes. A value of zero indicates that there is no pending change of state.

To get the current status of a service you use the GetStatus function:

```
GetStatus(HOST, SERVICE, STATUS)
```

This obtains the status of SERVICE on HOST, placing the information into the hash pointed to by STATUS. The returned hash contains a number of keys, as shown in Table 8-8.

The current status of a service can be verified against the constants shown in Table 8-9.

The following script uses the Win32::Service module to selectively start and stop services on a local or remote machine, presuming you have suitable privileges to do so.

```
#!perl -w
use Win32::Service;
use Getopt::Long;

my ($upserv,$downserv,$server,%services);

GetOptions("u=s" => \$upserv,
           "d=s" => \$downserv
```

TABLE 8-9

Current service
status constants.

Constant	Description
SERVICE_START_PENDING	The service is scheduled to start, but is waiting in the queue to be started.
SERVICE_STOP_PENDING	The service is scheduled to stop, but it is in the queue waiting to actually be stopped.
SERVICE_RUNNING	The service is currently active.
SERVICE_CONTINUE_RUNNING	The service is in the process of resuming since being paused.
SERVICE_PAUSE_PENDING	The service is waiting to be paused.
SERVICE_PAUSED	The service is currently paused.

```perl
               );
if (@ARGV)
{
    $server = $ARGV[0];
}
else
{
    $server = Win32::NodeName();
}
Win32::Service::GetServices($server,\%services);

print "Server $server\n";

if ($upserv)
{
    startservices(split(/,/,$upserv));
}
elsif ($downserv)
{
    stopservices(split(/,/,$downserv));
}
else
{
    listservices();
}

sub startservices
{
    my (@servicelist) = @_;
    for my $service (@servicelist)
    {
        if (defined($services{$service}))
        {
            print "Starting the $service service...";
            Win32::Service::StartService($server,$service);
            opstatus("start $service");
            sleep 5;
            print "$service: ",chkstatus($service);
        }
```

```perl
            else
            {
                print "ERROR: Service $service does not exist\n";
            }
        }
    }
}

sub stopservices
{
    my (@servicelist) = @_;
    for my $service (@servicelist)
    {
        if (defined($services{$service}))
        {
            print "Stopping the $service service...";
            Win32::Service::StopService($server,$service);
            opstatus("stop $service");
            sleep 5;
            print "$service: ",chkstatus($service);
        }
        else
        {
            print "ERROR: Service $service does not exist\n";
        }
    }
}

sub opstatus
{
    my ($opname) = @_;
    my $error=Win32::GetLastError();
    if ($error ne 0)
    {
        print("\n$opname: ", Win32::FormatMessage($error),"\n");
    }
}
sub chkstatus
{
    my ($service) = @_;
    my %status;
    Win32::Service::GetStatus($server,$service,\%status);
    if (defined($status{CurrentState})
        and $status{CurrentState} eq 4)
    {
        return "Started";
    }
    else
    {
        return "Stopped";
    }
}

sub listservices
{
    for my $service (sort keys %services)
    {
        print "$service: ",chkstatus($service),"\n";
    }
}
```

The script is relatively straightforward; you check or ascertain the node name that you are managing and then start or stop the specified service using the `Win32::Service::StartService` and `Win32::Service::StopService` functions. Note that you check the result of each command using the same `opstatus` function as before, which resolves the error reported by the function if there was a problem.

Also note that you wait between stopping or starting the service and then reporting the new status, in order to give the service time to start or stop accordingly. If you don't supply any arguments to the script, then it just reports the status of all the currently configured services for the machine, as in:

```
Alerter: Started
ClipBook Server: Stopped
Computer Browser: Stopped
DHCP Client: Stopped
Directory Replicator: Stopped
EventLog: Started
MGACtrl: Started
McAfee Alert Manager: Started
McAfee VirusScan Task Manager: Started
Messenger: Started
NT LM Security Support Provider: Started
Net Logon: Stopped
Network DDE: Stopped
Network DDE DSDM: Stopped
Norton SpeedDisk: Started
Norton Unerase Protection: Started
Plug and Play: Stopped
Protected Storage: Started
Remote Access Autodial Manager: Stopped
Remote Access Connection Manager: Stopped
Remote Access Server: Stopped
Remote Procedure Call (RPC) Locator: Stopped
Remote Procedure Call (RPC) Service: Stopped
Retrospect Remote Client: Started
Schedule: Stopped
Server: Stopped
Spooler: Started
TCP/IP NetBIOS Helper: Started
Telephony Service: Stopped
UPS: Stopped
Workstation: Started
```

If you try to start a service, you get this result:

```
C:\> ntserv.pl -u
Server INSENTIENT
Starting the Server service...

Server: Starter
```

System Administration

The Windows systems administration toolkits provide a programmable interface to create and manage machines. These include the configuration of users and groups and determining system and network information such as active disk drives and domain controllers. There are a number of different modules with different levels of support to the core services. A low-level interface accompanies the `Win32API::Net` module, which connects directly to the API exported by Windows for user and group administration.

The `Win32::NetAdmin` module is geared toward supplying network information, including domain servers and basic user information. The final module we'll look at is the `Win32::AdminMisc` module, written by Dave Roth. This is not supplied as standard with the ActivePerl distribution, but it probably should be, since it provides a number of functions not included in the standard library. The module provides the user with network interfaces offered by `Win32API::Net` and `Win32::NetAdmin`, as well as additional functions for determining network layout and system information, including a list of the disks and their storage space.

Like other parts of the Windows system, user and group information is shared across the network through a series of domain servers. These are not Internet domains (although see the "Domains and Windows 2000" sidebar), but NT domains. When a user logs in to their client machine, they are authorized via a domain server, and it's possible for a user to have different logins for different domains on a network.

Domains and Windows 2000

Under Windows NT, domains and the user information that they held were proprietary, with the only real interface being the Windows API. With Windows 2000, Microsoft introduced a new domain manager called the Active Directory, which has two effects. First of all, they changed the storage method for the database to be an LDAP database. LDAP, or Lightweight Directory Access Protocol, is a standard directory service that structures information in a hierarchical format and can store a variety of information from authorization data through to contact details and resources.

This means that the Windows 2000 domain not only holds information about users and groups, it also contains their e-mail addresses, details on printers and other network resources, and most importantly, details about their machine and configuration information.

The second change is also significant. Under Windows NT, a domain controller could hold information about a number of Internet domains and provide services through those domains to the LAN and Internet. However, there was never any correlation between a Windows NT domain and the Internet domains that it managed. With Windows 2000, the Internet domain is now the reference point—if you have a registered Internet domain, then you can use it as your Windows 2000 domain.

It's beyond the scope of this book to go through the details, but it offers far more flexibility than other systems and is better integrated with the OS, while actually using standard tools and technologies. I haven't yet investigated the possibility of communicating directly with a Windows 2000 LDAP database, although tools do exist on CPAN for accessing LDAP information from Perl.

It's best to think of Windows NT domains as logical collections of computers, with a central resource for authorizing users and user access. By sharing authorization across the domain, you can control the access to specific resources right across the network, across a number of servers using the same authority database. This is similar in principle, but frankly better implemented, than the NIS/NIS+ systems supported under Unix.

Under Windows NT, the domains are managed by a single primary domain controller (PDC)—this is the senior database host on which all information is stored. Other servers can be backup domain controllers (BDC). These have the ability to authorize a connection in the event that the PDC is unavailable. However, a BDC's database is a replica of the PDC. You can make changes (such as the password) to a BDC database, but these are communicated back to the PDC before being propagated to other BDCs within the network.

Under Windows 2000, the interface within Perl is identical, but the overall operation is slightly different. Now there is no "primary" domain controller. All servers that provide authorization information are considered peers of each other—they exchange information with each other directly. Furthermore, as described in the sidebar, Windows 2000 domains provide a close link between Windows NT domains and Internet domains.

NOTE. *All of the modules in this section provide an interface for managing Windows NT domains and will not work on Windows 95/98.*

Win32API::Net

The Win32API::Net module provides a complete interface to the underlying C++ functions for managing accounts with Windows NT. The module supports four main groups of functions for managing users, net groups, local groups, and finally, domain controller information.

It's worth noting that Windows NT domain accounts include not only the normal login accounts used by users but also accounts responsible for managing the domain, accounts that provide a conduit between two or more domains, and accounts for workstations and servers within the domain.

By default, the module does not export any names to the callers' namespace, so you will need to use fully qualified function names. Alternatively, during import you can specify the functions that you want to have exported using tags, as detailed in the following:

```
use Win32API::Net qw/:User/;       # imports User*() functions
use Win32API::Net qw/:Get/;        # imports Get*() functions
use Win32API::Net qw/:Group/;      # imports Group*() functions
use Win32API::Net qw/:LocalGroup/; # imports LocalGroup*() functions
```

Domain Functions In order to obtain user and group information, you must first know the domain controller for the domain that you want to manage. The Win32API::Net module provides a single function, GetDCName, which obtains this for:

```
Win32API::Net::GetDCName(MACHINE, DOMAIN, SERVER)
```

The function places the name of the domain controller into the scalar pointed to by SERVER for the MACHINE within the DOMAIN. For example:

```
use Win32API::Net;

unless(Win32API::Net::GetDCName('INCONTINENT','MCHOME',$server))
{
```

```
    die Win32::FormatMessage(Win32::GetLastError());
}

print "Domain Server: $server\n";
```

If you use empty strings or undef for the MACHINE and DOMAIN arguments, then the function returns the information for the current
machine. Alternatively, you can use the Win32::NodeName and
Win32::DomainName functions to get the information.

User Functions   The main function is the UserGetInfo function.
This returns the information about an individual user on a server. For
example:

```
UserGetInfo(SERVER, USER, LEVEL, HASH)
```

places the information for USER on SERVER into HASH, providing the list
of fields specified by LEVEL. For example:

```
use Win32API::Net;

Win32API::Net::GetDCName(Win32::NodeName,Win32::DomainName,$server);

Win32API::Net::UserGetInfo($server, Win32::LoginName(), 10, \%user);

print "Hello $user{fullName}\n";
```

The level of information returned by this and many of the functions is
controlled by a numerical "user level." In the example above, we've used
a level of 10, which returns the user name and comment information. If
you are only interested in particular pieces of user information, then you
can use the user level to define the number of keys returned. For example, you can use a level of zero to verify a user name, since the name you
supply as the second argument to the function should be the same as
that returned in the name key of the hash.

This is one of the main areas where Unix and Windows differ for user
information. In particular, the amount of information stored against a
single user by Windows is much more extensive and more readily available than under Unix. It's also available through a hash, rather than as
part of an array. The hash that is returned can also be used (or indeed
created) in order to update or create new users. See the UserSetInfo
function below for more information.

The list of levels supported by the module is shown in Table 8-10. The
Fields column lists the actual key name returned in the user hash. See
Table 8-11 for more information on what information each key means.

TABLE 8-10

User information
levels supported.

Level	Fields
0	name
1	comment, flags, homeDir, name, password, passwordAge, priv, scriptPath
2	acctExpires, authFlags, badPwCount, codePage, comment, countryCode, flags, fullName, homeDir, lastLogoff, lastLogon, logonHours, logonServer, maxStorage, name, numLogons, parms, password, passwordAge, priv, scriptPath, unitsPerWeek, usrComment, workstations
3	acctExpires, authFlags, badPwCount, codePage, comment, countryCode, flags, fullName, homeDir, homeDirDrive, lastLogoff, lastLogon, logonHours, logonServer, maxStorage, name, numLogons, parms, password, passwordAge, passwordExpired, primaryGroupId, priv, profile, scriptPath, unitsPerWeek, userId, usrComment, workstations
10	comment, fullName, name, usrComment
11	authFlags, badPwCount, codePage, comment, countryCode, fullName, homeDir, lastLogoff, lastLogon, logonHours, logonServer, maxStorage, name, numLogons, parms, passwordAge, priv, unitsPerWeek, usrComment, workstations
20	comment, flags, fullName, name, userId
21	Not supported
22	Not supported
1003	password
1005	priv
1006	homeDir
1007	comment
1008	flags
1009	scriptPath
1010	authFlags
1011	fullName
1012	usrComment
1013	parms
1014	workstations
1017	acctExpires
1018	maxStorage
1020	LogonHours, unitsPerWeek
1023	logonServer
1024	countryCode
1025	codePage
1051	primaryGroupId
1052	profile
1053	homeDirDrive

TABLE 8-11

User information fields.

Hash Key	Description
acctExpires	The number of seconds since the epoch when the account expires. A -1 indicates that the account never expires.
authFlags	A list of authorization flags that correspond to the basic level of authority that the user has. This level of authority is governed by the groups to which the user is a member. The module exports three functions that can be used to check against this value. The AF_OP_PRINT() constant indicates the user is a member of the printer operator group, AF_OP_SERVER() is a server operator, and AF_OP_ACCOUNTS() is an account operator.
badPwCount	The number of times that a user login has failed due to an incorrect password.
codePage	The code page (keyboard/character layout) that the user uses.
comment	The user comment.
countryCode	The country code that user uses.
flags	The flags for this user—these specify the password preferences and user privileges. See Table 8-12 for a list of valid values, which should be logically OR'd together.
fullName	The user's full name.
homeDir	The user's home directory, either specified as a simple directory (i.e., C:\User), or as a UNC to a server directory for the user. Can be an empty string.
homeDirDrive	The drive that the user's home directory should be mapped to.
lastLogoff	The time the user last logged off, supplied as the number of seconds since the epoch.
lastLogon	The time the user last logged on, supplied as the number of seconds since the epoch.
logonHours	The times at which the user can log on. This is an integer array of 21 elements, where each element accounts for 8 hours. Therefore, 3 elements refer to a single day. Each bit within each element refers to each individual hour that the user can log on. If unset (0), then the user is unable to log on for that hour. If the entire array is undefined, then there are no restrictions.
logonServer	The server to which the user will log on. This will always be '*' under Windows NT.
maxStorage	The maximum storage quota for the user.
name	The user name (login) for the user.
numLogons	The number of times the user has successfully logged in.
parms	A freeform list of parameters. Currently unused.

Hash Key	Description
password	The user's password. The value will be blank when getting user information.
passwordAge	The age of the current password, or more practically, the time since the password was last updated.
passwordExpired	Indicates whether the password has expired or not. When getting information, a 1 indicates that the password has expired. When setting information, supplying a value of 1 will immediately expire the password.
primaryGroupId	The ID of the primary group to which the user belongs.
priv	Use privilege flags. See Table 8-13 for information.
profile	The path to the user's profile information. Can either be a local directory path or a UNC.
scriptPath	The relative path to the script to be executed when the user logs on.
unitsPerWeek	Specifies the granularity of the logonHours element.
userId	The internal user ID used by the OS. This is automatically generated and cannot be modified.
usrComment	The User comment.
workstations	A comma-separated list of the workstations that this user is allowed to log on to. Note that the operating system only supports up to eight named workstations.

The user flags—stored in the flags key of the hash—determine information about the user that may not be immediately obvious elsewhere. For example, the fact that the password should not expire can be determined using the UF_DONT_EXPIRE_PASSWD flag, but the information is also available through the passwordExpired key of the hash. Also remember that the same hash is used for creating new users, and some of the flags are required on some platforms. The full list of flags, which are actually defined as functions, are given in Table 8-12.

You can determine the privileges for a user by examining the groups that they belong to. For quick authorization, it's probably easier to use the contents of the priv key and use the constants returned by the functions in Table 8-13.

To create a new account, or update an existing one, you will need to edit or create a hash matching the keys for the required level. Then you

TABLE 8-12

User account flags.

Flag	Description
UF_ACCOUNTDISABLE()	The account has been disabled.
UF_DONT_EXPIRE_PASSWD()	The password on this account should never expire.
HOMEDIR_REQUIRED()	A home directory should be specified for this account.
UF_INTERDOMAIN_TRUST_ACCOUNT()	The account is an interdomain trust account; these provide connectivity between two accounts to allow logins to be authorized across both domains.
UF_LOCKOUT()	The account has been locked out due to a security failure.
UF_NORMAL_ACCOUNT()	The account is a normal user account.
UF_PASSWD_CANT_CHANGE()	The password for this account cannot be changed except by an administrator.
UF_PASSWD_NOTREQD()	A password is not required for this account.
UF_SCRIPT()	The user account has a script associated with it. This must be set when creating the account on Windows NT.
UF_SERVER_TRUST_ACCOUNT()	The account represents a Windows NT BDC for the domain.
UF_TEMP_DUPLICATE_ACCOUNT()	The account is temporary and is allowed to access resources only within this domain, but not to trusted domains related to the current domain.
UF_WORKSTATION_TRUST_ACCOUNT()	The account is for a workstation or server within the domain.

TABLE 8-13

User privilege flags.

User Privilege	Description
USER_PRIV_ADMIN()	The account has administrative abilities.
USER_PRIV_GUEST()	The account is a guest account.
USER_PRIV_USER()	The account is a normal user account.

use the `Win32API::Net::UserSetInfo` function to save the information from the supplied hash into the user database. For example:

```
Win32API::Net::UserSetInfo(SERVER, USER, LEVEL, HASH, ERROR)
```

sets the information for `USER` on `SERVER`, using the information in the `HASH`. The `LEVEL` sets the fields that will be updated.

Errors when updating are placed into the scalar pointed to by the `ERROR` argument. For example, to force a user to enter a new password next time they connect:

```
use Win32API::Net;

unless (@ARGV)
{
    die "Usage:\n$0 user [user...]\n";
}

$node = Win32::NodeName();

$domain = Win32::DomainName();

foreach $user (@ARGV)
{
    Win32API::Net::GetDCName($node,$domain,$server);
    unless(Win32API::Net::UserGetInfo($server, $user, 2, \%user))
    {
        print STDERR "Error: $user not found on $server\n";
        next;
    }
    print "Resetting password for $user\n";
    $user{passwordExpired} = 1;

    unless(Win32API::Net::UserSetInfo($server, $user,
                                2, \%user, $error))
    {
        print STDERR "Error: Couldn't reset password\n";
    }
}
```

If you are updating specific fields, then you can use the scalar pointed to by `ERROR` as an indication of why the operation failed. You need to use the constants in Table 8-14. Note that the value of `ERROR` will only match the first error in the hash that was identified.

The remainder of the functions in the module provide quicker ways of updating specific information, adding new users or deleting them. For example:

```
UserAdd(SERVER, LEVEL, HASH, ERROR)
```

adds a new user account to `SERVER`, to the `LEVEL`, using the information

TABLE 8-14

Error constants for
the user functions.

Constant	Description
USER_ACCT_EXPIRES_PARMNUM	The expiration value for the user's account is incorrectly specified or absent.
USER_AUTH_FLAGS_PARMNUM	The authorization flags for the user are incorrect/invalid or absent.
USER_BAD_PW_COUNT_PARMNUM	The user's password count was badly specified or absent.
USER_CODE_PAGE_PARMNUM	The user's code page value was incorrectly specified or absent.
USER_COMMENT_PARMNUM	The user's comment was invalid.
USER_COUNTRY_CODE_PARMNUM	The user's country code was invalid.
USER_FLAGS_PARMNUM	The user's flags were invalid.
USER_FULL_NAME_PARMNUM	The user's full name was invalid.
USER_HOME_DIR_DRIVE_PARMNUM	The user's home directory drive was incorrectly specified or absent.
USER_HOME_DIR_PARMNUM	The home directory was incorrectly specified or absent.
USER_LAST_LOGOFF_PARMNUM	The last logoff value was incorrectly specified or absent.
USER_LAST_LOGON_PARMNUM	The last logon value was incorrectly specified or absent.
USER_LOGON_HOURS_PARMNUM	The logon hours field was incorrectly specified or absent.
USER_LOGON_SERVER_PARMNUM	The logon server for the user was incorrectly specified or absent.
USER_MAX_STORAGE_PARMNUM	The maximum storage value for the user was incorrectly specified or absent.
USER_NAME_PARMNUM	The user's name was incorrectly specified or absent.
USER_NUM_LOGONS_PARMNUM	The number of logons field was incorrectly specified or absent.
USER_PARMS_PARMNUM	The user parameters were incorrectly specified or absent.
USER_PASSWORD_AGE_PARMNUM	The password age was incorrectly specified or absent.
USER_PASSWORD_PARMNUM	The user's password was incorrectly specified or absent.
USER_PRIMARY_GROUP_PARMNUM	The user's primary group was incorrectly specified or absent.

Constant	Description
USER_PRIV_PARMNUM	The user's privileges were incorrectly specified or absent.
USER_PROFILE_PARMNUM	The user's profile was incorrectly specified or absent.
USER_SCRIPT_PATH_PARMNUM	The user's script path was incorrectly specified or absent.
USER_UNITS_PER_WEEK_PARMNUM	The units per week was incorrectly specified or absent.
USER_USR_COMMENT_PARMNUM	The user's comment field was incorrectly specified or absent.
USER_WORKSTATIONS_PARMNUM	The user's workstations field was incorrectly specified or absent.

supplied in HASH. Any errors in the hash are reported into the ERROR scalar. The following code:

```
UserChangePassword(SERVER, USER, OLD, NEW)
```

changes the password for USER on SERVER from OLD to NEW.
    The following:

```
UserDel(SERVER, USER)
```

deletes USER from SERVER.
    This code:

```
UserEnum(SERVER, ARRAY [, FILTER])
```

places the list of users on SERVER into the array pointed to by ARRAY. If the FILTER argument is specified, then the function only places those users that match the filter into the array. Multiple filters can be specified if you OR them together.
    Valid values for the FILTER are shown in Table 8-15:
    The following code:

```
UserGetGroups(SERVER, USER, ARRAY)
```

gets the list of valid groups for USER on SERVER, placing it into the array pointed to by ARRAY. This code:

```
UserGetLocalGroups(SERVER, USER, ARRAY [, FLAGS])
```

TABLE 8-15

Filters that can be used to select a list of users.

Filter Constant	Description
FILTER_TEMP_DUPLICATE_ACCOUNT()	Returns the list of temporary accounts that are duplicates of real accounts.
FILTER_NORMAL_ACCOUNT()	Returns the list of normal user accounts.
FILTER_INTERDOMAIN_TRUST_ACCOUNT()	Returns the list of accounts trusted for interdomain transfer.
FILTER_WORKSTATION_TRUST_ACCOUNT()	Returns the list of workstation accounts.
FILTER_SERVER_TRUST_ACCOUNT()	Returns the list of server accounts.

gets the list of local groups of which USER on SERVER is a member. The list is placed in ARRAY. FLAGS can use the optional LG_INCLUDE_DIRECT constant, which includes the list of groups of which the user is indirectly a member.

This code:

```
UserSetGroups(SERVER, USER, ARRAY)
```

sets the list of groups for USER on SERVER to that specified by the reference ARRAY.

Group Functions Group information is more limited than under Unix. Under Windows NT, users are members of groups; if you want to adjust group membership, then you need to use the user functions. There are, in fact, two levels of group: the global group and the local group.

The *global group* can contain only users and is accessible to anybody who has access to the domain. Global groups are often used where a networkwide group is required. For example, you might create a global Administrators group and then set each machine within the network to be controllable by any user in the Administrators group.

A *local group* is specific to a machine and can be made up of users and global groups. For example, we might create a local Administrators group that includes not only the global Administrators group but also a number of users who only have the ability to administer the local machine. The users in the local domain don't have the power to manage all the machines in the network, unless, of course, they are also members of the global Administrators group.

TABLE 8-16

Group levels.

Level	Fields
0	name
1	name, comment
2	name, comment, groupId, attributes
1002	comment
1005	attributes

Like the user functions, the group functions use a set of specific levels, as detailed in Table 8-16.

The fields of a group hash are the groups name, as it should be referred to and displayed, the groupId, which is the internal identifier for the group, the group comment, and the attributes, which are currently unused. The basic operation of these functions is identical to the user functions, so a summary of the functions is shown below.

```
GroupAdd(SERVER, LEVEL, HASH, ERROR)
```

adds the group, specified by the HASH using the fields up to the LEVEL, on the SERVER. Errors are placed into ERROR.

```
GroupAddUser(SERVER, GROUP, USER)
```

adds USER to GROUP on SERVER.

```
GroupDel(SERVER, GROUP)
```

deletes GROUP from SERVER.

```
GroupDelUser(SERVER, GROUP, USER)
```

deletes USER from GROUP on SERVER.

```
GroupEnum(SERVER, ARRAY)
```

places a list of groups into the array pointed to by ARRAY from SERVER.

```
GroupGetUsers(SERVER, GROUP, ARRAY)
```

places the list of users for GROUP on SERVER into the array pointed to by ARRAY.

```
GroupSetInfo(SERVER, GROUP, LEVEL, HASH, ERROR)
```

sets the fields of GROUP on SERVER from HASH. The list of specified fields is defined by LEVEL, and any errors are placed into ERROR.

```
GroupSetUsers(SERVER, GROUP, ARRAY)
```

sets the membership of GROUP on SERVER, using the list of users in ARRAY.

The errors returned when accessing and updating the groups can be matched against some predefined constants. GROUP_ATTRIBUTES_ PARMNUM indicates that the attributes field was absent. GROUP_COM- MENT_PARMNUM indicates that the comment field was absent or incor- rectly specified. GROUP_NAME_PARMNUM indicates that the name field was absent.

Local Group Functions   This series of functions supports access and updating of the local groups. It uses the same group fields and other information supported by the group functions.

```
LocalGroupAdd(SERVER, LEVEL, HASH, ERROR)
```

adds the group specified in HASH, using the fields LEVEL on SERVER. Errors are placed into ERROR.

```
LocalGroupAddMembers(SERVER, GROUP, ARRAY)
```

adds the users in ARRAY to GROUP on SERVER.

```
LocalGroupDel(SERVER, GROUP)
```

deletes the local GROUP on SERVER.

```
LocalGroupDelMembers(SERVER, GROUP, ARRAY)
```

deletes the list of users in ARRAY from GROUP on SERVER.

```
LocalGroupEnum(SERVER, ARRAY)
```

places the list of GROUPs on SERVER into ARRAY.

```
LocalGroupGetInfo(SERVER, GROUP, LEVEL, HASH)
```

gets the information for GROUP to LEVEL on SERVER, placing it into HASH.

```
LocalGroupGetMembers(SERVER, GROUP, ARRAY)
```

puts the list of members of GROUP on SERVER into ARRAY.

```
LocalGroupSetInfo(server, level, hash, error)
```

sets the information for the group defined in HASH, using the fields specified by LEVEL on SERVER. Errors are placed into ERROR.

Win32::NetAdmin

This module provides control over the users and groups on a system. The functions are similar to those supported by both the Win32API::Net and Win32::AdminMisc modules. On the whole, the functions supplied by Win32::NetAdmin are geared to solving specific problems, such as passwords or creating users. The amount to which you have access is significantly limited compared to that offered by the Win32API::Net module.

Domain Functions The Win32::NetAdmin module expands on the domain functions offered by Win32API::Net module by also allowing us to select specific servers within a network, or obtain a list of servers of a particular type. For example:

```
GetDomainController(MACHINE, DOMAIN, SERVER)
```

This is synonymous with the Win32API::Net::GetDCName function. It returns the name of the PDC for the specified MACHINE in DOMAIN, placing the name into SERVER.

The following code:

```
GetAnyDomainController(MACHINE, DOMAIN, SERVER)
```

returns the name of any domain controller (PDC or BDC) for the specified MACHINE in DOMAIN, placing the name into SERVER.

```
GetServers(SERVER, DOMAIN, FLAGS, SERVERS)
```

places a list of server names into the array or hash pointed to by SERVERS for the specified DOMAIN. If you use a hash, then the values contain the comment field for each server.

To select a specific list of servers, you can supply a value to the FLAGS argument. A value of undef will select all servers. Valid constants for use with the function are shown in Table 8-17, multiple values can be logically OR'd together.

TABLE 8-17

Valid constants for
server information.

Constant	Description
SV_TYPE_AFP	Servers supporting the AppleShare AFP protocol. Note that this will only list NT servers supporting AFP, along with AppleShare IP 6.x servers that have successfully registered with an NT server.
SV_TYPE_ALL	All server types.
SV_TYPE_BACKUP_BROWSER	Servers providing a backup browsing service (as used by the desktop Network Browser).
SV_TYPE_DFS	Servers supported by the distributed file system.
SV_TYPE_DIALIN	Machines that are currently connected via a dial-in service.
SV_TYPE_DIALIN_SERVER	Machines supporting a dial-in service.
SV_TYPE_DOMAIN_BAKCTRL	Backup domain controllers.
SV_TYPE_DOMAIN_CTRL	Domain controllers (backup or primary).
SV_TYPE_DOMAIN_MASTER	Primary domain controllers.
SV_TYPE_DOMAIN_MEMBER	Members of the current domain.
SV_TYPE_LOCAL_LIST_ONLY	Machines identified by browser. Use the value 0x40000000 rather than the constant.
SV_TYPE_MASTER_BROWSER	Servers providing the browsing service (as used by the desktop Network Browser).
SV_TYPE_NOVELL	Novell servers.
SV_TYPE_NT	Windows NT workstations or servers.
SV_TYPE_POTENTIAL_BROWSER	Servers that may be able to provide the browsing service (as used by the desktop Network Browser).
SV_TYPE_PRINT	Printers, or machines that are sharing a printer.
SV_TYPE_PRINTQ_SERVER	Servers offering printer queuing or spooling services.
SV_TYPE_SERVER	Any machine registered as a server.
SV_TYPE_SERVER_NT	Any machine registered as an NT server (including Windows 2000). You'll need to use a value 0x00008000, rather than the constant.
SV_TYPE_SERVER_OSF	Servers running the OSF/1 operating system.
SV_TYPE_SERVER_Unix	Servers running Unix that have registered with the network browser (i.e., Samba servers).
SV_TYPE_SERVER_VMS	Servers running the VMS operating system.

Constant	Description
SV_TYPE_SQLSERVER	Servers that provide connectivity to an SQL Server service.
SV_TYPE_TIMESOURCE	Servers that provide a networkwide time reference value.
SV_TYPE_WFW	Workstations running Windows for Workgroups (Windows 3.11).
SV_TYPE_WINDOWS	Workstations running any version of Windows. Use the value 0x00400000.
SV_TYPE_WORKSTATION	Machines which have been registered as workstations.
SV_TYPE_XENIX_SERVER	Servers running the XENIX operating system.

The folowing code:

```
GetTransports(SERVER, TRANSPORTS)
```

places a list of valid network transports into the array or hash pointed to by TRANSPORTS. If you specify a hash reference, then a hash of hashes is created and filled with all the data for the transports.

This code:

```
LoggedOnUsers(SERVER, USERS)
```

places a list of users currently logged into SERVER into the array or hash pointed to by USERS. If USERS is a hash reference, the value is a semi-colon-delimited list consisting of the user name, login domain, and server for each user.

This code:

```
GetAliasFromRID(MACHINE, RID, ALIAS)
GetUserGroupFromRID(MACHINE, RID, ALIAS)
```

places the name of an alias (local group) or user/group for the type specified in RID from MACHINE into the ALIAS scalar. This provides you with the ability to obtain the real name of the specific general entity. Valid values for RID are listed in Table 8-18.

TABLE 8-18

Getting aliases to
specific group
types.

RID Constant	Description
DOMAIN_ALIAS_RID_ACCOUNT_OPS	Alias to the local account operator group.
DOMAIN_ALIAS_RID_ADMINS	Alias to the local administrator group.
DOMAIN_ALIAS_RID_BACKUP_OPS	Alias to the local backup operators.
DOMAIN_ALIAS_RID_GUESTS	Alias to the local guest group.
DOMAIN_ALIAS_RID_POWER_USERS	Alias to the local power group.
DOMAIN_ALIAS_RID_PRINT_OPS	Alias to the local print operator group.
DOMAIN_ALIAS_RID_REPLICATOR	Replicator users (used to exchange domain information).
DOMAIN_ALIAS_RID_SYSTEM_OPS	Alias to the local system operator group.
DOMAIN_ALIAS_RID_USERS	Alias to the local user group.
DOMAIN_GROUP_RID_ADMINS	The domain's administrator group.
DOMAIN_GROUP_RID_GUESTS	The domain's guest group.
DOMAIN_GROUP_RID_USERS	The domain's user group.
DOMAIN_USER_RID_ADMIN	The domain's administrator user.
DOMAIN_USER_RID_GUEST	The domain's guest user.

For example, to get the name of the administrator for the current domain:

```
use Win32::NetAdmin;

Win32::NetAdmin::GetUserGroupFromRID('',
                DOMAIN_USER_RID_ADMIN,
                $alias);

print "Administrator for this domain is $alias\n";
```

User Functions   The user functions in the Win32::NetAdmin module provide direct access for specific areas of the user management:

```
UserCreate(SERVER, USERNAME, PASSWORD, PASSWORDAGE, PRIVILEGE,
        HOMEDIR, COMMENT, FLAGS, SCRIPTPATH)
```

creates a user on SERVER with the remaining arguments. The function returns False if the operation failed. The PASSWORDAGE should be supplied as the number of seconds since the epoch. The PRIVILEGE field is the same as the `priv` key in `Win32API::Net`. The other fields should be self-explanatory.

```
UserDelete(SERVER, USER)
```

deletes USER from SERVER.

```
UserGetAttributes(SERVER, USERNAME, PASSWORD, PASSWORDAGE, PRIVILEGE,
                  HOMEDIR, COMMENT, FLAGS, SCRIPTPATH)
```

gets the information for USERNAME from SERVER, placing the corresponding information into the arguments pointed to by the remaining arguments.

```
UserSetAttributes(SERVER, USERNAME, PASSWORD, PASSWORDAGE, PRIVILEGE,
                  HOMEDIR, COMMENT, FLAGS, SCRIPTPATH)
```

updates the user on SERVER with the properties of the specified arguments.

```
UserChangePassword(DOMAINNAME, USERNAME, OLDPASSWORD, NEWPASSWORD)
```

changes the password for USERNAME on DOMAINNAME. Because you are required to supply the old password as well as the new, this function can be used by any user.

```
UsersExist(SERVER, USERNAME)
```

returns True if USERNAME exists on SERVER.

```
GetUsers(SERVER, FILTER, USERREF)
```

fills the array pointed to by USERREF with the list of users from SERVER. If USERREF is a hash reference, then the hash contains user names and the corresponding full names. If FILTER is not blank, the list is restricted to those users starting with FILTER.

Group Functions   The group functions mimic the functions exported by `Win32API::Net`.

```
GroupCreate(SERVER, GROUP, COMMENT)
```

creates GROUP on SERVER, with a suitable COMMENT if nonblank.

```
GroupDelete(SERVER, GROUP)
```

deletes GROUP **on** SERVER.

```
GroupGetAttributes(SERVER, GROUP, COMMENT)
```

places the comment for GROUP **on** SERVER **into** COMMENT.

```
GroupSetAttributes(SERVER, GROUP, COMMENT)
```

sets the comment for GROUP **on** SERVER **from** COMMENT.

```
GroupAddUsers(SERVER, GROUP, USERS)
```

adds the list of USERS **to** GROUP **on** SERVER.

```
GroupDeleteUsers(SERVER, GROUP, USERS)
```

deletes the list of USERS **from** GROUP **on** SERVER.

```
GroupIsMember(SERVER, GROUP, USER)
```

returns True **if** USER **is a member of** GROUP **on** SERVER.

```
GroupGetMembers(SERVER, GROUP, USERS)
```

places the list of users that are members of GROUP **into the array pointed to by** USERS.

Local Group Functions   The local group functions control the groups specified on the local machine:

```
LocalGroupCreate(server, group, comment)
```

creates the local GROUP.

```
LocalGroupDelete(SERVER, GROUP)
```

deletes the local GROUP.

```
LocalGroupGetAttributes(SERVER, GROUP, COMMENT)
```

gets the comment for the local GROUP, **putting it into** COMMENT.

```
LocalGroupSetAttributes(SERVER, GROUP, COMMENT)
```

sets the comment for the local GROUP, from the value in COMMENT.

```
LocalGroupIsMember(SERVER, GROUP, USER)
```

returns True if USER is a member of the local GROUP.

```
LocalGroupGetMembers(SERVER, GROUP, USERS)
```

places the list of members of GROUP into the array pointed to by USERS.

```
LocalGroupGetMembersWithDomain(SERVER, GROUPNAME, USERS)
```

places a list of USERS that are members of GROUP into the array or hash pointed to by USERS. Unlike LocalGroupGetMembers, the user names include the domain name, in the form "DOMAIN\USERNAME."

```
LocalGroupAddUsers(SERVER, GROUP, USERS)
```

adds the list of USERS to the local GROUP.

```
LocalGroupDeleteUsers(SERVER, GROUP, USERS)
```

deletes the list of USERS from GROUP.

System Functions   The last function in the module is something of an oddity. It places the list of drives currently available on a remote server into an array.

```
GetServerDisks(SERVER, DRIVES)
```

The usefulness of this is beyond me, since it gives no more information than the drive letter on the machine. The Win32::AdminMisc::GetDrives provides a much more useful list, albeit only for local drives. See later in this chapter for more information.

Win32::AdminMisc

Dave Roth has done an excellent job in providing a single module that provides a mixture of functions across a range of different topics. These provide access to a number of purely administrative functions, from creating users, through to emulating other users, and even getting status information.

Because the module provides such a wide range of functions, they are listed here in logical groups.

Domain Functions   The domain functions here augment the functions offered in the other modules.

GetPDC   This function returns the primary controller for the current domain, or the domain specified in DOMAIN. If DOMAIN is a machine, it returns the PDC for that machine. For example:

```
GetPDC([DOMAIN]);
```

GetDC   This function returns the domain controller (backup or primary) of DOMAIN if specified, or the domain controller of the current domain if none is specified. It returns undef if the name of the domain controller cannot be determined. For example:

```
GetDC([DOMAIN]);
```

GetMachines   This function gets a list of machines according to a particular type. This is similar to Win32::NetAdmin::GetServers function. For example:

```
GetMachines(SERVER, TYPE, LIST [, PREFIX]);
```

populates LIST, which should be a reference to an array or hash, containing the names of computers matching TYPE. The TYPE should be one of UF_SERVER_TRUST_ACCOUNTS, which lists the domain server's machine accounts, UF_INTERDOMAIN_TRUST_ACCOUNT, which lists trusted accounts between machines, or UF_WORKSTATION_ TRUST_ACCOUNTS, for workstation accounts.

If specified, PREFIX restricts the list of machines returned to only those starting with PREFIX. This returns 1 if successful, or 0 on failure.

GetComputerName   This function returns the Windows NT node name for the current machine. Equivalent to the Win32::GetNodeName function. For example:

```
GetComputerName();
```

SetComputerName   This function sets the computer name to NAME. For example:

```
SetComputerName(NAME);
```

Using this on a machine within a domain will remove the machine from that domain (since it will no longer be a registered member of the domain). You'll need to re-create the machine's account on the PDC or BDC for the domain.

User/Group Functions   The user/group functions also work in a similar fashion to the functions to other modules. Note, however, that the `Win32::AdminMisc` module also provides you with the ability to logon as a separate user—something we looked at in Chapter 5.

`GetLogonName`   This function returns the name of the user this account is logged on as. For example:

```
GetLogonName();
```

This is not necessarily the same as the user under which the script is running, since you can masquerade as another user under Windows the same way you can with setuid scripts under Unix. This correctly reflects the login account rather than the current user value returned by `Win32::GetLogonName`.

`GetGroups`   This function returns a list of groups from a machine or domain according to a particular type and/or prefix. For example:

```
GetGroups([ MACHINE|DOMAIN ], TYPE, LIST [, PREFIX])
```

will return a list of user groups that are of `TYPE`, placing the information into the array or hash reference pointed to by `LIST`. `TYPE` can be one of `GROUP_TYPE_LOCAL` (returns an array), which lists only groups defined only on the specified machine, or `GROUP_TYPE_GLOBAL` (array), which lists all groups defined in the current domain. You can also set `GROUP_TYPE_ALL` (hash) to get a list of all the groups, local and global.

    The first parameter is either a server name, as in `"\\INSENTIENT"`, or a domain name, such as `"MCHOME"`. This value determines which machine will be used to determine the list of groups. If undefined, it uses the local machine. It returns a `0` if the search was unsuccessful, `1` otherwise.

`GetUsers`   This function returns the list of users logged into a server, filtering by a prefix if required. For example:

```
GetUsers(SERVER, PREFIX, LIST)
```

populates the array or hash pointed to by LIST with the users on SERVER, starting with the specified PREFIX. If PREFIX is empty, then all users are returned.

LogonAsUser   This function provides a similar level of ability as a setuid script. With this function you can masquerade as another user, providing you know the user name and password. For example:

```
LogonAsUser(DOMAIN, USER, PASSWORD [, LOGONTYPE])
```

The login is valid for the specified DOMAIN, USER, and PASSWORD. If DOMAIN is blank, then USER is assumed to be in the current user's domain. The valid optional types for LOGONTYPE are shown in Table 8-19.
    See Chapter 5 for a sample.

LogoffAsUser   This function logs the user off from an impersonated account (as initiated by LogonAsUser). For example:

```
LogoffAsUser([1|0])
```

If you supply a nonzero argument, the logoff is forced. Always returns 1.

RenameUser   This function changes the login name of a user on a server or domain. For example:

```
RenameUser(SERVER, USER, NEWUSER)
```

changes the name of USER on the specified SERVER to NEWUSER. The update will change throughout the user database, updating the user and group information. If SERVER is the name of a domain, the PDC is found

TABLE 8-19

Logon types for impersonating users.

Type	Description
LOGON32_LOGON_BATCH	Logs on as a noninteractive batch file.
LOGON32_LOGON_INTERACTIVE	Logs on as a normal interactive user.
LOGON32_LOGON_SERVICE	Logs on as a system service (under Windows NT).
LOGON32_LOGON_NETWORK	Logs on as a standard network user.

and the command sent to that machine. If SERVER is blank, it changes the name on the local machine.

SetPassword This function changes the password for a user. You must have administrative privileges to use this function. For example:

```
SetPassword(SERVER, USER, PASSWORD)
```

changes the password for USER on the domain server SERVER to PASS-WORD. SERVER can be the explicit name of a server or the name of a domain, in which case the primary domain controller will be searched. You must have administration privileges for this to work. The function returns 0 on failure. See the UserChangePassword function for a user-oriented version.

UserChangePassword This function changes the password for a user. This function can be used from a user script, because you also need the old password. For example:

```
UserChangePassword(DOMAIN, USER, OLDPW, NEWPW)
```

changes the password for USER in DOMAIN (or on the server DOMAIN) to NEWPW, provided that OLDPW matches the existing password. If DOMAIN is empty, it assumes the current local domain. If USER is empty, then it assumes the current user. Returns 0 if the password was not modified.

UserCheckPassword This function verifies a password for a user on a server or domain. For example:

```
UserCheckPassword(DOMAIN, USER, PASSWORD)
```

verifies that the password for USER within DOMAIN matches PASSWORD. If DOMAIN is empty, assumes the current local domain. If USER is empty, then it assumes the current user. Returns 0 if the password does not match.

UserGetAttributes Gets the user information for a specified user on a server or domain. For example:

```
UserGetAttributes(SERVER, USER, NAME, PASSWORD, PASSWORDAGE, PRIVS,
                  HOMEDIR, COMMENT, FLAGS, SCRIPTPATH);
```

gets the user information for the specified USER, placing the values into the remainder of the arguments supplied. If DOMAIN is empty, it assumes the current local domain. If USER is empty, then it assumes the current user. You should use the UserGetMiscAttributes, which provides a more familiar hash-based interface to the information. Returns 0 if the user could not be found.

UserSetAttributes This function sets the attributes for a given user. For example:

```
UserSetAttributes(SERVER, USER, NAME, PASSWORD, PASSWORDAGE, PRIVS,
                HOMEDIR, COMMENT, FLAGS, SCRIPTPATH)
```

sets the attributes for USER on SERVER to the specified values. You should use the UserSetMiscAttributes function, which not only provides a more user-friendly interface but also allows you to set significantly more options.

UserGetMiscAttributes This an expanded version of the UserGetAttributes function. It supports a similar interface to the Win32API::Net::UserGetInfo function by placing the user information into a hash. For example:

```
GetMiscAttributes(DOMAIN, USER, INFO)
```

places the attributes for USER in DOMAIN into the hash pointed to by INFO. The list of hash elements is shown in Table 8-20.
The valid user flags are listed in Table 8-21.

To determine whether a user flag is set, you must logically AND the value of USER_FLAGS with one of the constants in Table 8-21. To disable a flag, you must logically AND the flag with the two's complement of the constant. To turn on a value, you need to logically OR the user flags with the constant.

UserSetMiscAttributes This function sets the attributes for a user using a hash, as defined by Table 8-20. For example:

```
UserSetMiscAttributes(DOMAIN, USER, USERINFO)
```

sets the information in the hash USERINFO for USER in the domain DOMAIN. Refer to Tables 8-20 and 8-21 for details on the individual hash elements. This function returns 1 if the update was successful.

TABLE 8-20

User information fields.

Element	Description
USER_ACCT_EXPIRES	When the user account is set to expire. Specified by the number of seconds since the epoch.
USER_AUTH_FLAGS	Defines the abilities of the user, existing constants are as follows: AF_OP_PRINT—User has print operator privileges. AF_OP_COMM—User has communications operator privileges. AF_OP_SERVER—User has server operator privilege. AF_OP_ACCOUNTS—User has accounts operator privilege.
USER_BAD_PW_COUNT	The number of times the user has supplied a bad password. Note that this value is recorded individually by each backup domain controller; you will need to interrogate all BDCs and PDCs to get a complete value.
USER_CODE_PAGE	The code page of the user's language.
USER_COMMENT	The user's account comment.
USER_COUNTRY_CODE	The country code for the user's preferred language.
USER_FLAGS	A set of flags defining the current user account information. See Table 8-21.
USER_FULL_NAME	The user's full name.
USER_HOME_DIR	The user's home directory.
USER_HOME_DIR_DRIVE	The drive letter assigned to the user's home directory during logon.
USER_LAST_LOGOFF	The number of seconds since the epoch when the user last logged off. Note that this value is recorded individually by each backup domain controller; you will need to interrogate all BDCs and PDCs to get a complete value.
USER_LAST_LOGON	The number of seconds since the epoch when the user last logged on. Note that this value is recorded individually by each backup domain controller; you will need to interrogate all BDCs and PDCs to get a complete value.
USER_LOGON_HOURS	A string, 21 bytes in length, that specifies the times during which the user can log on. Each bit refers to a sequential hour in the week, with bit zero referring to Sunday, 0:00, to 0:59. You can extract the information using the vec function.

TABLE 8-20

Continued

Element	Description
USER_LOGON_SERVER	The name of the server to which logon requests are sent.
USER_MAX_STORAGE	The maximum disk quote available to the user.
USER_NAME	The user's account name.
USER_NUM_LOGONS	The number of times the user has successfully logged on to the server. Note that this value is recorded individually by each backup domain controller; you will need to interrogate all BDCs and PDCs to get a complete value.
USER_PARMS	A set of user-defined parameters. This information is used almost exclusively by Microsoft applications for some configuration information.
USER_PASSWORD	The encrypted version of the user's password.
USER_PASSWORD_AGE	The number of seconds since the password was last changed.
USER_PASSWORD_EXPIRED	Determines whether the user's password has expired.
USER_PRIMARY_GROUP_ID	The primary group to which the user belongs.
USER_PRIV	The privileges of the user: USER_PRIV_GUEST—Guest privileges. USER_PRIV_USER—Standard user privileges. USER_PRIV_ADMIN—Administration privileges.
USER_PROFILE	The path to the user's profile information.
USER_SCRIPT_PATH	The path to the user's logon script.
USER_UNITS_PER_WEEK	Defines the number of equal units into which the week is divided.
USER_USERID	The relative ID of the user.
USER_WORKSTATIONS	The list of workstations, separated by commas, into which the user is allowed to log in.

Internet Domain Names   Although some of the networking functions work as normal (see Chapter 7), the Win32::AdminMisc module also provides a series of functions that communicate directly with the Windows DNS system.

GetHostAddress   This function gets a host address using DNS, returning an IP address for the machine in the string NAME. For instance:

```
GetHostAddress(NAME)
```

TABLE 8-21

User flags.

Value	Description
UF_ACCOUNTDISABLE	The user's account is disabled.
UF_DONT_EXPIRE_PASSWD	The user's password should never expire.
UF_HOMEDIR_REQUIRED	The user requires a home directory (ignored under Windows NT).
UF_INTERDOMAIN_TRUST_ACCOUNT	This is an interdomain account, allowing one domain to have trust to another domain.
UF_LOCKOUT	The user account is currently locked out (disabled).
UF_NORMAL_ACCOUNT	The default account type.
UF_PASSWD_CANT_CHANGE	User cannot change his or her password.
UF_PASSWD_NOTREQD	User does not require a password.
UF_SCRIPT	The login script executed.
UF_SERVER_TRUST_ACCOUNT	This is a trusted server user account.
UF_TEMP_DUPLICATE_ACCOUNT	The account is a duplicate temporary account. This is usually created when the user's primary account is in another domain.
UF_WORKSTATION_TRUST_ACCOUNT	This is a trusted workstation user account.

GetHostName   This function gets a host name from the supplied IP ADDRESS. Note that the address should be in the dotted-quad string format, for example, 198.112.10.128.

gethostbyname   This function gets a host address using DNS, an alias to the GetHostAddress function. For example:

```
gethostbyname(NAME)
```

gethostbyaddr   This function gets a host name from the supplied IP ADDRESS, an alias to the GetHostName function. For instance:

```
gethostbyaddr(ADDRESS)
```

DNSCache   This function switches the local DNS cache on (1) or off (0). This can be useful if you suspect that an address is being returned incorrectly because the local cache is being used, instead of querying the name or address with one of the configured name servers. For example:

```
DNSCache([1|0])
```

returns the new status. If no argument is supplied, then no changes are made, but the status is still returned.

DNSCacheCount   This function returns the number of elements in the DNS cache. For example:

```
DNSCacheCount()
```

DNSCacheSize   This function sets the size of the DNS cache to `SIZE`, returning the new current size. For example:

```
DNSCacheSize([SIZE])
```

If the `SIZE` is not specified, it simply returns the current size.

System Information   These functions relate to getting information about the current machine.

GetDrives   This function returns a list of valid drive letters for the current machine. For instance:

```
GetDrives([TYPE])
```

The function is essentially equivalent to:

```
Win32::NetAdmin::GetServerDisks('',\@drives);
```

If `TYPE` is specified, then it only returns the drive letters of the specified type. The list of valid drive filters is shown in Table 8-22.
The function returns a list of drive letters, or an empty list if none of the specified types are found.

GetDriveType   This function returns an integer relating to the drive type for a specified drive letter. For example:

```
GetDriveType(DRIVE)
```

Refer to Table 8-22 for a list of constants to check against. On error it returns 0 if the test was unsuccessful, and 1 if the drive type couldn't be determined.

TABLE 8-22

Valid drive filters.

Constant	Description
DRIVE_FIXED	Any fixed media (hard drive).
DRIVE_REMOVABLE	Any removable media.
DRIVE_REMOTE	Any drive remotely mounted from another machine.
DRIVE_CDROM	Any CD-ROM drive.
DRIVE_RAMDISK	Any drive emulated within memory.

GetDriveSpace This function returns an array consisting of the total drive capacity and free space on the specified DRIVE. For example:

```
GetDriveSpace(DRIVE)
```

In addition to the drive letter, you can also explicitly request the information from a remote mount such as "\\Atuin\MC\", but note that you must add the trailing slash. It returns nothing if the information could not be determined.

For example, the following script produces output similar to the Unix df command:

```
use Win32::AdminMisc;

my @drives = Win32::AdminMisc::GetDrives();

printf("%-20s %9s %9s %2s\n",'Drive','Used','Free','%Used');

foreach my $let (@drives)
{
    %info = Win32::AdminMisc::GetVolumeInfo($let);
    my ($tot,$free) = Win32::AdminMisc::GetDriveSpace($let);
    $used = ($tot-$free)/1024;
    $usedpc = int($used/($tot/1024));
    printf("%-20s %9d %9d %%%02d\n",
            "$let $info{Volume}",
            $used,
            ($free/1024),
            $usedpc);
}
```

GetVolumeInfo This function returns extended information for a given drive letter or UNC name. For example:

```
GetVolumeInfo(DRIVE)
```

TABLE 8-23

Hash Elements
Returned by
GetVolumeInfo.

Element	Description
Volume	The volume label.
Serial	The serial number for the drive, in decimal (rather than hexadecimal).
MaxFileNameLength	The maximum number of characters in a file name.
SystemFlag	A combination of the following predefined constants:
	FS_CASE_IS_PRESERVED—The character case is preserved on the drive.
	FS_CASE_SENSITIVE—The drive supports case-sensitive filenames.
	FS_UNICODE_STORED_ON_DISK—Supports Unicode-formatted filenames.
	FS_PERSISTENT_ACLS—Stores and enforces access control lists.
	FS_FILE_COMPRESSION—The file system supports file-based compression (such as Windows NT file-based compression).
	FS_VOL_IS_COMPRESSED—Signifies that the drive is a compressed device (as created by Stacker or Windows).

returns a hash containing the current information for the specified drive (either C:\ or \\Atuin\MC. The elements of the hash are shown in Table 8-23.

SetVolumeLabel This function sets the volume label for a drive. For example:

```
SetVolumeLabel(DRIVE, LABEL)
```

sets the volume label for DRIVE to LABEL. Cannot be used on a UNC (since that would change the share name), only on a drive letter.

GetEnvVar The environment variables on a Windows NT machine can be modified within a process with the %ENV hash, but to modify the environment variables used for all processes, you need to use the *EnvVar functions from the Win32::AdminMisc module. These directly modify the environment variables configured through the System control panel (see Chapter 5). For example:

```
GetEnvVar(NAME [, TYPE])
```

returns the value of the environment variable NAME. If TYPE is specified, then it must be one of ENV_SYSTEM for a system variable or ENV_USER for a user variable. Returns undef if the variable could not be found.

SetEnvVar   This function sets the global environment variables. For example:

```
SetEnvVar(NAME, VALUE [, TYPE [, TIMEOUT]])
```

sets the value of the variable NAME to VALUE. If specified, creates the variable within the system variables (ENV_SYSTEM, the default) or user variables (ENV_USER). Changes are global and permanent, with the value change being broadcast to the other processes for a maximum of TIMEOUT seconds.

DelEnvVar   This function deletes system and environment variables. For example:

```
DelEnvVar(NAME [, TYPE] [, TIMEOUT]])
```

The NAME is the name of the environment variable, and the type is ENV_SYSTEM by default, but you can also use ENV_USER to delete a user environmental variable. The optional TIMEOUT specifies the number of seconds that the change notification should be broadcast. If the timeout value is reached, the variable is still deleted, but the broadcast will be aborted.

The function returns 1 if successful, or 0 on failure.

GetIdInfo   This function returns an array of information for the current thread/process. For example:

```
($pid, $tid, $ppriority, $tpriority, $cmd) = GetIdInfo();
```

The elements are the process ID, the thread ID, the process priority, the thread priority, and the command line used to execute the script.

GetMemoryInfo   This function returns a hash containing information about the current memory situation. For example:

```
GetMemoryInfo()
```

TABLE 8-24

Memory informa-
tion returned by
the GetMemory
Info function.

Element	Description
Load	Percentage load on the available memory.
RAMTotal	Total amount, in bytes, of physical RAM.
RAMAvail	Total amount, in bytes, of available physical RAM.
PageTotal	Total amount, in bytes, of paged RAM.
PageAvail	Total amount, in bytes, of available paged RAM.
VirtTotal	Total amount, in bytes, of virtual memory.
VirtAvail	Total amount, in bytes, of available virtual memory.

The list of keys and their meanings in the returned hash is shown in Table 8-24.

GetProcessorInfo   This function returns a hash of processor-related information, as shown in Table 8-25. For example:

```
GetProcessorInfo()
```

GetWinVersion   This function returns a hash defining the version information for the current Windows environment, as shown in Table 8-26. The syntax is as follows:

```
GetWinVersion()
```

ReadINI   The Windows INI files are configuration files used by many applications. The file is split into individual sections, and then within

TABLE 8-25

Information gained
from the
GetProcessor
Info function.

Element	Description
OEMID	The OEM (original equipment manufacturer) ID.
NumOfProcessors	The number of processors.
ProcessorType	Type of microprocessor.
ProcessorLevel	The level of processor (4=486, 5=586, etc.).
ProcessorRevision	The revision of the processor.
PageSize	The size of individual pages of memory (a page is the unit of information written swapped out to disk/virtual memory).

TABLE 8-26

Hash elements returned by `GetWinVersion`.

Element	Description
Major	The major release (for example, Windows NT 4).
Minor	The minor release.
Build	The build number.
Platform	One of `Win32s`, `Win32_95`, `Win32_NT`.
CSD	Currently installed service pack number.

each section, you get keyword/value pairs that relate to the actual configuration information. For example, here's a fragment for the WIN.INI file from a Windows NT machine:

```
[fonts]
[extensions]
[mci extensions]
[files]
[Mail]
CMC=1
CMCDLLNAME=mapi.dll
CMCDLLNAME32=mapi32.dll
```

The INI files have largely been replaced by the Windows Registry and are mostly only retained for 16-bit (Windows 3.x) compatibility.

The `ReadINI` function returns the value for a given configuration line within an INI file. For example:

```
ReadINI(FILE, SECTION, KEY)
```

retrieves the specified value for the specified KEY, from the corresponding SECTION or the INI FILE. If KEY is empty, it returns a list of all the keys in the section, and if both KEYS and SECTION are blank, it returns a list of sections.

WriteINI The `WriteINI` function updates an INI file. For example:

```
WriteINI(FILE, SECTION, KEY, VALUE)
```

writes the KEY/VALUE pair into the INI file referred to by FILE, into the section defined by SECTION. If VALUE is empty, the KEY is removed. If KEY is empty, all keys in SECTION are removed, and if SECTION is empty, all sections in the entire file are removed. Returns 1 if successful, and undef on failure.

Flag	Description
EWX_LOGOFF	Log the user off, but don't shut down windows. Applications will be asked to shut down gracefully.
EWX_POWEROFF	Shut down the machine, and switch off the power if power management is supported.
EWX_REBOOT	Shut down and reboot.
EWX_SHUTDOWN	Shut down the system, but don't power off or reboot.
EWX_FORCE	Log the user off, forcing applications to quit immediately.

Control Functions   The Win32::AdminMisc provides a single function that allows you to exit from a Windows session. The options provided are identical to the options offered when you choose Shutdown from the Start menu.

ExitWindows   Exits the current Windows session, using the method defined in the FLAG. Valid values are listed in Table 8-27. The syntax is as follows:

```
ExitWindows(FLAG)
```

The function returns 0 if the operation was unsuccessful, or nonzero if the instruction to exit Windows was accepted successfully.

Miscellaneous Functions   There are a number of functions within the Win32::AdminMisc module that cannot be categorized anywhere else.

ScheduleAdd   The Windows NT operating system provides a similar schedule service to the cron/at system supported under Unix. Unlike the Unix version, the schedule is much more specific. You can schedule entries at particular times and days of the month or week. The Win32::AdminMisc module does a good job of hiding the differences from the programmer. For example:

```
ScheduleAdd(MACHINE, TIME, DOM, DOW, FLAGS, COMMAND)
```

schedules COMMAND to be run at a particular date and time. The MACHINE is the machine on which the command should be run. The TIME is the time at which the command should be run. The DOM and DOW arguments define the day of the month and the day of week on which the command should be run. The day of the month is a bitset, each bit, starting at zero, referring to subsequent days of the month. You can either use vec to create this or use the power of 2 to create the correct value. Values can be OR'd together, such that 2**1 | 2**31 specifies the 1st and 31st of the month.

The DOW is also a bitset, but there are values predefined for MONDAY, TUESDAY, WEDNESDAY, THURSDAY, FRIDAY, SATURDAY, and SUNDAY. Values can be OR'd together to specify multiple days.

The FLAGS is a list of options used for creating the scheduled entry. Valid values are listed in Table 22-28.

The function returns a unique job number for the scheduled command.

ScheduleDel This function deletes a given job, using the job number. For example:

```
ScheduleDel(MACHINE, JOB [, MAXJOB])
```

deletes the job number JOB from the schedule for MACHINE. If MAXJOB is specified, it removes all jobs with IDs from JOB to MAXJOB.

ScheduleGet This function gets the schedule information for a given job ID. For instance:

```
ScheduleGet(MACHINE, JOB, JOBINFO)
```

	Flag	Description
TABLE 8-28 Flags for creating scheduled jobs.	JOB_RUN_PERIODICALLY	The job will be run every month on the specified days of the week and/or days of the week at the specified time.
	JOB_ADD_CURRENT_DATE	The job will run today at the specified time, or tomorrow if the current time is greater than TIME.
	JOB_EXEC_ERROR	Set if the last time the job was executed it failed.
	JOB_RUN_TODAY	Set when the job's time has yet to pass for the current day. Set irrespective of the DOM or DOW settings.
	JOB_NONINTERACTIVE	Set if the job is not allowed desktop interaction (a background job).

places the information about JOB on MACHINE into the hash reference pointed to by JOBINFO. The elements of the hash are Machine, Time, DOM, DOW, Flags, Command. **Refer to** ScheduleAdd **above for more information.**

ScheduleList   This function lists all of the scheduled events for a machine. For example:

```
ScheduleList(MACHINE [, LIST])
```

places a reference to a hash of hashes into the variable pointed to by LIST, defining the list of scheduled jobs for MACHINE. Returns the number of scheduled jobs on the machine, or undef if there was a problem.

GetStdHandle   This function returns a Perl handle to the Win32 handle used for one of the standard I/O channels. For example:

```
GetStdHanle(HANDLE)
```

returns a Win32 handle for the filehandle specified by HANDLE. HANDLE should be one of STD_INPUT_HANDLE, STD_OUTPUT_HANDLE, or STD_ERROR_HANDLE. **Returns** undef **on error.**

GetTOD   This functions gets the time of day on a machine, specified as the number of seconds since the epoch. It is similar to the Perl built-in time(), except that you can obtain the time of a remote machine. For example:

```
GetTOD(MACHINE)
```

returns the time of the specified MACHINE.

Administration Example

This script reads in the user data for a specific machine and/or domain and reports any inconsistencies or possible security traps in the information.

```perl
#!perl

use Win32::AdminMisc;
use Win32::NetAdmin;
use Getopt::Long;

my ($machine,$domain,@users,%attribs);

GetOptions("d=s" => \$domain);
```

```perl
$machine = Win32::NodeName();

$domain =Win32::DomainName()
    unless (defined($domain));

if (@ARGV)
{
    @users = @ARGV;
}
else
{
   Win32::NetAdmin::GetUsers(Win32::AdminMisc::GetDC($domain),
                             '',\@users);
}

if (@users)
{
    print "Domain: $domain\n";
}

for $user (sort @users)
{
    unless(Win32::AdminMisc::UserGetMiscAttributes($domain,
                                                   $user,
                                                   \%attribs))

    {
        opstatus();
    }
    else
    {
        if ($attribs{"USER_PASSWORD_EXPIRED"} == 1)
        {
        print "Error: $user : Password has expired\n";
        }
        if ($machine eq Win32::AdminMisc::GetDC($domain))
        {
            unless(-d $attribs{"USER_HOME_DIR"})
        {
            print("Error: $user : Home directory, ",
                $attribs{"USER_HOME_DIR"},
                " does not exist\n");
        }
    }
    if ($user !˜7E /Administrator/)
    {
        if ($attribs{"USER_PRIV"} == 2)
        {
            print("Warning: $user : User has ",
                "administrator privileges\n");
        }
        else
        {
            if ($attribs{"USER_AUTH_FLAGS"} & 1)
            {
                print("Warning: $user : User does not have ",
                    "administrator privileges but does ",
                    "have Print Admin privileges\n");
            }
            if ($attribs{"USER_AUTH_FLAGS"} & 4)
```

```perl
        {
            print("Warning: $user : User does not have ",
                  "administrator privileges but does ",
                  "have Server Admin privileges\n");
        }
        if ($attribs{"USER_AUTH_FLAGS"} & 8)
        {
            print("Warning: $user : User does not have ",
                  "administrator privileges but does ",
                  "have Accounts Admin privileges\n");
        }
      }
    }
    if ($attribs{"USER_PASSWORD_AGE"} > (31*24*60*60))
    {
        print("Error: $user : Password is more than ",
              "one month (31 days) old\n");
    }
    if ($attribs{"USER_BAD_PW_COUNT"} > 0)
    {
        print("Warning: $user : User has had ",
              $attribs{"USER_BAD_PW_COUNT"},
              " bad password attempts\n");
    }
  }
}

sub opstatus
{
    my $error=Win32::GetLastError();
    if ($error ne 0)
    {
        print("\nERROR: ", Win32::FormatMessage($error),"\n");
    }
}
```

You should be able to follow the execution fairly easily. First, you use the functions in the Win32::NetAdmin module to verify or resolve the supplied machine name, either for its validity or to determine the domain's primary controller. Then you use the UserGetAdminMiscAttributes function from Dave Roth's Win32::AdminMisc module to get the individual information for each user, before you go through and check individual components of the user's attributes.

## CHAPTER 9

Web
Development

Perl has for a long time been the language used to develop the sort of interactivity seen on most modern sites. This is because the web interface is largely text-based and therefore something that is handled very well by the Perl language, which was originally invented to parse and process text.

Web programming with Perl has been a cornerstone of the Perl language for so long that most people already know the issues surrounding the development of Perl-based CGI scripts. Therefore, in this chapter, we'll concentrate on some fundamentals, including the differences that lie between Unix and Windows environments when scripting with Perl.

We'll then move on to using the CGI module, which is bundled with all Perl distributions. The module makes CGI development and, more importantly, cross-platform CGI development significantly easier. It also makes producing HTML much easier by supporting its own set of functions that generate correctly formatted HTML for you.

The next section in this chapter concentrates on the PerlIS extension for IIS-compliant web servers. This significantly increases the speed of execution for your scripts, but there are some minor differences between the environment that might cause problems when executing certain types of Perl scripts. We'll also take a brief look at PerlEx, another extension that betters the 10 to 20x speed improvement of PerlIS to provide a 40 to 50x improvement when executing Perl-based CGI scripts.

The remainder of the chapter is given to PerlScript. PerlScript is an extension that allows you to use Perl as a scripting language embedded into HTML pages. This enables you to use Perl as an ASP (Active Server Page) scripting language in the same way as you can use Visual Basic. Better still, you can also use PerlScript to offer client-based scripting embedded into the pages, allowing you to develop Perl-based interactive pages just as you use JavaScript.

Fundamentals

Web programming is easy if you know how information is transferred from the client to the server, from the server to the script, and then from the script back to the client. The most important thing to remember is that the client is unintelligent—it sends a URL request to a web server. The request is made up of the URL that is requested, any form data supplied by the browser, and, optionally, a browser cookie.

The server takes this information and updates the environment according to the information supplied and then runs the script that was requested. This is the CGI, or Common Gateway Interface, stage; it's responsible for supplying the information received from the browser to the script. We'll look at the environmental information created for a CGI script below.

Once the CGI script starts, it processes the information supplied to it by the server, either by accessing environment variables or for large data streams from the client by reading the information supplied to the standard input. The information is always supplied in the same format, and the script must parse this information in order to extract the individual fields from the form data supplied.

The last stage is for the script to supply information back to the browser. The web server basically takes any output generated via the standard output from the browser and sends it to the client. The actual information that is supplied back is a two-stage process, consisting of a header and a body. The header is the HTTP header and indicates the format of the body being returned and additional information such as a web cookie. The body is the file itself. Normally, this is HTML, but it could be any type of file and image—say, a Zip file or even an application. It's up to the browser to interpret the file according to the file type you supplied in the HTTP header. In all cases, the script determines what file type is returned. The web server doesn't play any part in this process; it just provides a conduit for supplying the information from the script to the client browser over the TCP/IP connection.

To summarize:

1. The user's browser (the client) opens a connection to the server.
2. The user's browser requests a URL from the server.
3. The server parses the URL and determines whether a file is to be returned or whether it needs to run an external application. For this run-through we'll assume the latter.
4. The external application is called. This can be a binary executable, a batch file, a shell script, an *awk* script, or perhaps one written in Python. For us, though, we're only interested in Perl scripts.
5. Any additional information supplied by the user's browser, such as that from a form, is supplied to the application, either using an environment variable or by passing the data as a stream to the application's standard input.
6. Any output produced by the application is sent back directly to the user's browser.

As a general rule, there are few differences between developing on a Unix platform and Windows, but it's worth recapping and highlighting some of the differences that do exist.

Environment

The environment is used primarily as a way of supplying background information to the script that is being executed. It provides information such as the path accessed and the address and name of the client and server. You display the environment variables available within a script by using a simple `for` loop to list each environment back to the browser, for example:

```
print "Content-type: text/html\n\n";
foreach $key (sort keys %ENV)
{
    print "$key<br>\n$key: $ENV{$key}<br>\n";
}
```

This will output a list similar to the one that follows. This one has been stripped of the environment variables that would exist for any script:

```
CONTENT_LENGTH: 0
GATEWAY_INTERFACE: CGI/1.1
HTTP_ACCEPT: */*
HTTP_ACCEPT_LANGUAGE: en
HTTP_COOKIE:
HTTP_HOST: incontinent
HTTP_UA_CPU: PPC
HTTP_UA_OS: MacOS
HTTP_USER_AGENT: Mozilla/4.0 (compatible; MSIE 5.0; Mac_PowerPC)
HTTPS: off
LOCAL_ADDR: 198.112.10.125
PATH_INFO: /www/env.pl
PATH_TRANSLATED: D:\Shared\Websites\Incontinent\env.pl
REMOTE_ADDR: 198.112.10.134
REMOTE_HOST: 198.112.10.134
REQUEST_METHOD: GET
SCRIPT_NAME: /www/env.pl
SERVER_NAME: incontinent
SERVER_PORT: 80
SERVER_PORT_SECURE: 0
SERVER_PROTOCOL: HTTP/1.0
SERVER_SOFTWARE: Microsoft-IIS/5.0
```

For a description of what each environment variable holds, see Table 9-1.

TABLE 9-1

Environment
variables.

Variable	Description
CONTENT_LENGTH	The length of the query string supplied to the web server for processing by the CGI script.
GATEWAY_INTERFACE	The type and version number of the gateway interface being used. The type is generally CGI, and versions vary between web server software.
HTTP_ACCEPT	The list of MIME file types accepted by the browser. See the section on "HTTP Headers" later in this chapter for some examples of MIME types.
HTTP_ACCEPT_LANGUAGE	The (spoken) languages accepted by the browser. The format is a two-character string, with multiple languages being separated by commas.
HTTP_ACCEPT_CHARSET	The character set accepted by the browser.
HTTP_ACCEPT_ENCODING	A list of any additional encoding formats supported by the browser. All accept raw data, but more advanced browsers may also accept Gzip or compressed documents, which will be decompressed by the browser before display.
HTTP_COOKIE	The cookie returned by the browser. Cookies are used to store information within a browser about a particular site. See "Cookies" later in the chapter when we look at the CGI script.
HTTP_HOST	The name of the server host (without its domain).
HTTP_UA_CPU	The CPU type of the user agent (UA) that sent the request to the server.
HTTP_UA_OS	The OS of the user agent that sent the request.
HTTP_USER_AGENT	The full name of the user agent used to send the request. The format is a string consisting of the name, version number, and platform. Note that user agents can be browsers such as Internet Explorer, scripting systems like the LWP toolkit that we've already seen, or "robots" used by search engines to download pages. If you are examining the content of this variable, remember to check the entire variable for information. The name *Mozilla*, which traditionally referred to any Netscape browser, is now used by any browser that is considered Netscape-compliant, including Internet Explorer.
HTTPS	Contains the string on if the request (and response) is being encoded using the HTTPS protocol.
LOCAL_ADDR	The IP address, in the format of a dotted quad, of the web server.

(Continued)

TABLE 9-1

(Continued)

Variable	Description
PATH_INFO	The path to the CGI script as requested by the browser. This is essentially the path element of the URL (without host or domain information).
PATH_TRANSLATED	The full path to the actual script being executed. Note that this will almost certainly differ from the value of PATH_INFO.
QUERY_STRING	The query string, used with GET requests.
REMOTE_ADDR	The IP address of the client.
REMOTE_HOST	The hostname of the client. This is a resolved name (based on a reverse lookup of the IP address) and not the name that the browser identifies itself with.
REQUEST_METHOD	The method of the CGI request. Generally PUT, POST, GET, or similar.
SCRIPT_NAME	The name of the script being accessed by the browser. May be different to the PATH_INFO due to redirection or aliasing. This will also be the strict script name, not the entire path element supplied.
SERVER_NAME	The hostname of the server.
SERVER_PORT	The port number used to access the server.
SERVER_PORT_SECURE	The port number used for secure communication (HTTPS).
SERVER_PROTOCOL	The protocol and version number used to supply the request and response information.
SERVER_SOFTWARE	A string relating to the server software in use.

Note that some elements that you may be used to do not exist under the Windows environment. Notably, the DOCUMENT_ROOT is not defined; you'll need to use the PATH_INFO or PATH_TRANSLATED.

The Common Gateway Interface

The Common Gateway Interface, or CGI, is a set of standards that define how information is exchanged between the web server and a script. In fact, web applications are often called *CGI scripts*, but don't make the mistake of calling a CGI script simply *CGI*. The term CGI refers to the standards and isn't the name of an application.

The part of the process you need to worry about at this stage is the transfer of information from the browser, through the web server, to the CGI script. The reason you need to accept information is to enable you to process information entered into an HTML form or when a URL consists of additional information, for example:

```
http://www.foo.bar/main.cgi?sessionid=974863-849764-87478
```

Here we have a single field, `sessionid`, that has some information attached to it. Both a form and a URL can supply information to a script, and you need to be able to parse both forms.

When the user clicks on the Send button, the information will be transferred to the web server and then on to the CGI script. The CGI script to be used is defined within the HTML definition for the form. The information is transferred using one of two main methods, `GET` and `POST`. The difference between the two methods is directly attributable to how the information is transferred. With the `GET` method, the information is placed into the `QUERY_STRING` environment variable, and with the `POST` method, the information is sent to the standard input of the application that has been called. Other methods are supported for transferring information, but these are the main two that are used.

There are advantages and disadvantages to both methods. The `GET` method supports two ways of transferring information from the client. With `GET`, you can supply information either through HTML forms or through the use of an extended URL. If you remember, back at the start of this chapter we looked at the following URL:

```
http://www.foo.bar/main.cgi?sessionid=974863-849764-87478
```

The `main.cgi` is the name of a script, and the question mark indicates the start of the information that you want to supply to the script. This has major benefits because you can generate new URLs and include the information as links in normal HTML pages rather than using multiple forms. The limitation is that the `GET` method has a limited transfer size. Although there is officially no limit, most people try to keep `GET` method requests down to less than 1 KB (1024 bytes). Also note that because the information is placed into an environment variable, your OS might have limits on the size of either individual environment variables or the environment space as a whole.

The `POST` method has no such limitation. You can transfer as much information as you like within a `POST` request without fear of any truncation along the way. However, you cannot use a `POST` request to process an extended URL. For the POST method, the QUERY_LENGTH environment variable contains the length of the query supplied, and it can be used to ensure that you read the right amount of information from the standard input.

No matter how the data is supplied to the script, both methods use the same basic format. The information is supplied as name/value pairs, separated by ampersands (&). Each name/value pair is then also separated by an equal sign. For example, the following query string shows two fields, first and last:

```
first=Martin&last=Brown
```

Splitting these fields up is easy within Perl. You can use split to do the hard work for you and first split the name/value pairs, then convert the pairs into keys and values within a hash.

One final note, though, is that many of the characters you may take for granted are encoded so that the URL is not misinterpreted. Imagine what would happen if my name contained an ampersand or equal sign!

The encoding, like other elements, is very simple. It uses a percent sign, followed by a two-digit hex string that defines the ASCII character code for the character in question. So the string Martin Brown would be translated into

```
Martin%20Brown
```

where 20 is the hexadecimal code for ASCII character 32, the space. You may also find that spaces are encoded using a single + sign—the example that follows accounts for both formats.

Armed with all this information, you can use something like the following init_cgi function to access the information supplied by a browser. The function supports both GET and POST requests:

```
sub init_cgi
{
    my $length = $ENV{QUERY_LENGTH};
    my $query = $ENV{QUERY_STRING};
    my (@assign);

    if (defined($query))
    {
        @assign = split('&',$query);
    }
    elsif (defined($length) and $length > 0 )
    {
        sysread(STDIN, $_, $length);
        chomp;
```

```
        @assign = split('&');
    }
    foreach (@assign)
    {
        my ($name,$value) = split /=/;
        $value =~ tr/+/ /;
        $value =~ s/%([a-fA-F0-9][a-fA-F0-9])/pack("C", hex($1))/eg;
        if (defined($formlist{$name}))
        {
            $formlist{$name} .= ",$value";
        }
        else
        {
            $formlist{$name} = $value;
        }
    }
}
```

The steps are straightforward, and they follow the description. First of all, you access the query string, either by getting the value of the QUERY_STRING environment variable or by accepting input up to the length specified in QUERY_LENGTH, from standard input using the sysread function. Note that you must use this method rather than the <STDIN> operator because you want to ensure that you read in the entire contents, irrespective of any line termination. HTML forms provide multiline text-entry fields, and using a line input operator could lead to unexpected results.

Also, it's possible to transfer binary information using a POST method, and any form of line processing might produce a garbled response. Finally, it acts as a security check. Many denial of service attacks prey on the fact that a script accepts an unlimited amount of information while also tricking the server into believing that the query length is small or even unspecified. If you arbitrarily imported all the information provided, you could easily lock up a small server.

Once you have obtained the query string, you split it by an ampersand into the @assign array and then process each field/value pair in turn. For convenience, you place the information into a hash. The keys of the hash become the field names, and the corresponding values become the values as supplied by the browser. The most important trick here is the line

```
$value =~ s/%([a-fA-F0-9][a-fA-F0-9])/pack("C", hex($1))/eg;
```

This uses the functional replacement to a standard regular expression to decode the %xx characters in the query into their correct values.

To encode the information back into the URL format within your script, the best solution is to use the URI::Escape module by Gisle Aas.

This provides a function `uri_escape` for converting a string into its URL escaped equivalent. You can also use the `uri_unescape` to convert it back.

Using the above function, you can write a simple Perl script that reports the information provided to it by either method:

```
#!/usr/local/bin/perl -w

print "Content-type: text/html\n\n";

init_cgi();
print("Form length is: ", scalar keys %formlist, "<br>\n");

for my $key (sort keys %formlist)
{
    print "Key $key = $formlist{$key}<br>\n";
}
```

If you place this on a server and supply it a URL such as the following:

```
http://www.mcwords.com/cgi/test.cgi?first=Martin&last=Brown
```

the browser window reports this back:

```
Form length is: 2
Key first = Martin
Key last = Brown
```

Of course, most scripts do other things besides printing the information back. Either they format the data and send it on in an e-mail, or search a database, or perform a myriad of other tasks. What has been demonstrated here is how to extract the information supplied via either method into a suitable hash structure that you can use within Perl. How you use the information depends on what you are trying to achieve.

The process detailed here has been duplicated many times in a number of different modules. The best solution though is to use the facilities provided by the standard `CGI` module. This comes with the standard Perl distribution and should be your first point of call for developing web applications. We'll be taking a closer look at the `CGI` module later in this chapter.

HTTP Headers

The HTTP header is used to supply information back to the browser in relation to the file that is being sent back to the browser. HTTP header information can include detail on the file format, length, modification dates, and cookie data.

The HTTP header information is returned as follows:

```
Field: data
```

The case of the `Field` name is important, but otherwise, you can use as much white space as you like between the colon and the field data. A sample list of HTTP header fields is shown in Table 9-2.

TABLE 9-2

HTTP header fields.

Field	Meaning
Allow	A comma-delimited list of the HTTP request methods supported by the requested resource (script or program). Scripts generally support GET and POST; other methods include HEAD, POST, DELETE, LINK, and UNLINK.
Content-Encoding	The encoding used in the message body. Currently the only supported formats are Gzip and Compress. If you want to encode data this way, make sure you check the value of HTTP_ACCEPT_ENCODING from the environment variables.
Content-type	A MIME string defining the format of the file being returned.
Content-length	The length, in bytes, of the data being returned. The browser uses this value to report the estimated download time for a file.
Date	The date and time the message is sent. It should be in the format 01 Jan 1998 12:00:00 GMT. The time zone should be GMT for reference purposes; the browser can calculate the difference for its local time zone if it has to.
Expires	The date the information becomes invalid. This should be used by the browser to decide when a page needs to be refreshed.
Last-modified	The date of last modification of the resource.
Location	The URL that should be returned instead of the URL requested.
MIME-version	The version of the MIME protocol supported.
Server	The web server application and version number.
Title	The title of the resource.
URI	The URI that should be returned instead of the requested one.

The only field required when returning information is the Content-type, which must identify the format of the file you are returning. If you do not specify anything, the browser assumes you are sending back preformatted raw text, not HTML. The definition of the file format is by a MIME string. MIME is short for Multipurpose Internet Mail Extensions and is a slash-separated string that defines the raw format and a subformat within it. For example, text/html says the information returned is plain text, using HTML as a file format. Mac users will be familiar with the concept of file owners and types, and this is the basic model employed by MIME.

Other examples include application/pdf, which states that the file type is application (and therefore binary) and that the file's format is PDF, the Adobe Acrobat file format. (PDF stands for Portable Document Format.) Others you might be familiar with are image/gif, which states that the file is a GIF (Graphics Interchange Format) image file, and application/zip, which is a file compressed using the Zip algorithm.

This MIME information is used by the browser to decide how to process the file. Most browsers will have a mapping that says they deal with files of type image/gif so that you can place graphical files within a page. They may also have an entry for application/pdf, which either calls an external application to open the received file or passes the file to a plug-in that optionally displays the file to the user. For example, here's an extract from the file supplied by default with the Apache web server:

```
application/mac-binhex40          hqx
application/mac-compactpro        cpt
application/macwriteii
application/msword                doc
application/news-message-id
application/news-transmission
application/octet-stream          bin dms lha lzh exe class
application/oda                   oda
application/pdf                   pdf
application/postscript            ai eps ps
application/powerpoint            ppt
application/remote-printing
application/rtf                   rtf
application/slate
application/wita
application/wordperfect5.1
application/x-bcpio               bcpio
application/x-cdlink              vcd
application/x-compress
application/x-cpio                cpio
application/x-csh                 csh
application/x-director            dcr dir dxr
```

It's important to realize the significance of this one, seemingly innocent field. Without it, your browser will not know how to process the information it receives. Normally the web server sends the MIME type back to the browser, and it uses a lookup table that maps MIME strings to the file extensions shown in the list above. Thus, when a browser requests image.gif, the server sends back a Content-type field value of image/gif. Since a script is executed by the server rather than sent back verbatim to the browser, it must supply this information itself.

Here's an example of a script that makes use of the Content-type field to supply back a file based on its extension:

```perl
#!/usr/local/bin/perl5

use CGI;

my %mimetypes;
my $file_directory = "C:/download";

init_mime('mime.types');

my $filename = param('filename');

unless(defined($filename))
{
    respond("Error: Didn't get the info I was expecting");
}

respond("Error: File $filename isn't valid")
    if ($filename =~ /[!|\/\\$()]/);
my ($filext) = ($filename =~ /\.(.*)$/);

defined($mimetypes{$filext}) ?
    send_file($filename,$mimetypes{$filext}) :
    send_file($filename,'application/octet-stream');

sub init_mime()
{
    my ($file) = @_;
    open(MIME,"<$file")
        or respond('Error: Couldnt get any mime types');
    while(<MIME>)
    {
        next if (/^\#/);
        next if (length eq 0);
        my ($mime,@ext) = split(/\s+/);
        for my $ext (@ext)
        {
            $mimetypes{$ext} = $mime;
        }
    }
    close(MIME);
}

sub send_file
{
    my ($filename,$mimetype) = @_;
    my $buffer;
```

```
        open(FILE,"<$file_directory/$filename")
            or respond("Error: Can't find file");
        print "Content-type: $mimetype\n\n";
        while(sysread(FILE,$buffer,1024))
        {
            print $buffer;
        }
        close(FILE);
}

sub respond
{
    my $message = shift;
    print "Content-type: text/html\n\n";
    show_debug();
    print <<EOF;
<head>
<title>$message</title>
</head>
<body>
$message
</body>
EOF
        exit;
}
```

Other fields in Table 9-2 are optional but also have useful applications. The Location field can be used to automatically redirect a user to an alternative page. The existence of the Location field automatically instructs the browser to load the URL contained in the field's value. Here's another script that uses the earlier init_cgi function and the Location HTTP field to point a user in a different direction:

```
#!/usr/local/bin/perl
my %formlist;

sub init_cgi
{
    my $length = $ENV{QUERY_LENGTH};
    my $query = $ENV{QUERY_STRING};
    my (@assign);

    if (defined($query))
    {
        @assign = split('&',$query);
    }
    elsif (defined($length) and $length > 0 )
    {
        sysread(STDIN, $_, $length);
        chomp;
        @assign = split('&');
    }
    foreach (@assign)
    {
        my ($name,$value) = split /=/;
```

```
                           $value =~ tr/+/ /;
                           $value =~ s/%([a-fA-F0-9][a-fA-F0-9])/pack("C", hex($1))/eg;
                           if (defined($formlist{$name}))
                           {
                               $formlist{$name} .= ",$value";
                           }
                           else
                           {
                               $formlist{$name} = $value;
                           }
                   }
           }

           respond("Error: No URL specified")
               unless(defined($formlist{url}));

           open(LOG,">/usr/local/http/logs/jump.log")
               or respond("Error: A config error has occurred");

           print LOG (scalar(localtime(time)),
                       " $ENV{REMOTE_ADDR} $formlist{url}\n");
           close(LOG)
               or respond("Error: A config error has occurred");

           print "Location: $formlist{url}\n\n";

           sub respond
           {
               my $message = shift;
               print "Content-type: text/html\n\n";
               show_debug();
               print <<EOF;
           <head>
           <title>$message</title>
           </head>
           <body>
           $message
           </body>
           EOF
               exit;
           }
```

This is actually a version of a script used on a number of sites I have developed that allows you to keep a log of when a user clicks onto a foreign page. For example, you might have links on a page to another site, and you want to be able to record how many people visit this other site from your page. Instead of using a normal link within your HTML document, you could use the following CGI script:

```
<a href="/cgi/redirect.pl?url=http://www.mcwords.com">MCwords</a>
```

Every time users click on this link, they will still visit the new site, but you'll have a record of their leap off of your site.

The CGI Module

The CGI module is included with all Perl distributions and fills the two basic gaps that we've already discussed: parsing CGI requests and generating HTTP headers. The CGI module also provides functions that allow you to generate HTML in a pragmatic form that is generally more reliable than outputting your own text from within the Perl script.

We already know how to parse CGI information to extract the individual fields and data. The CGI module does the processing for us and makes the information available via a function that will return the info for a field on request. It also goes one stage further than the sample function above—fields that potentially contain more than one piece of information (checkboxes, list boxes, etc.) are available and return arrays rather than scalar values.

When outputting HTTP headers, the CGI module also supports a more pragmatic approach than the usual method of using print to output the HTTP header. Instead, there are a series of functions that output the base header and also allow you to embed cookie replies, redirections, and other information during the return of the header data.

Generating your own HTML and writing your own processing routines has its downsides. When it comes to HTML production, even the slightest imperfection in your code can cause problems. To give a classic example, one of the most popular HTML failures is caused by neglecting to add a </table> tag when generating tables. This not only fails to display the table but also the rest of the HTML in the file.

In addition to these features, the module also supports some of the more advanced features of CGI scripting. These include the support for uploading files via HTTP from the browser and supporting the parsing and generation of cookies—something we'll look at later in this chapter. For the designers among you, the CGI module also supports cascading style sheets and frames. Finally, it supports server push—a technology that allows a server to send new data to a client at periodic intervals. This is useful for pages and especially images that need to be updated. This has largely been superseded by the client-side RELOAD directive, but it still has its uses.

Let's look at an example that uses the main features of the CGI module. In this case, the script can be used for converting roman numerals into integer decimal numbers using the following script. It not only builds and produces the HTML form, but it also provides a method for processing the information supplied when the user fills in and submits the form.

```
#!/usr/local/bin/perl -w

use CGI qw/:standard/;

print header,
     start_html('Roman Numerals Conversion'),
     h1('Roman Numeral Converter'),
     start_form,
     "What's the Roman Numeral number?",
     textfield('roman'),p,
     submit,
     end_form,p,hr,p;

if (param())
{
    print(h3('The value is ',parse_roman(uc(param('roman')))),p,hr);
}

sub parse_roman
{
    $_ = shift;
    my %roman = ('I' => 1,
                 'V' => 5,
                 'X' => 10,
                 'L' => 50,
                 'C' => 100,
                 'D' => 500,
                 'M' => 1000,
                 );
    my @roman = qw/M D C L X V I/;
    my @special = qw/CM CD XC XL IX IV/;
    my $result = 0;

    return 'Invalid numerals' unless(m/[IVXLXDM]+/);

    foreach $special (@special)
    {
        if (s/$special//)
        {
            $result += $roman{substr($special,1,1)}
                          - $roman{substr($special,0,1)};
        }
    }
    foreach $roman (@roman)
    {
        $result += $roman{$roman} while s/$roman//;
    }
    return $result;
}
```

The first part of the script prints a form using the functional interface to the CGI module. It provides a simple text entry box, which you then supply to the parse_roman function to produce an integer value. If the user has provided some information, you use the param function to check this; the information is printed after a new form has been provided. You can see what a sample screen looks like in Figure 9-1.

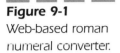

Figure 9-1

Web-based roman
numeral converter.

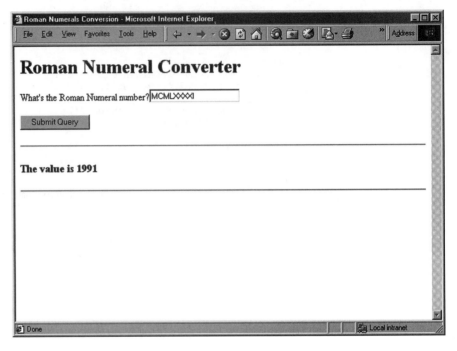

Because you are using the functional interface, you have to specify the routines or sets of routines that you want to import. The main set is :standard, which is what is used in this script. Other import sets define the functions exported by the module. They are logically grouped by either HTML standards or the information they process. For example, the form set imports functions suitable for form processing. Supported import sets are shown in Table 9-3.

Let's look a bit more closely at that page builder:

```
print header,
      start_html('Roman Numerals Conversion'),
      h1('Roman Numeral Converter'),
      start_form,
      "What's the Roman Numeral number?",
      textfield('roman'),p,
      submit,
      end_form,p,hr,p;
```

The print function is used, since that's how you report information back to the user. The header function produces the HTTP header. You can supply additional arguments to this function to configure other elements of the header, just as if you were doing it normally. You can also

TABLE 9-3

*CGI module import
sets.*

Import Set	Exported Symbols/Symbol Sets
html2	h1 h2 h3 h4 h5 h6 p br hr ol ul li dl dt dd menu code var strong em tt u i b blockquote pre img a address cite samp dfn html head base body Link nextid title meta kbd start_html end_html input Select option comment
html3	div table caption th td TR Tr sup sub strike applet Param embed basefont style span layer ilayer font frameset frame script small big
netscape	blink fontsize center
form	Textfield textarea filefield password_field hidden checkbox checkbox_group submit reset defaults radio_group popup_menu button autoEscape scrolling_list image_button start_form end_form start-form endform start_multipart_form isindex tmpFileName uploadInfo URL_ENCODED MULTIPART
cgi	param path_info path_translated url self_url script_name cookie dump raw_cookie request_method query_string accept user_agent remote_host remote_addr referer server_name server_software server_port server_protocol virtual_host remote_ident auth_type http use_named_parameters save_parameters restore_parameters param_fetch remote_user user_name header redirect import_names put Delete Delete_all url_param
ssl	https
cgi-lib	ReadParse PrintHeader HtmlTop HtmlBot SplitParam
html	html2 html3 netscape
standard	html2 html3 form cgi
push	Multipart_init multipart_start multipart_end
all	html2 html3 netscape form cgi internal

supply a single argument that defines the MIME string for the information you are sending back. For example:

```
print header('text/html');
```

If you don't specify a value, the text/html value is used by default. The remainder of the lines use functions to introduce HTML tagged text. You start with start_html, which starts an HTML document. In this case it takes a single argument—the page title. This returns the following string:

```
<HTML><HEAD><TITLE>Roman Numerals Conversion</TITLE>
</HEAD><BODY>
```

This introduces the page title and sets the header and body style. The `h1` function formats the supplied text in the header level-one style.

The `start_form` function initiates an HTML form. By default, it assumes you are using the same script; this is an HTML/browser feature, rather than a Perl CGI feature, and the `textfield` function inserts a simple text field. The argument supplied defines the name of the field as it will be sent to the script when the Submit button is pressed.

To specify additional fields to the HTML field definition, you pass the function a hash, where each key of the hash should be a hyphen-prefixed field name. Therefore, you could rewrite the preceding code as

```
textfield(-name => 'roman')
```

Other fields might include `-size` for the size of the text field on screen and `-maxlength` for the maximum number of characters accepted in a field.

Other possible HTML field types are `textarea`, for a large multiline text box, or `popup_menu`, for a menu field that pops up and provides a list of values when clicked. You can also use `scrolling_list` for a list of values in a scrolling box, as well as checkboxes and radio buttons with the `checkbox_group` and `radio_group` functions.

Returning to the example script, the `submit` function provides a simple Submit button for sending the request to the server, and finally the `end_form` function indicates the end of the form within the HTML text. The remaining functions `p` and `hr` insert a paragraph break and horizontal rule, respectively.

This information is printed out for every invocation of the script. The `param` function is used to check whether any fields were supplied to the script, either by a GET or POST method. It returns an array of valid field names supplied, for example:

```
@fields = param();
```

Since any list in a scalar context returns the number of elements in the list, this is a safe way of detecting whether any information was provided. The same function is then used to extract the values from the fields specified. In the example, there is only one field—roman—which contains the roman numeral string entered by the user.

The `parse_roman` function then does all the work of parsing the string and translating the roman numerals into integer values. I'll leave it up to the reader to determine how this function works.

This concludes our brief look into the use of the `CGI` module for speeding up and improving the overall processing of producing and parsing the information supplied on a form. Admittedly, it makes the process significantly easier. Just look at the previous examples to see the complications involved in writing a non-`CGI` module-based script.

Cookies

A *cookie* is a small discrete piece of information used to store information within a web browser. The cookie itself is stored on the client end rather than server end, and it can therefore be used to store state information between individual accesses by the browser, either in the same session or across a number of sessions. In its simplest form, a cookie might just store your name; in a more complex system, it provides login and password information for a website. This can be used by web designers to provide customized pages to individual users.

In other systems, cookies are used to store the information about the products you have chosen in web-based stores. The cookie then acts as your "shopping basket," storing information about your products and other selections.

In either case, the creation of a cookie and how you access the information stored in a cookie are server-based requests, since it's the server that uses the information to provide the customized web page, or that updates the selected products stored in your web basket. There is a limit to the size of cookie, and it varies from browser to browser. In general, a cookie shouldn't need to be more than 1024 bytes, but some browsers will support sizes as large as 16,384 bytes, and sometimes even more.

A cookie is formatted much like a CGI form field data stream. The cookie is composed of a series of field/value pairs separated by ampersands, with each field/value additionally separated by an equal sign. The content of the cookie is exchanged between the server and client when the client requests a URL. The server sends the cookie updates back as part of the HTTP headers, and the browser sends the current cookie contents as part of its request to the server.

Besides the field/value pairs, a cookie has a number of additional attributes. These are an expiration time, a domain, a path, and an optional secure flag. Attributes are as follows:

1. The expiration time is used by the browser to determine when the cookie should be deleted from its own internal list. As long as the expiration time has not been reached, the cookie will be sent back to the correct server each time you access a page from that server.

2. The definition of a valid server is stored within the domain attribute. This is a partial or complete domain name for the server that should be sent to the cookie. For example, if the value of the domain attribute is `.foo.com`, then any server within the foo.com domain will be sent the cookie data for each access.

3. The path is a similar partial match against a path within the web server. For example, a path of `/cgi-bin` means that the cookie data will only be sent with any requests starting with that path. Normally, you would specify `/` to have the cookie sent to all CGI scripts, but you might want to restrict the cookie data so it is only sent to scripts starting with `/cgi-public`, but not to `/cgi-private`.

4. The secure attribute restricts the browser from sending the cookie to unsecure links. If set, cookie data will only be transferred over secure connections, such as those provided by SSL (Secure Sockets Layer).

The best interface is to use the `CGI` module, which provides a simple functional interface for updating and accessing cookie information. For example, you can create a cookie like this:

```
$cookie = cookie(-name => 'SiteCookie',
                 -value => \%webvalues,
                 -expires => '+24h',
                 -path => '/',
                 -domain => '.foo.com'
                );
```

If you update the values of the cookie, then it must be supplied back to the user as part of the HTTP header, like this:

```
print header(-cookie => $cookie);
```

To access the values, call the `cookie` function without the `-values` argument:

```
my %cookie_values = cookie(-name => 'SiteCookie');
```

What you store and use the cookie for is entirely up to you. Most people employ cookies as a way of identifying people on the site without them having to log in. The complicated part—communicating cookie information between the script and browser—is handled through the CGI module.

Debugging and Testing CGI Applications

Although it sounds like an impossible task, sometimes you need to test a script without requiring or using a browser and web server. Certainly, if you switch warnings ON and use the strict pragma, your script may well die before reporting any information to the browser if Perl finds any problems. This can be a problem if you don't have access to the error logs on the web server, which is where the information will be recorded.

You may even find yourself in a situation where you do not have privileges or even the software to support a web service on which to do your testing. Any or all of these situations require another method for supplying a query to a CGI script and alternative ways of extracting and monitoring error messages from your scripts.

The simplest method is to supply the information that would ordinarily be supplied to the script via a browser using a more direct method. Because you know the information can be supplied to the script via an environment variable, all you have to do is create the environment variable with a properly formatted string in it. For example, you might use the following within a DOS prompt:

```
set QUERY_STRING=first=Martin&last=Brown
```

This is easy if the query data is simple, but what if the information needs to be escaped because of special characters? In this instance, the easiest thing is to grab a GET-based URL from the browser, or get the script to print a copy of the escaped query string, and then assign that to the environment variable. Still, this is not an ideal solution.

Alternatively, if you use the init_cgi function from earlier in this chapter, or the CGI module, you can supply the field name/value pairs as a string to the standard input. Both will wait for input from the keyboard before continuing if no environment query string has been set. However, this method still doesn't get around the problem of escaping characters and sequences, and it can be quite tiresome for scripts that expect a large amount of input.

All of these methods assume that you cannot (or do not want to) make modifications to the script. If you are willing to make modifications, then it's easier, and sometimes clearer, just to assign sample values to the form variables directly. For example, using the `init_cgi` function:

```
$formlist{name} = 'MC';
```

Or, if you are using the `CGI` module, then you need to use the `param` function to set the values. You can either use a simple functional call with arguments, such as this:

```
param('name','MC');
```

or you can use the hash format:

```
param(-name => 'name', -value => 'MC');
```

Just remember to unset these hard-coded values before you use the script; otherwise, you may have trouble using the script effectively.

For monitoring errors there are a number of methods available. The most obvious is to use `print` statements to output debugging information (remember that you can't use `warn`) as part of the HTML page. If you decide to do it this way, remember to output the errors *after* the HTTP header; otherwise, you'll get garbled information. In practice, your scripts should be outputting the HTTP header as early as possible anyway.

Another alternative is to use `warn`, and in fact `die`, as usual, but redirect `STDERR` to a log file. If you are running the script from the command line under Unix using one of the preceding techniques, you can do this just by using the normal redirection operators within the shell. For example:

```
C:\> roman.cgi 2>roman.err
```

You can also do this within the script by restating the association of `STDERR` with a call to the `open` function:

```
open(STDERR, ">error.log") or die "Couldn't append to log file";
```

Note that you don't have to do any tricks here with reassigning the old `STDERR` to point elsewhere; you just want `STDERR` to point to a static file.

One final piece of advice: If you decide to use this method in a production system, remember to print out additional information with the report so that you can start to isolate the problem. In particular, consider stacking up the errors in an array just using a simple push call, and then call a function right at the end of the script to dump out the date, time, and error log, along with the values of the environment variables. I've used a function similar to the one below to dump out the information at the end of the CGI script. The @errorlist array is used within the bulk of the CGI script to store the error lines:

```
sub error_report
{
    open (ERRORLOG, ">error.log") or die "Fatal: Can't open log $!";
    $old = select ERROR;
    if (@errorlist)
    {
        print scalar localtime,"\n\n";
        print "Environment:\n";
        foreach (sort %ENV)
        {
            print "$_ = $ENV{$_}\n";
        }
        print "\nErrors:\n";
        print join "\n",@errorlist;
    }
    select $old;
}
```

That should cover most of the bases for any errors that might occur. Remember to try and be as quick as possible though—the script is providing a user interface, and the longer users have to wait for any output, the less likely they are to appreciate the work the script is doing. I've seen some, for example, that post information on to other scripts and websites, and even some that attempt to send e-mail with the errors in. These can cause both delays and problems of their own. You need something as plain and simple as the print statements and an external file to ensure reliability; otherwise, you end up trying to account for and report errors in more and more layers of interfaces.

Developing with Perl for ISAPI/WSAPI

Perl for ISAPI is an extension for executing Perl scripts under web servers that support the Microsoft Internet Server Application Programming Interface, hence, ISAPI. ISAPI provides the necessary interface and extensions for supporting the CGI protocol used to exchange information between the client, the web server, and external scripts accessed through the browser.

The main benefit of ISAPI-based extensions is that functionality is loaded through a DLL rather than calling an external program. The DLL is located within the server's process space, so there's no need to allocate more memory or start a new process. Creating a new thread and executing Perl within that thread is a time-consuming process, and it also introduces overheads when you have to pass large volumes of data between the web server and the CGI script that you want to use.

The Perl for WSAPI is a similar solution, but it supports O'Reilly's WebSite Professional web server, rather than IIS-compliant web servers. In all respects, the two solutions work the same, with both offering significant speed and memory advantages over using Perl as an external CGI component.

Perl for ISAPI comes free with the standard ActivePerl package and should have been installed when you installed the ActivePerl package.

Programming with ISAPI

From a programming perspective, there is no difference between writing a normal CGI script and writing an ISAPI-compliant script. You can use exactly the same modules and extensions, and you can use the same techniques to extract form data and communicate information back to the user.

That said, there is one major difference regarding the naming of files. When you install ActivePerl, you will be asked whether you want to associate a particular extension with Perl for ISAPI scripts. The default is *.plx*, and the web server will automatically use CGI scripts with a *.plx* extension via the Perl for ISAPI DLL. Scripts that have a standard *.pl* extension will continue to be executed using the normal external Perl application.

You can change the configuration of the extensions and the use of Perl for ISAPI by changing the application mappings within IIS. If you want Perl scripts to be executed as a normal external application, then within the Application Extension Mapping dialog, use the full path to the Perl binary followed by %s %s, for example:

```
C:\Perl\bin\perl.exe %s %s
```

You can then set whatever extension you like to be mapped against the Perl application. The first %s is replaced by the full path to the script, and the second %s contains the script parameters. The ActivePerl installer uses *.pl* as a default, but you can use anything you like—*.cgi* is common on many hosted services.

If you want to use Perl for ISAPI then use the following line:

```
C:\Perl\bin\perlis.dll
```

Note that you don't need the arguments to the Perl for ISAPI DLL. Information about the script and its arguments are passed internally to the function exported by the Perl DLL. Again, assign the extension you want to use for Perl for ISAPI scripts. The default is *.plx*, and it should have been set up when you first installed ActivePerl.

Environment Variables

The environment variables under Perl for ISAPI are slightly different from those available under standard Perl CGI scripts. For a start, most of the environmental variables used to exchange information between the web server and the CGI script will appear to be nonexistent. If you try running the following script as a Perl for ISAPI script:

```
print "Content-type: text/html\n\n";

foreach $key (sort keys %ENV)
{
    print "$key: $ENV{$key}<br>\n";
}
```

you'll get a much reduced environment list:

```
ALLUSERSPROFILE: C:\Documents and Settings\All Users
COMMONPROGRAMFILES: C:\Program Files\Common Files
COMPUTERNAME: INCONTINENT
COMSPEC: C:\WINNT\system32\cmd.exe
NUMBER_OF_PROCESSORS: 1
OS: Windows_NT
OS2LIBPATH: C:\WINNT\system32\os2\dll;
PATH: C:\Perl\bin;C:\WINNT\system32;C:\WINNT;C:\WINNT\System32\Wbem
PATHEXT: .COM;.EXE;.BAT;.CMD;.VBS;.VBE;.JS;.JSE;.WSF;.WSH
PROCESSOR_ARCHITECTURE: x86
PROCESSOR_IDENTIFIER: x86 Family 6 Model 3 Stepping 3, GenuineIntel
PROCESSOR_LEVEL: 6
PROCESSOR_REVISION: 0303
PROGRAMFILES: C:\Program Files
SYSTEMDRIVE: C:
```

```
SYSTEMROOT: C:\WINNT
TEMP: C:\WINNT\TEMP
TMP: C:\WINNT\TEMP
USERPROFILE: C:\Documents and Settings\Default User
WINDIR: C:\WINNT
```

In fact, Perl for ISAPI doesn't populate the %ENV hash properly, but it does actually return information about specific environment variables when accessed. For example, the REQUEST_METHOD key will return the correct information. Unfortunately, the lack of a properly populated environment can make debugging difficult, so you will need to check for specific keys within the hash for the information you require.

There is one significant addition to the environment, however. The PERLXS key returns the environment under which the script is running. If the script is running as a normal CGI program, then the key does not exist, but under Perl for ISAPI the corresponding value contains PerlIS, and under Perl for WSAPI, it contains PerlWS.

Directories and Pathnames

When using Perl for ISAPI you cannot always be assured that there is a "current" directory, and therefore, using relative pathnames within your script should be avoided. However, under IIS 4.0 and above, the PATH_TRANSLATED environment variable should contain the full path to the script. This is the expanded version of the PATH_INFO variable, which contains the path accessed.

Threads and Extensions

Not all extensions available for Perl are written to be thread-safe. For standalone applications, this is not a serious consideration, and it therefore does affect scripts that are run as normal CGI scripts. However, scripts run through the PerlIS interface do potentially have problems, especially as it's highly likely that the script will be run a number of times simultaneously.

The problem arises because PerlIS loads DLLs and the scripts into the same memory space (which is where most of the speed improvement lies). Because some DLLs are not thread-aware, they use a global variable to store a piece of information. For example, imagine a DLL that stores the error number for the previous error in a global variable. If you have two scripts using the DLL, they will both access the same error variable—even though one script's function call may have worked and the other script's call failed.

The problem only affects Win32 extensions that make their own calls through DLLs to the Windows subsystems. The situation has improved recently. Most Windows DLLs are thread-compliant (since Windows itself is thread-based), and ActivePerl is now thread-compliant. Therefore, developing thread-safe scripts has become significantly easier.

If you are concerned about a script, or you are having problems with a particular script, then use Perl in its CGI rather PerlIS form to execute the problem script.

Spawning External Programs

Because Perl for ISAPI runs as a thread within the web server process and not as a separate process with its own threads, there can be potential problems spawning new applications directly from a Perl for ISAPI script. This is because you are attempting to load a program within the scope of the Web server's memory space (since it will be a child of the Perl script, which is in turn a thread of the web server).

Since you can do most things within the confines of Perl, this won't always be a problem. However, if you are worried about the need to call an external program, then use the Perl CGI rather than PerlIS DLL for executing that script.

PerlEx

PerlEx is an additional, chargeable extension from ActiveState that goes one stage further than PerlIS when it comes to improving the performance of your Perl scripts. When you access a normal Perl CGI script through your web server, the process goes something like this:

1. Start new process using Perl executable.
2. Perl compiles the script into the internal opcodes. (See "Compilation versus Interpretation" in Chapter 15 for more on opcodes.)
3. Perl executes the opcodes using the Perl virtual machine.

There are two bottlenecks here, the first is in Stage 1; loading a new copy of the Perl application each time you want to execute a Perl script is a time-consuming and resource-hungry endeavor. The second is in Stage 2; the process of compiling each script is relatively time-consuming as well.

PerlIS addresses the first problem by eliminating the need to load a Perl executable for each script. Instead, the Perl interpreter is loaded as a DLL into the same memory space as the web server. When you execute the script, the Perl interpreter is already loaded; the script only needs to be compiled and then executed.

PerlEx addresses the bottleneck at Stage 2. It's highly likely that for most sites the actual number of scripts is relatively small, but the number of times they are executed is quite high. Although the compilation time is relatively small—probably less than 10 percent of the total execution time of a script—when that same script is executed 10,000 times, you could be wasting hours of time each day recompiling the same static script.

PerlEx eliminates Stage 2. The first time the script is executed, it's stored in its compiled state, so that the next time the script is executed, the precompiled version is used. By eliminating Stages 1 and 2 of the execution process, you can improve the speed of your scripts by a claimed 48x.

PerlScript

PerlScript is an extension that comes with the standard ActivePerl distribution that exposes Perl as an ActiveX scripting engine, in the same way as VBScript, JavaScript, and others are exported. By using PerlScript, you can produce HTML pages that make use of server pages (ASP) while using the Perl language. PerlScript—through ActiveX—is supported on the server side by Microsoft's IIS 3.0 and higher or the Peer Web Services web server. For client-side scripting, PerlScript is available both within Internet Explorer and Windows Scripting Host (WSH), which is a scriptable component of 32-bit Windows operating systems. It's WSH that provides support for the Active Desktop built into recent versions of Internet Explorer.

ActiveX/ASP Introduction

For those people who have not used ASP scripting before, the path to script development is slightly different. For a start, you embed the scripting language and commands straight into the content of the web page. The Perl script is not a separate entity; instead, it becomes part of the HTML.

When the page is being served by a web server that supports ASP, the page is parsed and any scripted component executed via the correspon-ding scripting language. The interpreter is active for the entire page—so you can embed statements into the HTML at a number of points within the script. The resulting HTML page (with the script elements removed but merged with any output that the script produced) is then sent to the browser. The user need never know that they are accessing a page parsed by Perl. In fact, the only indication is that the page normally has an extension of *.asp*. We'll look at using server-side scripting shortly.

For client-side scripting, you can either supply the page from a web server or open the page locally. WSH or Internet Explorer will then parse the page and display it. The real difference is that the interpreter is active for the entire duration that the page is open within the browser. You can attach Perl functions to buttons and other elements, and the corresponding Perl code will be executed. This allows you to process forms and offer veri-fication using Perl within the page, without having to communicate with a web server. We'll be using the same basic script, only converted for client-side scripting, to demonstrate this effect later in this chapter.

In the remainder of this chapter, we'll be concentrating on how PerlScript can be used for ASP programming, but we won't look in detail at the vagaries of ASP. For an all-around guide to developing ASP scripts, consider the *Instant ASP Scripts*, by Greg Buczek (McGraw-Hill, 1999).

Migrating from VBScript to PerlScript

PerlScript exposes itself in an almost identical fashion to VBScript. However, instead of the normal VBScript objects, you need to use Perl scalar variables that point to those objects. You can see a list of the VBScript and corresponding PerlScript objects in Table 9-4.

Because the objects are standard Perl objects, you can access them as normal Perl objects. Instead of

```
Session("UserName")
```

use

```
$Session->{UserName}
```

TABLE 9-4

VBScript to
PerlScript
migration.

VBScript Object	PerlScript Object	Description
Session	$Session	Supports methods and properties relating to a specific visitor.
Response	$Response	Supports methods and properties for building a response to a user.
Request	$Request	Supports methods and properties that contain information about the request supplied by the client.
Server	$Server	Handles the creation of server components and server settings.
Application	$Application	Supports properties and methods for managing a web application, which is defined as a group of web pages.

For method calls, use:

```
$Session->Method();
```

Server-Side Scripting

In order to use server-side scripting, you must have ActivePerl and PerlScript installed on your server, but it is not required on the client side. As a general rule, ASP-based scripts operate in an identical fashion to a normal CGI script. The script is embedded within the HTML and parsed and executed before the final page is sent to the client. Pages that should be parsed by the ASP system should have the extension *.asp*.

To embed the script within your pages, you need to use one of two formats. The first uses an explicit tag:

```
<SCRIPT LANGUAGE = PerlScript RUNAT=Server>
...
</SCRIPT>
```

Note the classification of the language being used and the RUNAT option, which tells the web server that this code should be executed by the ASP host, not the client. This format is most useful when you want the script to act as an embedded CGI script with the script being executed once during the parsing of the page. The problem with these tags is that because they are individual start and end tags, embedding them within the HTML is more cumbersome and often makes the code look untidy, although it still functions in the same way.

The other method is to embed your script within <%...%> tags. The first call to these tags should name the language being used. Further script lines can be included just by using additional tags. For example:

```
<%@ LANGUAGE = PerlScript %>
<HTML>
<BODY>
<% $Response->write("Hello"); %>
</BODY>
</HTML>
```

In this instance we do not need to explicitly define the execution host; the use of <%...%> tags automatically implies server-side scripting.

The preceding example also demonstrates the other portion of server-side script—how the Perl script communicates back with the user. Unlike CGI scripts, you cannot use print, because there is no standard output for the embedding Perl interpreter. Instead, you must use the $Response object in combination with the write method to output the text that will be included in the page.

To actually get any information supplied in a request from the client, you need to access and parse the $Request object. The properties of this object include any client certificates, cookies, form elements, query strings (as normally supplied to a CGI), and any server variables that have been configured for this script or directory. The important one is the QueryString property. This contains three subproperties: Count, Item, and Key. The Count property contains the number of key/value pairs within the query string. The Item property contains the actual string. The Key property can be ignored. The format of the query string is identical to that supplied when using Perl as CGI, with key/value pairs separated by ampersands and the key and value separated by equal signs. See the init_cgi function earlier in this chapter for details on how to parse the contents into a hash.

As an example, here's the roman numerals converter written as ASP script:

```
<HTML>
<HEAD><TITLE>Roman Numerals Conversion</TITLE></HEAD>
<BODY BGCOLOR="#ffffff">
<Table>
<%@ LANGUAGE="PerlScript" %>
<%
my %param,$value;
```

```perl
if ($Request->{QueryString}->{Count})
{
    foreach $pair (split(/&/,$Request->{QueryString}->{Item}))
    {
        ($key, $val) = split(/=/,$pair);
        $param{$key} = $val;
    }
    $value = parse_roman($param{Input});
}

sub parse_roman
{
    $_ = uc($_[0]);

    my %roman = ('I' => 1,
                 'V' => 5,
                 'X' => 10,
                 'L' => 50,
                 'C' => 100,
                 'D' => 500,
                 'M' => 1000,
                 );
    my @roman = qw/M D C L X V I/;
    my @special = qw/CM CD XC XL IX IV/;
    my $result = 0;

    return 'Invalid numerals' unless(m/[IVXLXDM]+/);

    foreach $special (@special)
    {
        if (s/$special//)
        {
            $result += $roman{substr($special,1,1)}
                     - $roman{substr($special,0,1)};
        }
    }
    foreach $roman (@roman)
    {
        $result += $roman{$roman} while s/$roman//;
    }
    return $result;
}
%>
<Table>
<FORM ACTION="/www/romansrv.asp" Name="Roman">
<tr><td><b>Roman:</td><td><input name="Input" Type="Text"
  SIZE="24"></td></tr>
<tr><td><b>Decimal:</td><td><textarea rows=1 columns=24><%
  $Response->write($value); %></textarea></td></tr>
<tr><TD><INPUT TYPE="Submit" VALUE="Convert"></TD></tr>
</body>
</html>
```

The important parts here are the initial scripting element, which extracts the query string and parses it to obtain the roman numeral string to be converted, and the form at the bottom of the page. Because the Perl interpreter is used to parse all the scripting elements of the

Figure 9-2

Server-side roman numeral conversion with PerlScript.

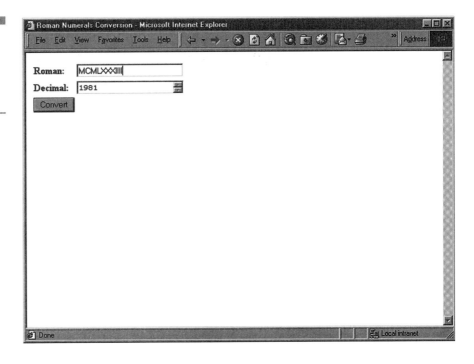

page, we can embed a single Perl statement to print out the converted value of the roman numeral string.

A sample window is shown in Figure 9-2.

Client-Side Perl Scripting

One of the more interesting elements of PerlScript is that it can also be used as a client-side scripting service. Since PerlScript exposes Perl as an ActiveX scripting engine, it can be used in any client that works as an ActiveX scripting host. In addition to IIS, this also includes Internet Explorer and the Windows Scripting Host. Unlike server-parsed scripts, however, the client must have ActivePerl and PerlScript installed, for the script to work. If you don't have them installed, the scriptable element will just be ignored by the browser.

Scripts that are embedded into pages that should be handled on the client side can have any extension. Since they are not parsed by the web server, they do not need a special extension. When actually embedding the script, you use the SCRIPT tag, but you don't qualify it as executing on the server side:

```
<SCRIPT LANGUAGE="PerlScript">
```

Normally, there is only one embedded script within the page, and it contains the hooks necessary to parse the information and format a suitable output page. More complex examples include an initial parsing section and then additional short sections to insert data parsed by the initial script into the HTML.

Field Communication   For most client-side script examples, you'll be using a form both to communicate with the user and also to communicate information back. Using the $Response->write() method will work, but it is often impractical, since you want the response to be placed back into a specific location.

You also need to obtain the information that the user has supplied by reading the information straight from the form. When you create a form and corresponding fields, all the different elements have names. The base object is $window and refers to the current browser or WSH window. Within the $window object you'll find window titles and other information, and most importantly the document object. This is the parsed version of the HTML document.

Within the document you can then access individual components. Forms are identified by their name, so we can access the form Roman using the following:

```
$form = $window->document->Roman;
```

Within the form, each field is accessible by its name, so to access a field called Input, and within the field object, you can obtain the configuration of the individual field. For input boxes, for instance, you can get or set the size and value by accessing the corresponding property. For example, to get the value of a field:

```
$source = $window->document->Roman->Input->{'Value'};
```

Other field types are available in the same way, and you can make any changes you like to the configuration of the form fields. To set a value, just use assignation to assign a value to the `Value` property:

```
$window->document->Roman->Input->{'Value'} = 99;
```

Button and Field Methods   To activate buttons, you use a different method. When you are creating a form field, the properties for that field can include the size and predefined value. In addition, there are a series of properties that specify the handlers for specific events. The events range from the click of a button to the pointer hovering over a specific field or other object. For example, to create an input field that uses a function to validate its content, you use the following:

```
<INPUT NAME="userName" onchange="validUserName(this.value)">
```

This explicitly names the function to be called when the contents of the field change.

There is also an implicit function that is called for certain events. For example, you do not need to explicitly define the function called when a button is pressed. Instead, just create a function with a suffix for the `onClick` event. For example:

```
sub Enter_onClick()
{
    $window->document->Roman->$form->Readout->{'Value'} = 99;
}
```

Some browsers define the function as `onclick`, so it's also a good idea to create a function that points to the real one:

```
sub Enter_onclick()
{
    Enter_onClick()
}
```

For more details on the abilities of embedded scripting and parsing, see the HTML documentation (available from http://www.w3c.org) or the Instant ASP Scripts book.

Roman Numerals Sample   Here's our familiar roman numerals example—only this time—it's written as a client-side script:

```
<HTML>
<HEAD><TITLE>Roman Numerals Conversion</TITLE></HEAD>
```

```perl
<BODY BGCOLOR="#ffffff">
<SCRIPT LANGUAGE="PerlScript">

sub parse_roman
{
    $_ = uc($_[0]);

    my %roman = ('I' => 1,
                 'V' => 5,
                 'X' => 10,
                 'L' => 50,
                 'C' => 100,
                 'D' => 500,
                 'M' => 1000,
                 );
    my @roman = qw/M D C L X V I/;
    my @special = qw/CM CD XC XL IX IV/;
    my $result = 0;

    return 'Invalid numerals' unless(m/[IVXLXDM]+/);

    foreach $special (@special)
    {
        if (s/$special//)
        {
            $result += $roman{substr($special,1,1)}
                        - $roman{substr($special,0,1)};
        }
    }
    foreach $roman (@roman)
    {
        $result += $roman{$roman} while s/$roman//;
    }
    return $result;
}

sub Enter_onClick()
{
    my $form = $window->document->Roman;
    $form->Readout->{'Value'} = parse_roman($form->Input->{'Value'});
}

sub Enter_onclick()
{
    Enter_onClick()
}

</SCRIPT>

<FORM ACTION="" Name="Roman">
<Table>
<tr><td><b>Roman:</td><td><input name="Input" Type="Text"
  SIZE="24"></td></tr>
<tr><td><b>Decimal:</td><td><input name="Readout" Type="Text"
  SIZE="24"></td></tr>
<tr><TD><INPUT NAME="Enter" TYPE="Button" VALUE="Enter"></TD></tr>
</body>
</html>
```

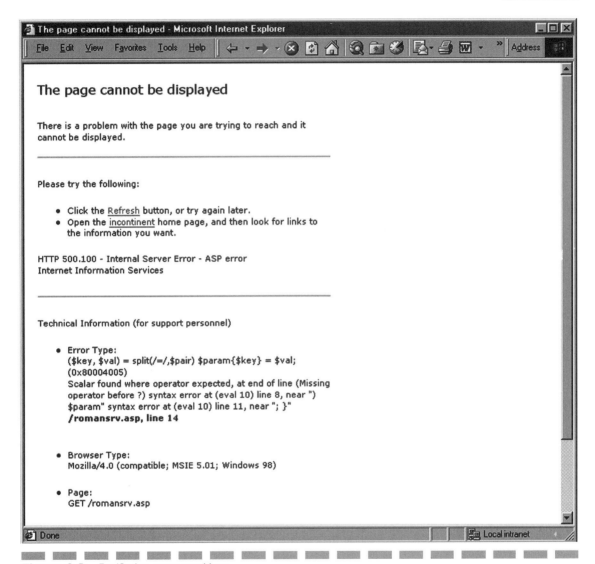

Figure 9-3 PerlScript error tracking.

The significant difference here is that there is no need to parse any information. All we have to do is access the contents of the form field directly. When the button is pressed, the `Enter_onClick` function is called, which accesses the field and calls the `parse_roman` function, placing the result back into the `Readout` form field.

Debugging PerlScript Scripts

When you access a page that makes use of PerlScript, the embedded script elements are parsed by the Perl interpreter just like any other script. If there are any compilation errors during this time, then they are displayed by the browser (through the server if using ASP scripts) before the content of the HTML page is also displayed. The information shown will include the line number and error, just as it would if running the script locally. You can see this more clearly in Figure 9-3.

For more esoteric errors within the script that are difficult to debug, you can either use the `$Response->write()` function or create a special debug field within the form that can contain your debugging output—just assign the error messages or debug details to the field during compilation.

## CHAPTER 10

Interface
Development

While it's true that the current push for interface development is centered around web rather than native interfaces, the command line, text (console), and traditional GUI (graphical user interface)–based interfaces still have some life left in them. For example, there is a distinct push at the moment for developing front ends to database systems using simple interface technologies such as Microsoft's Visual Basic (VB).

VB is not a general-purpose programming language. Although it has the ability to be used for a wide range of purposes, VB was designed to act as an interface development language to an underlying database supplied by Access, SQL Server, or another ODBC-compliant database.

Because Perl is a general-purpose development language, we can use it for more than designing interfaces—a Perl application can do almost anything. However, unlike VB, Perl does not come with a "standard" interface development environment. Instead, we need to use either a number of standard Perl modules or additional toolkits such as Win32::GUI and Tk.

The definition of a user interface is rather loose—you could consider the command line as a sort of user interface. We can even use the standard command console or DOS prompt (depending on whether you have Windows NT or 95/98) to offer an interface to your program. For simple applications, you can accept information on the command line or get user input from the STDIN file handle to get information from the keyboard. You can even create command-line interfaces using standard modules such as Term::Complete and Term::ReadLine.

If you want to display information in a more structured fashion, for example, a status display that outlines the current machine activity within a command prompt, then you need a different approach. You will need to be able to address different areas of the screen or perhaps even format different areas of text in different colors. ActivePerl provides this functionality using the Win32::Console—think of it as the Windows version of Unix curses interface for the command prompt.

To support a GUI to a Perl program, we need to look elsewhere. There are two choices available to us. The first uses the Win32::GUI module by Aldo Calpini. This module is a set of extensions that provide a direct interface to the GUI code used by other Windows applications. Using this module, you can create windows, scroll bars, buttons, and other artifacts, all within the confines of the Win32 environment. Development of this tool is sporadic and obviously not cross-platform compatible.

For a cross-platform solution, we need to use Tk. Tk is a platform-independent interface library. Tk provides a generic interface library that supports the basic elements of a GUI application such as windows, menus, and buttons. The advantage of Tk over the previous examples is that it is completely cross-platform compatible. You can write a program that uses Tk under Unix, transfer it to a Windows machine, and get exactly the same functionality and look and feel.

When porting a Unix application to Windows, or when developing a solution that needs to be used across the two platforms, Tk is the obvious solution—both programs will look and work identically with few, if any, modifications required to execute the application on each platform.

In this chapter we'll look at each of the possible solutions, starting with the use of the command line and moving up to full-blown application development using the Tk interface.

Text Interfaces

Most text-based interfaces fall into one of three different types—the command-line interface, the line interface, and the managed interface. A command-line interface works by accepting input and instructions from the command line and acting upon them. We've already seen a number of examples of the command-line interface in action. There are some pitfalls when using the command line under Windows compared to Unix, and we'll look at those in more detail shortly.

A line-based interface is just a simple line-by-line interaction. The program asks a question and then accepts some input from the user. These are more friendly than the command-line interfaces and may also be more familiar to some Windows users. Some of the oldest PC-based programs worked in this fashion. Although there are no Windows-specific tools for making that process easier, there are some generic Perl toolkits that can aid the process.

The final form is what we'll call the "managed interface." This uses the features of the command prompt or DOS window to allow the programmer to place characters in specific locations within a window. These are the same principles used by many DOS-based programs, and nearly all of the interface Unix programs such as Emacs, DOS Edit—even ScanDisk. The ActivePerl distribution comes with the `Win32::Console` module, which provides us with access to these features in a structured fashion.

Parsing Command-Line Arguments

The basics of accessing the command line should already be understood. Any information supplied on the command line is available within the `@ARGV` array. However, there are a number of minor differences between the information supplied to a Perl application under a Unix shell and the Win32 command prompt.

First and foremost, the command prompt handles arguments differently. You can try this out by using the following simple script:

```
foreach(my $i=0;$i<@ARGV;$i++)
{
    print "ARGV $i: $ARGV[$i]\n";
}
```

When you need to supply a space-separated string as an argument to a script, under Unix you can use either double or single quotes. Under Windows, only double quotes work, such that:

```
C:\>perl cltest.pl 'Hello World'
ARGV 0: 'Hello
ARGV 1: World'

C:\>perl cltest.pl "Hello World"
ARGV 0: Hello World
```

You should also remember that, historically, DOS has used /x for arguments, not -x. Although the difference is fairly minor, it may affect how your users try to use your application.

Also remember that command-line arguments that include file specifications are *not* processed by the Windows command interpreter. You can verify this using our test script:

```
C:\>perl cltest.pl *.pl
ARGV 0: *.pl
```

Ignoring these minor annoyances, the contents of the @ARGV array can be parsed in much the same way as you would parse it under Unix. There are two ways to process command-line arguments: either you process each argument manually, or you use one of Getopt::* modules to parse the command-line arguments for you.

To process the array manually, just examine the individual elements of the @ARGV array, for example:

```
for my $arg (@ARGV)
{
    $debug = 1 if ($arg eq '-d');
...
}
```

This is an incredibly time-consuming process if you want to handle a lot of options. A better solution is to use either the Getopt::Std or

`Getopt::Long` modules to parse the arguments for you. For example:

```
use Getopt::Long;

my %options;
GetOptions(\%options, 'file=s', '+debug');
```

will allow us to process a command line of the form:

```
C:\> perl cla.pl -debug -file=myfile.txt
```

placing the named arguments and their values into the keys of the `%options` hash. These modules are well documented elsewhere. See the online documentation for details on the `Getopt::Std` and `Getopt::Long` modules.

Developing a Line Interface

The majority of modern applications are based either on a GUI or on a secondary interface system, such as that provided when you develop a web-based application. The combination of HTML forms and the CGI scripts that parse them form the interface, albeit in an indirect fashion, as information is exchanged between the CGI, web server, and user's client.

There are times, however, when a command-line interface can be more practical. For example, when querying a database or a service that provides status information, accessing the individual elements by supplying commands can be a practical way of gaining access to the information without the GUI overhead. Furthermore, you can set up a Windows NT or Windows 2000 machine so that it acts as a Telnet server, which, of course, only offers a text interface.

The primary concern when developing a line-based interface is handling the input of commands. Although there are no specific tools for developing line interfaces, there are some modules supplied with the standard Perl library that will make it easier.

Text::Abbrev   This utility module takes a list of words (in our case, commands) and produces a hash that contains a list of abbreviations of the words you supply, which you can use within your application to identify the command that has been requested. For example:

```
use Text::Abbrev;
```

```
%abbrev = ();
abbrev(\%abbrev, qw/be bet better/);
```

will populate the %abbrev hash with

```
b       => be,
be      => be,
bet     => bet,
bett    => better,
bette   => better,
better  => better,
```

Term::ReadLine   This is a function library that supports the input of text in a line-by-line editable format. In addition to allowing the user to edit the information they input, Term::ReadLine also allows you to add commands to a command history so that previous commands can be reselected. The interface is object-based:

```
use Term::ReadLine;

$line = new Term::ReadLine 'Line Interface';
$input = $line->readline('Name? ');

print "Got $input\n";
```

By combining the two modules and using references to execute the function entered on the "command line," you can develop a complex interface that operates in a similar fashion to the command prompt or the Unix shell. For example:

```
use Term::ReadLine;
use Text::Abbrev;

@commands = qw/list help quit/;

sub list
{
    print "I could be printing a list\n";
}

sub help
{
    print "Supported commands:\n";
    print join(' ',@commands),"\n";
}

sub quit
{
    print "Quitting...\n";
    exit(0);
}

my %abbrev_cmd;
```

```
abbrev(\%abbrev_cmd, @commands);

$line = new Term::ReadLine 'Line Interface';
while(1)
{
    $selection = $line->readline("CLI> ");
    ($command,@arguments) = split / /,$selection,2;
    if (exists($abbrev_cmd{$command}))
    {
        $command = $abbrev_cmd{$command};
        if (defined(&$command))
        {
            &$command(@arguments);
        }
        else
        {
            print "$selection has not been defined yet\n";
        }
    }
}
```

If you run this script, you can see the effects—we don't have to enter the full command name, but we also get an editable line:

```
CLI> li
I could be printing a list
CLI>
CLI>
CLI> h
Supported commands:
list help quit
CLI> quit
Quitting...
```

Unfortunately, the keyboard shortcuts for selecting items from the history don't work, but it's still a practical way of getting commands from the user in a command-line style.

Using `Win32::Console`

The `Win32::Console` is similar in principle to a blank Xterm window—it's just a chunk of memory that Win32 reserves and uses to display the contents of a buffer within a window. It's a Win32 console that provides the basic window for the command prompt within Win 95/98 and NT. Any program can use a console; in fact, it's the console that is being used when you `print` from a Perl program executed on the command line. In both these cases, the console is automatically allocated.

When a console is created, it generates three buffers, one each for the familiar, standard input, standard output, and standard error filehandles. For programs executed using the command-line interface (the DOS prompt), these buffers are automatically created and associated with the program's normal file handles.

The console is bound directly to the buffers; printing to the buffer produces output in the window, and reading from the buffer accepts keyboard input just like the standard input. Beyond these simple functions, consoles also allow you to define color and position of the text that you output by modifying the contents of the buffer correctly. We can therefore use the buffer to provide an interface to the user.

There are some limitations. A process can only have one console, so we can't use the console system to create multiple windows. However, during a program's lifetime, it can destroy and create as many consoles as it requires. It's also possible to have multiple buffers—but only one buffer can be displayed at any time. This presents some interesting possibilities. For instance, you could have multiple "pages" of information displayed on screen, and all of the buffers could be updated. By pressing a key, the user could switch between each buffer, thereby displaying each page.

Managing Consoles   Two basic functions create and destroy consoles. The `Win32::Console::Alloc` function allocates a console to the current program. The function accepts no arguments and will return `True` if the allocation was successful. An `undef` value will be returned if the allocation failed (probably due to a pre-existing console):

```
Win32::Console::Alloc();
```

Note that for most Perl programs we do not need to allocate ourselves a console—it's done automatically by the Perl interpreter to enable the `STDIN`, `STDOUT`, and `STDERR` file handles to work as you would expect within the Perl language. The only exception to this rule is if you have spawned a process using the `DETACHED_PROCESS` flag—in this instance, no console is allocated to the process.

To destroy an allocated console, you use the `Win32::Console::Free` function. Like `Win32::Console::Alloc`, it takes no arguments and returns `True` if successful or `undef` on error.

Note that buffers are not directly related to consoles. Buffers are not destroyed or emptied when a console is destroyed; the two objects are completely separate. This means that buffers can survive beyond the life of a single console, although this is not necessarily guaranteed. If you do need to manually allocate and destroy multiple consoles, it's best to also delete the buffers and re-create them to ensure that the buffers operate correctly.

We'll return to the topic of buffers and how they can be used later. For now, let's concentrate on managing the console, whether it's been created for us or if we've created a new one.

Managing Console Buffers   Because Perl under Win32 automatically creates its own console when it is started, what we really need to know is how to create and manage the buffers that we will use to display and obtain information from the console. To set up a new buffer, you create a new Win32::Console object. This operates in two ways. The first accepts the name of an existing handle, associating the handle with the new buffer object:

```
$InputBuffer = new Win32::Console(HANDLE);
```

The HANDLE is one of a predefined set of constants that refer to the standard file handles. See Table 10-1 for details of the valid constants.

This form of the function call returns a new object that points to the corresponding standard file handle. This can be used to return the console to displaying normal print statements—we'll see exactly how this works when we look at creating new, unattached buffers in a moment.

To create a new buffer, we create a new object, supplying two optional arguments:

```
$buffer = new Win32::Console([ACCESSMODE [, SHAREMODE] ] );
```

The first, ACCESSMODE, defines the permissions to be used when reading and writing from the buffer. Just like files, you can select each buffer to be read-only, write-only, or both. If you do not specify any options, then the buffer is by default created as a read/write buffer.

TABLE 10-1

The handle definitions.

Constant	Description
STD_OUTPUT_HANDLE	Sets the new buffer to point to the default output handle (STDOUT), normally the screen.
STD_INPUT_HANDLE	Sets the new buffer to point to the default input handle (STDIN), normally the keyboard.
STD_ERROR_HANDLE	Sets the new buffer to point to the default error handle (STDERR), normally the screen.

TABLE 10-2

The buffer's
ACCESSMODE.

Constant	Description
GENERIC_READ	The buffer is read-only—we can read data from the console but cannot write to it (except when OR'd with GENERIC_WRITE).
GENERIC_WRITE	The buffer is writable—we can write to the console but cannot read from it (except when OR'd with GENERIC_READ).

Table 10-2 lists the constants that can be OR'd together to specify the buffer's mode.

The second argument, SHAREMODE, defines whether other processes can read and write to the buffer that you have created. If not specified, this argument defaults to read/write permissions to the shared buffer. It's unlikely that you should need to modify this setting, since Perl does not directly support the other functions and interfaces that would allow such sharing to take place; however, this information can be useful when developing Perl extensions where the sharing of the buffer information is required. See Table 10-3 for details on the constants you can use with this argument.

Remember that if you do not specify any arguments when creating the buffer object, then the buffer is read/write and shared read/write—in essence, just a basic buffer.

Before we go any further, let's look at a sample script that shows the basic operation of the console and how the use of different buffers adjusts what information is displayed. In this script we create five separate buffers. One is our generic STDOUT, which we need so that we can return to the normal operation of a script. The other four just display a single piece of information, the number of the current buffer, and a prompt that allows us to select an alternative buffer to be displayed.

```perl
#!perl -w

use strict;
use Win32::Console;
```

TABLE 10-3

The buffer's
SHAREMODE.

Constant	Description
FILE_SHARE_READ	The buffer is shared with read-only permissions; other processes can read the information stored within the buffer.
FILE_SHARE_WRITE	The buffer is shared with write permissions; other processes can modify the information stored in the buffer.

```
my %buffers;

$buffers{stdout} = new Win32::Console(STD_OUTPUT_HANDLE)
    or die "Can't create STDOUT buffer: $!, $^E\n";

$buffers{'1'} = new Win32::Console();
$buffers{'2'} = new Win32::Console();
$buffers{'3'} = new Win32::Console();
$buffers{'4'} = new Win32::Console();

my $buffer = '1';

while(1)
{
    $buffers{$buffer}->Write("This is buffer $buffer\n");
    $buffers{$buffer}->Write("Select [1,2,3,4,Q]: ");
    $buffers{$buffer}->Display();
    my $response = <STDIN>;
    chomp($response);
    if ($response =~ m/[1-4Qq]/)
    {
        last if ("\U$response" eq 'Q');
        $buffer = $response;
    }
}

$buffers{stdout}->Display();
print "Back to the standard output...quitting\n";
```

If you run the script in a DOS window, the contents of the window should be replaced with the prompt for buffer 1 (see also Figure 10-1):

```
This is buffer 1
Select [1,2,3,4,Q]:
```

Figure 10-1
The first buffer.

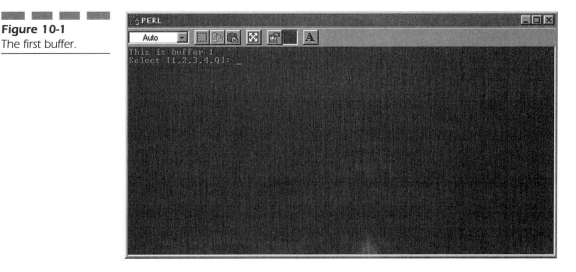

Figure 10-2
The second buffer.

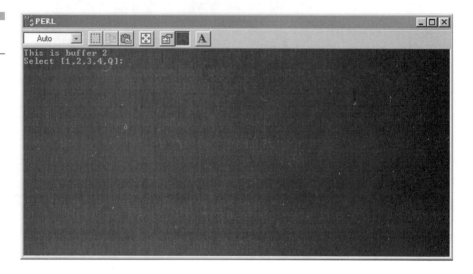

If you type in the number of an alternative buffer, you switch to that display—the entire window is emptied and the contents of the new buffer are displayed on screen (see also Figure 10-2):

```
This is buffer 2
Select [1,2,3,4,Q]:
```

If you go back to buffer 1, then the original message, your response, and the new message should be displayed (see also Figure 10-3):

```
This is buffer 1
Select [1,2,3,4,Q]: 2
This is buffer 1
Select [1,2,3,4,Q]:
```

The information in the buffer has not been emptied—we've simply added to it. You can see the effects more clearly in Figures 10-1 through to 10-4—including what is displayed when we finally exit the script by pressing "Q" (Figure 10-4).

Each buffer is treated individually. Switching the console to display a different buffer causes the contents of that buffer to be displayed on screen, while the contents of the buffers remain static.

Because buffers are just simple objects, to destroy them, we can either just let the object go out of scope (which automatically destroys it) or kill it off manually by assigning the buffer the undefined value:

```
undef $buffer;
```

Figure 10-3
The first buffer again.

NOTE.   *You can also call the* _CloseHandle() *method to the buffer; this is the method called when the object is destroyed. This is no different than calling* undef, *which is guaranteed to call the correct* Destroy *method even if the method name is changed in the future.*

Figure 10-4
Back to the standard output.

Setting the Display Buffer   It should be apparent from the example script above that you set the buffer to be displayed using the `Display` method to the required buffer. The method returns `True` if successful or `undef` on failure:

```
$buffer->Display();
```

Note that there is no way to display to the "standard output" again—in other words, what is displayed on screen before you switched the console to display the current buffer. The trick is to create a new object based on the current standard output:

```
$stdout = new Win32::Console(STD_OUTPUT_HANDLE);
$buffer->Display();
# Work within the new buffer
$stdout->Display();
# Change back to the standard output again
```

It's important to note here that it is the last active buffer that is then displayed within the console window. If you run Perl script that uses `Win32::Console` and do not display the standard output buffer before leaving the script, then the contents of the last buffer will remain on screen; it won't automatically return to the contents of the original DOS prompt buffer before you switched.

Modifying the Buffer Contents   There are two basic ways of writing text into a buffer. The first, `Write`, inserts text at the current cursor location. The second, `WriteChar`, inserts text at a specific location within the buffer. There is also a method for writing entire rectangular blocks of text to the buffer using the `WriteRect` method.

In addition, you can also clear the contents of the buffer using the `Cls` method, or you can fill a buffer with a specific character using the `FillChar` method. Finally, you can use `FillAttr` to fill a buffer with a character using a specific color.

WRITE   The `Write` function writes a piece of text to the buffer using the current cursor location as a starting point:

```
$buffer->Write(EXPR);
```

This writes EXPR to the console buffer. You can change the current cursor location before you write the information. The color used when writing will match the color specified by the `Attr` method—*not* the attributes set for the current location.

WRITECHAR WriteChar writes a string to the buffer at a specific location, using the colors set for that area within the buffer (as set by WriteAttr). The format of the method is as follows:

```
$buffer->WriteChar(DATA, X, Y);
```

The DATA is the string that you want to write, and X and Y the location within the buffer at which you want to start writing.

Remember, the WriteChar method only writes characters into the buffer; it does not overwrite, reset, or otherwise control the colors used to display the characters. See the WriteAttr method later in this chapter for information and examples.

CLS The Cls method clears the contents of the buffer, effectively emptying the contents. What it actually does is write a space to every character of the buffer and sets the attribute of each character to the default attributes configured when the buffer was created. Alternatively, the Cls method will accept an optional color attribute value to use for each character in the buffer.

For example, the following will merely clear the buffer:

```
$buffer->Cls();
```

while the line

```
$buffer->Cls(pack('c',(BACKGROUND_BLUE|FOREGROUND_WHITE)));
```

would clear the buffer, set the background to blue, and set the foreground to white. See the section "Writing with Color" later in the chapter for details on specifying color attributes.

FILLCHAR To fill a specific area of the screen with a single character, use the FillChar method:

```
$buffer->FillChar(CHAR, LENGTH, X, Y);
```

The CHAR is the single character that you want to use to fill, and LENGTH is the number of characters to be written. The X and Y arguments refer to the location at which the characters will start to be written. Remember that the information will be written sequentially to the buffer, wrapping from one line to the next if the number of characters extends beyond the end of a row.

Reading from a Console Buffer   There are two ways of reading information from a console. You can either read the contents of a buffer (which could include text entered by the user) or you can directly accept user input if you have created an input buffer.

To read an area of information from the buffer using the `ReadChar` method:

```
$data = $buffer->ReadChar(LENGTH, X, Y);
```

where LENGTH is the number of characters to read from the buffer, and X and Y the location at which to start reading information. Note that the information you read will be the text, not the attributes—use `ReadAttr` if you want to determine the color settings of a specific location within the buffer.

The `InputChar` method reads a specific number of characters from the keyboard, but only when used on a buffer that has been created with the `STD_INPUT_HANDLE` option:

```
$ibuffer = new Win32::Console(STD_INPUT_HANDLE);
$data = $ibuffer->InputChar(NUMBER);
```

The NUMBER is the number of characters to be read from the buffer. For example:

```
use Win32::Console;
$ibuffer = new Win32::Console(STD_INPUT_HANDLE);

print "Press N to continue, or Q to quit\n";
$data = $ibuffer->InputChar(1);
if (uc($data) eq 'N')
{
    print "Continuing...\n";
}
elsif (uc($data) eq 'Q')
{
    print "Quitting...\n";
    exit(1);
}
```

Note that the function should only return when it's read the specified number of characters from the user's keyboard.

Scrolling Text   The `Scroll` method allows you to scroll (move) a rectangle of information within a buffer. You supply the rectangle of the buffer that you want to move, its new location, the fill characters and attributes, and, optionally, a clipping rectangle.

```
$buffer->Scroll(LEFT, TOP, RIGHT, BOTTOM, COL, ROW, CHAR, ATTR
                [, CLIPLEFT, CLIPTOP, CLIPRIGHT, CLIPBOTTOM]);
```

The LEFT, TOP, RIGHT, and BOTTOM define the location of the top left and bottom right of the rectangle that you want to move. The COL and ROW is the location that you want the top left of the rectangle to be moved to. The CHAR and ATTR are the character and attribute that you want to use to fill the space left when the rectangle moves. Note that CHAR should be specified numerically, not as a single character. Use the ord or unpack functions to convert a single character into its numerical equivalent.

The following script demonstrates how to move a square from the top left to the bottom right of the buffer.

```
use Win32::Console;

$width = 80;
$height = 24;

$buffer = new Win32::Console();
$buffer->Size($width,$height);
$buffer->Display();

$buffer->Cls($FG_WHITE|$BG_BLUE);

$buffer->WriteChar("Hello",0,0);
$buffer->WriteChar("This is",0,1);
$buffer->WriteChar("a Box!",0,2);

$buffer->WriteChar("Created the Scrollbox",0,24);

sleep(5);

$buffer->Scroll(0,0,8,2,40,10,ord('*'),
                $FG_WHITE|$BG_RED,0,0,1000,1000);

$buffer->WriteChar("Moved the Scrollbox",0,24);

sleep(5);
```

NOTE.   *Due to a bug in the* Scroll *method, the default clipping path is 0,0,0,0, which means the method call will not do anything unless you explicitly supply the clipping rectangle. To get around the problem here, we've specified a suitably large rectangle for the clipping to be ignored.*

The clipping rectangle defines the area that will not be overwritten when the rectangle is moved. You can use a clipping rectangle to emulate a "scrollbox" by moving a rectangle of information in a direction that is clipped. To demonstrate what I mean, the following script scrolls an array of text within a box:

```perl
use Win32::Console;

$width = 80;
$height = 24;

@text = ('Once upon a time',
         'there was a little',
         'girl wearing a red',
         'cape. She was',
         'going to grandmas',
         'with some goodies.');

$buffer = new Win32::Console();
$buffer->Size($width,$height);
$buffer->Display();

$buffer->Cls($FG_WHITE|$BG_BLUE);

ScrollText($buffer,20,10,3,@text);

sub ScrollText
{
    my ($buffer,$col,$row,$lines,@text) = @_;

    my $width = 0;

    foreach $line (@text)
    {
        $width = length($line) if (length($line) > $width);
    }

    for($i=0;$i<$lines;$i++)
    {
        $buffer->WriteChar($text[$i],$col,($row+$i));
    }

    for(;$i < @text;$i++)
    {
        sleep(2);
        $buffer->Scroll($col,$row,($col+$width),($row+$lines),
                    $col,($row-1), ord(' '), $FG_WHITE|$BG_BLUE,
                    $col,$row,($col+$width),($row+$lines));
        $buffer->WriteChar($text[$i],$col,($row+$lines-1));
    }
}
```

When you run this script, a small box, just three lines high, will be created, and the text will be scrolled within it. Because we've set the clipping path to be the same size as the box that the text was originally created within, when we scroll the text, the top line of the rectangle is deleted.

Reading and Writing Rectangles   You can read and write rectangles of information to and from a buffer using the ReadRect and WriteRect methods. The ReadRect method reads a rectangle of information and returns the information as a binary string, containing the rectangle's characters and attributes:

```
$buffer = $buffer->ReadRect(LEFT, TOP, RIGHT, BOTTOM)
```

The parameters LEFT, TOP, RIGHT, and BOTTOM refer to the locations of the top left and bottom right corners of the rectangle. If the method fails, then the undef is returned.

The WriteRect method works in a similar fashion:

```
@result = $buffer->WriteRect(DATA, LEFT, TOP, RIGHT, BOTTOM)
```

The LEFT, TOP, RIGHT, and BOTTOM are as before, defining the top left and bottom right corners of the rectangle. The DATA should be a binary string as returned from a previous ReadRect call. The DATA will over-write the existing information (characters and attributes) within the buffer. The return value is a four-element array containing the coordinates of the rectangle that was written.

Because ReadRect and WriteRect can only be used in conjunction with each other, the use is limited to providing a way of moving rectangles of information around the buffer. They can also be used for copying text between buffers or for acting as a temporary storage for pop-up windows and other features when you need to remember the contents of a specific area of the screen.

Writing with Color   Writing a piece of text in color on the screen is somewhat more complicated. You actually have to write the text in two stages, first setting the color that you want to use, and then actually inserting the text. At the most basic level, you can use the Attr method, which sets the "current" color used when you write information using the Write method. For more complex needs, you use WriteAttr. This sets an area with a specific set of attributes, which you can then fill in with the required characters using the WriteChar method.

The Attr method is actually short for *attributes* and goes back to the days when you used attributes within the DOS window to change the color via the ANSI terminal support. The format of the method is as follows:

```
$buffer->Attr([ DATA ]);
```

If not supplied any arguments, then `Attr` returns the current attribute. If you supply a value, then the current color will be set to the supplied value. We'll look at the specifics of color definition in a moment. Once set, all characters written to the buffer with the `Write` method will use the current attributes.

To set the color for an area of text within the buffer, you use the `WriteAttr` method:

```
$buffer->WriteAttr(DATA [, X, Y]);
```

where `DATA` is a byte string of attributes. Each byte in the string sets the color attributes for one character within the buffer, so to color the word *Hello*, you would have to pass `WriteAttr` a string of 5 bytes. The `X` and `Y` are optional and specify the cursor location on screen for the attributes to be set. Note that this is a starting location, not a rectangle specification. If you supply a string that extends beyond the width of the buffer, then the text will wrap, just as with `WriteChar`. If you want to color a rectangle on the screen, you will need to use multiple calls to the `WriteAttr` method. Also be aware that if you don't supply the coordinates, the method assumes 0,0 (top left), which may not be the effect you had in mind.

Although this seems like a long-winded way of doing things, it's actually quite practical if you think about the complexities of specifying the color each time. By setting the attributes for individual colors within the buffer, we only have to worry about the process once. Adding text to the buffer does not affect the attributes; it'll automatically be colored correctly.

The actual attributes are specified using a combination of constants logically OR'd together. There are individual constants for the foreground and background colors—applying a foreground and background constant sets the color combination. Because `DATA` should be in the form of a byte string, it's best to use `pack` or `chr` to ensure we get a single byte of information, and then use string multiplication to color the number of characters we want. For example:

```
$buffer->WriteAttr(pack('c',(BACKGROUND_BLUE|FOREGROUND_WHITE)) x 5,
                   10,10);
$buffer->WriteChar("Hello",10,10);
```

See Table 10-4 for a list of the valid constants.

Note that you are actually mixing colors here, rather than explicitly setting named colors. For example, mixing FOREGROUND_RED and FOREGROUND_BLUE results in the color better known as magenta (purple). Adding intensity increases the brightness of the color, which can make quite a difference. If you compare normal white against bright white,

TABLE 10-4

Basic color constants.

Constants	Description
BACKGROUND_BLUE	Sets a blue background.
BACKGROUND_GREEN	Sets a green background.
BACKGROUND_RED	Sets a red background.
BACKGROUND_INTENSITY	Adds intensity (makes colors bright).
FOREGROUND_BLUE	Sets a blue foreground.
FOREGROUND_GREEN	Sets a green foreground.
FOREGROUND_RED	Sets a red foreground.
FOREGROUND_INTENSITY	Adds intensity (makes colors bright).

you'll actually notice that the default white color is more like 50 percent gray. The other point to remember is that specifying no color means black, so a specification of FOREGROUND_GREEN results in green on a black background.

Remembering all of the combinations can be a nightmare when you really just want to select a specific color by name. The Win32::Console actually defines a number of variables that contain equivalent definitions for foreground and background colors. The variables are as follows, and their meaning should be obvious:

$BG_BLACK	$FG_BLACK
$BG_BLUE	$FG_BLUE
$BG_BROWN	$FG_BROWN
$BG_CYAN	$FG_CYAN
$BG_GRAY	$FG_GRAY
$BG_GREEN	$FG_GREEN
$BG_LIGHTBLUE	$FG_LIGHTBLUE
$BG_LIGHTCYAN	$FG_LIGHTCYAN
$BG_LIGHTGREEN	$FG_LIGHTGREEN
$BG_LIGHTMAGENTA	$FG_LIGHTMAGENTA
$BG_LIGHTRED	$FG_LIGHTRED
$BG_MAGENTA	$FG_MAGENTA
$BG_RED	$FG_RED
$BG_WHITE	$FG_WHITE

TABLE 10-5

Quick colors and
their constant
equivalents.

Quick Color	Constant Equivalent
BLACK	
BLUE	BLUE
BROWN	RED|GREEN
CYAN	BLUE|GREEN
GRAY	INTENSITY
GREEN	GREEN
LIGHTBLUE	BLUE|INTENSITY
LIGHTCYAN	BLUE|GREEN|INTENSITY
LIGHTGREEN	GREEN|INTENSITY
LIGHTMAGENTA	RED|BLUE|INTENSITY
LIGHTRED	RED|INTENSITY
MAGENTA	RED|BLUE
RED	RED
WHITE	RED|GREEN|BLUE|INTENSITY

For convenience, listed in Table 10-5 are the colors defined in the quick access variables and their constant equivalents.

Note that there is one color that cannot be set using the quick color variables, and this is base white, instead of the "bright" white that is displayed with the $FG_WHITE/$BG_WHITE variables. The base white is probably more correctly defined as a light gray (somewhere between the $FG_GRAY and $FG_BLACK). This is actually the default color used in the console window and can be obtained using the combination RED|GREEN|BLUE.

The example below defines a new function, called ColorWrite, which accepts the buffer, text, color, and if desired, the coordinates where the text should be written. It sets the color and then writes the text, creating the correctly sized attribute byte string to ensure the text is colored properly.

```
#perl -w

use Win32::Console;

$buffera = new Win32::Console();

$buffera->Cls($FG_WHITE|$BG_BLUE);
```

```
ColorWrite($buffera,'This is a test B&W string');
ColorWrite($buffera,'This is a test placed color string',
          ($FG_WHITE|$BG_BLUE), 10,10);

$buffera->Display();

sleep(5);

sub ColorWrite($$;$$$)
{
    my $color = (FOREGROUND_RED|FOREGROUND_BLUE|FOREGROUND_GREEN);
    my ($buffer,$string);
    my ($row,$col) = (-1,-1);

    if (@_ == 2)
    {
        ($buffer,$string) = @_;
    }
    if (@_ == 3)
    {
        ($buffer,$string,$color) = @_;
    }
    if (@_ == 5)
    {
        ($buffer,$string,$color,$row,$col) = @_;
    }

    my $length = length($string);

    if ($row == -1)
    {
        $buffer->WriteAttr(pack('c',$color) x $length);
        $buffer->Write($string);
    }
    else
    {
        $buffer->WriteAttr(pack('c',$color) x $length,$row,$col);
        $buffer->WriteChar($string,$row,$col);
    }
}
```

If you need to, you can also read the current attributes for a specific
section of the screen using the ReadAttr method. This accepts the same
basic arguments as the WriteAttr method, except that the DATA is
instead replaced by a SIZE specification so you can decide how many
bytes to read from the screen:

```
$attributes = $buffer->ReadAttr(SIZE [, X, Y]);
```

The information returned is the byte string containing the attributes, or
undef if the attribute settings could not be determined. The returned byte
string can be used directly with the ReadAttr method to set the attributes
again. Although this seems pointless—you should probably know what

color a portion of the screen should be—it can be helpful when you want to modify the color slightly. For example, to highlight an area on the screen, you could read the attributes, add the FOREGROUND_INTENSITY constant, and you would have effectively emboldened the text portion. Here's a very simple and unelegant function to blink a region of text:

```perl
sub Blink
{
    my ($buffer, $row, $col, $length, $color, $repeat) = @_;
    $attributes = $buffer->ReadAttr($length,$row,$col);
    $highlight = $attributes;
    $highlight = join('',map { $_ = pack('c', unpack('c',$_)|$color) }
                    split(//,$highlight));

    for($i=0;$i<$repeat;$i++)
    {
        $buffer->WriteAttr($highlight,$row,$col);
        sleep(1);
        $buffer->WriteAttr($attributes,$row,$col);
        sleep(1);
    }
}
```

We have to jump through a few hoops in order to update the color, since we need to set the new value of each individual byte in the attribute byte string. Doing this effectively means using join and split with pack and unpack within a map statement to get the effect we want.

To actually use the function, specify the buffer, location, length and modification, and the number of repetitions:

```perl
Blink($buffer,40,10,9,FOREGROUND_INTENSITY,5);
```

Try the colortst.pl script on the CD to see the effect.

NOTE.   *Your* Win32::Console *module may be broken; specifically, the embedded call to the underlying attribute function is wrong. In this case, you need to add an extra argument to the call. I modified the function in my version of* Win32::Console *to read*

```perl
#=============
sub ReadAttr {
#=============
    my($self, $size, $col, $row) = @_;
    return undef unless ref($self);
    my $buffer;

    return(_ReadConsoleOutputAttribute($self->{'handle'}, \$buffer,
                                $size, $col, $row));
}
```

FILLATTR   Both ReadAttr and WriteAttr read and write the specified number of attributes from a specific location. When you want to set a block of text with a specific set of attributes, the problem is that you need to create an attribute string of the correct size. Although this gives you the flexibility of creating a string with different attributes in it, it is much more likely that you want to change a block of text to the same color. You can do this with the FillAttr command:

```
$buffer->FillAttr(COLOR, LENGTH, X, Y);
```

where COLOR is the color definition, LENGTH is the number of characters to be written to the buffer, and X and Y are the column and row at which to start writing. Like WriteAttr, this only writes attributes, not characters. If you want to write characters and attributes, you'll need to combine it with the FillChar method. For example, we could emulate the Cls method using both methods:

```
($width,$height) = %buffer->MaxWindow();
$buffer->FillAttr($FG_WHITE|$BG_BLACK,($width*$height),0,0);
$buffer->FillChar(' ',($width*$height),0,0);
```

Getting Buffer/Console Properties   You can get the properties of the console in relation to the current buffer by calling the Info method to the buffer. This returns an 11-element array that defines the current properties for the buffer and console.

```
($columns, $rows, $cursorcol, $cursorrow, $color, $bufleftcol,
 $buftoprow, $bufrightcol, $bufbotrow, $colwidth, $rowheight)
    = $buffer->Info();
```

Note that properties are largely buffer, rather than console dependent, so different buffers will return different information. See Table 10-6 for details on the information returned.

For example, to summarize the current buffer/console setting:

```
#perl -w

use Win32::Console;

$buffer = new Win32::Console(STD_OUTPUT_HANDLE);

($columns, $rows, $cursorcol, $cursorrow, $color, $bufleftcol,
 $buftoprow, $bufrightcol, $bufbotrow, $colwidth, $rowheight)
    = $buffer->Info();

print("Buffer size: $columns x $rows\n");
print("Cursor: $cursorcol,$cursorrow\n");
print("Color Setting: $color\n");
```

TABLE 10-6

Console properties
as returned by the
Info method.

Element	Description
$columns	The number of columns within the current buffer.
$rows	The number of rows within the current buffer.
$cursorcol	The column location of the cursor within the buffer.
$cursorrow	The row location of the cursor within the buffer.
$color	The current color that will be used to display the next piece of information to the buffer.
$bufleftcol	The value of the minimum (leftmost) column being displayed by the console within the current buffer.
$buftoprow	The value of the minimum (topmost) row being displayed by the console within the current buffer.
$bufrightcol	The value of the maximum (rightmost) row being displayed by the console within the current buffer.
$bufbotrow	The value of the maximum (bottommost) row being displayed by the console within the current buffer.
$colwidth	The maximum width of the current console.
$rowheight	The maximum height of the current console.

```
print("Console Coordinates: ",
     "$bufleftcol,$buftoprow $bufrightcol,$bufbotrow\n");
print("Console Size: $colwidth, $rowheight\n");
```

Configuring the Console I/O Properties   You can modify the properties of the current console in a number of ways, including setting the console size pragmatically within Perl. The basic console properties affect how the console treats different input and output character sequences.

The Mode method sets the properties for the console via the currently active buffer:

```
$mode = $buffer->Mode([MODE]);
```

The MODE is an optional bitmask, based on the constants shown below. If MODE is not supplied, then the method just returns the current properties for the console. The method returns the new mode, or undef on failure.

For example, the script below displays the current settings for the console:

```
#perl -w

use Win32::Console;
```

```
$buffer = new Win32::Console();

$mode = $buffer->Mode();

print "Echo Input\n" if ($mode & ENABLE_ECHO_INPUT);
print "Line Input\n" if ($mode & ENABLE_LINE_INPUT);
print "Mouse Input\n" if ($mode & ENABLE_MOUSE_INPUT);
print "Processed Input\n" if ($mode & ENABLE_PROCESSED_INPUT);
print "Processed Output\n" if ($mode & ENABLE_PROCESSED_OUTPUT);
print "Window Input\n" if ($mode & ENABLE_WINDOW_INPUT);
print "Wrap EOL\n" if ($mode & ENABLE_WRAP_AT_EOL_OUTPUT);
```

To explicitly set the properties for the console:

```
use Win32::Console;

$buffer = new Win32::Console();

$buffer->Mode(ENABLE_ECHO_INPUT || ENABLE_WINDOW_INPUT);
```

If you want to add properties to the current console settings, you need to get the current settings first and add the new properties:

```
use Win32::Console;

$buffer = new Win32::Console();

$mode = $buffer->Mode();

$buffer->Mode($mode || ENABLE_WINDOW_INPUT);
```

See below for a list of valid constants and their meanings.

ENABLE_ECHO_INPUT   Input to the buffer is echoed to the screen. With this enabled, when a user presses a character, it will be echoed to the screen, as well as being accepted by the process using a read, InputChar, or similar call. By default, this is actually switched off. This property can only be enabled when the ENABLE_LINE_INPUT property is also set.

ENABLE_LINE_INPUT   With this option enabled, input will only be accepted from the keyboard after the carriage return key is pressed. This is fine for line-interactive environments, but for those where you want to accept input of single characters (for example, to change buffers or select options), this option should be turned off. By default, this option is turned on.

Note that with both ENABLE_LINE_INPUT and ENABLE_ECHO_INPUT properties disabled, you can accept single characters from the keyboard without them being echoed to the screen. This is the perfect environment for an interactive interface.

ENABLE_MOUSE_INPUT   You can use the mouse to act as a cursor, providing the console window has the focus and the mouse pointer is within the window. The mouse naturally generates the equivalent key presses for the normal cursor keys. If this property is set, then the key presses generated by the individual mouse events are placed into the input buffer. Note that you must also disable the Quick Edit option with the DOS window properties for this to work.

ENABLE_PROCESSED_INPUT   Certain characters and character sequences are processed by the operating system rather than being passed on to the process controlling the console. These include the special sequences such as backspace, return, Ctrl-C, and others. With this option enabled, the OS will process the input, meaning that you will be unable to identify these special sequences. If this option is not specified, the special sequences will be passed to the input buffer of the process without any processing. This option is on by default.

ENABLE_PROCESSED_OUTPUT   If this property is enabled, then control characters output to the console such as the bell, carriage return, and linefeed will be interpreted by the operating system, rather than being sent native to the console. This only affects characters written to the console using the Write method. This option is on by default.

ENABLE_WINDOW_INPUT   If enabled, this property causes user changes to the console size to be placed into the current input buffer for the console. You can read this information using the normal buffer input techniques.

ENABLE_WRAP_AT_EOL_OUTPUT   Normally when you use Write and other buffer output methods—and indeed the print function—lines printed automatically wrap at the end of the line. This causes the whole buffer to scroll one line up in order to incorporate the additional text when you are on the last (bottommost) line in the buffer, also losing the top line. This is not very practical in situations where you are trying to very precisely lay out components on the screen. To get around this, you can set the ENABLE_WRAP_AT_EOL_OUTPUT property. When this property is set, the last character on the line is overwritten by the remainder of the characters sent to the buffer.

Setting the Console Title   The console title is the name that appears in the window title bar. By default, the operating system actually populates this with the name of the application being executed. Therefore, if you want to change the console to reflect a proper program name, you will need to use the `Title` method to a buffer:

```
$buffer->Title([TITLE]);
```

Note that there is no limit to the length of the string that is passed to the method. The method returns the title of the window.

Like other methods that modify the console, the window title is linked to the console, even though you set the value via a buffer object. This can lead to some confusion. You cannot set different window titles for different buffers automatically. The following script sets the title to "Other Window Title," irrespective of which buffer is displayed:

```
#perl -w

use Win32::Console;

$buffer = new Win32::Console(STD_OUTPUT_HANDLE);
$other = new Win32::Console();

$buffer->Title("Window Title");
$other->Title("Other Window Title");

$buffer->Display();
sleep(5);
$other->Display();
```

If you want to have a different window title displayed for each buffer, then you will need to make separate calls to `Title` when you make calls to `Display`.

Setting the Console Size   You can adjust the size of a console by using the `Size` method. For example, to set the size of the console buffer to 80x25 characters, set the window title and clear the screen:

```
use Win32::Console;
$console = new Win32::Console();
$console->Size(80,25);
$console->Title('Perl Console');
$console->Cls();
```

You can obtain the maximum size of the console window using the `MaxWindow` method. This calculates the maximum size by taking into account the current console font and the resolution of the screen being used:

```
my ($maxwidth, $maxheight) = $buffer->MaxWindow();
```

Using Tk

Often when developing applications on the Unix platform, you have one of three main interface possibilities: the command line, the GUI, and a web-based interface. The command-line interface is pretty basic and also, at least on the Unix platform, is fairly common. The X Windows system has been around for a number of years, but at the end of the day, most Unix users just use X Windows as a way of displaying multiple terminal windows on the screen. Let's face it: If someone asks to display a list of the files on a Unix machine, probably 90 percent of users would open a terminal and type ll.

Under a Windows platform, command-line interfaces are not so common. Although Windows was originally produced, essentially, as an extension to DOS (it even still retains DOS compatibility), the idea behind Windows was to protect the user from the "complex" command line. Sure, there are command-line programs—if you want, you can run a command prompt and type dir for old times' sake, but it's more likely you'll open Windows Explorer and display a graphical list of files.

We looked in detail in the previous chapter at how to use ActivePerl to produce web interfaces. Aside from some minor tricks, most of the fundamentals of the web programming process are identical on the two platforms. This is helped by Perl, which eliminates most of the complexity of the process of designing an interactive website. The rest of the complexity is HTML, which is not really a language and certainly isn't platform-dependent.

That just leaves us with the GUI interface. As a rule, GUI interfaces are not very popular within the Unix arena, although they do exist. There are many applications—StarOffice, Oracle, Netscape—all of which are built on the X Windows interface. Even so, GUI applications are still not very popular. Even Emacs retains a terminal-like interface when it is running as an X application.

We already know how to develop a GUI-based application under Windows. But you don't want to have two different interfaces—command line/terminal and GUI—to the same application when you are producing a cross-platform application. If you are building an application that requires cross-platform compatibility and a GUI interface, then your options are limited. The two GUI environments are very different and are based on two completely different technologies. Although many of the basic principles are the same—windows, buttons, checkboxes, and so on—you cannot directly program both. Developing two different interfaces within the same environment is time-consuming and to be more specific, time-wasting.

Although there are other toolkits for building GUIs, Tk has become the most respected of those available, largely because of its feature list and the professional-looking quality of the windows and interfaces it builds. The history of Tk is somewhat checkered, but this has not affected the overall development of Tk as an interface system.

Tk was originally developed by Dr. John Ousterhout, who was originally at the University of California, Berkeley before moving to Sun Microsystems. Ousterhout, Tk, and its sister scripting language Tcl are now part of a commercial development effort called *Scriptics*. The original Tcl and Tk projects are still free, while Scriptics also develops commercial products such as Tcl Pro.

Tk sits at a similar level to `Win32::Console` or `Win32::GUI`, except that the objects and entities you create are generated with the same function on both platforms (Unix and Win32) and generate the corresponding object on each platform (an X widget or a Win32 control). The role of Tk is to make the process of designing a user interface significantly easier. The core of the windowing system provides the methods and basis for simple operations and events such as opening windows and drawing lines and accepting input and actions from the keyboard and mouse.

Creating even a simple onscreen element such as a button or even a simple text pane originally involved hundreds of lines of code. The result was the development of individual elements of a GUI environment called *widgets*. A single widget can define a core element of the interface such as a button, scroll bar, and even more-complex elements such as scales and hierarchical lists, which themselves can be composed of other simpler widgets. Within Unix and the X Windows system, a number of different widget toolkits have been produced, including Motif, Athena, OpenWindows, and, of course, Tk.

Because of the natural relationship between widgets and objects, developing GUIs within a scripting language is incredibly easy, and Tk was originally developed in cooperation with the Tcl language. Tcl (short for Tool Command Language) is essentially a macro language for making development of complex programs within the shell easier. However, Tcl is itself difficult to use in comparison to Perl, Python, and other scripting languages, so efforts were made to support the Tk widgets directly within these languages.

The first real system was designed by Malcolm Beattie, who embedded a Tcl interpreter within a Perl layer to enable a connection between Perl and Tk. It was Nick Ing-Simmons who developed the now standard Perl/Tk interface by stripping the Tk system of its Tcl-specific code. On top of the base Tk functionality was built a generic porting layer, called *pTk*, which is now the basis for a number of Tk interfaces to scripting languages, including Perl, Python, Scheme, and Guile.

The result is Perl/Tk—an interface system that you access within Perl as the Tk module. This has been successfully supported on Unix for a number of years. At Sun, Tcl and Tk were ported to Windows and Mac OS, and although the Windows version of Perl/Tk has been available for some time, a Mac version has yet to materialize.

If you are serious about developing interfaces with Tk, or any other system, I suggest, for your, as well as your users' benefit, that you read a suitable human-computer interface book. I can heartily recommend all of Apple's texts; they are the basis for many of the best interfaces you will find. You may also want to check Alan Cooper's *About Face: The Essentials of User Interface Design*, (IDG Books, 1995) or the excellent introductory guide *The Elements of User Interface Design*, by Theo Mandel (Wiley, 1997).

Installing Tk under Windows

The best way to install Tk under Windows is to use either the basic Perl Package Manager (PPM) or the Visual Package Manager (VPM) that come with ActivePerl and the Perl Development Kit, respectively.

Within PPM, just typing

```
PPM> install Tk
```

should be enough to download and then install everything you need. See Chapter 12 for more details on using PPM and VPM to install packages.

Hello from Tk

Developing a user interface with Tk is a case of creating a number of nested objects. The first object you create is the main window for your application. The nested objects are the individual widgets that make up the user interface. A widget can be a button, text box, menu, or a variety of other components used to build up your interface within your window.

Once you have defined the individual widgets that make up the window, the script then goes into a loop, called the *event loop*. The script accepts events from the user and performs the commands and actions that were defined when the widgets were created. This is different from most other Perl scripts, which follow a logical process. However, unlike many Perl scripts, users control the execution and choose a number of different options, according to which button, text box, or other widget they manipulate.

The basic process for creating a Tk-based GUI application is as follows:

1. Create a window to hold all of your objects. The main window is generally known as *main* or *top-level*, although it could be called anything.

2. Create a number of widgets, defining their contents, actions, and other elements. In this example, a label, to hold a simple message, and a button, which when pressed will exit the script, are created.

3. Display and arrange the widgets within the window. This is frequently handled by the Packer geometry manager, although there are other managers available. The geometry manager supplies a function that allows you to control the orientation and spacing of the widgets within the window. Although you can exercise a certain amount of control, the geometry manager actually does a lot of the work for you. It makes decisions, based on your recommendations, about how to lay out the individual components.

4. Start the event loop. The main execution of the script has now finished, and the rest of the script will be driven by the events configured for individual widgets.

Here is a very quick Perl/Tk script that demonstrates this:

```
use Tk;

$main = MainWindow->new();
$main->title("Hello World!");

$label = $main->Label(text => 'Hello from Tk!');
$button = $main->Button();

$icon = $button->Photo(-file => 'icon.gif');
```

```
$button->configure(image => $icon,
                command => sub { exit; }
                );

$label->pack(side => 'left');
$button->pack(side => 'left',
                padx => 5
                );

MainLoop();
```

The result, when run, looks like Figure 10-5 on a Windows 98 machine. You can see the effects of the script quite clearly. As a comparison, you can see the same script executed on a Redhat Linux machine in Figure 10-6. The insides of the two windows are identical. It is only the window manager dressing for resizing the window, minimizing or maximizing the window, or closing it altogether that are different. The window decorations are specific to the platform and window manager, and any window you create within Tk will have these decorations.

There are five important elements that you should remember when developing Tk interfaces: windows, widgets, nesting, the geometry manager and callbacks.

Windows   The window is the main container for all widgets, and the only way in which you can develop an interface with Tk. Without a window, you cannot create a widget. It's possible to create a number of different "main" windows within the same application; you are not restricted to only one window as you are with the Win32::Console

Figure 10-5
The Hello from Tk window under Microsoft Windows.

Figure 10-6
The Hello from Tk
window under X
Windows/Linux.

interface. This makes Tk much more practical from an application development point of view—you can actually develop most of the basic artifacts that you would expect from a GUI interface. This includes not just the basic windows, but also floating palettes, pop-up boxes, and warning messages.

Widgets   It's also worth paying attention to how the individual widgets are created. You cannot create a widget outside of a window—a widget must be within a container of some kind. Most containers are windows, although you can have widgets that are containers for others. For example, the `Frame` widget can contain other widgets and is used to help confine one or more widgets within certain areas within your window. Furthermore, because the `Frame` is a widget itself, you can nest multiple frames to produce complex layouts.

Nesting   The nesting of widgets is another important principle. Within Microsoft Windows applications, each application window generally consists of two main areas. The very top of the window contains the menu bar, and the remainder of the window is given to either a single frame of other components or an interface that allows multiple windows to exist within the larger frame. For example, within Microsoft Word you can have multiple documents open that all share the same menu bar.

NOTE.   As an aside, the inclusion of a per-window menu bar is different in other environments. Mac OS is a prime example, where there is one menu bar that all applications share. When you switch applications, the contents of the menu bar changes. This makes the menu bar a completely separate item to deal with, almost as if it's within its own window.

The contents of a menu bar within a Windows application are somewhat limited. Although some applications feign certain abilities, most Windows menus are limited to simple operations. The menu bar is in fact a container widget. There is nothing special about the `MenuBar` object; it's largely based on the `Frame` widget. Into that `MenuBar` widget you place `MenuButtons`, and each `MenuButton` is made up of a number of menu items. However, unlike our typical Windows application, a Tk-based application can put anything into the menu item: buttons, checkboxes, radio buttons—in fact, any other widget you like.

Furthermore, because a `MenuBar` is just another widget, you can place menus anywhere within the window; you're not tied to just producing the menu at the top of the window. The combination of flexible menus and nested widgets within those menus is great for tool and color palettes or when you want to introduce a complex list of possibilities within a confined space.

I would be willing to argue that the nesting ability of the Tk interface system is perhaps the most powerful feature after Tk's cross-platform compatibility.

Geometry Management   Finally, you must not dismiss the need for a geometry manager. The geometry manager actually does a lot more than just organizing the layout of the individual widgets within the window. Because the geometry manager is also ultimately responsible for drawing the widgets on the screen (since only it knows where they should be drawn), it's the geometry manager that actually displays each widget.

If you didn't call the geometry manager, then no widgets would be displayed, because Tk doesn't inherently know where to display them—it only knows how to display them.

Callbacks   In our demonstration script, the main `Button` widget had a command property. This pointed to the function `exit` via an anonymous subroutine. This command is what's called a *callback*—because they call back a piece of code from another part of the script when you perform a certain action. In this case, when you clicked on the button, the script ended.

To fully understand callbacks and how the other elements of the Tk window work, we need to understand *event loops*.

Event Loops

The `MainLoop` function executes a simple loop that dispatches requests from the underlying windowing system to the corresponding widgets. For each event, the function defined in the command property is executed. However, it's the responsibility of the called function to perform its job and relinquish control as soon as possible, so as to allow other waiting events to execute.

For complex systems that are CPU-intensive, you will also need to make sure that you can effectively multitask between the different threads of execution so that you don't lock up the process while servicing an earlier event loop. For some applications and some systems, this will require you to manually divide a task into manageable chunks. This will allow the event loop to send requests to other callback functions. An alternative solution is to use a multithreaded application model.

Any system call that blocks is generally a bad idea within a GUI interface, since events in the event stack will not be processed while the system blocks. This is a particular issue on Windows systems, where the process blocking can actually freeze the whole machine (although it's not supposed to). The best method is to use something like select, which will do the job of multiplexing between open file handles for you. Unfortunately, this doesn't get around the problem of handling GUI and file events for you.

The MainLoop function is not configurable; it's impossible to supply your own version. The loop only exits when users click on the Close box within their windowed environment or when a call to exit is made. Without multithreaded support there will be no way for you either to use the select function or handle the data. The solution is to use the fileevent function. This notifies a callback function when the specified file handle is ready to accept or supply data. You use it much like you use any other callback function within the Tk environment:

```
open(DATA, "file.txt) or die "Can't open $!";
$label->fileevent(DATA, "readable", \&accept_data);
```

The callback function will be called, in this instance, when data is waiting to be read from the file and when an end-of-file is identified. The callback function will need to handle both these instances. For example:

```
sub accept_data
{
    if (eof(DATA))
    {
        $label->fileevent(DATA, "readable", undef);
        return;
    }
    else
    {
        $text .= <DATA>;
    }
}
```

Of course, this doesn't guarantee that the operator or function you have chosen will not block the process if there isn't as much information as it was expecting. You should be using nonblocking I/O for this sort of process anyway. See Chapter 6 in *Perl: The Complete Reference* for more information.

Event Bindings   Beyond the basic event bindings handled by the command property, it is possible to bind specific events, such as keypresses and mouse clicks, to other functions. This is how you make keys equate to specific function calls and provide shortcuts to commands and functions. Tk provides the bind function, which allows you to map these low-level events to corresponding functions. It is also the method employed by individual widgets when you define the command property. The format for the function is as follows:

```
$widget->bind(event, callback);
```

The event is the name of the event you want to bind and can include key presses or a mouse click (which is defined as a press and release). The bind function also supports more-complicated events such as a mouse click and drag, general mouse motion, the mouse pointer entering or leaving the windows, and whole window events like resizing and iconifying.

The event is defined as a string containing the sequence you want to map, which can be made up of one or more individual events called *event sequences*. For example, the code

```
$widget->bind("<z>", \&pressed_z);
```

maps the user pressing the Z key, without any modifier, to the function. Other possible values for event are

```
$widget->bind("<Control-z>", \&undo);
```

which occurs when the Ctrl key and Z are pressed at the same time, and

```
widget->bind("<Escape><Control-z>", \&redo);
```

which would call redo when the Esc key was pressed, followed by Ctrl and Z. For mouse clicks you would use

```
$widget->bind("<Button1>", \&redo);
```

Individual events are grouped into different classes called *modifiers*, *types*, and *details*. A modifier is a special key such as *Escape*, *Control*, *Meta*, *Alt*, and *Shift*. Mouse buttons are also grouped into this class, so you get *Button1*, *Button2*, *Double* for a double click, and *Triple* for a triple click. There is also a special modifier, *Any*, which matches all of the modifiers, including none.

The type of event is one of *KeyPress*, *KeyRelease*, *ButtonPress*, *ButtonRelease*, *Enter*, *Leave*, and *Motion*. Note that you can identify both a key press and its release, so you can configure a game, for example, to accept a certain key press and only stop processing when the key is finally released. The same is true of button presses and releases. Finally, the Leave option identifies when the pointer leaves the confines of a widget (useful for tear-off menus and pallettes), and *Motion* identifies when the pointer has been moved while a button and/or keyboard combination is pressed.

The detail class is only used for keyboard bindings and is a string defining the character that has been pressed. In addition, it also supports *Enter*, *Right*, *Delete*, *Backspace*, *Escape*, *F1*, the basic ASCII characters *A* to *Z*, and so on.

To make life easier, the Tk library also allows you to use abbreviations of the most common key presses so that `<KeyPress-z>` can be specified simply as `<z>` and `<Button1-ButtonPress>` as `<1>`.

In addition, the `Text` and `Canvas` widgets allow an even finer granularity on individual bindings, allowing you to attach a binding to a specific tag. The format of `bind` changes accordingly: The first argument now defines the tag to identify, and the second and third arguments define the binding and function to be called. Thus, you can create a binding for pressing the second button on a piece of tagged text:

```
$text->bind('word', '<2>', \&synonym_menu);
```

Obtaining Event Details   Since it's possible to bind any key or button sequence to a function, it's also possible to assign multiple bindings to a single handler. In these instances, the handler must be able to determine what key or button was pressed and where the cursor was at the time the event occurred. To obtain the event details, you use the `Ev` function, which extracts the information from the event itself, since it is the event that records the information about what was pressed and where.

The `Ev('k')` call returns the key code that triggered the event, as previously defined, and `Ev('x')` and `Ev('y')` return the x and y coordinates of the mouse pointer when the event was received. To use, you need to supply an array as the value to the function-binding argument:

```
$widget->bind("<Button1>", [\&redo, Ev('k')]);
```

The first element of the array reference is the function to be called, and further elements are the arguments to be passed to the function.

Widgets

To understand how the Tk system works, we'll take a brief look at the most commonly used widgets. There are many exceptions that are not listed due to space constraints. If you want more information, check the well-organized and voluminous documentation supplied with the Perl/Tk package.

The Core Widgets   The Tk library comes with a number of predefined widgets. Some are the basic building blocks of your typical GUI application, such as a `Button` or `Label`. Others are composites of other widgets. Table 10-7 lists the basic widgets that are supported by the Tk system.

One of the advantages of Tk is that because it supports such basic levels of widgets they can be combined or modified to build other widgets. For example, the `ScrolledText` widget is a combination of the `Scrollbar` and `Text` widgets that allows you to control what part of the `Text` widgets text is displayed according to the position of the `Scrollbar`.

At first, this makes Tk look far less practical than other more feature-rich toolkits. For example, unlike Windows and some of the Unix-based toolkits, Tk doesn't support a "standard" dialog box widget—you have to make one yourself. On the other hand, because you have to make it yourself, you can produce a custom version, perhaps including an error or reference number, something that the predefined toolkits wouldn't be able to support. The downside is that the development process can take longer—you spend a long time introducing the "standard" artifacts of a good GUI. However, the flexibility wins out in the end.

We'll take a closer look at some of the more commonly used widgets as we go through the rest of this chapter.

Generic Widget Properties   The configuration of individual widgets is controlled through a series of properties. All widgets have a set of properties that define everything from the existence of borders and colors to font styles and sizes. Individual specialized widgets also have properties for the unique elements that make up that widget. For example, a

TABLE 10-7

The basic widget
set.

Widget Class	Description
BitmapImage	A subclass of the Image widget for displaying bitmap images
Button	A simple push-button widget with similar properties to the Label widget
Canvas	A drawing area into which you can place circles, lines, text, and other graphic artifacts
CheckButton	A multiple-choice button widget, where each item within the selection can be selected individually
Entry	A single-line text entry box
Frame	A container for arranging other widgets
Image	A simple widget for displaying bitmaps, pixmaps (color bitmaps), and other graphic objects
Label	A simple box into which you can place message text (noneditable)
Listbox	A multiline list of selection choices
Menu	A list of menu selections that can be made up of Label, Message, Button, and other widgets
MenuButton	A menu (within a single menu bar) that lists the selections specified in a Menu object
Message	A multiline Label object (noneditable)
OptionMenu	A special type of Menu widget that provides a pop-up list of items within a selection
PhotoImage	A subclass of the Image widget for displaying full-color images
RadioButton	A multiple-choice button widget, where you can choose only one of multiple values
Scale	A slider that allows you to set a value according to a specific scale
Scrollbar	A slider for controlling the contents of another widget, such as Text or Canvas
Text	A multiline text widget that supports editable text that also can be tagged for display in different fonts and colors
Toplevel	A window that will be managed and dressed by the parent Window Manager
TriButton	An adaptation of the Button widget that allows it to support three different states instead of the normal bipolar on/off.

MenuButton widget has a property called state, which indicates whether the menu is active or disabled.

When you define a widget, you set the properties by specifying the property name and value as part of the hash that you supply to a widget method called configure. For example:

```
$label->configure(text="Hello World!\n", foreground = 'red');
```

The generic properties that are configurable for all widgets are shown in Table 10-8. Note that although the properties shown here are without leading hyphens (as required by Tk normally), you may need to add them. The Perl/Tk interface allows you to use specifications both with and without the hyphen prefix.

All widgets also support a number of methods for controlling and configuring their options. There are two basic methods. The first is `configure`, which allows you to set multiple properties on a widget object at once:

```
$label->configure(text  => 'Hello World!', foreground => 'red');
```

TABLE 10-8

Generic widget
properties.

Property	Description
font	The font name in X or Windows format.
background, bg	The color of the background, specified either by a name or hexadecimal RGB value.
foreground, fg	The color of the foreground, specified either by a name or hexadecimal RGB value.
text	The string to be displayed within the widget, using the foreground and font values specified.
image, bitmap	The image or bitmap file to be displayed within the widget.
relief	The style of the widget's border, which should be one of raised, sunken, flat, ridge, or groove.
borderwidth	The width of the relief border.
height	The height of the widget; specified in the number of characters for labels, buttons, and text widgets, and in pixels for all other widgets.
width	The width of the widget; specified in the number of characters for labels, buttons, and text widgets, and in pixels for all other widgets.
textvariable	The name of a variable to be used and/or updated when the widget changes.
anchor	Defines the location of the widget within the window, or the location of the text within the widget. Valid values are n, ne, e, se, s, sw, w, nw, or center.

The second, `cget`, returns the value of a specific property:

```
$color =  $label->cget('foreground');
```

SPECIFYING FONTS   Font values are traditionally specified in the XLFD (X Logical Font Description) format. This is a complex string consisting of 14 fields, each separated by a hyphen. Each field defines a different property. For example, the font

```
-sony-fixed-medium-r-normal—16-120-100-100-c-80-iso8859-1
```

defines a font from the "sony" foundry, the "fixed" family, of medium weight. It's a regular (rather than italic) font—identified by the `r`, and the width is normal. The size of the font is 16 pixels or 12 points high (point size is specified in tenths of a point, so the size specified is 120 rather than 12). The next two fields specify the resolution—in this instance, 100 pixels wide and 100 pixels high—with an overall character (`c`) width of 80. The last field is the registry or character locale name.

Usually, however, you can get away with specifying an asterisk or question mark as wildcards in particular fields so that you can request a more general font, and then let the Tk and windowing interface determine the correct font. You should be able to get away with specifying the foundry, family, weight, slant, and points fields. For example, to use 12-point Helvetica, you might use

```
$label->configure(font=>
                  '-adobe-helvetica-medium-r-*—*-120-*-*-*-*-*');
```

Obviously, this is quite a mouthful, and it doesn't really apply to the Windows font system, which is much simpler. The Tk libraries also accept the simpler Windows-style definition, which is also backward-compatible with the Unix Tk libraries. This definition includes the font name, point size, and weight. For example:

```
$label->configure(font => 'Helvetica 12 regular');
```

SPECIFYING COLORS   The X Windows system supports a file called rgb.txt, which maps red, green, and blue intensities to color names. This allows you to specify a color with a simple name. Here's a short extract from the beginning of a sample rgb.txt file:

```
255 250 250               snow
248 248 255               ghost white
```

```
248 248 255              GhostWhite
 47  79  79              DarkSlateGray
  0 191 255              DeepSkyBlue
 46 139  87              SeaGreen
178  34  34              firebrick
147 112 219              MediumPurple
```

Obviously, Windows does not use X Windows, but it still has access to the core set of colors as described above. If you want to be more specific, you can explicitly specify the RGB values precisely in the form #RGB, #RRGGBB, #RRRGGGBBB, and #RRRRGGGGBBBB, where the R, G, and B refer to an individual hexadecimal digit of the corresponding color's intensity.

For example, the GhostWhite color above could be described as #F8F8FF. For many situations, it may be easier to use sprintf to create the string:

```
$color = sprintf("#%02x%02x%02x",142,112,219);
```

SPECIFYING SIZES   When you are specifying the size for a specific widget parameter, there are a number of choices available to you, depending on the widget you are using. If the widget is of a graphical rather than textual base—for example, Canvas—then the size specification accepted by the height and width properties is in pixels. This also extends to labels and buttons that have a graphical rather than textual value. For all widgets that are text-based the specification is in characters, according to the size of the font being used to display the text.

IMAGES AND BITMAPS   Certain widgets support the use of images rather than text. For example, you can use an image in place of the text that would normally appear on a button. There are essentially two types of images—a two-color bitmap and a multicolored pixmap. In an effort to help improve performance, Tk considers an image to be a unique element. If it needs to be displayed in more than one place, you render it once and use the rendered image object as the source for the widget image. This means there are two steps to using an image within a widget.

The first step is to create the rendered image object. You use a different function to render individual image formats, although the return value from each function is always of the same type. To create an image object from an X Bitmap (XBM):

```
$image = $label->Bitmap(file => 'icon.xbm');
```

For an X Pixmap (XPM):

```
$image = $label->Pixmap(file => 'icon.xpm');
```

And for a GIF or Portable Pixmap (PPM) format, you need to use the Photo **constructor:**

```
$image = $label->Photo(file => 'icon.gif');
```

When you want to configure a particular widget with an image object, use the image **property:**

```
$label->configure(image => $image);
```

For bitmaps, the foreground and background properties of the widget control the foreground and background color of the bitmap.

Labels   A Label widget is the basic widget and provides a simple way of displaying a small text label within a window. It supports all the basic properties shown in Table 10-7. Because labels are such basic elements, they often form parts or the basis of many of the other widgets in the Tk toolkit.

Buttons   Button widgets are essentially just labels with an additional property, command, which is a pointer to a function that will be called when the button is pressed. The list of additional properties and methods beyond the base list are shown in Table 10-9.

You saw an example of both the label and button in the introductory script.

TABLE 10-9

Properties and methods for buttons.

Property	Description
command	A reference to the Perl function to be called when button is clicked with mouse button 1.

Method	Description
flash	Flashes the button briefly by reversing and resetting the foreground and background colors.
invoke	Starts the subroutine defined in the command property.

TABLE 10-10

Properties and
methods for radio
buttons.

Property	Description
command	A reference to the Perl function to be called when button is clicked with mouse button 1. The variable referred to by the variable property is updated with the value in the value property before the referenced subroutine is invoked.
variable	Takes a reference to a variable and updates with the value property when the button is clicked. When the value of the referenced variable matches the value property, the button is selected automatically.
value	Specifies the value to store within the variable pointed to by the variable property when the button is selected.

Method	Description
select	Selects the radio button and sets the variable to value.
flash	Flashes the button briefly by reversing and resetting the foreground and background colors.
invoke	Starts the subroutine defined in the command property.

Radio Buttons   The RadioButton widget is used to provide either a simple on/off button or to act as a toggle between several different options. The valid properties and methods for a radio button are shown in Table 10-10.

For example, the following script shows a very simple radio button that allows you to choose between different names:

```
use Tk;

$name = 'martin';

$main = MainWindow->new();

$main->Radiobutton(text   => 'Martin',
                   value => 'martin',
                   variable => \$name)->pack(side => 'left');
$main->Radiobutton(text   => 'Sharon',
                   value => 'sharon',
                   variable => \$name)->pack(side => 'left');
$main->Radiobutton(text   => 'Wendy',
                   value => 'wendy',
                   variable => \$name)->pack(side => 'left');

MainLoop();
```

Note that the same variable is used in each property definition, and so the information is shared. A change to the value will update the corre-

Figure 10-7
Tk radio buttons.

sponding radio button family with the correct selection. The resultant window is shown in Figure 10-7.

Check Buttons   A CheckButton widget, perhaps better known as a checkbox, depending on your background, is like a radio button, except that it is normally used to allow the user to select multiple checkboxes for a single option. The possible properties and methods for a CheckButton widget are shown in Table 10-11.

TABLE 10-11

Properties and methods for check buttons.

Property	Description
command	A reference to the Perl function to be called when button is clicked with mouse button 1. The variable referred to by the variable property is updated with the value in the value property before the referenced subroutine is invoked.
variable	Takes a reference to a variable and updates with the value property when the button is clicked. When the value of the referenced variable matches the value property, the button is selected automatically.
onvalue	Specifies the value to store within the variable pointed to by the variable property when the button is selected.
offvalue	Specifies the value to store within the variable pointed to by the variable property when the button is not selected.
indicatoron	If false (zero), then rather than displaying the checkbox indicator, it toggles the relief base property of the entire widget, effectively making the whole widget the check box.

Method	Description
select	Selects the checkbutton and sets the variable to value.
flash	Flashes the button briefly by reversing and resetting the foreground and background colors.
invoke	Starts the subroutine defined in the command property.
toggle	Toggles the selection state and values of the button on and off.

Text   A `Text` widget is a simple text box used for displaying multiple lines of text, unlike a label, which is really only useful for a small number of words on a single line. A `Text` widget becomes an editable entry box for information. It supports the `emacs` keyboard shortcuts for data entry and for moving around the box. In addition to the editing features of a `Text` widget, you can also "tag" individual pieces of text and change their properties. This allows you to create a fully featured text editor with multiple font, point size, and color support without any additional programming.

    `Text` widget methods take one or more index specifications as arguments. An argument can be an absolute number (base) or a relative number (base and modifier), and both are specified as strings. Supported base index specifications are shown below. Items in italics indicate the components of the index specification that you can modify. Anything else is a keyword.

line.*char*	Indicates the character at `char` characters across (left to right) and `line` lines down (top to bottom). The specification starts at zero for characters within a line, and 1 for lines within a text box.
end	The end of the text, as defined by the character just after the last newline.
insert	The location of the insertion cursor.
mark	The character just after the marker whose name is `mark`.
tag.first, *tag*.last	Used to specify the first and last characters of a tag.

    These index specifications can also be qualified with an additional modifier:

+*count* chars, -*count* chars, +*count* lines, -*count* lines	Adjust the base index specification by the `count` characters or lines.
wordstart, wordend, linestart, lineend	Adjust the index to point to the first character on the word or line specified by the index (`wordstart`, `linestart`) or to the character immediately after the word or line.

    A sample of supported properties and methods is shown in Table 10-12. For example, to insert a piece of text at the end of a text box:

```
$text->insert('Beginning!', 'end');
```

TABLE 10-12

Properties and methods for Text widgets.

Property	Description
tabs	The list of tab stops for the Text widget. Specification should be as a reference to a list of strings. Each string should be composed of a number defining the character location within the line, followed by l, c, or r for left, center, or right justification for the specified tab.
state	One of normal for a standard editable text box, or disabled for a non-modifiable text box.

Method	Description
insert(INDEX [, STRING [, TAG]] ...)	Insert STRING with an optional TAG at the specified INDEX.
delete(INDEX1 [,INDEX2])	Delete the character at INDEX1 or the text from INDEX1 to INDEX2.
get(INDEX1 [,INDEX2])	Get the character at INDEX1 or the text from INDEX1 to INDEX2.
index(INDEX)	Returns an absolute index for the corresponding INDEX supplied.
see(INDEX)	Returns True if the text at INDEX is visible.
markSet(NAME, INDEX)	Gives the text at INDEX the bookmark name NAME.
markUnset(NAME)	Unsets a bookmark NAME.

Or to insert the same piece of text at character 20 on line 5:

```
$text->insert('Beginning!', '5.20');
```

To specify and configure the tags, you need the methods and properties shown in Table 10-13.

For example, to create a simple tag:

```
$text->tagAdd('tagged', '1.0', '3.0');
```

This creates a tag called "tagged" from lines 1 through 3 inclusive. The tag name should be unique because you need it when configuring the options on an individual tag. Therefore, to change the text tagged with the name "tagged" to 24-point Times, boldfaced:

```
$text->tagConfigure('tagged', font => 'Times 24 Bold');
```

You can also use the tie function with a Text widget to tie the text

TABLE 10-13

Table methods and properties.

Method	Description
tagAdd(NAME [,INDEX1[.INDEX2]] ...)	Adds the tag NAME at the position specified in INDEX1 or bounded by INDEX1 and INDEX2.
tagRemove(NAME [,INDEX1[.INDEX2]] ...)	Removes the tag NAME from the character or range specified by INDEX1 and INDEX2, but does not delete the actual tag definition.
tagDelete(NAME)	Removes and deletes the tag NAME.
tagConfigure	Configures one or more properties for a tag.

Property	Description
-foreground, -background, -fgstipple, -bgstipple, -font	As for the basic properties.
-justify	Justification for the tagged text, one of center, left, and right.
-relief, -borderwidth	The border width and relief style.
-tabs	As for basic text properties, but applies only if the first character in that line also belongs to the same tag. You cannot add "subtabs" to a tagged block.
-underline	Underlines the tagged text.

box contents to a file handle. Once tied, you can print and read from the Text widget just like any other file handle. Thus, you can create a very simple text file viewer with code like this:

```
use Tk;

$main = MainWindow->new();
$main->title("Text Viewer");

$maintext = $main->Scrolled('Text');

open(SOURCE, "myfile.txt") or die "Can't open source";
tie(*TEXT, 'Tk::Text', $maintext);
print TEXT <SOURCE>;
close (SOURCE);

$maintext->pack();

MainLoop();
```

Entry   An `Entry` widget is essentially a single-line text box, and it inherits many of the same features and methods from the `Text` widget. However, because it's only a single line, the indexing and methods are much simpler. The indexing options are as follows:

number	An index into the widget's contents, starting with zero as the first character.
end	The end of the text.
insert	The position immediately after the insertion cursor.
sel.first, sel.last	Indicates the first and last character of a tag.

The supported properties and methods are shown in Table 10-14.

List Boxes   A `Listbox` widget enables you to create a list, from which you can select an individual item. It displays a list of strings, one per line, and all the strings displayed have the same characteristics. When you are creating the list, the easiest way to populate it is to create the

TABLE 10-14

Properties and methods for the `Entry` widget.

Property	Description
show	A simple Boolean option. If set, it displays * for each character entered and is primarily used for password entry. Note that although the characters are displayed in this manner, copying and pasting the contents of a "hidden" field will reveal the real contents.

Method	Description
get(INDEX)	Gets the string starting at INDEX.
insert(INDEX, STRING)	Inserts STRING at INDEX.
index(INDEX)	Returns an absolute index from a relative one.
selectionFrom(INDEX)	Sets the selection from INDEX to the end of the field.
selectionTo(INDEX)	Sets the selection from the beginning of the field to INDEX.
selection(FROM, TO)	Sets the selection to the characters starting at FROM and ending at TO.
selectionClear	Clears the selection.
selectionPresent	True if a selection is currently active.

widget and then use the `insert` method to add items to the list. The
`width` and `height` properties for the `Listbox` widget define the width
of the list box and the height in characters. Or you can specify values of
zero, which will cause the list box to grow to display all of the objects.

You can see an example of the `Listbox` widget in the following:

```
use Tk;

$main = MainWindow->new();

$list = $main->Listbox(height => 5,
                       width => 0)->pack();

$list->insert('end', qw/Martin Sharon Wendy Sharon Chris/);

MainLoop();
```

The result is shown in Figure 10-8. Note that you will need to use the
`bind` method shown earlier in this chapter to bind a particular operation
such as a double-click to a function. Within the function, you'll need to
use the `get` method to obtain the current selection.

You can refer to individual elements within a `Listbox` in a similar
fashion to selecting text within a `Textbox` widget. Specification is by a
string defining the row, row selection, or relative location within the list.
The details are shown below.

number	The index of the row, starting with zero for the first element.
end	Indicates the end of the current row.
active	Where the location cursor is currently positioned, and the active location appears underlined in the list view.
anchor	The anchor point of the selection.

The properties and methods supported by the `Listbox` widget are
shown in Table 10-15.

Menus   Menus are logically split into `Menubutton` widgets, which are
the menu names. The `Menubutton` widget then becomes a container
that holds the individual menu item widgets, which are split into different types to allow you to add normal menu items (actually just labels),
buttons, checkboxes, and radio buttons to your menus.

The normal method for creating a menu is as follows:

1. Create a menu bar frame, using the `Frame` widget, to hold individual menu buttons.

Figure 10-8
A Listbox widget
in action.

TABLE 10-15

Properties and
methods sup-
ported by the
Listbox widget.

Property	Description
height, width	The height and width of the list in rows and characters. If either is zero, then the widget resizes to incorporate all of the list elements.
selectMode	Defines the selection mode of the list, one of single, browse, multiple, or extended.

Method	Description
get(INDEX)	Gets the string, starting at INDEX.
insert(index, string)	Inserts STRING at INDEX.
delete(INDEX [, LAST])	Deletes the row at INDEX, or the rows between INDEX and LAST.
see(INDEX)	Brings the element INDEX into the current view.
selectionFrom(INDEX)	Selects all the rows from INDEX to the end of the list.
selectionTo(INDEX)	Selects all the rows from the beginning of the list to INDEX.
selection(FROM, TO)	Selects the rows starting at FROM and ending at TO.
selectionClear()	Clears the selection.
selectionPresent()	Returns True if there is an active selection.
curselection()	A list of the index values of all the selected items.

2. Create the individual menu buttons within the new frame.

3. Use the `MenuButton` widget methods to create the individual menu items.

Every method of the `MenuButton` widget supports the now familiar index format, although the index refers to the individual menu item:

number	The index of the menu item, starting at zero for the first item. When the menu is configured for tear-off, the first entry is a separator automatically inserted by the widget.
end, `last`	Indicates the last entry.
`active`	Where the location cursor is currently active.
`none`	Indicates that none of the menu options are active.
pattern	A pattern to be matched against all entries. This only matches exactly; regular expressions are supported.

Properties and methods for the `MenuButton` widget are shown in Table 10-16.

The configurable `options` supported for the methods in Table 10-16 work like all other properties and are listed in Table 10-17. Note that because you can have hierarchical menus, individual items can use further methods from Table 10-16.

For example, to create a simple Help menu, you might use a script like this:

```
use Tk;

$main = MainWindow->new();

$menu = $main->Frame()->pack(side => 'top');

$help_menu = $menu->Menubutton(text        => 'Help',
                               relief       => 'raised',
                               borderwidth => 2,
                               )->pack(side => 'left',
                                       padx => 2
                                       );

$help_menu->command('-label'    => 'About',
                    accelerator => 'Meta+A',
                    underline   => 0,
                    command     => sub { print "All about me\n" }
                    );

$help_menu->separator();

$help_menu->command('-label'    => 'Help Index',
```

TABLE 10-16

Menu item methods.

Property	Description
indicatorOn	If true, shows a small diamond to the right of the menu.
state	The state of the menu—one of normal, active, or disabled.

Method	Description
menu	Returns the underlying menu associated with this menu button.
command(OPTIONS)	Creates a standard menu item using the properties in OPTIONS.
separator(OPTIONS)	A separator.
radiobutton(OPTIONS)	A radio button menu item using the properties in OPTIONS.
checkbutton(OPTIONS)	A check button menu item using the properties in OPTIONS.
cascade(OPTIONS)	Inserts a new cascading (hierarchical) menu using the properties in OPTIONS.
add(TYPE, OPTIONS)	Adds a new menu of TYPE with OPTIONS.
delete(INDEX1 [, index2])	Deletes the menu item INDEX1 or the items from INDEX1 to INDEX2.
insert(INDEX1, TYPE, OPTIONS)	Inserts a menu item of TYPE with OPTIONS into the location INDEX1.
entryconfigure(INDEX, OPTIONS)	Changes the properties of the menu item according to OPTIONS pointed to by INDEX.
entrycget(INDEX)	Gets the configuration options for the menu item at INDEX.

```
                    accelerator => 'Meta+H',
                    underline   => 0,
                    command => \&draw_help_window(),
                    );

$help_menu->command('-label' => 'Help on Help',
                    command   => sub { print "Try Help Index\n" }
                    );

MainLoop();
```

The result can be seen in Figure 10-9.

Frame   A Frame widget is simply a container for other widgets. It's used when you need to create a complex layout that requires more-

TABLE 10-17

Menu item
properties.

Property	Description
indicatorOn	If true, places a small diamond next to the menu option, which allows an option to be toggled on and off by a menu.
selectColor	The color of the indicator, if indicatorOn is true.
tearOff	If true, the first element of the menu is a separator. Clicking on the separator "tears off" the menu into a separate top-level window. This is not always supported on all implementations.
label	The text to use for the menu item. This should be used in place of the normal text property.
underline	The index of a character to underline. This is used in combination with the accelerator property to indicate which keyboard shortcut should be used for this menu.
accelerator	Shows the string to be displayed, right justified, as the keyboard equivalent for the menu option. This doesn't bind the key to the command for you. You'll have to do that separately.
state	Status: normal, active, or disabled.
command	The reference of a subroutine to call when the menu item is selected.
value	The value of the attached radio button (see Table 10-10).
variable	The variable used to store value.
onvalue, offvalue	Identical to the options in Table 10-11 for check-button-style entries.

Figure 10-9
A simple Tk menu.

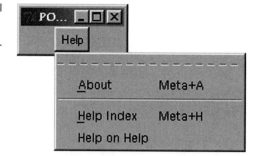

advanced geometry management than you can normally do with the available tools. The way it works is that you divide individual areas of the window into frames and pack the collection of objects into the frame. For example, you might create a new frame that contains the menu bar, which you gravitate to the top of the window, while the actual menu buttons within the menu bar are arranged horizontally. We'll see an example later in this chapter when we look at the Scale widget.

Scroll Bars   Scroll bars are available either as separate widgets, in which case you are responsible for managing the corresponding widget you are scrolling, or they can be automatically added to any suitable widgets. We'll deal with the automatic scroll bars first. To create an automatically scrolled widget, you use the special Scrolled widget method, and then specify the type of widget to create with a scroll bar.

For example, here's the line from the text viewer that creates a scrolled Text widget:

```
$maintext = $main->Scrolled('Text');
```

Internally, this creates a Frame widget that contains the main Text widget and the horizontal (and vertical) scroll bars. The reference returned actually refers to the newly created Frame widget.

Alternatively, you can create and manage your own scroll bars using the methods and properties in Tables 10-18 and 10-19. The methods in Table 10-19 allow you to set the current view within the widget to which you want to associate the scroll bar. The set function controls the current view, and the command property is called when the scroll bar is moved.

All widgets that are scrollable also support the methods and properties shown in Table 10-19. The properties define the functions and increments that the scroll bars control. The scrollbar widget automatically calls the correct method (xview or yview) to modify the display of the linked widget.

Scale   Scales are like thermometers. You define a size and range, and the widget displays a horizontal or vertical slider. The slider automatically has a label (if you've defined one) and tick marks to indicate individual divisions. You can see a sample in Figure 10-10, and we'll look at the code required to build this application shortly.

TABLE 10-18

Properties and methods for scroll bars.

Property	Description
command	A reference to a subroutine used to change the view in the widget.

Method	Description
set(FIRST, LAST)	Indicates the current view. The FIRST and LAST elements should be fractions between 0 and 1. For example, a value of 0.1 and 0.2 should indicate that the area between 10 percent and 20 percent of the item should be shown.
get	Returns the current scroll bar settings.

TABLE 10-19

Properties and methods for scrollable widgets.

Property	Description
xscrollincrement, yscrollincrement	The scrolling, x and y, will be done in the specified increments.
xscrollcommand, yscrollcommand	A reference to the function used to reposition the widget when the scroll bar is moved.

Method	Description
xview('moveto', FRACTION)	Moves the scrollbar to the location specified by fraction, which indicates the leftmost, or topmost, character or pixel. Note that the first argument is a constant.
yview('moveto', FRACTION)	
xview('scroll', NUMBER, WHAT)	Indicates that the view should be moved up or down, or left or right, for NUMBER increments. If WHAT is "units," then it is scrolled according to the increment in the properties xscrollincrement and yscrollincrement. If WHAT is "pages," then the widget is scrolled NUMBER pages.

TABLE 10-20

Properties and
methods for
Scale widgets.

Property	Description
command	Reference to a subroutine, which will be called when the scale's value is changed.
variable	Reference to a variable to be updated whenever the slider moves. Works like the variable base property; updating this value will also set the slider position.
width, length	The width and length of the scale in pixels (not characters).
orient	Allows you to select horizontal or vertical orientation.
from, to	The real range of values that the widget should scale from and to.
resolution	The value displayed and set into variable will always be a multiple of this number. The default is 1.
tickinterval	The spacing, in real values, between tick marks on the scale.
label	The label to be displayed to the top (horizontal) or left (vertical) scale.

Method	Description
set(VALUE)	Identical to modifying the value of variable.

The supported properties and methods are shown in Table 10-20.

Here's the script that generated Figure 10-10. It provides a simple tool for converting feet into meters and vice versa.

```
use Tk;

my ($feetscale, $metrescale) = (0,0);

$main = MainWindow->new();

$feetframe = $main->Frame()->pack(side => 'left');

$feetframe->Scale(command      => \&update_feet,
                  variable     => \$feetscale,
                  width        => 20,
                  length       => 400,
                  orient       => 'vertical',
                  from         => 0,
                  to           => 328,
                  resolution   => 1,
                  tickinterval => 25,
                  label        => 'Feet'
```

Figure 10-10

A Scale widget for converting feet into meters.

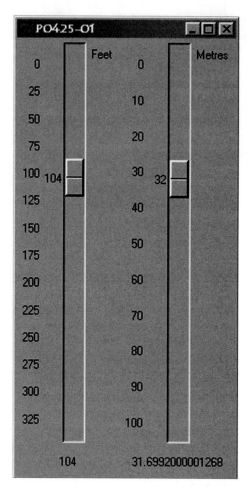

```
                            )->pack(side => 'top');

    $feetframe->Label(textvariable => \$feetscale)->pack(side => 'top',
                                                         pady => 5);

    $metreframe = $main->Frame()->pack(side => 'left');

    $metreframe->Scale(command      => \&update_metre,
                       variable      => \$metrescale,
                       width         => 20,
                       length        => 400,
                       orient        => 'vertical',
                       from          => 0,
                       to            => 100,
                       resolution    => 1,
                       tickinterval  => 10,
                       label         => 'Metres'
```

```
                       )->pack(side => 'top');

$metreframe->Label(textvariable => \$metrescale)->pack(side => top,
                                                       pady => 5);

MainLoop();

sub update_feet
{
    $metrescale = $feetscale/3.280839895;
}

sub update_metre
{
    $feetscale = $metrescale*3.280839895;
}
```

A `Frame` widget is used to specify two frames, side by side, and then within each frame, the scale and the floating-point value are shown one above the other.

Controlling Window Geometry

Throughout this chapter you've seen examples of the `pack` function, and you already know it is a required element of the window-building process. However, there are some tricks you can do with `pack` to aid in the arrangement of individual widgets within a window. Tk also supports two other methods of arranging widgets: the Placer and the Grid. You must use the same geometry manager within a single parent, although it's possible to mix and match individual geometry managers within multiple frames within a single window to suit your needs.

The Placer requires some careful planning to use properly, since you must specify the location of each widget within the window using x, y coordinates. This is the same system used within the `Bulletin Board` widget under Motif and Visual Basic, so people moving from these systems may be more comfortable with this system.

The Grid geometry manager uses a simple table layout, as you might use within a word processor or when designing web pages with HTML. Each widget is placed into a table cell, and you specify its location by defining the row and column in which the widget should appear. Individual widgets can span multiple rows and columns if necessary. As with the Placer geometry manager, you will need to give some careful thought regarding how to lay out your widgets in this system.

The Packer geometry manager is the one we've been using in this chapter, and it's the most practical if you do not want to think too much about the geometry management process. As such, it's the one we'll pay the most attention to in this chapter. If you want details on the systems, please see the documentation that comes with the Perl/Tk module.

Packer The Packer geometry manager is similar to Motif's `Form` widget and uses a much simpler system for defining the location of widgets within a frame of a window. Remember that the `pack` function is just that—it only provides the algorithm used to organize the layout of widgets. Individual calls to the `pack` method pack the corresponding widget into the next available space within the frame or window. This means that widgets are added to the window or frame in the order they are packed. This is similar to how you would pack a bag or fill a shelf: You start from a single point and add items until the space is all used up.

The algorithm works like this:

1. Given a frame, the packer attaches a widget to a particular side (top, bottom, left, or right).

2. The space used up by the widget is taken off from the space available in the frame. This area is called the *parcel*. If the widget does not fill the parcel completely (if it is wider or taller than the area sliced for the widget), then that space is essentially wasted. This is in fact the reason for supporting additional `Frame` widgets to make the best use of the space.

3. The next widget is then placed into the remaining space, and once again the widget can attach itself to the top or bottom of the available space.

4. Note that all widgets that specify a particular anchor point will be grouped together and share that space. Thus, if you specify multiple widgets with "left" anchor, they will be organized left-to-right within the frame. Once again, if you want to do more-complex layouts (as in the `Scale` widget example), you will need to create separate frames.

The available options to the packer method are shown in Table 10-21. Like other elements of the Tk system, options are specified as a hash to the `pack` method.

If you do not specify an option, the Packer geometry manager inserts widgets from top to bottom.

The `padx`, `pady`, `ipadx`, and `ipady` properties accept a string, rather than a numeric value. Depending on the value's suffix, the value is interpreted either as pixels, centimeters, inches, millimeters, or points. For

TABLE 10-21

Options to the
pack function.

Property	Description
side	The side of the frame to which the widget should be added. Should be one of left, right, top, or bottom.
fill	Specifies whether the widget should fill up the space in the parcel in the x or y direction accordingly. You can also specify both, to fill in both directions, or none, to prevent filling altogether. The ipadx or ipady options can be used to specify some additional blank padding space around the widget within the parcel.
expand	Specifies whether the widget should expand to take up all of the remaining space after the other widgets have been placed. This is useful for Textbox widgets where you are defining an outer menu and toolbar and want the main widget to take up all the remaining space.
padx, pady	The spacing between widgets, specified in pixels, millimeters, inches, or points. (See also Table 10-22.)
ipadx, ipady	The spacing around a widget that is "filling" the space provided by the parcel. Specified in pixels, millimeters, inches, or points. (See also Table 10-22.)

values other than pixels, the geometry manager will interrogate the window manager and determine the screen resolution and density to decide how many actual pixels to use—for example, on a typical Windows screen running at 96 dpi, a specification of 1i would introduce padding of 96 pixels. The valid suffixes are shown in Table 10-22.

Grid   The Grid geometry manager works in an identical fashion as tables within HTML. These individual widgets are placed into a grid of rows and columns. Individual widgets are confined to each cell within the grid, but individual cells can be made to span more than one row or column if required.

The grid function/method is the interface to the Grid manager. You specify the location of each widget according to the row and column in which it should appear. The final size of the grid is based on the maximum row and column that you specify. The properties for the grid function are shown in Table 10-23.

Placer   The Placer manager works slightly differently than the other two geometry managers. Whereas the Packer and Grid work on the basis of aligning widgets according to the other widgets on the page, the Placer allows you to specify very precisely where you want a widget to be

TABLE 10-22

Padding character suffixes.

Suffix	Description
none	Size is calculated in pixels.
c	Size is interpreted as onscreen centimeters.
i	Size is interpreted as onscreen inches.
m	Size is interpreted as onscreen millimeters.
p	Size is interpreted as printer's points (1 point is approximately 1/72 inch). This is the same unit as the point size used when specifying font sizes.

placed. The specification is based on the location and size of the window into which the widget is placed. If you consider each window to be similar to a cell with the Grid manager, you should get the idea. The widget is then placed into the window that is created. The specification for the size of the window itself is defined in relation to the widget's parent (either a Window or Frame or other container widget). Armed with this principle, you can specify either:

- The location (in pixels) and size of the window within the parent.
- The location and size of the window in relation to the parent.

TABLE 10-23

Properties for the Grid geometry manager.

Property	Value
column	The column in which to insert the widget.
columnspan	The number of columns that the widget should span within the grid.
row	The row in which to insert the widget.
rowspan	The number of rows that the widget should span within the grid.
sticky	Defines the side of the parent widget to which the widget will stick. Should be specified as zero or more of the characters n, s, e, or w. If none are specified, the widget becomes centered within its cell. If both n and s (or e and w) are specified, then the widget will stretch to fill the height (or width) of the cell. If all four are specified, then the widget grows to fill the entire cell.
padx, pady	The spacing between widgets, specified in pixels, millimeters, inches, or points. (See Table 10-22.)
ipadx, ipady	The spacing around a widget that is "filling" the space provided by the parcel. Specified in pixels, millimeters, inches, or points. (See Table 10-22.)

- A combination of the two—so you can have a fixed size but a variable location, or a fixed location but a variable size.

Thus you can have a widget centered within a parent that expands with the parent, increasing both the border and widget size. These options are incredibly useful for Canvas, Text, and other widgets where you want to expand the display area without affecting the other widgets within the window.

The interface to the Placer manager is via the place method to your widgets. The supported key/value pairs accepted by the function are shown in Table 10-24.

TABLE 10-24		
Properties for the Placer geometry manager.		

Property	Description
in	The widget (object) that the widget should be placed relative to. The value must be a valid widget object and must either be the window parent or a descendant of the window parent. You must also ensure that the widget and its parent are both descendants of the same window.
x, y	The x (horizontal) and y (vertical) coordinates to use as the anchor point for the widget. See Table 10-22 for a list of valid qualifiers for the number.
relx, rely	The relative x (horizontal) coordinate within the parent window. The number should be specified as a floating-point number, where 0.0 refers to the left edge of the parent, and 1.0 to the right edge; thus, the setting 0.5 would center the widget in the parent.
anchor	Defines which point of the window should be treated as the anchor point. Uses the normal N, NE, E, SE, S, SW, W, NW values.
width, height	Specifies the width or height of the window. See Table 10-22 for a list of valid values. Note that in both cases the measurement defines the outer width of the window, including any border.
relwidth, relheight	The relative width or height of the window compared to the size of the parent, where 0.5 means the window is half as big as the parent, and 1.0 means that the window and parent are the same width or height.
bordermode	One of inside (default), outside, or ignore. If set to inside, then the area for the window is calculated less any border on the parent. If outside, it includes the area set by the parent's border. If set to ignore, then the calculations are taken irrespective of the border size, making the entire parent window available for use.

NOTE.   *The* x, relx, y, *and* rely *settings can be combined. A value of* 0.5 *for* relx *and* 5 *for* x *would place the widget 5 pixels to the right of the center of the parent. The same is true for* width, relwidth, height, *and* relheight, *where a specification of* 1.0 *for* relwidth *and* 5 *for* width *would produce a window 5 pixels smaller than the parent.*

Easing the Process

If you are designing a relatively static window for your Perl script rather than one with many dynamic elements, you may find the SpecTcl application of some use. SpecTcl is a GUI designer, which is itself written in Tcl and Tk. The newer versions include the ability to design Tk-based user environments that generate the necessary code for Tcl, Java, HTML, and Perl. The Java 1.1, HTML, and Perl extensions are still experimental, but they will allow you to generate most of the required code to build your application.

SpecTcl will particularly appeal to people who have had the experience of using a visual interface development environment such as Access or Visual Basic. You lay out widgets of static pages by simply dragging and dropping the individual elements into a window and configuring the properties, such as fonts and colors, from lists of suitable values. SpecTcl creates all the Perl/Tk code for you; all you need to do is supply the callback functions and the rest of the support code to go with it.

For example, Figure 10-11 shows the SpecTcl application in action, in this case developing the basic layout for a calculator (actually based on a Python application, although SpecTcl doesn't currently support Python). When you have finished drawing and configuring all of the individual components, then you click on the Build icon, and the Perl code is generated.

Following is the code generated for our calculator application:

```perl
use Tk;

my $expression ='Welcome';

# interface generated by SpecTcl (Perl enabled) version 1.1
# from C:/Program Files/SpecTcl1.1/demo/calctest.ui
# For use with Tk400.202, using the gridbag geometry manager

sub evalexpression
{
    my $result;
    $result = eval($expression);
```

Figure 10-11
The SpecTcl application in action.

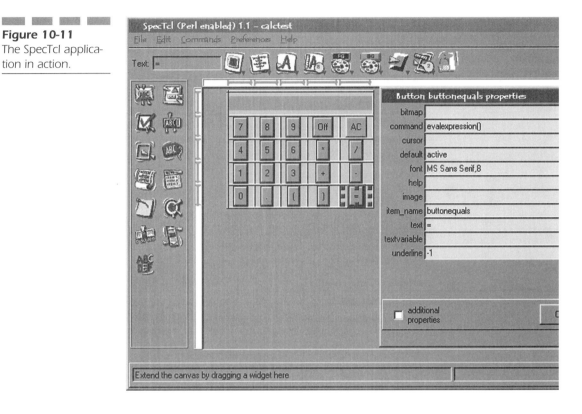

```perl
        if ($@)
        {
            $expression = $@;
        }
        else
        {
            $expression = $result;
        }
}

sub all_clear
{
    $expression = '';
}

sub insert
{
    $expression .= $_[0];
}

sub calctest_ui {
    my($root) = @_;

    # widget creation
```

```
my($expression) = $root->Entry (-textvariable => \$expression,);
my($button7) = $root->Button (-text => '7',);
my($button8) = $root->Button (-text => '8',);
my($button9) = $root->Button (-text => '9',);
my($buttonoff) = $root->Button (-text => 'Off',);
my($buttonAC) = $root->Button (-text => 'AC',);
my($button4) = $root->Button (-text => '4',);
my($button5) = $root->Button (-text => '5',);
my($button6) = $root->Button (-text => '6',);
my($buttontimes) = $root->Button (-text => '*',);
my($buttondivide) = $root->Button (-text => '/',);
my($button1) = $root->Button (-text => '1',);
my($button2) = $root->Button (-text => '2',);
my($button3) = $root->Button (-text => '3',);
my($buttonplus) = $root->Button (-text => '+',
my($buttonminus) = $root->Button (-text => '-',
my($button0) = $root->Button (-text => '0',);
my($buttonperiod) = $root->Button (-text => '.',);
my($buttonleft) = $root->Button (-text => '(',);
my($buttonright) = $root->Button (-text => ')',);
my($buttonequals) = $root->Button (-text => '=',);

# widget commands

$button7->configure(-command => sub { insert '7'; });
$button8->configure(-command => sub { insert '8'; });
$button9->configure(-command => sub { insert '9'; });
$buttonoff->configure(-command => sub { exit(); });
$buttonAC->configure(-command => \&all_clear);
$button4->configure(-command => sub { insert '4'; });
$button5->configure(-command => sub { insert '5'; });
$button6->configure(-command => sub { insert '6'; });
$buttontimes->configure(-command => sub { insert '*'; });
$buttondivide->configure(-command => sub { insert '/'; });
$button1->configure(-command => sub { insert '1'; });
$button2->configure(-command => sub { insert '2'; });
$button3->configure(-command => sub { insert '3'; });
$buttonplus->configure(-command => sub { insert '+'; });
$buttonminus->configure(-command => sub { insert '-'; });
$button0->configure(-command => sub { insert '0'; });
$buttonperiod->configure(-command => sub { insert '.'; });
$buttonleft->configure(-command => sub { insert '('; });
$buttonright->configure(-command => sub { insert ')'; });
$buttonequals->configure(-command => \&evalexpression);

# Geometry management

$expression->grid(-in => $root,
                  -column => '1',
                  -row => '1',
                  -columnspan => '5');
$button7->grid(-in => $root,
               -column => '1',
               -row => '2');
$button8->grid(-in => $root,
               -column => '2',
               -row => '2'
                    );
$button9->grid(-in => $root,
```

```
                             -column => '3',
                             -row => '2');
        $buttonoff->grid(-in => $root,
                         -column => '4',
                         -row => '2');
        $buttonAC->grid(-in => $root,
                        -column => '5',
                        -row => '2');
        $button4->grid(-in => $root,
                       -column => '1',
                       -row => '3');
        $button5->grid(-in => $root,
                       -column => '2',
                       -row => '3');
        $button6->grid(-in => $root,
                       -column => '3',
                       -row => '3');
        $buttontimes->grid(-in => $root,
                           -column => '4',
                           -row => '3');
        $buttondivide->grid(-in => $root,
                            -column => '5',
                            -row => '3');
        $button1->grid(-in => $root,
                       -column => '1',
                       -row => '4');
        $button2->grid(-in => $root,
                       -column => '2',
                       -row => '4');
        $button3->grid(-in => $root,
                       -column => '3',
                       -row => '4');
        $buttonplus->grid(-in => $root,
                          -column => '4',
                          -row => '4');
        $buttonminus->grid(-in => $root,
                           -column => '5',
                           -row => '4');
        $button0->grid(-in => $root,
                       -column => '1',
                       -row => '5');
        $buttonperiod->grid(-in => $root,
                            -column => '2',
                            -row => '5');
        $buttonleft->grid(-in => $root,
                          -column => '3',
                          -row => '5');
        $buttonright->grid(-in => $root,
                           -column => '4',
                           -row => '5');
        $buttonequals->grid(-in => $root,
                            -column => '5',
                            -row => '5');

        # Resize behavior management

        # container $root (rows)
        $root->gridRowconfigure(1, -weight  => 0, -minsize  => 30);
        $root->gridRowconfigure(2, -weight  => 0, -minsize  => 17);
```

```
$root->gridRowconfigure(3, -weight  => 0, -minsize  => 8);
$root->gridRowconfigure(4, -weight  => 0, -minsize  => 7);
$root->gridRowconfigure(5, -weight  => 0, -minsize  => 2);

# container $root (columns)
$root->gridColumnconfigure(1, -weight => 0, -minsize => 2);
$root->gridColumnconfigure(2, -weight => 0, -minsize => 13);
$root->gridColumnconfigure(3, -weight => 0, -minsize => 13);
$root->gridColumnconfigure(4, -weight => 0, -minsize => 30);
$root->gridColumnconfigure(5, -weight => 0, -minsize => 30);

# additional interface code
# end additional interface code

}

$main = MainWindow->new();
$main->title("Calculator");

calctest_ui($main);

MainLoop();
```

The amount of code generated is quite high when compared to that generated manually because the properties are created in separate sections (basic, then commands). Otherwise, the code generated works. The three functions used by the buttons have been added at the top, in addition to the glue code required to generate a window, and then they call the `MainLoop` function to kick the process off. You can see the finished product in Figure 10-12.

The code is primarily aimed at producing simple form-based windows for data entry and other similar static window development, although it may also provide you with enough base code to start you on your way with Tk development.

Development of the SpecTcl system has now stopped, since it was actually developed at Sun while the Tcl and Tk projects were being developed at the company. Even so, the package still remains solid, and for projects that require very quick development, it may provide an immediate solution without the manual labor.

You can download SpecTcl from Scriptics (www.scriptics.com). The SpecPerl portion of the development is handled by Mark Kvale, and you can download the latest version from http://www.keck.ucsf.edu/~~kvale/specPerl.

Win32::GUI

The `Win32::GUI` module, developed by Aldo Calpini, takes a different path to the development of a GUI than Tk. Tk works by creating a layer

Figure 10-12
Finished calculator, designed using SpecTcl.

that separates the underlying widget definition from the host GUI. When you create a Tk widget, it is the Tk library and designs that build the individual widget pixel by pixel. This means that between platforms the Tk interface looks the same—one of the main design points behind Tk.

When you compare a Tk interface to a native Win32 application, however, you will notice minor differences. For most applications the difference is not going to be significant enough for most users to quibble about the style, but you might want to develop an application within Perl that looks identical to a native application. This is where the Win32::GUI module fits in.

Like Tk, Win32::GUI allows you to build an interface, but unlike Tk, Win32::GUI uses the tools defined within the Windows operating system. This means that you are using the pop-up, menu, and other definitions from the Windows GUI libraries and not a compatibility-style interface, as offered by Tk.

You can get information on the Win32::GUI toolkit at http://dada.perl.it.

Beyond Compatibility

Although remaining compatible with the Unix and perhaps other versions of the Perl interpreter is good practice, there are times when you want to develop an application that uses features only available within the Windows environment. This is especially true when you are developing applications within Perl that you want to integrate into an existing environment, making use directly of the features of the Windows operating system.

Unix is often used through web and other applications as a server platform, rather than as a client platform. Windows, on the other hand, is primarily a client operating system. In the last chapter of this section, we will concentrate on three modules supplied as standard with the ActivePerl distribution that don't provide any compatibility with a Unix feature: `Win32::Clipboard`, `Win32::Sound`, and `Win32::OLE`. The `Win32::Clipboard` module provides access to the global clipboard available under Windows. The `Win32::Sound` module provides a generic interface for playing audio files from Perl.

The last module offers the greatest amount of flexibility. The `Win32::OLE` module allows you to communicate with another Windows application and control its operation. At the simplest level, this can be used to open a Word document and print it, all controlled from the Perl language. At the other end of the scale, the module can be used to provide interfaces to other sources of information that would otherwise be unavailable. For example, we can use `Win32::OLE` to extract information from a Word document without actually having to understand the format in which the document was stored.

Win32::Clipboard

The `Win32::Clipboard` is probably the simplest Windows module you can find. The module provides access to the contents of the clipboard. At the moment, the access is limited to text information only. To get the contents of the clipboard:

```
use Win32::Clipboard;

$clipboard = Win32::Clipboard();
```

The newly created object then supports three methods: `Get`, `Set`, and `Empty`. To return the current contents of the clipboard, you use the `Get` method:

```
$current = $clipboard->Get();
```

To set the contents to a new value, use the `Set` method:

```
$clipboard->Set("This is the clipboard contents");
```

To actually empty the contents of the clipboard, use `Empty`:

```
$clipboard->Empty();
```

Using `Win32::Sound`

Another artifact of the client, rather than the server-oriented approach, of the Windows OS is the multimedia abilities. Although these features have been in Unix for years, their accessibility is often questionable. This is largely because there is no standard for talking to a sound device. The SGI and Sun platforms both have sound hardware built in, but because they are platform-specific, support for these is limited (although the Python language actually supports a pretty good interface to both platforms, including the ability to output AIFF files directly).

Under Windows, there are three basic types of sound: system beeps, system events, and WAV files. The system beep is the simple beep (actually called a "ding" in recent Windows releases) given when no other sound has been configured. A system event sound is played when a particular event occurs. These are normally configured through the Sound control panel and are the event-specific sounds that occur when you open a window or receive an email.

A WAV file is the standard audio format supported by Windows. WAV files are used as the sounds for the default beep, system events, and many other sounds used on your machine, including those in other applications and games. The WAV format is fairly widely accepted, and you should be able to record and supply your own WAV files for use in your own applications.

The module supports a number of functions. The main function, however, is `Play`, which plays a sound, either the default beep, one of the preconfigured system event sounds, or a WAV file:

```
use Win32::Sound;

Win32::Sound::Play([SOUND [, FLAG]);
```

If not supplied any arguments, then the system beep is played. If supplied the first argument and it points to a WAV file, the function will play that file. However, if the first argument contains a string naming an existing event, the sound configured for that event will be played. For example, the line

```
Win32::Sound::Play('MailBeep');
```

will play the sound configured on the current machine when email is received. The exact list of system events supported on the current machine is specific to an individual user's profile. You can access this information by looking at the hash in the registry key HKEY_CURRENT_USER/AppEvents/Schemes/Apps/.Default. For example, the following script will find all of the system events configured for the current user, show the name of the file that is being used for the event, and then play the sound in question:

```
use Win32::TieRegistry(Delimiter => '/');
use Win32::Sound;

my $root = $Registry->{"CUser/AppEvents/Schemes/Apps/.Default"};

foreach $sound (sort keys(%{$root}))
{
    $sound =~ s|/$||;
    print "System Event: $sound\n";
    print "         File: ",$root->{$sound}->{'.Current/'}->{'/'},"\n";
    Win32::Sound::Play($sound);
}
```

Incidentally, if you have a machine that supports themes (Windows 98, Windows 2000), the sounds used for the different themes are also stored here—if you display the contents of the hash for a specific event. The following script accesses the registry and plays the different sounds for a particular event as supplied on the command line:

```
use Win32::TieRegistry(Delimiter => '/');
use Win32::Sound;

my $root = $Registry->{"CUser/AppEvents/Schemes/Apps/.Default"};

$sound = $ARGV[0];

if (@ARGV && exists($root->{$sound}))
{
    $sound =~ s|/$||;
    print "System Event: $sound\n";
    foreach $sub (keys %{$root->{$sound}})
    {
```

```
                    if ($sub =~ m/^[a-zA-Z.]/
                        && $root->{$sound}->{$sub}->{'/'})
                    {
                        $sub =~ s|/$||;
                        print("Playing $sub:",
                            $root->{$sound}->{$sub}->{'/'},"\n");
                        Win32::Sound::Play($root->{$sound}->{$sub}->{'/'});
                    }
                }
            }
            else
            {
                print "Not a valid event, please choose one of:\n";
                foreach $event (sort keys %{$root})
                {
                    $event =~ s|/$||;
                    print "$event\n";
                }
            }
```

For example, with this script you can now type

```
C:\> perl 03.pl SystemExit
```

and all the different sounds for the different themes you have installed on your machine will be played.

The optional FLAG parameter to the Win32::Sound::Play function specifies how the sound is played. Valid values are shown in Table 11-1. Note that if you do not specify any flags, then the process will block while the sound is played.

Flags can be OR'd together to combine their operation. If you do not specify a sound, or if the sound you specify cannot be found, then the

TABLE 11-1

Flags for playing sounds.

Flag	Description
SND_ASYNC	Sound is played asynchronously; the process does not block when the sound starts playing, and the function call returns immediately.
SND_LOOP	Sound loops repeatedly. You should specify SND_ASYNC as well; otherwise, the process will block completely.
SND_NODEFAULT	Does not play the default sound if the sound you specify cannot be found. The function returns immediately without playing any sound.
SND_NOSTOP	Causes the function to fail if a sound is currently playing. Without this option, a sound already playing will stop in order to play the newly supplied sound.

default Windows sound will be played instead, unless you specify the SND_NODEFAULT flag.

Once an asynchronous sound has started to play, you can stop it in two ways. The first is to call the function with the SND_NODEFAULT flags:

```
Win32::Sound::Play('',SND_NODEFAULT);
```

Alternatively, you can call the Win32::Sound::Stop function.

Automation and Data Sharing Using OLE

The Object Linking and Embedding (OLE) system is a core part of the Windows operating system. OLE is a high-level interface to the underlying Component Object Model (COM) system. COM is a software architecture built into Windows that allows components made by different software companies to be combined. COM defines the standard for communication between individual objects.

The COM system is the core of the operation. The different pieces of application software that you have installed on your machine are built using objects, and each object has its own properties and methods. The COM provides the underlying architecture that allows for these objects to be combined into single documents using systems such as OLE. For example, an Excel spreadsheet is a type of object, and this can be embedded, through OLE and COM, into a Word document.

When you want to edit the spreadsheet, you can edit it directly within Word, because the spreadsheet is an object with its own set of methods and abilities. It is OLE that provides the interaction between the functional components—the spreadsheet, Word document, and so on.

However, OLE and COM allow us to go much further than simply resolving information into strict objects with formats and methods. The OLE system also allows these objects to be controlled and automated, so we can pragmatically tell a single paragraph within a Word document to use a different style or insert data directly into an Excel spreadsheet.

This is where a scriptable language such as Visual Basic or Perl comes in. We can use the Win32::OLE module supplied with ActivePerl both to communicate with existing objects to exchange information and to tell a specific object to execute a particular method. For example, we can use Perl to open a Word document and then save it in a different format, just by connecting to the corresponding COM object and executing the right method, in this case, `Save`.

COM and DCOM

Before we look at the specifics of using the `Win32::OLE` module, we first need to understand how the Perl script talks to the COM object and then how that object is manipulated with the OLE interface. When a Perl script connects to a COM object it is called the *client*, or sometimes the *COM controller*. Through the `Win32::OLE` module, a request is made to create a new COM object or connect to an existing COM object. The application that provides the COM object is called the *COM server*. It is the COM object that provides the ability to use a particular type of object. When you open a COM object, one of two methods is used to interact with the object: either a DLL or other system library is loaded to use the object or an external application is executed to provide the interaction with the object.

One step beyond a local COM object is DCOM, for Distributed COM. The DCOM system allows you to connect to an object on a remote server. Because you connect to the object, the application or library used to interact with the object is actually opened on the server, not the client. You can use this to execute applications and interfaces on a remote server without having to provide any other form of communication between the client and the remote server; the COM system handles the communication.

A DCOM system is generally used where you want to share the load of executing a particular application across a number of servers, or where the security of the information is paramount. For example, imagine a web server that provides an interface to a database. There are three ways to communicate with the database: locally, remotely, and with DCOM. With a local system you have to run the database on the same machine as the web server, which obviously requires a suitable high-powered machine to support both operations.

With a remote system, the web server provides the client interface, while network connection to a database server handles the database work. The connection can either be handled through a normal socket connection, through a Windows pipe, or through another library such as the ODBC toolkit. Whichever way the interface is handled, the application itself runs on the web server, which still requires a powerful machine to serve both requests.

The final method is to use DCOM. When the CGI script executes, it connects, through DCOM, to a remote application and executes commands. The DCOM system handles the communication across the network, and the OLE interface handles the communication and control between the host application and the CGI script. Here the application overhead has been completely shunted to the "application server," while the web server is able to concentrate on what it does best—providing an interface between the user and the database.

The security of this last method is also much greater than the previous two methods. With a local method, once a user has made it into your web server (which needs to be accessible to the public), he or she has access to your database. With the remote system the client and server must be capable of communicating over traditional sockets, which still provides a path to your database server. By using DCOM we remove the requirement to support connectivity over the normal networking channels and in fact completely separate the process of executing statements and accessing data. Through DCOM we have only access to the methods and information supplied to us through the remote COM object.

The final benefit of DCOM is that because the application runs on a separate machine, we have better control over the loading of the servers that support the system. Clients can connect to a variety of application servers on the network, all especially configured purely for running the COM objects that support the service.

Using a COM Object

Let's look at a very simple Perl script that opens a Word document and then prints it:

```
use Win32::OLE;
$file = "./PW32-11.doc";

$document = Win32::OLE->GetObject($file);

if ($document)
{
    print "Printing out $file\n";
    $application = $document->{Parent};
    $application->{Visible} = 1;
    $application->PrintOut();
    $application->Quit();
}
```

Looking at this script, it appears as though there is a strict format to the way in which we use and interact with the COM object. In fact, the only piece of pure Perl code is the `GetObject` function call, which opens the document you specify using the correct COM object and library.

All of the rest of the process is actually the OLE/COM interface. The object that we create in Perl is a pointer to the COM object that was created to handle the document. This is one of the most important distinctions to understand. Although we access the object just like any other Perl object, we are in fact accessing the properties and methods of the COM object. Furthermore, it's not Perl that creates the COM object—that would require Perl to be a COM server. Instead, the Perl object is just an easy pointer to the object created by the system libraries that support the COM object we want to access.

The properties and methods that we use are defined within the COM object, not within Perl or the `Win32::OLE` module. There are no standards for the methods and properties that we'll find, since all objects and applications are different. However, there are some assumptions that we can make—for example, for most documents and objects, it's safe to assume that there will be a `Save` method, but the format and arguments to that method will be different for all objects.

If you want to know the different properties and methods available for a COM object, you will need to check the developer documentation for the corresponding application. For Microsoft products, the best source for information is the MSDN CD that comes with any of the Visual Studio products, including Visual Basic. Of course, if you already make use of COM and OLE within Visual Basic, you'll already know the methods and properties that you need to access.

Creating and Using COM Objects

There are three ways of accessing COM objects within Perl: creating a new object, connecting to an existing (open) object, or opening a persistent object. Each way involves a different method of access within the `Win32::OLE` module, and they each have their advantages and disadvantages. We'll look at each in turn, along with how we can access the objects.

Creating New Objects   OLE classes are the most compatible and reliable way of identifying and using COM objects. The OLE classes are structured according to the application and the objects defined within that application. For example, there is a top-level class called *Word*, within which you will find two objects—*Application* and *Document*. To create a new instance of the Word application, you would create a new object identified by `Word.Application`. Having access to the application gives you the ability to control the application at the top level, so you can do everything from accessing autotext entries to getting a list of all of the open documents. To create or open a Word document, you would use the `Word.Document` class.

To request a new object to be created, you need to create a new object with the `Win32::OLE` module using the `new` method. For example, to create a new Word document:

```
use Win32::OLE;

$document = new Win32::OLE('Word.Document');
```

The `new` method actually accepts two arguments:

```
$object = new Win32::OLE(CLASS [, DESTROY_METHOD]);
```

The `CLASS` is the name of the class to use when creating the new COM object. In our example above, it's a Word document. The class can either be a named class—for example, `Word.Application`—or a two-element array that opens an object on a remote machine. In either case, the class name can also be supplied as a GUID. We'll look at those other methods shortly.

The optional `DESTROY_METHOD` should be a reference to a Perl function that will ask the COM object to quit gracefully when the object is destroyed. For most situations the solution is to call the `Quit` method on the object. The function that is called is passed one argument—the object reference. For example, we might create a function like this:

```
sub Quit
{
    my $object = shift;
    $object->Quit();
}

my $object = new Win32::OLE('Word.Application',\Quit);
```

The function is required for most applications to ensure that the application instance is destroyed when the COM object is destroyed. Some programs (most significantly, Microsoft Office, especially Excel) do not quit when the object is destroyed and therefore start using up lots of resources as multiple copies of the application are open simultaneously without doing anything. To add insult to injury, these applications cannot be killed, even from the Task Manager, and the only way to reclaim the space is to reboot.

The return value of the function is a reference pointing to the COM object created by the OLE system. If you want to check whether the operation succeeded, either add a die statement to the new method, like this:

```
my $object = new Win32::OLE('Word.Application',\Quit)
    || die "Cant create OLE instance";
```

or check the return value:

```
my $object = new Win32::OLE('Word.Application',\Quit);
if ($object)
{
...
}
else
{
    die "Couldn't create OLE instance";
}
```

USING DISTRIBUTED OBJECTS You can also supply the CLASS argument as a two-element array. The first argument is the name of the server on which you want to open the object. This can be specified either as a UNC—for example, \\MCHOME\Insentient—or as a TCP/IP address, 'insentient.mchome.com'. The second element of the array is the name or GUID of the OLE class to open. For example, the following script opens an Excel application on the remote machine, puts some into the first object, and then saves the document:

```
use Win32::OLE;

$excel = new Win32::OLE(['incontinent','Excel.Application'],\&Quit)
    || die "Cannot create OLE instance";

$excel->{Visible} = 1;
$workbook = $excel->Workbooks()->Add();
$sheet = $workbook->Worksheets(1);
$sheet->{Name} = "My Workbook";

$range = $sheet->Range('A1');
$range->{Value} = 'Hello!!!';
$Workbook->SaveAs('myfile.xls');

sub Quit
{
    my $object = shift;
    $object->Quit();
}
```

Before you get worried about security, keep in mind that you can control from the remote server which machines, users, and applications a remote user has access to. The default security level allows only administrators or similar high-level personnel to execute a remote application.

To configure the access permissions on a machine, you need to run the `dcomcnfg` utility. This provides the interface for controlling access at the different levels to individual applications and OLE classes. Also note that under Windows 95/98, you will need to enable User-level share control in the Network control panel. Figure 11-1 shows the main panel of the control panel, which displays the list of valid OLE objects.

Figure 11-1
Configuring access to DCOM objects.

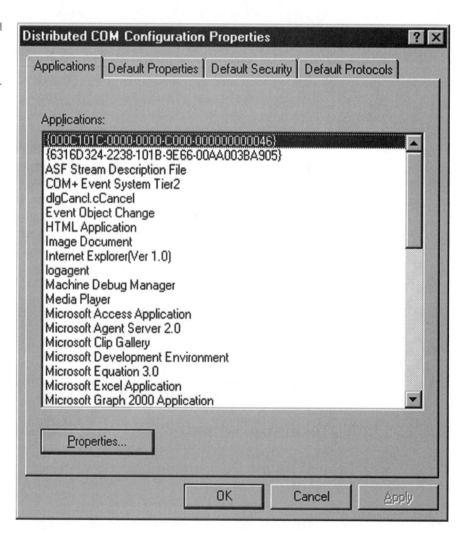

Distributed COM Configuration Properties

Applications | Default Properties | Default Security | Default Protocols

Applications:

{000C101C-0000-0000-C000-000000000046}
{6316D324-2238-101B-9E66-00AA003BA905}
ASF Stream Description File
COM+ Event System Tier2
dlgCancl.cCancel
Event Object Change
HTML Application
Image Document
Internet Explorer(Ver 1.0)
logagent
Machine Debug Manager
Media Player
Microsoft Access Application
Microsoft Agent Server 2.0
Microsoft Clip Gallery
Microsoft Development Environment
Microsoft Equation 3.0
Microsoft Excel Application
Microsoft Graph 2000 Application

Properties...

OK   Cancel   Apply

In the figure, you can see the list of applications. Control is limited to application level; it is not possible to restrict access to specific objects within an Application class. For all DCOM objects there are a set of default security, property, and transport options. You can also set individual applications with their set of configurations.

The security and property elements are obvious; the transport is not so clear. The transport property is the network protocol used to communicate with the DCOM object. By default it's set to the main network transport protocol—usually TCP/IP. If you want to provide access to DCOM over a specific protocol, then you will need to add the protocol in the Network control panel and then additionally configure the protocol in this utility. Note that the listed protocols are actually used in order; the top protocol is tried first, and if it fails, the next is attempted.

USING A GUID   When a class name is used, Windows will open the latest version of the object that is requested. For example, if you have Office 97 and Office 2000 on your machine and open the object `Word.Application`, then the Office 2000 version will be used. If you want to open a specific version of the installed objects, you can use a longer format that also specifies the version number. Office 97 included Word v7, so the string would be `Word.Application.7`. Of course, if you have Office 2000 installed, which includes Word v8, then the object creation will fail.

NOTE.   *Under Windows 98 and Windows 2000, you can find out what OLE classes have been installed on your machine using the System Information utility, available in the System Tools folder of the Start menu.*

If you want to be more specific about the version of an application that you want to create an instance of, you will need to use the GUID. The Global Unique Identifier is a hexadecimal string that refers to a single version of an application. For example, the GUID for Excel 5.0 is `{00020841-0000-0000-C000-000000000046}`, while the GUID of Excel 8.0 is `{00030000-0000-0000-C000-000000000046}`. The GUID is unique to every application but is constant across machines: the GUIDs above will work on all machines that have the software installed.

If you do look through the registry for these keys, the easiest way to find them is to start in `HKEY_CLASSES_ROOT`. After the entries relating to file extensions, you'll see a list of classes; these are actual root classes for the different GUIDs. For example, you'll see that Excel Worksheets, Charts, Workbooks, and other objects all have their own GUID. Unfortunately, this doesn't mean they are all OLE-accessible—you should choose the type of document that you want to create. Within each class entry you'll find a CLSID—the Class Identifier; this is the GUID. You may also find them called AppID (Application ID), IID (Interface ID), or UUID (Universally Unique ID).

You can use a GUID directly in place of the class name. For example:

```
$excel
    = new Win32::OLE(['{00030000-0000-0000-C000-
    000000000046}'],\&Quit)
        || die "Cannot create OLE instance";
```

Of course, the danger with a GUID is that for future compatibility you will need to keep modifying your script to take account of the new GUID of the latest version of the software. On the flip side, you can also be sure that the machine on which the application is running has the version that you want to use, because if the GUID has not been registered, then the COM object creation will fail.

Connecting to Existing Objects   If an instance of the application supporting a particular object is already running, then it is more efficient to connect to the existing object, rather than creating a new one. You do this using the GetActiveObject method:

```
$object = Win32::OLE->GetActiveObject(CLASS);
```

Once again, the CLASS argument can be an OLE class name, a GUID, or a two-element array to a machine and class name/GUID. For example, to connect to an open instance of Word and then save all of the open documents:

```
use Win32::OLE;

$word = Win32::OLE->GetActiveObject("Word.Application");

if ($word)
{
    $word->Documents->Save();
}
```

See the section on "Automating Microsoft Office" later in the chapter for more information on what you can control when connecting to an active object.

Opening a Persistent Object A persistent COM object is a file used to store a document. We've already seen an example of this when we first looked at how to print documents within Word from Perl. The basic format is as follows:

```
$object = Win32::OLE->GetObject(PATH);
```

where PATH is the path to the file that you want to open. For example, to open a Word document and then make it visible:

```
$document = Win32::OLE->GetObject($file);

if ($document)
{
    $application = $document->{Parent};
    $application->{Visible} = 1;
}
```

The method for choosing the COM object to use when opening a file is as follows:

1. First, the OLE system searches the open objects for a match for the specified file, using the extension as the key.
2. If not found, the OLE system searches the file's meta information for a GUID, which will then be used to open the file, assuming the GUID matches an installed OLE class.
3. If still unable to find a match, then the OLE system walks the registry looking through each GUID in HKEY_CLASSES_ROOT and checks the file type—a four-digit hexadecimal value—against the file.
4. If it still cannot be found, then the OLE system searches the file extensions logged in HKEY_CLASSES_ROOT for a match, and from there a matching GUID.

Other Methods and Functions

In addition to the base methods that are available for creating and accessing OLE objects, there is a range of additional functions that either control how the OLE interface is organized or provide additional information about the objects currently available within the OLE system.

Controlling the OLE Interface You can control how the interface to the OLE system is treated within the Perl environment. This is actually a feature of the OLE API, and it helps to control how simultaneous access to COM objects is controlled through the OLE interface. The base method for setting up the system is the `Initialize` method:

```
Win32::OLE->Initialize(INIT)
```

The `Initialize` method defines how the OLE interface and Perl are created within the application. The `INIT` argument is the method to use when communicating with the OLE API. The default option is to create an additional apartment (thread) for the Perl interpreter (available via the `COINIT_MULTITHREADED` constant) and the OLE interface. This allows for safe simultaneous access to a COM object.

This is the best option to use if you want to access objects that may already exist in memory (via the `GetActiveObject` or `GetObject` methods). If you are accessing a distributed object, it also ensures that your access to the object will not prevent access to the object by other OLE clients.

If you specify the `COINIT_APARTMENTTHREADED` constant, then the interface to the OLE system is made through a message queue system. Requests to modify, access, or operate on a specific object are placed into a message queue. If you set this option, then you must manually send the waiting messages from the queue to the COM object using the `SpinMessageLoop` method.

The `COINIT_OLEINITIALIZE` constant is similar in principle to the `COINIT_APARTMENTTHREADED` option, but it allows the COM object and OLE to support additional initialization abilities. This last option is often needed when an external OLE object uses a nonstandard object model, which then requires additional OLE components in order to execute properly.

Whatever option you use, the `Initialize` method should be called before any objects are created. If you also require the `Win32::OLE::Const` module, then you will need to put the method call into a `BEGIN` block. For example:

```
BEGIN
{

    use Win32::OLE;
    Win32::OLE->Initialize(COINIT_OLEINITIALIZE);

}
```

*NOTE. For more information on the single and multithreaded opera-
tion of OLE, see the "Processes and Threads" section of the* OLE
Programmer's Reference *supplied with MSDN or the Microsoft Visual
Studio products.*

The `SpinMessageLoop` method is required when operating in single-
threaded mode. For example:

```
Win32::OLE->SpinMessageLoop();
```

This retrieves all pending messages from the OLE message queue and
sends them on to their corresponding window destinations.

The `Uninitialize` method uninitializes the OLE system and effectively disables the OLE system until a new initialization call is made or
a new object is created:

```
Win32::OLE->Uninitialize();
```

Object Information   To determine the current type and class name of
an object, use the `QueryObjectType` method. In a list context, this
returns the type library name and the object's class name. In a scalar
context, it only returns the object's class name:

```
Win32::OLE->QueryObjectType(OBJECT);
```

If the information is unavailable, then it returns `undef`.

For example, the following script:

```
use Win32::OLE;

$word = new Win32::OLE("Word.Document");

if ($word)
{
    $paragraph = $word->Paragraphs(1);
    print Win32::OLE->QueryObjectType($paragraph),"\n";
}
```

will output `WordParagraph`.

To get a list of all the current objects, you can use the
`EnumAllObjects` method, which returns a count of the number
of objects currently in existence within the current Perl script. For
example:

```
$count = Win32::OLE->EnumAllObjects([CALLBACK]);
```

The CALLBACK should be a reference to a function or an anonymous function that will be called for each object found. The function is passed one argument, a reference to the object in question. For example, to print out the information about all objects within the current script, you might use this script, taken from the Win32::OLE documentation:

```
use Win32::OLE;

$Count = Win32::OLE->EnumAllObjects(sub {
    my $Object = shift;
    my $Class = Win32::OLE->QueryObjectType($Object);
    printf "# Object=%s Class=%s\n", $Object, $Class;});
```

Module Options   The Win32::OLE module supports three options that affect how the module operates. The values are retrieved or set using the Option method:

```
Win32::OLE->Option(EXPR);
```

If EXPR is a single argument, then it returns the value of that option:

```
$codepage = Win32::OLE->Option(CP);
```

If the argument is a hash or hash reference, then the option or options are set. For example:

```
Win32::OLE->Option(Warn => 3);
```

The valid options are shown in Table 11-2.

TABLE 11-2

Options for the
Win32::OLE
module.

Option	Description
CP	Defines the codepage that should be used to translate between the Perl string and Unicode string used internally by Windows. The default is CP_ACP for the ANSI codepage. You can also use CP_OEMCP, CP_MACCP, CP_UTF7, and CP_UTF8. The constants are not exported by default, so you will need to specifically import them.
LCID	The locale identifier used for all OLE calls. Valid LCID values are defined by the Win32::OLE::NLS module—see the module's documentation for more information.
Warn	Sets the warning level for all OLE operations. See the "Errors" section below for a description of the different warning levels.

Errors   The `Win32::GetLastError` function will not work, because the OLE API does not report its errors back to the operating system directly. Instead, there is a `LastError` method defined within the module that will return the last error from an OLE call:

```
Win32::OLE->LastError();
```

You can use this after any OLE operation, from creating a COM object to calling a method on a COM object.

You can also set a warning level, either by setting the value of the `Win32::OLE::Warn` variable or by using the `Option` method to set the value of the `Warn` variable. For example, the following two lines are identical:

```
$Win32::OLE::Warn = 3;
Win32::OLE->Option(Warn => 3);
```

The values for the `Warn` variable are shown in Table 11-3.

Method and Property Access   The normal approach for accessing a property of a COM object is using the normal Perl hash dereference:

```
$object->{Property};
```

or to access a method:

```
$object->Method(ARGS);
```

TABLE 11-3

Warning levels for the `Win32::OLE` module.

Value	Description
0	The default value. Errors are ignored by the module, and any OLE errors will return `undef` to the caller. You can use the `Win32::OLE->LastError` function to get the OLE error message generated.
1	A warning message is displayed using the `Carp::carp` function, provided warnings have been enabled on the command line (with the `-w` option) or with the `$^W` special variable.
2	A warning message is displayed using the `Carp::carp` function, irrespective of whether warnings have been switched on.
3	An error message is displayed using the `Carp::croak` function and the script terminates.

There are some limitations to these methods when compared to the Visual Basic abilities and compatibility that are addressed by the following functions and methods.

The `Invoke` method involves a specific method on the current object. The `Invoke` method is essentially identical to the normal Perl method call, but it allows you to call methods that would not normally be supported by Perl, including those with spaces and special characters:

```
Win32::OLE->Invoke(METHOD, ARGS)
```

This is equivalent to using `$oleobject->METHOD(ARGS)`.

To set a property, you can either use the notation above or the `SetProperty` method:

```
Win32::OLE->SetProperty(NAME, VALUE);
Win32::OLE->SetProperty(NAME, ARGS, VALUE);
```

The property has two forms. When passed a single argument, it sets the property NAME to VALUE. In the second form, it allows the property NAME with the arguments ARGS to be set to VALUE. This gets around the issue of being unable to access a property that has additional arguments using the hash dereference notation shown above.

The final format gets around the inability of the hash dereference technique when you want to set the property of an object to point to the value of another object. This is because Perl will assume that you want the property value to be the reference to the other object, not a copy of the object itself. The following code:

```
Win32::OLE->LetProperty(NAME, VALUE);
Win32::OLE->SetProperty(NAME, ARGS, VALUE);
```

sets the value of the property NAME to the value of the object pointed to by VALUE. Note that the function also supports the optional property arguments. See the `SetProperty` method for more information.

Support Modules

Beyond the base `Win32::OLE` module there are four submodules that provide additional functionality when communicating with COM objects. The `Win32::OLE::Const` module exports the constants required when communicating with many COM objects. The `Win32::OLE::Enum` module allows you to enumerate over collection objects (see "Automating

Microsoft Office" later in the chapter for more information on collection objects). The `Win32::OLE::NLS` module provides an interface to the multilanguage support offered by Windows and the OLE interface. The final module, `Win32::OLE::Variant`, allows you to convert strings and Perl object types into the object variants used by COM for numbers, dates, and other values.

`Win32::OLE::Const`   When you interface to an OLE application, you will often need to use a constant that is defined within the COM object's type library. These constants are unique to the type library for an application and change from version to version. As such, it's not possible to document or maintain a list within the `Win32::OLE` module. To get around this limitation, you can use the `Win32::OLE::Const` module. This will export the constants defined within a specific COM object's type library and expose those constants as Perl constants, which you can then use directly within a Perl script.

The format for using the module is as follows:

```
use Win32::OLE::Const (TYPELIB [,MAJOR [,MINOR [,LANGUAGE]]]);
```

The `TYPELIB` argument specifies the type library that you want to load. The value given is matched against a type library name using the regular expression `/^TYPELIB/`. You can therefore get away with `Microsoft Word` instead of `Microsoft Word 8.0 Type Library`. To match more loosely, supply a string with an embedded regex, for example:

```
use Win32::OLE::Const ('.*Excel');
```

The optional `MAJOR`, and `MINOR` select the major and minor version number of the application. For example, to select version 8.0 of Word:

```
use Win32::OLE::Const ('Microsoft Word', 8, 0);
```

Note that the specification matches against a minimum `MINOR` value. For example, specifying `4.3` would load version 4.3 through to 4.9 of an application's type library, but it would not load anything earlier than 4.2 or greater than 5.0.

The last argument, `LANGUAGE`, defines the language ID of the constants that should be imported. By specifying this argument, you can import constants with their localized name. The default is, of course, English. You can get a valid language ID from the `Win32::OLE::NLS` module.

As an alternative, you can import the module and then separately load the constants. This has the added advantage that the information is placed into a local hash, which can then be searched for a suitable constant. This interface is offered by the Load function:

```
$hash = Win32::OLE::Const->Load (TYPELIB [,MAJOR [,MINOR
  [,LANGUAGE]]]);
```

The arguments are as for the use statement above, except that TYPELIB accepts either a name or a Win32::OLE object, which allows you to load the constants for a specific object even if you don't know what the object type is.

Win32::OLE:Enum   Some object methods return collection objects rather than individual objects when called. For example, the Paragraphs method to a Word document object returns a collection object, which points to all of the paragraphs within a document. The normal method for working with a collection is to access the Count property and then count through the items. For example:

```
$maxpara = $document->Paragraphs()->{Count};
for($i=1;$i<$maxpara;$i++)
{
    $paragraph = $document->Paragraphs($i);
...
}
```

The problem is that we have to make multiple calls to the Paragraphs method in order to get the information, which is largely inefficient. Instead, we can use the Win32::OLE::Enum module to enable us to enumerate through the individual objects in a collection object just as if we were working through an array.

The operation of the enumeration system is similar to that of the keys, values, and each functions when accessing the elements of a hash. The current location within the list is stored, and each successive iteration of the enumeration object returns the next object in the list.

You create a new enumeration object with the new method:

```
$enumerate = Win32::OLE::Enum->new(OBJECT);
```

The OBJECT argument should be a reference to an existing collection object. The return value is a new Win32::OLE::Enum object.

To obtain an array whose elements each contain a reference to the corresponding object within the collection, you can use the All method:

```
$paragraphs = $document->Paragraphs();
$enum = new Win32::OLE::Enum($paragraphs);
@paragraphs = $enum->All();
```

Alternatively, you can call the method as a class method and automatically translate a collection object into an array:

```
$paragraphs = $document->Paragraphs();
@paragraphs = Win32::OLE::Enum->($paragraphs);
```

The `Next` method returns the next object within the collection. Generally, you use it within a `while` block to process through each object:

```
while ($paragraph = $enum->Next())
```

You can also supply the method a numerical argument that will return the specified number of objects back:

```
while (@paras = $enum->Next(5))
```

In a scalar context, only the last of the specified objects is returned. For example, the line

```
while ($paragraph = $enum->Next(5))
```

would only work through and select every fifth paragraph.

To reset the iteration counter back to the beginning of the list, use the `Reset` method:

```
$enum->Reset();
```

To skip over a number of elements in an enumeration, you can use the `Skip` method:

```
$enum->Skip([COUNT]);
```

This will skip over COUNT elements within the enumeration object. The method returns `True` if the method could skip or at least COUNT arguments. Otherwise, it returns `False`.

Note that not all the methods are supported by all the collection objects. This means that you will need to embed the method call in an `eval` block to ensure that the script does not unceremoniously exit when a method is not defined.

Win32::OLE::NLS The `Win32::OLE::NLS` module provides an interface to the National Language Support system and how the `Win32::OLE` module treats the NLS interface. There are some minor differences when using the OLE interface between languages—mostly related to the property names, which will sometimes use their localized, rather than English, names. There are also problems when passing information to applications that use English terms to describe elements. For example, the row/column specification is localized, and the functions used in Excel expressions are also localized.

See the `Win32::OLE::NLS` documentation for more information.

Win32::OLE::Variant You need to use the `Win32::OLE::Variant` module when you want to introduce values into a COM object that match a specific type. Ordinarily, the `Win32::OLE` module performs the conversion between the local Perl data type and the actual data type required by the COM object, which is called a *variant*. However, there are times when the automatic system will pass a value of the wrong type to the COM object. You can get around this by directly specifying the type of variable that should be passed to the COM object using the `Win32::OLE::Variant` module.

The module exports a number of functions, the most useful of which is `Variant`, and a series of constants that define the different data types. The format of the function is as follows:

```
$variant = Variant(TYPE, VALUE);
```

where `TYPE` is one of the types shown in Table 11-4, optionally with one of the data type flags shown in Table 11-5. The type flags should be logically `OR`'d with the variant data type. The `VALUE` is the Perl variable or constant that you want to convert.

For example, to convert a Perl floating-point constant into a currency variant:

```
$curvar = Variant(VT_CY,"3.99");
```

Note that the `Win32::OLE::Variant` module also defines a number of additional functions that allow more control over the variant data types. For example, you can create a date by converting a specific date string format, or you can control the precise details of how a currency value will be represented. Please refer to the `Win32::OLE::Variant` documentation for details.

TABLE 11-4

Valid variant data types.

Data Type	Description
VT_BOOL	A Boolean value.
VT_BSTR	A fixed-length, Unicode string.
VT_CY	A currency data type (consists of the currency flags—prefix character, separator, etc.—and a floating-point value).
VT_DATE	A date (accepts a variety of different date formats, including 21 Mar 1999 and 21/3/99).
VT_DISPATCH	A pointer to another Win32::OLE object.
VT_EMPTY	An empty value (not equivalent to undef).
VT_ERROR	An error value, used to return errors and results.
VT_I2	A 2-byte (short) signed integer.
VT_I4	A 4-byte (long) signed integer.
VT_R4	A 4-byte (float) floating-point value.
VT_R8	An 8-byte (double) floating-point value.
VT_UI1	An unsigned single character.
VT_UNKNOWN	An unidentified OLE object.
VT_VARIANT	A reference to another variant object.

Automating Microsoft Office

Although most applications support OLE, it's understandable that some of the best support comes from Microsoft and their Office product. It's possible with OLE to control the operation of Excel, Word, PowerPoint, and Project, and the level of access and supported methods is extensive. In essence, anything that you can perform inside the application can be

TABLE 11-5

Variant data type flags.

Flag	Description
VT_ARRAY	Indicates that the variant should represent an array of values. This will convert a Perl array to a variant array. Note that the Perl array should consist only of a particular type. Passing a mixed numerical/string array will not work.
VT_BYREF	The resulting variant should be a reference to the information, rather than a copy of the information.

controlled externally by Perl. Even if you don't want to use Microsoft Office with OLE, this section still provides some useful tips on using the OLE interface within Perl.

The OLE system mirrors the ability of the macro system built into the Office software, and this goes some way to demonstrating the level of flexibility offered by OLE. The macro system of Office uses the VBScript/VBA (Visual Basic for Applications) language to control the operation of the application. Within Perl, the control is very similar to programming with Visual Basic or its derivatives, and programmers familiar with the VB environment should be able to use the Perl interface without any problems. We've already seen some examples of the basic format, but let's recap. To call a method:

```
$object->Method([ARGS, ...])
```

To access a property:

```
$object->{Property}
```

To set a property:

```
$object->{Property} = EXPR;
```

You can, of course, nest properties/methods. For example, to access the property of an object returned by a method call:

```
$object->Method()->{Property}
```

Alternatively, to access an embedded property:

```
$object->{PropertyA}->{PropertyB};
```

In this section we'll look very quickly at using Word through the `Win32::OLE` interface. Many of the methods, properties, and principles that we'll look at here are shared across many applications. Even if you don't intend to connect to Word, the principles shown here should give you enough background information to get started with the OLE system.

Interfacing to Microsoft Word   Microsoft Word, like most other COM objects, uses a very structured format for the information stored within the documents that it creates. At the top level is the Word application. Within a Word application is a document, and within a document there are paragraphs, lists, tables, styles, and so on.

For example, to get a list of the documents in the currently active Word application:

```
use Win32::OLE;
#Get the connection to the Word Application
#This will make $word point to the Word Application
#object
$word = Win32::OLE->GetActiveObject("Word.Application");

#Providing we could connect
if ($word)
{
    # Get a count of the number of open documents
    $count = $word->Documents()->{Count};

    # Work through the list
    for($i=1;$i<$count;$i++)
    {
        # Create a Word.Document object
        $document = $word->Documents($i);
        # Get the documents name
        print $document->{Name},"\n";
    }
}
```

You should be able to follow this quite easily. The Documents method returns a collection object that contains all of the open documents. The Count property of the collection object is the number of open documents. If we supply an argument to the Documents method, then it returns a Document object that points to the corresponding document number. Then the Name property of the Document object contains the document's name.

Of course, once we're connected, we can do anything. We saw an example earlier where we saved all of the open documents:

```
use Win32::OLE;

$word = Win32::OLE->GetActiveObject("Word.Application");
if ($word)
{
    $count = $word->Documents()->{Count};
    for($i=1;$i<$count;$i++)
    {
        $document = $word->Documents($i);
        $document->Save();
    }
}
```

Other examples have been demonstrated elsewhere, such as the ability to print a document. However, for our final example, we'll look at a real script that was written as part of a series of scripts that I use when I'm writing an article or book.

As a writer, anything that saves me time is a bonus. This is particularly true when working through a document to fix inconsistencies in the formatting or appearance of individual components. The simple things, like checking the spelling of a specific term or verifying that a word is boldfaced rather than quoted, take significant amounts of time when it comes to editing and proofreading the document.

Normally, the method of verifying this pragmatically is to create a list of known words and then manually working through the document using the eye and brain as the check method. A better solution is to process contents of the file directly. In the past, I'd do this by saving the file as text, or maybe even HTML, and then processing the file with Perl to pick out the unusual or specific words or phrases of interest.

With OLE, however, we can go one stage further and actually access the information directly from the document. Yet we don't need to know the format of the Word document; we just use OLE to access the document directly.

Within Word, we already know that the individual components that go to make up a document are available individually. It is possible to actually access the contents of a document using OLE. The Text property of a Paragraph object contains the raw text that makes up the paragraph in question. Also contained within the Paragraph object is the style used to format the paragraph.

In this script I use both pieces of information to extract a text-based outline of the document in question. This is a vital part of the development and production process; we're not worried about page numbers at this stage, but knowing what topics have been covered and the general layout of the book is always a useful cross-reference for future chapters.

```
use Win32::OLE;
use Win32::OLE::Enum;

my @filelist;

while($arg = shift)
{
    if ($arg =~ m/(\?|\*)/)
    {
        push @filelist,glob($arg);
    }
    else
    {
        push @filelist,$arg;
    }
}

@ARGV = sort @filelist;
```

```perl
foreach $file (@ARGV)
{
    parse_outline($file);
}

sub parse_outline($)
{
    my ($file) = @_;

    $document = Win32::OLE->GetObject($file);
    unless ($document)
    {
        print STDERR "Couldn't creat OLE instance\n";
        return;
    }
    $paragraphs = $document->Paragraphs();
    $enumerate = new Win32::OLE::Enum($paragraphs);
    while(defined($paragraph = $enumerate->Next()))
    {
        $style = $paragraph->{Style}->{NameLocal};
        $text = $paragraph->{Range}->{Text};
        $text =~ s/[\n\r]//g;
        if ($style =~ m/^Heading (\d+)$/)
        {
            $indent = $1;
            $text =~ s/^\s*\(\d+\)//;
            print " " x ($indent*2),$text,"\n";
        }
        elsif ($text =~ m/^.*\(cn\)(.*)/i)
        {
            print "$1-";
        }
        elsif ($text =~ m/^.*\(ct\)(.*)/i)
        {
            print "$1\n";
        }
    }
}
```

The first part of the script accounts for the lack of command-line argument parsing into a list of files. The real meat is the `parse_outline` function, which works through each paragaph in the document, checks what the style is, and outputs a header accordingly. The header is indented with a set number of spaces according to the heading level. The rest of the function actually accounts for the formatting of the document used by Osborne/McGraw-Hill to identify the file contents. This also allows me to output the chapter number and title.

Running the script on the manuscript for this chapter, we start to get output like this:

```
Chapter 11 - Beyond Compatibility
  Win32::Clipboard
  Using Win32::Sound
Automation and Data Sharing using OLE
```

```
COM and DCOM
Using a COM Object
Creating and Using COM Objects
  Creating New Objects
    Using Distributed Objects
    Using a GUID
  Connecting to Existing Objects
  Opening a Persistent Object
Other Methods and Functions
  Controlling the OLE Interface
  Object Information
  Module Options
  Errors
  Method and Property Access
Support Modules
  Win32::OLE::Const
  Win32::OLE:Enum
  Win32::OLE::NLS
  Win32::OLE::Variant
Automating Microsoft Office
  Interfacing to Microsoft Word
```

Of course, there is much more to using OLE and COM objects than described here, but this is not really the place to go into the process in detail. The best guide is the *Microsoft Office / Visual Basic Programmer's Guide*, which contains extensive information on the different methods and properties of most of the COM objects available within Word, Excel, and other Office applications. The guide comes as part of Microsoft Developer Network (MSDN) documentation.

ActivePerl Development Tools

## CHAPTER 12

Perl Package Managers

Although developing your own modules and extensions to the Perl language can be fun, it can also be a waste of effort and a significant waste of time. To reduce the amount of duplication of effort, the CPAN archive was developed. CPAN, or the Comprehensive Perl Archive Network, is a collection of modules and scripts that can be downloaded and installed into your Perl distribution.

CPAN is a publicly developed network, but it's a testament to the quality of the modules that most of them have made it into either the baser module library supplied with Perl or the extension libraries supplied with the ActivePerl distribution. Modules released on CPAN are generally supplied in the same format, a selection of source files supplied with a Perl Makefile. This in turn produces a standard Makefile, which when used with the Unix `make` command and a standard C compiler, compiles and installs the module into the Perl distribution. To make the process even easier, the `CPAN` module, which comes standard with Perl, allows you to search the CPAN archives, then it downloads, compiles, and installs the module for you.

Under Unix the system works very well; however, under Windows there are a number of omissions from the standard OS toolkit. No C compiler is supplied as standard, nor is there a `make` utility to actually perform the build and installation. This also means that the `CPAN` module won't work properly.

ActiveState has supplied a solution in the form of the Perl Package Manager, which comes free with the ActivePerl distribution, and the Visual Package Manager, which comes with the Perl Development Kit.

Perl Package Manager

Instead of providing a suite of tools that allow you to install the standard CPAN modules onto your machine, the Perl Package Manager (PPM) approaches the solution from the other end. ActiveState and some other sites have specifically created packages that can be installed using the PPM, bypassing the normal Perl Makefile route offered by the packages on CPAN.

This only works because the Windows platform is standardized. The packages are prebuilt and compiled, bypassing the normal `make` stages required by other packages. All the PPM system has to do is download them and then install the extensions, modules, and documentation into the Perl directory tree.

NOTE. *In order to use most of the features of PPM, you must be connected to the Internet. If you don't have access, then you will need an account. If you use a dial-up connection, make sure the connection is open before querying a remote server or downloading and installing a package.*

PPM Commands

PPM is available in two ways: you can either use it as a command-line tool or as an interactive interface. In its command-line format, you use the ppm program, followed by the command you want to run and any options. For example, to verify the installed packages:

```
C:\> ppm verify
```

In its interactive form, you start the ppm program and then enter commands into the PPM prompt:

```
C:\> ppm
PPM interactive shell (1.1.1) - type 'help' for available commands.
PPM> verify
```

The command-line approach is useful when you want to automatically upgrade or verify an installation. The interactive format is more useful when you're not entirely sure what you are looking for. You can do searches and install multiple packages without having to continually load new versions of the PPM application.

search   The search command searches a repository for matching packages. The format of the command for the command line is as follows:

```
ppm search [—searchtag=abstract|author|title] [—case|nocase]
           [—location=LOCATION] [PATTERN]
```

In its interactive form, the command looks like this:

```
search [/abstract|/title|/author] [/location LOCATION] [PATTERN]
```

The PATTERN is a regular expression to be used to match against the list of packages. If PATTERN is not specified, then all the available packages are listed. Note that because it's a regular expression, you can enter complex searches. For example:

```
search ^[A-F].*
```

You can also restrict your search to a particular location within the package definition—the default is to search the package name and title. The options are to search the `abstract`, `title`, or `author`. In addition, you can search a specific repository using the `location` option (see "Package Repositories" later in this section for more information).

The `case` and `nocase` options are limited to the command-line version and allow you to specify case-sensitive on non-case-sensitive pattern matching. For case sensitivity settings within the interactive interface, see the `set` command later in this section.

For example, to search the current repository for the Tk library, which we looked at in Chapter 10, you might use the following:

```
PPM> search Tk
Packages available from http://www.ActiveState.com/packages:
Tk            [800.018] Tk - a Graphical User Interface Toolkit
Tk-GBARR      [1.03   ] A collection of Tk widgets.
Tk-JPEG       [2.013  ] JPEG format loader for Photo image type.
Tk-Multi      [0.3    ] A set of Tk composite widget to allow you to
                        manage
                        several scrolled Text windows in your Toplevel
                        window.
Tk-ObjScanner [1.017  ] Tk composite widget object scanner
```

Alternatively, to specifically search for modules by Graham Barr from the command line:

```
C:\WINDOWS>ppm search —searchtag=author BARR
Packages available from http://www.ActiveState.com/packages:
Convert-BER [1.26] Encode and decode objects as described by
                   ITU-T standard X.209 (ASN.1) using Basic
                   Encoding Rules (BER)
Errno       [1.09] System errno constants
FindBin     [1.04] Locate directory of original perl script
MailTools   [1.12] A set of perl modules related to mail Applications
Tie-Dir     [1.02] class definition for reading directories via a
                   tied hash
TimeDate    [1.08] Date formatter and parser; timesone
                   manipulation routines.
Tk-GBARR    [1.03] A collection of Tk widgets.
libnet      [1.06] libnet is a collection of Perl modules which
                   provides a simple and consistent programming
                   interface (API) to the client side of various
                   protocols used in the internet community.
perl-ldap   [0.11] A library of modules implementing an LDAP client.
```

query   The `query` command lists the modules currently installed. The format of the command on the command line is as follows:

```
ppm query [—searchtag=abstract|author|title] [—case|nocase] [PATTERN]
```

In its interactive form, the command looks like this:

```
search [/abstract|/title|/author] [PATTERN]
```

The format is essentially the same as the search function, except that it operates only on the packages installed locally. See the notes for search regarding the case and nocase options. If PATTERN is not supplied, then the command lists all of the packages currently installed. For example:

```
PPM> query
Archive-Tar            [0.072 ] module for manipulation of tar
archives.
Compress-Zlib          [1.03  ] Interface to zlib compression library
HTML-Parser            [2.23  ] SGML parser class
MIME-Base64            [2.11  ] Encoding and decoding of base64
strings
PPM                    [1.1.1 ] Perl Package Manager: locate, install,
                                upgrade software packages.
URI                    [1.04  ] Uniform Resource Identifiers (absolute
                                and relative)
Win32-AuthenticateUser [0.01  ]
Win32-Resource         [0.10  ]
XML-Element            [0.10  ] Base element class for XML elements
XML-Parser             [2.27  ] A Perl module for parsing XML docu-
ments
libwin32               [0.15.1] Win32-only extensions that provides a
                                quick migration path for people
                                wanting
                                to use the core support for win32 in
                                perl 5.004 and later.
libwww-perl            [5.45  ] Library for WWW access in Perl
```

If you supply a PATTERN then it will display the description for matching packages:

```
PPM> query URI
URI [1.04] Uniform Resource Identifiers (absolute and relative)
```

install Once you have selected your package with search to download and install the package, you need to use the install command:

```
ppm install [-location=LOCATION] PACKAGE [PACKAGE2 ...]
```

In its interactive form, the command looks like this:

```
install [/location LOCATION] PACKAGE [PACKAGE2 ...]
```

For example, to install the Tk package, which we needed for Chapter 10, you might use

```
PPM> install Tk
Install package 'Tk?' (y/N): y
Retrieving package 'Tk'...
...
Installing C:\Perl\site\lib\Tk.pm
Installing C:\Perl\bin\ptked
Installing C:\Perl\bin\ptked.bat
Installing C:\Perl\bin\ptksh
Installing C:\Perl\bin\ptksh.bat
Installing C:\Perl\bin\widget
Installing C:\Perl\bin\widget.bat
Writing C:\Perl\site\lib\auto\Tk\.packlist
PPM>
```

The output has been edited here for brevity, but you can see that the package is automatically downloaded (by the LWP toolkit) and then installed. If a LOCATION is supplied, then the location is used as the download point, instead of the default. In addition, if there are any packages or modules on which the package you are installing depends, then they will also be installed by this command.

remove   The remove command, as its name suggests, removes an installed package:

```
ppm remove PACKAGE [PACKAGE2 ...]
```

In its interactive form, the command looks like this:

```
remove PACKAGE [PACKAGE2 ...]
```

Care should be taken with this command, since it will remove a package without checking dependencies. For example:

```
PPM> remove Tk
Remote pacakge 'Tk?' (y/N): y
```

Be especially careful if you remove the LWP toolkit, since that will actually disable the package manager's ability to download new packages and install them. If you want to upgrade to a new package, use the verify command.

verify   The verify command is a sort of combination of the search, query, and install commands. It checks the currently installed packages against the packages on the repositories, comparing version numbers. If the versions on a repository are later than those currently installed, you are notified of the fact. You can also have the packages immediately updated to the latest version using the upgrade option:

```
ppm verify [-location=LOCATION] [-upgrade] [PACKAGE [PACKAGE2 ...]]
```

In its interactive form, the command looks like this:

```
verify [/location LOCATION] [/upgrade] [PACKAGE [PACKAGE2 ...]]
```

For example, to simply check the current status of the installed packages:

```
PPM> verify
Package 'URI' is up to date.
Package 'Archive-Tar' is up to date.
Error verifying Win32-Resource: Could not locate a PPD file for
  Win32-Resource
Package 'XML-Element' is up to date.
Package 'libwin32' is up to date.
Package 'Compress-Zlib' is up to date.
Package 'MIME-Base64' is up to date.
Package 'XML-Parser' is up to date.
An upgrade to package 'libwww-perl' is available.
An upgrade to package 'PPM' is available.
Error verifying Win32-AuthenticateUser: Could not locate a PPD
  file for Win32-AuthenticateUser
An upgrade to package 'HTML-Parser' is available.
```

To automatically upgrade a package:

```
PPM> verify /upgrade PPM
Upgrade package PPM? (y/N): y
Installing C:\Perl\html\lib\site\PPM.html
Installing C:\Perl\html\lib\site\XML\PPD.html
Installing C:\Perl\html\lib\site\XML\PPMConfig.html
Installing C:\Perl\htmlhelp\pkg-PPM.chm
Installing C:\Perl\htmlhelp\pkg-PPM.hhc
Installing C:\Perl\lib\PPM\RelocPerl.pm
Installing C:\Perl\lib\PPM.pm
Installing C:\Perl\lib\XML\PPD.pm
Installing C:\Perl\lib\XML\PPMConfig.pm
Installing C:\Perl\lib\XML\RepositorySummary.pm
Installing C:\Perl\bin\ppm.pl
Writing C:\Perl\lib\auto\PPM\.packlist
Package PPM upgraded to version 1,1,2,0
PPM>
```

━━ ━━ ━━ ━━ ━━ ━━ ━━ ━━ ━━ ━━ ━━ ━━ ━━ ━━ ━━ ━━

WARNING. PPM's upgrade operation is somewhat unruly and can occasionally refuse to update a package, and using the verify upgrade *commands without any packages is definitely not recommended. Hopefully, these bugs will be fixed in the near future.*

set   The `set` command allows you to configure the environment during an interactive session. Although the command is available on the command line, the effects won't be felt until you save them and restart the session. See Table 12-1 for a list of the configurable options.

Once you have set up a number of options, you can save the configuration using the `set save` command. This will update the configuration information stored in C:\Perl\site\lib\PPM.XML. Alternatively, you can try editing the file yourself. Look for the line that starts with `OPTIONS` within the PPM.XML file.

Other Commands   Three other commands, `exit`, `quit`, and `help` are supported by the interactive interface. The `exit` and `quit` commands should be self-explanatory. The `help` command returns brief help information.

Package Repositories

When you use the `search`, `install`, or `verify` commands, the information about the packages is checked against a package repository. This is a website that holds the actual package files and also supports the scripts necessary to return specific information about the packages that are available. The default repository is held at the ActiveState corporation and is one of the largest package repositories.

You can configure additional repositories to use both on the command line and through the interactive interface. At the moment, the number of repositories is limited, but over time the number is expected to increase as more Windows-specific modules and precompiled compatible packages are made available.

Remote Repositories   To use a remote repository, you need to supply the URL of the repository to the `location` option of the command:

```
ppm install —location=http://rto.dk/packages/ VRML
```

or within the interactive interface:

```
search /location http://rto.dk/packages/
```

The default repository is ActiveState, and a list of all the active sites is shown in Table 12-2.

TABLE 12-1

Options for the
Perl Package
Manager.

Command	Description
set	Displays the current settings.
set build DIRECTORY	Changes the directory used to build packages before installation. The default is C:\TEMP.
set case [Yes|No]	Sets searches to be case-sensitive. Default is for searches to be non-case-sensitive.
set clean [Yes|No]	If set (the default), then packages successfully installed from the Build directory will be deleted once the installation is complete.
set confirm [Yes|No]	If set (the default), then the install, remove, and upgrade commands will always confirm before continuing.
set force_install [Yes|No]	If set (the default), then a package will be installed even if its dependencies cannot be followed and installed.
set more NUMBER	Paginates the display by NUMBER lines. If set to zero (the default), then no paging will occur.
set repository NAME LOCATION	Adds a repository to the list repositories for this session. The NAME is the name by which this repository will be referred, and LOCATION is the URL or directory from which to download packages.
set repository /remove NAME	Removes the repository NAME from the list of repositories.
set root DIRECTORY	Sets the installation directory to DIRECTORY.
set save	Saves current options as defaults.
set trace LEVEL	Sets the debugging level: The default is 1, which outputs brief progress messages; the maximum value is 4; and a value of 0 indicates that no tracing should occur.
set tracefile FILE	The file to use when logging debug information.
set verbose [Yes|No]	If set (the default), then the query and search commands will display additional detail.

Local Repositories If you want to install the same package on a number of machines, it's obviously very time-consuming (and possibly expensive) to download the package a number of times. You can use a local repository to store the packages and then use this repository when searching, updating, or installing files.

TABLE 12-2

PPM repositories.

Repository	URL
ActiveState	http://www.activestate.com/packages
Jan Krynicky	http://jenda.krynicky.cz/perl
Roth Consulting	http://www.roth.net/perl/packages/
Achim Bohnet	http://www.xray.mpe.mpg.de/~ach/prk/ppm
RTO	http://rto.dk/packages/gf

To use a local package, you need to download the package file from one of the repositories in Table 12-2. Usually these are available as ZIP files (see http://www.activestate.com/packages/zips/). Once extracted, the ZIP file should contain a README, a PPD file (which contains the package definition), and an x86 directory in which the actual package files are stored in a Gzipped Tar archive.

To install the package immediately, you can just change to the new directory and type:

```
ppm install PACKAGE
```

where `PACKAGE` is the name of the package that you want to install. PPM will automatically use the local version of the package. More usefully, you can create your own repository with its own library of packages by using the following steps:

1. Create a new directory, preferably on a network drive, to hold the new packages. Create another directory inside this one called x86.

2. Copy the PPD file to the new directory.

3. Copy the contents of the x86 directory from the package's ZIP file to the x86 directory created in Step 1.

Once you have all the packages copied into the directory, you can use PPM to install them. For example, if the repository is in a directory called PPM on the shared E: drive:

```
ppm install —location=e:\PPM VRML
```

or within the interactive interface:

```
search /location e:\ppm
```

Creating Your Own PPM Packages

As we've already seen, a PPM package really just consists of a PPD file, which contains the necessary definitions used by the PPM system and an archive of the normal contents of a Perl module as it would be downloaded from CPAN. We already know that CPAN modules include the Perl source files and a file called Makefile.PL. Like the normal Makefile the Perl Makefile.PL contains the necessary definitions required to build your package using the MakeMaker module that comes with all Perl distributions.

Makefile.PL is actually just a Perl script that calls a function called WriteMakefile, which is exported by the MakeMaker module. MakeMaker does all of the complicated stuff, accounting for the local Perl installation and operating system, and in turn generates a Makefile that can be used by a make utility such as dmake or nmake to build the source files into a Perl module.

The MakeMaker tool is far too complicated to go into too much detail at this stage (see Chapter 20 of *Perl: The Complete Reference* for more information). At its most basic level, however, you can use the following template:

```
use ExtUtils::MakeMaker;

WriteMakefile(
    'NAME' => 'MyModule',
    'VERSION_FROM' => 'MyModule.pm',
    ($] ge '5.005') ? (
        'AUTHOR' => 'Me (me@me.org)',
        'ABSTRACT' => 'Does my stuff',
    ) : (),
);
```

Obviously, you will need to replace the values of the NAME, VERSION_FROM, AUTHOR, and ABSTRACT arguments to reflect the name of your module.

Normally at this point we'd package up the source files and this Makefile.PL file into a distributable package. However, we need to perform the build process on behalf of end users, since we cannot guarantee they will have the utilities required to extract the file themselves. To do this, type

```
C:\> perl Makefile.PL
C:\> nmake
```

(If you don't have a copy of nmake (which comes with Visual Studio), you can download it from ftp://ftp.microsoft.com/Softlib/MSLFILES/nmake15.exe.)

This will go through the build process, creating the directory structure used by the PPM system when installing the module into its final location. Normally, this would be handled by a make or similar utility. You might see output like the following, although it will depend on the make utility you are using:

```
mkdir blib
mkdir blib/lib
mkdir blib/arch
mkdir blib/arch/auto
mkdir blib/lib/auto
mkdir blib/man3
copy MyModule.pm blib/lib/MyModule.pm
```

You now need to package the blib directory up using tar and gzip. You can get these utilities from a variety of places—ActiveState recommends http://www.itribe.net/virtunix/.

For example:

```
C:\> tar cvf MyModule.tar blib
C:\> gzip MyModule.tar
```

This will create a file called MyModule.tar.gz. The final step is to create the PPD file that specifies the package information required by PPM. The MakeMaker utility places the necessary steps into the Makefile, so we can type

```
C:\> nmake ppd
```

The resulting file should be called MyModule.PPD, and it will look something like this:

```
<SOFTPKG NAME="MyModule"VERSION="1,0,0,0">
   <TITLE>MyModule</TITLE>
   <ABSTRACT>Does my stuff</ABSTRACT>
   <AUTHOR>Me (me@me.org)</AUTHOR>
   <IMPLEMENTATION>
      <OS NAME="MSWin32" />
      <ARCHITECTURE NAME="MSWin32-x86-object" />
      <CODEBASE HREF="" />
   </IMPLEMENTATION>
</SOFTPKG>
```

The file is actually in XML format and defines all of the information required by PPM when you search a repository. You will need to change the value of the CODEBASE property to point to the location of the source package file. If you want to follow the format of others you put the MyModule.tar.gz file in an x86 directory, and then zip the whole lot up into a file that you can supply to ActiveState or one of the other repositories.

Visual Package Manager

If you want a simpler and interactive interface to downloading and installing packages, you can use the Visual Package Manager (VPM). This comes as part of the Perl Developers Kit, a chargeable extra to the ActivePerl distribution. The VPM works by starting a web server on the local machine through which you access the information that is normally provided through PPM. VPM and PPM are at the core identical; the difference is that VPM offers a web-based interface to the package management process in place of the command line or text interface service offered by PPM.

To start the VPM service, choose the VPM program from the Perl Development Kit folder on the Start menu. This will start the VPM Server process and open a browser window connected to the local server.

NOTE. You may have to log in to the VPM service in order to use it. Under Windows 95/98, use your normal network login to open the connection. Under Windows NT or Windows 2000, you may need to use an administrator password to update the packages successfully. Talk to your systems administrator if you don't have the necessary privileges.

There are four pages controlling the VPM service that relate to the different commands available within PPM.

Verify

The Verify page is the main interface to the VPM system. It takes over from the verify and query commands in PPM. See Figure 12-1 for a sample.

The Verify page provides a list of all of the packages currently installed. A common feature throughout all of the pages is that the pack-

Figure 12-1

The Verify page in VPM.

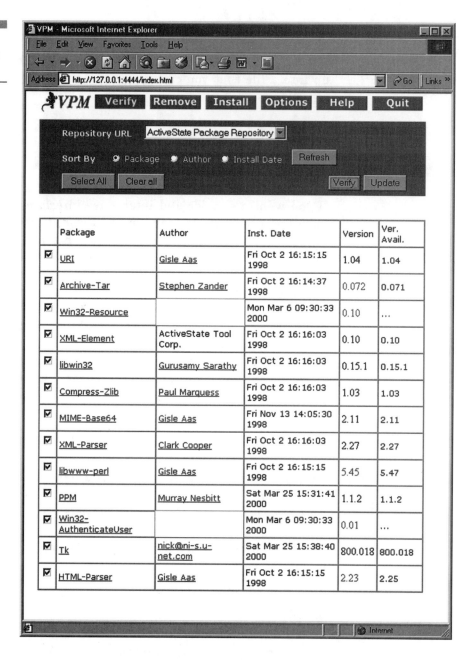

ages are hyperlinks. Clicking on the package name will provide detailed information about the package you have selected.

If you click on any of the modules listed and then press the Verify button, the module version numbers will be checked against the modules available on the repository shown at the top of the page, in the same way as the `verify` command in PPM. Clicking on the Update button will download and install any packages that are out of date. This is the same as the `/update` option with the `verify` command in PPM.

Quick buttons are provided to select or deselect all of the modules, and you can select a different repository using the pop-up. See the information on the Options page for details on how to expand the repository list.

Remove

The Remove page provides a direct interface to the `remove` command in PPM. You can see from the sample window in Figure 12-2 that the list of modules currently installed is listed within the page.

Selecting any of the installed modules and pressing the Remove button will remove them from the system.

Install

The Install page lists all of the packages available on a repository. Unfortunately, we lose the ability to search for packages when using VPM, but like the other pages, actually performing an installation is as straightforward as selecting the package you want to install and clicking a button. You can see a sample list in Figure 12-3.

When you first switch to the Install page, the list of packages is not shown. You need to click on the Refresh button next to the Repository pop-up to actually display the list. Once the list appears, click on the packages you want to install, and then use the Install These Packages button to actually install the packages you have selected.

Options

The Options window allows you to configure the same options as supported by the PPM system, albeit in a more friendly format. You can see the Options page in Figure 12-4.

To add new repositories, enter the repository name and the URL or directory location of the repository, and then click on the Add button. To remove an existing entry, select it from the list, and click on the Remove button. Note that the changes you make in this page will be saved. The next time you use the VPM system, you will have access to the same list of repositories.

Figure 12-2

The Remove page in VPM.

Figure 12-3

The Install page in VPM.

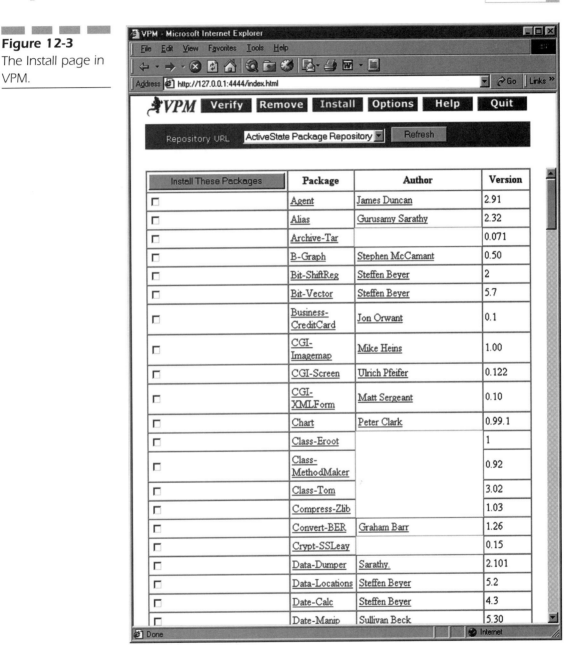

Figure 12-4

The Options page in VPM.

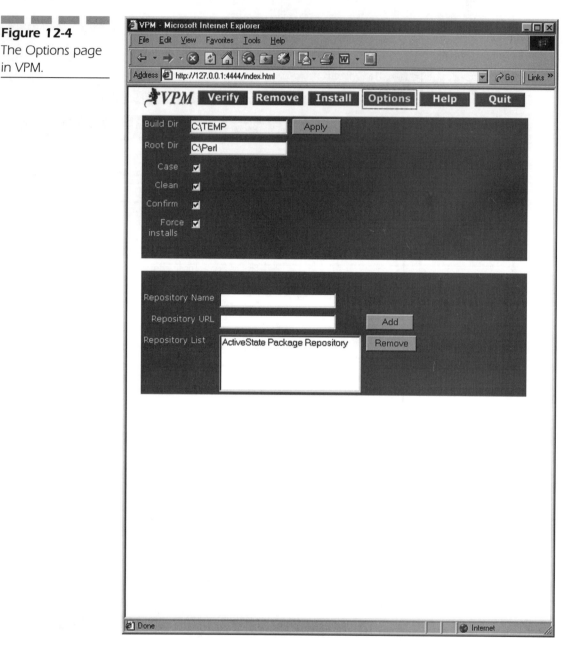

Quitting

To quit the VPM system, you *must* click on the Quit button in the browser window. This is because this will correctly shut down the server process that supports the VPM system. If you close the browser window, the VPM server will still be running, which may present problems when you come to restart or shut down your machine or open a new VPM process.

## CHAPTER 13

ActiveState Perl Debugger

It's a sad fact that most programs have bugs in them, and that finding those bugs is probably one of the longest parts of the programming process. Perl is not notorious for its bugs, but its free and easy format can sometimes help to breed a simple bug into something much more complex. You therefore need something to trace those bugs and determine the root of the problem. This is where debuggers come in.

Perl comes with its own standard debugger that uses a rather raw text-based interface, but is nonetheless very functional and should help to trace bugs easily. You can get to this debugger with ActivePerl by using the -d switch on the command line, for example:

```
C:\> perl -d script.pl
```

We won't cover the debugger at this point, since it's already covered both in the `perldebug` manual page, and also in a number of books. See Appendix A for some examples.

Although there is actually nothing wrong with the text-based debugger, for many Windows-based programmers it will feel a little restrictive and complicated to use. The ActiveState Perl Debugger (APD), which comes with the Perl Development Kit, provides a GUI interface to a debugger that will be familiar to Visual Studio and other integrated development environments.

The Debugger Interface

Once you have installed the Perl Development Kit, the APD replaces the default debugger installed as part of the core Perl distribution. This means that to actually start the APD you use the same command line option:

```
C:\> perl -d script.pl
```

There is unfortunately no way of using the standard Perl debugger once the ActiveState version has been installed. The default ActivePerl debugger window can be seen in Figure 13-1.

Once started, the debugger automatically opens your script and executes any `use` statements and any BEGIN blocks. The starting location for the script is therefore the first statement that would ordinarily be executed by the compiler *after* the compilation process.

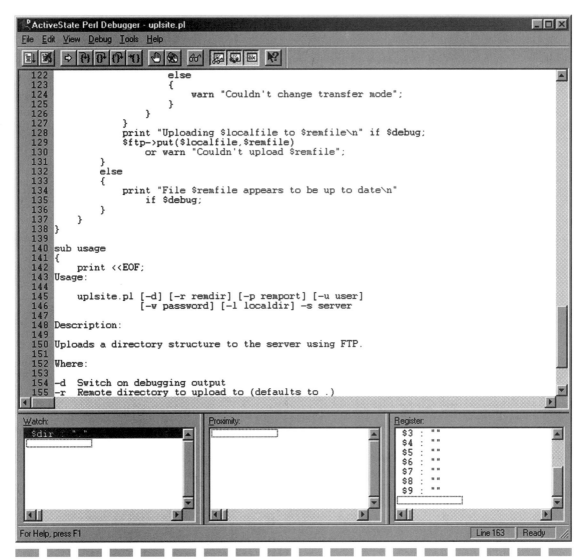

Figure 13-1   The ActiveState Perl debugger.

By default, the window is split into four areas, the main source window, which shows the source script currently being debugged, and the Watch, Proximity, and Register panels, which show information about the current state of execution.

Note that any changes that you make to the configuration of the Perl debugger are permanent. The next time you use the debugger the same watches, window, and tools will be available to you.

The Source Panel

The source panel shows the source for the currently executing statement. Initially this will show the script you are debugging, but if your script also imports any external modules, then the debugger will trace through to those modules, also showing their source. You can always tell what file you are currently debugging by looking at the window title—this will always show the path of the file.

Within the source panel, the left-hand side shows the line numbers for the file being debugged. Although the line numbers seem trivial, they are handy when you want to set breakpoints. We will look at these in more detail later.

The yellow arrow shows the statement/line that will be executed next, not the statement that has just been executed. The blue arrow shows the location of the current "cursor" used when creating new breakpoints and bookmarks.

We will cover the actual execution process of the script later.

Figure 13-2
Setting syntax colors.

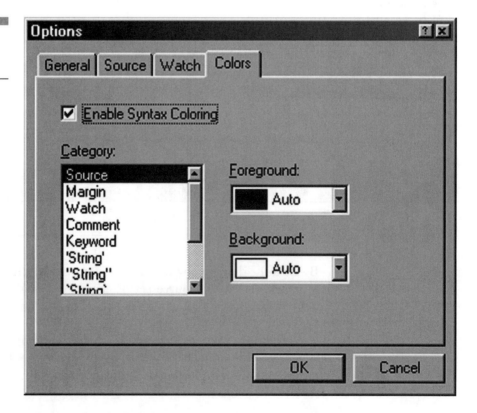

Syntax Colorization

So that you can easily identify elements while looking at the source code, it is colored according to the individual components that make up each statement. You can configure the coloring used by using the Colors panel of the Options window, available from the Tools menu. You can see an example in Figure 13-2.

To enable syntax coloring, you need to check the Enable Syntax Coloring checkbox. If the box is left unchecked, then all the text is shown with a black foreground and white background.

For ease of use, each component of a script can be colorized individually, and for each component you can set the foreground and background color. You can see a list of the components recognized by the debugger in Table 13-1.

TABLE 13-1

Syntax colorization.

Component	Description
Source	The default color for the source not otherwise colored according the other components
Margin	The color of the margin along the left side of the window used to list the line numbers
Watch	The colors used to display the contents of the Watch, Proximity, and Registers panels
Comments	The colors used for comments in the code. Comments are identified using the normal comment rules: all text after a # sign that does not immediately follow a $ sign up to the end of line. Embedded POD document is also color using the same settings.
Keyword	Sets the color for any keywords in the source code. The debugger comes with a predefined number of keywords that match the list of keywords supported by Perl. You can edit the list of the keywords by editing the keywords.txt file installed in the debugger directory.
`'String'`	Sets the color used for single-quoted strings, whether they are identified by the ' single quote character, or matching the q// operator.
`"String"`	Sets the color used for double-quoted strings, whether they are identified by the " double-quote character or matching the qq// operator.
`` `String` ``	Sets the color used for backquoted strings, whether they are identified by the ' backquote character or matching the qx// operator.
`Match`	Sets the color used to identify regular expression matches. A match expression is identified by the // operator or the m// operator.
Substitution	Sets the color used to identify substitution expressions. A substitution expression is identified by the s/// operator.
Translation	Sets the color used to identify translation expression. A translation expression is identified either by the tr/// or y/// operators.

To actually change the color, select the component from the left-hand list and then select the foreground and background colors from the pop-up menus on the right. Clicking the OK button at any time will accept all the changes that you've made, while clicking Cancel will forget any of the changes.

Colorizing code only changes the color of what is displayed, no other modification is made. Although this may seem like an obvious statement, there are times when it might be convenient for the latter to happen. For example, I often use the debugger with the comment component set to white on both the foreground and background. This effectively hides the comments from the program, useful if I'm debugging my own code when the comments don't add to my understanding. Unfortunately, it also has the effect of introducing blank areas within the debugger source window.

Source Options

The Source panel from the Options item in the Tools menu allows you to configure the look and feel of the main source panel. There are five options: You can control the fonts, tab size, watch, and break tip display, and the use of line numbers.

The Set Font option allows you to set the font style and size used to display the source code. The Tab Size is the number of spaces used to replace each tab used as indent within the code. The default is a value of 4 (as used in this book).

WatchTips and BreakTips define whether the information about a watch or breakpoint is shown in a tooltip when the cursor points to a watched variable or breakpoint.

The Display Line Numbers option defines whether line numbers are shown in the left-hand margin. Note that this does not affect the display of the current statement arrow or breakpoints, only the line numbers.

The Registers

The register simulates the operation of the register panel in a normal debugging tool. Perl doesn't actually use internal registers, even within the Perl virtual machine, but there are some global variables that can have an effect on the overall execution of your script. For example, the $\_$ variable, which is used as the scratchpad throughout your script, is often the default variable used by many functions and operators if you fail to supply any arguments.

TABLE 13-2

Registers displayed by the debugger.

Register	Description
$_	The scratchpad variable
$.	The current line within the file currently being used
$&	The string match by the last successful pattern match
$`	The string preceding the information matched by the last pattern match
$'	The string following the information matched by the last pattern match
$1..$9	The variables used to store the result of the corresponding parentheses from the last regular expression match

The register panel therefore lists the core global variables used by the Perl interpreter. The list of variables displayed is shown in Table 13-2.

The entries listed in Table 13-2 are the defaults, you can add your own list of registers to be watched by right-clicking within the register window. The menu provides three options; you can add, modify, or update the watches within the list. The changes you make are permanent; the next time you open and use the debugger the list of watches will be as you last used them. You can reset the list of register watches to the default by clicking the Reset button in the Watch panel under tools and options when configuring debugging options.

Watches are a common feature of the debugger, see the section on the "Watches" panel later in this chapter for details on adding watches to the register panel.

You can hide the register window by selecting Hide from the pop-up menu displayed when you right-click within the register panel or by selecting the Register option from the View menu.

Proximity Panel

The proximity panel displays the values of the variables surrounding the current line. You cannot configure the variables that are displayed, nor can you control how the variables that are listed are displayed. You can, however, control how many lines above and below the current line are examined to determine which variables to monitor.

To adjust the proximity properties, select the Options item from the Tools menu. This will present the Options window. If you switch to the Watch tab, seen here in Figure 13-3, you can see the configurable

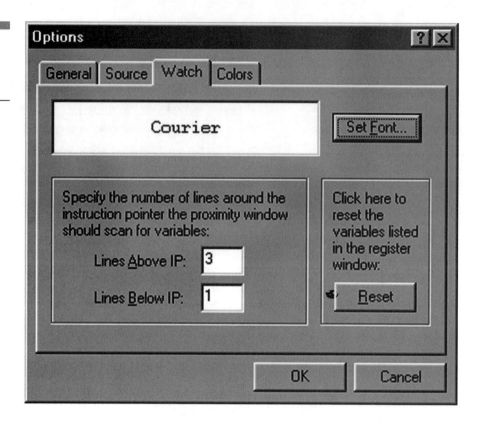

options. The lines above and below the next line in the execution control
how many lines are monitored by the proximity panel.

The other options allow you to reset the list of watches displayed in
the Register panel and to set the font used in all three watch panels. The
setting of this font does not affect the display of the main window, only
the panels.

Watches

The Watch panel allows you to set specific variables to be watched at all
times. This bypasses the normal register display and the proximity display. The information listed within the Watch panel remains, no matter
where you are within the execution of the script being debugged.

To add a new watch, you can either right-click on a variable in the
proximity panel and select Copy to Watch, or right-click within the
Watch panel.

Watches (either in the Watch or Register panel) are not simply static variables; the statement used when creating a new watch is evaluated just like any other Perl statement. This means that they can be used in complex expressions, or you can embed expressions and functions into the watch to format the variable that you want to watch in a more human-readable format.

For example, when watching an array you might want to use

```
join(', ', @array)
```

as the watch statement. If you want to get even more creative, you can also enter multiline or block-based statements. Here's one that monitors a hash:

```
foreach $key (sort keys %hash) { $string .= "$key -> $hash{$key}\n" }
  $string
```

The only problem with all watches is that because the source for the watch is displayed within the panel, long watch statements like the one above may not be displayed properly. This is not a significant problem, but it can be a constant frustration!

Watches are always evaluated using the current context. This means that if you switch to a block or function that uses a variable with the same name, the local variable will be displayed. Special care should be taken if you use a scalar to hold a reference to another data type, because the watch may not evaluate properly.

Executing Statements

Once you have opened the script you want to debug, you will need to decide how to execute it. There are two basic methods offered by all debuggers: stepping and breakpoints.

Stepping

When you step through a script you execute each line individually. For each step, the current line is executed and then execution immediately stops until you execute the next statement. The ActiveState debugger supports four step commands: Step Into, Step Over, Step Out, and Run to Cursor.

- *Step Into* executes the current statement, following the execution of any functions or methods found within the statement. Execution goes as far as calling the function or method, and bypassing any variable initialization, and stops at the first executable statement within the called function.

- *Step Over* executes the current statement. Any functions or methods that are called are executed without being processed by the debugger, so execution stops on the next executable statement within the current file.

- *Step Out* continues execution until the current function or method ends. Execution stops at the next executable statement, either within the next function call of the current line from the calling script or to the next statement of the caller.

- *Run to Cursor* is similar in principle to breakpoints, except that execution only continues as far as the line prior to the one pointed to by the cursor. Breakpoints are still honored, so execution will stop at a breakpoint that lies between the current line and the cursor line.

The advantage of stepping over breakpoints is that it allows you to monitor each line individually. This is particularly useful when you want to study a sequence or each iteration of a loop in detail.

Breakpoints

Breakpoints offer a different approach. Instead of laboriously stepping through each line of a script you can set a breakpoint at a future point in the script and the start execution. The debugger will execute all of the lines up until the given breakpoint. In addition, you can also set a breakpoint to be triggered only when a variable matches a certain condition.

For example, imagine you are having trouble within a loop, but only when the loop counter reaches 1000, you can set a breakpoint to be triggered when the counter value is greater than or equal to 1000. The loop will parse and execute 1000 times, and then the debugger will halt to allow you to process each individual line until you trace the problem.

To create a breakpoint, move the cursor to the line on which you want to set the breakpoint and then press F9, right-click and select Toggle Breakpoint or select it from the Edit menu. The option is a toggle, so you can use the same process to remove an existing breakpoint.

Alternatively, you can insert a breakpoint at a specific line using the Insert Breakpoint option. This allows you to select the line on which the

Figure 13-4
Editing all break-
points.

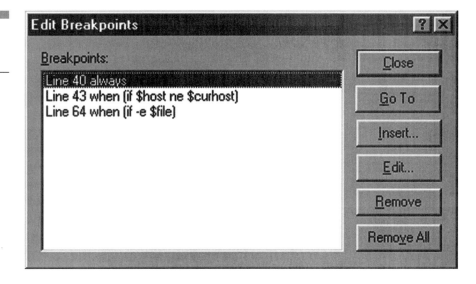

breakpoint should occur (it defaults to the current cursor line) and to enter a condition to use in order to trigger the breakpoint. The condition should be in the same format as conditions used in `if`, `while`, and other control statements; if the result of the condition is a positive integer, then it is treated as a success and triggers the breakpoint and halts execution.

To edit all of the breakpoints that you have configured, choose the Edit Breakpoints option. This will provide you with a list of all the breakpoints, as seen in Figure 13-4.

Pressing F5 will start execution and it will only stop when execution reaches a breakpoint, otherwise the entire script will execute. For most scripts it's a good idea to insert a couple of breakpoints just to allow you to interrupt processing of the script so that you can monitor what is going on.

Debug Tools

Over and above the watches, proximity lists, and registers you can also get immediate information about the script being debugged by using the Quick Eval, Dump Variable, and Call Stack options from the Debug menu. These provide information about variables and the stack trace for the current statement, according to the context of the current line.

Quick Eval

The Quick Eval option allows you to execute any Perl statement within the context of the script being debugged. You have access to all of the variables defined within the current debugger location within the script. For a more permanent view on the statement that you enter you can click the Add Watch button.

Dump Variable

The Dump Variable option dumps the contents of a variable into a scrollable box. For very large variables this is vital because it enables you to view the entire contents without the restrictions enforced by the individual panels.

Unlike the other watches, you cannot supply a statement to be evaluated, only a variable or variable component (i.e., an array or hash element). The debugger displays the variable formatted according to the variables type and content. The actual dump is handled by the `Data::Dumper` module.

Call Stack

The Call Stack option displays a trace of the function calls used to reach the current statement and information about how those functions were called. The actual output is handled by the `caller` function, a function built into the Perl compiler. The Call Stack option uses the extended version of the `caller` function described below.

If you want to use the `caller` function in your own programs, the information on using the function is included here. The data returned by the `caller` function includes details about the subroutine (or `eval` or `require`) statement:

```
caller EXPR
caller
```

In a scalar context, it simply returns the package name. In a simple list context, the function returns the package name, filename, and line of the caller of the current subroutine, `eval`, or `require` statement:

```
($package, $filename, $line) = caller;
```

If EXPR is specified, `caller` returns extended information. The value of EXPR should be the number of frames on the stack to go back to before the current one. That is, if you specify a value of 1, the parent subroutine information will be printed, a value of 2 will print the grandparent subroutine, and so on. The information returned is

```
($package, $filename, $line, $subroutine,
$hasargs, $wantarray, $evaltext, $is_require) = caller($i);
```

The `$evaltext` and `$is_require` values are only returned when the subroutine being examined is actually the result of an `eval()` statement.

As an example, examine the script below:

```perl
sub bar
{
    Top::top();
}

bar();

package Top;

sub top
{
    my $level = 0;
    print "Top of the world, Ma!\n";
    while (((($package, $file, $line,
            $subname, $hasargs, $wantarray) = caller($level++)))
    {
        $hasargs    = $hasargs    ? 'Yes' : 'No';
        if (defined($wantarray))
        {
            $wantarray = 'Yes';
        }
        else
        {
            $wantarray = 'No';
        }
        print <<EOF;
Stack:
        Package: $package
           File: $file
           Line: $line
     Subroutine: $subname
  Has Arguments?: $hasargs
    Wants Array?: $wantarray
EOF
    }
}
```

When executed, the resultant information shows the stack trace for the `top` function, including its original call from `main` and from the `bar` function:

```
Top of the world, Ma!
Stack:
            Package: main
               File: ./././t.pl
               Line: 5
         Subroutine: Top::top
     Has Arguments?: Yes
       Wants Array?: No
Stack:
            Package: main
               File: ./././t.pl
               Line: 8
         Subroutine: main::bar
     Has Arguments?: Yes
       Wants Array?: No
```

The information provided should enable you to pinpoint the location within a script. If you want to report the information to a log, you may want to introduce a wrapper function like this one:

```
sub callerlog
{
    my $reference = shift;
    open(DATA,">caller.log") || return;
    print DATA join(' ',@_),":$reference\n";
    close(DATA);
}
```

Then to call the function, you would use a line such as

```
callerlog("Writing data",caller());
```

to report the information for the current stack trace. Note that you can't directly use the information from `callerlog`, since that will introduce its own frame of information at location zero within the stack. You could, however, use a modified form of the `callerlog` function that returns the stack trace from frame one onward:

```
sub callerlog
{
    my $reference = shift;
    my $level = 1;
    while (((@data) = caller($level++)))
    {
        print join(' ',@data),":$reference\n";
    }
}
```

Bookmarks

You can introduce a bookmark into any piece of code. A bookmark operates like an Internet bookmark: it allows you to go straight to a location within a script file at any time. This can be useful when you want to jump to a particular function that is called regularly and monitor its status.

To set a new bookmark, use the mouse to select the line (as marked by the blue arrow) and then select Toggle Bookmark (Ctrl-F2). This is a toggle, so you can also use it to remove the bookmark from an individual line. To view a bookmark use the Next (F2) and Previous Bookmark (Shift-F2) items from the Edit menu.

NOTE   *Bookmarks are also retained after the debugger completes execution. To clear all bookmarks, select Remove All Bookmarks (Ctrl-Shift-F2) from the Edit menu.*

Using Tools

You can configure a number of tools that you can access directly from the debugger. These can be used to open the script you are debugging in an editor, or to execute the script directly, or through another tool—perhaps a Web browser if you are developing a Web-based interface.

To configure the tools available within the debugger, choose the Customize option from the Tools menu. You'll get a window like the one shown in Figure 13-5.

To set up a new tool, click the left-most button at the top of the window, and then enter the tools name, as it will appear in the menu. If you prefix the name with an ampersand, then the command will be given a menu shortcut using the normal letter prefix. The first nine tools are always available as Alt-#, where # is the number from 1 to 9. You can configure which tool appears at the top of the list (and therefore has a shortcut of Alt-1) by selecting the tool item and then using the up and down arrow buttons to adjust its position.

The Command configures the program that will be executed when the tool is selected. You can use the Browse button to select the program using a normal file dialog box. The Command box must only contain the path to a program; if you want to add arguments, you must use the Arguments box.

Figure 13-5
Customizing tools.

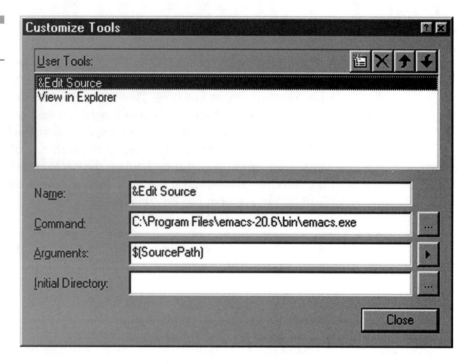

The Arguments box allows you to introduce additional arguments to be appended to the line during execution. You can place any text into this box, but the tool is most useful when you use one of the predefined arguments supplied by the debugger tool. You can see a list of the arguments and their descriptions in Table 13-3.

TABLE 13.3

Custom tool variables.

Argument	Description
SourcePath	The full path to the source file currently being debugged. Note that this is the current debug file, not necessarily the script that you were originally debugging.
SourceDirectory	The directory component of the current file's path
SourceName	The name (without extension) of the current file
SourceExtension	The extension (with leading period) of the current file
CurrentDirectory	The current directory. This is the directory in which the debugger was started, not the current directory within the execution of the script.
CurrentLine	The line number of the statement being debugged
CurrentText	The text of the current line being debugged

Note that the Source Extension argument includes the period used to separate the base name and its extension. For example, when debugging a CGI script, you might create a Tool with the following properties:

```
Name: View in Explorer
Command: C:\Program Files\Internet Explorer\Iexplore.exe
Arguments: incontinent/www/$(SourceName)$(SourceExtension)
```

The final entry allows you to configure the directory in which execution starts. Although not useful (or necessary) for editing files, it can be useful if you want to create a tool that executes the script outside of the confines of the debugger.

14

Creating Standalone Applications

The normal way of distributing Perl-based applications is to supply the Perl scripts and use a Perl interpreter installed on the local machine. There are two downsides to this from a developer's point of view. The first is that people could potentially steal the code that you have written, possibly even passing it off as their own code. Although this is not a serious consideration for some users (especially since Perl is free), it can cause problems when the scripts are being deployed in a commercial product.

The second downside is that it places additional requirements onto the user when installing the software. By requiring other software to be installed—even when it's as easy as installing ActivePerl—you are complicating the process and opening yourself up to all sorts of possible complications that may be completely unrelated to the scripts you have distributed.

Visual Basic and C++ programmers are accustomed to being able to distribute standalone applications that work and operate like other applications installed on the Windows machine. These programs don't rely on anything—except perhaps the standard Windows libraries and extensions.

A compiler called `perlcc`, supplied with Perl, takes a Perl script, compiles it into the internal instructions used by the Perl interpreter—called *opcodes*—and then encapsulates the opcodes into C source, which can then be compiled with a standard C compiler. The whole thing is then bonded with the standard Perl libraries in order to produce a final executable.

For a variety of reasons, `perlcc` does not work under Windows at the moment. Although the modules that are used to support the back-end portion of the compiler system operate under Windows, the front-end script doesn't work properly, and it still requires a C compiler—not a standard Windows tool.

PerlApp

There is a solution called PerlApp that comes with the Perl Development Kit. It uses a similar approach to the problem of producing standalone Perl applications. However, rather than converting them to the C source and compiling them, it embeds the code into a small Windows application. This allows you to distribute the application just like it was any other Windows application. All you have to do is double-click on it or call the program name in a command window.

NOTE. *The current version of PerlApp (v1.2 at this writing) only works on Windows NT machines. However, applications built with PerlApp, even dependent ones, will work on all platforms.*

Application Modes

PerlApp creates two types of application: dependent and freestanding. The dependent form just embeds the Perl script into a very small application file. When executed, the application makes calls to the Perl libraries (the Perl interpreter is actually located within a DLL installed with ActivePerl and the PDK) to actually execute the script. This makes the applications very small—the overhead is about 7 Kb over and above the size of the application. The execution is also very fast; with such a small overhead, there is little code that needs to be loaded and the script starts almost instantaneously.

The downside to the dependent method is that it requires ActivePerl, PDK, and any additional modules that your script uses to be installed on each machine on which you want to run the application. Within your local network this is probably not a problem, but if you want to distribute the application elsewhere, it adds extra levels of complication—something we were hoping to avoid by compiling a standalone application in the first place.

The freestanding application is the solution. This embeds the Perl script into an application that also includes the Perl interpreter, any modules on which the Perl script relies, and any DLLs required by those modules. The result is an application that can be run on any Windows machine, whether it has Perl installed or not.

The application is much larger: There's now an overhead of about 820 Kb, and that's before you add any modules or DLLs required by the script. Because of the size, the application also takes much longer to load, but it can be distributed without ever having to worry about whether the end user has Perl.

Building Scripts into Applications

The interface to PerlApp is a command-line application that takes your Perl script as its input and generates the application (actually an EXE file). Before we look at the specifics, a small tip. The PerlApp interface is actually handled by a Perl script. Therefore, the normal method of execution is as follows:

```
C:\> perl perlapp.pl myscript.pl
```

If you use the supplied `pl2bat` utility, you can make the PerlApp script into a more handy application. You'll find the PerlApp script in the `bin` directory of the base Perl installation—normally C:\Perl. You'll therefore need to do the following:

```
C:\> cd \perl\bin
C:\Perl\bin> pl2bat perlapp.pl
```

The `Perl\bin` directory should already be in your `PATH`, so the new interface to PerlApp should work from any location. We'll assume from here on that you've performed these steps.

The basic format for the command is as follows:

```
perlapp [-d[ependent] | -f[reestanding]
        -s[cript]=SRC
        [-e[xe]=EXEFILE]
        [-c[lean]]
        [-a[dd]=MODULES]
        [-i[nfo]=LIST]
        [-g[ui]]
        [-v[erbose]]
        [SCRIPT]
```

For example, to create a freestanding application:

```
C:\> perlapp -f myscript.pl
```

Note that the default is to create a dependent application.

The effect of the different command-line options is shown in Table 14-1.

For example, to create a dependent application that includes the `IO::Socket` module:

```
C:\> perlapp -d -v -a=IO::Socket httpserv.pl
Using httpserv.pl for script name
Input script name: httpserv.pl
Output exe name: httpserv.exe
Exe Mode: Perl Dependent
Creating dependent executable
```

Libraries and Dependencies

When you build a new application with PerlApp in dependent mode, the new application includes only the original script. Any of the modules or

TABLE 14-1

Options when cre-
ating applications
with PerlApp.

Option	Description
-a[dd]=MODULES	Adds the supplied MODULES to the file that is created. See the section "Libraries and Dependencies" for more information.
-c[clean]	Cleans up the files used during the build process.
-d[ependent]	Creates a dependent application.
-e[xe]=EXEFILE	Creates the application with EXENAME. If you don't specify anything, then the script creates the application with the same basename (i.e., without the extension) as the source script. Note that the = character can be replaced by a space.
-f[reestanding]	Creates a freestanding application.
-g[ui]	Builds an application that does not rely on a command console to operate. If you want to create this type of application, then you need to use Win32::Console to create your own consoles, or use Tk. See Chapter 10 for more information on developing alternative interfaces to Perl applications.
-i[nfo]=LIST	Add the version information specified in LIST to the application that is created. This information is the same as that returned by the Win32::AdminMisc::GetFileInfo function—see Chapter 4 for more information. The LIST should be in the form of name/value pairs separated by an equals sign, with each pair separated by semicolons. See Table 14-2 for a list of valid options.
-s[cript]=SRC	Uses SRC as the source script for the application. Uses SCRIPT (the first script supplied on the command line) if this is not specified. Note that the = character can be replaced by a space.
-v[erbose]	Generate verbose output about the production process.

DLLs that are required by the script are not included in the final application; they must exist on the host on which you want to execute the application. There is no way to override this operation—even using the -add command-line option will not include the modules in the final application.

When creating applications that are freestanding, PerlApp includes any modules imported using the use or require statements and any DLLs on which they rely. Furthermore, module dependencies are followed, so if a module you import in your script in turn imports another module, then that module is also included. For example, the sample script:

```
use Win32::Internet;

print 'Doin Nothing\n';
```

TABLE 14-2

Application infor-
mation to be
appended to the
file.

Option	Description
comments	Comments about the file contents.
companyname	The name of the company that generated the application.
filedescription	A simple description of the application's purpose/abilities.
fileversion	The file version number in the form $W.X.Y.Z$, where each number is in the range $0-65535$ and the X, Y, and Z elements are optional, defaulting to zero.
internalname	The internal name used by the application.
legalcopyright	The copyright notice for the file.
legaltrademarks	Any trademarks relevant to the application.
originalfilename	You should set this to the name of the script that was used as the source of the application.
productname	The name of the overall product to which this application belongs.
productversion	The product version number in the form $W.X.Y.Z$, where each number is in the range $0-65535$ and the X, Y, and Z elements are optional, defaulting to zero. Note that this can be a different number than fileversion.

imports the Win32::Internet module, the Exporter module, and others, as you can see from the output it generates:

```
Adding Module: C:/Perl/lib/Exporter.pm
Adding Module: C:/Perl/site/lib/Win32/Internet.pm
Adding Module: C:/Perl/lib/vars.pm
Adding Module: C:/Perl/lib/AutoLoader.pm
Adding Module: C:/Perl/lib/DynaLoader.pm
Adding Module: C:/Perl/lib/auto/DynaLoader/dl_expandspec.al
Adding Module: C:/Perl/lib/auto/DynaLoader/dl_findfile.al
Adding Module: C:/Perl/lib/auto/DynaLoader/dl_find_symbol_anywhere.al
Adding Module: C:/Perl/lib/auto/DynaLoader/autosplit.ix
Adding Binary: C:/Perl/site/lib/auto/Win32/Internet/Internet.dll
```

However, note that although we know that Win32::Internet relies
on the WININET.DLL Windows library, it's not included in the final
application. DLLs are followed to only one level. If all DLL dependencies
were followed, then the resulting application would end up including the
entire Windows library set!

Furthermore, there is one additional exception. Modules imported using require that rely on the name of a variable to define the module to be imported will not work. For example, the following script:

```
$mymodule = "Win32::Internet";
require $mymodule;
```

will compile into a final application without warning, but when you try to execute it, the following occurs:

```
C:\>t.exe
Can't locate Win32::Internet in @INC (@INC contains: .
C:\TEMP\t\{29BAE3F0-0586-11D4-B33C-005056AD0A87}\) at (eval 1) line
110.
```

To get around this, supply the name of the module that is required using the -add command-line option:

```
C:\> perlapp -freestanding -add=Win32::Internet
```

This will force the module (and its dependencies and DLLs) to be added to the final executable, even though PerlApp cannot determine the dependencies at compile time.

SECTION

Visual Basic Migration Guide

## CHAPTER 15

A Difference of Approach

The last section of the book will concentrate on helping existing Visual Basic programmers migrate from programming with VB to Perl. If you are a VB programmer and have taken a look at some of the earlier chapters, you will probably have already noticed that the basic sequence and execution of the two languages is actually very similar. In fact, many of the functions, operators, and statements that you already use under VB will work under Perl, albeit with a few minor differences.

Even though there are similarities, it should also be obvious even to the casual observer that there are some quite significant differences. In this chapter we'll look first at the ethos of the two languages, and then at the basic differences between each language in a number of key areas.

The remainder of the chapters in this section will concentrate on how to develop your applications using Perl and how the different Perl elements differ from the VB equivalents. Perl is different enough from VB that a straight migration is not possible. VB and Perl work in two completely different ways, and Perl will feel very different to the average VB programmer. We'll therefore concentrate on how to program in Perl, rather than how to migrate your applications to the Perl platform.

Visual Basic's Approach

Unsurprisingly, as the name suggests, Visual Basic is a very visually oriented language. Although it is a general-purpose tool that can be used for a variety of different projects, its primary use is in the development of front ends for databases. The entire language is geared toward working as the back end to an interface, and therefore, most of the functions and abilities of the language center around the user interface and the display and formatting of information. Although there are functions that will help to convert and manipulate data, it is not the language's focus, and this can sometimes be a frustrating limitation.

There are other aspects to the language. For example, a subset of VB, Visual Basic for Applications, is used as an embedded macro language in many of Microsoft's applications, including Word and Excel, and as a base scripting language for Access. As a macro language, VB becomes an integral part of the package, allowing you to automate components and to interface from one application to another.

VB is also a core part of the Windows operating system and is often used as a solution to the problem of scripting Windows. By using VB in combination with Object Linking and Embedding (OLE) and the COM interface, it's possible to use VB both to control another application and to act as a conduit for communication between applications or other user interfaces.

Web development is a case in point. You can use VB as an ASP scripting component both for general scripting within your interface and also to allow the easy presentation of information from a database to a web browser. In all these instances, it is the OLE interaction that provides the functionality for VB.

Anatomy of a VB Application

Let's look at the anatomy and makeup of a typical VB application. A Visual Basic application is composed of a number of objects. The objects mimic the physical representation of the application as it would appear on screen. By definition, each object consists of data and code. These two components make up the visual elements that you see on screen—the buttons, list boxes, and other entities that compose the interface of the application you are developing.

Within a VB application, these objects are placed into a form, which becomes the definition of the appearance and behavior of your application. For each form in an application, there is a corresponding form module that contains the definition and code that allows the form to operate.

In addition to the definition of the form, the form module also contains event procedures. The event procedures process the events that take place within the application. These include handling a button when it is pressed or displaying a dialog to select a file. Finally, forms can contain general procedures that are executed when the form is initialized or that can be called by other event-driven procedures. These are the generic procedures that do most of the general processing of information within the application. Code that is not form-related is placed into a standard module that is generally used to contain code that will be executed from a number of the different event procedures, or that contains an object or class definition to be shared by the other elements of the application.

The final application is then compiled into an application, with all of the units linked together to produce a standalone executable. Take, for example, the Hello World application. Under Visual Basic, Hello World consists of a form that displays the message and a series of code fragments that initialize the application and display the form, along with our "Hello World" message to the screen.

Perl's Approach

Perl has its roots in the Unix operating system, a largely text-driven operating system, both from the point of view of the interface and the type of information that is frequently dealt with. Although it's unfair to pigeonhole Perl as a text-processing language—it does a lot more than that—text processing was its original purpose. Because of this, Perl has some very strong data-handling features, and the majority of its abilities are geared to processing information of some kind.

Perl is therefore less visually oriented; it doesn't come with a development environment, and you are not limited to tying your applications to a GUI interface. Perl also becomes much more practical when you want to create a quick application or utility to do a specific task. There is less overhead and there are fewer rules about how the program is developed and organized.

Beyond its built-in functions that provide extensive data handling and manipulation, file and network access, and interfaces to the underlying OS, Perl also supports the ability to import additional modules to extend the facilities offered by Perl. Modules are very flexible and can either be made up of further Perl statements or C/C++ extensions to provide Perl with interfaces to standard system libraries. For example, all of the modules we've looked at in the first section of this book are actually supported by a C extension to Perl that interfaces to the Windows libraries.

Anatomy of a Perl Application

Because Perl does not work from the basis of a visual interface, the general program structure is much cleaner and quicker to produce. You actually use a simple text editor to produce your Perl application, and the entire development is driven by the contents of this one text file—it defines the objects, variables, and methods you use, and can even be used to develop a visual application with a suitable extension module. The base script also specifies which modules and libraries should be imported and used by the application.

This is probably the most fundamental difference—the "script" that you write defines everything about the application. There is no "project" file as there is in VB, and it's not necessary to compartmentalize the different features of your applications into different modules. Although this may make the process sound unstructured, it actually allows the programmer much more freedom and enables you to make programs and applications as free-form or structured as you like.

Perl is also not based around the premise of objects and classes. You can develop a Perl application without having to use objects. This does not mean that Perl does not support object-based development. Perl does have a very strong object development system that builds on the ease of use of the rest of the programming.

In fact, the ease of use is the common theme in all Perl programs; programmers can be as messy or tidy in their code development as they like. There are no restrictions or guides to how you program, but there is nothing to stop you from formulating a style or using the features of the Perl interpreter to help enforce some of the more casual programming techniques.

Compilation versus Interpretation

Another difference that some programmers have difficulty in conceptualizing is that Perl is not a compiled language—at least not in the true sense. The traditional way to create a VB application is to create a new VB project in the VB development environment and compile it into a final application. A single project can consist of multiple modules, but each module in the module is bonded (linked) during the compilation process into a final application.

Perl works differently. At its heart, Perl is an interpreted language, but with a slight twist. With an interpreted language, the interpreter reads the original source code and interprets each of the statements in order to perform the different operations. Each line of the source is executed one by one, directly by the interpreter and without the initial compilation stage. This has some advantages: Because there is no compilation process, the development of interpreted code should be significantly quicker. Interpreted code also tends to be smaller and easier to distribute. The disadvantages are that the original source must be supplied in order to execute the program, and an interpreted program is generally slower than a compiled executable because of the way the code is executed.

Perl fits neither of these descriptions in the real sense. The internals of Perl are such that the individual elements of a script are compiled into a tree of *opcodes*. Opcodes are similar in concept to the machine code that normal applications are compiled to. However, whereas machine code is executed directly by hardware, opcodes are executed by a virtual machine. The opcodes are highly optimized objects designed to perform a specific function. This is similar but not identical to the way Java works.

In essence, at the time of executing a Perl script, it is compiled into opcodes, which in turn are executed via a virtual machine. This enables Perl to provide all the advantages of a scripting language in combination with the fast execution of a compiled program. There is a little bit of overhead with a program that works in this fashion, since the script must be compiled on the fly each time the script is executed. However, the other benefits far outweigh this problem. For most scripts, the compilation process takes less than a second even with hundreds, even thousands, of lines.

Perl Basics

To create your first Perl script, open up a text editor—Notepad will do fine—and type in the following:

```
print "Hello World\n";
```

Save the file, and give it an extension of *.pl*. This isn't required, but it will help you to identify the file as a Perl script. For example, you might call the file test.pl.

Now open a DOS command prompt, change to the directory in which you saved the file and type the following:

```
C:\> perl test.pl
```

It should print out this:

```
Hello World
```

before returning you to the DOS prompt. The Perl interpreter opens the script, parses the contents, and executes the script. Then when the script ends, the interpreter exits and puts you back at the prompt.

Programmers familiar with VB and other languages will spot a few things about the script:

■ *There is no preamble.*   Unlike other languages, Perl doesn't require any form of preamble or initialization. You can just start writing your code statements.

- *There is no termination.* There's no indication of where the script ends. Actually, the script terminates when the interpreter reaches the end of the executable statements.

- *There is no compilation stage.* As we've already seen (see the "Compilation versus Interpretation" section earlier in this chapter), Perl interprets the code more or less as it goes along. It doesn't need to be separately compiled first.

- *There is no "main."* Execution of the script starts on the first line of the source script file and continues until no more statements can be executed. The execution can still jump to other parts of the source. Perl still supports functions and can call functions in external modules, but you do not have to define a special function or area as the "main" execution core of the application.

If you look a bit closer, you should be able to see some other artifacts of the Perl language. Like other languages such as C, but unlike Visual Basic, lines must be terminated by a semicolon. Perl takes everything up to a semicolon (unless the semicolon is part of a quoted string) as the Perl statement. This allows you to spread statements over more than one line. Therefore, the scripts

```
print
'Hello World\n';
```

and

```
print 'Hello
World\n';
```

will also work. The second example will actually print out the following:

```
Hello
World
```

since the newline is embedded within a quoted string.

The `print` keyword is actually a function, and this script demonstrates another difference when compared to other languages. Parentheses around function arguments are optional in Perl and only really necessary when writing a complex statement.

Let's look at a more typical example. This one takes in your name and then prints the result back to you, using a function to print the message:

```
print 'Welcome to the Greeting program!\n';
```

```
while(1)
{
    print "Enter your name: ";
    $name = <STDIN>;
    last if ($name eq 'exit');
    chomp($name);
    print_message($name);
}

sub print_message
{
    my ($name) = @_;

    print "Hey, nice to see you $name!\n";
}
```

Here you can see that the first line to be executed is the `while` loop. Then execution moves on to the initial welcome, which asks you for your name, gets the text you type, and then calls the function to print out a greeting message. When the loop exits (because you supply the name `exit`), then there are no more valid statements to execute directly—the rest of the script contains function definitions.

Further Reading

The next three chapters in this section look at how to use Perl for programming. Starting in Chapter 16 we look at the basics of Perl statements, operators, and Perl's base variable types. In Chapter 17 we look at how to create Perl functions, how to use and create your own Perl modules, and at how Perl implements objects. The final chapter in this section takes a closer look at Perl's built-in functions and how they can be used to process information, communicate with the user, and read and write files.

For a more specific guide to migrating VB function calls to their Perl equivalents, see Appendix C. The appendix includes details on all Visual Basic 6 functions, as well as details on an equivalent Perl function. If there isn't a direct equivalent, then an alternative solution is given, if possible. You'll also find a quick guide to the Perl built-in functions supported in ActivePerl.

## CHAPTER 16

Variables, Operators, and Statements

There are three basic building blocks that make up any language: variables, operators, and statements.

Variables

The supported variable types is one of the core areas in which Visual Basic and Perl differ. Visual Basic makes use of a wide range of data types that are used to store different values. There are individual types for integers, floating-point values, currencies, dates, objects, and other data types. There is also a catch-all variant data type that can be used to store most data types without requiring any form of conversion when it is used within other statements.

Perl, on the other hand, supports a single base data type—the scalar. Scalars hold any type of information, from integers and bytes up to strings, floats, and references to other variables. Scalars are the basic building blocks for all data stored within Perl. Perl also supports two further types, the array and the hash, both of which are based on the scalar data type.

TABLE 16-1

Visual Basic and
Perl data types.

VB Data Type	Stores	Perl Equivalent
Integer	Integer numbers	Scalar
Long Integer	Long integers	Scalar
Single	Single-precision floating point	Scalar
Double	Double-precision floating point	Scalar
Currency	Single-precision floating point	Scalar
Byte	Single byte of information	Scalar
String	String of characters or bytes	Scalar
Boolean	True or false value	Scalar
Date	Date and time	Scalar (as seconds since the epoch)
Object	Any object or object reference	Scalar
Variant	Any system-defined data type	Scalar
Array	Array (sequence) of a data type	Array

The significance of this terminology difference is that unlike VB, where an array is of a fixed type, Perl creates an array of scalars. Since a scalar can hold any type of information, a Perl array is capable of storing a list of numbers, strings, bytes, references, and other data; you are not restricted to a single type. As a general rule, arrays do generally hold a list of strings or numbers, but the flexibility remains.

The hash is a much more complex structure. You may have come across the data type before, but it may have been called a *dictionary*. Hashes work a bit like arrays, except that instead of a numerical index to access individual elements, hashes use scalars. By using a scalar, you can access elements in the hash using a number, string, reference, or other information. The only requirement is that the index—called the *key*—is unique within the hash.

Table 16-1 shows a list of the Visual Basic data types and their Perl equivalents (which happen to be scalar in almost every case).

Before we move on to the specifics of how to use the different Perl variable types, let's look at some of the other basic differences between Visual Basic and Perl when using variables.

Variable Declaration and Naming

Within Visual Basic you must define a variable and its type before the variable is used. For example, to define a variable as the `Double` type, you use

```
Dim Amt As Double
```

before the fragment of code that expects to use the variable. The exception is the variant type, which does not have to be specified; variables must still be declared, but failure to specify the type forces the variable to be of the `Variant` type.

With Perl, variables can be created on the fly; they do not need to be declared before you use them. For example, the following script works correctly even though the variables have not been declared beforehand:

```
$denominator = 3;
$numerator = 4;
$fraction = $denominator/$numerator;
$message = 'Hello World!';
```

You should also notice that the variables have the $ character preceding their name. This indicates to Perl that the type of variable that we are accessing is a scalar variable.

Also note that there is no definition of what the variable contains. Perl assigns the value—in the preceding cases an integer, a float (from the calculation), and a string to each scalar—and it automatically makes a decision about how to store the information. Without getting into the internal details of how data is stored by Perl, internally it creates a scalar of a specific type (integer, float, or string), but it exposes the variable to the programmer as only one type—the scalar. When the scalar is used, Perl knows its type, and either it uses that type directly or converts the internal type so that it is compatible with the required value.

For example, in the following calculation, the $denominator and $numerator variables are created as integers. However, when the two are used in the calculation, they are converted to floating-point values, so that the return value is a floating value (0.75).

```
$denominator = 3;
$numerator = 4;
$fraction = $denominator/$numerator;
```

The conversion is automatic and doesn't require any intervention by the programmer. Furthermore, the conversion also happens when you use a numerical scalar in a string—but we'll see some examples of that later.

All variables within Perl have a leading character that defines their type and how they should be accessed. The @ sign indicates that you are accessing the entire array, and the % sign indicates an entire hash. Each variable type has its own name space. Therefore, the following lines:

```
$var = 'Hello';
@var = (1,2);
%var = ();
```

create three individual variables: one a scalar, one an array, and another a hash.

To actually extract the information from an array or hash, you need to access the information as a scalar variable. This is something we'll return to when we take a closer look at the individual Perl variable types.

Constant Values

Perl supports the same basic constant values as Visual Basic. Constant values are the numbers and strings hard-coded into the application's source code, not the special Constants supported by VB.

Numbers   Numbers can be supplied as simple numeric values. The following are all valid numerical constants being assigned to scalar variables:

```
$integer = 99;
$float = 3.141592654;
$bigfloat = 3.4762476E+38;
```

Perl stores all integers as `long integers` internally, so you have the same range ($2^{32} - 1$) as available in Visual Basic. All floating-point values are stored as `double` internally, so all floating-point values have the same range as VB `Double`. Note, however, that you cannot use the `mmmmDeee` notation to supply a double precision value—use the `mmmmEeee` notation.

Strings   Strings in Perl are of variable sizes, and there is no actual limit to the size of a string (or indeed any variable) in Perl, other than the limit of the memory of the machine. Perl will even allow you to create a 16-Mb scalar—if you really needed it.

Perl strings are of two basic types: the raw and the interpolated string. A single-quoted string is a raw string. For example, the line

```
$string = 'Hello World';
```

works as you would expect. A double quoted string, on the other hand, is also referred to as an *interpolated string*. Interpolated strings have their values evaluated before they are returned. This allows you to embed special characters, such as newlines, tabs, and so on, and to embed the values of other variables. For example:

```
$name = 'Martin C Brown';
$msg = 'Hello $name\n';
$realmsg = 'Hello $name\n';
```

The value of `$msg` would be printed as

```
Hello $name\n
```

without any trailing newline (the `\n` character). However, the value of `$realmsg` would be printed as

```
Hello Martin C Brown
```

including a trailing newline character.

Interpolation makes printing out and creating strings for use in your

TABLE 16-2

Embedded control characters.

Sequence	Character Inserted
\t	Tab
\n	Newline
\r	Carriage return
\f	Form feed
\a	Alarm (bell)
\e	Escape
\b	Backspace
\0##	Octal character
\x##	Hex character
\c[	Control character

software much easier. Instead of using concatenation or Format function to format the data and produce a string, interpolation allows you to embed the variables straight into a string.

The special characters interpreted with an interpolated string are shown in Table 16-2.

Data Conversion   It's also worth noting, as mentioned before, that scalars are automatically converted between the necessary formats in order to achieve the desired results. For example, the following code:

```
$value = '123';
print $value + 1, '\n';
```

would print out a value of 124. Perl automatically converts the string value into a number before applying the operator and adding 1 to the value.

Beyond Numbers and Strings

Perl also supports one final special value for a scalar. The undefined value, undef, can be used to identify certain error conditions and the existence, or otherwise, of information in arrays and hashes. The undef is most widely used as a return value from a function that would otherwise supply a value of zero that could be genuine. For example, the location of the file pointer within a file handle could genuinely be at zero, so the `tell` function returns the `undef` value if the location cannot be determined.

You do not have to predefine variables; they will automatically be created when first used. Their initial value will be null, either `" "` for a string or 0 (zero) for a number. Depending on where you use them, a scalar (and other types of variables) will be interpreted automatically as strings, numbers, or as a boolean (true or false) value. Different operators and functions expect and return different scalar values.

Byte Value The Visual Basic `Byte` data type is a binary format used when reading and writing files, calling DLLs and other situations where raw rather than string information is required. The Perl scalar data type will hold raw binary data—in fact, the internal string data type is actually based on the same unsigned character type.

Null and Empty Values The VB `Null` value usually indicates a lack of information for a given function call. The `Empty` value indicates that a variant data type has never been assigned any value; the variable is empty.

Perl uses the undefined value, available via the `undef` keyword, to indicate an undefined (empty) variable. All variables that are declared but not assigned a value contain the undefined value. The `undef` is also frequently used to indicate that there is no information available. It therefore fulfills the role of both the `Null` and `Empty` values.

The undefined value is also a good way of emptying a scalar variable without actually destroying the variable:

```
$value = '99';
$value = undef;
```

The `$value` scalar can still be checked and used within a statement, but it no longer contains a useful value. You can see the effects of the `undef` value on boolean tests next.

Boolean Values The `Boolean` data type in VB allows you to support a simple flip-flop value in a variable. Since a boolean actually stores the value as an integer—`zero` is false, and `1` is true—you can use the Perl scalar data type to hold boolean data.

Table 16-3 shows the logical assumptions that Perl makes about the different data values.

TABLE 16-3

Values and their
logical equivalents.

Value	Logical Value
Negative number	True
Zero	False
Positive number	True
Empty string	False
Non-empty string	True
Undefined value	False

To check for the undefined value, you can use the `defined` function. This returns a positive integer (`True`) if the variable contains a valid value, or `zero` (`False`) if the variable equals the `undef` value.

Dates   There is no special `Date` data type built into Perl. Instead, Perl uses a special long-integer value to refer to a specific date and time. The value is calculated as the number of seconds that have elapsed since the epoch, which is defined under Windows as the number of seconds since 00:00:00 on January 1, 1970 UTC. If you know the number of seconds that have elapsed since the epoch, you can then calculate the current date and time. For example, at the time I write this, the current time counter (as supplied by the Perl `time` function) is 956073429, which equates to a date and time of Tue Apr 18 16:57:09 2000.

See Appendix C for details on how to extract individual date and time values from the epoch value, as well as some tricks for migrating from the VB functions to Perl.

Arrays

Before we move on and look at arrays, you need to understand Perl lists. To understand lists, consider the following definitions:

■ A *list* is an ordered set of scalar data

■ An *array* is a variable that holds a list

Lists can be specified by enclosing a sequence of scalars separated by commas and enclosed in parentheses. For example, the following are all examples of lists:

```
(1,2,3)
(1,'two','three')
($a,$b,$c)
```

Note that the second example is a list of mixed types; as mentioned before, you are not limited in Perl to an array of integers or characters. The empty list obviously contains no elements and is defined by an empty pair of parentheses:

```
()
```

You can also use the qw operator, which is short for "quote word." This is a special operator that allows you to create a list of words without the use of commas or quote characters. In fact, it takes any whitespace (space, tab, newline) as a separator between values, so we can create a list of days like this:

```
@days = qw/Monday
           Tuesday
           Wednesday
           Thursday
           Friday
           Saturday
           Sunday
           /;
```

Lists are also used when supplying information to a function and can be used when assigning values to variables. We'll see some examples of this later.

Populating Arrays   Arrays are just lists stored in a variable. To create an array, you assign a list of values to an array variable:

```
@array = (1,2,3);
```

The individual scalars of an array are referred to as *elements*, and each element is referenced by a number. For example, you can use an array to store a list of days of the week, starting with Sunday:

```
@days = ('Sun', 'Mon', 'Tue', 'Wed', 'Thu', 'Fri', 'Sat');
```

The first element of an array is element 0, the second element has an index of 1, the third, 2, and so on. This may not be a problem if you are using the array to hold a list of values. However, if you are using the array as an indexed list of values, then it's unlikely you want to refer to an entry with a value of 0. The following example populates an array with a list of months:

```
@months = qw/Jan Feb Mar Apr May Jun Jul Aug Sep Oct Nov Dec/;
```

The problem should be obvious: month three, which should be March, will be stored in the array as April. You can solve this either by using the direct notation in the previous code, never specifying a value for index 0 (not recommended), or by using the special JUNK placeholder with the qw operator:

```
@months = qw/JUNK Jan Feb Mar Apr May Jun Jul Aug Sep Oct Nov Dec/;
```

This will correctly reference month three as March.

You can also assign the elements of arrays to arrays, for example, to append a new value to an existing array:

```
@array = (1,2,3);
@array = (@array,4);
```

or to insert a new value before an array:

```
@array = (0,@array);
```

If you want to find out the number of elements in an array, you have two possible methods. The $#months notation returns the index of the largest element in the array. This will always be one less than the actual number of elements. However, use of this is deprecated. To get the number of elements in an array, use the @months variable in a scalar context—that is, when Perl is expecting a scalar not a list value. For example:

```
$size = @months;
```

You can enforce scalar context by prefixing the array with the scalar keyword. This is vital when an operator or a function accepts a list value. The print function is a good example. This accepts a list of information. Therefore, the following line:

```
print ('The number of elements is ',@months,'\n');
```

actually outputs

```
The number of elements is JUNKJanFebMarAprMayJunJulAugSepOctNovDec
```

If we prefix @months with scalar, however, as in the following:

```
print ("The number of elements is ",scalar @months,"\n");
```

then we get the expected answer of 13:

```
The number of elements is 13
```

Array Element Access   To access the information stored in an array, you need to specify the index element that you want to access. Indexes start at zero, so to access the first element from the array, you would use

```
@days = ("Sun", "Mon", "Tue", "Wed", "Thu", "Fri", "Sat");
$days[0];
```

Note that the leading character is now a $ sign, not an @ sign. This is because we are asking Perl to access a scalar not an array value. The square brackets are used to indicate the element from the array that we want to access.

Assignment works in the same way, so the following:

```
$days[2] = "Holiday";
```

now makes the third element of the @days array equal the string Holiday.

Sometimes it's also necessary to refer to elements of an array from the last, rather than the first, element. Perl allows you to extract elements from an array in reverse order by specifying a negative number. An index of -1 indicates the last element of an array. This code

```
print $days[-1];
```

outputs Sat, and this code

```
print $days[-6];
```

will display Mon.

It's also possible to use a statement to select an element from the array. For example:

```
$month = 3;
@months = qw/JUNK Jan Feb Mar Apr May Jun Jul Aug Sep Oct Nov Dec/;
print $months[$month-1];
```

would print out Feb. The statement in the square brackets is evaluated as the value of the array index.

Finally, you can also access slices of an array by supplying a list of elements that you want to access within the square brackets. Because we are accessing an array rather than an individual value, you must use the @ notation. Hence:

```
print @months[3,6,9,12],"\n";
```

would output MarJunSepDec. You can use the .. operator to select a range of numbers. For example:

```
print @months[3..6,9,12],"\n";
```

would output MarAprMayJunSepDec.

Note that the return value in both cases is a new list, which we could assign to a new array:

```
@mymonths = @months[3..6,9,12];
```

Lists and Assignment   Lists can be used without assigning them to arrays. For example, consider the following code:

```
($a, $b, $c) = (1, 2, 3);
```

There are two lists here—the one on the left-hand side of the equals sign contains a list of scalar variables, and the one on the right contains a list of numeric constants. The two lists are of the same size, and so the single line shown previously actually equates to a sequence such as:

```
$a = 1;
$b = 2;
$c = 3;
```

Each element of the left-hand list is assigned the corresponding value of the element on the right-hand list. This is another of the common tricks in Perl that makes working with large volumes of information much easier. The trick works with any list or array, for example, the localtime function converts an epoch time value into a list of individual component values (hour, month, year, etc.). The information is returned as a list, and we can use list assignment to extract the individual elements from the list to individual scalar variables:

```
($sec,$min,$hour,$mday,$mon,$year,$wday,$yday,$isdst) =
localtime(time);
```

List Element Access   The same notation used above for accessing elements in an array will also work on lists. This is called *subscript notation*. For example, we might want to access the first and last elements from a list:

```
@mydays = (qw/Mon Tue Wed Thu Fri Sat Sun/)[0,-1];
```

Note the use of parentheses around the list we are creating. This indicates to Perl that you want to access the item as a list. The same trick works for function calls too. For example, to extract only the time element from the list returned by localtime:

```
($sec, $min, $hour) = (localtime(time))[0..2];
```

Hashes

One of the limitations with arrays is that the information is stored sequentially, using a numeric index reference. This causes problems when you have to delete, insert, and update information in an array, because you must reorganize the sequence each time you make a change. Furthermore, you need to know what information is stored in each index location in order to update the information. This makes using arrays for anything other than simple lists very complex.

A better alternative for managing complex list data is a hash. A hash uses strings as the index values instead of the arbitrary integer value. This means that a hash has no sense of order (there is no natural progression of the index values), and there is no first or last addressable element. Conversely, it also means that additional values can be added to the hash without requiring you to reorganize the list contents.

The real advantage though is that you can refer to an element of a hash by name instead of by number. Let's look at an example. Imagine you want the reverse of the earlier months array—that is, you want to return a number based on a month name. You can use a hash, with the month names as the index (or key) of the hash and the month number as the corresponding value.

■ ■ ■ ■ ■ ■ ■ ■ ■ ■ ■ ■ ■ ■ ■ ■ ■ ■

NOTE.   Hashes are often called associative arrays, *because a string index is associated with a scalar value. However, this is too long for general use, and the name hash is quicker and easier to use.*

Because the keys to a hash are not automatically implied, you must supply the key as well as the value when you are populating a hash. It is still possible to assign a list to a hash, but Perl interprets alternate elements of the list as keys and values. For example, to populate a hash with short day names as the keys and corresponding long names as the values, you could use

```
%longday = ("Sun", "Sunday", "Mon", "Monday", "Tue", "Tuesday",
            "Wed", "Wednesday", "Thu", "Thursday", "Fri", "Friday",
            "Sat", "Saturday");
```

However, this is not only very difficult to understand but also unclear as to exactly what is being achieved. Perl provides an alternative operator for defining the key and value pairs—the => operator. The operator is just an alias for the comma, but it makes the syntax much clearer, enabling you to identify both the key and corresponding value. You can therefore rewrite the previous hash population statement as the following:

```
%longday = ("Sun" => "Sunday",
            "Mon" => "Monday",
            "Tue" => "Tuesday",
            "Wed" => "Wednesday",
            "Thu" => "Thursday",
            "Fri" => "Friday",
            "Sat" => "Saturday"
           );
```

If you refer to the entire hash using %longday, then it will be converted back to a list of key and value pairs as in the first example. The alternative is to use the keys and values functions, which return the appropriate keys or values of an entire hash as a list. In both cases the list is in arbitrary order, and there is no guarantee that two sequential calls to list the hash contents will produce the list in the same order. In these cases you can use the sort or reverse functions to place a suitable order on the lists. When used in a list context, the reverse of the above assignment occurs. The hash is resolved into a simple list with keys and values appearing as pairs of elements.

To access the elements from a hash, you need to use the scalar notation. For example, to get the long name of Mon:

```
print $longday{Mon};
```

The dollar sign indicates to Perl that you are accessing a scalar variable, and the curly brackets indicate the value is a component of a hash. The value you supply in the curly brackets is used as the key that you want to access. The key is automatically quoted—although for some complex strings you may need to manually quote the key.

Getting Key/Value Pairs Because a single element of a hash consists of two strings—the key and the value—you cannot use the same functions or tricks with hashes that you can with arrays. For that reason, there are a number of functions that support accessing key/value pairs individually or obtaining entire lists of all the keys or values in a hash.

```
each HASH
```

The each function allows you to iterate over all the key/value pairs in a hash sequentially. There is no facility for sorting, and the information is returned in a random order. Since it only returns two arguments, it can be used to iterate through very large lists in a loop without Perl creating large temporary lists to store keys or values. When the end of the hash is reached, it returns a null list and is therefore safe to be used within loops. For example:

```
while (($key, $value) = each(%hash))
{
    print "$key=$value\n";
}
```

Alternatively, in a scalar context, it returns only the key:

```
while ($key = each(%hash))
{
    print "$key=$hash{$key}\n";
}
```

The same iterator (and, therefore, sequence and position within the hash) is used for every call to each. If you want to start back at the beginning of a hash, you must reevaluate the entire hash, which is easiest to do as:

```
%hash;
```

Alternatively, you can use the keys function, which also resets the iterator to the start of the list:

```
keys %hash;
```

While within the iterator loop, you shouldn't add elements to the hash, since this will only confuse the `each` function. You can, however, delete elements from the list using `delete`.

Getting a List of Hash Keys   The `keys` function returns a list of all the keys in a hash:

```
keys HASH
```

The order of the keys returned is random, actually sharing the same order as the `each` function. The typical use is within a loop:

```
foreach (keys %hash)
{
    print "$_=$hash{$_}\n";
}
```

Since the function returns a simple list of the keys, you can use the `sort` function to sort the list of keys (and therefore, presumably, the information stored therein). This is usually employed directly within a loop:

```
foreach (sort keys %hash)
```

However, don't be tempted to do this:

```
foreach (sort keys %oldhash)
{
    $newhash{$_} = $oldhash{$_};
}
```

and expect `%newhash` to contain an ordered list of key/value pairs. It won't. It will just contain a copy of `%oldhash` and will return a random list of key/value pairs when accessed again.

Either way, you should always be careful when using the `keys` function on large hashes (such as a DBM file), since it will return a suitably large list. This may cause a problem if you are running short of memory. In this case it's probably best to use `each`, although be aware that you can't sort `each` pairs.

Getting a List of Hash Values   The equivalent of `keys` for the values stored in the hash is the `values` function. The following code:

```
values HASH
```

returns a list of all the values within a hash. The order is the same as that returned by the `keys` and `each` functions. Note that accessing the values does exactly that: The key/value pair works in one direction; the key refers to the value. You cannot determine the key related to an individual value.

If you want to sort on the values within a hash, you must use the block or subroutine format of the `sort` command and compare the values of the hash. The `$a` and `$b` variables refer to the two keys of the hash being compared in the following example:

```
foreach (sort { $hash{$a} cmp $hash{$b} } keys %hash)
```

Or if you are comparing numerical values:

```
foreach (sort { $hash{$a} <=> $hash{$b} } keys %hash)
```

Checking for a Specific Hash Key   Perl will return the undefined value (`undef`) if the key you are accessing from the hash does not exist. This is not always very useful, since it's possible that the key does exist, but its corresponding value contains `undef`. To get around this, you can use the `exists` function, which returns `True` if the key exists in the hash—irrespective of what the corresponding value may equal.

For example:

```
exists($longday{Mon});
```

should return `True`, while

```
exists($longday{Muggle});
```

will return `False`.

Deleting a Hash Key/Value Pair   If you have a hash and want to delete a hash element, the immediate temptation is to use the undefined value:

```
$hash{'key'} = undef;
```

However, all this does is assign the undefined value to the key `key`. The key still exists within the hash, and it will still be returned by the `each` and `keys` functions. To delete the key/value pair, you need to use the `delete` function:

```
delete LIST
```

This deletes the hash elements specified by LIST, removing both the keys and their corresponding values.

For example, to empty the entire hash, you use

```
while ($key = each %hash)
{
    delete $hash{$key};
}
```

although it's quicker just to empty it with a simple assignment:

```
%hash = ();
```

If you use delete on elements of $ENV hash, then it modifies the current environment. This can be useful to remove environment variables for the current process, which will also affect all called and forked commands via functions such as open or system.

If you use delete on hash elements of a hash tied to an external DBM database (or other tied structure), the data is permanently removed from the tied source. See the section "Using tie" later in this chapter.

Hash Sizes   In a scalar context, a hash returns a string that defines the number of allocated blocks (called *buckets*) and used blocks in the entire hash structure. If you want to obtain the number of elements in the hash, then you need to count the number of keys contained in the hash. Since the keys function returns a list, you'll need to enforce scalar context on the function to ensure that you get a numerical value. For example:

```
print "The number of items is: ",scalar keys (%longday),"\n";
```

If you just use scalar context on a hash, then it returns a string that defines the size of the storage blocks used to store the data.

Quoting Mechanisms

Perl supports two types of quoting: the customary (preferred) format and the alternative functional generic style. Different quote operators imply different evaluations, and only some interpolate values and variables.

TABLE 16-4

Perl quotes.

Customary	Generic	Meaning	Interpolates
' '	q//	Literal	No
" "	qq//	Literal	Yes
` `	qx//	Command	Yes
()	qw//	Word list	No
//	m//	Pattern match	Yes
s///	s///	Substitution	Yes
y///	tr///	Translation	No

For example, the customary noninterpolated string quote is the single quote:

```
$string = 'Hello World';
```

which is equivalent to:

```
$string = q/Hello World/;
```

The quotes are summarized in Table 16-4.

Built-in Variables

Perl supports a number of built-in variables that supply information about the Perl environment or that control the way that Perl handles the input and output of information. These built-in variables form a core part of the Perl programming language. A number of them are used or populated for almost every statement.

We'll look in this section at some of the most regularly used variables and how they are used. All the variables use a special mnemonic as an identifier; for example, the `$\` variable contains the default output record separator and was selected because you would normally use `\n` at the end of a printed line.

You can use English names by importing the `English` module by placing

```
use English;
```

TABLE 16-5

Perl and English
variable names.

Perl	English
@_	@ARG
$_	$ARG
$&	$MATCH
$'	$PREMATCH
$'	$POSTMATCH
$+	$LAST_PAREN_MATCH
$.	$INPUT_LINE_NUMBER
	$NR
$/	$INPUT_RECORD_SEPARATOR
	$RS
$|	$OUTPUT_AUTOFLUSH
$,	$OUTPUT_FIELD_SEPARATOR
	$OFS
$\	$OUTPUT_RECORD_SEPARATOR
	$ORS
$"	$LIST_SEPARATOR
$;	$SUBSCRIPT_SEPARATOR
	$SUBSEP
$?	$CHILD_ERROR
	$! $OS_ERROR
	$ERRNO
$@	$EVAL_ERROR
$0	$PROGRAM_NAME
$]	$PERL_VERSION
$^T	$BASETIME
$^W	$WARNING
$^X	$EXECUTABLE_NAME
$^O	$OSNAME

at the beginning of your Perl script. See Chapter 17 for more details on how to use modules in Perl. The full list of English names can be seen in Table 16-5.

$_   This is the default input and pattern searching space. For many functions and operations, if no specific variable is specified, the default input variable $_ will be used. For example:

```
$_ = "Hello World\n";
print;
```

would print the "Hello World" message. The $_ is also the default variable populated when you read information from a file, and it is the default variable processed when you use a regular expression.

Perl will automatically use the default space in the following situations even if you do not specify it:

- Unary functions, such as ord and int
- All file tests except -t, which defaults to STDIN
- Most of the functions that support lists as arguments (see Appendix B)
- The pattern matching operations m//, s///, and tr/// when used without an =~ operator
- The default iterator variable in a for or foreach loop, if no other variable is supplied
- The implicit operator in map and grep functions
- The default place to store an input record when reading from a file handle.

$<digits>   This variable contains the regular expression specified within the corresponding parentheses from the last regular expression match.

$&   This variable contains the string matched by the last successful pattern match.

$'   This contains the string preceding the information matched by the last pattern match.

$'   This contains the string following the information matched by the last pattern match.

$+   This defines the last bracket match by the last regular expression search pattern.

$.   This contains the current input line number of the last file from which you read. This can be either the keyboard or an external file or other file handle (such as a network socket).

$/   This defines the current input record separator. When reading information from a file in a loop, information is generally read on a record-by-record basis, where individual records are separated by a specific character. By default, the character is the newline/carriage return used to terminate each line in a text file.

$| By default, all output is buffered. This means all information to be written is stored temporarily in memory and periodically flushed, if the value of $| is set to zero. If it is set to nonzero, the STDOUT file handle will be automatically flushed after each write operation.

$,   This variable defines the default output separator for the print series of functions. By default, print outputs the comma-separated fields you specify without any delimiter. You can set this variable to commas, tabs, or any other value to insert a different delimiter.

$ This defines the default output record separator. Ordinarily, print outputs individual records without a standard separator, and no trailing newline or other record separator is output.

$"   This defines the separator inserted between elements of an array output within a double-quoted string. The default is a single space.

$?   This defines the status returned by the last external command (via backticks or system) or the last pipe close. This is the value returned by wait, so the true return value is $? > 8, and $? & 127 is the number of the signals received by the process, if appropriate.

$!   This variable returns the error number or error string, according to the context in which it is used. This is equivalent to the errno value and can be used to print the error number or error string when a particular system or function call has failed.

$^E This contains extended error information for operating systems other than Unix. Under Unix the value equals the value of $!. We'll look more closely at the use of this variable when we study the use of Perl as a cross-platform development solution.

$@ This defines the error message returned by the Perl interpreter when Perl has been executed via the eval function. If null, then the last eval call executed successfully.

$$ This defines the process number of the Perl interpreter executing the current script.

$0 This defines the name of the file containing the script currently being executed.

$] This defines the version + patchlevel/1000 of the Perl interpreter. This variable can be used to determine the version number of Perl being used, and therefore what functions and abilities the current interpreter supports.

$^D This defines the value of the current debugging flags.

$^H This defines the status of syntax checks enabled by compiler hints, such as use strict.

$^O This defines the operating system name, as determined via the configuration system during compilation.

$^T This defines the time at which the script started running, defined as the number of seconds since the epoch.

S^X This defines the name of the Perl binary being executed, as determined via the value of C's argv[0].

@ARGV The @ARGV array contains the list of the command-line arguments supplied to the script. Note that the first value, at index zero, is the first argument, not the name of the script.

@INC This defines the list of directories that Perl should examine when importing modules via the do, require, or use constructs (see the section "use and require" in Chapter 5).

@_   Within a subroutine (or function), the @_ array contains the list of parameters supplied to the function.

%INC   This defines the list of the files that have been included via do or require. The key is the file you specified, and the value is the actual location of the imported file.

%ENV   This defines the list of variables as supplied by the current environment. The key is the name of the environment variable, and the corresponding value is the variable's value. Setting a value in the hash changes the environment variable for child processes.

%SIG   The keys of the %SIG hash correspond to the signals available on the current machine. The value corresponds to how the signal will be handled. You use this mechanism to support signal handlers within Perl.

Operators

Most of the operators that you are used to with Visual Basic work unchanged. There are, however, some minor differences. Perl makes much more use of operators for simple statements, comparisons, and numeric and logical operations, whereas Visual Basic tends to use functions for the same operation.

For example, Visual Basic uses the And operator when doing a logical AND operation, whereas Perl uses the && operator. Other Perl operators are outlined in the next section, with comparisons to their Visual Basic equivalents where relevant.

Numeric Operators

The first numeric operators are the increment (++) and decrement (--) operators. When used in front of a statement, the statement is incremented or decremented before being used. When used after a statement, the value is incremented or decremented after the entire statement has been evaluated. For example:

```
$var = 23;
print ++$var,"\n";
```

prints a value of 24, but the script

```
$var = 23;
print $var++,"\n";
```

prints a value of 23. If you print the value of $var now, you should get 24:

```
print $var,"\n";
```

The increment operator has one other trick up its sleeve. When used with an alphabetical or alphanumeric value, the increment is executed as a string, incrementing each character within its range:

```
print ++('Az');        #prints 'Ba'
print ++('a0');        #prints 'a1'
```

The decrement operator does not work in the same way.

The available numeric operators are summarized in Table 16-6.

String Operators

The equivalent of + for strings is the period. Using a period concatenates two strings. For example:

```
$string = 'Hello' . ' ' . 'World!';
print $string,"\n";
```

would print out the familiar "Hello World!" message.

TABLE 16-6

Numeric operators.

Operator	Action
+	Adds the two statements.
–	Subtracts the statement on the right from the statement on the left.
*	Multiplies the statement on the right by the statement on the left.
/	Divides the statement on the left by the statement on the right.
**	Exponential—the statement on the left is raised to the power of the statement on the right.
%	Returns the modulus of two numbers. The *modulus* is the integer remainder when the left statement is divided by the right statement. For example, 8 % 3 is 2.

There is also a multiplication operator for strings, x, which allows you to repeat a string for the specified number of times. The string is taken from the left of the operator, and the multiplication value is taken from the right. So:

```
print '=' x 80;
```

would print a row of equal signs 80 characters wide.

Equality and Relational Operators

Being able to test the equality of two statements is important. This ability enables you to produce test statements and make decisions based on the results of the test.

Also useful is the ability to compare the relation between two statements (particularly strings). Table 16-7 lists equality and relational operators.

It is important to appreciate the difference between comparing numbers and strings. The tests

```
$var = 1;
print "Right!" if ($var == 1);
```

and

```
$var = 1;
print "Wrong!" if ($var eq 1);
```

are not testing the same thing, although both work.

The easiest way to remember which operator to use is that numeric comparisons use special characters; string comparisons use words.

Logical Operators

Logical operators allow you to compare and evaluate logical (boolean) expressions. See Table 16-8 for the list of logical operators supported. In a list context, the logical operators are evaluated right statement first. Care must be taken, therefore, if using logical operators in function calls.

It is worth noting that logical operators in Perl return the last value

TABLE 16-7

Equality and rela-
tional operators.

Operator	Action
<	Returns True if the left statement is numerically less than the right statement.
>	Returns True if the left statement is numerically greater than the right statement.
<=	Returns True if the left statement is numerically less than or equal to the right statement.
>=	Returns True if the left statement is numerically greater than or equal to the right statement.
==	Returns True if the left statement is numerically equal to the right statement.
!=	Returns True if the left statement is numerically not equal to the right statement.
<=>	Returns -1, 0, or 1, depending on whether the left statement is numerically less than, equal to, or greater than the right statement.
lt	Returns True if the left statement is stringwise less than the right statement.
gt	Returns True if the left statement is stringwise greater than the right statement.
le	Returns True if the left statement is stringwise less than or equal to the right statement.
ge	Returns True if the left statement is stringwise greater than or equal to the right statement.
eq	Returns True if the left statement is stringwise equal to the right statement.
ne	Returns True if the left statement is stringwise not equal to the right statement.
cmp	Returns -1, 0, or 1 depending on whether the left statement is stringwise less than, equal to, or greater than the right statement.

TABLE 16-8

Logical operators.

Operator	VB Equivalent	Action
&&	And	Logical AND. The evaluation returns true only if both the left and right statements are logically true.
||	Or	Logical OR. The evaluation returns true if one or the other of the statements is true.
!	Not	Logical NOT. The evaluation returns the opposite of the statement on the right.

evaluated. This is different from C, in which individual statements must be encapsulated within parentheses to evaluate multiple statements simultaneously. For example, the following statement is a practical way of discovering a user's login name:

```
$login = $ENV{'USER'} || $ENV{'LOGNAME'} || getlogin();
```

Each statement is evaluated, and the one that returns a value will be assigned to the $login variable. This is far more practical and certainly easier to read.

If you prefer, you can use and and or in place of && and ||. However, they have a much lower precedence, which means they can safely be used in list contexts. For example,

```
unlink 'rod', 'jane', 'freddy' || die "Error deleting files";
```

would actually evaluate the result of the die statement against the value of 'freddy', which is not the desired result. You would instead have to write that statement as

```
unlink('rod', 'jane', 'freddy') || die "Error deleting files";
```

Using or, you can return to the previous format:

```
unlink 'rod', 'jane', 'freddy' or die "Error deleting files";
```

As a rule you should use || and && in preference to or and and.

Bitwise Operators

You can perform bitwise operations on scalars to operate on individual bits within the value. There are three main bitwise operators: AND (&), OR (|), and exclusive OR (^). The & operator returns two statements ANDed together bit by bit.

You can also shift numbers by a number of bits left and right using the shift operators << and >>, respectively. You will need to know binary mathematics to understand it fully, but we'll demonstrate with a quick example:

```
print 1 << 4,"\n";
```

The last bitwise operator is ~, which returns the bitwise negation, or 1's complement, of a number.

Range Operator

The range operator (..) allows you to define a range between the left and right statements. The result of using the operator depends on the context. In a list context, it returns an array of values from the right operator to the left in steps of one element. For example, to extract elements 4 to 5 from an array, you might use

```
print $months[3..5];
```

You also use it within for and foreach loops:

```
for(1..1000) {
...
}
```

If the operands are strings, Perl makes use of the auto-increment feature; so you can refer to the entire uppercase alphabet with

```
@alphabet = ('A' .. 'Z');
```

Or to get a list of days of the month with leading zeros, you can use:

```
@days = ('01' .. '31');
```

In a scalar context, the .. operator acts as a toggle. The range operator is false as long as the left statement is false. Once the left statement is true, the range operator also becomes true. The operator then stays true until the right statement becomes true, at which point the range operator becomes false, and so the process continues. This can be used to toggle between two states where the range between the scalars is relevant. The example given in the documentation is that of a mail message, which is logically divided into a message header and a message body. You could therefore use the following fragment to parse an e-mail message:

```
while(<>)
{
    $in_header = 1 ../^$/;
    $in_body = /^$/ .. eof();
}
```

Assignment Operators

The standard assignment operator is the equal sign (=). It assigns the result of the evaluation of the statement on the right side to the statement on the left. For example:

```
$var = 15;
```

assigns the value of 15 to the variable $var. This works in an identical fashion to Visual Basic. Note that like VB, the expression on the right-hand side of the equals is evaluated before being assigned to the variable on the left. For example, to add 15 to our existing variable, you use

```
$var = $var +15;
```

Perl also allows you to shorten this to

```
$var += 15;
```

The full list of operators which work in this fashion can be seen in Table 16-9.

TABLE 16-9

Assignment operators.

Operator	Operation
a += b	Adds B to A
a -= b	Subtracts B from A
a .= b	Concatenates B to A
a *= b	Multiplies A by B
a /= b	Divides A by B
a %= B	Modulus of A/B
a **= B	Raises A to the exponent B
a x= B	Multiplies the string A by B times
a &= b	A bitwise ANDed with B
a |= b	A bitwise OR'd with B
a ^= b	A bitwise XOR'd with B
a <<= B	Shifts A to the left B times
A >>= B	Shifts A to the right B times

Comma Operator

The comma (,) is the list operator. In a scalar context it evaluates the statement on the left, disposes of the value, and then evaluates and returns the result of the right statement. This allows you to write fragments like this:

```
print "Hello\n", exit;
```

The `print` statement is executed, and the result (which would return `True` if the print was successful) is disposed of before the exit statement is executed.

The `=>` operator is just a synonym for the comma operator but is most useful when using arguments that come in pairs—for example, hash index and value arguments.

Loops and Control Statements

Visual Basic supports a number of loops and control statements such as `while` and `if`, and many of these can be transferred directly to your Perl scripts with little modification. However, Perl identifies code blocks differently, and the format of each statement is slightly different in Perl.

Code Blocks

In Visual Basic, control and loop statements have a specific format. Take the `If` statement, for example. The typical format is as follows:

```
If condition Then
...
End If
```

The indented portion contains the statements executed when the condition resolves to `True`, and the statement block is terminated because of the `End If` keywords; the indentation is not mandatory but is enforced by the VB IDE.

Within Perl, individual code blocks are defined by a pair of braces. For example, this is a simple code block:

```
{
    print "Hello World!\n";
}
```

For an `if` statement, this translates into

```
if condition
{
    print "Hello World!\n";
}
```

The braces start and terminate the code block for the statement. The braces are required; they tell the Perl interpreter the start and end of the code block. We'll see more examples as we go through the different control statements supported by Perl.

Labels   All blocks and loop statements can have an optional label. This way you can label a code block and then jump to that code block at any point within the program. Note that this is different from a function: A labeled block does not return to the caller once the block has been executed and evaluated. We'll see examples of how to use labels and labeled blocks later in this chapter.

Conditional Statements

Perl supports two basic conditional statements. The `if` statement is essentially identical to the Visual Basic version. There are five different formats for the `if` statement in Perl:

```
if (EXPR)
if (EXPR) {BLOCK}
if (EXPR) {BLOCK} else {BLOCK}
if (EXPR) {BLOCK} elsif (EXPR) {BLOCK} ...
if (EXPR) {BLOCK} elsif (EXPR) {BLOCK} ...else {BLOCK}
```

The first format will be new to most Visual Basic programmers. It allows you to execute a single statement only if a specific condition exists. For example:

```
print "Happy Birthday!\n" if ($date == $today);
```

In this instance the message will only be printed if the expression evaluates to a true value.

The second format is the more traditional conditional statement:

```
if ($date == $today)
{
   print "Happy Birthday!\n";
}
```

This produces the same result as the previous example, but because the condition can be followed by a code block, you can insert additional statements and expressions.

The third format allows for exceptions to the primary condition. If the expression evaluates to True, then the first block is executed; otherwise (else), the second block is executed:

```
if ($date == $today)
{
   print "Happy Birthday!\n";
}
else
{
   print "Happy Unbirthday!\n";
}
```

The fourth form allows for additional tests if the first expression does not return True. The elsif can be repeated an infinite number of times to test as many different alternatives as are required:

```
if ($date == $today)
{
   print "Happy Birthday!\n";
}
elsif ($date == $christmas)
{
   print "Happy Christmas!\n";
}
```

Finally, the fifth form allows for both additional tests and a final exception if all the other tests fail:

```
if ($date == $today)
{
   print "Happy Birthday!\n";
}
elsif ($date == $christmas)
{
   print "Happy Christmas!\n";
}
else
{
```

```
    print "Happy Unbirthday!\n";
}
```

Perl also supports the `unless` statement, which is the logical opposite of `if`. In essence, where `if` executes a block when the statement resolves to true, the `unless` statement executes the block only when the condition resolves to `False`. For example:

```
print "Happy Unbirthday!\n" unless ($date == $today);
```

is equivalent to

```
print "Happy Unbirthday!\n" if ($date != $today);
```

However, if you want to make multiple tests, there is no `elsunless`, and therefore no equivalent to the `elsif` statement. It is more sensible to use `unless` only in situations where there is a single statement or code block; using `unless` and `else` or `elsif` only confuses the process. For instance, the following is a less elegant solution to the above `if...else` example:

```
unless ($date != $today)
{
    print "Happy Unbirthday!\n";
}
else
{
    print "Happy Birthday!\n";
}
```

although it achieves the same result.

The final conditional statement is actually an operator—the conditional operator. It is equivalent to the `Iif` Visual Basic function. The format for the operator is as follows:

```
(expression) ? (statement if true) : (statement if false)
```

For example, we can emulate the above example:

```
($date == $today) ? print "Happy Birthday!\n" : print
  "Happy Unbirthday!\n";
```

Because Perl implements the test as an operator, it can be incorporated directly into expressions where you would otherwise require statements. This means you can compound the preceding example to the following:

```
print "Happy ", ($date == $today) ? "Birthday!\n" : "Unbirthday!\n";
```

Loops

Perl supports four main loop types: `while`, `until`, `for`, and `foreach`. The Perl `while` loop is synonymous with the Visual Basic `While...Wend` loop and has three forms:

```
while EXPR
LABEL while (EXPR) BLOCK
LABEL while (EXPR) BLOCK continue BLOCK
```

The first format allows simple statements to be executed. The expression is evaluated first, and then the statement is evaluated. For example:

```
$linecount while !eof();
```

The exception to this rule is when the `while` condition is combined with a preceding `do {}` block, as in:

```
do
{
    $calc += ($fact*$ivalue);
} while $calc <100;
```

In this case the code block is executed first, and the conditional expression is only evaluated at the end of each loop iteration. Note this is identical to the `Do...Done` block in Visual Basic.

The second two forms of the `while` loop repeatedly execute the code block as long as the result from the conditional expression is true. For example:

```
while ($i < 50)
{
    $i++;
}
```

If the optional `continue` block is included, then it is executed after the main code block, and when the execution skips to the next iteration as part of a loop control statement (see the "Loop Control" section coming up next). In general practice, continue blocks are not used, but they are included to allow us to reproduce a `for` loop using a `while` loop.

The inverse of the `while` loop is the `until` loop, which evaluates the conditional expression and reiterates over the loop only when the expression returns `False`. Once the expression returns `True`, the loop ends. In the case of a `do...until` loop, the conditional expression is only evaluated at the end of the code block. In an `until (EXPR) BLOCK` loop, the expression is evaluated before the block executes. Using an `until` loop, you could rewrite the above example as follows:

```
do
{
   $calc += ($fact*$ivalue);
} until $calc >= 100;
```

The Perl `for` loop is basically identical to the VB `For...Next` loop. The format of the `for` loop is as follows:

```
LABEL for (EXPR; EXPR; EXPR) BLOCK
```

Thus, you can write a loop to iterate 100 times like this:

```
for ($i=0;$i<100;$i++)
{
...
}
```

You can place multiple variables into the expressions using the standard list operator (the comma):

```
for ($i=0, $j=0;$i<100;$i++,$j++)
```

Thus, the `for` loop is much more flexible than the Visual Basic, where you would require two nested loops to achieve the same result. Furthermore, the expressions are optional, so you can create an infinite loop like this:

```
for(;;)
{
...
}
```

The last loop type is the `foreach`, again, essentially identical to the `Foreach...Next` VB loop. The Perl version has a format like this:

```
LABEL foreach VAR (LIST) BLOCK
LABEL foreach VAR (LIST) BLOCK continue BLOCK
```

For example, you can iterate over an array using a normal `for` loop:

```
for ($index=0;$index<=@months;$index++)
{
   print "$months[$index]\n";
}
```

This is messy because you're manually selecting the individual elements from the array and using an additional variable, $index, to extract the information. Using a foreach loop, you can simplify the process:

```
foreach (@months)
{
   print "$_\n";
}
```

Perl has automatically separated the elements, placing each element of the array into the default input space—the $_ variable. Each iteration of the loop will take the next element of the array. The list can be any expression, and you can supply an optional variable for the loop to place each value of the list into. To print out each word on an individual line from a file, you could use the following:

```
while (<FILE>)
{
   chomp;
   foreach $word (split)
   {
      print "$word\n";
   }
}
```

The foreach loop can even be used to iterate through a hash, provided you return the list of values or keys from the hash as the list:

```
foreach $key (keys %monthstonum)
{
   print "Month $monthstonum{$key} is $key\n";
}
```

NOTE. *Unlike VB, in Perl the* for *and* foreach *keywords are synonymous. You can use either keyword to use either type of loop. However, as with other parts of the Perl language, you should use them as listed here so that it is obvious to readers of your source code what you are trying to achieve.*

Loop Control   There are three loop control keywords: next, last, and redo. The next keyword skips the remainder of the code block, forcing the loop to proceed to the next value in the loop. For example:

```
while (<DATA>)
{
    next if /^#/;
}
```

would skip lines from the file if they started with a hash symbol. This is the standard comment style under Unix. If there is a continue block, it is executed before execution proceeds to the next iteration of the loop.

The `last` keyword ends the loop entirely, skipping the remaining statements in the code block, as well as dropping out of the loop. This is best used to escape a loop when an alternative condition has been reached within a loop that cannot otherwise be trapped. For example:

```
while (<DATA>)
{
    last if ($found);
}
```

would exit the loop if the value of `$found` was true, regardless of whether the end of the file had actually been reached. The `continue` block is not executed.

The `redo` keyword reexecutes the code block without reevaluating the conditional statement for the loop. This skips the remainder of the code block and also the `continue` block before the main code block is reexecuted. This is especially useful if you want to reiterate over a code block based on a condition that is unrelated to the loop condition. For example, the following code would read the next line from a file if the current line terminates with a backslash:

```
while(<DATA>)
{
    if (s#\\$#)
    {
        $_ .= <DATA>;
        redo;
    }
}
```

In all cases the loop control keyword affects the current (innermost) loop. You can supply an optional label, at which point the keyword will affect the corresponding named block. This allows you to nest and control loops:

```
OUTER:
while(<DATA>)
{
    chomp;
```

```
@linearray=split;
foreach $word (@linearray)
{
    next OUTER if ($word =~ /next/i)
}
}
```

This would skip the current input line from the file if there was a word
next in the input line while allowing the remainder of the words from
the file to be processed.

Perl considers all the keywords here to be operators, rather than functions or statements. This allows you to use them in an expression as you
would any other operator, rather than using them in more simple statements.

Emulating case or switch   The only missing function supplied in VB
but not supported by Perl is the switch function. However, you can use
a number of different methods to emulate the same functionality. The
most obvious is to use an if...elsif...else combination. However,
this can be difficult to follow and complex to debug.

A more elegant solution is to use a labeled code block with loop control
operators. For example:

```
SWITCH: {
    if ($date == $today) { print "Happy Birthday!\n";   last SWITCH; }
    if ($date != $today) { print "Happy Unbirthday!\n"; last SWITCH; }
    if ($date == $xmas)  { print "Happy Christmas!\n";  last SWITCH; }
}
```

This is not as strange as it appears once you realize that you can use
the loop control operators last, next, and redo within any block. This
also means you could write to the same script as

```
SWITCH: {
    print "Happy Birthday!\n",   last SWITCH if ($date == $today);
    print "Happy Unbirthday!\n", last SWITCH if ($date != $today);
    print "Happy Christmas!\n",  last SWITCH if ($date == $xmas);
}
```

Or for a more formatted solution:

```
SWITCH: {
    ($date == $today)     && do {
                                print "Happy Birthday!\n";
                                last SWITCH;
                            };
    ($date != $today)     && do {
                                print "Happy Unbirthday!\n";
```

```
                                          last SWITCH;
                          };

  ($date == $xmas)        && do {
                                          print "Happy Christmas!\n";
                                          last SWITCH;
                          };
}
```

Note that in this last example you could exclude the label. The do {}
blocks are not loops, and so the last command would ignore them and
instead drop out of the parent SWITCH block.

## CHAPTER 17

Functions, Modules, and Object Orientation

Most applications are split into a combination of functions, which help to structure your application and make it easier to manage. Visual Basic applications are also split into form modules, which make up the individual windows and interfaces, and extension modules, which provide core code and shared functions and objects used by the rest of the application.

Within Perl, individual scripts are split into functions, and the application can be logically divided into a number of packages. Each package has its own namespace—similar in principle to the modules within a VB project. Perl also provides a suite of additional functions and libraries beyond the built-in libraries in the form of modules. These are actually just Perl scripts that have some additional code added to them to export the functions to the calling script. Perl also uses modules to provide object-oriented facilities—you define new object classes within a module, and the module includes the object creator code, definition, and associated methods.

Functions

Within Visual Basic you use the `Function` keyword to define a new function. The format of the definition also specifies the availability of the function to other functions and modules, the arguments that the function accepts, and if necessary, the return value. Let's have a look at the format of the `Function` definition in VB:

```
[Static] [Private] Function function-name [(arguments)]
[As type] [Static var [,var]...] [Dim var [,var]...]
[statements]
[function-name = expression]
[Exit Function]
End Function
```

The availability of the function is defined by its location in a package or module. We'll look at the effects of packages and modules later in this chapter. We'll also look at the definition of variables within a code block—in this case a function—in the section called "Scoping."

For the moment, let's assume that you want to create a basic function in Perl that doesn't accept any arguments and doesn't return anything. The basic format for creating the function is as follows:

```
sub NAME
{
}
```

The sub keyword tells Perl that you are defining for a Perl a new subroutine. Don't worry about the terminology; Perl doesn't distinguish between a function and a subroutine. In Perl, all functions and subroutines are declared using the sub keyword. The only difference, even in Visual Basic, between a subroutine and a function is that a subroutine does not return a value, but a function does.

For example, let's define a function that prints the "Hello World" message:

```
sub hw
{
    print 'Hello World\n';
}
```

That's it. To actually use a function, just supply the function name:

```
hw();
```

The brackets are actually optional—just check the call to print in the function definition. You could just do the following:

```
hw;
```

However, the use of brackets ensures that when you supply multiple arguments to the function, they are clearly grouped together. The function calling here works for any function, whether it's been defined within the current script, as one of the built-in functions, or as a function imported from an external module.

Passing Arguments

Perl has a very simple attitude toward function arguments. In Visual Basic, you must list the arguments that you expect to be supplied to the function when it is called. You also need to define the argument types, and you are limited to calling the function with that many arguments; if there are three arguments in the definition, then you must supply three arguments when you call the function.

Perl is much more relaxed. Aside from the fact there are no different argument types, all arguments will be scalars, even if they are scalar references, arrays of scalars, or hashes. The decision to accept arguments is entirely up to you, and Perl doesn't place any restrictions on the defined arguments, their types, or how many you need to supply when the function is called. (There is an exception, however. See the "Function Prototypes" section later in this chapter.)

Any arguments supplied to the function are available within this special @_ array variable. To access any arguments, you need to access the individual elements of the array. For example, an add function that accepts two arguments might look something like this:

```
sub add
{
    $first_num  = $_[0];
    $second_num = $_[1];
    print 'The value is: $first_num+$second_num\n';
}
```

The first argument supplied to the function is placed into the first element of the @_ array, the second argument into the second, and so on. To call this function, you use the following:

```
add(1,2);
```

You could also omit an argument:

```
add(1);
```

which would just print 1. Perl doesn't complain about this, either when compiling or executing the script. You could even call it without any arguments; Perl would still execute the function without complaining. Any arguments not supplied will result in the elements of the @_ array having a value of undef—the undefined value. To determine how arguments have been supplied, you can, of course, access the @_ array in a scalar context (see Chapter 16).

Although the long format in the preceding code has been used to extract the elements of the supplied arguments into local variables, it's more normal to use the list assignment syntax. For example:

```
sub add
{
    ($first_num, $second_num) = @_;
    print 'The value is: $first_num+$second_num\n';
}
```

The list assignment also has the advantage that we can extract a variable number of arguments. For example, consider the function definition:

```
sub add
{
```

```
    ($first_num, $second_num, @rest_of_nums) = @_;
}
```

The $first_num and $second_num variables will contain the first two arguments supplied to the function; the @rest_of_nums array will contain any additional arguments supplied. Finally, the same format can be used to get a hash from the caller:

```
sub printhash
{
    my (%hash) = @_;
    foreach my $key (sort keys %hash)
    {
        print '$key = $hash{$key}\n';
    }
}
```

However, the above definition assumes that you have supplied an even number of arguments. Perl will convert a hash into a list when supplied as normal in a function call. The list will be composed of alternate elements—the first is the key, the second the value, the third the next key, and so on. When extracting the data, the opposite will happen. If Perl doesn't see an even number of arguments being assigned to a hash, then it raises an error.

You can also get arguments from the @_ array by using the shift function. This returns the first argument (element zero) supplied and removes it from the array, so subsequent calls to the shift function return the next argument supplied. This allows you to easily parse multiple arguments without worrying about how many they are. You just use a loop:

```
sub add
{
    $ret;
    while($value = shift)
    {
        $ret += $value;
    }
    return($ret);
}
```

Now you can call the add function with any number of arguments:

```
print add(3,34,55,5,98,43),'\n';
```

Incidentally, if you pass more arguments than the function extracts, the additional arguments are ignored. They are still supplied in the @_

array, but unless you actually extract or use those elements, then the information is useless. If you only take the first 2 arguments out of the 20 supplied, that's your business.

Return Values

Perl also has a relaxed attitude toward return values. Within Visual Basic, you assign a value to the function within the function definition, and this is the value returned to the caller. To force a function return, you have to specify an Exit function; otherwise, the remainder of the statements are also executed.

Perl allows you to return as many or as few values as you require. You can return a scalar, a number of scalars, an array, or a hash; however, the values will always be returned as a list. It's up to you to extract the return values in a suitable manner. We saw some examples in the last chapter.

Perl always returns the value of the last evaluated statement in a function definition. For example, if we wanted to convert our add function to return the value of two numbers added together, we might write it as:

```
sub add
{
    ($first,$second) = @_;
    $first+$second;
}
```

Now we can modify the function call to the following:

```
print add(1,2),'\n';
```

If you want to force the return of a different value from a function, you need to use the return keyword:

```
sub max
{
    ($first,$second) = @_;
    return $first if ($first>$second);
    return $second;
}
```

The return keyword does two things, first it sets the return value. Then, it immediately returns from the function. This is effectively equivalent to the VB process of setting the value and calling the Exit function. So in our preceding example:

```
print max(2,1),'\n';
print max(5,6),'\n';
```

would output 2 and 6.

To return multiple values, just supply them to the `return` statement:

```
return 1,2;
```

Remember that the list is implied, but it's clearer if you use brackets:

```
return (1,2);
```

Contexts

Because of Perl's freeform format and its ability to accept and return multiple values, Perl has an additional feature called *context*. You already have seen mention of this when we discussed accessing an array in scalar context. The context of a function or statement is defined as the type of return value that is expected. This means that you can have a function that returns different values based on whether the caller is expecting a single scalar value or a list of values.

This can be confusing, since most other languages support only one type of return value. In fact, it's very practical, because it reduces the amount of code required to achieve different results. Here's an example from the built-in Perl functions that shows the flexibility:

```
my $timestr = localtime(time);
```

In this example, we're obviously only expecting a single value, and therefore, we've implied scalar context on the function. In a scalar context, the function returns a formatted date and time string. Conversely, the following statement:

```
($sec,$min,$hour,$mday,$mon,$year,$wday,$yday,$isdst) =
  localtime(time);
```

obviously expects a list of values, and so the function will work in a list context. In a list context, the `localtime` function returns the individual components that make up the date and time. We can now use the returned values to build our own string, instead of relying on the default value returned in a scalar context.

In order to discover the context in which a function has been called, you need to use the `wantarray` function. This returns `True` if the function has been called in a list context, `False` otherwise. Consider the following script, which prints a scalar or list-based message, depending on how the hw function was called:

```
sub hw
{
    if (wantarray)
    {
        return('Hello','World','\n');
    }
    else
    {
        return 'Hello World\n';
    }
}

$scalarmsg = hw();
$listmsg = join('-',hw());

print 'Scalar is $scalarmsg';
print 'List is $listmsg';
```

The list context is implied here because the join function expects a list as the second argument. If you run this program, you get

```
Scalar is Hello World
List is Hello—World—
```

which we know to be correct and is the result we expected.

Perl identifies list context either because you've specified a list of scalars, an array variable, or a hash variable to assign the returned values to. There is no hash context—see the notes in the preceding sections on argument and return values for details on using hashes with functions.

You can force a function to return a scalar value with the scalar keyword. This forces the context of the function to be recognized as a scalar, not a list value. To use, just place the scalar function before the statement or expression that you want to be forced into scalar context:

```
my $time = scalar localtime;
```

This is especially important when you want to supply the scalar value of a variable or function call to another function. Because functions can potentially accept multiple arguments, they automatically imply list context on any embedded function calls. For example, with the localtime function, the line

```
print localtime();
```

will actually print a list of all of the values returned by the `localtime` function when operating in list context, because the `print` function (and indeed any function) expects a list of values. To print out a formatted date and time string:

```
print scalar localtime();
```

Function Prototypes

The function definition in Visual Basic automatically implies the number of arguments the function expects and also what type of arguments to expect. We already know that Perl doesn't use the same rules when defining a function, but it does provide an extension to the function definition that allows you to specify this information either separately or when the function is created.

Argument and return type definitions have some benefits when programming because they ensure that your function arguments and return types are checked. Many programming bugs are introduced by people trying to supply the wrong value or argument type to a function, and the VB definition format for a function helps to eliminate those problems, since differences between the definition's expectations and any function calls are highlighted during the compilation process.

Perl's system is called function prototypes, and it works by specifying the argument types and return value as part of the function definition. Currently, these additional specifications are optional, and this is unlikely to change, since doing so would upset many existing scripts:

```
sub syswrite($$$;$)
```

You specify the function arguments by using the special characters that precede normal variables as indicators of the variable type expected. In the preceding example, the dollar signs signify that scalar values are expected. The @ and % characters, as expected, specify arrays and hashes. However, except in the case noted below, unbackslashed entries gobble up all the remaining arguments, regardless of the rest of the prototype.

Any backslash quoted character signifies that the argument absolutely must start with that character. For example, \@ would require that the function call specify a list as the first argument. A semicolon separates the required arguments from optional arguments in the prototype. The semicolon is used to distinguish between the arguments that are required and those that are optional.

TABLE 17-1

Sample prototype
declarations.

Declaration	Example Call
sub mylink ($$)	mylink $old, $new
sub myvec ($$$)	myvec $var, $offset, 1
sub myindex ($$;$)	myindex &getstring, 'substr'
sub mysyswrite ($$$;$)	mysyswrite $buf, 0, length($buf) - $off,
sub myreverse (@)	myreverse $a, $b, $c
sub myjoin ($@)	myjoin ':', $a, $b, $c
sub mypop (\@)	mypop @array
sub mysplice (\@$$@)	mysplice @array, @array, 0, @pushme
sub mykeys (\%)	mykeys %{$hashref}
sub myopen (*;$)	myopen HANDLE, $name
sub mypipe (**)	mypipe READHANDLE, WRITEHANDLE
sub mygrep (&@)	mygrep { /foo/ } $a, $b, $c
sub myrand ($)	myrand 42
sub mytime ()	Mytime

Table 17-1 shows a full list of the supported prototype definitions.
Don't worry if you don't understand all the tricks used here. Remember
that Perl does not enforce prototypes, but if you are worried about passing the wrong type, you are free to use them.

In the last three examples in Table 17-1, Perl treats the declarations
slightly differently. The mygrep function is passed as a true list operator,
interpreting the following arguments as elements of a list and not as further arguments to the original mygrep function. The myrand function
behaves like a true unary operator, and the mytime function is treated
as a function with no arguments at all. This means you can get away
with statements like

```
mytime +2
```

and you'll end up with the return value of mytime added to the static
value, instead of Perl calling mytime with an argument of +2.

You should be careful when specifying prototypes, since many of the
options imply the context in which the function should return and, in
turn, the function-specific utilities such as wantarray. In general, there-

fore, you should use prototypes only on new functions, rather than retro-fitting them to functions you have already written. This will prevent the effects of imposing a scalar context on a function that is expecting to return in a list context. For example, consider a function with a single argument:

```
sub printmsg($)
{
    print 'Message: ', shift, '\n';
}
```

Calling this function with an argument that returns a single element list wouldn't produce the same results. The call

```
printmsg(@message);
```

would actually print a value of 1, since the scalar prototype has imposed that the list argument supplied be converted to a scalar.

In the case of a list, the scalar value of a list variable is the number of elements in the list. Worse, using a function such as `split`, which uses the context in which it is called to determine where it puts its results, would cause a more serious problem. If used as the argument to the pro-totype function, `split` would execute in the scalar context, messing up your @_ argument list.

Packages

Aside from modules and forms, there is no logical way of dividing up a Visual Basic application into logical units. Although this is not really a serious constraint, Perl's different approach and the extensible nature of the language mean that we need some way of compartmentalizing different functions and variables within the Perl interpreter.

Packages provide a mechanism for breaking up the code that makes up a Perl application into more manageable segments and also lays the foundation for the development of modules that extend Perl's functionality. The main principle behind packages in Perl is to protect the name-space of one section of code from another, therefore helping to prevent functions and variables from overwriting each other's values. Despite what you may have seen up to now, there is no such thing as a global variable—all *user* variables are created within the realms of a package. There is a default package, `main`, which is where your script normally lies, any variables created in the root level of the `main` package are global variables, equivalent in principle to VB's `Public` variables.

You can change the current package to another by using the `package` keyword. The current package determines what symbol table is consulted when a user makes a function call or accesses a variable. The current package name is determined at compile time and runtime. This is because certain operations such as dereferencing require Perl to know what the "current" package is. Any `eval` blocks are also executed at runtime, and the current package will directly affect the symbol table to which the `eval` block has access.

All identifiers (except those declared with `my` or with an absolute package name) are created within the symbol table of the current package. The package definition remains either until another package definition occurs or until the block in which the package was defined terminates. You can intersperse different package names in the same file and even specify the same package multiple times within multiple files. The `package` declaration only changes the default symbol table. For example, in the following code both the `add` and `subtract` functions are part of the `Basemath` package, even though the `square` function has been inserted within a `Multimath` package:

```
package Basemath;

sub add { $_[0]+$_[1] }

package Multimath;

sub square { $_[0] *= $_[0] }
package Basemath;

sub subtract { $_[0]-$_[1] }
```

The preceding is probably not a good example of when a `package` is normally defined. Normally, the first statement within a new file would be used to define the package name for a module that would be imported via the `use` or `require` statement. Of course, there is nothing to stop you from using a `package` statement anywhere you would use any other statement.

You can reference a symbol entry from any package by specifying the full package and symbol name. The separator between the package and symbol entry is the double colon. You could refer to the `add` function above as `Basemath::add`. If you are referring to a variable, you place the character for the variable type before the package name, for example, `$Basemath::PI`. The main package can either be specified directly, as in

$main::var, or you can ignore the name and simply use $::var.

You can also nest package names in order to create a package hierarchy. Using the math module again, you might want to split it into three separate packages. The main Math package contains the constant definitions, with two nested packages: Math::Base and Math::Multi. The hierarchy does not introduce any additional symbol tables, so the variable $Math::Multi::var is not simply accessible as $Multi::var. You either need to change the current package with a package statement or refer to the variable with its full name. See the "Variable Scope" section later in this chapter for more details on how Perl handles variables and their availability to other functions and modules.

The symbol table is the list of active symbols (functions, variables, objects) within a package. Each package has its own symbol table, and with some exceptions, all the identifiers starting with letters or underscores are stored within the corresponding symbol table for each package. This means that all other identifiers, including all of the special punctuation-only variables such as $_, are stored within the main package. Other identifiers that are forced to be within the main package include STDIN, STDOUT, STDERR, %ARGV, ARGVOUT, %ENV, @INC, and %SIG.

BEGIN and END

Before we move on and look at Perl modules, it's worth taking a brief look at the BEGIN and END code blocks. These are special code blocks (see Chapter 16) in a package that act as initializers and finalizers. They are defined like this:

```
BEGIN { print 'Start!\n' };
END   { print 'End!\n'   };
```

A BEGIN block is executed as soon as possible after it has been defined. This means that the code within a BEGIN block is executed at the time of compilation (see Chapter 15), rather than the time of execution. You can have multiple BEGIN blocks that are executed in the order they were defined. You can use a BEGIN block to import functions and values from other modules so that the objects required by the rest of the package are defined at the point the block is parsed. This can be especially useful if you are using the function prototyping and declarations seen earlier in this chapter. If a function has been defined such that it is interpreted as an operator, or with a specific prototyping format, then it will need to exist before Perl interprets the rest of the package.

An END routine is the opposite: It is executed as late as possible. In practice, this means that an END block is executed at the point the parser and interpreter are about to exit. This is the case even if the reason for the failure is a die function call or through the normal execution of a script.

END blocks are executed in reverse order—that is, the last END block specified will be the first to be executed. The following program doesn't do quite what we want, although it's pretty close:

```
BEGIN { print 'Eanie\n' }
die 'Meanie\n';
END { print 'Miney\n' }
END { print 'Mo\n' }
```

You should not assume that the main program code has been executed in an END block. Care is needed to ensure you don't try to use a variable or function in an END block that has not otherwise been defined, although you should be doing this kind of checking in the main body of the script anyway.

Modules

A Perl module is essentially just a file that contains a number of functions and variables that are available for importing into another script. They work in an identical fashion to the generic modules that you create in a VB project. Perl comes with an extensive library of modules that provide all sorts of different facilities.

You can also define your own modules in order to organize your own projects. Before we look at the process of defining modules, we will instead look at the process of importing existing modules into your own scripts and projects.

use and require

With Visual Basic, incorporating an existing module is a case of adding the module to the list of modules within the project. Because Perl scripts are executed using the contents of a text file, we need a different method for including modules into our scripts.

When you import a module, you can use one of two keywords: use or require. The difference between the two is that a require statement imports the functions into their own namespaces, according to the `package` definition. The `use` statement, however, imports the functions and variables into the current package. The `require` method is a relatively unused format, so we'll concentrate instead on the `use` statement, since it's how you'll most likely use modules.

The general format of the `use` statement is as follows:

```
use Module;
```

or

```
use Module LIST;
```

The first form imports all of the symbols that have been configured within the module to be exported by default. The second form allows you to specify the functions and variables that you selectively want to import from the module. For example, the line

```
use MyMathLib qw/add square/;
```

would cause only the `add` and `square` functions to be exported from the `MyMathLib` module. We'll look at how to configure these two options from within the module itself shortly.

What actually happens when you use the `use` statement is that Perl uses `require` to import the packages from the specified file into their own namespace. Then Perl calls a special `import` function defined within the module to import the functions and variables into the namespace of the current package.

To compare this process against the `require` statement, you would have to do something like this:

```
BEGIN
{
    require 'Module.pm';
    Module->import();
}
```

Alternatively, you may not wish to import any symbols from the module, in which case you can use

```
use MyMathLib ();
```

or its `require` equivalent:

```
BEGIN { require MyMathLib; }
```

You can see from the preceding example that important difference: the `require` statement reads in the specified module, but it does not call the `import` method. This has the effect that symbols defined within another package do not update the current package's symbol table—for example:

```
require Cwd;
$pwd = Cwd::getcwd();
```

as opposed to:

```
use Cwd;
$pwd = getcwd();
```

One other significant difference between `require` and `use` is that `use` statements are interpreted and executed at the time the file is parsed. But `require` statements import modules at runtime, which means you can supply a variable name to a `require` statement based on other elements of your program.

Perl modules are just scripts—text files with suitable code for exporting their objects, functions, and variables. They also have a special extension, *.pm*, to indicate that the file is a Perl module. You'll also notice from many of the latter examples that we are not specifying the full filename. By specifying a filename, we imply the full name and location of the file. If you do not specify the name in quotes and leave off the extension, both `require` and `use` imply the *.pm* extension.

The path used to determine the location of the files imported this way is the `@INC` array. This can be updated to allow other paths to be taken into account. The paths specified are the top directories. You can further subdivide modules into other subdirectories for clarity, in which case you must specify the relative pathname for the module you want to import, using the double colon notation in place of your operating system's pathname separator. For example:

```
use File::Basename;
```

actually imports the File\Basename.pm file.

The `use` and `require` statements also serve one final purpose—they provide a mechanism for controlling how the interpreter compiles and executes its code. For example, the `use strict` pragma demands stricter processing on the syntax and use of variables and functions within your script. The pragmas are beyond the scope of this book; see *Perl: The Complete Reference* for more details (see Appendix A).

Creating Your Own Modules

Creating your own module consists of more steps than just changing the file's extension to .pm. Once you have developed your own library of functions, you need to do the following to convert the script into a Perl module:

1. Change the filename and add the *.pm* extension.
2. Define a new package, using the filename as the package name.
3. Insert the code necessary to export your functions and variables to calling scripts.
4. Ensure that the new module returns a true value (1) when imported.

As an example, we'll convert our mathematical functions into a `MyMathLib` module. We already know how to create a new package—you use the `package` statement. Therefore, the file should look like this:

```
package MyMathLib;

sub add
{
    $_[0]+$_[1]
}
sub square
{
    $_[0] *= $_[0]
}
sub subtract
{
    $_[0]-$_[1]
}
```

If you copy that into a file called MyMathLib.pm, we've completed the first two steps. Note that the package name and filename are identical (aside from the extension). This is important because the `use` statement

```
use MyMathLib;
```

will open the file MyMathLib.pm, and for the package `MyMathLib` within that file—if it cannot find the MyMathLib package within the file, the import process fails.

Exporting Symbols   To configure the module to export its symbols, we need to create a function called `import`, which will be called by the importing script. Writing this function is not easy, so the Perl libraries provide a solution. The `Exporter` module provides a simple `import` function that can be used within your modules. The `Exporter` module uses two main variables, the @EXPORT and EXPORT_OK arrays. These arrays define the list of variables and functions that you want to export from your module.

To use the Exporter module, you need to include the following at the top of our module file:

```
package MyMathLib;
require Exporter;
@ISA       = qw/Exporter/;
@EXPORT    = qw/add subtract/;
@EXPORT_OK = qw/square/;
```

We need to require the Exporter module because we don't want to import the symbols into our package—only provide access to them. The @ISA array is actually a Perl artifact; it defines the list of modules to use when searching for a class definition to inherit from. We need this because we are actually going to inherit rather than import the import function from the Exporter module.

The Exporter's import function uses a number of variables defined within the calling package to specify which functions will be exported. The @EXPORT array contains the variables to be exported when the calling package does not specify any functions. For example, the line

```
use MyMathLib;
```

will import the add and subtract functions but *not* square into the script.

The @EXPORT_OK array lists the functions that can be selectively imported. In other words,

```
use MyMathLib qw/add square/;
```

imports add and square into the script.

Returning a True Value   In all cases, irrespective of how the module is imported into your program, the module must return a true value; otherwise, the import process assumes there was an error. You can do this in a number of different ways. Complex modules may wish to decide on the status of other elements before they return a successful import. The most usual solution however is to place

```
1;
```

at the end of your module.

The result after all of this is that our math library file should look like this:

```
package MyMathLib;
require Exporter;
@ISA       = qw/Exporter/;
@EXPORT    = qw/add subtract/;
@EXPORT_OK = qw/square/;

sub add
{
    $_[0]+$_[1]
}
sub square
{
    $_[0]  *= $_[0]
}
sub subtract
{
    $_[0]-$_[1]
}

1;
```

Variable Scope

By default, all variables are created as global variables within the confines of the current package, even if they are defined within a function or other code block. Perl actually supports two localization keywords: my and local. The my keyword defines a variable or list of variables as local within the current code block and is basically equivalent to the Private keyword in Visual Basic.

For example, consider the following code. Although a variable $var has been defined as global within the package, because a localized variable is defined within the function, it is the value of that variable that is printed:

```
$var = 'Hello World\n';


sub hw
{
```

```
    my $var = 'Hello Core\n';
    print $var;
}

hw();
print $var;
```

When run, this produces

```
Hello Core
Hello World
```

Note that when using my, multiple variables must be enclosed in parentheses:

```
my ($one, $two);
```

The local keyword is slightly different. Although it localizes a variable to the current block, it will also create a local copy of a global variable (if it exists) and localize it into the local scope. This means that it can be used to modify the scope of an existing global variable. A commonly used trick is to localize the record separator variable in order to allow you to read the entire contents of a file into a scalar variable:

```
{ local $/; $file = <DATA>; }
```

The global $/ variable has not been modified, and the default value of the copy is undef rather than the default \n character. See Chapter 18 for more information on using files.

There is another difference between the two keywords: local variables are dynamically scoped, and my variables are lexically scoped. Dynamically scoped variables are available both to the local block and to the functions called from within the block in which the variables are declared. Lexically scoped variables are truly localized to the current block—the variable is truly hidden from the outside world. This is true even if the function calls itself; a new localized variable is created for use by the new instance of the function.

This means that you can call a function within a code block that accesses a variable declared local, but a variable declared with my will not be found. As a general rule, you should use my over local. The my keyword produces the result most people expect and is a direct equivalent of the Private declaration in VB.

One final advantage is that the my keyword can be used in place to declare a variable within loops and other functions and operators. For example, you may want to localize the loop variable:

```
foreach my $key (keys %hash)
```

The $key variable will be localized to the foreach block, which guarantees that the $key variable you are accessing within the block is the one you want, not a variable defined elsewhere.

Objects

Perl's approach to objects is slightly different from VB. Unlike VB, Perl was never designed with object orientation in mind, which means that the functionality has been added to the language, rather than being a core component. There is no reason to use objects within Perl. In fact, for many processes, Perl is easier to work with using a non-object-oriented approach.

That said, many of Perl's more modern features, particularly those supported by the modules that come with the standard library and those available from CPAN, use Perl's object system. The core of the object system is the package. A package defines a new Perl class and, in conjunction with the built-in bless function, provides everything we need to support object orientation in Perl.

For any object-based language there are three main terms—object, class, and method:

- Within Perl, an *object* is merely a reference to a data type that knows what class it belongs to. The object is stored as a reference in a scalar variable. Because a scalar only contains a reference to the object, the same scalar can hold different objects in different classes. When a particular operation is performed on an object, the corresponding method is called, as defined within the class.

- A *class* within Perl is a package that contains the corresponding methods required to create and manipulate objects.

- A *method* within Perl is a subroutine, defined with the package. The first argument to the method is an object reference or a package name, depending on whether the method affects the current object or the class.

References

The Perl scalar allows you to create references, or pointers, to other data types. A *reference* is just a token that tells Perl to look for information in a section of memory. Because Perl does not support a built-in object data type, it uses references to point to areas of memory that contain the object information.

To create a reference, you need to create a scalar variable that points to a specific piece of information. That information can be another scalar, an array, or a hash. Perl uses the \ operator to mean "reference to." Therefore, we can create a reference to a scalar using the following:

```
$scalar = 'Hello World\n';
$ref = \$scalar;
```

To access the information within a reference, we need to *dereference* the variable. Dereferencing tells Perl to look at the memory location for information, not at the variable that holds the reference. For example, to dereference our scalar variable:

```
print $$ref;
```

The leading $ sign tells Perl to dereference a scalar variable from the reference contained in $ref.

The same format is used when we want to update the information:

```
$$ref = 'Goodbye World\n';
```

References can also point to arrays. You can use two formats for creating a reference to an array. Either you can create a reference to a named array:

```
@array = qw/Hello World/;
$ref   = \@array;
```

or you can imply a reference :

```
$ref   = [ 'Hello', 'World' ];
```

The use of square brackets (as used when accessing elements of an array) creates a new anonymous array, which returns a reference. The reference is then assigned to the $ref scalar.

With a referenced array, you need to dereference it by specifying the @ symbol when you want to access the whole array:

```
print join(' ', @$ref);
```

When accessing an element of the array, you need to use the infix operator, ->:

```
print $ref->[0];
```

In this case we print out the first element (at index zero) from the array reference.

The same basic principles apply when creating hashes:

```
%hash = ('Name' => 'Martin',
         'Hair' => 'Brown');
$ref = \%hash;                    # Creates a reference to %hash
$ref = {'Name' => 'Martin',
        'Hair' => 'Brown'};       # Creates a reference to an anon hash
print (keys %$ref);               # Prints the keys of the hash
print $ref->{Name};               # Prints out a single element of
                                  #   anon hash
```

When you are accessing reference information, there are times when the reference variable name is ambiguous. To get around this problem, you can place curly brackets around the reference and prefix it with the required dereference data type. For example, the preceding dereferences could be rewritten as:

```
print ${$ref};
print join(' ', @{$ref});
print (keys %{$ref});
```

This is actually clearer, particularly when accessing complex data.

Because a reference is a pointer to another data type, it can be used to implement complex data structures such as two-dimensional arrays. The first dimension contains an array of scalars, with each scalar as a reference to a new array. For example, the following array maps out a tic-tac-toe board:

```
@tictactoe = ( ['X','O','O'],
               ['O','O','X'],
               ['O','X','X']
             );
```

This creates a nested set of arrays within a parent array, @tictactoe. To print out the bottom right corner, use the following:

```
print $tictactoe[2][2];
```

Alternatively, you can place the whole lot into a reference:

```
$tictactoe = [ ['X','O','O'],
               ['O','O','X'],
               ['O','X','X']
             ];
```

Note the use of the square brackets around the nested arrays, which indicates to Perl that you are creating an anonymous array and you need to return a reference to it. You assign the reference to the $tictactoe scalar, and to access the bottom right corner:

```
print $tictactoe[2][2];
```

Note the semantics here. Shouldn't you have dereferenced $tictactoe somehow?

Perl automatically assumes you are dereferencing if you use pairs of brackets together. Perl knows that this indicates a structure to a list of references, whether that's a hash or an array, so the infix operator (or block names) are implied. This doesn't prevent you from using them if you want to. The following lines are all equal:

```
print $tictactoe[2][2];
print $tictactoe->[2][2];
print $tictactoe[2]->[2];
print $tictactoe->[2]->[2];
```

Like many other similar features, this is a direct attempt to improve the overall readability of the code. The first format looks cleaner and should appeal to C programmers, since this is the same format used in C for multidimensional arrays. The other formats would perhaps make more sense to a hardened Perl programmer, and they help if you are particularly bothered about the notation of one reference point to another.

Other complex structures work the same way; you can create complex structures that are arrays of hashes, hashes of arrays, arrays of arrays, and hashes of hashes. Since an array or hash is made up of scalars, you can create any level of any structure, nested in any way you like.

Consider the following nested hash of arrays of hashes, which emulates a database that supports multiple tables:

```
%db = (
        contacts => [
                        { 'name'  => 'Martin',
                          'email' => 'mc@mcwords.com' },
                        { 'name'  => 'Bob',
                          'email' => 'bob@bob.com' },
                        ],
        appointments => [
                        { 'Date'  => '22/3/98',
                          'Time'  => '10:30',
                          'Title' => 'Dentist' },
                        { 'Date'  => '5/5/98',
                          'Time'  => '00:00',
                          'Title' => 'Birthday' },
                        ]
        );
```

To make the process of building complex structures easier, you can also copy references so that a particular element points to some other part of the structure. For example, you might want to create a new appointment and add a new field—say, an array of contacts who will attend the meeting:

```
%appt = ( 'Date' => '4/5/1999',
          'Time' => '10:30',
          'Title' => 'Production Meeting',
          'Members' => [ $db{'contacts'}[0], $db{'contacts'}[1] ]
          );

push @{$db{'appointments'}}, \%appt;
```

The new Members element of the hash contains an array, which has two references to the two contacts created in the preceding code. You can access their e-mail addresses directly with the following:

```
print ${$db{appointments}[2]{Members}[0]}{email},'\n';
```

But note that because it's a reference, an assignation like this

```
${$db{appointments}[2]{Members}[0]}{email} = 'foo@goo.bar';
```

updates the value of the contact's record directly. Therefore, both

```
print ${$db{appointments}[2]{Members}[0]}{email},'\n';
```

and

```
print $db{contacts}[0]{email},'\n';
```

print out the new *foo@goo.bar* e-mail address.

For more details on using complex structures, see *Perl: The Complete Reference*.

Creating and Using Objects

Perl objects are based on references, and you can create a Perl object that is based on a scalar, array, or hash reference, or even a nested structure. That said, most Perl objects are actually based on hash references, since they provide the most flexible way of storing and accessing different pieces of information.

As you already know from VB programming, when creating an object, you need to supply a *constructor*. Perl handles the need for a constructor by defining a subroutine within a package that returns an object reference. The object reference is created by *blessing* a reference to the package's class. For example:

```
package Vegetable;
sub new
{
    my $object = {};
    return bless $object;
}
```

this code creates a new package, Vegetable, with a single method, new, which is the default name for an object constructor. The new method returns a reference to a hash, defined in $object, which has been blessed using the bless function into an object reference.

You can now create a new Vegetable object by using this code:

```
$carrot = new Vegetable;
```

Note here that a hash is used as the base data type for the object. This is not required. You could use any of the available data types as the base for an object. Hashes are the normal receptacle only because you are usually constructing records where you want to be able to identify individual fields by name.

The use of bless defines the difference between a normal reference and an object reference. An object is a reference that has been blessed into a particular class, whereas a reference is just a reference to another entity.

If you want to initialize the object with some information before it is returned, you can put that into the subroutine itself. (The following example takes the data from the supplied arguments):

```
sub new
{
    my $object = {@_};
    return bless $object;
}
```

which can now populate when you create a new object:

```
$carrot = new Vegetable('Color' => 'Orange', 'Shape' => 'Carrot-
like');
```

You don't have to use the information supplied to the new method as a hash. The subroutine can take any arguments and process them as you require. Here's the same constructor, but this time it assumes you are supplying the information in the arguments to the constructor function:

```
sub new
{
    my $object = {};
    $object->{'Color'   => $_[0],
              'Shape'   => $_[1]
             };
    bless $object;
    return $object;
}
```

Normally, of course, you'd check the contents of the arguments before you started blindly filling in the details, but the process is essentially the same.

If you want to call your own initialization routine on a newly blessed object, you use

```
sub new
{
    my $object = {};
    bless $object;
    $object->_define();
    return $object;
}
```

The use of a leading underscore on the method _define is a convention used to indicate a private rather than public method. Here's a quick example of the function:

```
sub _define
{
    my $self = shift;
```

```
    $self->{'State'}        = 'Raw';
    $self->{'Composition'}  = 'Whole';
}
```

Don't worry too much about the semantics for a second, we'll cover that shortly.

For inheritance purposes, you will need to use a two-argument call to bless. The second argument should be the class into which you are blessing the object, and you can derive this from the first argument to the constructor method. For example, to explicitly define the above object into the Vegetable class:

```
sub new
{
    my $class = shift;
    my $object = {};
    return bless $object, $class;
}
```

The reason you need this is that methods execute within the confines of their base class, not their derived class. Thus, if you were to create a new class Fruit, which inherited methods from Vegetable, a call to the new constructor would bless an object into the Vegetable rather than the Fruit class. Using the above format with the two-argument version of bless ensures that the new object is part of the Fruit method.

Methods

We'll start with a reminder: an object is a blessed reference, but a reference is just a pointer to a data structure. When writing methods, it's important to understand this distinction. Within the confines of the class package and corresponding methods, you use the object as if it was a reference (which it is), but outside the class package, you use it as an object.

There is no special way within Perl to define a method, since a method is just a function defined within the class package. The only difference between a normal subroutine and a method is that the method should accept at least one argument, the contents of which will be the object you want to manipulate. There are no complications to creating the method. All you need to do is define the function, and Perl will handle the rest. See the section "Classes and Inheritance" later in the chapter for some exceptions, but otherwise this definition stands.

There are two types of methods: class and instance. A *class* method is one that affects the entire class. You've already seen some examples of this: The constructor subroutine is an example of a class method. The first argument a class method receives is the name of the class. This is ignored by most functions, since they already know to which class (package) they belong. However, as you've already seen in the previous section, it is sometimes necessary to identify the class.

An *instance* method is a function that operates on a specific object. It should accept at least one argument, which is the object on which you want to operate. For example, the boil method for our Vegetable object modifies the State element of the object's hash to boiled:

```
sub boil
{
    my $self = shift;
    $self->{'State'} = 'Boiled';
}
```

You take the first argument off with shift and then modify the object's contents. Note that the name of the variable that you store the reference in is called $self. This is an accepted standard, although there is no reason why you can't call it something else. The use is convention, rather than law. Remember that an object is just a reference to a particular data type, so you can modify the hash "object" just as you would any other reference.

To use this method, you use the infix operator to select the method to use on a particular object. For example:

```
$carrot = new Vegetable('Color' => 'Orange', 'Shape' = 'Carrot-like');
$carrot->boil;
```

The State field of the hash has now been updated.

You can also accept arguments to the method:

```
sub boil
{
    my $self = shift;
    $self->{'State'} = 'Boiled';
    if (@_ == 1)
    {
        $self->{'Composition'} = shift;
    }
}
```

thus allowing you to define how the vegetable will be before it's boiled:

```
$carrot->boil('Chopped');
```

You can also create a method that behaves differently based on what information it is supplied in that first argument. The way to do this is to use `ref` to identify whether or not the method was supplied a reference to an object:

```
sub new
{
    my $self = shift;
    my $type = ref($self) || $self;
    return bless {}, $type;
}
```

If the return value of the `ref` is a valid reference, then it's safe to assume you should be blessing an object. If `ref` returns `False`, then the argument is not an object but a class name.

Method Calls   There are two ways of invoking a method. The first format looks like this:

```
METHOD CLASS_OR_INSTANCE LIST
```

This is the format you've used for creating objects, for example:

```
new Vegetable('Color' => 'Orange', 'Shape' = 'Carrot-like');
```

In this case, `new` is the method, `Vegetable` is the class (and indicates to Perl the package to search for the `new` method), and the list is the optional list of arguments that will be passed to the method after the initial class name. The same format can be used for methods on existing objects:

```
boil $carrot 'Chopped';
```

This actually makes more sense (providing your methods and classes are suitably defined). The preceding line is equal to the earlier example, which uses the second syntax format:

```
CLASS_OR_INSTANCE->METHOD(LIST)
```

For our carrot, this means using this line to get it chopped and boiled:

```
$carrot->boil('Chopped');
```

Note that this second method requires parentheses around the arguments to the method because this syntax cannot be used as a list operator. This means you must be careful with the first format. It assumes that the first parenthesis defines the start of the arguments, and the matching closing parenthesis ends the argument list.

Note also that in both cases you can explicitly define the method/class you want to use with the normal qualification:

```
$carrot->Vegetable::boil('Chopped');
```

Finally, you can use a scalar variable to hold the name of a method to call, providing you use the `infix` operator form of the method call:

```
$method = 'boil';
$carrot->$method('Chopped');
```

This won't work with other constructs, so don't attempt to use a function call or other expression here. It won't be parsed properly, and Perl will report an error.

Accessing Object Data   At the risk of repeating myself yet again, an object is just a reference that knows what class it belongs to. This means you can access an element of the object by using reference notation. For example, to print the status of one of our `Vegetable` objects, you could use a line like this:

```
print $carrot->{'State'},'\n';
```

The same is true of any other data structure you decide to use. There is no need to create a subroutine to do it for you.

Classes and Inheritance

A class is just a package. You can inherit methods from a parent class in a new class through the use of the `@ISA` array. Note that you cannot automatically inherit data. Perl leaves that decision to you. Since an object is a reference, you should be able to copy the information over easily, or just copy references in the new object to allow access to the inherited object's data. Since the normal base data type for an object is a hash, copying "fields" is a case of accessing the corresponding hash elements. See the previous sections for more information.

You may recall that earlier in this chapter when we were looking at creating modules we said `@ISA` was used to define the list of base classes on which the package relies. This is in fact the array used for inheriting methods. When you call a method on an object, Perl first looks for it within the package class. It then follows the inheritance tree based on the root classes (packages) defined in @ISA. For each class (package) defined in the array, Perl follows the inherited classes defined in that package's @ISA array, and so on, until the complete tree has been followed. It then moves on to the next one. This allows you to inherit, almost by assumption, the methods defined in the packages specified in the @ISA array and, in turn, any methods defined within the base classes of those packages.

This is how you can identify the list of packages specified in @ISA as base classes, and how the interpretation of the @ISA array becomes "is-a," since a new object "is-a" member of the specified base classes.

The full path followed for method inheritance is actually slightly more complex, and the full list is as follows:

1. Perl searches the class of the specified object for the specified object.

2. Perl searches the classes defined in the object class's @ISA array.

3. If no method is found in Steps 1 or 2, then Perl uses an AUTOLOAD subroutine, if one is found in the @ISA tree.

4. If a matching method still cannot be found, then Perl searches for the method within the UNIVERSAL class (package) that comes as part of the standard Perl library.

5. If the method still hasn't been found, then Perl gives up and raises a runtime exception.

You can force Perl to examine the base class's @ISA list first by specifying the SUPER pseudoclass within the base class package, as in the following:

```
$carrot->SUPER::fry();
```

This would automatically force Perl to look in the @ISA classes rather than in the local class for the fry method. This can only be used within the base class package. You cannot use it on an object outside of the base class; so it's only of any use to object programmers rather than object users.

Destructors and Garbage Collection

If you have programmed using objects before, then you will be aware of the need to create a "destructor" to free the memory allocated to the object when you have finished using it. Perl does this automatically for you as soon as the object goes out of scope.

You may want to provide your own destruction mechanism, however. This is sometimes necessary if you are using objects to define network connectivity or to update tied persistent data (see "Using tie" below), or if you are using other objects that access external information. You will need to close the connections to these external sources politely, and for that, you need to define a special method called DESTROY. This method will be called on the object just before Perl frees the memory allocated to it. In all other respects, the DESTROY method is just like any other, and you can do anything you like with the object in order to close it properly.

A DESTROY method is absolutely essential in situations where you have objects that refer to nested structures (objects within objects), or when you have inherited information from another class. In these instances you will need to destroy the nested references yourself as part of the special DESTROY method.

## CHAPTER 18

Manipulating Data

For the last chapter in our migration guide, we will look at how Perl works when manipulating different types of information. The primary method of communication between Perl and the user is the filehandle. There are filehandles that communicate with the screen and keyboard, and filehandles also provide interfaces to files, network sockets, and other communication pipes. Unlike other languages, Perl is much more flexible about how you use and communicate with these devices. Unless you specifically want to work with files in a binary format, there are really only two functions you need to know—the `print` and the `<FILEHANDLE>` operators.

In its basic format, Perl does not provide any form of visual or graphical interface. However, you can use the Tk toolkit to provide a windows-based interface to your applications. You'll need to understand how to manipulate hashes and use objects to use some of the more advanced features. The approach you use will also need to be different. Programs developed using the Tk interface are completely script-driven. The production of windows, widgets, controls, and other window artifacts is controlled entirely from the confines of the Perl script, just like other parts of the Perl programming process. Unlike VB, there is no separate "form" module, but tools do exist for developing the interface in a VB fashion. See Chapter 10 for more information on programming with Tk.

In this chapter, we'll start by looking at how to handle errors within Perl before looking at how you can communicate with the user and files. We'll then move on to the specifics of manipulating different pieces of information within Perl, from splitting and combining strings to formatting information for printing. The last section looks at regular expressions—a feature that may be new to some VB programmers.

For a more detailed guide to Visual Basic functions and their Perl equivalents, see Appendix C.

Error Handling

VB provides a specific mechanism for handling errors by allowing the programmer to install a specific error-handling routine. The VB interpreter calls the function when an error occurs, and normally you use the function to identify the problem and either try to rectify it, or warn the user that an error has occurred.

Within Perl, rather than using a single function to process any errors, you use "traps" around individual statements to identify an error and either report it there and then, or call a function to handle the problem. The system works because the majority of functions that don't otherwise return a result return `True` when they are successful and `0` if there was a failure.

For example, the `open` function, which we'll see later in this chapter, works in this way. There are two ways you can trap errors. The first is to use an `if` or `unless` statement:

```
if (open(FILE, 'myfile.txt'))
{
    print "Opened the file\n";
}
else
{
    warn "Didn't open the file\n";
}
```

We'll have a look at the `warn` function in a moment. Generally, it makes more sense to use the `unless` statement, since this automatically implies that the following code block should only be executed on failure:

```
unless(open(FILE, 'myfile.txt'))
{
    warn "Didn't open the file\n";
}
```

The code also reads more clearly—think of the above as "unless the open function works...."

The other method is to use the logical OR operators, `||` or OR. These provide what is called a *short circuit operation*—for example, the statement

```
open(FILE, 'myfile.txt') || warn "Didn't open the file\n";
```

To understand how this works, you need to understand how the logical OR operators work. A logical OR basically looks like this:

```
a || b;
```

The definition of logical OR says that the statement should return 1 if either a or b has a value of 1; otherwise it returns a value of 0. Within Perl (and other languages), this is interpreted as "If a returns `True`, return `True` without evaluating b. Otherwise, evaluate b and return that value."

This means that the statement on the left of the OR operator is evaluated. If the result is true, there is no need to execute statement b, because it won't affect the return value. However, if statement a returns False, then we need to execute statement b to determine the return value of the entire statement.

So, in our example:

```
open(FILE, 'myfile.txt') || warn "Didn't open the file\n";
```

If the open function returns True, then nothing happens. If it returns False (i.e., the file fails to open), then we execute the warn statement.

The OR operator works in the same way, but because it has the lowest precedence, you can use it in situations where you have not used parentheses around a function call, or where the split is not clear. For example:

```
open FILE, 'myfile.txt' or warn "Didn't open the file\n";
```

As a general rule, it's good practice to use the OR operator in preference to ||, since it will always do what you expect.

Error Codes and Messages

When reporting an error, it's useful to supply the error that was returned by the operating system so that the problem can be identified. For example, when opening a file, the error could be caused by a lack of the file's existence or the user's privileges not allowing them to access the file. Perl uses the special $! variable to hold the error number or error string for the last system error that occurred.

For example, we could update our open error message to:

```
open FILE, 'myfile.txt' or warn "Didn't open the file: $!\n";
```

Whether the variable returns a numerical value or a string depends on the context in which it is used. If Perl is expecting a numerical value, then the variable returns the numerical error code. When called in a string context, the variable returns a string. The $! will return an error string in this instance, since we've embedded it into a double-quoted string.

The warn and die Functions

Using print to print out your messages is fine, but it doesn't actually highlight the message as an error; it just appears as another message.

You can get around this by using the `warn` or `die` functions:

```
warn LIST
die LIST
```

In both cases, the functions print out the value of the `LIST` you supply and raise an exception to the Perl interpreter. The exception doesn't have an effect in normal usage, but it will raise an error during an `eval` block. (The use and effect of `eval` is beyond the scope of this book; see *Perl: The Complete Reference* for more information.)

The only difference between the two functions is that `warn` only raises an exception and prints the error message to the standard error filehandle; `die` also calls `exit`, which causes a script to exit prematurely.

```
open FILE, 'myfile.txt' or warn "Didn't open the file: $!\n ";
open FILE, 'myfile.txt' or die "Didn't open the file: $!\n ";
```

If you fail to supply any arguments to the `warn` function, then the message `Warning: Something's wrong` is printed. When using `die`, if the value of `LIST` does not end in a newline, Perl adds the current script and line number to the message that is printed. It's a good idea in these situations to ensure you append `stopped` or a similar message to the value of `LIST`. This will print a more sensible message when the script and line number information is appended.

If you want to use the script name and line numbers within your error messages, you can use the special tokens `__FILE__` and `__LINE__`, respectively. For example:

```
chdir('C:/windows')
    or die "Can't change dir in ",__FILE__," line ", __LINE__, "\n";
```

If you failed to change the directory, this would print

```
Can't change dir in adduser.pl line 35
```

Working with Files

Visual Basic uses the notion of unique numbers when communicating with files. This is generally a good system, but it requires an on-the-ball programmer to remember which file number refers to which file, or the use of a structure to hold the information for you. The numbering system is actually inherited from the OS libraries, which use file numbers (called *file descriptors*) to identify the files opened by the system.

Perl uses the same system libraries, but instead of exposing the file numbers to the programmer, it uses a special structure called a filehandle to refer to the files that you open. Filehandles are really a special type of variable, and like variables they have names rather than numbers. The actual names can be of mixed case—just like variables—but according to convention, they are generally specified in uppercase. This helps to distinguish them from function names, since unlike the other variables used in Perl, they don't have a special character to identify them.

As far as Perl is concerned, all operating systems support three basic filehandles: STDIN, STDOUT, and STDERR. The exact interpretation of the filehandle and the device or file it is associated with depend on the OS and the Perl implementation. Table 18-1 shows the relationship between Perl filehandles and the underlying C file descriptors.

NOTE.   *Perl also supports two further filehandles:* ARGV *and* DATA. *See Chapter 11 of* Perl: The Complete Reference *for more information.*

We'll see some examples of how you can use these filehandles later.

Opening and Closing Files

All file data is exchanged through the use of a filehandle, which associates an external data source (a file, network socket, external program, pipe) with an internal data structure (the filehandle). The method with which you associate the filehandle differs depending on the type of external data source, although many of the functions used to access the data available with the filehandle are the same. For files, you use the open

TABLE 18-1

Standard perl file-handles.

Perl Filehandle	C File Descriptor	Associated Device	Access Mode
STDIN	0	Keyboard	Write-only
STDOUT	1	Monitor	Read-only
STDERR	2	Monitor	Write-only

function to open ordinary files and the `sysopen` function to handle more complex opening procedures. The `close` function is used to close any open filehandle, regardless of how it was opened.

open

The `open` function is almost certainly one of the most complicated to understand when you first approach the Perl language. The basic format of the command is as follows:

```
open FILEHANDLE, EXPR
```

The `FILEHANDLE` is the name that you want to use to refer to the opened file. For example, you might use `FILE` or `DATA`. The `EXPR` is more complex. Perl takes the value supplied, interpolates the string where necessary, and then strips any leading or trailing white space. The resultant string is then examined for special characters at the start and end of the string that define the mode and type of file to be opened.

The basic operators are the greater-than/less-than signs. The syntax is taken from the Unix shell, which uses a less-than sign to pass file contents to the standard input of a command. So, within Perl, to open the file you use

```
open(DATA, "<file.txt");
```

The use of a single < sign indicates that you want to open the file for read-only access—you cannot use the same filehandle to update the file without reassociating the filehandle with a suitable write or read/write statement. This is essentially equivalent to the following:

```
Open "file.txt" for Input access Read As 10
```

In VB, aside from the obvious lack of a numerical definition, the `Input` and `Read` arguments are implied by the single < character.

To write to a file, you use the greater-than sign:

```
open(DATA, ">file.txt");
```

This example actually truncates the file before opening it for writing, which may not be the desired effect. If you want to open a file for reading and writing, you put a plus sign before the > or < characters.

For example, to open a file for updating without truncating it:

```
open(DATA, "+<file.txt");
```

To truncate the file first:

```
open DATA, "+>file.txt";
```

This also demonstrates a basic principle of any programming: You must be able to track and trace errors. Perl has a simple but effective method of error checking that we'll see in various examples throughout the rest of the book.

In both of the previous cases, the file has been opened for updating, but the file pointer that describes the current position within the file is at the start. If you want to immediately append to a file, you can also use Unix shell-style operators:

```
open(DATA, ">file.txt");
```

A double >> opens the file for appending, placing the file pointer at the end, so that you can immediately start appending information. However, you can't read from it unless you also place a plus sign in front of it:

```
open(DATA, "+>>file.txt");
```

The list of available expressions and their VB equivalents are shown in Table 18-2. This is not a complete list of the supported options; see the manual pages or *Perl: The Complete Reference* for more details.

TABLE 18-2

Options for opening files.

Perl Expression	VB Expression	Result
"filename"	for Input Access Read	Opens the file for reading only.
"<filename"	for Input Access Read	Opens the file for reading only.
">filename"	for Output Access Write	Truncates and opens the file for writing.
"+<filename"	for Random Access Read Write	Opens the file for reading and writing.
"+>filename"	for Random Access Read Write	Truncates and opens the file for reading and writing.
">>filename"	for Append Access Read Write	Opens a file for read/write access, but places the file pointer at the end of the file.

Note that Perl doesn't distinguish between random and append access as VB does; if you have opened a file for read/write access using any of the methods in Table 18-2, then Perl allows you to move freely within the file and update the contents.

Also note that by default, all files are opened in a binary format—it's up to the functions and operators that you use to determine how the information is interpreted when you read from the file. See the discussion on the `<FILEHANDLE>` operator and `read` functions in the upcoming sections for more information.

close

To close a filehandle and therefore disassociate the filehandle from the corresponding file, you use the `close` function:

```
close FILEHANDLE
close
```

If no `FILEHANDLE` is specified, then it closes the currently selected file handle (see `select` in Appendix C). It returns `True` only if it could successfully flush the buffers and close the file. If you have been writing to a file, then `close` can be used as an effective method of checking that information has been successfully written. For example:

```
open(DATA,"+<data.txt") || die "Can't open data.txt";
    #do some work
close(DATA) || die "Couldn't close file properly";
```

However, if you are not worried about the file condition (for example, you are reading from a file), you do not need to close a filehandle before reassigning the filehandle to a new file. The `open` function implicitly closes the previous file before opening the new one, but be warned that there is no way of guaranteeing the file status in this way.

Reading and Writing Filehandles

Once you have an open filehandle, you need to be able to read and write information. There are a number of different ways of reading and writing data, although it's likely you'll stick to one or two methods that you find you prefer.

The <FILEHANDLE> operator

The main method of reading the information from an open filehandle is the <FILEHANDLE> operator. In a scalar context, it returns a single line from the filehandle. For example:

```
print "What is your name?\n";
$name = <STDIN>;
print "Hello $name\n";
```

By using the STDIN filehandle, which is always defined within a new script, you can read information from the keyboard. Note that the value of $name contains the entire line from the file, including the trailing newline character. You'll need to use chop or chomp to strip the newline from the end.

Also note that the line returned by the function only contains a newline, even though files under Windows are normally terminated by a carriage-return/newline character pair. Perl automatically does the translation for you to make migrating Unix scripts to Windows easier—see the binmode function later in this chapter for more information on reading data in binary mode.

More usually, you use the <FILEHANDLE> operator within a while statement:

```
while(<DATA>)
{
...
}
```

This actually implies a special operation within Perl—each line of the <DATA> filehandle will be placed into the $_ special variable, and the loop continues until the end of the file is reached.

You can also use the <FILEHANDLE> operator in a list context, where it returns a list of lines from the specified filehandle. For example, to import all the lines from a file into an array:

```
open(DATA,"<import.txt") or die "Can't open data";
@lines = <DATA>;
close(DATA);
```

NOTE. *Although this operation looks dangerous, Perl lets you go ahead and read the entire contents of a file into a single variable. Perl dynamically allocates all of the memory it needs. The only limitation is the amount of physical and virtual memory your machine has.*

Although it appears that <FILEHANDLE> only reads in lines from the file, you can specify a different record separator using the $/ or $INPUT_RECORD_SEPARATOR variable. You can therefore use the $/ variable and <FILEHANDLE> operator to read in character-delimited records from a file. For example, you could use Perl to read information from a file where the individual records are separated by ~ characters:

```
$/ = '~';
while (<FILE>)
{
...
}
```

You can also use the $/ variable and the local keyword to allow you to read the entire contents of a file into a scalar variable, using the first form of the operator:

```
{
    local $/;
    $file = <FILE>;
}
```

By using local, we are creating a local and empty version of the $/ variable. Without a character to use to separate each record in the source file, we read in the entire contents, and because there is no separator, it returns the contents as a single scalar.

getc

The getc function returns just a single character from the specified FILEHANDLE, or STDIN if none is specified:

```
getc FILEHANDLE
getc
```

If there was an error, or the filehandle is at the end of the file, then undef is returned instead. Unfortunately, because of the buffering on filehandles, you can't use it effectively to get nonbuffered single characters. See Chapter 10 for some alternatives.

read

Whereas the <FILEHANDLE> operator reads data from a filehandle using the input record separator, the read function reads a block of information from the buffered filehandle:

```
read FILEHANDLE, SCALAR, LENGTH, OFFSET
read FILEHANDLE, SCALAR, LENGTH
```

The length of the data read is defined by LENGTH, and the data is placed at the start of SCALAR if no OFFSET is specified. Otherwise, data is placed after OFFSET bytes in SCALAR, allowing you to append information from the filehandle to the existing scalar string. The function returns the number of bytes read on success, 0 at end of file, or undef if there was an error.

This function can be used to read fixed-length records from files, just like the system fread() function on which it is based. However, it must be used in combination with print and seek to ensure that the buffering system works correctly without overwriting existing data. For a more reliable method of reading and writing fixed-length data, see the sysread function in Appendix C.

print

For all the different methods used for reading information from filehandles, the main function for writing information back is the print function. Unlike C, in Perl, print is not just used for outputting information to the screen; it can be used to print information to any open filehandle. This is largely due to the way Perl structures its internal data. Because scalars are stored precisely, without using the traditional null termination seen in other languages, it's safe to use the print function to output both variable and fixed-length information. For example:

```
print FILEHANDLE LIST
print LIST
print
```

━━ ━━ ━━ ━━ ━━ ━━ ━━ ━━ ━━ ━━ ━━ ━━ ━━ ━━ ━━ ━━

WARNING.   *The most common error a new Perl programmer makes is to place a comma between the* FILEHANDLE *and* LIST. *This often causes undesired results, because to the* print *function, the comma makes* FILEHANDLE *the first element of the* LIST *to be evaluated and printed.*

The print function prints the evaluated value of LIST to FILEHANDLE, or to the current output filehandle (STDOUT by default). For example:

```
print "Hello World!\n";
```

or:

```
print "Hello", $name, "\nHow are you today?\n";
```

which prints

```
Hello Martin
How are you today?
```

Note that `LIST` rather than string interpolation is used in the last example. You can achieve the same result using a here document with the `print` function:

```
print <<EOT;
Hello $name
How are you today?
EOT
```

Because the argument to the `print` function is a `LIST`, the individual elements of the list are evaluated before the results are passed to `print`, which then outputs the values. You need to be careful when incorporating a `print` statement within a larger statement, especially one that itself uses a `LIST` context. For example, the line

```
print "Hello ", print "How are you today?";
```

actually prints

```
How are you today?Hello 1
```

The second element to the `print` function is evaluated first, resulting in the message, and then the resulting list values are output by `print`, which explains the 1—the return value from the nested `print` function.

To get around this problem, you can use parentheses to enclose the list of values for `print`:

```
print("Hello "),print "How are you today?";
```

which correctly outputs the message `Hello How are you today?`

However, care should be taken with the parentheses, since you can also get unexpected results:

```
print (1+2)*3, "\n";
```

Only the first calculation is printed, since the parser assumes the parentheses specify the `LIST` to the `print` function. The remaining values are ignored, since they no longer form part of a valid expression. Perl doesn't produce an error, because you are still defining valid Perl code—even the values of the list are never used.

The correct way to write the preceding equation is

```
print(((1+2)*3),"\n");
```

If no LIST is specified, then the print function prints out the value of $_.

printf

Although print is incredibly useful, it suffers from a lack of format. The Perl parser decides how a particular value is printed. This means that floating-point numbers are printed as such, when you may wish to restrict the number of places past the decimal point that the number is printed. Alternatively, you may wish to left- rather than right-justify strings when you print them:

```
printf FILEHANDLE FORMAT, LIST
printf FORMAT, LIST
```

Within VB, there is no direct way of printing and formatting information with one function—you need to use the Format and Print functions together to produce a formatted string. With Perl, printf allows you to do both at the same time. There is also a sprintf function, which is identical to printf except that it returns a formatted string instead of printing the string directly to the screen.

The printf and sprintf functions use a formatting string as the first element and format the remaining values in the list according to the format specified in the format string. Each format is called a *format conversion* and is made up of an initial percent sign, followed by some optional flags, and finally a single character that defines how the value in the list is printed. Each format conversion string relates to the corresponding value in the remainder of the argument list.

For example, the statement

```
printf "%d\n", 3.1415126;
```

only prints the number 3. The %d conversion format determines that an integer should be printed. Alternatively, you can define a "currency" format like this:

```
printf "The cost is $%6.2f\n",499;
```

TABLE 18-3

Conversion formats for `printf` and `sprintf`.

Format	Result
%%	A percent sign.
%c	A character with the given ASCII code.
%s	A string.
%d	A signed integer (decimal).
%u	An unsigned integer (decimal).
%o	An unsigned integer (octal).
%x	An unsigned integer (hexadecimal).
%X	An unsigned integer (hexadecimal using uppercase characters).
%e	A floating-point number (scientific notation).
%E	A floating-point number (scientific notation using E in place of e).
%f	A floating-point number (fixed decimal notation).
%g	A floating-point number (%e of %f notation according to value size).
%G	A floating-point number (as %g, but using E in place of e when appropriate).
%p	A pointer (prints the memory address of the value in hexadecimal).
%n	Stores the number of characters output so far into the next variable in the parameter list.
%i	A synonym for %d.
%D	A synonym for C %ld.
%U	A synonym for C %lu.
%O	A synonym for C %lo.
%F	A synonym for C %f.

which would print

```
The cost is $499.00
```

The `printf` function accepts the format conversions in Table 18-3.

Perl also supports flags that optionally adjust the output format. These are specified between the % and conversion letter, as shown in Table 18-4.

If you do not require a specific output format, you should use `print` in preference to `printf`, as it's faster and less prone to errors induced by the format string.

TABLE 18-4

Formatting flags for `printf`/ `sprintf` conversion formats.

Flag	Result
space	Prefix positive number with a space.
+	Prefix positive number with a plus sign.
-	Left-justify within field.
0	Use zeros, not spaces, to right-justify.
#	Prefix nonzero octal with `0` and hexadecimal with `0x`.
number	Minimum field width.
.number	Specify precision (number of digits after decimal point) for floating-point numbers.
l	Interpret integer as C type "long" or "unsigned long."
h	Interpret integer as C type "short" or "unsigned short."
V	Interpret integer as Perl's standard integer type.

Locating Your Position within a File

When reading and writing files using the standard line-based or record-based methods, you are normally processing individual records in sequence—outputting or formatting the results as you read in the entire file in sequence. However, if you are accessing fixed-length information—for example, a database—you are likely to require access to the information in a more random fashion. In order for this to work correctly, you need to be able to discover your current location and set a new location within the file.

tell

The seek function is equivalent to the VB `Loc` function; it returns your current location within a file:

```
tell FILEHANDLE
tell
```

This returns the position of the file pointer, in bytes, within FILEHANDLE if specified, or the current default selected filehandle if none is specified. The function returns undef if there is a problem getting the file position information, since a value of 0 could just indicate that you're at the start of the file.

seek

The seek function is equivalent to the VB Seek function and positions the file pointer to the specified number of bytes within a file:

```
seek FILEHANDLE, POSITION, WHENCE
```

The function uses the fseek system function, and you have the same ability to position relative to three different points: the start, end, and current position. You do this by specifying a value for WHENCE. The possible values are 0, 1, and 2 for positions relative to the start, current, and end of the file. If you import the IO::Seekable module, you can use the constants SEEK_SET, SEEK_CUR, and SEEK_END, respectively.

A value of 0 sets the positioning relative to the start of the file. For example, the line

```
seek DATA, 256, 0;
```

sets the file pointer to the 256th byte in the file. Using a value of 1 sets the position relative to the current position; so the line

```
seek DATA, 128, 1;
```

moves the file point onto byte 384, while the line

```
seek DATA, -128, SEEK_CUR;
```

moves back to byte 256.

A WHENCE value of 2 moves the file relative to the end of the file, and the value of POSITION is generally specified as a negative number. You can move to a point 80 bytes from the end of the file using a line like this:

```
seek DATA, -80, SEEK_END;
```

It's worth noting that the seek function resets the end-of-file condition. You can use the SEEK_CUR constant with a WHENCE value of 0 to achieve this, since the overall effect is to move nowhere. If you were to use the SEEK_SET or SEEK_END function, you'd have to use the tell function to discover the current location.

Miscellaneous File Control Functions

There are a few functions that do not conveniently fall into one of the sections we have already discussed. They are functions that primarily control the operation or control of a filehandle, or they may return some additional information for a specific filehandle.

binmode

On older operating systems, there is a distinction between textual and binary files. The difference occurs because Perl converts automatically between external file formats that contain two characters for line separation. We already know that Windows uses CR LF (carriage return/newline) to terminate lines, which Perl translates internally to LF, converting them back when information is written. For example:

```
binmode FILEHANDLE
```

This obviously causes a problem when opening files for binary access, since you will lose information in the internal representation and can corrupt the files due to the conversion process. To get around this problem, you can use the binmode function, which forces Perl to ignore line termination, thus preventing it from doing any form of conversion. To use it, open a filehandle and then call the binmode function with the new filehandle. For example:

```
open(DATA,"+<input.bin") or die "Couldn't open the file input.bin\n";
binmode(DATA) or die "Couldn't set binary mode on input.bin\n";
...
```

The binmode function returns the usual True/False on success/failure. Once set, there is no way to unset binary mode short of closing the filehandle and reopening it, although you're unlikely to want to change the format of an open file anyway.

eof

Although all functions and operators that read information automatically detect the end-of-file condition and return a suitable error code to the user, it is sometimes necessary to check the status outside of such a test. The eof function supports this action:

```
eof FILEHANDLE
```

If `eof` is specified with a `FILEHANDLE`, then it checks whether the next read from the specified filehandle will return an end-of-file condition. The function returns `True` if the end-of-file condition exists or `undef` otherwise.

Working with Strings

Once you've opened your file, you need to be able to parse the information within the file and extract the information contained within each line. Some of Perl's strongest features are in its ability to easily extract and work with string-based information.

Simple String Modifications

There are some simple modifications built into Perl as functions that may be more convenient and quicker than using the regular expressions we will cover later in this chapter. The four basic functions are `lc`, `uc`, `lcfirst`, and `ucfirst`. They convert a string to all lowercase, all uppercase, or only the first characters to lower- or uppercase, respectively:

```
lc EXPR
lc
lcfirst EXPR
lcfirst
uc EXPR
uc
ucfirst EXPR
ucfirst
```

In each case, the `$_` variable is modified if you do not specify an expression. The most obvious use of these functions is to change the case of a supplied expression when displaying or formatting text. You can also use the `lc` and `uc` functions to "normalize" a string so that when you are doing comparisons, or using a variable as the key to a hash element, every string is the same upper- or lowercase.

When you read in data from a file handle using a `while` or other loop and the `<FH>` operator, the trailing newline on the file remains in the string that you import. It's often the case that you are processing the data contained within each line and do not want the newline character. The `chop` function can be used to strip the last character off of any expression:

```
while(<FH>)
{
    chop;
...
}
```

The only danger with the `chop` function is that it strips the last character from the line irrespective of what the last character was.

The `chomp` function works in combination with the `$/` variable when reading from filehandles. It is the record separator that is attached to the records you read from a filehandle, which is by default set to the newline character. The `chomp` function works by removing the last character from a string only if it matches the value of `$/`. To do a safe strip from a record of the record separator character, just use it in place of `chop`:

```
while(<FH>)
{
    chomp;
...
}
```

Using `chomp` is a much safer option, as it guarantees that the data of a record will remain intact, irrespective of the last character type.

Substrings

Within Visual Basic, strings are generally stored as arrays of characters. To access an individual character from a string, you just directly access the character number within the array. Because Perl does not use the same system for storing strings, we need to use a different method.

To access an individual character within a string, you need to determine the location of the character within the string and access that element of the array. Perl does not support this option, because often you are not working with the individual characters within the string, but the string as a whole.

Two functions, `index` and `rindex`, can be used to find the position of a particular character or string of characters within another string:

```
index STR, SUBSTR, POSITION
index STR, SUBSTR
rindex STR, SUBSTR, POSITION
rindex STR, SUBSTR
```

The `index` function works the same way as the VB `InStr` function and returns the first position of SUBSTR within the string STR or - 1 if the string cannot be found. If the POSITION argument is specified, then the search starts from that many characters in the string (from the beginning). The rindex function is equivalent to the VB InStrRev function, it returns the opposite of the index function—the last occurrence of SUBSTR in STR or - 1 if the substring could not be found. If POSITION is specified, then it starts from that many characters from the end of the string.

The substr function can be used to extract a substring from another string based on the position of the first character and the number of characters you want to extract. This is the same as the Left$ and Right$ functions in VB, but combined into a single function within Perl:

```
substr EXPR, OFFSET, LENGTH, REPLACEMENT
substr EXPR, OFFSET, LENGTH
substr EXPR, OFFSET
```

The EXPR is the string that is being extracted from. Data is extracted from a starting point of OFFSET characters from the start of EXPR or, if the value is negative, that many characters from the end of the string. The optional LENGTH parameter defines the number of characters to be read from the string. If it is not specified, then all characters to the end of the string are extracted. Alternatively, if the number specified in LENGTH is negative, then that many characters are left off the end of the string. For example, the script

```
$string = 'The cat sat on the mat';
print substr($string,4),"\n";
print substr($string,4,3),"\n";
print substr($string,-7),"\n";
print substr($string,4,-4),"\n";
```

should print

```
cat sat on the mat
cat
the mat
cat sat on the
```

The last example is equivalent to

```
print substr($string,4,14),"\n";
```

But it may be more effective to use the first form if you have used the rindex function to return the last occurrence of a space within the string.

You can also use `substr` to replace segments of a string with another string. With the four-argument version of the command, the REPLACE-MENT argument is the string that you want to use as the replacement text. For example:

```
substr($string,4,3,'dog');
print "$string\n";
```

Alternatively, the `substr` function can also work as an assignable value, so you can replace the characters in the expression you specify with another value. For example, the statement

```
substr($string,4,3) = 'dog';
print "$string\n";
```

should print the dog sat on the mat, because we replaced the word cat, starting at the fourth character and lasting for three characters.

The assignment works intelligently, shrinking or growing the string according to the size of the string you assign, so you can replace dog with computer programmer like this:

```
substr($string,4,3) = 'computer programmer';
print "$string\n";
```

Specifying values of zero allows you to prepend strings to other strings by specifying an OFFSET of 0, although it's arguably easier to use concatenation to achieve the same result. Appending with `substr` is not so easy; you cannot specify beyond the last character, although you could use the output from `length` to calculate where that might be. In these cases a simple

```
$string .= 'programming';
```

is definitely easier.

split

When reading files that contain delimited data, you need to extract each field from the record by splitting the text on the delimited character. You could do this with the `index` and `substr` functions, but Perl provides a much cleaner solution in the form of the `split` function. The `split` function separates a scalar or other string expression into a list, using a regular expression. For example:

```
split /PATTERN/, EXPR, LIMIT
split /PATTERN/, EXPR
split /PATTERN/
split
```

If you do not specify a pattern, then `split` splits `$_`, using white space as the separator pattern. This also has the effect of skipping the leading white space in `$_`. For reference, white space includes spaces, tabs (vertical and horizontal), line feeds, carriage returns, and form feeds.

The `PATTERN` can be any standard regular expression (see "Regular Expressions" later in this chapter). You can use quotes to specify the separator, but you should instead use the match operator and regular expression syntax—the forward slash is the default operator recognized by Perl.

If you specify a `LIMIT`, then it only splits for `LIMIT` elements. If there is any remaining text in `EXPR`, it is returned as the last element with all characters in text. Otherwise, the entire string is split, and the full list of separated values is returned. If you specify a negative value, Perl acts as if a huge value has been supplied and splits the entire string, including trailing null fields.

For example, to split a line from a CSV (comma-separated value) file by the commas used to identify the individual fields:

```
while (<CSV>)
{
    @fields = split /,/;
}
```

NOTE.   *You cannot use this to extract data from CSV files exported by Excel and similar software, since they also quote information that could contain a comma. You'll need to use a regular expression match to extract the information from those files.*

You can also use all of the normal list and array constructs to extract and combine values:

```
print join(" ",split /:/),"\n";
```

and even extract only select fields:

```
print "User: ",(split /:/)[0],"\n";
```

If you specify a null string, it splits EXPR into individual characters, such that

```
print join('-',split(/ */, 'Hello World')),"\n";
```

produces

```
H-e-l-l-o-W-o-r-l-d
```

Note that the space is ignored.

join

When you use the print function to print an array, the value of $, is used to separate the individual elements:

```
$, = '::';
print @array,"\n";
```

The default value for $, is nothing, and you should be aware that if you specify the array within double quotes, the value used is always a space.
    When you want to create a new scalar containing a list of separated elements, you have to use the join function:

```
join EXPR, LIST
```

This combines the elements of LIST, returning a scalar where each element is separated by the value of EXPR to separate each element. Note that EXPR is a simple expression, not a regular expression:

```
print join(', ',@users);
```


sort

With any list data, whether contained in an array or returned by another function, it can be useful to sort the contents. Doing this manually is a complex process, so Perl provides a built-in function that takes a list and returns a lexically sorted version. For practicality, it also accepts a function or block that can be used to create your own sorting algorithm.

For example:

```
sort SUBNAME LIST
sort BLOCK LIST
sort LIST
```

Both the subroutine and block (which is an anonymous subroutine) should return a value—less than, greater than, or equal to zero—depending on whether the two elements of the list are less than, greater than, or equal to each other. The two elements of the list are available in the $a and $b variables.

For example, to do a standard lexical sort:

```
sort @array;
```

Or to specify an explicit lexical subroutine:

```
sort { $a cmp $b } @array;
```

To perform a reverse lexical sort:

```
sort { $b cmp $a } @array;
```

All the preceding examples take into account the differences between upper- and lowercase. You can use the lc or uc functions within the subroutine to ignore the case of the individual values. The individual elements are not actually modified; it only affects the values compared during the sort process:

```
sort { lc($a) cmp lc($b) } @array;
```

If you know you are sorting numbers, you need to use the <=> operator:

```
sort { $a <=> $b } @numbers;
```

Alternatively, to use a separated routine:

```
sub lexical
{
    $a cmp $b;
}
sort lexical @array;
```

reverse

On a sorted list you can use sort to return a list in reverse order by changing the comparison statement used in the sort. However, it can be quicker, and more practical for unsorted lists, to use the `reverse` function:

```
reverse LIST
```

In a list context the function returns the elements of `LIST` in reverse order. This is often used with the `sort` function to produce a reverse sorted list:

```
foreach (reverse sort keys %hash)
{
...
}
```

In a scalar context it returns a concatenated string of the values of `LIST`, with all bytes in opposite order. This also works if a single element list or a scalar is supplied, such that

```
print scalar reverse("Hello World"),"\n";
```

produces

```
dlroW olleH
```

Regular Expressions

Using the functions we've seen so far for finding your location within a string and updating that string are fine if you know precisely what you are looking for. Often, however, what you are looking for is either a range of characters or a specific pattern, perhaps matching a range of individual words, letters, or numbers separated by other elements. These patterns are impossible to emulate using the `substr` and `index` functions because they rely on using a fixed string as the search criteria.

Identifying patterns instead of strings within Perl is as easy as writing the correct regular expression. A *regular expression* is a string of characters that define the pattern or patterns you are viewing. Of course, writing the correct regular expression is the more difficult part. There are tricks to make the format of a regular expression easier to read, but there is no easy way of making a regular expression easier to understand!

The syntax of regular expressions in Perl is very similar to what you will find within other regular expressions—supporting programs, including that built into Microsoft Word's "pattern matching" replacement tool. The characters used are slightly different, but many of the basic principles are the same.

The basic method for applying a regular expression is to use the pattern binding operators =~ and !~. The first operator is a test and assignment operator. In a test context (called a *match* in Perl), the operator returns True if the value on the left-hand side of the operator matches the regular expression on the right. In an assignment context (substitution), it modifies the statement on the left based on the regular expression on the right. The second operator, !~, is for tests only and is the exact opposite: It returns True only if the value on the left does not match the regular expression on the right.

The statements on the right-hand side of the two test and assignment operators must be regular expression operators. There are two regular expression operators within Perl—m// (match) and s/// (substitute) The match operator, m//, is used to match a string or statement to a regular expression. For example, to match the word *foo* against the scalar $bar, you might use a statement like this:

```
if ($bar =~ m/foo/)
```

Provided the delimiters in your statement with the m// operators are forward slashes, you can omit the leading m:

```
if ($bar =~ /foo/)
```

However, you must use m// if you want to specify delimiters other than the forward slash. This can be useful if your regular expression contains the forward slash that would otherwise need escaping.

For example, let's imagine you want to check on whether the $dir variable contains a particular directory. The delimiter for directories is the forward slash and would look messy if you had to escape each occurrence:

```
if ($dir =~ /\/usr\/local\/lib/)
```

By using a different delimiter, you can use a much clearer regular expression:

```
if ($dir =~ m(/usr/local/lib))
```

You can, in fact, use any character as a delimiter—even letters and numbers. Just remember that the aim is to make the code easier to understand.

It's also worth noting that the entire match statement (including the $~) actually returns all of the elements that match in the regular expression. The following example attempts to match a time specified in hours, minutes, and seconds using colons as separators:

```
my ($hours, $minutes, $seconds) = ($time =~ m/(\d+):(\d+):(\d+)/);
```

This example uses grouping and a character class to specify the individual elements. The groupings are the elements in standard parentheses, and each one will match (we hope) in sequence, returning a list that has been assigned to the hours, minutes, and seconds variables. The rest of this chapter will cover all the details of this.

There is also a simpler version of the match operator—the ?PATTERN? operator. This is basically identical to the m// operator except that it only matches once. To match the same pattern/operator sequence again, you must use the reset operator. The operator works as a useful optimization of the matching process when you want to search a set of data streams, but only want to match once within each stream.

The substitution operator, s///, is more complex than the match operator, although the basic principles remain the same. The first "argument" within the delimiters is the regular expression that we are looking for. The second argument to the delimiters is a specification for the text or regular expression that we want to replace the found elements with. For example, you may remember from the preceding substr definition that you could replace a specific number of characters within a string by using assignment, as in

```
$string = 'The cat sat on the mat';
$start  = index($string,'cat',0);
$end    = index($string,' ',$start)-$start;
substr($string,$start,$end) = 'dog';
```

You can achieve the same result with a regular expression:

```
$string = 'The cat sat on the mat';
$string =~ s/cat/dog/;
```

Note that we have managed to avoid the process of finding the start and end of the string we want to replace. This is a fundamental part of understanding the regular expression syntax. A regular expression will match the text anywhere within the string. You do not have to specify the starting point or location within the string, although it is possible to do so if that's what you want. Taking this to its logical conclusion, we can use the same regular expression to replace the word *cat* with *dog* in any string, irrespective of the location of the original word:

```
$string = 'Oscar is my cat';
$string =~ s/cat/dog/;
```

The $string variable now contains the phrase Oscar is my dog, which is factually incorrect, but it does demonstrate the ease with which you can replace strings with other strings.

Here's a more complex example that we will return to later. In this instance, we need to change a date in the form 03/26/1999 to 19990326. Using grouping again, we can change it very easily with a regular expression:

```
$date = '03/26/1999';
$date =~ s#(\d+)/(\d+)/(\d+)#\3\1\2#;
```

This example also demonstrates the fact that you can use delimiters other than the forward slash for substitutions too. Just like the match operator, the character used is the one immediately following the s. Alternatively, if you specify a naturally paired delimiter such as a brace, then the replacement expression can have its own pair of delimiters:

```
$date =~ s{(\d+)/(\d+)/(\d+)}
          {\3\1\2}x;
```

There are also some functions that accept regular expressions as arguments. In these instances, the format is the same as for a match operator without the leading m. For example:

```
my @words = split(/ /,$sentence);
```

The delimiters are still required to tell Perl that the argument is a regular expression. The regular expression also uses exactly the same format as the operators, and we'll examine this next.

Regular Expression Elements

The regular expression engine is responsible for parsing the regular expression and matching the elements of the regular expression with the string supplied. Depending on the context of the regular expression, different results will occur: A substitution replaces character sequences, for example.

The regular expression syntax is best thought of as a little language in its own right. It's very powerful, and an incredible amount of ability is compacted into a very small space. Like all languages though, a regular expression is composed of a number of discrete elements, and if you understand those individual elements, you can understand the entire regular expression.

For most characters and character sequences, the interpretation is literal, so a substitution to replace every occurrence of cat with dog can be as simple as

```
s/cat/dog/;
```

Additional functionality is provided by a number of metacharacters. These have special meaning within the context of a regular expression, and they are summarized in Table 18-5.

The first metacharacter is the backslash. If it is followed by an alphanumeric character, it has special meaning, which we'll examine shortly. If what follows is a metacharacter, the backslash acts as an escape and forces the regular expression engine to interpret the following character as a literal. To insert a backslash, for example, you would use a double backslash:

```
m/\\/;
```

TABLE 18-5

Regular expression metacharacters.

Metacharacter(s)	Description
\	Treats the following metacharacter as a real character, ignoring any associations with a Perl regular expression metacharacter. Known as the escape character.
^	Matches from the beginning of the string (or the line if /m modifier is in place).
$	Matches from the end of the string (or the line if /m modifier is in place).
.	Matches any character except the newline character.
|	Allows you to specify alternate matches within the same regexp. Known as the OR operator.
( )	Groups expressions together.
[]	Looks for a set of characters.

The ^ metacharacter matches the beginning of the string. The line below would only return `True` if the character sequence `cat` were present at the beginning of `$string`:

```
if ($string =~ /^cat/)
```

Note that I've used *character sequence* in the description above. This is because regular expressions take the characters specified literally as they are written. So the above test would not only match "cat is a furry animal" but also "cationic surfactant" and "caterpillar," and indeed, any string whose first three characters are *c*, *a*, and *t*. You'll see later how to refine the search.

The `$` operator matches the end of the string:

```
if ($string =~ /cat^/)
```

So, the above example only matches when the `cat` character sequence is at the end of the string being matched.

The . (period) character is a wildcard and matches any single character (except the newline) in a string. The expression

```
if ($string =~ /c.t/)
```

would therefore match any sequence of `c` followed by any character and then `t`. This would, for example, match "cat" or "cot," or indeed, words such as "acetic" and "acidification."

The | character is just like the standard or bitwise `OR` within Perl. It specifies alternate matches within a regular expression or group. For example, to match `cat` or `dog` in the expression, you might use

```
if ($string =~ /cat|dog/)
```

You can group individual elements of an expression together in order to support complex matches. Searching for two people's names could be achieved with two separate tests like this:

```
if (($string =~ /Martin Brown/) ||
    ($string =~ /Sharon Brown/))
```

You could write this more efficiently in a single regular expression like this:

```
if ($string =~ /(Martin|Sharon) Brown/)
```

The use of grouping here is vital. By using a group, the code looks for `Martin  Brown` **or** `Sharon  Brown` because the `OR` operation simply works on either side of the | metacharacter. Had you written

```
if ($string =~ /Martin|Sharon Brown/)
```

the regular expression would match either `Martin` **or** `Sharon  Brown`, which may or may not be what you want. In general, the use of grouping with the | metacharacter follows the same rules as the logical operators elsewhere in Perl.

Finally, as you've already seen in the previous examples, groupings have special results when used with both the match and substitution operators. In either case, each grouping is given a number, in the sequence of each leading open parenthesis. With a match operator, the resulting match for each group is returned as a list:

```
my ($hours, $minutes, $seconds) = ($time =~ m/(\d+):(\d+):(\d+)/);
```

Each group is also recorded in the special variables $1, $2, $3, and so on, so the preceding example could be rewritten as

```
$time =~ m/(\d+):(\d+):(\d+)/;
my ($hours, $minutes, $seconds) = ($1, $2, $3);
```

In the case of substitution, each matched group is also available as a replacement. So, using the preceding date string example:

```
$date = '03/26/1999';
$date =~ s#(\d+)/(\d+)/(\d+)#$3$1$2#;
```

Each element of the date is placed into the temporary variables, so the month (group 1) is in \1, the day is in group 2, and the year is in group 3. To convert to the number format, you just need to specify each element in the desired order—in this example, year, month, day. The resulting string is `19990326`. The matched groups are perpetual—that is, you can also access each matched group outside of the substitution expression. Obviously, the next regular expression executed resets all of the values.

When working with nested groups, you must remember that the numbering system keys on the first opening parenthesis, as demonstrated by the following code:

```
$date = '03/26/1999';
$date =~ s#((\d+)/(\d+)/(\d+))#Date \1 = \4\2\3#;
print "$date\n";
```

This prints

```
Date 03/26/1999 = 19990326
```

The first parenthesis matches the whole date string; the nested parentheses then match the individual year, month, and day of the date.

The final metacharacter(s) are the [] parentheses. These allow you to specify a list of values for a single character. This can be useful if you want to find a name that may or may not have been specified with a leading capital letter:

```
if ($name =~ /[Mm]artin/)
```

Within the [] metacharacters you can also specify lists, such as a-z for all lowercase characters, 0-9 for numbers, and so on. If you want to specify a hyphen, use a backslash within the class to prevent Perl from trying to produce a range. If you want to match a right square bracket (which would otherwise be interpreted as a character class), use a backslash or place it first in the list, for example [[]].

Beyond the metacharacters above, you can also use special backslashed character sequences to specify assertions and specific characters for the regular expression. For example, there are sequences to match the beginning and end of a word, and also sequences to match alphanumeric and nonalphanumeric characters. The sequences are shown in Table 18-6.

Many entries in Table 18-6 should be self-explanatory, although some warrant special consideration.

The \w and \W sequences match alphanumeric characters and nonalphanumeric characters, respectively. So, to split up a string on its words, you might use a regular expression like this:

```
($worda, $wordb, $wordc) = $string =~ /(\w+)\W+(\w+)\W+(\w+)/;
```

This checks for an alphanumeric string of one or more characters followed by a string of nonalphanumeric characters. The nonalphanumeric string matches spaces, punctuation, and tabs; and by specifying a multiplier, you can catch any number of these in sequence.

If you want to match white space—that is, spaces and tabs—use the \s sequence. This is best used when trying to import the contents of a text file that has fields separated by multiple spaces, tabs, or a combination of both. The inverse will catch anything that is not white space, even punctuation.

TABLE 18-6

Regular expression
character patterns.

Sequence	Purpose
\w	Matches an alphanumeric character (including _).
\W	Matches a nonalphanumeric character.
\s	Matches a white-space character (spaces, tabs).
\S	Matches a non-white-space character.
\d	Matches a digit.
\D	Matches a nondigit character.
\b	Matches a word boundary.
\B	Matches a non—word boundary.
\A	Matches only the beginning of a string.
\Z	Matches only at the end of a string.
\G	Matches where previous m//g operation left off (only works with /g modifier).
\t	Specifies a tab.
\n	Specifies a newline.
\r	Specifies a carriage return.
\f	Specifies a form feed.
\a	Specifies an alarm (bell).
\e	Specifies an escape.
\b	Specifies a backspace.
\033	Specifies an octal character.
\x1B	Specifies a hex character.
\c[	Specifies a control character.
\l	Makes the next character lowercase.
\u	Makes the next character uppercase.
\L	Specifies lowercase till \E.
\U	Specifies uppercase till \E.
\E	Ends case modification.
\Q	Quotes (disables) regular expression metacharacters till \E.

The \d sequence forces identification of the character as a digit. The match is strict, such that if you want to match periods or commas often used to separate elements of numbers, then you must specify them additionally within a set:

```
if ('23,445.33' =~ m/([\d,.]+)/)
```

A *word boundary* is defined as any character that would, in your locality, act as a word separator. In English, this means spaces and punctuation but does not include hyphens or underscores.

In many of the preceding examples, you'll see a quantifier—a special character or sequence that defines the number of times the previous sequence or character appears. Using a quantifier, you can specify that a sequence must appear a minimum or maximum number of times, or that a character can repeat indefinitely until the next regular expression element. Table 18-7 shows the supported quantifiers.

The * and + operators match 0 or more, or 1 or more items. By using a pattern of /.*/, you can match everything (although this seems rather pointless), or with /.+/, you can match nothing. The brace specifications allow you to specify a range of repetitions. Following are some examples and equivalencies:

```
m/.{0}/;      #Matches no characters
m/.{1,}/;      #Matches any character at least once, equivalent to /.+/
m/\d{2,4}/; #Matches any digit at least two and a maximum of four times
```

In Table 18-7 entries in the left-hand (Maximal) column will match the maximum number of times. This means that the quantifier will soak up all the characters it can before it attempts the next match in the reg-

TABLE 18-7

Regular expression
pattern quantifiers.

Maximal	Minimal	Purpose
*	*?	Matches 0 or more items.
+	+?	Matches 1 or more items.
?	??	Matches 0 or 1 items.
{n}	{n}?	Matches exactly n times.
{n,}	{n,}?	Matches at least n times.
{n,m}	{n,m}?	Matches at least n times but no more than m times.

ular expression. The Minimal column shows the sequence that will match the minimum number of times before the next element of the regular expression is matched. The following code demonstrates the effect:

```
$string = "There was a food shortage in foodham";
print "Maximal:",($string =~ /(.*)foo/),"\n";
print "Minimal:",($string =~ /(.*?)foo/),"\n";
```

If you run this, the result is

```
Maximal:There was a food shortage in
Minimal:There was a
```

You can modify the overall effect of the regular expression match using a number of modifiers. Some apply to both the match and substitution operators and are shown in Table 18-8.

Although referred to here as /x modifiers, they do, of course, follow the characters used to parenthesize the entire expression. For example, the regular expression s#/#:#x may use a hash character for separation, but it still has the /x modifier invoked.

The /g modifier forces a match or substitution to occur globally within the string. For example, using s/foo/bar/g will replace all occurrences of foo with bar. Without this operator, only the match for foo will be replaced with bar. In a list context, the m//g returns a list of values matched by any parenthesized elements of the regular expression, or if no parentheses are specified, then it returns a list of all the matches.

TABLE 18-8

Perl regular expression modifiers for matching and substitution.

Modifier	Description
g	Matches/replaces globally every occurrence within a string, not just the first.
i	Makes the match case-insensitive.
m	Specifies that if the string has newline or carriage return characters, the ^ and $ operators (in Table 18-5) match the start and end of the string, rather than individual lines.
o	Evaluates the expression only once.
s	Allows use of . to match a newline character.
x	Allows you to use white space in the expression for clarity.
e	Evaluates replacement string as an expression (substitution only).

In a scalar `m//g` statement, this means that the pattern match iterates through the string and returns `True` (the value of the match). Repetitive matches using the same regular expression and string return each occurrence of the match. If you modify the string in any way, the start position is reset to the beginning of the string. You can use the `pos` function to return the position of where the last `m//g` match left off. Here's an example that counts sentences ending in a period, question mark, or exclamation mark:

```
$/ = "";
while ($para = <>)
{
    while ($para =~ /[a-z]['")]*[.!?]+['")]*\s/g)
    {
        $sentences++;
    }
}
print "Sentence count: $sentences\n";
```

The `/i` modifier ignores case in the regular expression search. Thus, the expression `/foo/i` will match `foo`, `FOO` and indeed, `Foo`. For a more specific case match, use the set, `[]`, expression, as in `/[fF]oo/`, which will match only `Foo` and `foo`.

If the string you are trying to match contains multiple lines, it should be classed as a multiline string using the `/m` modifier. Without this specification, the `^` and `$` metacharacters will match the beginning and end of the entire string. With this modifier, they match the beginning and end of individual lines within the string. If you still want to match the beginning and end of the entire string, use the `\A` and `\Z` qualifiers.

If the match pattern that you specify includes variables, they will be interpolated as normal into the regular expression each time the pattern is evaluated. You can restrict the evaluation of the pattern to occur only once with the `/o` modifier. This lets you tell Perl that you will not be modifying the values of the variables during the script. This can improve performance, since it avoids runtime compilations of the expression. The problem is that with this modifier, even if you do change the values, Perl won't take any notice of them. You should therefore make sure that the value you are interpolating will not change; otherwise, you may not get the response you expect.

By default, the `.` metacharacter does not match a newline character in a string. In most cases this is the behavior you want. However, if you are matching a multiline string, perhaps with the `/m` modifier as well, then you may want the period to match a newline character. The `/s` operator enables this behavior.

The final modifier that affects both matches and substitution is the /x modifier. Regular expressions can be very complicated when written down as a single line. For example, it's not immediately obvious what this regular expression is doing:

```
$matched =~ /(\S+)\s+(\S+)\s+(\S+)\s+\[(.*)\]\s+"(.*)"\s+(\S+)\s+(\S+)/;
```

However, by specifying the /x modifier, you can insert white space and even newlines and comments into the regular expression to make the expression clearer and easier to understand. The preceding example actually processes a standard web log and could be rewritten as:

```
matched - /(\S+)     #Host.
         \s+         #(space separator)
         (\S+)       #Identifier
         \s+         #(space separator)
         (\S+)       #Username
         \s+         #(space separator)
         \[(.*)\]    #Time
         \s+         #(space separator)
         "(.*)"          #Request
         \s+         #(space separator)
         (\S+)       #Result
         \s+         #(space separator)
         (\S+)       #Bytes sent
         /x;
```

Although it takes up more editor and page space, it is much clearer what you are trying to achieve.

The /e modifier allows you to specify a replacement text that will be evaluated as an expression (a standard Perl expression, not a regular expression). This is basically equivalent to an eval, but the expression is syntax-checked at compile time rather than at execution time. By using a combination of grouping and the expression modifier, you can perform specific functions on individual elements of a string. The following example is a typical regular expression used to extract the "quoted" elements of a URL during CGI programming. Quoted elements within a URL are expressed as the ASCII value of the character to be quoted, preceded by a percent sign:

```
$value =~ s/%([a-fA-F0-9][a-fA-F0-9])/pack("C", hex($1))/eg;
```

Note that you have to use the $1 syntax. The \1 syntax only works within a regular expression, which the function above is not strictly a part of.

Supporting Functions

When you've performed a match, you can find the location within the string at the point where the regular expression stopped checking for new matches within an m//g regular expression:

```
pos SCALAR
post
```

The pos function returns the location for SCALAR if specified or $_ if no scalar is specified. For example:

```
$string = "The food is in the salad bar";
$string =~ m/foo/g;
print pos($string),"\n";
```

should print a value of 7—the number of characters read before the match operator stopped looking for new entries (because there weren't any).

In Table 18-6 you should have noticed the \Q sequence, which prevented the regular expression engine from interpreting metacharacters or sequences as special values within a regular expression. This effect is actually achieved by the general Perl function quotemeta:

```
quotemeta EXPR
quotemeta
```

The function replaces any nonalphanumeric (that is not matching [a-zA-Z0-9]) character with a backslash version. For example, the string

```
print quotemeta "[Foobar!]";
```

will return

```
\[Foobar\!\]
```

If you do not specify an expression, then the value of $_ will be quoted instead.

Translation

Translation is similar, but not identical, to the principles of substitution. Unlike regular expressions, translation is used to convert characters. For instance:

```
tr/SEARCHLIST/REPLACEMENTLIST/cds
y/SEARCHLIST/REPLACEMENTLIST/cds
```

The translation replaces all occurrences of the characters in SEARCH-LIST with the corresponding characters in REPLACEMENTLIST. For example, using the original version of the string we have been using in this chapter:

```
$string =~ tr/a/o/;
print "$string\n";
```

The script prints out The cot sot on the mot. Standard Perl ranges can also be used, allowing you to specify ranges of characters either by letter or numerical value. To change the case of the string, you might use

```
$string =~ tr/a-z/A-Z/;
```

in place of the uc function. The tr operator only works on a scalar or single element of an array or hash; you cannot use it directly against an array or hash. You can also use it with any reference or function that can be assigned to—for example, to convert the word *cat* from the string to uppercase, you could do

```
substr($string,4,3) =~ tr/a-z/A-Z/;
```

Unlike regular expressions, the SEARCHLIST and REPLACEMENTLIST arguments to the operator do not need to use the same delimiters. As long as the SEARCHLIST is naturally paired with delimiters such as parentheses or braces, the REPLACEMENTLIST can use its own pair. This makes the conversion of forward slashes clearer than the traditional regular expression search:

```
$macdir = tr(/)/:/;
```

The same feature can be used to make certain character sequences seem clearer, such as the one that follows, which converts an 8-bit string into a 7-bit string, albeit with some loss of information:

```
tr [\200-\377]
   [\000-\177]
```

Three modifiers are supported by the tr operator, as seen in Table 18-9.

TABLE 18-9

Modifiers to the
tr operator.

Modifier	Meaning
c	Complement SEARCHLIST.
d	Delete found but unreplaced characters.
s	Squash duplicate replaced characters.

The /c modifier changes the replacement text to be the characters not specified in SEARCHLIST. You might use this to replace characters other than those specified in the SEARCHLIST with a null alternative. For example:

```
$string = 'the cat sat on the mat.';
$string =~ tr/a-zA-Z/-/c;
print "$string\n";
```

replaces any noncharacter with a hyphen.

The /d modifier, in addition to performing a standard translation, also deletes any characters defined in SEARCHLIST that do not have a corresponding translation in REPLACEMENTLIST. For example:

```
$string = 'the cat sat on the mat.';
$string =~ tr/a-z/b/d;
print "$string\n";
```

translates the character a to b, and then deletes the characters that do not have a translation—this actually results in the translation deleting the characters b-z from the original string. This gives a resultant string of b b   b. Note as well that the . character remains unchanged, because it wasn't defined in the SEARCHLIST. It becomes even clearer if we use a mixed-case statement:

```
$string = 'The Cat Sat on the Mat';
$string =~ tr/at/b/d;
print "$string\n";
```

which produces the string The Cb Sb on he Mb. The a has been translated to b, and the t deleted.

The last modifier, /s, removes the duplicate sequences of characters that were replaced; so

```
tr/a-zA-Z/ /s;
```

replaces any alphanumeric characters with a single space.

If you do not specify the REPLACEMENTLIST, Perl uses the values in SEARCHLIST. This is most useful for doing character-class-based counts, something that cannot be done with the length function. For example, to count the alphanumeric characters in a string:

```
$cnt = $string =~ tr/a-zA-Z0-9//s;
```

If you use the /c option, you can count the opposite—that is, the characters not defined in REPLACEMENT list:

```
$cnt = $string =~ tr/a-zA-Z0-9//cs;
```

In all cases, the tr operator returns the number of characters changed (including those deleted).

Appendixes

Appendix A

Resource Guide

Your main port of call for further information should be the supplied documentation, but there are other places that you can look for information about using Perl on Windows. Because the main version of Perl under Windows is supported by ActiveState, a visit to their website will yield some information of use—although most of it is included with the documentation that is installed when you first install the interpreter.

Since its release, Perl has been heavily supported on the Internet, with numerous Usenet newsgroups, websites, and e-mail mailing lists for you to choose from. Whatever you are looking for about Perl, the chances are it's on the Internet somewhere. For more traditional methods, there are literally hundreds of books out there to choose from.

In this appendix I've tried to include the resources that I use most often when programming Perl—it includes a mixture of desktop and computer-based sources.

Online Documentation

The ActiveState installers all include a full set of online documentation that can be viewed with any suitable Web browser. You'll need something that is able to display frames to see the documentation properly: Netscape Communicator/Navigator 4.x or Internet Explorer 4.x or above.

The documentation installed includes

- Complete guide to the ActivePerl applications, release notes, an installation guide, and information on using the Perl Package Manager (PPM) to install additional third-party modules.

- ActivePerl component guide to the different ActivePerl application packages.

- A Frequently Asked Questions (FAQ) section that covers both Win32-specific queries and compatibility queries when you are moving from the Unix platform.

- HTML versions of all the core Perl documentation normally supplied with the Unix version of the Perl interpreter, including the FAQ sections.

- HTML versions of all the POD documentation included within the Perl standard library.

- Documentation for all the Win32 modules supplied as standard with the ActivePerl distribution.

631

You can access the documentation through the Start menu.

Other Applications

Although the Win32 distributions come with a huge amount of documentation, they often fail to mention many of the intricacies of programming the Windows platform. All of the documentation supplied takes a number of liberties and assumes an awful lot about the readers' knowledge of the Windows platform.

The best source for further information about what some of the features, functions, and constants really mean is the Microsoft Developer Network documentation that comes with any of the Visual Studio development products. If you don't have access to a Visual Studio product, you can try the online Developer Network site on the Web. See below for details on how to access the site.

Printed Material

Although it's impossible to list all the books, journals, and other publications that promote Perl as a programming language, there are some standard books that all Perl programmers should probably keep on their bookshelf.

Books

***Perl Annotated Archives*. Brown, M. C. 1999. Berkeley, CA: Osborne McGraw-Hill**

The Annotated Archives series takes real-world scripts, and then annotates them on a line-by-line basis to demonstrate the semantics of the Perl language, and the algorithms and tricks required to complete the program. The title includes scripts for processing text files and logs, using Perl for networking. There is even a special section on developing and managing websites using Perl. The book should help both beginners and advanced users, and it is an excellent companion to *Perl: The Complete Reference*.

***Perl: Complete Reference.* Brown, M. C. 1999. Berkeley, CA: Osborne McGraw-Hill**

Perl: The Complete Reference is a complete guide to programming in Perl. Everything from the simple semantics of the language through to writing a cross-platform compatible script, writing extensions, and even the new Perl compiler and threads options are included.

***Perl Programmers Reference.* Brown, M. C. 1999. Berkeley, CA: Osborne McGraw-Hill**

A condensed version of *Perl: The Complete Reference*, this contains a quick reference guide to the features you will probably use most often within Perl. This includes the semantics, built-in functions, the standard Perl library, and the Perl debugger.

***Cross-Platform Perl.* Johnson, E. F. 1996. Foster City, CA: IDG Press**

This book concentrates on creating code that can be easily transported between Unix and NT hosts. Special attention is given to scripts that deal with systems administration and websites, although the book covers a wide range of other topics.

***Perl 5 Interactive Course: Certified Edition.* Orwant, J. 1997. Corte Madera, CA: Waite Group**

This book is a thorough guide to Perl 5 programming, taking the reader through a series of different tasks and topics that range from building basic scripts to the proper use of variables, functions, and Perl-style regular expressions.

***Learning Perl on Win32 Systems.* Schwartz, R. L., E. Olson, and T. Christiansen. 1997. Sebastopol, CA: O'Reilly**

This is a modified version of the *Learning Perl* title, customized to include information about using Perl on Windows systems. Unfortunately, it is now out of date and fails to mention many of the features now present in ActivePerl and other Windows-specific builds.

***Advanced Perl Programming.* Srinivasan, S. 1997. Sebastopol, CA: O'Reilly**

This book is an excellent guide to data modeling, networking, and the Tk widget interface. It also covers the internal workings of Perl, which will help the advanced programmer write more efficient and smaller code, while providing all the information necessary for extending Perl with external C code.

Programming Perl. **2d ed. Wall, L., T. Christiansen, and R. L. Schwartz. 1996. Sebastopol, CA: O'Reilly**

Written by the three modern Perl architects, this is the definitive guide to Perl programming. This is what most people refer to as the "Camel" book, since that is the picture used on the front.

Perl Cookbook. **Wall, L., T. Christiansen, and N. Torkington. 1998. Sebastopol, CA: O'Reilly**

This cookbook of recipes for programming in the Perl language is written by the same team as the classic Camel book and is based on two chapters from the original first edition.

Journals

Most of the pertinent and up-to-date information is distributed over the various websites and newsgroups on the Internet. However, there are some magazines and other periodicals that contain example scripts and guides to different styles and methods of programming.

The Perl Journal　A periodical devoted entirely to Perl, *The Perl Journal* covers a wide range of topics from basic principles for beginners to the advanced topics of Perl internals. The Journal also includes book and product reviews and guides to writing better Perl.

SunExpert Magazine　Although this magazine is aimed at Unix (specifically Unix and AIX), this magazine often includes examples of text processing and includes a regular column written by Aeleen Frisch on integrating Windows and Windows NT into a Unix environment called NTegration. This often includes script examples that help to bridge the gap between the two platforms.

Web Resources

Although Perl's history is rooted in a simple reporting language, it became rapidly apparent that it could be used as a suitable language for CGI programming, and there are therefore a vast number of websites dedicated to Perl. The main site is at www.perl.com and is sponsored by O'Reilly. This is the home of Perl and is a good place to start looking for more information.

If you don't find what you are looking for under one of the sites in Table A-1, try visiting Yahoo (www.yahoo.com) or AltaVista (www.altavista. digital.com). The former lists hundreds of sites within its directory.

TABLE A-1 *Perl websites.*

Site	Description
www.perl.org	Originally the home of the Perl Institute, this is now the home of the Perl Mongers, a group of individual local organizations that meet to discuss Perl and Perl programming.
www.perl.com	Now the home of Perl, and sponsored by O'Reilly, this should be your first port of call for Perl information and resources. The site is managed by the main Perl development team, which includes Larry Wall, Tom Christiansen, and Randal L Schwartz, among others. As well as providing the usual links and other information about Perl, the site also supports a magazine format, with guest editorial and regular articles covering different aspects of Perl programming.
www.cpan.org	The Comprehensive Perl Archive Network (CPAN) is an online library of scripts, modules, and extensions to Perl. The organization can sometimes leave something to be desired, and it can take you some time to find what you want, but, it's undoubtedly the best all-round resource for Perl modules and scripts.
www.ActiveState.com	ActiveState is the home of Perl under Win32, and you can download installers for all the different distributions available from ActiveState. You can also download 30-day trial licenses of the commercial Perl development tools.
www.roth.net/perl	This site is maintained by Dave Roth, the author of the `Win32::AdminMisc` and `Win32::ODBC` modules. The site also includes some general information and tips about programming Perl under Win32.
dada.perl.it	Aldo Calpini develops the `Win32::GUI` and is also a general Perl consultant. This site is a mixture of information about his own modules and other Win32-related modules and extensions.
www.scriptics.com	The home of the Tk interface builder and Tcl programming language. You can download the necessary installers and libraries from this site to enable Tk on your machine. You'll need to use the PPM utility to install the Tk module.
www.perl.com/CPAN-local/ ports/win32/Standard/x86/	This is Gurusamy Sarathy's archive of the standard ActivePerl Win32 extensions modified so that they work with the core distribution.
www.bybyte.de/jmk/	Jutta Klebe's site for the `Win32::PerfLib` interface module.
www.gonefishing.org/techstuff/	The home of the `Win32::FileSecurity` extension.
www.geocities.com/Silicon Valley/Way/6278/perl-win32-database.html	Matt Sergeant's Database FAQ—an excellent resource for database programming within Perl when using the Win32::ODBC driver.

TABLE A-2

Perl FTP sites.

Server Name	Directory
coombs.anu.edu.au	/pub/perl/CPAN/src/5.0
ftp.cis.ufl.edu	/pub/perl/CPAN/src/5.0
ftp.cs.ruu.nl	/pub/PERL/perl5.0/src
ftp.funet.fi	/pub/languages/perl/CPAN/src/5.0
ftp.metronet.com	/pub/perl/source
ftp.netlabs.com	/pub/outgoing/perl5.0
sinsite.doc.ic.ac.uk	/pub/computing/programming/languages/perl/perl.5.0
sungear.mame.mu.oz.au	/pub/perl/src/5.0

FTP Sites

If you are looking for a specific module, script, or idea, then it's best to visit the CPAN archives (see Table A-1), because the CPAN system will automatically take you to a local FTP site. However, if all you want to do is browse around the available files, or download the entire contents, then try some of the sites in Table A-2.

Mailing Lists

Mailing lists fall into two distinct categories: announcements or discussions. If the list is for announcements, you are not allowed to post to the group. These tend to be low volume and are useful for keeping in touch with the direction of Perl. If it's a discussion list, you can post and reply to messages just as you would in a Usenet newsgroup. These are higher-volume lists, and the number of messages can become unmanageable very quickly.

Saying that, a discussion list is likely to have the experts and users in it that are able to answer your questions and queries with authority.

General Mailing Lists

Perl Institute Announce   This list carries announcements from the Perl Institute on general Perl issues. To subscribe, send e-mail to majordomo@perl.org with `subscribe tpi-announce` in the body of the message.

Perl-Unicode (from the Perl Institute)   This list is concerned with issues surrounding Unicode and Perl at both porting and using levels. To subscribe, send e-mail to majordomo@perl.org with `subscribe perl-unicode` in the body of the message.

Perl5-Porters   If you are porting Perl or Perl modules or want to help in the development of the Perl language in general, you should be a member of this discussion list. Don't join if you are just interested. This is a high-volume, highly technical mailing list. To subscribe, send e-mail to majordomo@perl.org with `subscribe perl5-porters` in the body of the message.

Windows-Specific Mailing Lists

Windows Users   The Perl-Win32-Users mailing list is targeted for Perl installation and programming questions. There are two versions: standard and digest. To subscribe to the standard version, send e-mail to ListManager@ActiveState.com with `SUBSCRIBE Perl-Win32-Users` in the body of the message. To subscribe to the digest version, send e-mail to ListManager@ActiveState.com with `DIGEST Perl-Win32-Users` in the body of the message.

Windows Announce   This mailing list is for announcements of new builds, bugs, security problems, and other information. To subscribe to the standard version, send e-mail to ListManager@ActiveState.com with `SUBSCRIBE Perl-Win32-Announce` in the body of the message. To subscribe to the digest version, send e-mail to ListManager@ActiveState.com with `DIGEST Perl-Win32-Announce` in the body of the message.

Windows Web Programming   This focuses on using Perl as a CGI programming alternative on Windows NT servers. To subscribe to the standard version, send e-mail to ListManager@ActiveState.com with `SUBSCRIBE Perl-Win32-Web` in the body of the message. To subscribe to the digest version, send e-mail to ListManager@ActiveState.com with `DIGEST Perl-Win32-Web` in the body of the message.

Windows Admin   Here you will find information and discussion on using Perl for administering and managing Windows 95 and NT machines. To subscribe to the standard version, send e-mail to ListManager@ActiveState.com with `SUBSCRIBE Perl-Win32-Admin` in the body of the message. To subscribe to the digest version, send e-mail to ListManager@ActiveState.com with `DIGEST Perl-Win32-Admin` in the body of the message.

Newsgroups

To reach a more general Perl audience, you might want to post a question or announcement to one of the many Perl newsgroups. These are avail-

TABLE A-3

Perl-friendly newsgroups.

Newsgroup	Description
comp.infosystems.www.authoring.cgi	Deals with using Perl as a tool for writing CGI programs. This is a general CGI discussion group; it is not specifically targeted at Perl users. However, it does provide a lot of useful information on extracting, receiving, and returning information from Web servers and clients.
comp.lang.perl.announce	Used to announce news from the Perl world. This includes new book releases, new version releases, and occasionally major Perl module releases.
comp.lang.perl.misc	A general discussion forum for Perl. Everything from queries about how best to tackle a problem to the inside machinations of Perl are discussed here. Some of the discussion can get quite technical and be more biased to someone interested in the internal Perl workings, but it still represents the best port of call if you are having trouble with a problem or Perl script.
comp.lang.perl.modules	This was set up to specifically discuss the use and creation of Perl modules. Unlike comp.lang.perl.misc, you should only find problems related to modules in this group. If you are having trouble with something downloaded from CPAN, this is the best place to start asking questions.
comp.lang.perl.tk	Tk is a toolkit that provides a set of functions to support a graphical user interface (GUI) within Perl. Tk was originally developed in combination with Tcl (Tool command language) but has been massaged to work with other scripting systems, including Perl.

able on more ISP's Usenet news servers, and many will be happy to add them to their list if you ask nicely; the list is summarized in Table A-3.

You may also want to refer to "Joseph's Top Ten Tips for Answering Questions Posted to comp.lang.perl.misc," available at http://www.5sigma.com/perl/topten.html. This will provide you with some hints and tips on how best to make use of the question-and-answer nature of many of these groups. The site is a little tongue-in-cheek, but still a good resource.

Appendix B
Tk Quick Reference

This appendix is a quick guide to the properties and methods supported by the most commonly used widgets in the Tk module. This is not a complete or exhaustive guide to the features of the Tk interface library. Refer to the document that comes with the Perl/Tk module for more information. For examples on using the Tk module, see Chapter 10.

The Basic Widget Set

The list of Tk widgets supported through the Perl/Tk interface is given in Table B-1.

TABLE B-1

A selection of widgets supported by Perl/Tk.

Widget Class	Description
BitmapImage	A subclass of the Image widget for displaying bitmap images.
Button	A simple push-button widget with similar properties to the Label widget.
Canvas	A drawing area into which you can place circles, lines, text, and other graphic artifacts.
CheckButton	A multiple-choice button widget, where each item within the selection can be selected individually.
Entry	A single-line text entry box.
Frame	A container for arranging other widgets.
Image	A simple widget for displaying bitmaps, pixmaps (color bitmaps), and other graphic objects.
Label	A simple box into which you can place message text (noneditable).
Listbox	A multiline list of selection choices.
Menu	A list of menu selections that can be made up of Label, Message, Button, and other widgets.
MenuButton	A menu (within a single menu bar) that lists the selections specified in a Menu object.

(Continued)

TABLE B-1

(Continued)

Widget Class	Description
Message	A multiline `Label` object (noneditable).
OptionMenu	A special type of `Menu` widget that provides a pop-up list of items within a selection.
PhotoImage	A subclass of the `Image` widget for displaying full-color images.
Radiobutton	A multiple-choice button widget, where you can choose only one of a multiple of values.
Scale	A slider that allows you to set a value according to a specific scale.
Scrollbar	A slider for controlling the contents of another widget, such as `Text` or `Canvas`.
Text	A multiline text widget that supports editable text that can also be tagged for display in different fonts and colors.
Toplevel	A window that will be managed and dressed by the parent window manager.
Tributton	An adaptation of the `Button` widget that allows it to support three different states instead of the normal bipolar on/off.

Screen Units

A *screen unit* is used to describe the padding or size of a widget according to a fixed reference value such as the physical length. You should supply the numerical size and then append one of the characters shown in Table B-2.

Generic Methods and Properties

These generic widget properties are inherited by all widgets. The exact list of inherited properties varies with each widget, and the effect of a given property may vary according to the widget in use. See Table B-3 for the list of properties and Table B-4 for the base methods inherited by most widget classes.

TABLE B-2

Screen units supported by the Tk library.

Suffix	Description
None	Size is calculated in pixels.
c	Size is interpreted as onscreen centimeters.
i	Size is interpreted as onscreen inches.
m	Size is interpreted as onscreen millimeters.
p	Size is interpreted as printer's points (1 point is approximately 1/72 inch). This is the same unit as the point size used when specifying font sizes.

TABLE B-3

Generic widget properties.

Property	Description
activebackground	The background color used for active widgets.
activeforeground	The foreground color used for active widgets.
anchor	Defines the location of the widget within the window or the location of the text within the widget. Valid values are n, ne, e, se, s, sw, w, nw, or center.
background, bg	The color of the background, specified either by a name or hexadecimal RGB value.
bitmap	The image or bitmap file to be displayed within the widget.
borderwidth	The width of the relief border.
cursor	The cursor to display when using the widget.
disabledforeground	The foreground color used for disabled widgets.
font	The font name in X or Windows format.
foreground, fg	The color of the foreground, specified either by a name or hexadecimal RGB value.
height	The height of the widget in pixels or characters, according to widget type.
highlightbackground	The color used when a widget does not have input focus.
highlightcolor	The color used when a widget has input focus.
highlightthickness	The thickness of the rectangle drawn around the outside of the widget when it has input focus.
image	The image or bitmap file to be displayed within the widget.

(Continued)

TABLE B-3

(Continued)

Property	Description
justify	The justification for the widget, one of left, center, or right.
padx	The additional pixels to be placed around the left- and right-hand side of the widget.
pady	The additional pixels to be placed around the top and bottom of the widget.
relief	The style of the widget's border, which should be one of raised, sunken, flat, ridge, or groove.
takefocus	If set to 1, indicates that the widget should take focus when switching between widgets with the Tab and Shift-Tab keys.
text	The string to be displayed within the widget, using the foreground and font values specified.
textvariable	The name of a variable to be used and/or updated when the widget changes.
underline	Defines the integer index of the character within the label property to underline.
width	The width of the widget; specified in the number of characters for labels, buttons, and text widgets, and in pixels for all other widgets.
wraplength	For widgets that perform word wrapping, this defines the maximum line length.

TABLE B-4

Generic methods inherited by most widgets.

Method	Description
configure(PROPERTIES)	Configure the widget using the properties supplied.
cget(PROPERTY)	Return the currently configured value for the specified PROPERTY.

Button

This widget is a simple button used to execute a function. Table B-5 gives the widget properties, and Table B-6 gives the widget methods supported in addition to the generic properties and methods.

TABLE B-5

Additional proper-
ties supported by
Button widgets.

Property	Description
command	A reference to the Perl function to be called when the button is clicked with mouse button 1.
default	Specifies the default state of the button, either normal, active, or disabled. The active state draws the button in a platform-specific format for a default button. The normal state is a normal button, and the disabled state shows the button as disabled (grayed out).
state	Specifies the state of the button, either normal, active, or disabled. In normal state, the foreground and background properties are used to display the button. Also, in normal state, the activeForeground and activeBackground properties are used. The disabled state uses the disabledForeground and background colors.

TABLE B-6

Additional methods
supported by
Button widgets.

Method	Description
flash	Flashes the button briefly by reversing and resetting the foreground and background colors.
invoke	Starts the subroutine defined in the command property.

CheckButton

The CheckButton is the square checkbox widget that supports more than one concurrent selection, unlike radio buttons, which only allow one selection within a group. Table B-7 lists the widget-specific properties, and Table B-8 lists the widget's properties.

Entry

An Entry widget is a simple entry box used to get a string from the user. Through the validate property you can verify the entry contents. Tables B-9 and B-10 show the widget-specific properties and methods.

TABLE B-7

CheckButton
widget properties.

Property	Description
command	A reference to the Perl function to be called when the button is clicked with mouse button 1. The variable referred to by the variable property is updated with the value in the value property before the referenced subroutine is invoked.
indicatoron	If false (zero), then rather than displaying the checkbox indicator, it toggles the relief base property of the entire widget, effectively making the whole widget the checkbox.
offvalue	Specifies the value to store within the variable pointed to by the variable property when the button is not selected.
onvalue	Specifies the value to store within the variable pointed to by the variable property when the button is selected.
selectcolor	The background color to use when the button is selected.
selectimage	The image to display when the button is selected.
variable	Takes a reference to a variable and updates with the value property when the button is clicked. When the value of the referenced variable matches the value property, the button is selected automatically.

TABLE B-8

CheckButton
widget methods.

Method	Description
deselect	Deselects the button and sets the widget's variable to the off value.
flash	Flashes the button briefly by reversing and resetting the foreground and background colors.
invoke	Starts the subroutine defined in the command property.
select	Selects the check button and sets the widget's variable to the on value.
toggle	Toggles the selection state and values of the button on and off.

Index specifications within the text widget use the formats shown in Table B-11.

Label

The Label widget uses the generic properties and methods shown in Tables B-3 and B-4.

TABLE B-9

Entry widget
properties.

Property	Description
show	A simple Boolean option. If set, it displays * for each character entered and is primarily used for password entry. Note that although the characters are displayed in this manner, copying and pasting the contents of a "hidden" field will reveal the real contents.
invalidcommand	A reference to the function that should be called when the function specified in the validatecommand property returns 0.
state	The initial state of the widget. If disabled, then the widget's value cannot be changed. If set to normal, then the widget operates normally.
validate	Specifies the mode in which validation should occur. It defaults to none, which means that no validation occurs. If set to focus, focusin, focusout, key, or all, then validation will occur when the widget has focus, when the focus is switched to the widget, when the focus is switched from the widget, whenever a key is pressed, or under all conditions, respectively.
validatecommand	A reference to a function that should be called to validate the contents of the widget. The function should return 0 if validation failed, and 1 if it succeeded. A value of undef disables the feature.

TABLE B-10

Entry widget
methods.

Method	Description
get(INDEX)	Gets the string starting at INDEX.
index(INDEX)	Returns an absolute index from a relative one.
insert(INDEX, STRING)	Inserts STRING at INDEX.
selection(FROM, TO)	Sets the selection to the characters starting at FROM and ending at TO.
selectionClear	Clears the selection.
selectionFrom(INDEX)	Sets the selection from INDEX to the end of the field.
SelectionPresent	True if a selection is currently active.
selectionTo(INDEX)	Sets the selection from the beginning of the field to INDEX.

TABLE B-11

Entry widget addressing formats.

Specification	Description
end	The end of the text.
insert	The position immediately after the insertion cursor.
number	An index into the widget's contents, starting with 0 as the first character.
sel.first, sel.last	Indicates the first and last character of a tag.

Listbox

The Listbox widget is a list of values, as used to display file lists or selection lists. The additional widget properties are shown in Table B-12 and the methods in Table B-13.

Individual elements within the listbox can be accessed using the index formats shown in Table B-14.

Menu

A menu is merely an anchor point for a number of menu items. A menu item can be another Label, Checkbutton, Radiobutton, or Menu object. Menus and menu items share many of the same properties and methods, as shown here in Tables B-15 and B-16.

TABLE B-12

Listbox widget properties.

Property	Description
selectMode	Defines the selection mode of the list, one of single, browse, multiple, or extended. In single or browse mode, at most, one element can be selected from the listbox list at any one time. In browse mode, you can also drag the item within the list. If the selection mode is multiple or extended, more than one item can be selected. In multiple mode, clicking on an item modifies its selected state. In extended mode, you can select multiple items by clicking and dragging a selection.

TABLE B-13

Listbox widget
methods.

Method	Description
curselection()	A list of the index values of all the selected items.
delete(INDEX [, LAST])	Deletes the row at INDEX, or the rows between INDEX and LAST.
get(INDEX)	Gets the string, starting at INDEX.
insert(index, string)	Inserts STRING at INDEX.
see(INDEX)	Brings the element INDEX into the current view.
selection(FROM, TO)	Selects the rows starting at FROM and ending at TO.
selectionClear()	Clears the selection.
selectionFrom(INDEX)	Selects all the rows from INDEX to the end of the list.
selectionPresent()	Returns True if there is an active selection.
selectionTo(INDEX)	Selects all the rows from the beginning of the list to INDEX.

TABLE B-14

Listbox widget
addressing
formats.

Specification	Description
active	Where the location cursor is currently positioned and the active location appears underlined in the list view.
anchor	The anchor point of the selection.
end	Indicates the end of the current row.
number	The index of the row, starting with 0 for the first element.

You can access a specific menu item using its index location or using one of the shortcuts shown in Table B-17.

Radiobutton

A radio button is like a check button, except that within a group of radio buttons, only one button can be selected at any one time. The properties and methods for the Radiobutton widget are shown in Tables B-18 and B-19.

TABLE B-15

Menu and menu
item widget
properties.

Property	Description
accelerator	Shows the string to be displayed, right-justified, as the keyboard equivalent for the menu option. This doesn't bind the key to the command for you. You'll have to do that separately.
command	The reference of a subroutine to call when the menu item is selected.
indicatoron	If true, places a small diamond next to the menu option, which allows an option to be toggled on and off by a menu.
label	The text to use for the menu item. This should be used in place of the normal text property.
onvalue, offvalue	Identical to the options in Table B-7 for check-button-style entries.
selectcolor	The color of the indicator, if indicatoron is true.
state	Status: normal, active, or disabled.
tearoff	If true, the first element of the menu is a separator. Clicking on the separator "tears off" the menu into a separate top-level window. This is not always supported on all implementations.
underline	The index of a character to underline. This is used in combination with the accelerator property to indicate which keyboard shortcut should be used for this menu.
value	The value of the attached radio button (see Table B-18).
variable	A reference to the variable used to store value.

Scale

The Scale widget provides a simple slider that can be used to set a numerical value for a variable. Sliders use a scale, calculated using the maximum and minimum values and their physical onscreen size. Changing the value of the Scale widget's variable will adjust its position. Other properties and Scale methods are shown in Tables B-20 and B-21.

Scrollbar Widget

Scroll bars are modifications of the Scale widget, used to control the display area of another widget. As such, a Scrollbar widget has its own

TABLE B-16

Menu and menu item widget methods.

Method	Description
activate(INDEX)	Changes the state of the item pointed to by INDEX to be active.
add(TYPE, PROPERTIES)	Adds a new menu item of type TYPE to the menu, using the properties supplied in the hash or key/value pair PROPERTIES. The TYPE must be one of cascade, checkbutton, command, radiobutton, or separator.
clone(PARENT, TYPE)	Creates a clone of the menu as a child of PARENT. The TYPE should be one of normal, menubar, or tearoff.
delete(INDEX1, INDEX2)	Deletes the menu items between INDEX1 and INDEX2.
entrycget(INDEX [,PROPERTY])	Gets the properties for the menu item at INDEX. If PROPERTY is supplied, then the value of the specified property will be returned instead of a hash of all the properties.
entryconfigure(INDEX [,PROPERTIES])	Configures the menu item at INDEX with the properties supplied in PROPERTIES.
index(INDEX)	Returns the numerical index that points to INDEX.
insert(INSERT, TYPE, PROPERTIES)	Identical to the add method, except that it inserts a new item *before* the item pointed to by INDEX.
invoke(INDEX)	Invokes the action (as configured by the command property) for the menu item at INDEX.
post(X,Y)	Displays the menu on the screen at the root window coordinates given by X and Y.
postcascade(INDEX)	Displays the submenu associated with the cascade entry at INDEX.
type(INDEX)	Returns the type of menu item at INDEX.
unpost()	Unposts (removes) the menu from the display.
yposition(INDEX)	Returns the Y coordinate within the menu window of the topmost pixel for the menu item at INDEX.

TABLE B-17

Menu and menu
item index
formats.

Specification	Description
number	The index of the menu item, starting at zero for the first item. When the menu is configured for tear-off, the first entry is a separator automatically inserted by the widget.
end, last	Indicates the last entry.
active	Where the location cursor is currently active.
none	Indicates that none of the menu options are active.
pattern	A pattern to be matched against the label property of all entries. This only matches exactly; regular expressions are supported.

TABLE B-18

Radiobutton
widget properties.

Property	Description
command	A reference to the Perl function to be called when button is clicked with mouse button 1. The variable referred to by the variable property is updated with the value in the value property before the referenced subroutine is invoked.
indicatoron	If set to 1, places an indicator next to the item. If set to 0, then the whole widget is sunken when the widget has been selected.
selectimage	Specifies the image to be displayed when the item is selected.
state	Specifies the state of the button, either normal, active, or disabled. In normal state, the foreground and background properties are used to display the button. In normal state, the activeForeground and activeBackground properties are used. The disabled state uses the disabledForeground and background colors.
value	Specifies the value to store within the variable pointed to by the variable property when the button is selected.
variable	Takes a reference to a variable and updates with the value property when the button is clicked. When the value of the referenced variable matches the value property, the button is selected automatically.

TABLE B-19

Radiobutton
widget methods.

Method	Description
deselect	Deselects the radio button and sets the variable to an empty string.
flash	Flashes the button briefly by reversing and resetting the foreground and background colors.
invoke	Starts the subroutine defined in the command property.
select	Selects the radio button and sets the variable to value.

TABLE B-20

Scale widget
properties.

Property	Description
bigincrement	The size of the large increments, defaults to 1/10th of the range of the scale.
command	Reference to a subroutine, which will be called when the scale's value is changed.
digits	An integer specifying how many significant digits should be returned when converting a scale value to a string.
from	The real range of values that the widget should scale from.
label	The label to be displayed to the top (horizontal) or left (vertical) scale.
length	The length of the scale in pixels.
orient	Allows you to select horizontal or vertical orientation.
resolution	The value displayed and set into variable will always be a multiple of this number. The default is 1.
showvalue	If true, then the current value of the slider will be displayed.
sliderlength	The size of the slider, measured in screen units.
sliderrelief	The relief to use when displaying the slider.
state	Defines the state of the slider bar. The normal format will display the slider normally. The active format will force the display of the slider to use the color defined by activebackground. If disabled, then the slider cannot be changed.
tickinterval	The spacing, in real values, between tick marks on the scale.
to	The real range of values that the widget should scale to.
variable	Reference to a variable to be updated whenever the slider moves. Works like the variable base property; updating this value will also set the slider position.
width	The width of the scale in pixels.

TABLE B-21

Scale widget
methods.

Method	Description
set(VALUE)	Identical to modifying the value of variable.
get([X,Y])	If no arguments are supplied, then it returns the current slider value. If supplied the coordinates, then it returns the value of the slider if it were at the given coordinates.

TABLE B-22

`Scrollbar`
widget properties.

Property	Description
`activerelief`	Specifies the relief to use when displaying the active selection within the scroll bar.
`command`	A reference to a subroutine used to change the view in the widget.
`elementborderwidth`	The width of the borders to be drawn around the scroll bar (including the arrows and slider).

properties and methods—shown in Tables B-22 and B-23. Widgets that inherit the `Scrollbar` widget (such as the special `ScrolledText` widget) also inherit the properties and methods shown in Tables B-24 and B-25.

Text

The `Text` widget is a multiline text-entry widget suitable for displaying large volumes of text. The text can be edited, and using *tags,*

TABLE B-23

`Scrollbar`
widget methods.

Method	Description
`get`	Returns the current scroll bar settings.
`set(FIRST, LAST)`	Indicates the current view. The `FIRST` and `LAST` elements should be fractions between `0` and `1`. For example, a value of `0.1` and `0.2` should indicate that the area between 10 percent and 20 percent of the item should be shown.

TABLE B-24

Additional properties for scrollable widgets.

Property	Description
`xscrollcommand, yscrollcommand`	A reference to the function used to reposition the widget when the scroll bar is moved.
`xscrollincrement, yscrollincrement`	The scrolling, `x` and `y`, will be down in the specified increments.

TABLE B-25

Additional methods
for scrollable
widgets.

Method	Description
`xview('moveto', FRACTION)` `yview('moveto', FRACTION)`	Moves the scroll bar to the location specified by `fraction`, which indicates the leftmost, or topmost, character or pixel. Note that the first argument is a constant.
`xview('scroll', NUMBER, WHAT) yview('scroll', NUMBER, WHAT)`	Indicates that the view should be moved up or down, or left or right, for NUMBER increments. If WHAT is "units", then it is scrolled according to the increment in the `xscrollincrement` and `yscrollincrement` properties. If WHAT is "pages", then the widget is scrolled NUMBER pages.

selected areas of text can be formatted in different fonts, line spacing, and other artifacts. See Tables B-26 and B-27 for the main widget properties.

Table B-28 shows the acceptable formats for defining a tag location. To configure tags within a Text widget, you need to use the methods shown in Table B-29. All tags also inherit the properties shown in Table B-30.

TABLE B-26

Text widget
properties.

Property	Description
`spacing1`	Specifies additional spacing to be inserted before each line within the Text widget. Specification should be in screen units (see Table B-2).
`spacing2`	Specifies additional spacing to be inserted between each line of a wrapped paragraph within the Text widget. Specification should be in screen units (see Table B-2).
`spacing3`	Specifies additional spacing to be added after each line within the text widget. Specification should be in screen units (see Table B-2).
`state`	One of `normal` for a standard editable text box, or `disabled` for a non-modifiable text box.
`tabs`	The list of tab stops for the Text widget. Specification should be as a reference to a list of strings. Each string should be composed of a number defining the character location within the line, followed by `1`, `c`, or `r` for left, center, or right justification for the specified tab.

TABLE B-27

Text widget methods.

Method	Description
delete(INDEX1 [,INDEX2])	Delete the character at INDEX1 or the text from INDEX1 to INDEX2.
get(INDEX1 [,INDEX2])	Get the character at INDEX1 or the text from INDEX1 to INDEX2.
index(INDEX)	Returns an absolute index for the corresponding INDEX supplied.
insert(INDEX [, STRING [, TAG]] ...)	Insert STRING with an optional TAG at the specified INDEX.
markSet(NAME, INDEX)	Gives the text at INDEX the bookmark NAME.
markUnset(NAME)	Unsets a bookmark NAME.
see(INDEX)	Returns true if the text at INDEX is visible.

TABLE B-28

Tag index formats.

Specification/Qualifier	Description
line.char	Indicates the character at char characters across (left to right) and line lines down (top to bottom). The specification starts at 0 for characters within a line, and 1 for lines within a text box.
end	The end of the text, as defined by the character just after the last newline character.
insert	The location of the insertion cursor.
mark	The character just after the marker whose name is mark.
tag.first, tag.last	Used to specify the first and last characters of a tag.
+count chars, -count chars, +count lines, -count lines	Adjust the base index specification by the count characters or lines.
wordstart, wordend, linestart, lineend	Adjust the index to point to the first character on the word or line specified by the index (wordstart, linestart) or to the character immediately after the word or line.

TABLE B-29

Text tag methods
and properties.

Method	Description
tagAdd(Name [,INDEX1[.INDEX2]] ...)	Adds the tag NAME at the position specified in INDEX1 or bounded by INDEX1 and INDEX2.
tagConfigure	Configures one or more properties for a tag.
tagDelete(NAME)	Removes and deletes the tag NAME.
tagRemove(NAME [,INDEX1[.INDEX2]] ...)	Removes the tag NAME from the character or range specified by INDEX1 and INDEX2, but it does not delete the actual tag definition.

TABLE B-30

Tag properties.

Property	Description
background	The color to use for the background of the characters defined by the tag.
bgstipple	The bitmap to use for the background. If not specified, then a solid fill is used.
borderwidth	The width of the border to draw around the background of the tagged text.
data	A reference to a variable that will be used as the content of the tagged text.
elide	If set to 1, text covered by the tag is not displayed (but still takes up screen space).
fgstipple	The bitmap to use for the foreground of the tagged text.
font	The font to use for the tagged text.
justify	The justification for the tagged text.
lmargin1	The indentation for the first line of the tagged text. Specification should be in pixels, according to the distance between the first character of the line and the left inner edge of the widget.
lmargin2	The indentation for subsequent lines of a wrapped section of tagged text.
offset	The vertical offset of the text from the baseline. A positive value would create a superscript, while a negative value would create a subscript tagged section.

(Continued)

TABLE B-30

(Continued)

Property	Description
overstrike	If set to 1, will cause the tagged text to be displayed with a single line drawn through the middle of the characters.
relief	The relief format for the background of a tagged text portion.
rmargin	The right margin for a tagged piece of text. Specification should be in pixels, according to the distance between the last character of the line and the right inner edge of the widget.
spacing1	Specifies additional spacing to be inserted before each line within the Text widget. Specification should be in screen units (see Table B-2).
spacing1	Specifies additional spacing to be inserted before each line within the Text widget. Specification should be in screen units (see Table B-2).
spacing2	Specifies additional spacing to be inserted between each line of a wrapped paragraph within the Text widget. Specification should be in screen units (see Table B-2).
spacing2	Specifies additional spacing to be inserted between each line of a wrapped paragraph within the Text widget. Specification should be in screen units (see Table B-2).
spacing3	Specifies additional spacing to be added after each line within the Text widget. Specification should be in screen units (see Table B-2).
spacing3	Specifies additional spacing to be added after each line within the Text widget. Specification should be in screen units (see Table B-2).
state	One of normal for a standard editable text box, or disabled for a nonmodifiable text box.
state	If set to 1, the tagged text will be hidden. This means that it is not displayed and does not appear on screen, but its display attributes and contents can still be modified.
tabs	The list of tab stops for the Text widget. Specification should be as a reference to a list of strings. Each string should be composed of a number defining the character location within the line, followed by 1, c, or r for left, center, or right justification for the specified tab.
tabs	A list of tab stops for the line, along the same lines as the base tabs property for a Text widget.
underline	If set to 1, draws an underline beneath all the characters of the tagged text.
wrap	Should be one of none, char, or word to define where the lines wrap according to the width of the widget.

Widget Geometry

Widget placement within a window is controlled by three geometry managers. You cannot mix geometry management within a single container (window, Frame, or other container widget), but you can mix and match geometry managers within the same parent. For example, a window with two frames could be managed by the Packer Manager, with the first frame using the Grid Manager and the second using the Placer Manager.

Note that you *must* use a geometry manager in order for a widget to be placed and displayed on screen. Without geometry management, a widget will not appear on screen.

Packer

The Packer Manager is accessible through the pack function or pack method to an existing widget. The Packer places widgets according to their side affinity and the remaining space after previous widgets have been placed. See Chapter 10 for more information. Configuration of the manager is via the properties shown in Table B-31.

TABLE B-31

Packer geometry management.

Property	Description
expand	Specifies whether the widget should expand to take up all of the remaining space after the other widgets have been placed. This is useful for Textbox widgets where you are defining an outer menu and toolbar and want the main widget to take up all the remaining space.
fill	Specifies whether the widget should fill up the space in the parcel in the x or y direction accordingly. You can also specify both to fill in both directions, or none to prevent filling altogether. The ipadx or ipady options can be used to specify some additional blank padding space around the widget within the parcel.
ipadx, ipady	The spacing around a widget that is "filling" the space provided by the parcel. Specified in pixels, millimeters, inches, or points (see Table B-2).
padx, pady	The spacing between widgets, specified in pixels, millimeters, inches, or points (see Table B-2).
side	The side of the frame to which the widget should be added. Should be one of left, right, top, or bottom.

TABLE B-32

Properties for the
grid geometry
manager.

Property	Value
column	The column in which to insert the widget.
columnspan	The number of columns that the widget should span within the grid.
ipadx, ipady	The spacing around a widget that is "filling" the space provided by the parcel. Specified in pixels, millimeters, inches, or points (see Table B-2).
padx, pady	The spacing between widgets, specified in pixels, millimeters, inches, or points (see Table B-2).
row	The row in which to insert the widget.
rowspan	The number of rows that the widget should span within the grid.
sticky	Defines the side of the parent widget to which the widget will stick. Should be specified as zero or more of the characters n, s, e, or w. If none are specified, the widget becomes centered within its cell. If both n and s (or e and w) are specified, then the widget will stretch to fill the height (or width) of the cell. If all four are specified, then the widget grows to fill the entire cell.

Grid

The Grid Manager places widgets according to a table format, with each widget being placed into a cell. The format is similar to the tables used in HTML. Properties for the manager are shown in Table B-32 and are set using the grid function/method.

Placer

The Placer Geometry Manager places widgets at an exact X/Y coordinate within a parent widget. This is similar to the system operated by Visual Basic for placing controls within a window. Operation is via the place function/method and the accepted properties are shown in Table B-33.

TABLE B-33

Properties for the Placer Geometry Manager.

Property	Description
anchor	Defines which point of the window should be treated as the anchor point. Uses the normal n, ne, e, se, s, sw, w, nw values.
bordermode	One of inside (default), outside, or ignore. If set to inside, then the area of the window is calculated less any border on the parent. If outside, it includes the area set by the parent's border. If set to ignore, then the calculations are taken irrespective of the border size, making the entire parent window available for use.
in	The widget (object) that the widget should be placed relative to. The value must be a valid widget object and must either be the window parent or a descendant of the window parent. You must also ensure that the widget and its parent are both descendants of the same window.
relwidth, relheight	The relative width or height of the window compared to the size of the parent, where 0.5 means the window is half as big as the parent, and 1.0 means that the window and parent are the same width or height.
relx, rely	The relative x (horizontal) coordinate within the parent window. The number should be specified as a floating-point number, where 0.0 refers to the left edge of the parent, and 1.0 to the right edge; thus, the setting 0.5 would center the widget in the parent.
width, height	Specifies the width or height of the window. See Table B-2. Note that in both cases the measurement defines the outer width of the window, including any border.
x, y	The x (horizontal) and y (vertical) coordinates to use as the anchor point for the widget. See Table B-2.

Appendix C

Visual Basic/Perl Function and Operator Migration Reference

This appendix is a rough guide for Visual Basic programmers, which takes the VB operators and functions and details the Perl equivalent, or a Perl-based solution to the problem. Note the first definition is for the Visual Basic equivalent, then a comparable Perl equivalent is given. The section at the end of the appendix provides a brief guide to the Perl functions supported under Windows.

Some general notes:

- Due to the inherent variable type differences, many of the functions in the VB set are data-type specific; alternatives and compatible functions and types have been given where possible.

- All built-in Perl functions are lowercase, not mixed case or uppercase. The most common errors when migrating from VB are to use identically named functions but specify mixed case.

- Don't expect an identically named function to work in the same manner on both languages.

- Remember that Perl functions can return different values based on their context—that is, what is expected to be returned, a single value, or a list of values.

- References include references to earlier chapters and to the function guide given in the second half of this appendix.

!

```
recordset!field
```

Database Field Access—Used to indicate a single database field when using a record set object.

Perl Equivalent

No direct. Access to individual fields within a database query is handled according the database interface or driver that you are using. For example, with `Win32::ODBC` the closest equivalent is to use the `DataHash` function to return an entire record as a hash, with keys referring to the individual fields. For example, you might do this:

```
# Some select Statements
...
while($db->FetchRow())
{
    my %record = $db->DataHash()
    print $record{ID},"\n";
...
}
```

Once the data has been retrieved, you can use standard hash notation to retrieve specific fields from the record.

References

Chapter 3

#

```
variable#
```

Double operator—Sets a variable to be a double (floating point).

Perl Equivalent

There is no way within Perl to set a scalar variable to a specific type. The scalar type holds integers, floats, and strings. However, if you are assigning value to a variable, internally, Perl will use a suitable data type. For example:

```
$int = 99;
$float = 12.3;
```

Perl automatically converts between types.

References

Chapter 16

#DATE#/#TIME#

```
#datetime#
```

Used to introduce a date or time constant, where datetime is a date or time string.

Perl Equivalent

None. Perl does not have an internal data type for storing dates or times as strings. However, there are a number of tricks you can use to convert a date or time string into a suitable value. The first is to use a strict format for a date that can easily be extracted or printed suitable for use elsewhere. For example, you can store a date as a string DDMM YYYY, using `sprintf` and the `localtime` function to create the string:

```
my ($day, $mon, $year) = (localtime())[3..5];
$year += 1900;
$mon++;

$date = sprint("%02d%02d%04d",$day, $mon, $year);
```

Now the information can be stored in a string. To extract the information back into a normal date, use a regular expression:

```
$date =~ s/(..)(..)(....)/$1\/$2\/$3/;
```

This will convert the date string back to a normal string.

NOTE. *If you use the format YYYYMMDD, the date string becomes an integer value that can be sorted to produce a list in date order. You can still use the same tricks to format and extract the date into a useful format.*

The other solution is to use the `Time::Local` module to convert a list of variables relating to a date and time back into the long integer used internally by the time system. The format of the function is as follows:

```
use Time::Local;

$time = timelocal(SEC, MIN, HOURS, MDAY, MON, YEAR);
```

such that:

```
use Time::Local;

$time = time;

print "Time!" if ($time == (timelocal((localtime)[0..5])));
```

References

localtime, gmtime, time

#CONST

```
#Const constname = expression
```

Conditional compilation constant, makes constname **equal** expression valid within the current VB module.

Perl Equivalent

There is no way to introduce a constant in this way during compilation time, since Perl does not use the same execution model. Instead, use a normal variable:

```
$constant = expression
```

Alternatively, use the const pragma. Perl will optimize the constant during the compilation/execution stage.

References

Chapter 16

#if...#else...#endif

```
#if
...
#else
...
#endif
```

Conditional compilation—Evaluated and executed only during the compilation stage. Used to select portions of code to be executed or to assign different values to constants.

Perl Equivalent

No direct Perl equivalent because of the difference in execution model. The nearest approximation is to use a BEGIN block, which will be executed during the compilation stage. For example:

```
BEGIN
{
    if (EXPR)
    {
    ...
    }
}
```

$

```
a$
```

Sets the type of a variable to be a string.

Perl Equivalent

None—Use simple assignation to assign a scalar to hold a string value. For example:

```
$string = 'Hello, this is a string';
```

References

Chapter 16

%

```
a%
```

Sets the type of a variable to be an integer.

Perl Equivalent

None—Use simple assignation to assign a scalar to hold an integer value, i.e.:

```
$value = 99;
```

Note that if you want to force a floating-point value to be converted to an integer, you can use the int function, which simply removes the fractional component, or use sprintf, which will round the value according to the normal numerical rules.

References

Chapter 16

&

```
a & b
```

Concatenates strings a and b together.

Perl Equivalent

The period operator will concatenate two strings together, the equivalent of the example given above in Perl would be as follows:

```
EXPR . EXPR
```

where EXPR is any valid variable or constant. You can also use the combine and assign operator, . =, to concatenate a variable or constant to the end of an existing scalar, for example:

```
$string = 'Hello';
$string .= 'World!';
print "$string\n";
```

The last form shows the final method, interpolating variables and constants into a quoted string creates a new string.

NOTE.   *Unlike the VB* & *operator, you can mix and match any variable scalar variable within the concatenation. Perl will automatically convert between numerical and string formats. However, you cannot concatenate arrays or hashes using this operator.*

References

Chapter 16

'

```
' comment
```

Introduces a comment into your code.

Perl Equivalent

Use the hash sign, #. For example:

```
# comment
```

References

Chapter 15

*

```
a * b
```

Multiplication operator for multiplying two numerical expressions or values together.

Perl Equivalent

Perl also uses the * as a numerical multiplication operator.

References

Chapter 16

+

```
a + b
```

Addition operator, for adding two numerical expressions or values together.

Perl Equivalent

Perl also uses the + as a numerical addition operator.

References

Chapter 16

+

```
a + b
```

String addition operator—Adds (concatenates) two string types together.

Perl Equivalent

Use the period operator.

References

Chapter 16

–

```
a - b
-b
```

Subtraction or negation operator.

Perl Equivalent

Perl uses the same operator:

```
$b = $a - 1;
```

References

Chapter 16

/

```
a / b
```

Division operator.

Perl Equivalent

The Perl / operator performs the same function. However, integers and floating-point values are automatically converted, and the return value will be in the appropriate type. For example:

```
$a = 4 / 2;
```

will make $a an integer scalar, while

```
$a = 4 / 3;
```

will make $a a floating-point scalar.

If you want to force an integer calculation, use the int function around the expression. If you want the modulus of an expression, use the Perl % operator.

References

Chapter 16

<

```
a < b
```

Less-than operator, returns True if the value of a is less than the value of b.

Perl Equivalent

Perl uses the same operator for numerical comparisons. However, if you are comparing strings, use the lt operator:

```
'Hello' lt 'hello'
```

References

Chapter 16

<=

```
a <= b
```

Less-than or equal to operator, returns True if the value of a is less than or equal to the value of b.

Perl Equivalent

Perl uses the same operator for numerical comparisons. However, if you are comparing strings, use the le operator:

```
'Hello' le 'hello'
```

References

Chapter 16

< >

```
a <> b
```

Nonequality operator. Returns `True` if a does not equal b.

Perl Equivalent

For numerical comparisons, use the `!=` operator:

```
$a != $b
```

For string comparisons, use the `ne` operator:

```
$a ne $b
```

References

Chapter 16

=

```
a = b
```

Equality operator, returns `True` if a equals b.

Perl Equivalent

Use the `==` operator for numerical values, and the `eq` operator for strings:

```
$a == $b
$a eq $b
```

References

Chapter 16

>

```
a > b
```

Greater-than operator. Returns `True` if a is greater than b.

Perl Equivalent

Perl uses the same operator for numerical values, but uses gt for string comparisons.

References

Chapter 16

>=

```
a >= b
```

Greater-than or equal to operator. Returns True if a is greater than or equal to b.

Perl Equivalent

Use the >= operator for numerical comparisons, and the ge operator for strings.

References

Chapter 16

?

```
? a
```

Prints the expression a to the current or Immediate window.

Perl Equivalent

Use the print function, which sends output to the current DOS window, or the currently selected filehandle.

References

Chapter 16

\

```
a \ b
```

Integer division operator.

Perl Equivalent

No direct equivalent. However, you can use the `int` function in combination with the / division operator:

```
$a = int($b/2);
```

References

Chapter 16

^

```
a ^ b
```

Exponent operator, raises a to the power of b.

Perl Equivalent

Perl uses the `**` operator:

```
$a = 2**4;
```

References

Chapter 16

Abs

```
Abs(num)
```

Returns the absolute (positive) value of a number.

Perl Equivalent

Use the `abs` function:

```
$value = abs($number);
```

References

abs

AddressOf

```
AddressOf procName
```

Returns the address of a function or procedure so that it can be used in a callback.

Perl Equivalent

There is no functional equivalent, but you can use the \ backslash operator to return a reference to any object, including a function. However, you must ensure that you type the object to which you are referring. For example, you must use the ampersand prefix before a function to refer to a code reference:

```
sub hw
{
    print "Hello World\n";
}

$function = \&hw;
```

References

Chapter 17

And

```
a And b
```

Logical AND, returns the logical result of two comparisons logically combined, or the bitwise result of two expressions.

Perl Equivalent

There are two equivalent operators. For logical operations, use the && operator:

```
1 && 0;
```

To perform a bitwise combination of two numbers, use the & operator:

```
15 & 8;
```

References

Chapter 16

AppActivate

```
AppActivate title [, wait]
```

Changes the currently active application to `title`.

Perl Equivalent

No direct equivalent, since Perl is not interface-oriented. However, if you are using Tk as your interface, you can use the focus method on an entry widget to change the input `focus` to that widget.

   If you are using the `Win32::Console` module, then you need to use the `Display` method to display the current buffer object within the console:

```
$buffer->Display();
```

References

Chapter 10

Array

```
Array(arglist)
```

Creates an array based on the elements listed in `arglist`.

Perl Equivalent

You can create an array using the list operator, which comes in two formats. The first is to use parentheses to list the elements:

```
@array = ('Brown', 'Smith', 'Jones');
```

   Alternatively, use the qw operator, which will automatically split a list of words into an array using white space. For example:

```
@array = qw/Brown Smith Jones/;
```

References

Chapter 16

Asc

```
Asc(val)
```

Returns the ASCII value of the first character of `val`.

Perl Equivalent

Use the `ord` function:

```
ord('A');
```

References

`ord`, `chr`

Atn

```
Atn(val)
```

Returns the arctangent of `val`.

Perl Equivalent

You will need to import the `Math::Trig` module and use the `atan` function:

```
use Math::Trig;
print atan(3.141);
```

Beep

```
Beep
```

Plays the simple error beep.

Perl Equivalent

No direct equivalent. However, you can use the `Win32::Sound` module to play the default Windows error sound:

```
use Win32::Sound;

Win32::Sound::Play();
```

References

Chapter 11

Call

```
Call name [argumentlist]
```

Calls a system or user defined procedure.

Perl Equivalent

Since Perl does not distinguish between system and user procedures and functions, you can call all functions using the same format:

```
subname [ARGUMENTS]
subname([ARGUMENTS])
```

where `subname` is the function name and `ARGUMENTS` are the optional arguments.

References

Chapter 17

CallByName

```
CallByName(object, procName, callType, [arglist])
```

Enables runtime binding of a method or property. The method or property specified by the string `procName` will be executed on the `object`.

Perl Equivalent

Perl uses references to perform the same operation. For example:

```
sub hw
{
    print "Hello World\n";
}

$function = 'hw';

&$function;
```

Here, the $function variable contains the name of the function, which is dereferenced with the & operator to force the execution of the function named by the string in $function. You can also pass arguments:

```
&$function('Hello World');
```

References
Chapter 17

CByte

```
CByte(expression)
```

Converts an expression to a byte data type. This takes up a single byte in memory.

Perl Equivalent

You can use the pack function to convert information into a strict format. However, there is no way to enforce a piece of information to be encoded into a single byte. For example, to assign a single character to be stored within a short integer (which is 2 bytes, or 16 bits long):

```
$byte = pack('S',256);
```

To enforce information to be placed into a single byte, you can use the vec function. This will store numerical values within a string by specifying the number of bits to use within the string for storing a value. For example, to place a value into a byte:

```
vec($byte,0,8) = 128;
```

References
pack, vec

CCur

```
CCur(expression)
```

Converts expression into a currency type.

Perl Equivalent

None; Perl has no currency data type.

CDbl

```
CDbl(expression)
```

Converts `expression` into a double (floating-point) value.

Perl Equivalent

Not necessary; Perl will automatically convert a value into a suitable type during calculations.

CDec

```
CDec(expression)
```

Converts a number to a decimal (base 10) format.

Perl Equivalent

None. If you need to convert a hexadecimal or octal number or string into decimal format, you can use the `hex` function:

```
hex(0755);
hex(0x7bef);
```

References

```
hex
```

ChDir

```
Chdir(expression)
```

Changes the current directory to `expression`.

Perl Equivalent

Use the `chdir` function, which operates in an identical fashion:

```
chdir('temp');
```

References

Chapter 4

ChDrive

```
ChDrive(expression)
```

Changes the current drive to `expression`.

Perl Equivalent

There is no direct equivalent, but you can use the `chdir` function under Windows to perform the same function:

```
chdir('C:');
```

References

Chapter 4

Choose

```
Choose(index%, expression1 [, expression2])
```

Returns the result of the expression at `index%`.

Perl Equivalent

There is no directly equivalent function; however, you can use subscript notation on a list of expressions to return an individual value. For example, the line

```
$selection = ('Fred', 'Wilma', 'Barney')[1];
```

would return `Wilma`.

References

Chapter 16

Chr, Chr$

```
Chr(asciicode%)
Chr$(asciicode%)
```

Returns the ASCII character corresponding to the number supplied by
`asciicode`.

Perl Equivalent

Use the `chr` function, which works in an identical fashion:

`chr(EXPR)`

References

`chre, ord`

ChrB, ChrB$

```
ChrB(asciicode%)
ChrB$(asciicode%)
```

Returns the ASCII character corresponding to the number supplied by
`asciicode` as a single byte.

Perl Equivalent

No equivalent; use the `chr` function.

References

`chr, ord`

ChrW, ChrW$

```
ChrW(asciicode%)
ChrW$(asciicode%)
```

Returns the character code for a multibyte character.

Perl Equivalent

No equivalent; Use the `chr` function. If you need Unicode character conversion, Perl does support the Unicode system, but the support is incom-
plete. See the `utf8` manual entry for information.

References

`chr, ord`

CInt

`CInt(expr)`

Converts `expr` to an integer.

Perl Equivalent

Use the `int` function:

`int(4/3);`

Note that no rounding occurs—this merely strips the fractional component.

References

`int`

CLng

`CLng(expr)`

Converts `expr` to a long integer.

Perl Equivalent

Perl doesn't distinguish between standard and long integers. Use the `int` function.

References

`int`

Close

`Close [#][filenumber%][, [#][filenumber%]]`

Close the file *filenumber*, or all open files if no arguments are supplied.

Perl Equivalent

You can only close a specific file handle using the Perl `close` function:

`close(FILEHANDLE);`

However, you do not have to explicitly close files; they will automatically be closed when the file handle goes out of scope or the script exits.

References

Chapter 4

Command

```
Command
```

Returns the arguments passed to the application when it was executed.

Perl Equivalent

Perl automatically populates the @ARGV array with the contents of the command line. Each individual word from the command line is in an individual element of the @ARGV array. For example, the line

```
C:\> perl script.pl -l option -i option
```

would have an @ARGV array of

```
('-l', 'option', '-i', 'option')
```

If you want to be able to parse options like the ones above, see the GetOpt::Long module.

CommitTrans

```
CommitTrans
```

Commits transactions to a database.

Perl Equivalent

No direct equivalent. See Chapter 3 for details on using the Win32::ODBC module with transaction processing.

References

Chapter 3

Const

```
[Global] Const name = expression [ name = expression]
```

Declare a variable as a constant.

Perl Equivalent

You can use the `constant` pragma (actually just another module) to create constant values. For example:

```
use constant PI => 3.141592654;
```

You can use any expression as the value, and you can call `use constant` as many times as you require. Therefore, the following will also work:

```
use constant PI => 22/7;
use constant USER => Win32::LoginName();
```

Cos

```
Cos(angle)
```

Returns the cosine of an angle (in radians).

Perl Equivalent

Use the `cos` function:

```
cos(EXPR);
```

References

cos

CreateObject

```
CreateObject(class [, server])
```

Creates a new object of type `class` either on the local machine or on the remote `server`.

Perl Equivalent

The actual method for creating new objects depends on the class definition; however, as a general rule, you use the `new` method with a class. For example, to create a new `IO::Socket` object:

```
$socket = IO::Socket->new(Domain => 'INET');
```

Or to create a new `LWP::UserAgent` object:

```
my $ua = new LWP::UserAgent;
```

It's not possible to create a new Perl object on a remote machine, but you can use Perl and the `Win32::OLE` module to create remote instances of a COM object. To do this, use an array as the first argument when creating a new object. For example:

```
use Win32::OLE;

$excel = new Win32::OLE(['incontinent','Excel.Application'],\&Quit)
    || die "Cannot create OLE instance";
```

References

Chapter 11

CSng

```
CSng(expression)
```

Converts an `expression` into a single-precision floating-point value.

Perl Equivalent

CStr

```
CStr(expression)
```

Converts any data type to a string.

Perl Equivalent

Not generally required, since Perl will automatically convert to a string as required. To very simply convert a scalar variable into a string, use interpolation and embed the variable into a quoted string:

```
$string = "$variable";
```

If you want to convert an expression, then use `sprintf` and supply the expression as the first argument to the function:

```
$string = sprintf(45*34);
```

With `sprintf`, you can also format the information. See Chapter 22 for more information on the function.

If you want to convert an array to a string, you can use the `join` function. This is the logical opposite of the `split` function. The first argument takes the string to interpolate between each element, and the remaining elements are the array that you want to format:

```
@array = qw/34 tins dogfood/;
$string = join(' ',@array);
```

For hashes, you'll need to use a loop:

```
foreach $key (sort keys %hash)
{
    $string .= "$key = $hash{$key}\n";
}
```

For more complex structures, you will need to develop your own formats for converting them into strings.

References

Chapter 16, `join`, `sprintf`

CurDir, CurDir$

```
CurDir$([drive$])
CurDir([drive$])
```

Returns the current directory, or the current directory for the drive specified by `drive$`.

Perl Equivalent

There is no built-in function; for Windows-only development, you can use the `Win32::GetCwd` function:

```
use Win32;
print Win32::GetCwd();
```

Alternatively, you can use the `getcwd` function, which comes as part of the `Cwd` module:

```
use Cwd;
print getcwd();
```

The Win32 module is more reliable under Windows and will also return the current directory in Windows (backslash) rather than Unix (forward slash) format.

CVar

```
CVar(expression)
```

Converts the given `expression` to a Variant data type.

Perl Equivalent

No equivalent. Since for most basic data—numbers, strings, characters—Perl will automatically convert any variable. There is no need for a separate variant data type.

CVDate

```
CVDate(expression)
```

Converts `expression` to a date data type.

Perl Equivalent

Perl does not have a strict date data type. For most purposes, dates are stored as the number of seconds that have elapsed since the epoch. See the #DATE# entry for details on converting individual date components into a more usable value.

CVErr

```
CVErr(errornum)
```

Creates an error object based on the error number in `errornum`.

Perl Equivalent

Perl handles built-in errors through the use of a global variable. The $! variable holds the error number or error string for the last error that occurred. In a numerical context, the variable will return the corresponding error number, whereas in a string context, it will return the corresponding error text:

```
print 0+$!; Returns error number
print $!; Returns
```

For OS-specific errors, you can use the $^E variable, but it's more reliable to use the Win32::GetLastError function to return the error number and Win32::FormatMessage function to convert the error number into a text string.

References

Chapter 18

Date

```
Date = date
```

Sets the system date to the value of date.

Perl Equivalent

No equivalent. There is no standard way of setting the system date from within Perl. In theory, it should be possible to set the date by communicating directly with the external date command, but this is not recommended.

Date, Date$

```
Date
Date$
```

Returns the current date as a date type or string type.

Perl Equivalent

Perl has an internal function that returns the number of seconds since the epoch called time. This is equivalent to the global Now variable supported in Visual Basic. You can supply the return value from this to the localtime or gmtime functions—if you don't supply a value, then the functions automatically use the time value. Both functions return a list of individual date and time values in a list context, or a simple string representation of the date and time in a scalar context. The difference between the two functions is that localtime returns the time of the current machine according to the current time zone, whereas gmtime returns the Greenwich time—that is, with no time zone adjustment.

In a scalar context, the format of the date and time string returned is as follows:

```
Sat Apr  1 11:56:51 2000
```

For example, to get a date string:

```
$datetime = localtime();
```

Or, to print the date and time:

```
print scalar localtime();
```

Note that you need to use the scalar keyword to ensure that the localtime function operates in a scalar rather than a list context.

In a list context, it returns the following information:

```
#  0    1    2    3    4    5    6    7    8
($sec,$min,$hour,$mday,$mon,$year,$wday,$yday,$isdst) = localtime(time);
```

Note that the information return is not in a ready-to-use format. The value of $mon starts at zero for January, and $year is the number of years since 1900.

To extract only the date, use a subscript on the function:

```
($mday, $mon, $year) = (localtime())[3..5];
$mon += 1;
$year += 1900;

print sprintf("%d/%d/%d",$mday, $mon, $year);
```

To print out the date with a month string, use an array to hold the month data:

```
@months = qw/Jan Feb Mar Apr May Jun Jul Aug Sep Oct Nov Dec/;
($mday, $mon, $year) = (localtime())[3..5];
$year += 1900;

print sprintf("%d %s %d",$mday, $months[$mon], $year);
```

TABLE C-1

Interval
conversions.

Interval	Description
yyyy	Year
q	Quarter
m	Month
y	Day of year
d	Day
w	Weekday
ww	Week
h	Hour
n	Minute
s	Second

References

```
localtime, gmtime, time
```

DateAdd

```
DateAdd(interval$, number%, dateVar)
```

Adds a specific value to an existing date variable. The `interval$` argument is the type of value to be added; valid values are shown in Table C-1.

Perl Equivalent

There isn't a direct equivalent, but you can add values to Perl time references to create new values. The following script actually emulates the VB `DateAdd` function:

```
use Time::Local;

sub DateAdd
{
    my ($interval, $number, $time, $sec,
        $min, $hour, $mday, $mon, $year);

    if (@_ <= 3)
    {
        if (@_ == 2)
```

```
        {
            $time = time();
            ($interval, $number) = @_;
        }
        else
        {
            ($interval, $number, $time) = @_;
        }
        ($sec,$min,$hour,$mday,$mon,$year)
            = (localtime($time))[0..5];
    }
    else
    {
        ($interval, $number, $time, $sec,
         $min, $hour, $mday, $mon, $year) = @_;
    }

    $year += $number if ($interval eq 'yyyy');
    if (($interval eq 'q') || ($interval eq 'm'))
    {
        $mon += $number if ($interval eq 'm');
        $mon += ($number*3) if ($interval eq 'q');
        if ($mon > 11)
        {
            $year += int ($mon/12);
            $mon = $mon % 12;
        }
    }

    $newtime = timelocal($sec,$min,$hour,$mday,$mon,$year);

    $newtime += ($number*24*60*60) if (($interval eq 'y') ||
                                       ($interval eq 'd') ||
                                       ($interval eq 'w'));
    $newtime += ($number*7*24*60*60) if ($interval eq 'ww');
    $newtime += ($number*60*60) if ($interval eq 'h');
    $newtime += ($number*60) if ($interval eq 'n');
    $newtime += $number if ($interval eq 's');
    return $newtime;
}
```

To use, supply the interval type and the number to be added. If you don't supply a time value, then the current time will be used. Alternatively, you can supply either an epoch value or the seconds, minutes, hours, day of the month, month, and year, in the same format as that returned by localtime.

For example:

```
print scalar localtime(DateAdd('ww',3)),"\n";
```

generates

```
Sat Apr 22 13:50:51 2000
```

DateDiff

```
DateDiff(interval$,date1,date2 [,firstdayofweek [,firstweekofyear]])
```

Returns the number of intervals between `date1` and `date2`.

Perl Equivalent

There's no built-in equivalent, but you can use `localtime` in combination with comparing the two epoch values. The following script emulates the `DateDiff` function:

```
use Time::Local;

sub DateDiff
{
    my ($interval,$datea,$dateb) = @_;

    $timeval = $dateb-$datea;

    return int($timeval/(7*24*60*60)) if ($interval eq 'ww');
    return int($timeval/(24*60*60))
        if ($interval eq 'w' || $interval eq 'd' || $interval eq 'y');
    return int($timeval/(60*60)) if ($interval eq 'h');
    return int($timeval/(60)) if ($interval eq 'n');
    return $timeval if ($interval eq 's');

    my ($sec,$min,$hour,$day,$mon,$year)
        = (localtime($timeval))[0..5];

    $year -= 70;

    return int(($year*12)+$mon) if ($interval eq 'm');
    return int((($year*12)+$mon)/3) if ($interval eq 'q');
    return $year if ($interval eq 'yyyy');
    my $return;
}
```

Note that we have to take into account the year. This is because Perl treats time values as the number of seconds since the epoch, which is midnight on 1st Jan 1970, but the actual number of years returned by `localtime` is quoted as the number of years since 1900.

DatePart

```
DatePart(INTERVAL$,DATE)
```

Returns the interval part of the supplied DATE value.

Perl Equivalent

Use the `localtime` or `gmtime` function, and select the element you want. For example, to get the day of the week:

```
my ($dayofweek) = (localtime())[6];
```

References

`localtime`

DateSerial

```
DateSerial(year%, month%, day%)
```

Returns a date type for the supplied date values.

Perl Equivalent

Use the `timelocal` function from the `Time::Local` module.

DateValue

```
DateValue(string)
```

Converts STRING to a date data type.

Perl Equivalent

There is no built-in equivalent, but the `Date::Parse` module (available from CPAN) takes standard date strings and converts them into an epoch value:

```
use Date::Parse;
$time = str2time("1st Apr 2000 20:00:01");
```

Day

```
Day(date)
```

Returns the day of the month for `date`.

Perl Equivalent

Use the fourth element from the values returned by `localtime`:

```
my ($day) = (localtime())[3];
```

References

localtime, gmtime, time

DDB

```
DDB(cost@, salvage@, life%, period% [, factor])
```

Calculates the depreciation of an item according to its COST.

Perl Equivalent

None. See the `Math::Financial` module for some financial functions and extensions to the Perl language.

Declare

```
Declare Sub Procname Lib Libname$ ...
```

Creates a local reference to a procedure or function from an external library.

Perl Equivalent

With Perl, when you use a module, it generally imports the functions that you want into the local namespace, in a similar fashion to `Declare`. There are occasions when modules only export functions when you specifically request them. In those situations, you need to supply a list of functions or function sets that you want to import.

References

Chapter 17

DefBool

```
DefBool letterrange
```

Defines all variables starting with `letterrange` as boolean data types.

Perl Equivalent

None.

DefByte

```
DefByte letterrange
```

Defines all variables starting with `letterrange` as byte data types.

Perl Equivalent

None.

DefCur

```
DefCur letterrange
```

Defines all variables starting with `letterrange` as currency data types.

Perl Equivalent

None.

DefDate

```
DefDate letterrange
```

Defines all variables starting with `letterrange` as date data types.

Perl Equivalent

None.

DefDbl

```
DefDbl letterrange
```

Defines all variables starting with `letterrange` as double data types.

Perl Equivalent

None.

DefDec

```
DefDec letterrange
```

Defines all variables starting with `letterrange` as decimal data types.

Perl Equivalent

None.

DefInt

```
DefInt letterrange
```

Defines all variables starting with `letterrange` as integer data types.

Perl Equivalent

None.

DefLng

```
DefLng letterrange
```

Defines all variables starting with `letterrange` as long data types.

Perl Equivalent

None.

DefObj

```
DefObj letterrange
```

Defines all variables starting with `letterrange` as object data types.

Perl Equivalent

None.

DefSng

`DefSng letterrange`

Defines all variables starting with `letterrange` as single data types.

Perl Equivalent

None.

DefStr

`DefStr letterrange`

Defines all variables starting with `letterrange` as string data types.

Perl Equivalent

None.

DefVar

`DefVar letterrange`

Defines all variables starting with `letterrange` as variant data types.

Perl Equivalent

None.

DeleteSetting

`DeleteSetting appname, section [,key]`

Deletes the registry entry (according to the supplied `key` and `section`) or the entire section (according to `section`) for the application `appname`.

Perl Equivalent

No built-in equivalent. However, you can use the `Win32API::Registry` or `Win32::TieRegistry` modules to do the work for you.

References

Chapter 8

Dim

```
Dim [Shared] name [As [New] type] [, ...]
```

Declare a new variable name as the data type type.

Perl Equivalent

You do not have to predeclare Perl variable before you use them. However, if you do want to initialize a variable, just assign the data to it:

```
$string = "Hello World\n";
```

To declare a variable within a specific scope, use the my keyword:

```
my $string = "Hello World\n";
```

References

Chapter 16

Dir, Dir$

```
Dir(pattern$ [, attributes])
Dir$(pattern$ [, attributes])
Dir
Dir$
```

Returns the first file matching the PATTERN, and then subsequent calls without any arguments return the next file matching the PATTERN.

Perl Equivalent

For a simpler approach, use the glob function to return a list of files matching a given pattern:

```
@files = glob("*.pl");
```

For a similar approach as the VB function, use the opendir functions:

```
opendir (DIR, '.') or die "Couldn't open directory, $!";
while ($file = readdir DIR)
{
    print "$file\n";
}
close DIR;
```

References

Chapter 4

Do...Loop

```
Do [While | Until condition] [statements] [Exit Do] [statements] Loop
Do [statements] Loop [While|Until condition]
```

Cycles through a loop until the necessary condition is met.

Perl Equivalent

Perl supports the while **and** until **loops. Both are of the same format:**

```
do
{
...
} [while|until] CONDITION
```

Like the VB equivalent, you can also test at the beginning of the loop, but only with the while loop:

```
while CONDITION
{
...
}
```

References

Chapter 16

DoEvents

```
DoEvents()
DoEvents
```

Provides a pause for other system events to process during the execution of a loop.

Perl Equivalent

Not strictly necessary, Perl does not tie up system resources while executing.

End

```
End [Function | If | Select | Sub | Type]
```

Terminates the script, function, If statement, or other definition.

Perl Equivalent

To terminate the execution of a script, use the exit function:

```
exit;
```

You can supply an optional argument that will be the return value to supply to the calling program.

Functions, test statements, and other statement blocks are terminated by braces. For example:

```
if (1)
{
...
}
```

References

Chapter 16

Enum

```
Enum setName
    constName1 = val1
    constName1 = val2
End Enum
```

Enumerates a set of constants.

Perl Equivalent

None, use the const pragma:

```
use const PI => 3.141592654;
```

Environ, Environ$

```
Environ$(entry-name$ | entry-position%)
Environ(entry-name$ | entry-position%)
```

Returns information on the current environment.

Perl Equivalent

The %ENV hash contains the environment of the current application. To access, supply the environment variable's name as the key of the hash:

```
$path = $ENV{PATH};
```

References

Chapter 5

EOF

```
EOF(file-number)
```

Returns the end-of-file condition for the given file-number.

Perl Equivalent

The eof function works in an identical fashion. However, you must supply the eof function the filehandle. For example:

```
eof(FILE);
```

References

Chapter 4

Eqv

```
a Eqv b
```

Returns the logical equivalence between A and B; effectively the same as a bitwise AND operation on the two elements.

Perl Equivalent

The & operator is the bitwise AND operator:

```
$a & $b
```

References

Chapter 16

Erase

```
Erase Arrayname [, arrayname]
```

Empties the array `Arrayname`.

Perl Equivalent

To empty the contents of an array or hash in Perl, just assign an empty list to the variable:

```
@array = ();
%hash  = ();
```

References

Chapter 16

Err Object

```
Err.Clear
Err.Raise
```

The `Err` object contains all of the information about a specific error. The `Clear` method clears the current error, and the `Raise` method raises an error of a specific type. The `Description` and `Number` properties of the `Err` object contain the error text and number, respectively.

Perl Equivalent

There is no error object; nor is there any way of raising or clearing a specific error. To get the error number of the last error to occur, you need to access the `$!` variable in a numerical context. The error message text is accessible when `$!` is accessed in a string context.

References

Chapters 8 and 18

Error

```
Error errorcode%
```

Generates an error of the type `errorcode`.

Perl Equivalent

None.

Error, Error$

```
Error$[(errorcode%)]
Error[(errorcode%)]
```

Returns the error string for the given `errorcode`.

Perl Equivalent

Use `$!` in a string context:

```
print $!;
```

References

Chapter 16

Event

```
[Public] Event procedurename [arglist]
```

Creates a user-defined event, designed to handle a specific occurrence.

Perl Equivalent

None. Although it is theoretically possible to trace events using signals, the list of supported signals under Windows is limited, and even under Unix is fixed. In theory, you could use the `Win32::Event` module to support a similar system.

References

Chapter 6

Exit

```
Exit Do
Exit For
Exit Sub
Exit Function
```

Exits the current operation before the conditions are complete.

Perl Equivalent

Within a function, you need to use the `return` keyword to immediately return before the function would naturally end. For example:

```
sub greet
{
    my ($msg) = @_;
    if ($msg)
    {
        print "$msg\n";
        return;
    }
    print "No Message!\n";
}
```

Within any other type of loop, you can use the `last` keyword:

```
while(<STDIN>)
{
    last if (m/\./);
}
```

References

Chapter 16

Exp

```
Exp(power)
```

Raises the base of the natural logarithm e to the power of `power`.

Perl Equivalent

Use the `exp` function:

```
print exp(10);
```

References

exp

False

False

The constant used to identify a false result or value.

Perl Equivalent

As a general rule, 0 indicates false within Perl. However, the undef value is also treated as false within Perl.

References

Chapter 16

FileAttr

FileAttr(filenumber% [, infotype%])

Returns the current mode of the file. The return value of the mode is an integer and can be a combination of input (1), output (2), random (4), append (8), binary (32).

Perl Equivalent

None. It's not possible to determine the mode in which a file handle has been opened, even when using the IO::Handle module.

References

Chapter 4

FileCopy

FileCopy source$, dest$

Copies the file from source to dest.

Perl Equivalent

There is no built-in function, but the `File::Copy` module allows you to copy or move files from one location to another:

```
use File::Copy;
copy('source', 'dest');
move('source', 'dest');
```

You can use the same module to copy an open file handle. Just supply it with a reference to a glob for the filehandle. In other words:

```
copy(\*SOURCE, 'dest');
```

FileDateTime

```
FileDateTime(filename$)
```

Returns the date and time when a file was last modified.

Perl Equivalent

Use the `stat` function to extract the modification time for a given file, and then use the `localtime` function to convert the returned integer into a real date and time:

```
my ($modtime) = (stat($file))[9];
my ($sec,$hours,$min,$mday,$mon,$year) = (localtime($modtime))[0..5];
$mon++;
$year += 1900;
```

References

Chapter 4

FileLen

```
FileLen(filename$)
```

Returns the length of `filename` in bytes.

Perl Equivalent

Use the `-s` test to determine the file size:

```
$size = (-s $file);
```

References

Chapter 4

Filter

```
Filter(ARRAY, PATTERN [, INCLUDE [, COMPARE]])
```

Filters ARRAY, returning a new array containing only the objects which match PATTERN.

Perl Equivalent

The grep function allows you to perform regular expression matches against any list:

```
@filtered = grep /[A-Z]*/, @array;
```

References

grep

Fix

```
Fix(numericExpression)
```

Similar to Int, but for negative numbers, it returns the first negative number greater than or equal to the passed value. Int returns the first negative number less than or equal to the passed value.

Perl Equivalent

None.

For Each...Next

```
For Each ELEMENT In GROUP [statements] Next [element]
```

Iterates through each ELEMENT in GROUP.

Perl Equivalent

Use the foreach loop:

```
foreach ELEMENT (LIST)
```

References

Chapter 16

For...Next

```
For COUNTER = STARTVALUE To ENDVALUE [Step INCREMENT]
```

Iterates through a loop from STARTVALUE to ENDVALUE, jumping in INCREMENT increments.

Perl Equivalent

Use the for loop:

```
for(EXPRA; EXPRB; EXPRC)
```

where EXPRA is the initialization for the counter variable, EXPRB is the test condition, and EXPRC is the statement for incrementing the counter. For example, the statement

```
for($i=0;$i<50;$i++)
```

would set up a loop for 50 iterations with an increment of 1, while

```
for($i=10;$i<500;$i+=2)
```

would set up a loop starting at 10 and stopping when $i reaches 500, with an increment of 2.

References

Chapter 16

Format, Format$

```
Format$(numericExpression, editPattern$)
```

Returns a string version of numericexpression formatted according to editpattern.

Perl Equivalent

You can use the sprintf function to return a string formatted according to a given layout. For example, to format a floating-point number with two digits:

```
$string = sprintf("%.2f",3.141592654);
```

References

`sprintf`, `printf`

FormatCurrency

```
FormatCurrency(numericExpression [,numDecimalPlaces
  [, includeleaddigit [, useparensfornegs [, groupdigits]]]])
```

Formats a currency variable into the specified format.

Perl Equivalent

There is no direct equivalent, since Perl doesn't support the currency data type. You can use the `sprintf` function on a floating-point value to format the value according to precision, lead digits, and any numerical formatting.

For a more direct comparison, you can use the `Math::Currency` module, available from CPAN. For example, the following code formats a value for the German Deutschmark:

```
use Math::Currency;
Math::Currency->format({
                    PREFIX    =>  '',
                    SEPARATOR =>  ' ',
                    DECIMAL   =>  ',',
                    POSTFIX   =>  ' DM'
                    });
$deutschmark = Money(12345.67);
```

FormatDateTime

```
FormatDateTime(date [, namedFormat])
```

Formats a date/time in one of the predefined formats.

Perl Equivalent

You'll need to use the `localtime` or `gmtime` functions to convert a time value into its separate components, and then format the individual elements according to the style you want.

References

```
localtime, gmtime
```

FormatNumber

```
FormatNumber(numericExpression [, numDecimalPlaces
   [, includeleaddigit [,useparensfornegs [, groupdigits]]]])
```

Formats a number according to the given format.

Perl Equivalent

Use the `sprintf` function to format the numerical value according to your needs. For example, to output an eight-digit integer, prefixed with zeros:

```
$string = sprintf("%08d",9);
```

References

```
sprintf, printf
```

FormatPercent

```
FormatPercent(numericExpression [, numdecimalplaces
   [, includeleaddigit [,useparensfornegs [,groupdigits]]]])
```

Formats a numerical value as a percentage value.

Perl Equivalent

Use `sprintf` or `printf` to format the numerical component, and use the `%%` format string to introduce a percent sign into the resultant string. For example:

```
printf("%.2f%%",56.4);
```

References

```
sprintf, printf
```

FreeFile

```
FreeFile
```

Returns the next valid free file number.

Perl Equivalent

Not required. Perl will automatically use the next available file number for you. In fact, you don't even need to worry about file numbers:

```
open(DATA,"file.txt");
```

References

Chapter 4

FreeLocks

```
FreeLocks
```

Allows background processing to take place when using dynamic sets to ensure that the sets remain current.

Perl Equivalent

Not required.

Friend

```
Friend procedureName
```

Makes `procedureName` publicly available within the project, but does not publish the procedure outside of the project.

Perl Equivalent

No direct equivalent. Functions are automatically available within the current package, but to publicize a function from within a module to other scripts and modules that use the module, you need to use the `Exporter` module to export the function. For example:

```
require Exporter;
@ISA = 'Exporter';
@EXPORT = qw(helloworld);
@EXPORT_OK = qw(hellomoon);
```

The `@EXPORT` array contains a list of functions and variables that will be imported by the caller by default, whereas `@EXPORT_OK` lists the functions that can be imported if specifically requested.

References

Chapter 17

Function...End Function

```
[Static] [Private] Function Function-name [(arguments)]
...
End Function
```

Defines a function within a module of form.

Perl Equivalent

Use the sub keyword to define a new function:

```
sub function
{
...
}
```

To extract any arguments supplied to the function, you need to access the individual elements of the @_ array. The first argument passed will be in $_[0]. You can extract a list of arguments using a list assignment:

```
sub function
{
    my ($arga, $argb, $argc) = @_;
...
}
```

To return a value from a function, use the return keyword:

```
sub function
{
    return "Hello World!";
}
```

References

Chapter 17

FV

```
FV(rate!, numperiods%, payment@, presentvalue@, whendue%)
```

Returns the future value of an annuity.

Perl Equivalent

No direct equivalent. You can, however, use the `Math::Financial` module to calculate the value for you.

Get

```
Get [#]filenumber% [, postition&], recordbuffer
```

Retrieves information from an open file and places it into a variable.

Perl Equivalent

Once you have opened a file, you can use a number of different methods to access data from the file. If you are reading the file line by line, you can use the `<FILEHANDLE>` operator to extract a single line from a file:

```
$line = <FILE>;
```

To get a specific number of bytes from a file, use the `sysread` function. For example, to read 80 bytes from a file:

```
sysread FILE, $buffer, 80;
```

References

Chapter 4

GetAllStrings

```
GetAllSettings(appName, section)
```

Gets all the settings for an application from the registry.

Perl Equivalent

No built-in equivalent, but you can use the `Win32::Registry` module. For example, to open a root registry key that points to Microsoft software:

```
$HKEY_LOCAL_MACHINE->Open('Software\Microsoft',$msroot);
```

References

Chapter 8

GetAttr

```
GetAttr(fileName$)
```

Returns the attributes of a given file.

Perl Equivalent

Use the `stat` function to get basic information, or use one of the `-X` file tests to get more specific information about the file's type and accessibility. To access the Windows attributes of a file, use the `Win32::File::GetAttributes` function.

References

Chapter 4

GetAutoServerSettings

```
object.GetAutoServerSettings([progID], [classID])
```

Retrieves the OLE registry condition of an ActiveX component.

Perl Equivalent

None.

GetObject

```
GetObject([pathName] [,className])
```

Returns a reference to a current object or creates the object if unavailable.

Perl Equivalent

Use the `GetObject` constructor within the `Win32::OLE` module. For example:

```
use Win32::OLE;

$document = Win32::OLE->GetObject("PW32-11.doc");
```

References

Chapter 11

GetSetting

```
GetSetting(appName, section, key [,default])
```

Reads a key setting from the application's area of the Windows registry.

Perl Equivalent

Use the `Win32::Registry` module to obtain the information.

References

Chapter 8

Global

```
Global name [As [New] type][, name [As [New] type]]
```

Declares a variable as globally available to all forms and modules in a project.

Perl Equivalent

None; all variables are declared as global unless specified otherwise using the `my` or `local` keywords. However, note that global variables are global only within the package scope.

References

Chapter 17

GoSub...Return

```
GoSub LineLabel | Linenumber
```

Jumps to a piece of code from within a subroutine or function.

Perl Equivalent

You can use the `goto` keyword to go to a labeled piece of code. However, you cannot return to the caller. Unless you have a specific reason for using `goto`, you should use a function call instead.

References

```
goto
```

GoTo

```
Goto [Linelabel | Linenumber]
```

Jump execution to another part of the application.

Perl Equivalent

Use a function or, if absolutely necessary, the goto keyword.

References

```
goto
```

Hex, Hex$

```
Hex(numericExpression)
```

Converts a number to its hexadecimal equivalent.

Perl Equivalent

Use sprintf to convert a number to hexadecimal format:

```
$hex = sprintf("%x",99);
```

The Perl hex function does the opposite; it takes a hexadecimal string and converts it into its decimal equivalent.

References

```
sprintf
```

Hour

```
Hour(dateVariant)
```

Returns the hour portion of a date and time value.

Perl Equivalent

Use the second element from the list returned by gmtime or localtime.

```
$hour = (localtime(time))[2];
```

References

localtime, gmtime, time

If...Then...Elsif...End If

```
If condition-1 Then
    [actions-1]
[ElsIf condition-2 Then]
    [actions-2]
[Else]
    [else-actions]
End If
```

Allows for the conditional execution of statements.

Perl Equivalent

Perl uses an identical if...elsif...else keyword set. There is no pending End If statement; the statement ends after the last block definition. For example:

```
if (1)
{

}
elsif (2)
{

}
else
{

}
```

References

Chapter 16

IIf

```
IIf(expression, valueIfTrue, valueIfFalse)
```

Simple If test that returns one of two values based on whether expression returns True.

Perl Equivalent

The Perl ?...:... statement provides the same functionality:

```
(expression) ? valueIfTrue : valueIfFalse;
```

For example:

```
(1) ? 'true' : 'false';
```

References

Chapter 16

Imp

```
a Imp b
```

Returns the logical implication from two values.

Perl Equivalent

None.

Implements

```
Implements name
```

Activates a specified interface or class as implemented within a class module.

Perl Equivalent

None. Use the method call format to call a method on an individual object:

```
$object->method();
```

References

Chapter 17

Input

```
Input #filenumber, var1 [,var2]
```

Returns a string from the open stream of an input or binary file.

Perl Equivalent

Since Input# reads a single line of information from a file, use the Perl <FILEHANDLE> operator:

```
$line = <FILE>;
```

References

Chapter 4

Input, Input$

```
Input$(inputlength%, [#]filenumber%)
```

Reads a specified number of characters from an open file.

Perl Equivalent

Use the `read` function to place information into a scalar:

```
read FILE, $buffer, 1024;
```

References

```
read, sysread
```


InputB, InputB$

```
InputB$(inputlength%, [#]filenumber%)
```

Reads a specified number of bytes from an open file.

Perl Equivalent

You'll need to use the `sysread` function to read raw binary data from a file without any form of character or line translation. You'll need to use `sysopen` rather than `open` to open the file:

```
sysopen DATA, "data.raw", O_RDWR;
sysread DATA, $buffer, 1024;
```

References

Chapter 4, `sysopen`, `sysread`

InputBox, InputBox$

```
InputBox$(msg$ [, [title$][, [default$][,xpos%, ypos%]]])
```

Presents an input dialog box that allows the user to enter text information.

Perl Equivalent

No direct equivalent. However, you can produce your own dialog box when working within the Tk environment.

References

Chapter 10

InStr

```
InStr([startpos&,] string1$, pattern$)
```

Returns the first position within `string1` that `pattern` occurs.

Perl Equivalent

Use the `index` function, which equates to:

```
index string1, pattern [, startpos]
```

References

`index`

InStrRev

```
InStrRev([startpos&,] string1$, pattern$)
```

Returns the first position within `string1` that `pattern` occurs starting from the end of the string.

Perl Equivalent

Use the `rindex` function, which equates to:

```
rindex string1, pattern [, startpos]
```

References

`rindex`

Int

```
Int(numericExpression)
```

Returns the integer value of `numericExpression`.

Perl Equivalent

Use the `int` function, which works in an identical fashion.

References

`int`

IPmt

```
IPmt(rate!, currentPeriod%, totalPeriods%, presentValue@
    [, FutureValue@, whenDue%])
```

Returns the interest rate per period calculated from an annuity.

Perl Equivalent

No built-in function, but the `Math::Financial` package provides an identical function.

IRR

```
IRR(valuesArray(), guess!)
```

Returns the return rate of a series of payments or receipts.

Perl Equivalent

No built-in function, but the `Math::Financial` package provides an identical function.

Is

```
a Is b
```

Compares two objects.

Perl Equivalent

There is no built-in function for comparing the values of objects. You'll have to create your own function that checks the properties of the two objects to determine their equality.

IsArray

IsArray(varName)

Returns True if varName holds a reference to an array.

Perl Equivalent

Use the ref function, which should return the string ARRAY if the reference you supply points to an array.

References

ref

IsDate

IsDate(variant)

Returns True if variant contains a valid date.

Perl Equivalent

None; there is no built-in date type in Perl.

IsEmpty

IsEmpty(varName)

Returns True if varName is empty.

Perl Equivalent

Use the defined function to determine whether a variable has been supplied a value.

References

Chapter 16, defined

IsError

IsError(varName)

Returns True if varName is an error.

Perl Equivalent

None; there is no built-in error type in Perl.

IsMissing

IsMissing(argName)

For procedures that allow optional arguments, this returns True if the optional argument was not supplied to the function.

Perl Equivalent

None; Perl handles the passing of arguments to functions differently.

References

Chapter 17

IsNull

IsNull(varName)

Returns True if varName holds a null value.

Perl Equivalent

The defined function will return True if the supplied variable has a valid value.

References

Chapter 16, defined

IsNumeric

IsNumeric(varName)

Returns True if varName is a numeric value.

Perl Equivalent

There is no built-in function, but you can use regular expressions to determine the contents:

```
print "Numeric" if ('234' =~ m/^[0-9]+$/);
```

You need to check the entire string by using the ^ and $ characters to define the start and end of the string.

References

Chapter 18

IsObject

```
IsObject(varName)
```

Returns True if varName is an object.

Perl Equivalent

Use the ref function, which should return the string REF variable you supply as a reference to a variable.

References

ref

Join

```
Join(array [, delimiter])
```

Concatenates strings contained in an array into a single string.

Perl Equivalent

If you only want to concatenate strings, use the . operator:

```
$string = 'Hello' . 'World!';
```

Alternatively, if you want to join together an array with an optional delimiter, use the Perl join function:

```
$string = join(' ',@array);
```

References

Chapter 18, join

Kill

```
Kill filename$
```

Deletes the file specified.

Perl Equivalent

Use the `unlink` function:

```
unlink("file.txt");
```

References

Chapter 4

LBound

```
LBound(arrayname [, dimension%])
```

Returns the lowest subscript available within an array.

Perl Equivalent

The lowest subscript available in any Perl array is always zero. There is a way to modify this, but the method is not recommended.

LCase, LCase$

```
LCase$(expression$)
```

Returns an all-lowercase string.

Perl Equivalent

The `lc` function returns a lowercase version of a string:

```
$lowercase = lc("UPPER");
```

The `lcfirst` function returns a string with only the first character converted to lowercase. Alternatively, you can use the `\L` escape code within an interpolated string:

```
print "\LUPPER\E";
```

which will print upper.

References
Chapter 18

Left, Left$

```
Left$(expression$, Length&)
```

Returns a string containing the first Length characters from expression.

Perl Equivalent
Use the substr function, the basic format is as follows:

```
substr EXPR, OFFSET, LEN
```

So the equivalent call would be:

```
substr expression, 0, Length;
```

References
Chapter 18, substr

Len

```
Len(variable-name)
```

Returns the length in characters of the supplied string.

Perl Equivalent
The length function provides the same functionality.

References
length

LenB

```
LenB(variable-name)
```

Returns the length of a string in bytes.

Perl Equivalent

The length function returns the number of characters/bytes in a given string or expression. Although Perl does provide Unicode (and therefore multibyte) character support, for most situations length will return the figure you expect. If you want to work with Unicode characters, check the perlunicode manual page that comes with the ActivePerl distribution.

References

length

Let

```
Let variablename = expression
```

Sets a variable to a particular value.

Perl Equivalent

Perl just uses the = operator to assign a value:

```
$string = "Hello World";
```

References

Chapter 16

Like

```
a Like b
```

Compares the string a with the pattern b.

Perl Equivalent

Use Perl regular expressions and the =~ operator to check a string against a match statement:

```
if ($string =~ /.*cat.*/)
{
...
}
```

References

Chapter 18

Line Input

```
Line Input #filenumber%, variable
```

Reads a single line from a sequential file.

Perl Equivalent

Use the `<FILEHANDLE>` operator:

```
$line = <DATA>;
```

References

Chapter 4

Load

```
Load form-name
```

Loads a form or control object but doesn't show it.

Perl Equivalent

None.

LoadPicture

```
LoadPicture(pircturefile$)
```

Loads a picture from the specified file for manipulation within a picture or image control.

Perl Equivalent

None. If you want to display a picture within a Tk object, you first need to create an icon object using the file information, and then assign that to the `image` property of the widget you are creating. For example:

```
$icon = $button->Photo(-file => 'icon.gif');
$button->configure(image => $icon);
```

References

Chapter 10

LoadResData

```
LoadResData(index,format)
```

Loads resource data from a resource file.

Perl Equivalent

None; Perl doesn't use resource files.

LoadResPicture

```
LoadResPicture(index,format)
```

Loads a picture from a resource file.

Perl Equivalent

None; Perl doesn't use resource files.

LoadResString

```
LoadResString(index)
```

Loads a string from a resource file.

Perl Equivalent

None; Perl doesn't use resource files.

Loc

```
Loc(filenumber%)
```

Returns the current location within a file.

Perl Equivalent

The `tell` function returns the current location within a filehandle:

```
$location = tell(DATA);
```

References

Chapter 4, `tell`

Lock...Unlock

```
Lock [#]filenumber% [,startpos&][ To endpos&]:
[statements] : Unlock [#]filenumber%[.startpos&] [ to endpos&]
```

Locks or unlocks access to parts of a file to prevent other processes from writing files that are open within the current process.

Perl Equivalent

None. There are file-locking techniques built into Perl, but many rely on Unix features. See Chapter 4 for an extensive discussion on file locking techniques supported under Windows.

References

Chapter 4

LOF

```
LOF([#]filenumber%)
```

Returns the length of a current open file.

Perl Equivalent

You can use the `-s` test on any filename to determine the file size. The file doesn't have to open. For example:

```
$size = -s "file.txt";
```

References

Chapter 4

Log

```
Log(numericExpression)
```

Returns the logarithmic value for a given expression.

Perl Equivalent

The `log` function performs the same basic calculation.

References

`log`

LSet

```
LSet resultvariable = sourcevariable
```

Left-justifies a string within the destination and fills the remainder with spaces.

Perl Equivalent

You need to use the `%s` with a negative width specification and the `sprintf` function. Because Perl doesn't use fixed-length strings, it's the format definition that defines the length of the resultant string. For example, to left-justify a 5-character word in a 10-character string:

```
$result = sprintf("%-10s",'Hello');
```

If you used a positive width, the string would be right-justified. In both cases, the string is padded with spaces.

References

`sprintf`, `printf`

LTrim, LTrim$

```
LTrim$(stringExpression$)
```

Returns a substring with the leading spaces from left to right removed from the passed string.

Perl Equivalent

The easiest approach is to use a regular expression to remove the spaces:

```
$string = '     Hello';
$string =~ s/^ *//g;
```

The ^ character tells the regular expression engine to search from the beginning of the string.

References

Chapter 18

Me Property

```
Me
```

Returns execution to the currently active form.

Perl Equivalent

None. Even with Tk, there is no need to return execution to the form, since it works on an event, rather than code, basis.

References

Chapter 10

Mid, Mid$

```
Mid$(stringExpression$, start& [, length&]) [= substString$]
```

Returns a substring from the string stringExpression starting at character start for length characters. If supplied, substString is used to replace the extracted text.

Perl Equivalent

The substr function performs the same operation. Both functions use the same basic syntax:

```
substr EXPR, OFFSET, LEN [, REPLACEMENT]
```

To extract a portion of a string:

```
$newstring = substr 'The Cat Sat', 4,3;
```

To replace a portion of a string:

```
$newstring = substr 'The Cat Sat', 4,3, 'Dog';
```

The replacement string does not have to be the same size, so you could write

```
$newstring = substr 'The Cat Sat', 4,3, 'Octopus';
```

References

substr

Minute

```
Minute(dateVariant)
```

Returns the minute portion of a date.

Perl Equivalent

Use the second element returned by the localtime or gmtime function:

```
($minute) = (localtime(time()))[1];
```

References

localtime, gmtime, time

MIRR

```
MIRR(valuesArray(), financeInterestRate!, reinvestmentInternalRate!)
```

Returns the modified internal rate of return.

Perl Equivalent

None

MkDir

```
MkDir(directory$)
```

Creates a new directory.

Perl Equivalent
Use the mkdir function:

```
mkdir("C:\Perltemp");
```

References
Chapter 4

Mod

```
a Mod b
```

Returns the modulus (remainder) of a divided by b.

Perl Equivalent
Use the % operator:

```
print 8 % 6, "\n";
```

References
Chapter 16

Month

```
Month(dateVariant)
```

Returns the month portion of a date.

Perl Equivalent
Use the fifth element returned by localtime or gmtime:

```
($month) = (localtime(time()))[4];
```

Remember that the month value returned starts at 0 for January, so you'll need to add 1 to the value returned to get a true month number.

References

localtime, gmtime, time

MonthName

MonthName(num [, abbreviate])

Returns the name for a specified month, or its abbreviated value.

Perl Equivalent

There's no built-in definition of month names; you'll need to compile your own month arrays:

```
@months = qw/JUNK
            January
            February
            ...
            December/;
($month) = (localtime(time()))[4];
$month++;
print "It's $months[$month]\n";
```

References

localtime, gmtime, time

MsgBox

MsgBox(message$ [, boxtype%][, windowtitle$])

Presents a message box to the screen and provides a mechanism for allowing input.

Perl Equivalent

None. You'll need to build your own message box using Tk, or use one of the many message box types produced by other people.

References

Chapter 10

Name

```
Name oldname As newname
```

Renames a file or directory from `oldname` to newname.

Perl Equivalent

Use the `rename` function:

```
rename "file.txt", "new.data";
```

References

Chapter 4

Not

```
Not expression
```

Logical negation.

Perl Equivalent

Use the `!` operator:

```
if (!$value)
...
```

Remember that for `if` tests it's clearer if you use

```
unless ($value)
...
```

instead of the `!` operator.

References

Chapter 16

Now

```
Now
```

Returns the current date and time.

Perl Equivalent

The `time` function returns a numerical value suitable for passing to `localtime` or `gmtime`.

References

`localtime, gmtime, time`

NPer

```
NPer(interestRate!, periodicPayment@, presentValue@
    [, futureValue@, whenDue%])
```

Returns the number of periods in an annuity.

Perl Equivalent

None. See the `Math::Financial` module for a similar function.

NPV

```
NPV(discountRate, valuesArray())
```

Returns the net present value based on payments, receipts, and discount rate.

Perl Equivalent

None. See the `Math::Financial` module for a similar function.

Oct, Oct$

```
Oct$(numericExpression)
```

Converts a number to its octal equivalent.

Perl Equivalent

You need to use the `sprintf` function to convert a decimal into an octal value:

```
$octal = sprintf("%o",14);
```

References

oct, sprintf, printf

On Error...

```
On Error GoTo error-handler
```

Installs an error handler routine for responding and acknowledging errors raised in your code.

Perl Equivalent

Perl uses a different system for identifying errors. See the discussion in Chapter 18 for more details.

References

Chapter 18

On...GoSub

```
On numericExpression GoSub Line1 [, Line 255]
```

Jumps to one of the list subroutines based on the value of numericExpression.

Perl Equivalent

The easiest way to implement this is to use multiple if statements:

```
functiona() if ($value = 2);
...
```

However, you can make the process even easier if you create an array, or even a hash that contains a list of functions, and then you use references to call the function. For example:

```
@functions = qw/get set/;
$function = $functions[0];
&{$function}(argument);
```

The leading & tells Perl to treat the `$function` as the name of the function call.

For an even safer alternative, you need to use a typeglob and examine the symbol table:

```
if (defined($main::{$function}))
{
    *code = \$main::{$function};
    &code(arguments);
}
```

The `$main::{$function}` checks that the function named in the string `$function` exists within the main package. Then `*code` creates a typeglob that points to the real function, and then we explicitly use `code` as a function by prefixing it with an & character.

References

Chapter 17

On...GoTo

```
On numericExpression GoTo Line1 [, Line255]
```

Changes execution to a subroutine based on the value of a numeric index.

Perl Equivalent

See the discussion on the `On...GoSub` function.

Open

```
Open filename$ [for mode] [Access access] [locktype] As
   [#]filenumber [Len=recordLength]
```

Opens a file for reading or writing.

Perl Equivalent

The `open` function:

```
open(DATA, "data.txt);
```

See the detailed discussion in Chapter 18 for more details on how to use files.

References

Chapters 4 and 18

Option Base

```
Option Base 0 | 1
```

Sets the default lower bound for arrays.

Perl Equivalent

There is a solution to this problem under Perl, but its use is to be thoroughly avoided as it could potentially break other areas of Perl code.

Option Compare

```
Option Compare (Binary|Text)
```

Sets the default comparison method for strings.

Perl Equivalent

The basic string comparisons operators, such as eq and gt operate in what VB calls a binary fashion. To operate in a case-insensitive mode, you need either to convert the strings during comparison using regular expressions, for example:

```
if ("\U$string\E" eq 'HELLO')
...
```

OR just regular expressions and specify the /i option:

```
if ($string =~ /hello/i)
...
```

References

Chapter 18

Option Explicit

```
Option Explicit
```

Requires that all variables be explicitly defined before use.

Perl Equivalent

The use strict pragma requires that all variables are defined before they are used:

```
use strict;
```

Option Private

```
Option Private Module
```

Prevents the method of a module being referenced from outside it.

Perl Equivalent

The only way to prevent access to a function within a Perl module is to omit it from either the @EXPORT or @EXPORT_OK variables.

References

Chapter 17

Or

```
a Or b
```

Logical OR.

Perl Equivalent

You can use either the || or OR operators to perform a logical OR operation in Perl. The difference is that OR has a lower precedence and can therefore be used without the use of brackets in certain situations without affecting the evaluation of the line.

References

Chapter 16

Partition

```
Partition(number&, startRange&, endRange&, interval&)
```

Returns a string denoting where the passed number occurs within the given range.

Perl Equivalent

None. You would need to develop your own function to calculate the value.

Pmt

```
Pmt(interestRate!, numberOfPayments%,
    presentValue@ [, futureValue@, whenDue%])
```

Returns a payment value for an annuity.

Perl Equivalent

None. Use the Math::Financial module.

PPmt

```
Pmt(interestRate!, whichPeriod%, totalPeriods%,
    presentValue@ [, futureValue@, whenDue%])
```

Returns the principal payment value for an annuity.

Perl Equivalent

None. Use the Math::Financial module.

Print

```
Print #filenumber [[Spc(n)|Tab(m)] expression [;|,]...]
```

Writes data to a specified sequential file.

Perl Equivalent

The print and printf functions allow you to write directly to an open file by supplying the file handle as the first argument:

```
print DATA "Hello World\n";
```

However, note that the first argument is not separated from the expression to be printed by a comma.

References

Chapters 4 and 18, `print`

Private

```
Private [Function|Sub|variableName]
```

Makes the entity private to the current form, module, or routine.

Perl Equivalent

None. If you want to hide an entity from the outside world within a module, omit the entity from the `@EXPORT` and `@EXPORT_OK` variables.

References

Chapter 17

Property Get/Let/Set

```
[Public|Private] [Static] Property Get name
[(arglist)] [As type] [statements] [Exit Property]
End Property
```

The `Property Get/Set/Let` functions allow you to minimize the direct accessibility of properties for individual objects.

Perl Equivalent

None. You cannot stop a programmer from accessing a property stored within an object if he or she knows the property name. There is, however, nothing to stop you from developing functions that access properties.

References

Chapter 18

Public

```
Public [Function|Sub|variablename]
```

Makes the named entity publicly available to other modules and forms.

Perl Equivalent

None. You'll need to declare the variable within the package to make it globally accessible within the package. To make a function or variable publicly accessible outside a module, just add it to the @EXPORT or @EXPORT_OK **arrays.**

References

Chapter 17

Put

```
Put [#]filenumber%, [position&], variablename
```

Writes variablename to a file.

Perl Equivalent

The print and printf functions allow you to write any expression to a file:

```
print DATA $string;
```

References

print

PV

```
PV(interestRate!, totalPeriods%, payment@ [, futureValue@, whenDue%])
```

Returns the present value of an annuity.

Perl Equivalent

None. Use the Math::Financial **module.**

QBColor

```
QBColor(color-number%)
```

Provides quick access to the simple colors supported within the QuickBasic system.

Perl Equivalent

None. However, most of the textual definitions of the colors will work within the Tk system.

References

Chapter 10

RaiseEvent

```
RaiseEvent eventName [(arglist)]
```

Simulates an event occurrence for user-created events.

Perl Equivalent

None. Perl does not directly support an event system. When developing with Tk, you can initiate different events in different ways according to the widgets (controls) you have created.

Randomize

```
Randomize [seed]
```

Initializes the random-number generator.

Perl Equivalent

The srand function initializes the random-number generator in Perl, and it too will accept an optional argument as a seed value. However, unlike the Randomizer VB function, the Perl srand function is automatically called before the first call to rand if it hasn't already been called.

References

srand, rand

Rate

```
Rate(totalperiods%, payment@, presentValue@
      [,futureValue@, whenDue%, guess!])
```

Returns the interest rate per period calculated from an annuity.

Perl Equivalent

None. Use the `Math::Financial` module.

ReDim

```
ReDim [Preserve] name[subscript-range][As type]
      [, namesubscript-range [ As type]]
```

Redimensions an array.

Perl Equivalent

Not required. Perl automatically resizes arrays for you; there are no limits to the size or dimension of an array in Perl.

Rem

```
Rem comment
```

Makes any following text invisible to the compiler.

Perl Equivalent

Perl uses the # symbol:

```
# This is a comment
print "Hello World\n" # Print a message
```

References

Chapter 16

Replace

```
Replace(str, find, replaceWith [,start [,count [,compare]]])
```

Replaces the text find with replaceWith within the string str.

Perl Equivalent

Use the regular expression system:

```
$string =~ s/find/replaceWith/;
```

References

Chapter 18

Reset

```
Reset
```

Closes all open files.

Perl Equivalent

None. There is no direct way of closing all the open files. Active file handles are automatically closed when the file handle goes out of scope, or when the script terminates, so you do not need to specifically close a file.

Resume

```
Resume [[0] | Next | line-number | line-label]
```

Resumes execution after an error-handling routine has completed.

Perl Equivalent

None. If you've installed a function that handles an error within Perl, just use the return keyword to return execution to the point of the function call.

References

```
return
```

Return

```
Return
```

Returns from a GoSub call within a subroutine.

Perl Equivalent

Perl uses the same return keyword. The only difference is that return can also be used to supply the return value from a function.

References

Chapter 17, return

RGB

```
RGB(red%, green%, blue%)
```

Returns a Long value representing the three RGB values supplied.

Perl Equivalent

None. When programming with Tk, you have to convert decimal RGB values into a hexadecimal string:

```
$color = sprintf("#%02x%02x%02x",142,112,219);
```

References

Chapter 10

Right, Right$

```
Right$(expression$, Length&)
```

Returns a string containing the amount of the right portion of the passed string.

Perl Equivalent

Use the substr function with a negative value to extract characters from the right-hand end of a string:

```
$string = 'Hello World';
$world = substr $string,-5;
```

References

substr

RmDir

```
RmDir dirname$
```

Removes the specified empty directory.

Perl Equivalent

The rmdir function performs the same operation.

References

Chapter 4, rmdir

Rnd

```
Rnd [(numericExpression)]
```

Returns a random number between 0 and 1.

Perl Equivalent

The rand function returns a random number, but allows you to specify the upper range in integers. For example, the call

```
$random = rand(100);
```

would return an integer random number between 0 and 100.

References

rand

Rollback

```
Rollback
```

Aborts the currently pending database operations—that is, modifications are not committed to the database.

Perl Equivalent

None. Although when working with the `Win32::ODBC` module, you can call the `Transact` method with the `SQL_ROLLBACK` constant to rollback a transaction on a database connection that supports it. For example:

```
$db->Transact(SQL_ROLLBACK);
```

References

Chapter 3

Round

```
Round(num [,numDecimalPlaces])
```

Rounds the passed `num` value to the specified number of decimal places.

Perl Equivalent

No direct equivalent, but you can use the `%f` format to the `printf` or `sprintf` functions to round a number:

```
$round = sprintf("%.2f",3.5);
```

The number after the period defines the number of decimal places.

References

`sprintf`, `printf`

RSet

```
Rset resultvariable = sourcevariable
```

Right-justifies a string, padding the characters with spaces.

Perl Equivalent

The `%s` format to the `sprintf` function automatically right-justifies a string. You'll need to supply the width of justification. For example, to right-justify to 20 characters:

```
$string = sprintf("%20s", 'Hello World');
```

References

sprintf, printf

RTrim, RTrim$

RTrim$(stringExpression)

Returns a substring with the trailing spaces from the right removed from the passed string.

Perl Equivalent

Use a regular expression substitution to strip the trailing spaces from a string:

```
$string =~ s/ *$/;
```

References

Chapter 18

SavePicture

SavePicture objectReference, picturefile$

Saves the image stored in a picture or image control.

Perl Equivalent

None.

SaveSetting

SaveSetting appName, section, key, setting

Writes an entry into the Windows Registry.

Perl Equivalent

You can use the Win32::Registry to access and update values in the Windows Registry.

References
Chapter 8

Second

```
Second(dateVariant)
```

Returns the seconds portion of the date and time variable passed to it.

Perl Equivalent
Accesses the first element of the list returned by either the `gmtime` or `localtime` functions:

```
($second) = (localtime(time()))[0];
```

References
`localtime, gmtime, time`

Seek

```
Seek [#]filenumber%, position&
```

Seeks to the `position` within the specified file.

Perl Equivalent
The `seek` function will seek to a specific location within a filehandle:

```
seek DATA, 1024, 0;
```

References
Chapters 4 and 18

Select Case

```
Select Case expression
    Case expression1
        [statements]
    ...
End Select
```

Executes a group of statements based on the value of `expression`.

Perl Equivalent

There is no `case` statement supported within Perl. You will need to use a series of `if...elsif` statements to provide the same functionality. See Chapter 16 for more information on other techniques for emulating `case` statements.

References

Chapter 16

SendKeys

```
SendKeys keystrokes$[, wait%]
```

Sends keystrokes to the active window.

Perl Equivalent

None. If you are using Tk, you can introduce key events to an application manually.

References

Chapter 10

Set

```
Set objectVariableName = [New] objectExpression
```

Creates a reference to an object.

Perl Equivalent

Use the \ (backslash) operator to identify a reference to a variable:

```
$string = "Hello World";
$reference = \$string;
```

Since all objects are accessed through the use of references to variables, all objects are in fact references. The exact statement will depend on how the object has been implemented, but the preferred method is as follows:

```
$ftp = new Net::FTP();
```

References

Chapter 16

SetAttr

```
SetAttr fileName$, attributeBits%
```

Sets the attributes of a file given a proper filename and path.

Perl Equivalent

Use the `Win32::File::SetAttributes` module:

```
Win32::File::SetAttributes(FILE, ATTR);
```

References

Chapter 4

SetDefaultWorkspace

```
SetDefaultWorkspace userName$, password$
```

Sets the default user name and password for accessing secure databases.

Perl Equivalent

When using the `Win32::ODBC` module, how you specify the user name and password depends on the driver you are using and the configuration of the DSN.

References

Chapter 3

Sgn

```
Sgn(numericExpression)
```

Returns the sign (+/-) of the number passed to it.

Perl Equivalent

None, but you can use a simple `if` statement to work it out:

```
print "Negative" if ($value < 0);
print "Positive" if ($value >= 0);
```

This assumes that you want to take 0 as a positive value, which is the default in Perl.

Shell

```
Shell(programname$ [, mode%])
```

Executes `programname`.

Perl Equivalent

There are a variety of ways to execute programs from Perl. The best way is to use the `system` function:

```
system('dir');
```

If you want to capture the output from the command, use backticks:

```
$directory = `dir`;
```

References

Chapters 5 and 6

Show Method

```
window.Show
```

Makes the current window visible.

Perl Equivalent

No direct equivalent. You can raise or move the current focus of a widget within a Tk window, but this does not guarantee to make the current window visible.

References

Chapter 10

Sin

```
Sin(angle)
```

Returns the sine of an angle specified in radians.

Perl Equivalent
The `sin` function performs the same calculation.

References
```
sin
```

SLN

```
SLN(initialCost@, salvageValue@, lifeSpan%)
```

Returns the value for a single period of straight line depreciation.

Perl Equivalent
None. The `Math::Financial` module, available from CPAN, contains a suite of financial functions.

Space, Space$

```
Space(number%)
```

Returns a string containing the number of spaces specified.

Perl Equivalent
Use string multiplication:

```
$blank = ' ' x 20;
```

References
Chapter 16

Spc

```
Spc(number%)
```

Adds spaces for formatting when working with the `Print` function.

Perl Equivalent

None. Either use string multiplication (see `Space`) or the `printf` function to format the string with leading or trailing space padding.

References

`sprintf, print`

Split

```
Split(str [,delimit [,count [,compare]]])
```

Splits a string on a fixed delimiter, up to a specified number of times.

Perl Equivalent

The `split` function provides the same functionality but allows you to supply a regular expression, rather than a simple character, on which to split the string. For example:

```
@split = split /,/,$string;
```

A third optional argument will limit the split to a specific number of elements.

References

Chapter 18, `split`

Sqr

```
Sqr(numericExpression)
```

Returns the square root of a given number.

Perl Equivalent

The `sqrt` function performs an identical calculation.

References

`sqrt`

Static

```
Static name [As type][, name [As type]]...
```

Makes a variable persistent even after the function has completed.

Perl Equivalent

None. If you store a value in a global, rather than local, variable, its value will remain between function calls, but you will need to ensure that other functions do not modify the variable.

Stop

```
Stop
```

Halts the execution of a program.

Perl Equivalent

The `exit` function will immediately halt the execution of a Perl script. It can also be used to return an exit value to the calling program, which could be trapped. Just supply the exit value:

```
exit 1;
```

Str, Str$

```
Str$(numericExpression)
```

Converts an expression to a string.

Perl Equivalent

Perl will automatically convert any numerical expression to a string when required; there is no need for a separate function. If you want to format the expression, use the `printf` or `sprintf` functions.

References

Chapter 16, `sprintf`

StrComp

```
StrComp(string1$, string2$ [, compareType%])
```

Compares two strings.

Perl Equivalent

The eq operator compares two strings for their equality, and the gt, lt, ge, le compare two strings according to whether they are greater than, less than, greater than or equal to, or less than or equal to each other. The ne operator tests for nonequality. For example, the following test returns True:

```
if ('Hello' eq 'Hello')
```

References

Chapter 16

StrConv

```
StrConv(str, convertType [,LCID])
```

Converts a string between character sets, or for simple conversions such as upper- or lowercase.

Perl Equivalent

Rather than a single function, Perl provides a number of methods for converting a string to different cases. The lc and uc convert an entire string to lower- or uppercase. The lcfirst and ucfirst functions convert only the first character of the entire string converted to lower- or uppercase.

You can also use translation to convert entire strings from lowercase to uppercase. For example, to convert from lowercase to uppercase:

```
$string =~ tr/a-z/A-Z/;
```

To convert the first letter of each word to uppercase, you'll need to split the string, convert each word, and recombine. For example:

```
sub ucfirstwords
{
    ($string) = @_;
    $newstring = join(' ', map { $_ = ucfirst($_) } split(/
      /,$string));
}
```

Now you can call `ucfirstwords`:

```
print ucfirstwords("the cat sat on the mat");
```

which should produce The Cat Sat On The Mat.

References

Chapter 18, `uc`, `ucfirst`, `lc`, `lcfirst` `map`, `join`

StrReverse

```
StrReverse(str)
```

Reverses the string that is passed to it.

Perl Equivalent

The `reverse` function will reverse an array, but not a scalar. So to reverse a string, we need to split the string into an array and then join it back. If you specify an empty regular expression and string to `split` and `join`, respectively, you achieve the desired result:

```
$reverse = join('',reverse(split(//,"The Cat Sat on the Mat")));
```

References

`join`, `split`, `reverse`

String, String$

```
String$(number&, character$)
```

Creates a string of `character` repeated `number` of times.

Perl Equivalent

Use string multiplication:

```
$astring = 'a' x 20;
```

You can multiply any string. For example, it can be more than one character:

```
$catstring = 'cat' x 20;
```

References

Chapter 16

Sub...End Sub

```
Sub...End Sub
```

Creates a new subroutine.

Perl Equivalent

The `sub` keyword creates a new function. Perl does not distinguish between functions and subroutines, nor does it rely on the subroutine definition to determine the accepted arguments or return values.

References

Chapter 17

Switch

```
Switch(expression1, value [... expression7, value7])
```

Evaluates the expressions and returns the corresponding value for the first expression that returns `True`.

Perl Equivalent

None. You'll need to use the `if` statement to evaluate each expression.

References

Chapter 16

SYD

```
SYD(initialCost@, salvageValue~, Lifespan%, period%)
```

Returns the sum depreciation of an asset.

Perl Equivalent

None. See the `Math::Financial` module.

Tab

```
Tab([column%])
```

Adds a tab to the formatting for a `Print` statement.

Perl Equivalent

You can directly introduce a tab into any string using the `\t` escape character:

```
print "\tTabbed text";
```

To insert multiple tabs, use string multiplication:

```
print "\t" x 5 . "Tabbed text";
```

References

Chapter 16

Tan

```
Tan(angle)
```

Returns the tangent of an angle specified in radians.

Perl Equivalent

There is no built-in equivalent, but the `POSIX` module supplied with Perl does provide the `tan` function:

```
use POSIX;
print tan(3.141592654);
```

Time

```
Time(time-string$)
```

Sets the current system time.

Perl Equivalent

None. You would have to call the DOS `time` command to set the system time.

Time$

```
Time$
```

Returns a string that contains the current system time.

Perl Equivalent

No direct equivalent, although you can use the `localtime` or `gmtime` functions in a scalar context to get a date and time string. If you want purely a time string, you'll need to extract the elements from a `localtime` or `gmtime` function call and assemble the string yourself:

```
($sec, $min, $hour) = (localtime(time()))[0..2];
$time = "$hour:$min:$sec";
```

References

`localtime, gmtime, time`

Timer

```
Timer
```

Returns the number of seconds that have elapsed since midnight.

Perl Equivalent

None. The VB `Timer` function is generally used to time system operation. You can do the same operation using the `time` function, which returns the number of seconds since the epoch. By comparing two time values, you can calculate the number of seconds that have elapsed. For example:

```
$start = time();
foreach($i;$i<=1000000;$i++)
{
    sin($i);
}
$end = time();
print "I took ", ($end-$start), "seconds\n";
```

References

time

TimeSerial

TimeSerial(hour%, minute%, second%)

Returns a time based on the serial parameters passed.

Perl Equivalent

To convert the individual time and date values into an epoch value, you need to use the Time::Local module:

$time = timelocal(SEC, MIN, HOURS, MDAY, MON, YEAR);

Note that you will need to take 1 off of the month value and 1900 off the year value if it is expressed in normal format. If you are using the values returned by a localtime or gmtime call, then no modification of the values will be required.

References

localtime, gmtime, time

TimeValue

TimeValue(timestring$)

Returns a date and time value based on the supplied time string.

Perl Equivalent

None. See the preceding discussion on Timer for more information on how to convert a time to the epoch value used by Perl.

Trim, Trim$

Trim$(Stringexpression)

Returns a string with the leading and trailing spaces removed.

Perl Equivalent

You'll need to use a regular expression to string the leading and trailing spaces:

```
$string =~ s/^ *(.*?) *$//;
```

References

Chapter 18

True

```
True
```

Returns a logical true value.

Perl Equivalent

In Perl, any nonzero value is treated as a true value whether negative or positive.

References

Chapter 16

Type...End Type

```
Type typename element As type [element As type] : : End Type
```

Creates a user-defined variable type.

Perl Equivalent

None. You cannot create your own variable types within Perl, but this is not normally a problem because Perl doesn't differentiate between different variable types. If you want to store multiple values in a single variable, use a hash.

TypeName

```
TypeName(varName)
```

Returns a string of the variable type passed to the function.

Perl Equivalent

The `ref` function returns an uppercase string that defines the variable type supplied to it. For example:

```
print ref($string);
```

will print SCALAR.

References

```
ref
```

UBound

```
UBound(arrayname [,dimension%])
```

Returns the highest subscript available within an array.

Perl Equivalent

To determine the length of an array, use `@array` in a scalar context:

```
$length = scalar @array;
```

You can then use that value to determine the lowest available array index. However, if you are determining the value so that you can add a new element or array to an existing array, it's easier to use the `push` function to add the new elements:

```
push @array,@elements;
```

This adds `@elements` to the end of the `@array` variable.

References

Chapter 16

UCase, UCase$

```
UCase$(expression)
```

Returns a completely uppercase string.

Perl Equivalent

The uc function returns a string converted to uppercase.

References

uc

Unload

```
Unload form-name
Unload control-name
```

Unloads a form or control object from memory.

Perl Equivalent

None.

Val

```
Val(string$)
```

Converts a string to its numerical value.

Perl Equivalent

Perl automatically converts strings to their numerical value as required. For example:

```
$value = 29 + "31";
```

will result in a value of 60.

References

Chapter 16

Value Property

```
object.Value
```

Holds or sets the value for a specific control property.

Perl Equivalent

To obtain the property value of an object, you need to access the named property stored within the objects hash. For example:

```
$object->{property};
```

References

Chapter 17

VarType

```
VarType(variant)
```

Returns the type of variable stored in the passed reference.

Perl Equivalent

The `ref` function will return a string relating to the type of variable passed to it. If the variable is a reference, it returns REF.

References

```
ref
```

WeekDay

```
WeekDay(dateVariant)
```

Returns the weekday portion of the passed date variable.

Perl Equivalent

The seventh element returned by the `localtime` or `gmtime` functions contains the numeric index of the current day of the week:

```
($weekday) = (localtime(time()))[6];
```

The weekday value is in the range 0 to 6, rather than the 1 to 7 returned by `WeekDay`, but the week still runs from Sunday to Saturday.

References

```
localtime, gmtime, time
```

WeekdayName

```
WeekdayName(weekDay [, abbr[, firstDayoftheWeek]])
```

Returns a string or abbreviated string for the given day of the week.

Perl Equivalent

You'll need to populate your own array with the information:

```
@weekdayname = qw/Sunday Monday Tuesday Wednesday
                  Thursday Friday Saturday/;
($weekday) = (localtime(time()))[6];
print $weekdayname[$weekday];
```

References

`localtime`, `gmtime`, `time`

While...Wend

```
While condition:
[statements]
Wend
```

Cycles through a loop until the necessary condition fails to resolve to true.

Perl Equivalent

The `while` statement performs the same function:

```
while(statement)
{
...
}
```

References

Chapter 16

Width

```
Width #fileNumber, width%
```

Sets the output width for the given file.

Perl Equivalent

If you want to restrict the width of output to a file, either use `printf` with fixed calculated format, or use `substr` to extract a given number of characters from a string before sending the output to a file. For example:

```
$output = substr $string, 0, 80;
print DATA $output;
```

References

Chapter 18

With...End With

```
With object [statements] End With
```

Executes the given statements for a specific object.

Perl Equivalent

No direct equivalent. You'll need to use a loop or function call to conduct the individual operations on any given object. Since an object is always a reference, you can supply the reference to a function. For example:

```
sub processobject
{
    my ($object) = @_;

    $object->method();
    $object->methodb();
}
```

Now you can execute the same method calls on any object you supply:

```
processobject($object);
```

Of course, the object will need to support the given methods to work properly.

References

Chapter 17

Write

```
Write #filenumber [, var1] [, var2] ...
```

Writes data to the specified file.

Perl Equivalent

The `print` and `printf` function will write information to a file if you supply the filehandle as the first argument:

```
print DATA $string;
```

Note that there is no comma between the filehandle and data that you want to write.

References

Chapter 18, `print`, `printf`

XOR

```
a Xor b
```

Exclusive OR.

Perl Equivalent

The `^` and `xor` operators both perform an exclusive OR operation. The `xor` operator has a lower precedence, however, and can be used in situations where `^` would be ambiguous.

References

Chapter 16

Year

```
Year(dateVariant)
```

Returns the year portion of a passed `Date` type.

Perl Equivalent

The sixth element returned by the `gmtime` and `localtime` functions is the year:

```
($year) = (localtime(time()))[5];
```

You will need to add 1900 to the value to get a four-digit date.

References

`localtime, gmtime, time`

Perl Function Reference

Note that this is intended as a quick reference for the arguments and values returned by each function. For a full discussion on how to use the function in a script, please refer to the corresponding chapter.

Note that in all cases, unless otherwise noted, the functions return either zero or `undef` on failure. Most functions will also set the value of `$!` to the corresponding system error number returned.

-X

```
-X FILEHANDLE
-X EXPR
-X
```

File test, where `X` is one or more of the letters listed in Table C-2. The function takes one operator, either a filename or a `FILEHANDLE`. The function tests the associated file to see if the selected option is true. If `EXPR` and `FILEHANDLE` are omitted, the function tests `$_`, except for `-t`, which tests `STDIN`.

Returns

0 if false

1 if true

Special conditions exist for some operators; see Table C-2.

abs

```
abs EXPR
abs
```

Returns the absolute value of `EXPR`, or `$_` if omitted.

TABLE C-2

File tests.

Test	Result
-r	File is readable by effective uid/gid.
-w	File is writable by effective uid/gid.
-x	File is executable by effective uid/gid.
-o	File is owned by effective uid.
-R	File is readable by real uid/gid.
-W	File is writable by real uid/gid.
-X	File is executable by real uid/gid.
-O	File is owned by real uid.
-e	File exists.
-z	File has zero size.
-s	File has nonzero size (returns size in bytes).
-f	File is a plain file.
-d	File is a directory.
-l	File is a symbolic link.
-p	File is a named pipe (FIFO), or FILEHANDLE is a pipe.
-s	File is a network socket.
-b	File is a block special file.
-c	File is a character special file.
-t	File is opened to a tty (terminal).
-u	File has setuid bit set.
-g	File has setgid bit set.
-k	File has sticky bit set.
-T	File is a text file.
-B	File is a binary file (opposite of -T).
-M	Age of file in days when script started.
-A	Time of last access in days when script started.
-C	Time of last inode change when script started.

Returns

Absolute value.

atan2

```
atan2 Y,X
```

Returns the arctangent of Y/X in the range π to $-\pi$.

Returns

Floating-point number

binmode

```
binmode FILEHANDLE
```

Sets the format for FILEHANDLE to be read from and written to as binary on the operating systems that differentiate between the two. Files that are not in binary have CR LF sequences converted to LF on input and LF to CR LF on output. This is vital for operating systems that use two characters to separate lines within text files (MS-DOS), but has no effect on operating systems that use single characters (Unix, Mac OS, QNX).

Returns

undef on failure or invalid FILEHANDLE

1 on success

bless

```
bless REF, CLASSNAME
bless REF
```

Tells entity referenced by REF it is now an object in the CLASSNAME package, or the current package if CLASSNAME is omitted.

Returns

The reference REF

caller

```
caller EXPR
caller
```

Returns the context of the current subroutine call; returns the caller's package name in a scalar context. Returns the package name, filename, and line within file in a list context, as in

```
($package, $filename, $line) = caller;
```

If EXPR is specified, `caller` returns extended information, relative to the stack trace. That is, if you specify a value of 1, the parent subroutine information will be printed; a value of 2, the grandparent subroutine; and so forth. The information returned is

```
($package, $filename, $line, $subroutine,
 $hasargs, $wantarray, $evaltext, $is_require) = caller($i);
```

The $evaltext and $is_require values are only returned when the subroutine being examined is actually the result of an eval() statement.

Returns

undef on failure

Basic information (list) in a list context with no expression

Extended information (list) in a list context with an expression

chdir

```
chdir EXPR
chdir
```

Changes the current working directory to EXPR, or user's home directory if none specified.

Returns

0 on failure

1 on success

chmod

```
chmod MODE, LIST
```

Changes the mode of the files specified in LIST to the MODE specified. The value of MODE should be in octal.

Returns

0 on failure

Integer, number of files successfully changed

chomp

```
chomp EXPR
chomp LIST
chomp
```

Removes the last character if it matches the value of $/ from EXPR, each element of LIST, or $_ if no value is specified. Note that this is a safer version of the chop function, since it only removes the last character if it matches $/. Removes all trailing newlines from the string or strings if in paragraph mode (when $/ = " ").

Returns

Integer, number of bytes removed for all strings

chop

```
chop EXPR
chop LIST
chop
```

Removes the last character from EXPR, each element of LIST, or $_ if no value is specified.

Returns

The character removed from EXPR, or from last element of LIST

chr

```
chr EXPR
chr
```

Returns the character represented by the numeric value of EXPR, or $_ if omitted, according to the current character set.

Returns

Character

close

```
close FILEHANDLE
close
```

Closes `FILEHANDLE`, flushing the buffers, if appropriate, and disassociating the `FILEHANDLE` with the original file, pipe, or socket. Closes the currently selected filehandle if none is specified.

Returns

0 on failure

1 if buffers were flushed and the file was successfully closed

closedir

```
closedir DIRHANDLE
```

Closes the directory handle `DIRHANDLE`.

Returns

0 on failure

1 on success

continue

```
continue BLOCK
```

Not a function. This is a flow control statement that executes `BLOCK` just before the conditional for the loop is evaluated.

Returns

Nothing

cos

```
cos EXPR
cos
```

Returns the cosine of EXPR, or $_ if EXPR is omitted. The value should be expressed in radians.

Returns

Floating-point number

defined

```
defined EXPR
defined
```

Returns TRUE if EXPR has a value other than the undef value, or $_ if EXPR is not specified. This can be used with many functions to detect a failure in operation, since they return undef if there was a problem. A simple boolean test does not differentiate between FALSE, zero, an empty string, or the string 0, which are all equally false.

If EXPR is a function or function reference, then it returns True if the function has been defined. When used with entire arrays and hashes, it will not always produce intuitive results. If a hash element is specified, it returns True if the corresponding value has been defined, but does not determine whether the specified key exists in the hash.

Returns

0 if EXPR has not been defined

1 if EXPR has been defined

delete

```
delete LIST
```

Deletes the specified keys and associated values from a hash. Deleting from the $ENV hash modifies the current environment, and deleting from a hash tied to a DBM database deletes the entry from the database file.

Returns

undef if the key does not exist

Each value associated with the corresponding key that was deleted

die

```
die LIST
```

Prints the value of LIST to STDERR and calls exit with the error value contained in $!. If $! is zero, then it prints the value of ($? > 8) (for use with backtick commands). If ($? > 8) is zero, then the exit status value returned is 255.

Inside an eval, the value of LIST is inserted in the $@ variable, and the eval block exits with an undefined value. You should therefore use die to raise an exception within a script.

If the value of LIST does not end in a newline, then Perl adds the current script and input line number to the message that is printed. If LIST is empty and $@ already contains a value, then the string "\t... propagated" is appended, and if LIST is empty, the string Died is printed instead.

Returns

Nothing

do

do EXPR

If EXPR is a subroutine, executes the subroutine using the supplied arguments; otherwise, uses EXPR as a filename and executes the contents of the file as a Perl script.

Returns

undef if file is not accessible

0 on failure (not a Perl script)

1 on success

each

each HASH

In a list context, returns a two-element list referring to the key and value for the next element of a hash, allowing you to iterate over it. In a scalar context, returns only the key for the next element in the hash. Information is returned in a random order, and a single iterator is shared among each—keys and values. The iterator can be reset by evaluating the entire hash or by calling the keys function in a scalar context.

Returns

In a list context, null array at end of hash

In a scalar context, undef at end of hash

In a list context, key and value for the next element of a hash

In a scalar context, key only for the next element of a hash

eof

```
eof FILEHANDLE
eof()
eof
```

Returns True if the next read on the specified FILEHANDLE will return end of file, or if FILEHANDLE is not currently associated with an open file. If FILEHANDLE is not specified, it returns the condition for the last accessed file.

If the eof() format is used, it checks the input status of the list of files supplied on the command line and hence allows you to detect the end of the file list, instead of the end of the current file.

Normally, you should never need to use eof, since all filehandle-compatible functions return false values when no data remains or if there was an error.

Returns

undef if FILEHANDLE is not at end of file

1 if FILEHANDLE will report end of file on next read

eval

```
eval EXPR
eval BLOCK
```

Evaluates EXPR at execution time as if EXPR was a separate Perl script. This allows you to use a separate, perhaps user-supplied, piece of Perl script within your program. An eval EXPR statement is evaluated separately each time the function is called.

The second form evaluates BLOCK when the rest of the script is parsed (before execution).

In both cases, the evaluated EXPR or BLOCK have access to the variables, objects, and functions available within the host script.

Returns

Value of last evaluated statement in EXPR or BLOCK

exec

exec LIST

Executes a system command (directly, not within a shell) and never returns to the calling script, except on error. The first element of LIST is taken as the program name; subsequent elements are passed as arguments to the command executed.

You should use system if you want to run a subcommand as part of a Perl script.

Returns

0 only if the command specified cannot be executed

exists

exists EXPR

Returns True if the specified hash key exists, regardless of the corresponding value.

Returns

0 if hash element does not exist
1 if hash element does exist

exit

exit EXPR
exit

Evaluates EXPR, exits the Perl interpreter, and returns the value as the exit value. Always runs all END{} blocks defined in the script (and imported packages) before exiting. If EXPR is omitted, then the interpreter exits with a value of 0. Should not be used to exit from a subroutine, either use eval and die or use return.

Returns

Nothing

exp

```
exp EXPR
exp
```

Returns e (the natural logarithm base) raised to the power of EXPR, or $_ if omitted.

Returns

e raised to the power

fileno

```
fileno FILEHANDLE
```

Returns the file descriptor number (as used by C and POSIX functions) of the specified FILEHANDLE. This is generally useful only for using the select function and any low-level tty functions.

Returns

undef if FILEHANDLE is not open

File descriptor (numeric) of FILEHANDLE

fork

```
fork
```

Forks a new process using the fork() system call. Any shared sockets or filehandles are duplicated across processes. You must ensure that you wait on your children to prevent "zombie" processes from forming.

Returns

undef on failure to fork

Child process ID to parent on success

0 to child on success

format

```
format NAME =
 picture line
 LIST
...
```

Declares a picture format for use by the `write` function.

Returns

Nothing

formline

```
formline PICTURE, LIST
```

An internal function used by the `format` function and related operators. It formats LIST according to the contents of PICTURE into the output accumulator variable $^A. The value is written out to a filehandle when a write is done.

Returns

1 (always)

getc

```
getc FILEHANDLE
getc
```

Reads the next character from FILEHANDLE (or STDIN if none specified), returning the value.

Returns

`undef` on error or end of file

Value of character read from FILEHANDLE

gethostbyaddr

```
gethostbyaddr ADDR, ADDRTYPE
```

Contacts the system's name-resolving service, returning a list of information for the host ADDR of type ADDRTYPE, as follows:

```
($name, $aliases, $addrtype, $length, @addrs)
```

The @addrs array contains a list of packed binary addresses. In a scalar context, returns the host address.

Returns

undef on error in scalar context

Empty list on error in list context

Host name in scalar context

Host information array in list context

gethostbyname

```
gethostbyname NAME
```

Contacts the system's name-resolving service, returning a list of information for NAME, as follows:

```
($name, $aliases, $addrtype, $length, @addrs)
```

The @addrs array contains a list of packed binary addresses. In a scalar context, returns the host address.

Returns

undef on error in scalar context

Empty list on error in list context

Host address in scalar context

Host information array in list context

getlogin

```
getlogin
```

Returns the user's name, as discovered by the system function getlogin().

Returns

undef **on failure**

User's login name

getnetbyaddr

getnetbyaddr ADDR, ADDRTYPE

In a list context, returns the information for the network specified by ADDR **and type** ADDRTYPE:

($name, $aliases, $addrtype, $net)

In a scalar context, returns only the network address.

Returns

undef **on error in scalar context**

Empty list on error in list context

Network address in scalar context

Network address information in a list context

getnetbyname

getnetbyname NAME

In a list context, returns the information for the network specified by NAME:

($name, $aliases, $addrtype, $net)

In a scalar context, returns only the network address.

Returns

undef **on error in scalar context**

Empty list on error in list context

Network address in scalar context

Network address information in a list context

getpeername

getpeername SOCKET

Returns the packed socket address of the remote host attached via SOCKET.

Returns

undef on error

Packed socket address

getprotobyname

getprotobyname NAME

Translates the protocol NAME into its corresponding number in a scalar context, and its number and associated information in a list context:

($name, $aliases, $protocol_number)

Returns

undef on error in a scalar context

Empty list in a list context

Protocol number in a scalar context

Protocol information in a list context

getprotobynumber

getprotobynumber NUMBER

Translates the protocol NUMBER into its corresponding name in a scalar context, and its name and associated information in a list context:

($name, $aliases, $protocol_number)

Returns

undef on error in a scalar context

Empty list in a list context

Protocol name in a scalar context

Protocol information in a list context

getservbyname

```
getservbyname NAME, PROTO
```

Translates the service NAME and for the protocol PROTO, returning the service number in a scalar context, and the number and associated information in a list context:

```
($name, $aliases, $port_number, $protocol_name)
```

Returns

undef on error in a scalar context

Empty list in a list context

Service number in a scalar context

Service information in a list context

getservbyport

```
getservbyport PORT, PROTO
```

Translates the service number PORT and for the protocol PROTO, returning the service name in a scalar context, and the name and associated information in a list context:

```
($name, $aliases, $port_number, $protocol_name)
```

Returns

undef on error in a scalar context

Empty list in a list context

Service name in a scalar context

Service information in a list context

getsockname

```
getsockname SOCKET
```

Returns a packed address of the local end of the network socket SOCKET.

Returns

undef **on error**

Packed address of local socket

getsockopt

getsockopt SOCKET, LEVEL, OPTNAME

Gets the socket options set on SOCKET, at the socket implementation level LEVEL for the option OPTNAME. Some sample values for OPTNAME at a socket level are given in Table C-3. The values are defined in the Socket package.

Returns

undef **on error**

Option value

TABLE C-3

Options for getsockopt.

OPTNAME	Result
SO_DEBUG	Get status of recording of debugging information.
SO_REUSEADDR	Get status of local address reuse.
SO_KEEPALIVE	Get status of keep connections alive.
SO_DONTROUTE	Get status of routing bypass for outgoing messages.
SO_LINGER	Get status of linger on close if data is present.
SO_BROADCAST	Get status of permission to transmit broadcast messages.
SO_OOBINLINE	Get status of out-of-band data in band.
SO_SNDBUF	Get buffer size for output.
SO_RCVBUF	Get buffer size for input.
SO_TYPE	Get the type of the socket.
SO_ERROR	Get and clear error on the socket.

glob

```
glob EXPR
glob
```

Returns a list of files matching EXPR as they would be expanded by the standard Bourne shell. If the EXPR does not specify a path, uses the current directory. If EXPR is omitted, the value of $_ is used.

Returns

Empty list on error

List of expanded filenames

gmtime

```
gmtime EXPR
gmtime
```

Returns a list of values corresponding to the date and time as specified by EXPR, or date and time returned by the time function if EXPR is omitted, localized for the standard Greenwich mean time. The values returned are as follows:

```
#  0    1    2    3    4    5    6    7    8
($sec,$min,$hour,$mday,$mon,$year,$wday,$yday,$isdst) = gmtime(time);
```

   The array elements are numeric, taken from the system struct tm. The value of $mon has a range of 0..11, $wday has a range of 0..6 (Sunday-Saturday), and $year is returned as the number of years from 1900; so 2010 is 110.

Returns

In a scalar context, returns a formatted string

In a list context, returns a list of time values

goto

```
goto LABEL
goto EXPR
goto &NAME
```

The first form causes the current execution point to jump to the point referred to as LABEL. A goto in this form cannot be used to jump into a loop or external function—you can only jump to a point within the same scope. The second form expects EXPR to evaluate to a recognizable LABEL. In general, you should be able to use a normal conditional statement or function to control the execution of a program, so its use is deprecated.

The third form substitutes a call to the named subroutine for the currently running subroutine. The new subroutine inherits the argument stack and other features of the original subroutine; it becomes impossible for the new subroutine even to know that it was called by another name.

Returns

Nothing

grep

```
grep BLOCK LIST
grep EXPR, LIST
```

Similar to the standard Unix grep command. However, the selection process is more widespread and limited to regular expressions. Evaluates the BLOCK or EXPR for each element of LIST, returning the list of elements that the block or statement returns True.

Returns

In a scalar context, number of times the expression returned True

In a list context, list of matching elements

hex

```
hex EXPR
hex
```

Interprets EXPR as a hexadecimal string and returns the value, or converts $_ if EXPR is omitted.

Returns

Numeric value

index

```
index STR, SUBSTR, POSITION
index STR, SUBSTR
```

Returns the position of the first occurrence of SUBSTR in STR, starting at the beginning, or from POSITION if specified.

Returns

-1 on failure

Position of string

int

```
int EXPR
int
```

Returns the integer element of EXPR, or $_ if omitted. The int function does not do rounding. If you need to round a value up to an integer, you should use sprintf.

Returns

Integer

join

```
join EXPR, LIST
```

Combines the elements of LIST into a single string using the value of EXPR to separate each element. Effectively the opposite of split.

Returns

Joined string

keys

```
keys HASH
```

Returns all the keys of the HASH as a list. The keys are returned in random order but, in fact, share the same order as that used by values and each. You can therefore use the `keys` function to reset the shared iterator for a specific hash.

Returns

List of keys

`kill`

```
kill EXPR, LIST
```

Sends a signal of the value `EXPR` to the process IDs specified in `LIST`. If the value of `EXPR` is negative, it kills all processes that are members of the process groups specified. You can also use a signal name if specified in quotes. The precise list of signals supported is entirely dependent on the system implementation, but Table C-4 shows the main signals that should be supported by all POSIX-compatible operating systems.

Returns

Nothing

TABLE C-4

POSIX-compatible
signals.

Name	Effect
SIGABRT	Aborts the process
SIGARLM	Alarm signal
SIGFPE	Arithmetic exception
SIGHUP	Hang up
SIGILL	Illegal instruction
SIGINT	Interrupt
SIGKILL	Termination signal
SIGPIPE	Writes to a pipe with no readers
SIGQUIT	Quit signal
SIGSEGV	Segmentation fault
SIGTERM	Termination signal
SIGUSER1	Application-defined signal 1
SIGUSER2	Application-defined signal 2

last

```
last LABEL
last
```

Not a function. The `last` keyword is a loop control statement that immediately causes the current iteration of a loop to become the last. No further statements are executed, and the loop ends. If LABEL is specified, then it drops out of the loop identified by LABEL instead of the currently enclosing loop.

Returns

Nothing

lc

```
lc EXPR
lc
```

Returns a lowercased version of EXPR, or $_ if omitted.

Returns

String

lcfirst

```
lcfirst EXPR
lcfirst
```

Returns the string EXPR or $_ with the first character lowercased.

Returns

String

length

```
length EXPR
length
```

Returns the length, in bytes, of the value of EXPR, or $_ if not specified.

Returns

Integer

local

```
local LIST
```

Sets the variables in LIST to be local to the current execution block. If more than one value is specified, you *must* use parentheses to define the list. You may wish to use my instead, as it's a more specific form of localization.

Returns

Nothing

localtime

```
localtime EXPR
```

In a list context, converts the time specified by EXPR, returning a nine-element array with the time analyzed for the current local time zone. The elements of the array are

```
#    0    1    2     3      4     5     6      7     8
($sec,$min,$hour,$mday,$mon,$year,$wday,$yday,$isdst) =
  localtime(time);
```

If EXPR is omitted, uses the value returned by time.

In a scalar context, returns a string representation of the time specified by EXPR, roughly equivalent to the value returned by ctime().

Returns

In a scalar context, returns a formatted string

In a list context, returns a list of time values

log

```
log EXPR
log
```

Returns the natural logarithm of EXPR, or $_ if omitted.

Returns

Floating-point number

m//

```
m//
```

Match operator. Parentheses after initial m can be any character and will be used to delimit the regular expression statement.

Returns

0 on failure to match

1 on success

List of values in a grouped regular expression match

map

```
map EXPR, LIST
map BLOCK LIST
```

Evaluates EXPR or BLOCK for each element of LIST, locally setting $_ to each element. Returns the evaluated list.

Returns

List of values

mkdir

```
mkdir EXPR,MODE
```

Makes a directory with the name and path EXPR using the mode specified by MODE (specified as an octal number).

Returns

0 on failure

1 on success

my

```
my LIST
```

Declares the variables in LIST to be local within the enclosing block. If more than one variable is specified, all variables must be enclosed in parentheses.

Returns

Nothing

next

```
next LABEL
next
```

Not a function. Causes the current loop iteration to skip to the next value or next evaluation of the control statement. No further statements in the current loop are executed. If LABEL is specified, then execution skips to the next iteration of the loop identified by LABEL.

Returns

Nothing

no

no MODULE LIST

no MODULE

If MODULE supports it, then no calls the unimport function defined in MODULE to unimport all symbols from the current package, or only the symbols referred to by LIST. Has some special meanings when used with pragmas.

Returns

Nothing

oct

```
oct EXPR
oct
```

Returns EXPR, or $_ if omitted, interpreted as an octal string. Most often used as a method for returning mode strings as octal values.

Returns

Octal value

open

```
open FILEHANDLE, EXPR
open FILEHANDLE
```

Opens the file specified by EXPR, associating it with FILEHANDLE. If EXPR is not specified, then the filename specified by the scalar variable of the same name as FILEHANDLE is used instead. The format of EXPR defines the mode in which the file is opened, as shown in Table C-5.

You should not ignore failures to the open command, so it is usually used in combination with warn, die, or a control statement.

If you are looking for the equivalent of the system function open(), see sysopen.

Returns

0 on failure

1 on success

opendir

```
opendir DIRHANDLE, EXPR
```

Opens the directory EXPR, associating it with DIRHANDLE for processing, using the readdir function.

Returns

0 on failure

1 on success

TABLE C-5

Options for opening files.

Expression	Result
`"filename"`	Opens the file for reading only.
`"<filename"`	Opens the file for reading only.
`">filename"`	Truncates and opens the file for writing.
`">filename"`	Opens the file for appending (places pointer at end of file).
`"+<filename"`	Opens the file for reading and writing.
`"+>filename"`	Truncates and opens the file for reading and writing.
`"|command"`	Runs the command and pipes the output to the filehandle.
`"command|"`	Pipes the output from file handle to the input of command.
`"-"`	Opens STDIN.
`">-"`	Opens STDOUT.
`"<&FILEHANDLE"`	Duplicates specified FILEHANDLE or file descriptor if numeric for reading.
`">&FILEHANDLE"`	Duplicates specified FILEHANDLE or file descriptor if numeric for writing.
`"<&=N"`	Opens the file descriptor matching N, essentially identical to C's fdopen().
`"|-" and "-|"`	Opens a pipe to a forked command.

ord

```
ord EXPR
ord
```

Returns the ASCII numeric value of the character specified by EXPR, or $_ if omitted.

Returns

Integer

pack

```
pack EXPR, LIST
```

Evaluates the expressions in LIST and packs it into a binary structure specified by EXPR. The format is specified using the characters shown in Table C-6.

TABLE C-6

pack format
characters.

Character	Description
@	Null fill to absolute position.
a	An ASCII string, will be null padded.
A	An ASCII string, will be space padded.
b	A bitstring (ascending bit order).
B	A bitstring (descending bit order).
c	A signed char value.
C	An unsigned char value.
d	A double-precision float in the native format.
f	A single-precision float in the native format.
H	A hex string (high nibble first).
h	A hex string (low nibble first).
i	A signed integer value.
I	An unsigned integer value.
l	A signed long value.
L	An unsigned long value.
N	A long in "network" (big endian) order.
n	A short in "network" (big endian) order.
p	A pointer to a null-terminated string.
P	A pointer to a structure (fixed-length string).
s	A signed short value.
S	An unsigned short value.
u	A unencoded string.
V	A long in "VAX" (little endian) order.
v	A short in "VAX" (little endian) order.
w	A BER compressed integer.
x	A null byte.
X	Back up a byte.

Each character may be optionally followed by a number, which specifies a repeat count. A value of * repeats for as many values remaining in LIST. Values can be unpacked with the unpack function.

Returns

Formatted string

package

```
package NAME
package
```

Changes the name of the current symbol table to NAME. The scope of the package name is until the end of the enclosing block. If NAME is omitted, there is no current package, and all function and variable names must be declared with their fully qualified names.

Returns

Nothing

pipe

```
1pipe READHANDLE, WRITEHANDLE
```

Opens a pair of connected communications pipes: READHANDLE for reading and WRITEHANDLE for writing.

Returns

0 on failure

1 on success

pop

```
pop ARRAY
pop
```

Returns the last element of ARRAY, removing the value from the list. If ARRAY is omitted, it pops the last value from @ARGV in the main program and the @_ array within a subroutine. The opposite of push, which when used in combination, allows you to implement "stacks."

Returns

undef if list is empty

Last element from the array.

pos

```
pos EXPR
pos
```

Returns the position within EXPR, or $_, where the last m//g search left off.

Returns

Integer

print

```
print FILEHANDLE LIST
print LIST
print
```

Prints the values of the expressions in LIST to the current default output file handle, or to the one specified by FILEHANDLE. If LIST is empty, the value in $_ is printed instead. Because print accepts a list of values, every element of the list will be interpreted as an expression. You should therefore ensure that if you are using print within a larger LIST context, you enclose the arguments to print in parentheses.

Returns

0 on failure

1 on success

printf

```
printf FILEHANDLE FORMAT, LIST
```

```
printf FORMAT, LIST
```

Prints the value of LIST interpreted via the format specified by FORMAT to the current output filehandle, or to the one specified by FILEHANDLE. Effectively equivalent to

```
print FILEHANDLE sprintf(FORMAT, LIST)
```

Remember to use print in place of printf if you do not require a specific output format. The print function is more efficient. Table C-7 shows the list of accepted formatting conversions.

Perl also supports flags that optionally adjust the output format. These are specified between the % and conversion letter, as shown in Table C-8.

Returns

0 on failure

1 on success

prototype

```
prototype EXPR
```

Returns a string containing the prototype of function or reference specified by EXPR, or undef if the function has no prototype.

Returns

undef if no function prototype

String

push

```
push ARRAY, LIST
```

Pushes the values in LIST on to the end of the list ARRAY. Used with pop to implement stacks.

Returns

Number of elements in new array

TABLE C-7

Conversion formats
for prinitf.

Format	Result
%%	A percent sign.
%c	A character with the given ASCII code.
%s	A string.
%d	A signed integer (decimal).
%u	An unsigned integer (decimal).
%o	An unsigned integer (octal).
%x	An unsigned integer (hexadecimal).
%X	An unsigned integer (hexadecimal using uppercase characters).
%e	A floating-point number (scientific notation).
%E	A floating-point number (scientific notation using E in place of e).
%f	A floating-point number (fixed decimal notation).
%g	A floating-point number (%e of %f notation according to value size).
%G	A floating-point number (as %g, but using E in place of e when appropriate).
%p	A pointer (prints the memory address of the value in hexadecimal).
%n	Stores the number of characters output so far into the next variable in the parameter list.
%I	A synonym for %d.
%D	A synonym for C %ld.
%U	A synonym for C %lu.
%O	A synonym for C %lo.
%F	A synonym for C %f.

quotemeta

```
quotemeta EXPR
quotemeta
```

Returns the value of EXPR or $_ with all nonalphanumeric characters
backslashed.

Returns

String

TABLE C-8

Formatting flags for printf conversion formats.

Flag	Result
space	Prefix positive number with a space.
+	Prefix positive number with a plus sign.
-	Left-justify within field.
0	Use zeros, not spaces, to right-justify.
#	Prefix nonzero octal with 0 and hexadecimal with 0x.
number	Minimum field width.
.number	Specify precision (number of digits after decimal point) for floating-point numbers.
l	Interpret integer as C type "long" or "unsigned long."
h	Interpret integer as C type "short" or "unsigned short."
V	Interpret integer as Perl's standard integer type.

rand

```
rand EXPR
rand
```

Returns a random fractional number between zero and the positive number EXPR, or 1 if not specified. Automatically calls srand to seed the random-number generator unless it has already been called.

Returns

Floating-point number

read

```
read FILEHANDLE, SCALAR, LENGTH, OFFSET
read FILEHANDLE, SCALAR, LENGTH
```

Tries to read LENGTH bytes from FILEHANDLE into SCALAR. If OFFSET is specified, then reading starts from that point within the input string, up to LENGTH bytes. Uses the equivalent of the C fread() function. For the equivalent of the C read() function, see sysread.

Returns

undef **on error**

0 **at end of file**

Number of bytes read

readdir

readdir DIRHANDLE

In a scalar context, returns the next directory entry from the directory associated with DIRHANDLE. In a list context, returns all of the remaining directory entries in DIRHANDLE.

Returns

undef **on failure in scalar context**

Empty list on failure in list context

Filename in scalar context

List of filenames in list context

readline

readline EXPR

Reads a line from the filehandle referred to by EXPR, returning the result. If you want to use a FILEHANDLE directly, it must be passed as a typeglob. In a scalar context, only one line is returned; in a list context, a list of lines up to end of file is returned. Ignores the setting of the $/ or $INPUT_RECORD_SEPARATOR variable. You should use the <> operator in preference.

Returns

undef, **or empty list, on error**

One line in scalar context

List of lines in list context

readlink

readlink EXPR
readlink

Returns the pathname of the file pointed to by the link EXPR, or $_ if EXPR is not specified.

Returns

undef on error

String

readpipe

```
readpipe EXPR
```

Executes EXPR as a command. The output is then returned, as a multi-line string in scalar text, or with the line returned as individual elements in a list context.

Returns

String in scalar context

List in list context

redo

```
redo LABEL
redo
```

Restarts the current loop without forcing the control statement to be evaluated. No further statements in the block are executed (execution restarts at the start of the block). A continue block, if present, will not be executed. If LABEL is specified, execution restarts at the start of the loop identified by LABEL.

Returns

Nothing

ref

```
ref EXPR
ref
```

Returns a True value if EXPR, or $_, is a reference. The actual value returned also defines the type of entity the reference refers to. The built-in types are:

REF
SCSLAR
ARRAY
HASH
CODE
GLOB

Returns

0 if not a reference

1 if a reference

rename

```
rename OLDNAME, NEWNAME
```

Renames the file with OLDNAME to NEWNAME. Uses the system function rename(), and so it will not rename files across file systems or volumes.

Returns

on success

require

```
require EXPR
require
```

If EXPR (or $_ if EXPR is omitted) is numeric, then it demands that the script requires the specified version of Perl in order to continue. If EXPR or $_ are not numeric, it assumes that the name is the name of a library file to be included. You cannot include the same file with this function twice. The included file must return a true value as the last statement.

This differs from use in that included files effectively become additional text for the current script. Functions, variables, and other objects are not imported into the current namespace, so if the specified file includes a package definition, then objects will require fully qualified names.

Returns

Nothing

reset

```
reset EXPR
reset
```

Resets (clears) all package variables starting with the letter range specified by EXPR. Generally only used within a continue block or at the end of a loop. If omitted, resets ?PATTERN? matches.

Returns

1 (always)

return

```
return EXPR
return
```

Returns EXPR at the end of a subroutine, block, or do function. EXPR may be a scalar, array, or hash value; context will be selected at execution time. If no EXPR is given, returns an empty list in list context, undef in scalar context, or nothing in a void context.

Returns

List, interpreted as scalar, array, or hash, depending on context

reverse

```
reverse LIST
```

In a list context, returns the elements of LIST in reverse order. In a scalar context, returns a concatenated string of the values of LIST, with all bytes in opposite order.

Returns

String in scalar context

List in a list context

rewinddir

```
rewinddir DIRHANDLE
```

Sets the current position within the directory specified by DIRHANDLE to the beginning of the directory.

Returns

Nothing

rindex

```
rindex STR, SUBSTR, POSITION
rindex STR, SUBSTR
```

Operates similar to index, except it returns the position of the last occurrence of SUBSTR in STR. If POSITION is specified, returns the last occurrence at or before that position.

Returns

undef on failure

Integer

rmdir

```
rmdir EXPR
rmdir
```

Deletes the directory specified by EXPR, or $_ if omitted. Only deletes the directory if the directory is empty.

Returns

0 on failure

1 on success

s///

```
s/PATTERN/REPLACE/
```

This is the regular expression substitution operator. Based on the regular expression specified in PATTERN, data is replaced by REPLACE. Like m//, the delimiters are defined by the first character following s.

Returns

0 on failure

Number of substitutions made

scalar

`scalar EXPR`

Forces the evaluation of EXPR to return a value in a scalar context.

Returns

Scalar

seek

`seek FILEHANDLE,POSITION,WHENCE`

Positions the file pointer for the specified FILEHANDLE. seek is basically the same as the `fseek()` C function. The position within the file is specified by POSITION, using the value of WHENCE as a reference point, as follows:

sets the new position to the current position plus POSITION bytes within the file.

2 sets the new position to POSITION bytes, relative to the end of the file.

If you prefer, you can use the constants SEEK_SET, SEEK_CUR, and SEEK_END, provided you have imported the IO::Seekable or POSIX modules.

If you are accessing a file using syswrite and sysread, you should use sysseek because of the effects of buffering.

The seek function clears the EOF condition on a file when called.

Returns

0 on failure

1 on success

seekdir

`seekdir DIRHANDLE, POS`

Sets the current position within DIRHANDLE to POS. The value of POS must be a value returned by telldir.

Returns

0 on failure

1 on success

select

```
select FILEHANDLE
select
```

Sets the default filehandle for output to FILEHANDLE, setting the filehandle used by functions such as print and write if no filehandle is specified. If FILEHANDLE is not specified, then it returns the name of the current default filehandle.

Returns

Previous default filehandle if FILEHANDLE specified

Current default filehandle if FILEHANDLE was not specified

select

```
select RBITS, WBITS, EBITS, TIMEOUT
```

Calls the system function select() using the bits specified. The select function sets the controls for handling nonblocking I/O requests. Returns the number of filehandles awaiting I/O in scalar context, or the number of waiting filehandles and the time remaining in a list context.

TIMEOUT is specified in seconds but accepts a floating-point instead of an integer value. You can use this ability to pause execution for milliseconds instead of the normal seconds available with sleep and alarm by specifying undef for the first three arguments.

Returns

The number of filehandles awaiting I/O in a scalar context

The number of filehandles and time remaining in a list context

setsockopt

setsockopt SOCKET, LEVEL, OPTNAME, OPTVAL

Sets the socket option OPTNAME with a value of OPTVAL on SOCKET at the specified LEVEL. You will need to import the Socket module for the valid values for OPTNAME shown in Table C-9.

Returns

undef on failure

1 on success

shift

shift ARRAY

shift

Returns the first value in an array, deleting it and shifting the elements of the array list to the left by one. If ARRAY is not specified, shifts the @_ array within a subroutine, or @ARGV otherwise. shift is essentially identical to pop, except values are taken from the start of the array instead of the end.

TABLE C-9

Socket options.

OPTNAME	Description
SO_DEBUG	Enable/disable recording of debugging information.
SO_REUSEADDR	Enable/disable local address reuse.
SO_KEEPALIVE	Enable/disable keep connections alive.
SO_DONTROUTE	Enable/disable routing bypass for outgoing messages.
SO_LINGER	Linger on close if data is present.
SO_BROADCAST	Enable/disable permission to transmit broadcast messages.
SO_OOBINLINE	Enable/disable reception of out-of-band data in band.
SO_SNDBUF	Set buffer size for output.
SO_RCVBUF	Set buffer size for input.
SO_TYPE	Get the type of the socket (get only).
SO_ERROR	Get and clear error on the socket (get only).

Returns

undef if the array is empty

First element in the array

shutdown

shutdown SOCKET, HOW

Disables a socket connection according to the value of HOW. The valid values for HOW are identical to the system call of the same name. A value of 0 indicates that you have stopped reading information from the socket. A 1 indicates that you've stopped writing to the socket. A value of 2 indicates that you have stopped using the socket altogether.

Returns

0 on failure

1 on success

sin

sin EXPR
sin

Returns the sine of EXPR, or $_ if not specified.

Returns

Floating point

sleep

sleep EXPR
sleep

Pauses the script for EXPR seconds, or forever if EXPR is not specified. Returns the number of seconds actually slept. Can be interrupted by a signal handler, but you should avoid using sleep with alarm, since many systems use alarm for the sleep implementation.

Returns

Integer, number of seconds actually slept

sort

```
sort SUBNAME LIST
sort BLOCK LIST
sort LIST
```

Sorts LIST according to the subroutine SUBNAME or the anonymous sub-routine specified by BLOCK. If no SUBNAME or BLOCK is specified, then sorts according to normal alphabetical sequence. If BLOCK or SUBNAME is specified, then the subroutine should return an integer less than, greater than, or equal to zero according to how the elements of the array are to be sorted.

Returns

List

splice

```
splice ARRAY, OFFSET, LENGTH, LIST
splice ARRAY, OFFSET, LENGTH
splice ARRAY, OFFSET
```

Removes the elements of ARRAY from the element OFFSET for LENGTH elements, replacing the elements removed with LIST, if specified. If LENGTH is omitted, removes everything from OFFSET onward.

Returns

undef if no elements removed in a scalar context

Last element removed in a scalar context

Empty list in a list context

List of elements removed in a list context

split

```
split /PATTERN/, EXPR, LIMIT
split /PATTERN/, EXPR
```

```
split /PATTERN/
split
```

Splits a string into an array of strings, returning the resultant list. By default, empty leading fields are preserved, and empty trailing fields are deleted.

In a scalar context, returns the number of fields found and splits the values into the @_ array using ?? as the pattern delimiter. If EXPR is omitted, splits the value of $_. If PATTERN is also omitted, it splits on white space (multiple spaces, tabs). Anything matching PATTERN is taken to be a delimiter separating fields and can be a regular expression of one or more characters.

If LIMIT has been specified and is positive, splits into a maximum of that many fields (or fewer). If LIMIT is unspecified or zero, splitting continues until there are no more delimited fields. If negative, then split acts as if an arbitrarily large value has been specified, preserving trailing null fields.

A PATTERN of a null string splits EXPR into individual characters.

Returns

Integer, number of elements in scalar context

List of split elements

sprintf

```
sprintf FORMAT, LIST
```

The sprintf function uses FORMAT to return a formatted string based on the values in LIST. Essentially identical to printf, but the formatted string is returned instead of being printed. The sprintf function is basically synonymous with the C sprintf function, but Perl does its own formatting; the C sprintf function is not used (except for basic floating-point formatting).

The sprintf function accepts the same format conversions as printf (see Table C-7). Perl also supports flags that optionally adjust the output format. These are specified between the % and conversion letter and are the same as those for printf (see Table C-8).

Returns

undef **on error**

Preformatted string according to FORMAT and LIST.

sqrt

```
sqrt EXPR
sqrt
```

Returns the square root of EXPR, or $_ if omitted.

Returns

Floating-point number

srand

```
srand EXPR
srand
```

Sets the seed value for the random-number generator to EXPR, or to a random value based on the time, process ID, and other values if EXPR is omitted.

Returns

Nothing

stat

```
stat FILEHANDLE
stat EXPR
stat
```

Returns a 13-element array giving the status info for a file, specified by either FILEHANDLE, EXPR, or $_. The list of values returned is shown in Table C-10. If used in a scalar context, returns 0 on failure, and 1 on success.

Returns

0 on failure in scalar context

1 on success in scalar context

Empty list on failure in list context

List of status on success values in list context

TABLE C-10

Values returned by `stat`.

Element	Description
0	Device number of file system.
1	Inode number.
2	File mode (type and permissions).
3	Number of (hard) links to the file.
4	Numeric user ID of file's owner.
5	Numeric group ID of file's owner.
6	The device identifier (special files only).
7	File size, in bytes.
8	Last access time since the epoch.
9	Last modify time since the epoch.
10	Inode change time (*not* creation time!) since the epoch.
11	Preferred block size for file system I/O.
12	Actual number of blocks allocated.

study

```
study EXPR
study
```

Takes extra time to study EXPR in order to improve the performance on regular expressions conducted on EXPR. If EXPR is omitted, uses $_. The actual speed gains may be very small, depending on the number of times you expect to search the string. You can only study one expression or scalar at any one time.

Returns

Nothing

sub

```
sub NAME BLOCK
sub NAME
sub BLOCK
```

Not a function. This is a keyword that signifies the start of a new subroutine definition. With NAME and BLOCK, it is a named function and definition. With only NAME (and optional prototypes), it is simply a declaration. With only BLOCK, it is an anonymous subroutine.

Returns

Nothing

substr

```
substr EXPR, OFFSET, LEN, REPLACEMENT
substr EXPR, OFFSET, LEN
substr EXPR, OFFSET
```

Returns a substring of EXPR, starting at OFFSET within the string. If OFFSET is negative, starts that many characters from the end of the string. If LEN is specified, returns that number of bytes, or all bytes up until end of string if not specified. If LEN is negative, leaves that many characters off the end of the string. If REPLACEMENT is specified, replaces the substring with the REPLACEMENT string.

If you specify a substring that passes beyond the end of the string, then it returns only the valid element of the original string.

Returns

String

sysopen

```
sysopen FILEHANDLE, FILENAME, MODE, PERMS
sysopen FILEHANDLE, FILENAME, MODE
```

Equivalent to the underlying C and operating system call open(). Opens the file specified by FILENAME, associating it with FILEHANDLE. The MODE argument specifies how the file should be opened. The values of MODE are system-dependent, but some values are historically set. Values of 0, 1, and 2 mean read-only, write-only, and read/write, respectively. The supported values are available in the Fcntl module. Note that FILENAME is strictly a filename; no interpretation of the contents takes place, and the mode of opening is defined by the MODE argument.

If the file has to be created, and the O_CREAT flag has been specified in MODE, then the file is created with the permissions of PERMS. The value of PERMS must be specified in traditional Unix-style hexadecimal. If PERMS is not specified, then Perl uses a default mode of 0666.

Returns

0 on failure

1 on success

sysread

```
sysread FILEHANDLE, SCALAR, LENGTH, OFFSET
sysread FILEHANDLE, SCALAR, LENGTH
```

Tries to read LENGTH bytes from FILEHANDLE, placing the result in SCALAR. If OFFSET is specified, then data is written to SCALAR from OFFSET bytes, effectively appending the information from a specific point. If OFFSET is negative, it starts from the number of bytes specified counted backwards from the end of the string. This is the equivalent of the C/operating system function read(). Because it bypasses the buffering system employed by functions like print, read, and seek, it should only be used with the corresponding syswrite and sysseek functions.

Returns

undef on error

0 at end of file

Integer, number of bytes read

sysseek

```
sysseek FILEHANDLE, POSITION, WHENCE
```

Sets the position within FILEHANDLE according to the values of POSITION and WHENCE. This function is the equivalent of the C function lseek(), so you should avoid using it with buffered forms of FILEHANDLE. This includes the <FILEHANDLE> notation and print, write, seek, and tell. Using it with sysread or syswrite is okay, since they too ignore buffering.

The position within the file is specified by POSITION, using the value of WHENCE as a reference point, as follows:

0 sets the new position to POSITION.

1 sets the new position to the current position plus POSITION.

2 sets the new position to EOF plus POSITION.

If you prefer, you can use the constants SEEK_SET, SEEK_CUR, and SEEK_END, respectively, provided you have imported the IO::Seekable or POSIX module.

Returns

undef on failure

A position of 0 is returned as the string 0 but true

Integer, new position (in bytes) on success

system

```
system PROGRAM, LIST
system PROGRAM
```

Executes the command specified by PROGRAM, passing LIST as arguments to the command. The script waits for execution of the child command to complete before continuing. If PROGRAM is the only argument specified, then Perl checks for any shell metacharacters and, if found, passes PROGRAM unchanged to the user's default command shell. If there are no metacharacters, then the value is split into words and passed as an entire command with arguments to the system execvp function.

The return value is the exit status of the program as returned by the wait function. To obtain the actual exit value, divide by 256. If you want to capture the output from a command, use the backticks operator.

Returns

Exit status of program as returned by wait

syswrite

```
syswrite FILEHANDLE, SCALAR, LENGTH, OFFSET
syswrite FILEHANDLE, SCALAR, LENGTH
```

Attempts to write LENGTH bytes from SCALAR to the file associated with FILEHANDLE. If OFFSET is specified, then information is read from

OFFSET bytes in the supplied SCALAR. This function uses the C/operating system write() function, which bypasses the normal buffering. You should therefore avoid using functions such as print and read in conjunction with this function.

Returns

undef on error

Integer, number of bytes written

tell

```
tell FILEHANDLE
tell
```

Returns the current position (in bytes) within the specified FILEHANDLE. If FILEHANDLE is omitted, then it returns the position within the last file accessed.

Returns

Integer, current file position (in bytes)

telldir

```
telldir DIRHANDLE
```

Returns the current position within the directory listing referred to by DIRHANDLE.

Returns

Integer

tie

```
tie VARIABLE, CLASSNAME, LIST
```

Ties the VARIABLE to the package class CLASSNAME that provides implementation for the variable type. Any additional arguments in LIST are passed to the constructor for the entire class. Typically used to bind hash variables to DBM databases.

Returns

Reference to tied object

tied

tied VARIABLE

Returns a reference to the object underlying the tied entity VARIABLE.

Returns

undef if VARIABLE is not tied to a package

time

time

Returns the number of seconds since the epoch (00:00:00 UTC, January 1, 1970, for most systems; 00:00:00, January 1, 1904, for Mac OS). Suitable for feeding to gmtime and localtime.

Returns

Integer, seconds since epoch

times

times

Returns a four-element list giving the user, system, child, and child system times for the current process and its children.

Returns

User, system, child, child system times as integer

tr///

tr/SEARCHLIST/REPLACEMENTLIST/

Not a function. This is the transliteration operator; it replaces all occurrences of the characters in `SEARCHLIST` with the characters in `REPLACEMENTLIST`.

Returns

Number of characters replaced or deleted

truncate

truncate FILEHANDLE, LENGTH

Truncates (reduces) the size of the file specified by `FILEHANDLE` to the specified `LENGTH` (in bytes). Produces a fatal error if the function is not implemented on your system.

Returns

undef if the operation failed

1 on success

uc

uc EXPR
uc

Returns an uppercased version of `EXPR`, or $_ if not specified.

Returns

String

ucfirst

ucfirst EXPR
ucfirst

Returns the value of `EXPR` with only the first character uppercased. If `EXPR` is omitted, then uses $_.

Returns

String

umask

```
umask EXPR
umask
```

Sets the umask (default mask applied when creating files and directories) for the current process. Value of EXPR must be an octal number. If EXPR is omitted, simply returns the previous value.

Returns

Previous umask value

undef

```
undef EXPR
undef
```

Undefines the value of EXPR. Use on a scalar, list, hash, function, or typeglob. Use on a hash with a statement such as undef $hash{$key}; actually sets the value of the specified key to an undefined value. If you want to delete the element from the hash, use the delete function.

Returns

undef

unlink

```
unlink LIST
unlink
```

Deletes the files specified by LIST, or the file specified by $_ otherwise.

Returns

Number of files deleted

unpack

```
unpack FORMAT, EXPR
```

Unpacks the binary string EXPR using the format specified in FORMAT.

Basically reverses the operation of `pack`, returning the list of packed values according to the supplied format.

You can also prefix any format field with a `%<number>` to indicate that you want a 16-bit checksum of the value of EXPR, instead of the value.

Returns

List of unpacked values

unshift

```
unshift ARRAY, LIST
```

Places the elements from LIST, in order, at the beginning of ARRAY.

Returns

Number of new elements in ARRAY

untie

```
untie VARIABLE
```

Breaks the binding between a variable and a package, undoing the association created by the `tie` function.

Returns

0 on failure

1 on success

use

```
use MODULE LIST
use MODULE
```

Imports all the functions exported by MODULE, or only those referred to by LIST, into the namespace of the current package. Effectively equivalent to

```
BEGIN
{
    require "Module.pm";
    Module->import();
}
```

Also used to impose compiler directives (pragmas) on the current script, although essentially these are just modules anyway.

Note that a `use` statement is evaluated at compile time. A `require` statement is evaluated at execution time.

Returns

Nothing

utime

`utime ATIME, MTIME, LIST`

Sets the access and modification times specified by `ATIME` and `MTIME` for the list of files in `LIST`. The values of `ATIME` and `MTIME` must be numerical. The inode modification time is set to the current time.

Returns

Number of files updated

values

`values HASH`

Returns the list of all the values contained in `HASH`. In a scalar context, returns the number of values that would be returned. Uses the same iterator, and therefore order, used by the `each` and `keys` functions.

Returns

Number of values in scalar context

List of values in list context

vec

`vec EXPR, OFFSET, BITS`

Treats the string in `EXPR` as a vector of unsigned integers and returns the value of the bit field specified by `OFFSET`. `BITS` specifies the number of bits reserved for each entry in the bit vector. This must be a power of two from 1 to 32.

Returns

Integer

wait

`wait`

Waits for a child process to terminate, returning the process ID of the deceased process. The exit status of the process is contained in $?.

Returns

-1 if there are no child processes

Process ID of deceased process

waitpid

`waitpid PID, FLAGS`

Waits for the child process with ID `PID` to terminate, returning the process ID of the deceased process. If `PID` does not exist, then it returns - 1. The exit status of the process is contained in $?.

If you import the POSIX module, you can specify flags by name, although all Perl implementations support a value of zero. Table C-11 lists the flags supported under Solaris. You will need to check your implementation for the flags your OS supports.

Returns

-1 if process does not exist

Process ID of deceased process

wantarray

`wantarray`

Returns True if the context of the currently executing function is looking for a list value. Returns False in a scalar context.

TABLE C-11

Flags for
`waitpid`.

Flag	Description
WIFEXITED	Wait for processes that have exited.
WIFSIGNALED	Wait for processes that received a signal.
WNOHANG	Nonblocking wait.
WSTOPSIG	Wait for processes that received STOP signal.
WTERMSIG	Wait for processes that received TERM signal.
WUNTRACED	Wait for processes stopped by signals.

Returns

`undef` **if no context**

0 **in scalar context**

1 **in list context**

warn

`warn LIST`

Prints the value of LIST to STDERR. Basically the same as the die function except that no call is made to the exit and no exception is raised within an `eval` statement. This can be useful to raise an error without causing the script to terminate prematurely.

If the variable `$@` contains a value (from a previous eval call) and LIST is empty, then the value of `$@` is printed with `\t...caught` appended to the end. If both `$@` and LIST are empty, then `Warning: Something's wrong` is printed.

Returns

Nothing

write

```
write FILEHANDLE
write
```

Writes a formatted record, as specified by `format` to `FILEHANDLE`. If `FILEHANDLE` is omitted, then writes the output to the currently selected default output channel. Form processing is handled automatically, adding new pages, headers, footers, and so on, as specified by the format for the filehandle.

Returns

0 on failure

1 on success

y///

`y/SEARCHLIST/REPLACEMENTLIST/`

Identical to the `tr///` operator; translates all characters in `SEARCHLIST` into the corresponding characters in `REPLACEMENTLIST`.

Returns

Number of characters modified

Appendix D

Windows Error Constants and Descriptions

This appendix includes a list of all the constants exported by `Win32::WinError` for which a valid description of the error exists. Constants and errors are logically grouped by the API that would normally return the error code corresponding to the constants in this appendix. See Chapter 8 for information on using these constants.

NOTE. *Some constants include* %x *strings, which are used by the error system to insert relevant data.*

Standard Error Codes

The error codes in Table D-1 are the core error codes that can be returned by any function call within the Win32 libraries.

TABLE D-1

Standard `Win32` errors.

Constant	Error Text/Description
E_ABORT	Operation aborted.
E_ACCESSDENIED	Access is denied.
E_FAIL	Unspecified error.
E_HANDLE	The handle is invalid.
E_INVALIDARG	The parameter is incorrect.
E_NOINTERFACE	No such interface supported.
E_NOTIMPL	Not implemented.
E_OUTOFMEMORY	Not enough storage is available to complete this operation.
E_POINTER	Invalid pointer.
E_UNEXPECTED	Unexpected failure.
NOERROR	The operation completed successfully.
NO_ERROR	The operation completed successfully.
SEVERITY_ERROR	Incorrect function.
SEVERITY_SUCCESS	The operation completed successfully.
S_FALSE	Incorrect function.
S_OK	The operation completed successfully.

Generic Network/Access Errors

Because the domain/network management and associated systems form such a large part of the Windows environment, there are an equally large number of generic errors. These all relate to user access and ability problems, or directly to the underlying network code errors, including identification of protocol and hardware errors. Other errors are related to storage and file system problems.

Table D-2 shows the valid constants, along with their descriptions.

TABLE D-2

Generic user/network errors.

Constant	Error Text/Description
ERROR_ACCESS_DENIED	Access is denied.
ERROR_ACCOUNT_DISABLED	Logon failure; account currently disabled.
ERROR_ACCOUNT_EXPIRED	The user's account has expired.
ERROR_ACCOUNT_LOCKED_OUT	The referenced account is currently locked out and may not be logged on to.
ERROR_ACCOUNT_RESTRICTION	Logon failure; user account restriction.
ERROR_ACTIVE_CONNECTIONS	Active connections still exist.
ERROR_ADAP_HDW_ERR	A network adapter hardware error occurred.
ERROR_ADDRESS_ALREADY_ASSOCIATED	The network transport endpoint already has an address associated with it.
ERROR_ADDRESS_NOT_ASSOCIATED	An address has not yet been associated with the network endpoint.
ERROR_ALIAS_EXISTS	The specified local group already exists.
ERROR_ALLOTTED_SPACE_EXCEEDED	No more memory is available for security information updates.
ERROR_ALREADY_ASSIGNED	The local device name is already in use.
ERROR_ALREADY_EXISTS	Cannot create a file when that file already exists.
ERROR_ALREADY_REGISTERED	The service is already registered.
ERROR_ALREADY_RUNNING_LKG	The system is currently running with the last-known-good configuration.
ERROR_ALREADY_WAITING	The specified printer handle is already being waited on.

Constant	Error Text/Description
ERROR_ARENA_TRASHED	The storage control blocks were destroyed.
ERROR_ARITHMETIC_OVERFLOW	Arithmetic result exceeded 32 bits.
ERROR_ATOMIC_LOCKS_NOT_SUPPORTED	The file system does not support atomic changes to the lock type.
ERROR_AUTODATASEG_EXCEEDS_64k	The operating system cannot run this application program.
ERROR_BADDB	The configuration registry database is corrupt.
ERROR_BADKEY	The configuration registry key is invalid.
ERROR_BAD_ARGUMENTS	The argument string passed to DosExecPgm is not correct.
ERROR_BAD_COMMAND	The device does not recognize the command.
ERROR_BAD_DESCRIPTOR_FORMAT	A security descriptor is not in the right format (absolute or self-relative).
ERROR_BAD_DEVICE	The specified device name is invalid.
ERROR_BAD_DEV_TYPE	The network resource type is not correct.
ERROR_BAD_DRIVER	The specified driver is invalid.
ERROR_BAD_DRIVER_LEVEL	The system does not support the command requested.
ERROR_BAD_ENVIRONMENT	The environment is incorrect.
ERROR_BAD_EXE_FORMAT	%1 is not a valid Win32 application.
ERROR_BAD_FORMAT	An attempt was made to load a program with an incorrect format.
ERROR_BAD_IMPERSONATION_LEVEL	Either a required impersonation level was not provided, or the provided impersonation level is invalid.
ERROR_BAD_INHERITANCE_ACL	The inherited access control list (ACL) or access control entry (ACE) could not be built.
ERROR_BAD_LENGTH	The program issued a command but the command length is incorrect.
ERROR_BAD_LOGON_SESSION_STATE	The logon session is not in a state that is consistent with the requested operation.
ERROR_BAD_NETPATH	The network path was not found.

(Continued)

TABLE D-2

(Continued)

Constant	Error Text/Description
ERROR_BAD_NET_NAME	The network name cannot be found.
ERROR_BAD_NET_RESP	The specified server cannot perform the requested operation.
ERROR_BAD_PATHNAME	The specified path is invalid.
ERROR_BAD_PIPE	The pipe state is invalid.
ERROR_BAD_PROFILE	The network connection profile is corrupt.
ERROR_BAD_PROVIDER	The specified network provider name is invalid.
ERROR_BAD_REM_ADAP	The remote adapter is not compatible.
ERROR_BAD_THREADID_ADDR	The address for the thread ID is not correct.
ERROR_BAD_TOKEN_TYPE	The type of the token is inappropriate for its attempted use.
ERROR_BAD_UNIT	The system cannot find the device specified.
ERROR_BAD_USERNAME	The specified user name is invalid.
ERROR_BAD_VALIDATION_CLASS	The validation information class requested was invalid.
ERROR_BEGINNING_OF_MEDIA	Beginning of tape or partition was encountered.
ERROR_BOOT_ALREADY_ACCEPTED	The current boot has already been accepted for use as the last-known-good control set.
ERROR_BROKEN_PIPE	The pipe has been ended.
ERROR_BUFFER_OVERFLOW	The filename is too long.
ERROR_BUSY	The requested resource is in use.
ERROR_BUSY_DRIVE	The system cannot perform a JOIN or SUBST at this time.
ERROR_BUS_RESET	The I/O bus was reset.
ERROR_CALL_NOT_IMPLEMENTED	This function is only valid in Win32 mode.
ERROR_CANCELLED	The operation was canceled by the user.
ERROR_CANCEL_VIOLATION	A lock request was not outstanding for the supplied cancel region.
ERROR_CANNOT_COPY	The copy API cannot be used.

Constant	Error Text/Description
ERROR_CANNOT_FIND_WND_CLASS	Cannot find window class.
ERROR_CANNOT_IMPERSONATE	Unable to impersonate via a named pipe until data has been read from that pipe.
ERROR_CANNOT_MAKE	The directory or file cannot be created.
ERROR_CANNOT_OPEN_PROFILE	Unable to open the network connection profile.
ERROR_CANTOPEN	The configuration registry key could not be opened.
ERROR_CANTREAD	The configuration registry key could not be read.
ERROR_CANTWRITE	The configuration registry key could not be written.
ERROR_CANT_ACCESS_DOMAIN_INFO	Indicates a Windows NT server could not be contacted or that objects within the domain are protected such that necessary information could not be retrieved.
ERROR_CANT_DISABLE_MANDATORY	The group may not be disabled.
ERROR_CANT_OPEN_ANONYMOUS	Cannot open an anonymous-level security token.
ERROR_CAN_NOT_COMPLETE	Cannot complete this function.
ERROR_CAN_NOT_DEL_LOCAL_WINS	The local WINS cannot be deleted.
ERROR_CHILD_MUST_BE_VOLATILE	Cannot create a stable subkey under a volatile parent key.
ERROR_CHILD_NOT_COMPLETE	The %1 application cannot be run in Win32 mode.
ERROR_CHILD_WINDOW_MENU	Child windows cannot have menus.
ERROR_CIRCULAR_DEPENDENCY	Circular service dependency was specified.
ERROR_CLASS_ALREADY_EXISTS	Class already exists.
ERROR_CLASS_DOES_NOT_EXIST	Class does not exist.
ERROR_CLASS_HAS_WINDOWS	Class still has open windows.
ERROR_CLIPBOARD_NOT_OPEN	Thread does not have a clipboard open.
ERROR_CLIPPING_NOT_SUPPORTED	The requested clipping operation is not supported.
ERROR_CONNECTION_ABORTED	The network connection was aborted by the local system.

(Continued)

TABLE D-2

(Continued)

Constant	Error Text/Description
ERROR_CONNECTION_ACTIVE	An invalid operation was attempted on an active network connection.
ERROR_CONNECTION_COUNT_LIMIT	A connection to the server could not be made because the limit on the number of concurrent connections for this account has been reached.
ERROR_CONNECTION_INVALID	An operation was attempted on a nonexistent network connection.
ERROR_CONNECTION_REFUSED	The remote system refused the network connection.
ERROR_CONNECTION_UNAVAIL	The device is not currently connected, but it is a remembered connection.
ERROR_CONTROL_ID_NOT_FOUND	Control ID not found.
ERROR_COUNTER_TIMEOUT	A serial I/O operation completed because the timeout period expired. (The IOCTL_SERIAL_XOFF_COUNTER did not reach zero.)
ERROR_CRC	Data error (cyclic redundancy check).
ERROR_CURRENT_DIRECTORY	The directory cannot be removed.
ERROR_DATABASE_DOES_NOT_EXIST	The database specified does not exist.
ERROR_DC_NOT_FOUND	Invalid device context (DC) handle.
ERROR_DEPENDENT_SERVICES_RUNNING	A stop control has been sent to a service that other running services are dependent on.
ERROR_DESTROY_OBJECT_OF_OTHER_THREAD	Cannot destroy object created by another thread.
ERROR_DEVICE_ALREADY_REMEMBERED	An attempt was made to remember a device that had previously been remembered.
ERROR_DEVICE_IN_USE	The device is in use by an active process and cannot be disconnected.
ERROR_DEVICE_NOT_PARTITIONED	Tape partition information could not be found when loading a tape.
ERROR_DEV_NOT_EXIST	The specified network resource or device is no longer available.
ERROR_DIRECTORY	The directory name is invalid.
ERROR_DIRECT_ACCESS_HANDLE	Attempt to use a file handle to an open disk partition for an operation other than raw disk I/O.

Constant	Error Text/Description
ERROR_DIR_NOT_EMPTY	The directory is not empty.
ERROR_DIR_NOT_ROOT	The directory is not a subdirectory of the root directory.
ERROR_DISCARDED	The segment is already discarded and cannot be locked.
ERROR_DISK_CHANGE	Program stopped because alternate diskette was not inserted.
ERROR_DISK_CORRUPT	The disk structure is corrupt and non-readable.
ERROR_DISK_FULL	There is not enough space on the disk.
ERROR_DISK_OPERATION_FAILED	While accessing the hard disk, a disk operation failed even after retries.
ERROR_DISK_RECALIBRATE_FAILED	While accessing the hard disk, a recalibrate operation failed even after retries.
ERROR_DISK_RESET_FAILED	While accessing the hard disk, a disk controller reset was needed, but even that failed.
ERROR_DLL_INIT_FAILED	A dynamic link library (DLL) initialization routine failed.
ERROR_DOMAIN_CONTROLLER_NOT_FOUND	Could not find the domain controller for this domain.
ERROR_DOMAIN_EXISTS	The specified domain already exists.
ERROR_DOMAIN_LIMIT_EXCEEDED	An attempt was made to exceed the limit on the number of domains per server.
ERROR_DOMAIN_TRUST_INCONSISTENT	The name or security ID (SID) of the domain specified is inconsistent with the trust information for that domain.
ERROR_DRIVE_LOCKED	The disk is in use or locked by another process.
ERROR_DUPLICATE_SERVICE_NAME	The name is already in use as either a service name or a service display name.
ERROR_DUP_DOMAINNAME	The workgroup or domain name is already in use by another computer on the network.
ERROR_DUP_NAME	A duplicate name exists on the network.
ERROR_DYNLINK_FROM_INVALID_RING	The operating system cannot run this application program.

(Continued)

Constant	Error Text/Description
ERROR_EAS_DIDNT_FIT	The extended attributes did not fit in the buffer.
ERROR_EAS_NOT_SUPPORTED	The mounted file system does not support extended attributes.
ERROR_EA_ACCESS_DENIED	Access to the extended attribute was denied.
ERROR_EA_FILE_CORRUPT	The extended attribute file on the mounted file system is corrupt.
ERROR_EA_LIST_INCONSISTENT	The extended attributes are inconsistent.
ERROR_EA_TABLE_FULL	The extended attribute table file is full.
ERROR_END_OF_MEDIA	The physical end of the tape has been reached.
ERROR_ENVVAR_NOT_FOUND	The system could not find the environment option that was entered.
ERROR_EOM_OVERFLOW	Physical end of tape encountered.
ERROR_EVENTLOG_CANT_START	No event log file could be opened, so the event logging service did not start.
ERROR_EVENTLOG_FILE_CHANGED	The event log file has changed between reads.
ERROR_EVENTLOG_FILE_CORRUPT	The event log file is corrupt.
ERROR_EXCEPTION_IN_SERVICE	An exception occurred in the service when handling the control request.
ERROR_EXCL_SEM_ALREADY_OWNED	The exclusive semaphore is owned by another process.
ERROR_EXE_MARKED_INVALID	The operating system cannot run %1.
ERROR_EXTENDED_ERROR	An extended error has occurred.
ERROR_FAILED_SERVICE_CONTROLLER_ CONNECT	The service process could not connect to the service controller.
ERROR_FAIL_I24	Fail on INT 24.
ERROR_FILEMARK_DETECTED	A tape access reached a filemark.
ERROR_FILENAME_EXCED_RANGE	The filename or extension is too long.
ERROR_FILE_CORRUPT	The file or directory is corrupt and non-readable.
ERROR_FILE_EXISTS	The file exists.

Constant	Error Text/Description
ERROR_FILE_INVALID	The volume for a file has been externally altered such that the opened file is no longer valid.
ERROR_FILE_NOT_FOUND	The system cannot find the file specified.
ERROR_FLOPPY_BAD_REGISTERS	The floppy disk controller returned inconsistent results in its registers.
ERROR_FLOPPY_ID_MARK_NOT_FOUND	No ID address mark was found on the floppy disk.
ERROR_FLOPPY_UNKNOWN_ERROR	The floppy disk controller reported an error that is not recognized by the floppy disk driver.
ERROR_FLOPPY_WRONG_CYLINDER	Mismatch between the floppy disk sector ID field and the floppy disk controller track address.
ERROR_FULLSCREEN_MODE	The requested operation cannot be performed in full-screen mode.
ERROR_FULL_BACKUP	The backup failed. Check the directory that you are backing the database to.
ERROR_GENERIC_NOT_MAPPED	Generic access types were contained in an access mask that should already be mapped to nongeneric types.
ERROR_GEN_FAILURE	A device attached to the system is not functioning.
ERROR_GLOBAL_ONLY_HOOK	This hook procedure can only be set globally.
ERROR_GRACEFUL_DISCONNECT	The network connection was gracefully closed.
ERROR_GROUP_EXISTS	The specified group already exists.
ERROR_HANDLE_DISK_FULL	The disk is full.
ERROR_HANDLE_EOF	Reached end of file.
ERROR_HOOK_NEEDS_HMOD	Cannot set nonlocal hook without a module handle.
ERROR_HOOK_NOT_INSTALLED	The hook procedure is not installed.
ERROR_HOST_UNREACHABLE	The remote system is not reachable by the transport.
ERROR_HOTKEY_ALREADY_REGISTERED	Hot key is already registered.

(Continued)

TABLE D-2

(Continued)

Constant	Error Text/Description
ERROR_HOTKEY_NOT_REGISTERED	Hot key is not registered.
ERROR_HWNDS_HAVE_DIFF_PARENT	All handles to windows in a multiple-window position structure must have the same parent.
ERROR_ILL_FORMED_PASSWORD	Unable to update the password. The value provided for the new password contains values that are not allowed in passwords.
ERROR_INCORRECT_ADDRESS	The network address could not be used for the operation requested.
ERROR_INC_BACKUP	The backup failed. Was a full backup done before?
ERROR_INFLOOP_IN_RELOC_CHAIN	The operating system cannot run %1.
ERROR_INSUFFICIENT_BUFFER	The data area passed to a system call is too small.
ERROR_INTERNAL_DB_CORRUPTION	Unable to complete the requested operation because of either a catastrophic media failure or a data structure corruption on the disk.
ERROR_INTERNAL_DB_ERROR	The local security authority database contains an internal inconsistency.
ERROR_INTERNAL_ERROR	The security account database contains an internal inconsistency.
ERROR_INVALID_ACCEL_HANDLE	Invalid accelerator table handle.
ERROR_INVALID_ACCESS	The access code is invalid.
ERROR_INVALID_ACCOUNT_NAME	The name provided is not a properly formed account name.
ERROR_INVALID_ACL	The access control list (ACL) structure is invalid.
ERROR_INVALID_ADDRESS	Attempt to access invalid address.
ERROR_INVALID_AT_INTERRUPT_TIME	Cannot request exclusive semaphores at interrupt time.
ERROR_INVALID_BLOCK	The storage control block address is invalid.
ERROR_INVALID_BLOCK_LENGTH	When accessing a new tape of a multi-volume partition, the current blocksize is incorrect.
ERROR_INVALID_CATEGORY	The IOCTL call made by the application program is not correct.

Constant	Error Text/Description
ERROR_INVALID_COMBOBOX_MESSAGE	Invalid message for a combo box because it does not have an edit control.
ERROR_INVALID_COMPUTERNAME	The format of the specified computer name is invalid.
ERROR_INVALID_CURSOR_HANDLE	Invalid cursor handle.
ERROR_INVALID_DATA	The data is invalid.
ERROR_INVALID_DATATYPE	The specified datatype is invalid.
ERROR_INVALID_DOMAINNAME	The format of the specified domain name is invalid.
ERROR_INVALID_DOMAIN_ROLE	This operation is only allowed for the primary domain controller of the domain.
ERROR_INVALID_DOMAIN_STATE	The domain was in the wrong state to perform the security operation.
ERROR_INVALID_DRIVE	The system cannot find the drive specified.
ERROR_INVALID_DWP_HANDLE	Invalid handle to a multiple-window position structure.
ERROR_INVALID_EA_HANDLE	The specified extended attribute handle is invalid.
ERROR_INVALID_EA_NAME	The specified extended attribute name was invalid.
ERROR_INVALID_EDIT_HEIGHT	Height must be less than 256.
ERROR_INVALID_ENVIRONMENT	The environment specified is invalid.
ERROR_INVALID_EVENTNAME	The format of the specified event name is invalid.
ERROR_INVALID_EVENT_COUNT	The number of specified semaphore events for DosMuxSemWait is not correct.
ERROR_INVALID_EXE_SIGNATURE	Cannot run %1 in Win32 mode.
ERROR_INVALID_FILTER_PROC	Invalid hook procedure.
ERROR_INVALID_FLAGS	Invalid flags.
ERROR_INVALID_FLAG_NUMBER	The flag passed is not correct.
ERROR_INVALID_FORM_NAME	The specified form name is invalid.
ERROR_INVALID_FORM_SIZE	The specified form size is invalid
ERROR_INVALID_FUNCTION	Incorrect function.

(Continued)

TABLE D-2

(Continued)

Constant	Error Text/Description
ERROR_INVALID_GROUPNAME	The format of the specified group name is invalid.
ERROR_INVALID_GROUP_ATTRIBUTES	The specified attributes are invalid or incompatible with the attributes for the group as a whole.
ERROR_INVALID_GW_COMMAND	Invalid GW_* command.
ERROR_INVALID_HANDLE	The handle is invalid.
ERROR_INVALID_HOOK_FILTER	Invalid hook procedure type.
ERROR_INVALID_HOOK_HANDLE	Invalid hook handle.
ERROR_INVALID_ICON_HANDLE	Invalid icon handle.
ERROR_INVALID_ID_AUTHORITY	The value provided was an invalid value for an identifier authority.
ERROR_INVALID_INDEX	Invalid index.
ERROR_INVALID_LB_MESSAGE	Invalid message for single-selection list-box.
ERROR_INVALID_LEVEL	The system call level is not correct.
ERROR_INVALID_LIST_FORMAT	The DosMuxSemWait list is not correct.
ERROR_INVALID_LOGON_HOURS	Logon failure; account logon time restriction violation.
ERROR_INVALID_LOGON_TYPE	A logon request contained an invalid logon type value.
ERROR_INVALID_MEMBER	A new member could not be added to a local group because the member has the wrong account type.
ERROR_INVALID_MENU_HANDLE	Invalid menu handle.
ERROR_INVALID_MESSAGE	The window cannot act on the sent message.
ERROR_INVALID_MESSAGEDEST	The format of the specified message destination is invalid.
ERROR_INVALID_MESSAGENAME	The format of the specified message name is invalid.
ERROR_INVALID_MINALLOCSIZE	The operating system cannot run %1.
ERROR_INVALID_MODULETYPE	The operating system cannot run %1.
ERROR_INVALID_MSGBOX_STYLE	Invalid message box style.
ERROR_INVALID_NAME	The filename, directory name, or volume label syntax is incorrect.

Constant	Error Text/Description
ERROR_INVALID_NETNAME	The format of the specified network name is invalid.
ERROR_INVALID_ORDINAL	The operating system cannot run %1.
ERROR_INVALID_OWNER	This security ID may not be assigned as the owner of this object.
ERROR_INVALID_PARAMETER	The parameter is incorrect.
ERROR_INVALID_PASSWORD	The specified network password is not correct.
ERROR_INVALID_PASSWORDNAME	The format of the specified password is invalid.
ERROR_INVALID_PIXEL_FORMAT	The pixel format is invalid.
ERROR_INVALID_PRIMARY_GROUP	This security ID may not be assigned as the primary group of an object.
ERROR_INVALID_PRINTER_COMMAND	The printer command is invalid.
ERROR_INVALID_PRINTER_NAME	The printer name is invalid.
ERROR_INVALID_PRINTER_STATE	The state of the printer is invalid.
ERROR_INVALID_PRIORITY	The specified priority is invalid.
ERROR_INVALID_SCROLLBAR_RANGE	Scroll bar range cannot be greater than 0x7FFF.
ERROR_INVALID_SECURITY_DESCR	The security descriptor structure is invalid.
ERROR_INVALID_SEGDPL	The operating system cannot run %1.
ERROR_INVALID_SEGMENT_NUMBER	The system detected a segment number that was not correct.
ERROR_INVALID_SEPARATOR_FILE	The specified separator file is invalid.
ERROR_INVALID_SERVER_STATE	The security account manager (SAM) or local security authority (LSA) server was in the wrong state to perform the security operation.
ERROR_INVALID_SERVICENAME	The format of the specified service name is invalid.
ERROR_INVALID_SERVICE_ACCOUNT	The account name is invalid or does not exist.
ERROR_INVALID_SERVICE_CONTROL	The requested control is not valid for this service.

(Continued)

Constant	Error Text/Description
ERROR_INVALID_SERVICE_LOCK	The specified service database lock is invalid.
ERROR_INVALID_SHARENAME	The format of the specified share name is invalid.
ERROR_INVALID_SHOWWIN_COMMAND	Cannot show or remove the window in the way specified.
ERROR_INVALID_SID	The security ID structure is invalid.
ERROR_INVALID_SIGNAL_NUMBER	The signal being posted is not correct.
ERROR_INVALID_SPI_VALUE	Invalid system-wide (SPI_*) parameter.
ERROR_INVALID_STACKSEG	The operating system cannot run %1.
ERROR_INVALID_STARTING_CODESEG	The operating system cannot run %1.
ERROR_INVALID_SUB_AUTHORITY	The subauthority part of a security ID is invalid for this particular use.
ERROR_INVALID_TARGET_HANDLE	The target internal file identifier is incorrect.
ERROR_INVALID_THREAD_ID	Invalid thread identifier.
ERROR_INVALID_TIME	The specified time is invalid.
ERROR_INVALID_USER_BUFFER	The supplied user buffer is not valid for the requested operation.
ERROR_INVALID_VERIFY_SWITCH	The verify-on-write switch parameter value is not correct.
ERROR_INVALID_WINDOW_HANDLE	Invalid window handle.
ERROR_INVALID_WINDOW_STYLE	The window style or class attribute is invalid for this operation.
ERROR_INVALID_WORKSTATION	Logon failure; user not allowed to log on to this computer.
ERROR_IOPL_NOT_ENABLED	The operating system is not presently configured to run this application.
ERROR_IO_DEVICE	The request could not be performed because of an I/O device error.
ERROR_IO_INCOMPLETE	Overlapped I/O event is not in a signaled state.
ERROR_IO_PENDING	Overlapped I/O operation is in progress.
ERROR_IRQ_BUSY	Unable to open a device that was sharing an interrupt request (IRQ) with other devices. At least one other device that uses that IRQ was already opened.

Constant	Error Text/Description
ERROR_IS_JOINED	An attempt was made to use a JOIN or SUBST command on a drive that has already been joined.
ERROR_IS_JOIN_PATH	Not enough resources are available to process this command.
ERROR_IS_JOIN_TARGET	A JOIN or SUBST command cannot be used for a drive that contains previously joined drives.
ERROR_IS_SUBSTED	An attempt was made to use a JOIN or SUBST command on a drive that has already been substituted.
ERROR_IS_SUBST_PATH	The path specified is being used in a substitute.
ERROR_IS_SUBST_TARGET	An attempt was made to join or substitute a drive for which a directory on the drive is the target of a previous substitute.
ERROR_ITERATED_DATA_EXCEEDS_64k	The operating system cannot run %1.
ERROR_JOIN_TO_JOIN	The system tried to join a drive to a directory on a joined drive.
ERROR_JOIN_TO_SUBST	The system tried to join a drive to a directory on a substituted drive.
ERROR_JOURNAL_HOOK_SET	The journal hook procedure is already installed.
ERROR_KEY_DELETED	Illegal operation attempted on a registry key that has been marked for deletion.
ERROR_KEY_HAS_CHILDREN	Cannot create a symbolic link in a registry key that already has subkeys or values.
ERROR_LABEL_TOO_LONG	The volume label you entered exceeds the label character limit of the target file system.
ERROR_LAST_ADMIN	The last remaining administration account cannot be disabled or deleted.
ERROR_LB_WITHOUT_TABSTOPS	This listbox does not support tab stops.
ERROR_LISTBOX_ID_NOT_FOUND	The listbox identifier was not found.
ERROR_LM_CROSS_ENCRYPTION_REQUIRED	A cross-encrypted password is necessary to change this user password.

(Continued)

TABLE D-2

(Continued)

Constant	Error Text/Description
ERROR_LOCAL_USER_SESSION_KEY	No encryption key is available. A well-known encryption key was returned.
ERROR_LOCKED	The segment is locked and cannot be reallocated.
ERROR_LOCK_FAILED	Unable to lock a region of a file.
ERROR_LOCK_VIOLATION	The process cannot access the file because another process has locked a portion of the file.
ERROR_LOGIN_TIME_RESTRICTION	Attempting to log in during an unauthorized time of day for this account.
ERROR_LOGIN_WKSTA_RESTRICTION	The account is not authorized to log in from this station.
ERROR_LOGON_FAILURE	Logon failure; unknown user name or bad password.
ERROR_LOGON_NOT_GRANTED	Logon failure; the user has not been granted the requested logon type at this computer.
ERROR_LOGON_SESSION_COLLISION	The logon session ID is already in use.
ERROR_LOGON_SESSION_EXISTS	Cannot start a new logon session with an ID that is already in use.
ERROR_LOGON_TYPE_NOT_GRANTED	Logon failure; the user has not been granted the requested logon type at this computer.
ERROR_LOG_FILE_FULL	The event log file is full.
ERROR_LUIDS_EXHAUSTED	No more local user identifiers (LUIDs) are available.
ERROR_MAPPED_ALIGNMENT	The base address or the file offset specified does not have the proper alignment.
ERROR_MAX_THRDS_REACHED	No more threads can be created in the system.
ERROR_MEDIA_CHANGED	Media in drive may have changed.
ERROR_MEMBERS_PRIMARY_GROUP	The user cannot be removed from a group because the group is currently the user's primary group.
ERROR_MEMBER_IN_ALIAS	The specified account name is already a member of the local group.
ERROR_MEMBER_IN_GROUP	Either the specified user account is already a member of the specified group or the specified group cannot be deleted because it contains a member.

Constant	Error Text/Description
ERROR_MEMBER_NOT_IN_ALIAS	The specified account name is not a member of the local group.
ERROR_MEMBER_NOT_IN_GROUP	The specified user account is not a member of the specified group account.
ERROR_METAFILE_NOT_SUPPORTED	The requested metafile operation is not supported.
ERROR_META_EXPANSION_TOO_LONG	The global filename characters * or ? are entered incorrectly or too many global filename characters are specified.
ERROR_MOD_NOT_FOUND	The specified module could not be found.
ERROR_MORE_DATA	More data is available.
ERROR_MORE_WRITES	A serial I/O operation was completed by another write to the serial port. (The IOCTL_SERIAL_XOFF_COUNTER reached zero.)
ERROR_MR_MID_NOT_FOUND	The system cannot find message for message number 0x%1 in message file for %2.
ERROR_NEGATIVE_SEEK	An attempt was made to move the file pointer before the beginning of the file.
ERROR_NESTING_NOT_ALLOWED	Can't nest calls to LoadModule.
ERROR_NETLOGON_NOT_STARTED	An attempt was made to log on, but the network logon service was not started.
ERROR_NETNAME_DELETED	The specified network name is no longer available.
ERROR_NETWORK_ACCESS_DENIED	Network access is denied.
ERROR_NETWORK_BUSY	The network is busy.
ERROR_NETWORK_UNREACHABLE	The remote network is not reachable by the transport.
ERROR_NET_WRITE_FAULT	A write fault occurred on the network.
ERROR_NOACCESS	Invalid access to memory location.
ERROR_NOLOGON_INTERDOMAIN_TRUST_ACCOUNT	The account used is an interdomain trust account. Use your global user account or local user account to access this server.
ERROR_NOLOGON_SERVER_TRUST_ACCOUNT	The account used is a server trust account. Use your global user account or local user account to access this server.

(Continued)

TABLE D-2

(Continued)

Constant	Error Text/Description
ERROR_NOLOGON_WORKSTATION_TRUST_ ACCOUNT	The account used is a computer account. Use your global user account or local user account to access this server.
ERROR_NONE_MAPPED	No mapping between account names and security IDs was done.
ERROR_NON_MDICHILD_WINDOW	Cannot process a message from a window that is not a multiple document interface (MDI) window.
ERROR_NOTIFY_ENUM_DIR	A notify change request is being completed and the information is not being returned in the caller's buffer. The caller now needs to enumerate the files to find the changes.
ERROR_NOT_ALL_ASSIGNED	Not all privileges referenced are assigned to the caller.
ERROR_NOT_CHILD_WINDOW	The window is not a child window.
ERROR_NOT_CONNECTED	This network connection does not exist.
ERROR_NOT_CONTAINER	Cannot enumerate a noncontainer.
ERROR_NOT_DOS_DISK	The specified disk or diskette cannot be accessed.
ERROR_NOT_ENOUGH_MEMORY	Not enough storage is available to process this command.
ERROR_NOT_ENOUGH_QUOTA	Not enough quota is available to process this command.
ERROR_NOT_ENOUGH_SERVER_MEMORY	Not enough server storage is available to process this command.
ERROR_NOT_JOINED	The system tried to delete the JOIN of a drive that is not joined.
ERROR_NOT_LOCKED	The segment is already unlocked.
ERROR_NOT_LOGON_PROCESS	The requested action is restricted for use by logon processes only. The calling process has not registered as a logon process.
ERROR_NOT_OWNER	Attempt to release mutex not owned by caller.
ERROR_NOT_READY	The device is not ready.
ERROR_NOT_REGISTRY_FILE	The system has attempted to load or restore a file into the registry, but the specified file is not in a registry file format.

Constant	Error Text/Description
ERROR_NOT_SAME_DEVICE	The system cannot move the file to a different disk drive.
ERROR_NOT_SUBSTED	The system tried to delete the substitution of a drive that is not substituted.
ERROR_NOT_SUPPORTED	The network request is not supported.
ERROR_NO_BROWSER_SERVERS_FOUND	The list of servers for this workgroup is not currently available.
ERROR_NO_DATA	The pipe is being closed.
ERROR_NO_DATA_DETECTED	No more data is on the tape.
ERROR_NO_IMPERSONATION_TOKEN	An attempt has been made to operate on an impersonation token by a thread that is not currently impersonating a client.
ERROR_NO_INHERITANCE	Indicates an ACL contains no inheritable components.
ERROR_NO_LOGON_SERVERS	There are currently no logon servers available to service the logon request.
ERROR_NO_LOG_SPACE	System could not allocate the required space in a registry log.
ERROR_NO_MEDIA_IN_DRIVE	No media in drive.
ERROR_NO_MORE_FILES	There are no more files.
ERROR_NO_MORE_ITEMS	No more data is available.
ERROR_NO_MORE_SEARCH_HANDLES	No more internal file identifiers available.
ERROR_NO_NETWORK	The network is not present or not started.
ERROR_NO_NET_OR_BAD_PATH	No network provider accepted the given network path.
ERROR_NO_PROC_SLOTS	The system cannot start another process at this time.
ERROR_NO_QUOTAS_FOR_ACCOUNT	No system quota limits are specifically set for this account.
ERROR_NO_SCROLLBARS	The window does not have scroll bars.
ERROR_NO_SECURITY_ON_OBJECTZ	Unable to perform a security operation on an object that has no associated security.
ERROR_NO_SHUTDOWN_IN_PROGRESS	Unable to abort the system shutdown because no shutdown was in progress.

(Continued)

TABLE D-2

(Continued)

Constant	Error Text/Description
ERROR_NO_SIGNAL_SENT	No process in the command subtree has a signal handler.
ERROR_NO_SPOOL_SPACE	Space to store the file waiting to be printed is not available on the server.
ERROR_NO_SUCH_ALIAS	The specified local group does not exist.
ERROR_NO_SUCH_DOMAIN	The specified domain did not exist.
ERROR_NO_SUCH_GROUP	The specified group does not exist.
ERROR_NO_SUCH_LOGON_SESSION	A specified logon session does not exist. It may already have been terminated.
ERROR_NO_SUCH_MEMBER	A new member could not be added to a local group because the member does not exist.
ERROR_NO_SUCH_PACKAGE	A specified authentication package is unknown.
ERROR_NO_SUCH_PRIVILEGE	A specified privilege does not exist.
ERROR_NO_SUCH_USER	The specified user does not exist.
ERROR_NO_SYSTEM_MENU	The window does not have a system menu.
ERROR_NO_TOKEN	An attempt was made to reference a token that does not exist.
ERROR_NO_TRUST_LSA_SECRET	The workstation does not have a trust secret.
ERROR_NO_TRUST_SAM_ACCOUNT	The SAM database on the Windows NT server does not have a computer account for this workstation trust relationship.
ERROR_NO_UNICODE_TRANSLATION	No mapping for the Unicode character exists in the target multibyte code page.
ERROR_NO_USER_SESSION_KEY	There is no user session key for the specified logon session.
ERROR_NO_VOLUME_LABEL	The disk has no volume label.
ERROR_NO_WILDCARD_CHARACTERS	No wildcards were found.
ERROR_NT_CROSS_ENCRYPTION_REQUIRED	A cross-encrypted password is necessary to change a user password.
ERROR_NULL_LM_PASSWORD	The NT password is too complex to be converted to a LAN Manager password. The LAN Manager password returned is a NULL string.

Constant	Error Text/Description
ERROR_OPEN_FAILED	The system cannot open the device or file specified.
ERROR_OPEN_FILES	This network connection has files open or requests pending.
ERROR_OPERATION_ABORTED	The I/O operation has been aborted because of either a thread exit or an application request.
ERROR_OUTOFMEMORY	Not enough storage is available to complete this operation.
ERROR_OUT_OF_PAPER	The printer is out of paper.
ERROR_OUT_OF_STRUCTURES	Storage to process this request is not available.
ERROR_PARTIAL_COPY	Only part of a `Read/WriteProcessMemory` request was completed.
ERROR_PARTITION_FAILURE	Tape could not be partitioned.
ERROR_PASSWORD_EXPIRED	Logon failure; the specified account password has expired.
ERROR_PASSWORD_MUST_CHANGE	The user must change his or her password before logging on the first time.
ERROR_PASSWORD_RESTRICTION	Unable to update the password because a password update rule has been violated.
ERROR_PATH_BUSY	The path specified cannot be used at this time.
ERROR_PATH_NOT_FOUND	The system cannot find the path specified.
ERROR_PIPE_BUSY	All pipe instances are busy.
ERROR_PIPE_CONNECTED	There is a process on other end of the pipe.
ERROR_PIPE_LISTENING	Waiting for a process to open the other end of the pipe.
ERROR_PIPE_NOT_CONNECTED	No process is on the other end of the pipe.
ERROR_POPUP_ALREADY_ACTIVE	Pop-up menu already active.
ERROR_PORT_UNREACHABLE	No service is operating at the destination network endpoint on the remote system.

(Continued)

TABLE D-2

(Continued)

Constant	Error Text/Description
ERROR_POSSIBLE_DEADLOCK	A potential deadlock condition has been detected.
ERROR_PRINTER_ALREADY_EXISTS	The printer already exists.
ERROR_PRINTER_DELETED	The specified printer has been deleted.
ERROR_PRINTER_DRIVER_ALREADY_ INSTALLED	The specified printer driver is already installed.
ERROR_PRINTER_DRIVER_IN_USE	The specified printer driver is currently in use.
ERROR_PRINTQ_FULL	The printer queue is full.
ERROR_PRINT_CANCELLED	Your file waiting to be printed was deleted.
ERROR_PRINT_MONITOR_ALREADY_ INSTALLED	The specified print monitor has already been installed.
ERROR_PRINT_PROCESSOR_ALREADY_ INSTALLED	The specified print processor has already been installed.
ERROR_PRIVATE_DIALOG_INDEX	Using private DIALOG window words.
ERROR_PRIVILEGE_NOT_HELD	A required privilege is not held by the client.
ERROR_PROCESS_ABORTED	The process terminated unexpectedly.
ERROR_PROC_NOT_FOUND	The specified procedure could not be found.
ERROR_PROTOCOL_UNREACHABLE	The remote system does not support the transport protocol.
ERROR_READ_FAULT	The system cannot read from the specified device.
ERROR_REC_NON_EXISTENT	The name does not exist in the WINS database.
ERROR_REDIRECTOR_HAS_OPEN_HANDLES	The redirector is in use and cannot be unloaded.
ERROR_REDIR_PAUSED	The specified printer or disk device has been paused.
ERROR_REGISTRY_CORRUPT	The registry is corrupt. The structure of one of the files that contains registry data is corrupt, or the system's image of the file in memory is corrupt, or the file could not be recovered because the alternate copy or log was absent or corrupt.

Constant	Error Text/Description
ERROR_REGISTRY_IO_FAILED	An I/O operation initiated by the registry failed unrecoverably. The registry could not read in, write out, or flush one of the files that contain the system's image of the registry.
ERROR_REGISTRY_RECOVERED	One of the files in the registry database had to be recovered by use of a log or alternate copy. The recovery was successful.
ERROR_RELOC_CHAIN_XEEDS_SEGLIM	The operating system cannot run %1.
ERROR_REMOTE_SESSION_LIMIT_EXCEEDED	An attempt was made to establish a session to a network server, but there are already too many sessions established to that server.
ERROR_REM_NOT_LIST	The remote computer is not available.
ERROR_REQUEST_ABORTED	The request was aborted.
ERROR_REQ_NOT_ACCEP	No more connections can be made to this remote computer at this time because there are already as many connections as the computer can accept.
ERROR_RESOURCE_DATA_NOT_FOUND	The specified image file did not contain a resource section.
ERROR_RESOURCE_LANG_NOT_FOUND	The specified resource language ID cannot be found in the image file.
ERROR_RESOURCE_NAME_NOT_FOUND	The specified resource name cannot be found in the image file.
ERROR_RESOURCE_TYPE_NOT_FOUND	The specified resource type cannot be found in the image file.
ERROR_RETRY	The operation could not be completed. A retry should be performed.
ERROR_REVISION_MISMATCH	Indicates two revision levels are incompatible.
ERROR_RING2SEG_MUST_BE_MOVABLE	The code segment cannot be greater than or equal to 64 KB.
ERROR_RING2_STACK_IN_USE	The ring 2 stack is in use.
ERROR_RPL_NOT_ALLOWED	Replication with a nonconfigured partner is not allowed.
ERROR_RXACT_COMMIT_FAILURE	An internal security database corruption has been encountered.

(Continued)

TABLE D-2

(Continued)

Constant	Error Text/Description
ERROR_RXACT_INVALID_STATE	The transaction state of a registry sub-tree is incompatible with the requested operation.
ERROR_SAME_DRIVE	The system cannot join or substitute a drive to or for a directory on the same drive.
ERROR_SCREEN_ALREADY_LOCKED	Screen already locked.
ERROR_SECRET_TOO_LONG	The length of a secret exceeds the maximum length allowed.
ERROR_SECTOR_NOT_FOUND	The drive cannot find the sector requested.
ERROR_SEEK	The drive cannot locate a specific area or track on the disk.
ERROR_SEEK_ON_DEVICE	The file pointer cannot be set on the specified device or file.
ERROR_SEM_IS_SET	The semaphore is set and cannot be closed.
ERROR_SEM_NOT_FOUND	The specified system semaphore name was not found.
ERROR_SEM_OWNER_DIED	The previous ownership of this semaphore has ended.
ERROR_SEM_TIMEOUT	The semaphore timeout period has expired.
ERROR_SEM_USER_LIMIT	Insert the diskette for drive %1.
ERROR_SERIAL_NO_DEVICE	No serial device was successfully initialized. The serial driver will unload.
ERROR_SERVER_DISABLED	The server is currently disabled.
ERROR_SERVER_HAS_OPEN_HANDLES	The server is in use and cannot be unloaded.
ERROR_SERVER_NOT_DISABLED	The server is currently enabled.
ERROR_SERVICE_ALREADY_RUNNING	An instance of the service is already running.
ERROR_SERVICE_CANNOT_ACCEPT_CTRL	The service cannot accept control messages at this time.
ERROR_SERVICE_DATABASE_LOCKED	The service database is locked.
ERROR_SERVICE_DEPENDENCY_DELETED	The dependency service does not exist or has been marked for deletion.

Constant	Error Text/Description
ERROR_SERVICE_DEPENDENCY_FAIL	The dependency service or group failed to start.
ERROR_SERVICE_DISABLED	The specified service is disabled and cannot be started.
ERROR_SERVICE_DOES_NOT_EXIST	The specified service does not exist as an installed service.
ERROR_SERVICE_EXISTS	The specified service already exists.
ERROR_SERVICE_LOGON_FAILED	The service did not start due to a logon failure.
ERROR_SERVICE_MARKED_FOR_DELETE	The specified service has been marked for deletion.
ERROR_SERVICE_NEVER_STARTED	No attempts to start the service have been made since the last boot.
ERROR_SERVICE_NOT_ACTIVE	The service has not been started.
ERROR_SERVICE_NOT_FOUND	The specified service does not exist.
ERROR_SERVICE_NO_THREAD	A thread could not be created for the service.
ERROR_SERVICE_REQUEST_TIMEOUT	The service did not respond to the start or control request in a timely fashion.
ERROR_SERVICE_SPECIFIC_ERROR	The service has returned a service-specific error code.
ERROR_SERVICE_START_HANG	After starting, the service hung in a start-pending state.
ERROR_SESSION_CREDENTIAL_CONFLICT	The credentials supplied conflict with an existing set of credentials.
ERROR_SETCOUNT_ON_BAD_LB	LB_SETCOUNT sent to nonlazy listbox.
ERROR_SETMARK_DETECTED	A tape access reached the end of a set of files.
ERROR_SHARING_BUFFER_EXCEEDED	Too many files opened for sharing.
ERROR_SHARING_PAUSED	The remote server has been paused or is in the process of being started.
ERROR_SHARING_VIOLATION	The process cannot access the file because it is being used by another process.
ERROR_SHUTDOWN_IN_PROGRESS	A system shutdown is in progress.
ERROR_SIGNAL_PENDING	A signal is already pending.

(Continued)

TABLE D-2

(Continued)

Constant	Error Text/Description
ERROR_SIGNAL_REFUSED	The recipient process has refused the signal.
ERROR_SOME_NOT_MAPPED	Some mapping between account names and security IDs was not done.
ERROR_SPECIAL_ACCOUNT	Cannot perform this operation on built-in accounts.
ERROR_SPECIAL_GROUP	Cannot perform this operation on this built-in special group.
ERROR_SPECIAL_USER	Cannot perform this operation on this built-in special user.
ERROR_SPL_NO_ADDJOB	An `AddJob` call was not issued.
ERROR_SPL_NO_STARTDOC	A `StartDocPrinter` call was not issued.
ERROR_SPOOL_FILE_NOT_FOUND	The spool file was not found.
ERROR_STACK_OVERFLOW	Recursion too deep; stack overflowed.
ERROR_STATIC_INIT	The importation from the file failed.
ERROR_SUBST_TO_JOIN	The system tried to `SUBST` a drive to a directory on a joined drive.
ERROR_SUBST_TO_SUBST	The system tried to substitute a drive to a directory on a substituted drive.
ERROR_SUCCESS	The operation completed successfully.
ERROR_SWAPERROR	Error performing inpage operation.
ERROR_SYSTEM_TRACE	System trace information was not specified in your CONFIG.SYS file, or tracing is disallowed.
ERROR_THREAD_1_INACTIVE	The signal handler cannot be set.
ERROR_TLW_WITH_WSCHILD	Cannot create a top-level child window.
ERROR_TOKEN_ALREADY_IN_USE	The token is already in use as a primary token.
ERROR_TOO_MANY_CMDS	The network BIOS command limit has been reached.
ERROR_TOO_MANY_CONTEXT_IDS	During a logon attempt, the user's security context accumulated too many security IDs.
ERROR_TOO_MANY_LUIDS_REQUESTED	Too many local user identifiers (LUIDs) were requested at one time.

Constant	Error Text/Description
ERROR_TOO_MANY_MODULES	Too many dynamic link modules are attached to this program or dynamic link module.
ERROR_TOO_MANY_MUXWAITERS	`DosMuxSemWait` did not execute; too many semaphores are already set.
ERROR_TOO_MANY_NAMES	The name limit for the local computer network adapter card was exceeded.
ERROR_TOO_MANY_OPEN_FILES	The system cannot open the file.
ERROR_TOO_MANY_POSTS	Too many posts were made to a semaphore.
ERROR_TOO_MANY_SECRETS	The maximum number of secrets that may be stored in a single system has been exceeded.
ERROR_TOO_MANY_SEMAPHORES	Cannot create another system semaphore.
ERROR_TOO_MANY_SEM_REQUESTS	The semaphore cannot be set again.
ERROR_TOO_MANY_SESS	The network BIOS session limit was exceeded.
ERROR_TOO_MANY_SIDS	Too many security IDs have been specified.
ERROR_TOO_MANY_TCBS	Cannot create another thread.
ERROR_TRANSFORM_NOT_SUPPORTED	The requested transformation operation is not supported.
ERROR_TRUSTED_DOMAIN_FAILURE	The trust relationship between the primary domain and the trusted domain failed.
ERROR_TRUSTED_RELATIONSHIP_FAILURE	The trust relationship between this workstation and the primary domain failed.
ERROR_TRUST_FAILURE	The network logon failed.
ERROR_UNABLE_TO_LOCK_MEDIA	Unable to lock the media eject mechanism.
ERROR_UNABLE_TO_UNLOAD_MEDIA	Unable to unload the media.
ERROR_UNEXP_NET_ERR	An unexpected network error occurred.
ERROR_UNKNOWN_PORT	The specified port is unknown.
ERROR_UNKNOWN_PRINTER_DRIVER	The printer driver is unknown.
ERROR_UNKNOWN_PRINTPROCESSOR	The print processor is unknown.

(Continued)

Constant	Error Text/Description
ERROR_UNKNOWN_PRINT_MONITOR	The specified print monitor is unknown.
ERROR_UNKNOWN_REVISION	The revision level is unknown.
ERROR_UNRECOGNIZED_MEDIA	The disk media is not recognized. It may not be formatted.
ERROR_UNRECOGNIZED_VOLUME	The volume does not contain a recognized file system. Please make sure that all required file system drivers are loaded and that the volume is not corrupt.
ERROR_USER_EXISTS	The specified user already exists.
ERROR_USER_MAPPED_FILE	The requested operation cannot be performed on a file with a user-mapped section open.
ERROR_VC_DISCONNECTED	The session was canceled.
ERROR_WAIT_NO_CHILDREN	There are no child processes to wait for.
ERROR_WINDOW_NOT_COMBOBOX	The window is not a combo box.
ERROR_WINDOW_NOT_DIALOG	The window is not a valid dialog window.
ERROR_WINDOW_OF_OTHER_THREAD	Invalid window; belongs to other thread.
ERROR_WINS_INTERNAL	WINS encountered an error while processing the command.
ERROR_WRITE_FAULT	The system cannot write to the specified device.
ERROR_WRITE_PROTECT	The media is write protected.
ERROR_WRONG_DISK	The wrong diskette is in the drive. Insert %2 (Volume Serial Number: %3) into drive %1.
ERROR_WRONG_PASSWORD	Unable to update the password. The value provided as the current password is incorrect.

Clipboard Errors

These error codes are returned when accessing or setting the clipboard using the Win32::Clipboard module. The list of valid constants is shown in Table D-3.

TABLE D-3

Clipboard error constants.

Constant	Error Text/Description
CLIPBRD_E_BAD_DATA	Data on clipboard is invalid.
CLIPBRD_E_CANT_CLOSE	CloseClipboard failed.
CLIPBRD_E_CANT_EMPTY	EmptyClipboard failed.
CLIPBRD_E_CANT_OPEN	OpenClipboard failed.
CLIPBRD_E_CANT_SET	SetClipboard failed.

OLE/COM Errors

The structure of the Windows OLE system and the COM interface is quite complex, and a variety of errors can be generated at a number of locations, from the origin of the COM object creation, through to the data conversion between the COM object and the caller.

Generic OLE Errors

The errors in Table D-4 are generic OLE errors, raised when an object is created, accessed, or when connecting to an existing COM object.

TABLE D-4

Generic OLE errors.

Constant	Error Text/Description
OLE_E_ADVISENOTSUPPORTED	This implementation doesn't take advises.
OLE_E_BLANK	Uninitialized object.
OLE_E_CANTCONVERT	Not able to convert object.
OLE_E_CANT_BINDTOSOURCE	Not able to bind to the source.
OLE_E_CANT_GETMONIKER	Not able to get the moniker of the object.
OLE_E_CLASSDIFF	Linked object's source class has changed.
OLE_E_ENUM_NOMORE	Can't enumerate any more, because the associated data is missing.
OLE_E_FIRST	Invalid OLEVERB structure.
OLE_E_INVALIDHWND	Invalid window handle.

(Continued)

Constant	Error Text/Description
OLE_E_INVALIDRECT	Invalid rectangle.
OLE_E_NOCACHE	There is no cache to operate on.
OLE_E_NOCONNECTION	There is no connection for this connection ID.
OLE_E_NOSTORAGE	Not able to perform the operation because object is not given storage yet.
OLE_E_NOTRUNNING	Need to run the object to perform this operation.
OLE_E_NOT_INPLACEACTIVE	Object is not in any of the in-place active states.
OLE_E_OLEVERB	Invalid OLEVERB structure.
OLE_E_PROMPTSAVECANCELLED	User canceled out of Save dialog.
OLE_E_STATIC	Object is static; operation not allowed.
OLE_E_WRONGCOMPOBJ	compobj.dll is too old for the ole2.dll initialized.

Object Creation Errors

The errors in Table D-5 highlight problems creating the environment necessary to create or connect to an existing COM object within the current OLE interface apartment. A failure at this point generally indicates a problem initializing the OLE system, the DLL that supports the COM object, or the network transport required to communicate with a COM object on another machine.

TABLE D-5

OLE initialization errors.

Constant	Error Text/Description
CO_E_ALREADYINITIALIZED	CoInitialize has already been called.
CO_E_APPDIDNTREG	Application was launched, but it didn't register a class factory.
CO_E_APPNOTFOUND	Application not found.
CO_E_APPSINGLEUSE	Application cannot be run more than once.
CO_E_BAD_PATH	Bad path to object.
CO_E_CANTDETERMINECLASS	Class of object cannot be determined.
CO_E_CLASSSTRING	Invalid class string.
CO_E_CLASS_CREATE_FAILED	Attempt to create a class object failed.

Constant	Error Text/Description
CO_E_DLLNOTFOUND	DLL for class not found.
CO_E_ERRORINAPP	Some error in application program.
CO_E_ERRORINDLL	Error in the DLL.
CO_E_FIRST	CoInitialize has not been called.
CO_E_IIDSTRING	Invalid interface string.
CO_E_INIT_CLASS_CACHE	Unable to initialize class cache.
CO_E_INIT_MEMORY_ALLOCATOR	Get memory allocator failure.
CO_E_INIT_ONLY_SINGLE_THREADED	There was an attempt to call CoInitialize a second time while single threaded.
CO_E_INIT_RPC_CHANNEL	Unable to initialize RPC services.
CO_E_INIT_SCM_EXEC_FAILURE	Failure attempting to launch OLE service.
CO_E_INIT_SCM_FILE_MAPPING_EXISTS	The OLE service file mapping already exists.
CO_E_INIT_SCM_MAP_VIEW_OF_FILE	Unable to map view of file for OLE service.
CO_E_INIT_SCM_MUTEX_EXISTS	The OLE service mutex already exists.
CO_E_INIT_SHARED_ALLOCATOR	Get shared memory allocator failure.
CO_E_INIT_TLS	Thread local storage failure.
CO_E_INIT_TLS_CHANNEL_CONTROL	Could not allocate thread local storage channel control.
CO_E_INIT_TLS_SET_CHANNEL_CONTROL	Cannot set thread local storage channel control.
CO_E_INIT_UNACCEPTED_USER_ALLOCATOR	The user-supplied memory allocator is unacceptable.
CO_E_LAST	Object has been released.
CO_E_NOTINITIALIZED	CoInitialize has not been called.
CO_E_OBJISREG	Object is already registered.
CO_E_OBJNOTCONNECTED	Object is not connected to server.
CO_E_OBJNOTREG	Object is not registered.

(Continued)

Constant	Error Text/Description
CO_E_OBJSRV_RPC_FAILURE	OLE service could not communicate with the object server.
CO_E_RELEASED	Object has been released.
CO_E_SCM_ERROR	OLE service could not bind object.
CO_E_SCM_RPC_FAILURE	RPC communication failed with OLE service.
CO_E_SERVER_EXEC_FAILURE	Server execution failed.
CO_E_SERVER_STOPPING	Object server is stopping when OLE service contacts it.
CO_E_WRONGOSFORAPP	Wrong OS or OS version for application.

Method Call Errors

These errors, shown in Table D-6, relate to problems calling methods and accessing the information and objects returned by a COM method call.

TABLE D-6

COM object method call.

Constant	Error Text/Description
DISP_E_ARRAYISLOCKED	Memory is locked.
DISP_E_BADCALLEE	Invalid callee.
DISP_E_BADINDEX	Invalid index.
DISP_E_BADPARAMCOUNT	Invalid number of parameters.
DISP_E_BADVARTYPE	Bad variable type.
DISP_E_EXCEPTION	Exception occurred.
DISP_E_MEMBERNOTFOUND	Member not found.
DISP_E_NONAMEDARGS	No named arguments.
DISP_E_NOTACOLLECTION	Does not support a collection.
DISP_E_OVERFLOW	Out of present range.
DISP_E_PARAMNOTFOUND	Parameter not found.
DISP_E_PARAMNOTOPTIONAL	Parameter not optional.
DISP_E_TYPEMISMATCH	Type mismatch.
DISP_E_UNKNOWNINTERFACE	Unknown interface.
DISP_E_UNKNOWNLCID	Unknown language.
DISP_E_UNKNOWNNAME	Unknown name.

TABLE D-7

Date/type
conversion errors.

Constant	Error Text/Description
EPT_S_CANT_CREATE	The endpoint mapper database could not be created. Indicates a failure to communicate with the DLL needed for data conversion.
EPT_S_CANT_PERFORM_OP	The server endpoint cannot perform the operation.
EPT_S_INVALID_ENTRY	The entry is invalid.
EPT_S_NOT_REGISTERED	There are no more endpoints available from the endpoint mapper.

Data/Type Conversion Errors

The endpoint database contains information on how to translate COM object data types into their local equivalent. Errors can occur both at the client (Perl) end and at the server end. Error constants and their descriptions are listed in Table D-7.

Object Storage Errors   The errors shown in Table D-8 indicate a problem with storing a COM object or with allocating the resources required to initiate an instance of the COM object.

TABLE D-8

Object storage
errors.

Constant	Error Text/Description
DV_E_DVTARGETDEVICE	Invalid DVTARGETDEVICE structure.
DV_E_DVTARGETDEVICE_SIZE	tdSize parameter of the DVTARGETDEVICE structure is invalid.
DV_E_FORMATETC	Invalid FORMATETC structure.
DV_E_LINDEX	Invalid lindex.
DV_E_NOIVIEWOBJECT	Object doesn't support IViewObject interface.
DV_E_STATDATA	Invalid STATDATA structure.
DV_E_STGMEDIUM	Invalid STDGMEDIUM structure.
DV_E_TYMED	Invalid tymed.

TABLE D-9

COM facility errors.

Constant	Error Text/Description
FACILITYCONTROL	The environment is incorrect or unable to support the requested facility.
FACILITYDISPATCH	The system cannot find the file specified.
FACILITYITF	The system cannot open the file.
FACILITYNULL	The operation completed successfully.
FACILITYRPC	Incorrect function. Usually indicates an inability to communicate with a remote COM object.
FACILITYSTORAGE	The system cannot find the path specified.
FACILITYWIN32	The storage control blocks were destroyed.
FACILITYWINDOWS	Not enough storage is available to process this command.

Facility Errors   A COM facility is the system service that provides access to a specific COM object. The errors detailed in Table D-9 indicate a problem when working with a specific facility to support the object.

COM Method/Property Errors

Table D-10 lists the constants relating to errors raised when calling methods and supplying method arguments for the current COM object.

TABLE D-10

COM method errors.

Constant	Error Text/Description
OLEOBJ_E_FIRST	No verbs for OLE object.
OLEOBJ_E_INVALIDVERB	Invalid verb for OLE object.
OLEOBJ_E_NOVERBS	No verbs for OLE object.
OLEOBJ_S_CANNOT_DOVERB_NOW	Verb number is valid but verb cannot be done now.
OLEOBJ_S_FIRST	Invalid verb for OLE object.
OLEOBJ_S_INVALIDHWND	Invalid window handle passed.
OLEOBJ_S_INVALIDVERB	Invalid verb for OLE object.
OLE_E_ADVF	Invalid advise flags.

OLE/COM Object Name Errors

Moniker errors indicate a problem opening and creating new COM objects. The list of constants is defined in Table D-11.

TABLE D-11

Moniker (object naming) errors.

Constant	Error Text/Description
MK_E_CANTOPENFILE	Moniker cannot open file.
MK_E_CONNECTMANUALLY	Moniker needs to be connected manually.
MK_E_ENUMERATION_FAILED	Moniker could not be enumerated.
MK_E_EXCEEDEDDEADLINE	Operation exceeded deadline.
MK_E_FIRST	Moniker needs to be connected manually.
MK_E_INTERMEDIATEINTERFACE NOTSUPPORTED	Intermediate operation failed.
MK_E_INVALIDEXTENSION	Bad extension for file.
MK_E_LAST	Moniker could not be enumerated.
MK_E_MUSTBOTHERUSER	User input required for operation to succeed.
MK_E_NEEDGENERIC	Moniker needs to be generic.
MK_E_NOINVERSE	Moniker class has no inverse.
MK_E_NOOBJECT	No object for moniker.
MK_E_NOPREFIX	No common prefix.
MK_E_NOSTORAGE	Moniker does not refer to storage.
MK_E_NOTBINDABLE	Moniker is not bindable.
MK_E_NOTBOUND	Moniker is not bound.
MK_E_NO_NORMALIZED	Moniker path could not be normalized.
MK_E_SYNTAX	Invalid syntax.
MK_E_UNAVAILABLE	Operation unavailable.
MK_S_HIM	Common prefix is input moniker.
MK_S_ME	Common prefix is this moniker.
MK_S_MONIKERALREADYREGISTERED	Moniker is already registered in running object table.
MK_S_REDUCED_TO_SELF	Moniker reduced to itself.
MK_S_US	Common prefix is both monikers.

TABLE D-12

Registry errors.

Constant	Error Text/Description
REGDB_E_CLASSNOTREG	Class not registered.
REGDB_E_FIRST	Could not read key from registry.
REGDB_E_IIDNOTREG	Interface not registered.
REGDB_E_INVALIDVALUE	Invalid value for registry.
REGDB_E_KEYMISSING	Could not find the key in the registry.
REGDB_E_READREGDB	Could not read key from registry.
REGDB_E_WRITEREGDB	Could not write key to registry.

Registry Errors

Table D-12 lists the constants relating to errors when accessing registry entries through the `Win32::APIRegistry`, `Win32::Registry`, and `Win32::TieRegistry` modules.

Remote Procedure Call Errors

Remote procedure calls (RPCs) are used through Windows to support many of the services and interaction between services, both on the local machine and remotely to other machines on the network. See Table D-13 for a list of error constants relating to RPC problems.

TABLE D-13

RPC errors.

Constant	Error Text/Description
RPC_E_ATTEMPTED_MULTITHREAD	Attempted to make calls on more than one thread in single-threaded mode.
RPC_E_CALL_CANCELED	Call was canceled by the message filter.
RPC_E_CALL_REJECTED	Call was rejected by callee.
RPC_E_CANTCALLOUT_AGAIN	There is no second outgoing call on same channel in DDE conversation.
RPC_E_CANTCALLOUT_INASYNCCALL	The caller is dispatching an asynchronous call and cannot make an outgoing call on behalf of this call.

Constant	Error Text/Description
RPC_E_CANTCALLOUT_INEXTERNALCALL	It is illegal to call out while inside message filter.
RPC_E_CANTCALLOUT_ININPUTSYNCCALL	An outgoing call cannot be made since the application is dispatching an input-synchronous call.
RPC_E_CANTPOST_INSENDCALL	The caller is dispatching an intertask SendMessage call and cannot call out via PostMessage.
RPC_E_CANTTRANSMIT_CALL	The call was not transmitted properly; the message queue was full and was not emptied after yielding.
RPC_E_CHANGED_MODE	Cannot change thread mode after it is set.
RPC_E_CLIENT_CANTMARSHAL_DATA	The client (caller) cannot marshall the parameter data—low memory, etc.
RPC_E_CLIENT_CANTUNMARSHAL_DATA	The client (caller) cannot unmarshall the return data—low memory, etc.
RPC_E_CLIENT_DIED	The caller (client) disappeared while the callee (server) was processing a call.
RPC_E_CONNECTION_TERMINATED	The connection terminated or is in a bogus state and cannot be used any more. Other connections are still valid.
RPC_E_DISCONNECTED	The object invoked has disconnected from its clients.
RPC_E_FAULT	RPC (remote procedure call) could not call the server or could not return the results of calling the server.
RPC_E_INVALIDMETHOD	The method called does not exist on the server.
RPC_E_INVALID_CALLDATA	A call control interfaces was called with invalid data.
RPC_E_INVALID_DATA	Received data is invalid; could be server or client data.
RPC_E_INVALID_DATAPACKET	The data packet with the marshalled parameter data is incorrect.
RPC_E_INVALID_PARAMETER	A particular parameter is invalid and cannot be (un)marshalled.
RPC_E_NOT_REGISTERED	The requested interface is not registered on the server object.

(Continued)

TABLE D-13

(Continued)

Constant	Error Text/Description
RPC_E_OUT_OF_RESOURCES	Could not allocate some required resource (memory, events, etc.).
RPC_E_RETRY	The object invoked chose not to process the call now. Try again later.
RPC_E_SERVERCALL_REJECTED	The message filter rejected the call.
RPC_E_SERVERCALL_RETRYLATER	The message filter indicated that the application is busy.
RPC_E_SERVERFAULT	The server threw an exception.
RPC_E_SERVER_CANTMARSHAL_DATA	The server (callee) cannot marshall the return data—low memory, etc.
RPC_E_SERVER_CANTUNMARSHAL_ DATA	The server (callee) cannot unmarshall the parameter data—low memory, etc.
RPC_E_SERVER_DIED	The callee (server [not server application]) is not available and disappeared; all connections are invalid. The call may have executed.
RPC_E_SERVER_DIED_DNE	The callee (server [not server application]) is not available and disappeared; all connections are invalid. The call did not execute.
RPC_E_SYS_CALL_FAILED	System call failed.
RPC_E_THREAD_NOT_INIT	CoInitialize has not been called on the current thread.
RPC_E_UNEXPECTED	An internal error occurred.
RPC_E_WRONG_THREAD	The application called an interface that was marshalled for a different thread.
RPC_S_ADDRESS_ERROR	An addressing error occurred in the remote procedure call server.
RPC_S_ALREADY_LISTENING	The RPC server is already listening.
RPC_S_ALREADY_REGISTERED	The object universal unique identifier (UUID) has already been registered.
RPC_S_BINDING_HAS_NO_AUTH	The binding does not contain any authentication information.
RPC_S_BINDING_INCOMPLETE	The binding handle does not contain all required information.
RPC_S_CALL_CANCELLED	The server was altered while processing this call.
RPC_S_CALL_FAILED	The remote procedure call failed.

Constant	Error Text/Description
RPC_S_CALL_FAILED_DNE	The remote procedure call failed and did not execute.
RPC_S_CALL_IN_PROGRESS	A remote procedure call is already in progress for this thread.
RPC_S_CANNOT_SUPPORT	The requested operation is not supported.
RPC_S_CANT_CREATE_ENDPOINT	The endpoint cannot be created.
RPC_S_COMM_FAILURE	Communications failure.
RPC_S_DUPLICATE_ENDPOINT	The endpoint is a duplicate.
RPC_S_ENTRY_ALREADY_EXISTS	The entry already exists.
RPC_S_ENTRY_NOT_FOUND	The entry is not found.
RPC_S_FP_DIV_ZERO	A floating-point operation at the RPC server caused a division by zero.
RPC_S_FP_OVERFLOW	A floating-point overflow occurred at the RPC server.
RPC_S_FP_UNDERFLOW	A floating-point underflow occurred at the RPC server.
RPC_S_GROUP_MEMBER_NOT_FOUND	The group member was not found.
RPC_S_INCOMPLETE_NAME	The entry name is incomplete.
RPC_S_INTERFACE_NOT_FOUND	The interface was not found.
RPC_S_INTERNAL_ERROR	An internal error occurred in a remote procedure call.
RPC_S_INVALID_AUTH_IDENTITY	The security context is invalid.
RPC_S_INVALID_BINDING	The binding handle is invalid.
RPC_S_INVALID_BOUND	The array bounds are invalid.
RPC_S_INVALID_ENDPOINT_FORMAT	The endpoint format is invalid.
RPC_S_INVALID_NAF_ID	The network address family is invalid.
RPC_S_INVALID_NAME_SYNTAX	The name syntax is invalid.
RPC_S_INVALID_NETWORK_OPTIONS	The network options are invalid.
RPC_S_INVALID_NET_ADDR	The network address is invalid.
RPC_S_INVALID_OBJECT	The object universal unique identifier (UUID) is the nil UUID.
RPC_S_INVALID_RPC_PROTSEQ	The RPC protocol sequence is invalid.
RPC_S_INVALID_STRING_BINDING	The string binding is invalid.

(Continued)

TABLE D-13

(Continued)

Constant	Error Text/Description
RPC_S_INVALID_STRING_UUID	The string universal unique identifier (UUID) is invalid.
RPC_S_INVALID_TAG	The tag is invalid.
RPC_S_INVALID_TIMEOUT	The timeout value is invalid.
RPC_S_INVALID_VERS_OPTION	The version option is invalid.
RPC_S_MAX_CALLS_TOO_SMALL	The maximum number of calls is too small.
RPC_S_NAME_SERVICE_UNAVAILABLE	The name service is unavailable.
RPC_S_NOTHING_TO_EXPORT	No interfaces have been exported.
RPC_S_NOT_ALL_OBJS_UNEXPORTED	There is nothing to unexport.
RPC_S_NOT_CANCELLED	Thread is not canceled.
RPC_S_NOT_LISTENING	The RPC server is not listening.
RPC_S_NOT_RPC_ERROR	The error specified is not a valid Windows RPC error code.
RPC_S_NO_BINDINGS	There are no bindings.
RPC_S_NO_CALL_ACTIVE	There is not a remote procedure call active in this thread.
RPC_S_NO_CONTEXT_AVAILABLE	No security context is available to allow impersonation.
RPC_S_NO_ENDPOINT_FOUND	No endpoint was found.
RPC_S_NO_ENTRY_NAME	The binding does not contain an entry name.
RPC_S_NO_INTERFACES	No interfaces have been registered.
RPC_S_NO_MORE_BINDINGS	There are no more bindings.
RPC_S_NO_MORE_MEMBERS	There are no more members.
RPC_S_NO_PRINC_NAME	No principal name registered.
RPC_S_NO_PROTSEQS	There are no protocol sequences.
RPC_S_NO_PROTSEQS_REGISTERED	No protocol sequences have been registered.
RPC_S_OBJECT_NOT_FOUND	The object universal unique identifier (UUID) was not found.
RPC_S_OUT_OF_RESOURCES	Not enough resources are available to complete this operation.
RPC_S_PROCNUM_OUT_OF_RANGE	The procedure number is out of range.
RPC_S_PROTOCOL_ERROR	A remote procedure call protocol error occurred.

Constant	Error Text/Description
RPC_S_PROTSEQ_NOT_FOUND	The RPC protocol sequence was not found.
RPC_S_PROTSEQ_NOT_SUPPORTED	The RPC protocol sequence is not supported.
RPC_S_SEC_PKG_ERROR	A security-package-specific error occurred.
RPC_S_SERVER_TOO_BUSY	The RPC server is too busy to complete this operation.
RPC_S_SERVER_UNAVAILABLE	The RPC server is unavailable.
RPC_S_STRING_TOO_LONG	The string is too long.
RPC_S_TYPE_ALREADY_REGISTERED	The type universal unique identifier (UUID) has already been registered.
RPC_S_UNKNOWN_AUTHN_LEVEL	The authentication level is unknown.
RPC_S_UNKNOWN_AUTHN_SERVICE	The authentication service is unknown.
RPC_S_UNKNOWN_AUTHN_TYPE	The authentication type is unknown.
RPC_S_UNKNOWN_AUTHZ_SERVICE	The authorization service is unknown.
RPC_S_UNKNOWN_IF	The interface is unknown.
RPC_S_UNKNOWN_MGR_TYPE	The manager type is unknown.
RPC_S_UNSUPPORTED_AUTHN_LEVEL	The requested authentication level is not supported.
RPC_S_UNSUPPORTED_NAME_SYNTAX	The name syntax is not supported.
RPC_S_UNSUPPORTED_TRANS_SYN	The transfer syntax is not supported by the RPC server.
RPC_S_UNSUPPORTED_TYPE	The universal unique identifier (UUID) type is not supported.
RPC_S_UUID_LOCAL_ONLY	A UUID that is valid only on this computer has been allocated.
RPC_S_UUID_NO_ADDRESS	No network address is available to use to construct a universal unique identifier (UUID).
RPC_S_WRONG_KIND_OF_BINDING	The binding handle is not the correct type.
RPC_S_ZERO_DIVIDE	The RPC server attempted an integer division by zero.
RPC_X_BAD_STUB_DATA	The stub received bad data.
RPC_X_BYTE_COUNT_TOO_SMALL	The byte count is too small.
RPC_X_ENUM_VALUE_OUT_OF_RANGE	The enumeration value is out of range.
RPC_X_INVALID_ES_ACTION	Invalid operation on the encoding/decoding handle.

(Continued)

TABLE D-13

(Continued)

Constant	Error Text/Description
RPC_X_NO_MORE_ENTRIES	The list of RPC servers available for the binding of auto handles has been exhausted.
RPC_X_NULL_REF_POINTER	A null reference pointer was passed to the stub.
RPC_X_SS_CANNOT_GET_CALL_HANDLE	The stub is unable to get the remote procedure call handle.
RPC_X_SS_CHAR_TRANS_OPEN_FAIL	Unable to open the character translation table file.
RPC_X_SS_CHAR_TRANS_SHORT_FILE	The file containing the character translation table has fewer than 512 bytes.
RPC_X_SS_CONTEXT_DAMAGED	The context handle changed during a remote procedure call.
RPC_X_SS_HANDLES_MISMATCH	The binding handles passed to a remote procedure call do not match.
RPC_X_SS_IN_NULL_CONTEXT	A NULL context handle was passed from the client to the host during a remote procedure call.
RPC_X_WRONG_ES_VERSION	Incompatible version of the serializing package.
RPC_X_WRONG_STUB_VERSION	Incompatible version of the RPC stub.

Storage (File System) Errors

The error constants in Table D-14 can be used to identify problems when storing information. Errors relate both to failures on the local file system and on the structures and interfaces to other services that rely on the file system and memory for storage.

Data Type Conversion/Naming Errors

Conversion between data formats within the internal operations of Windows can be trapped using the constants seen in Table D-15. Some of these relate to errors loading Windows components, including the OLE system. Others can indicate problems when setting the environment for Windows components to operate.

TABLE D-14

Storage errors.

Constant	Error Text/Description
MEM_E_INVALID_LINK	An allocation chain contained an invalid link pointer.
MEM_E_INVALID_ROOT	An invalid root block pointer was specified.
MEM_E_INVALID_SIZE	The requested allocation size was too large.
STG_E_ABNORMALAPIEXIT	An API call exited abnormally.
STG_E_ACCESSDENIED	Access denied.
STG_E_CANTSAVE	Can't save.
STG_E_DISKISWRITEPROTECTED	Disk is write-protected.
STG_E_EXTANTMARSHALLINGS	Illegal operation called on object with extant marshallings.
STG_E_FILEALREADYEXISTS	%1 already exists.
STG_E_FILENOTFOUND	%1 could not be found.
STG_E_INSUFFICIENTMEMORY	There is insufficient memory available to complete operation.
STG_E_INUSE	Attempted to use an object that is busy.
STG_E_INVALIDFLAG	Invalid flag error.
STG_E_INVALIDFUNCTION	Unable to perform requested operation.
STG_E_INVALIDHANDLE	Attempted an operation on an invalid object.
STG_E_INVALIDHEADER	The file %1 is not a valid compound file.
STG_E_INVALIDNAME	The name %1 is not valid.
STG_E_INVALIDPARAMETER	Invalid parameter error.
STG_E_INVALIDPOINTER	Invalid pointer error.
STG_E_LOCKVIOLATION	A lock violation has occurred.
STG_E_MEDIUMFULL	There is insufficient disk space to complete operation.
STG_E_NOMOREFILES	There are no more entries to return.
STG_E_NOTCURRENT	The storage has been changed since the last commit.
STG_E_NOTFILEBASEDSTORAGE	Illegal operation called on non-file-based storage.
STG_E_OLDDLL	The compound file %1 was produced with a newer version of storage.
STG_E_OLDFORMAT	The compound file %1 was produced with an incompatible version of storage.

(Continued)

TABLE D-14

(Continued)

Constant	Error Text/Description
STG_E_PATHNOTFOUND	The path %1 could not be found.
STG_E_READFAULT	A disk error occurred during a read operation.
STG_E_REVERTED	Attempted to use an object that has ceased to exist.
STG_E_SEEKERROR	An error occurred during a seek operation.
STG_E_SHAREREQUIRED	Share.exe or equivalent is required for operation.
STG_E_SHAREVIOLATION	A share violation has occurred.
STG_E_TOOMANYOPENFILES	There are insufficient resources to open another file.
STG_E_UNIMPLEMENTEDFUNCTION	That function is not implemented.
STG_E_UNKNOWN	An unexpected error occurred.
STG_E_WRITEFAULT	A disk error occurred during a write operation.
STG_S_CONVERTED	The underlying file was converted to compound file format.

TABLE D-15

Type conversion errors.

Constant	Error Text/Description
TYPE_E_AMBIGUOUSNAME	Ambiguous name.
TYPE_E_BADMODULEKIND	Wrong module kind for the operation.
TYPE_E_BUFFERTOOSMALL	Buffer too small.
TYPE_E_CANTCREATETMPFILE	Error creating unique TMP file.
TYPE_E_CANTLOADLIBRARY	Error loading type library/DLL.
TYPE_E_CIRCULARTYPE	Circular dependency between types/modules.
TYPE_E_DLLFUNCTIONNOTFOUND	Function not defined in specified DLL.
TYPE_E_DUPLICATEID	Duplicate ID in inheritance hierarchy.
TYPE_E_ELEMENTNOTFOUND	Element not found.
TYPE_E_INCONSISTENTPROPFUNCS	Inconsistent property functions.
TYPE_E_INVALIDID	Incorrect inheritance depth in standard OLE hmember.
TYPE_E_INVALIDSTATE	Invalid forward reference, or reference to uncompiled type.

Constant	Error Text/Description
TYPE_E_INVDATAREAD	Old format or invalid type library.
TYPE_E_IOERROR	I/O error.
TYPE_E_LIBNOTREGISTERED	Library not registered.
TYPE_E_NAMECONFLICT	Name already exists in the library.
TYPE_E_OUTOFBOUNDS	Invalid number of arguments.
TYPE_E_QUALIFIEDNAMEDISALLOWED	Qualified name disallowed.
TYPE_E_REGISTRYACCESS	Error accessing the OLE registry.
TYPE_E_SIZETOOBIG	Size may not exceed 64 K.
TYPE_E_TYPEMISMATCH	Type mismatch.
TYPE_E_UNDEFINEDTYPE	Bound to unknown type.
TYPE_E_UNKNOWNLCID	Unknown LCID.
TYPE_E_UNSUPFORMAT	Old format or invalid type library.
TYPE_E_WRONGTYPEKIND	Type mismatch.

INDEX

ABOUT THE AUTHOR

Martin Brown is the author of *Perl Annotated Archives*, *Perl: The Complete Reference, Perl Programmer's Reference*, and *Python: The Complete Reference* for Osborne. He is a former IT manager and freelance consultant with 15 years of multi-platform administration and programming experience, specializing in Perl development. Martin is now a full-time writer and consultant.